W9-ASG-125

SEP 1970
RECEIVED
OHIO DOMINICAN
COLLEGE LIBRARY
COLUMBUS, OHIO

22-38

Readings
in Child
Development
and Personality

Under the Editorship of Wayne H. Holtzman and Gardner Murphy

Readings in Child Development and Personality

SECOND EDITION

Paul Henry Mussen

John Janeway Conger

Jerome Kagan

Harper & Row, Publishers
New York, Evanston, and London

READINGS IN CHILD DEVELOPMENT AND PERSONALITY, Second Edition
Copyright © 1965, 1970 by Paul H. Mussen, John J. Conger, and Jerome Kagan

Printed in the United States of America. All rights reserved. No part of this book
may be used or reproduced in any manner whatsoever without written permission
except in the case of brief quotations embodied in critical articles and reviews. For
information address Harper & Row, Publishers, Incorporated, 49 East 33rd Street,
New York, N.Y. 10016.

Library of Congress Catalog Card Number: 71-86991

136.7
M989r
2d ed.

Contents

v

71365

Part II.   EARLY LANGUAGE AND COGNITIVE DEVELOPMENT

Part III.   FAMILIAL INFLUENCES ON SOCIALIZATION
AND PERSONALITY DEVELOPMENT

Part IV.   EXTRAFAMILIAL INFLUENCES ON PERSONALITY DEVELOPMENT

Part V.   THE SCHOOL AS AN AGENT OF SOCIALIZATION

Preface
to the First Edition

Part of the excitement of studying child development stems from the fact that the field is undergoing a period of unprecedented growth. Able investigators are being attracted by the challenges of the field in increasing numbers. As research techniques grow more sophisticated, empirical knowledge expands, and new facts replace older opinions. New concepts and theories are proposed, and these, in turn, stimulate the search for further knowledge of growth and development, and the factors affecting them.

As a result, books written a decade ago often seem hopelessly out of date. The student's understanding of the field, and his interest in it, increase in depth and breadth if, in addition to textbook summaries of various theories and research findings, he is exposed to primary sources illustrating recent developments in the field.

The present volume of readings was designed to make readily available a set of essays and empirical papers, most of them written recently, representing current theory and knowledge in the field of child development. A relatively small number of articles is included but, in the editors' opinion, these reflect major problem areas of the field, fundamental theoretical concepts and issues, basic research methods, and some of the most important research findings. A wide variety of topics is included: genetic and constitutional factors in development, critical periods, effects of infantile experience, dynamics of socialization during the preschool and early school years, relationships between personality and intelligence, problems of identity in adolescence, cognitive styles, and delinquency.

The editors regard human growth as a continuous process and they view the development of personality and behavior as the result of continuing interactions between the organism and its psychological, social, and physical environment. Consequently, the sections of the book are arranged according to successive stages of development, and most of the articles emphasize antecedent-consequent relationships. The editors' introductions to the sections, describing the major substantive and theoretical issues characterizing each stage of development, provide a general context for the illustrative articles presented.

We gratefully acknowledge our indebtedness to the authors and publishers who granted us permission to reprint their articles in this volume. They are given credit in the footnotes at the beginning of each selection. Dr. Douglas Kenny offered us many valuable criticisms and suggestions about the selection of articles. We also wish to thank Miss Audrey Smolin and Mrs. Doris Simpson who prepared the manuscript for publication.

P. H. M.
J. J. C.
J. K.

Preface
to the Second Edition

Study of developmental processes has accelerated remarkably during the last half decade as concern with the growth and development of children has attracted the interest of greater numbers of students, scientists, individual citizens, and political groups. Not only are we discovering the vital social necessity of providing for all children and adolescents the capability and motivation to enter actively into, and to contribute to, a complex, rapidly changing world; we are also discovering better ways to do so. It has become clear, for example, that important aspects of psychological development occur well before the child ever enters school, and some of the problems shown by children growing up in deprived social environments seem traceable to experiences encountered during the first few years of life. Furthermore, empirical research with primates in the laboratory, as well as in field settings, has been remarkably consonant with the results obtained from children. As a result, modern psychology is witness to a remarkable degree of agreement on concepts and hypotheses which, in turn, lead to a more optimistic search for major theoretical statements that might clarify the complicated and enigmatic processes that characterize human development.

The rapid advances in our knowledge about the infant, about biological and cognitive development, and about the role of social structure on the behavior of children and adolescents make a book of readings or a textbook obsolete in a very short time. This second edition of *Readings in Child Development and Personality* therefore is not issued prematurely. The present set of readings was designed to contain some of the important empirical papers upon which large sections of the textbook were based. Most of these articles have been written during the last five years. Those that were not are regarded by the editors as classic papers which still contain a valid message. The book is organized both longitudinally and topically. This edition, in contrast with the earlier version, places heavier emphasis on biological and cognitive factors in the first years of life, and the importance of social learning theory for the growth sciences. The national concern with the cognitive and personality characteristics of deprived children growing up in urban areas is reflected in several new papers, and timely articles on adolescence engage the issues of student protest, alienation, sexuality, and new value systems.

Many of the papers reflect a major conceptual change that has occurred in recent years. We now view the mind of the child as active and constructive rather than as an empty blackboard, a *tabula rasa,* upon which the message of experience is written. We see the infant and young child as a highly structured organism trying to make sense of his experience, not as a piece of clay passively molded by social forces.

The editors' introductions to the parts summarize the substantive theoretical issues therein and give a brief précis of the empirical message contained in each paper.

We acknowledge our indebtedness to the authors and publishers who have granted us permission to reprint their articles. Each is given credit in the footnote at the beginning of each selection. We wish to thank Doris C. Simpson, Nancy Smith, and Dorothy Townsend who helped to prepare this manuscript for publication.

P. H. M.

J. J. C.

J. K.

part I
Biological
and Environmental
Factors
in Development
in the First
Two Years

The young infant's psychological capabilities and his overt behaviors are a function of many factors, including his genetic constitution, and events that occur during the pregnancy and delivery periods. Many biological factors, both genetic and nongenetic, affect the child's reactions to his environment and, therefore, influence his learning and future personality development. One of the major problems of developmental psychology is to understand the relative contributions of heredity, prenatal processes, and early experiential factors to the totality that is called the child's psychological organization.

The first paper in this part, by I. I. Gottesman of the University of Minnesota, discusses the genetic aspects of intellectual performance, with special emphasis on differences in IQ between black and white children. Despite the fact that the IQ scores of black children are, on the average, 10 to 15 points lower than those of whites, this fact is not necessarily proof of genetic differences in intellectual potential. Professor Gottesman notes that many identical twins, with the same genetic constitution, differ appreciably in IQ score—their scores differing by as much as 20 points. Professor Gottesman suggests that we should not think of the contribution of heredity as determining a certain expected norm of reaction. Genetic constitution fixes a wide range of intellectual ability. Within this general range a particular child's genetic makeup can lead to any of a large variety of different kinds of intellectual profiles, depending on the specific environment in which he is raised. Although Professor Gottesman acknowledges the importance of genetic differences in psychological processes, he concludes that study of the available evidence suggests that differences in IQ score between black and white children in the United States appear to be primarily associated with differences in their environmental conditions and advantages.

The second paper, by Dr. Braine and his colleagues, focuses on a specific type of disadvantage, prematurity, and considers the physical and psychological consequences of premature birth. Infants whose birth weight is under 5½ pounds are typically classified as premature. Premature infants are exposed to dangers that are absent or less frequent in full-term infants. Two of these dangers are increased vulnerability to illness and retarded mental and motor growth. Unfortunately, there are many more premature births among disadvantaged lower-class than among middle-class families. This investigation of premature births in a New York City hospital indicates that the premature child has a slower rate of mental and motor development during the first year. The detrimental effects of prematurity are more serious both among boys, rather than girls, and among the most underprivileged members of the society. Thus a premature male born to severely underprivileged parents runs the highest risk of physical disease and psychological retardation.

One of the consequences of early disease or maturational retardation could be slower rates of learning during the first year of life. Dr. Hanuš Papoušek's careful study of learning in young infants is extremely important for developmental psychologists because it demonstrates that the young infant is capable of learning new responses from the first days of his life. The older the infant the more quickly he will learn a conditioned response. The dramatic differences between 1- and 90-day-old infants in ease of learning a conditioned reaction reflects the rapid maturation of the central nervous system during the first 3 months of life.

In addition to overt conditioned responses, infants also learn perceptual structures. By observing the world around them, they learn more about it and note the structure of external events.

The fourth study in this series, by Dr. Robert L. Fantz and Sonia Nevis, inquires into the perceptual dynamics of the infant. Research studies suggest that during the first year of life, meaning and contrast are important in controlling the events infants will attend to or study. Moreover, the research demonstrates that children who grow up in typical families, in contrast to institutions, show more precocious mental development. In general, it would appear that during the opening years of life the infant's distribution of attention is primarily a function of the stimulus properties of the object. In the fourth and fifth month, the infant's attention begins to come under the control of his past experience with the objects in his world.

The second group of papers in this part has to do with the important experiences the infant encounters that begin to control more complex aspects of his behavior. The first one, by Dr. Burton L. White of Harvard University demonstrates that stimulation of the infant during the first 3 months of life facilitates the acquisition of a tendency to attend to, and explore, the environment and fosters precocious sensorimotor coordinations. The development of sensorimotor coordination in the young infant is malleable, and can be changed by modifying the environment at the proper time.

The second paper in this series is a report of the more recent work on primates by Drs. Harry and Margaret Harlow of the University of Wisconsin. For many years the Harlows have been working on the effects of different rearing environments on the development of the primate and many of their findings seem relevant for the human infant. The investigators believe that there are stages in the affectional system of the monkey. One of the important systems involves the attachment of the infant to the mother, followed by a disattachment stage and then by a stage of maternal separation or rejection. This initial attachment of the monkey to another monkey, usually the mother, is necessary for normal social development. Monkeys raised in isolation are extremely deviant in their social behavior and sometimes appear extremely withdrawn, frightened, and emotionally labile.

The infant's social development is reflected in his social responsiveness, and the smile is one of the cues mothers use in recognizing this sociability. The paper by Dr. Jacob Gewirtz of the National Institutes of Health deals with the interesting and provocative response of the human smile. Research on many populations suggests that most human infants who are raised by human beings show a very strong tendency to smile to a human face somewhere between 3 and 5 months, with a clear peak at 4 months of age. Dr. Gewirtz has studied groups of infants in Israel some of whom were raised in typical families, others in a Kibbutz, and still others in a residential institution. All of the infants tended to show the same strong tendency to smile at a human face at 4 months of age. However, after 4 months of age the children who remained with their families showed much more smiling to faces than those who were raised in a Kibbutz or in an institution. It would appear that the 4-month-smile seems to be a maturational event requiring only contact with human faces during the earliest months. Frequency of smiling after this age seems to be a function of the frequency and quality of the child's experience with people and, therefore, more likely to be a social response.

The final two papers are closely related and involve reports of studies of mother-child interaction. Dr. Howard A. Moss of the National Institute of Mental Health has been concerned for many years with this interaction during the first year of life. He has discovered that the mother's behavior toward her infant changes dramatically between 2 weeks and 12 weeks of age as a function, in part, of the child's increasing maturity. The child needs the mother much less at 3 months than he did at 2 weeks and, therefore, the mother tends to be less nurturant. Moreover, mothers act differently toward daughters than they do toward sons. They are more likely to stress the musculature of their sons and stimulate them excessively. They are much more likely to imitate their daughter's babbling. As early as 3 months of age, American parents have already begun to treat their children differently as a function of the sex of their child.

The final paper by H. R. Schaffer and Peggy E. Emerson of the University of Strathclyde in Scotland is concerned with differences in infants' preference for physical contact. Some infants like to cuddle; others seem to resist it or not like it very much. The noncuddlers do not seem to find physical contact satisfying. The cuddlers of course receive much more maternal contact than the noncuddlers and therefore should develop a stronger affectionate bond with the mother. Thus the child's temperament makes as important a contribution to his own social development as the mother's behavior toward the child. The relationship between parent and child is a kind of ballet, with each partner contributing his own personality and dispositions to the form of the behavior each shows toward the other.

Biogenetics of Race and Class

I. I. Gottesman
UNIVERSITY OF MINNESOTA

GENETIC ASPECTS OF RACE DIFFERENCES
IN INTELLECTUAL PERFORMANCE

[The] difficulties of defining a race or of assigning a person to a particular race, such as the Negro, are formidable. . . . Similar difficulties are encountered when psychologists attempt to define a concept of intelligence (Liverant, 1960; Maher, 1963). Such a concept is necessary for an understanding of human behavior since individuals differ in their rate of acquisition of responses under similar learning conditions. Caution is required when

Reprinted from *Social class, race, and psychological development,* edited by Martin Deutsch, Irwin Katz, & Arthur B. Jensen, pp. 25–51. Copyright © 1968 by Holt, Rinehart and Winston, Inc. Reprinted by permission of Holt, Rinehart and Winston, Inc. Abridged by the omission of the first 14 pages with the permission of the author. Omitted sections are titled "Race Taxonomy"; "Who Is the Negro American?"; and "Natural Selection and the Origin of Race Relations."

anyone tries to explain the differences observed between mean IQs of whites and Negroes when the only variables in their study are IQ and race. Intelligent behavior, as with every response, is multiply determined, and unless all the *relevant* variables are matched except race, no valid explanations can be made. Even a cursory glance at the literature about changes in IQ (for example, Anastasi, 1958; Tyler, 1965) reveals a vast number of statistically significant correlates of IQ. Among them are basal metabolism rate, EEG alpha frequency, height, weight, anxiety level, race and warmth of examiner, father's occupation and years of schooling, mother's attitude toward achievement, home cultural level, mother's concern with language development, degree of anoxia at birth, the desire to master intellectual skills, and others too numerous to mention. It should be obvious that IQ tests do not directly measure innate gene-determined intellectual capacity but do measure current intellectual performance as defined by a particular culture or at least by its psychologists.

In looking at the literature on Negro-white differences in measured IQ (for example, Kennedy et al., 1963) in children from the same area, one will rarely find the Negroes higher, sometimes find them no different, but most often find them lower. It is a well-known fact that when tested on Army Alpha, some groups of northern Negroes made higher averages than some groups of southern whites, but that white soldiers consistently scored higher than Negro soldiers from the same region. Evidence from the classical studies by Klineberg and Lee shows that educational opportunity and not selective migration accounts for these kinds of results. A typical finding is that samples of northern Negro children have a mean IQ of 90 on the Stanford-Binet (Higgins and Sivers, 1958) compared to the normative sample (which excluded Negroes) mean of 100. In a well-designed study of 1800 elementary school Negro children representative of all those in Florida, Georgia, Alabama, Tennessee, and South Carolina (Kennedy et al., 1963), a mean IQ on the 1960 revision of the Stanford-Binet of 80.7 was obtained. The distributions of the Negro and Binet normative samples are given in Fig. 1.

What kinds of concrete meanings can be attached to the observed differences of 10 IQ points between northern Negroes and whites and 20 IQ points between southeastern Negroes and whites? As a result of a kind of overselling of the practical uses of IQ tests, professionals and laymen alike appear to invest test scores with an undeserved aura of permanence and profound significance. An exposure to data on the construct validity of intelligence tests and susceptibility to change of IQs (Maher, 1963; Hunt, 1961) would help temper this naive enthusiasm. It is too easy to forget the operations by which an IQ is computed. For example, on the 1937 Binet test the answer to a question is most often worth two months of mental-age credit; the answer to one question is thus good for 2 or 3 IQ points. Given two eight-year-old children with IQs of 90 and 100, the latter has been able to answer five more questions correctly than his classmate. It should be obvious that when an IQ test has fewer total questions than the Binet, each correct answer is worth proportionately more than 2 or 3 IQ points.

Another way to gain perspective on the practical meaning of 10 or 20 IQ

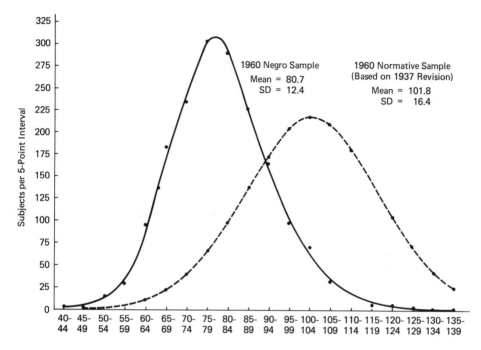

Fig. 1. The IQ distributions of normative white and southeastern Negro school children. (After Kennedy et al., 1963)

points is to look at the means for certain physically handicapped groups. In a survey of the results of intelligence test results with deaf children, Louttit (1957) recognizes that an over-all generalization may not be justifiable in the light of the unknown sampling errors; Pintner's conclusion is apparently endorsed; that is, the most probable average IQ is 86 on specially designed non-language group tests. Some studies are reported where the mean IQs are in the 70s and 80s.

Louttit also reports Hayes' survey of intelligence in blind children attending residential schools. Mean IQs measured on a special test ranged from 92 to 108, but the percentage of children with IQs 70 and below ranged from 4 percent to 19 percent. Only 2 percent of normal children on the Binet score less than IQ 70. In the Kennedy et al. sample of Negro school children 18.4 percent of the total group had Binet IQs less than 70. That such discrepancies primarily represent a form of over-all stimulus deprivation, somewhat like the sensorily handicapped rather than "genetic inferiority," is strongly suggested by the manner in which the mean IQs drop solely as a function of age (read exposure to an inadequate environment). While the mean IQ of the six-year-old group was 84, that of the thirteen-year-olds has dropped to 65; the proportion of IQs below 70 in these two extremes of the Kennedy et al. sample was 8.8 percent and 66.7 percent respectively.

A vast clinical and experimental literature has grown up documenting the importance of early experience for later development for both animals and man (Hunt, 1961; Brackbill, 1964). This literature strongly suggests that perceptual and stimulus deprivation of a rather subtle nature is capable of handicapping subsequent development. None of these statements should be taken to mean that true mental deficiency can be *cured* by a program of enriched education. One of the goals of this section is to explain Negro-white differences in IQ, rather than to explain them away.

Another way to gain perspective about the meaning of a 10 or 20 IQ point difference is to look at the data on within-pair differences in intelligence for identical (*MZ*) and fraternal (*DZ*) twins. The reason why these data are important to the issue of race differences in intelligence is that some people have interpreted the mean differences observed between white and Negro American samples as sufficient evidence of "genetic inferiority" or of differential capacity for intelligence. Since identical twins have no difference in their genes (they come from one egg which has split in two) any differences between them must be due to the environment, either prenatally or postnatally. If we construct two samples of identical genetic constitution by taking the brighter of each pair of identical twins in one group and the less bright in the other, what kind of mean IQ difference do we find? Even though the gene pools do not differ and even though each of the two groups has been raised under more or less the same regime, the mean difference amounts to 6 IQ points for the sample of fifty pairs studied by Newman et al. (1937). The range of within-pair differences was 0 to 20 points. Thus, even when gene pools are *known* to be matched, appreciable differences in mean IQ can be observed that could only have been associated with environmental differences.

A better appreciation of the influence of the environment on IQ can be gained from looking at the two unique samples of thoroughly described identical twins who have been reared apart and thus in discriminably different environments. Such data are crucial to understanding the range of intelligence which can be manifested by persons of the same genetic background. In the nineteen pairs of identical twins reared apart studied by Newman et al. (1937), the average intrapair difference on the Binet was 8 IQ points. The range of differences was 1 to 24 points! A very similar picture is given in a remarkably large sample of thirty-eight pairs of identical twins reared apart and studied by Shields (1962). When the tests used in this larger study are converted into IQ point equivalents (Shields and Gottesman, 1965), the average intrapair difference for the identicals is 14 points on a verbal IQ test and 10 points on a nonverbal test. The corresponding differences for a control sample of thirty-four identical pairs reared together, which Shields studied with the same instruments, were 9 IQ points for both tests. At least 25 percent of the sample of identicals reared apart had within-pair IQ point differences exceeding 16 points on at least one of the tests.[1]

---

[1] Some of the differences across experiments are the result of differing numbers of items in the tests. The fewer the items, the more IQ points an answer is worth.

It is obvious from looking at the data on identical twins that individuals with exactly the same genetic constitution can differ widely on the phenotypic trait we measure with IQ tests and label intelligence. The differences observed so far between whites and Negroes can hardly be accepted as sufficient evidence that with respect to intelligence, the Negro American is genetically less endowed. Should anyone choose to apply in a practical fashion the data obtained thus far on race differences in IQ, the procedure would be extremely inaccurate. From a consideration of the problems of overlapping distributions and different "base rates" of Negroes and whites in the United States population (compare Meehl and Rosen, 1955), it is possible to illustrate the practical futility of predicting race from a knowledge of IQ.

Let us use in our example the facts that 2 percent of the white standardization sample on the Binet obtain scores less than IQ 70 as contrasted with the 18 percent reported for the large representative sample of southeastern Negro elementary-school children described above. There are approximately 180 million whites and 20 million so-called Negroes in the United States at this time. If we choose to blindly label all individuals with tested IQs under 70 as Negro, the consequences are as follows: 3.6 million Negroes are accurately classified as to their race, but 3.6 million whites are misclassified as Negroes. In the United States, using IQ under 70 as a criterion, you would be wrong 50 percent of the time if you were to use IQ as an indicator of race. You would be wrong more frequently than this if you were to use a higher cutting score, such as IQ 80. With this score you could accurately identify 10.4 million Negroes, but you would also label 14.4 million whites as members of the Negro race. Inasmuch as an individual's IQ does not permit you to identify his race accurately, so also his race does not permit you to estimate his intelligence with sufficient accuracy.

The Dialectics of Heredity and Environment

If the reader wishes to conclude at this point that the contribution of genetics to variation in IQ is negligible, he has read too much into the above attempts at explaining Negro-white differences in IQ. The complexities of the issues involved in a satisfactory understanding of how nature works together with nurture to produce a trait and trait variability can only be broached in this chapter. More complete introductions can be found in the writings of the behavior geneticists (Fuller and Thompson, 1960; Gottesman, 1963*b;* Hirsch, 1962; and McClearn, 1964). Such authors make clear a crucial distinction between the concepts of *genotype* and *phenotype.* Genotype refers to the totality of factors that make up the genetic complement of an individual. Phenotype refers to the totality of physically or chemically observable characteristics of an individual that result from the interaction of his genotype with his environment. Environment must be broadly defined to include not only intrauterine and postnatal conditions but also a host of molecular factors within and between the embryonic cells (Waddington, 1957).

Different genotypes may have the same phenotype, and different phenotypes may be displayed by the same genotypes. A lack of clarity is perpetuated in discussions of individual differences by a failure to specify the environmental circumstances when describing the phenotype of genes. And conversely, the attribution of an effect to an environmental manipulation may be misleading unless the genotype is specified.

Genetically identical Himalayan rabbits, for example, reared under ordinary conditions have a white body with black extremities. When reared in a warm cage, they do not show the black pigment (Sinnott et al., 1958). Phenotypically white rabbits and phenotypically white-plus-black rabbits look different, while having the same genetic constitution, just because the environments to which they have been exposed were different. In an experiment by Freedman (1958) we have a very informative example of the interaction of heredity and environment in four breeds of dogs. Half of each litter was reared under "indulgent" conditions and the other half, "disciplined." Members of these highly inbred litters were as similar to each other as identical twins. At eight weeks of age each pup was tested for inhibition of eating after the person who had reared it had punished it for eating and then left the room. Basenjis ate as soon as the trainer left the room regardless of whether they had been raised in the indulged or disciplined environment. Both groups of Shetland sheep dogs refused the food over the whole test period of eight days. For these two genotypes then, the method of training had no effect, but the two breeds responded in opposite fashion. Beagles and fox terriers, however, divided themselves up neatly according to the method of training; the indulged beagles and terriers were more easily inhibited by the punishment. Freedman concluded that it was the strong constitutional attraction to the trainer interacting with the indulgent treatment that enhanced the effectiveness of later punishment for the beagles and terriers.

One further example from the experimental animal psychology literature emphasizes the crucial need to specify both environments and genotypes. The experiment will also serve as a bridge to a conceptual model of when it is appropriate to emphasize heredity, when it is appropriate to emphasize environment, and when it is appropriate to emphasize their interaction with respect to variability in a trait. Cooper and Zubek (1958) reared six groups of rats who were the thirteenth-generation descendants of animals selected for their ability to solve maze problems. One group each of genetically bright and genetically dull rats (as inferred from their breeding) were reared under three markedly different early environmental regimes.[2] An *enriched* environment was provided by slides, tunnels, balls, bells, and so on, and the cages faced a design-covered wall. A *restricted* environment was provided for the two genotypes by only a food box and water pan with the cages facing a gray wall. Control groups of the brights and dulls were reared in the *natural habitat* of a laboratory rat. At 65 days of age each of the six groups were tested for

_____

[2] Analogous experiments with children cannot ethically be done. Those few children reported in the literature who have been severely neglected cannot be assumed to have been like the average child *before* their exposure to deprivation, for example, feral children.

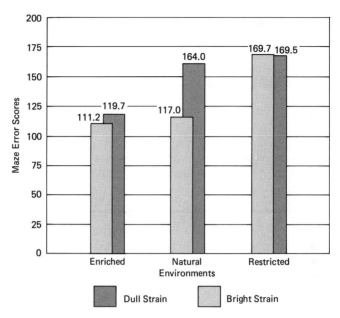

Fig. 2. Maze error scores of genetically bright and dull rats reared in three different environments. (After Pettigrew, 1964)

their problem-solving ability on the Hebb-Williams maze. The results are given in Fig. 2. An enriched early environment led to a considerable improvement over the natural-habitat performance of the dulls but had little noticeable effect upon the brights. [A similar phenomenon has been observed in comparing the effects of preschool attendance on lower- and middle-class children (McNemar, 1945).] A restricted early environment increased the errors of the brights by about 44 percent, but had little or no effect on the dulls.

Under the restricted conditions the results were what might have been expected. Even the animals with the genetic potential for superior performance were prevented from developing their potential by the environmental handicaps. The dull animals were already performing poorly in what was for other animals an adequate environment and had no room for an even poorer performance. It is more difficult to account for the failure of the brights to improve their performance under the enriched conditions. The bright animals would be expected to make better use of the stimulation (Hebb, 1949) with their presumably better cerebral functioning. The authors suggest that the maze test may have been inappropriate for discriminating among levels of superior functioning. That is, if an IQ test had a ceiling of 120, individuals who might score higher than that still obtain scores of 120. Another possibility was that there was not a linear relationship between error reduction and environment. In other words, it might have been much more difficult for the brights to reduce their errors from 120 to 100 than for the dulls to reduce their errors from 165 to 145 even though the absolute reduction was 20 points in each case.

These three experiments with rabbits, dogs, and rats permit us to make some important theoretical generalizations. Given uniformity of trait-relevant environment, almost all the observed phenotypical variance in a trait must stem from variability in the genotypes. Given uniformity in that part of the genotype relevant to the trait under consideration, almost all the observed phenotypical trait variance must stem from variability in the environments. Given heterogeneity for both genotypes and environments—the situation which prevails for human populations—the observed trait variability must be attributed to some combination of genetic and environmental variances.

The question of how much of intelligence is due to heredity and how much to environment is meaningless since neither agent alone can produce the trait. Such phrasing of the question is an important cause of the stalemate that has stifled progress in psychology over the past fifty years. Two answerable questions should be posed in the contemporary concern with the roles played by nature *and* nurture in human behavior: (1) How much of the variability observed within a group of individuals in a specified environment on a particular trait measure is attributable to hereditary differences among them, and (2) how modifiable by systematic environmental manipulation is the phenotypic expression of a trait. A further question is of crucial importance to the basic understanding of human behavior, but it must be deferred until such time as molecular geneticists, developmental biologists, and developmental psychologists are ready to collaborate. This is the question of *how* heredity interacts with the environment to produce trait variation (see Antastasi, 1958*b*). There are no genes *for* any behavior or other phenotypic trait. Genes exert their influence on behavior through their effects at the molecular level of organization. Enzymes, hormones, and neurons may be considered as the sequence of complex path markers between the genes and a behavioral characteristic (Fuller, 1957; Thompson, 1957).

For our purposes then, the best way to conceptualize the contribution of heredity to a trait such as intelligence is to think of heredity as determining a norm of reaction (Dobzhansky, 1955), or of heredity fixing a reaction range. Within this framework, a genotype determines an indefinite but nonetheless circumscribed assortment of phenotypes. Each phenotype corresponds to one of the possible environmental regimes to which the genotype could be exposed. Fuller (1954) has said that heredity is the capacity to utilize an environment in a particular way. Fig. 3 is a schematic presentation of the concept of reaction range for the phenotypic trait of IQ.

Each curve in Fig. 3 can be thought of as representing the response of samples of individuals homogeneous for four different levels of genetic potential who have been exposed to environments ranging from restricted through "natural" to enriched. Allen (1961) has noted that the most probable phenotype of some genotypes may be a deviant one. These genotypes, for

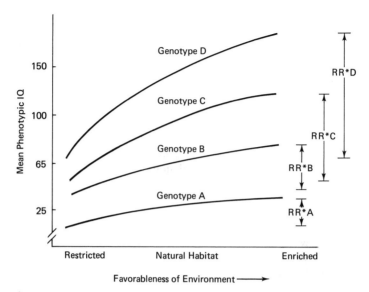

Fig. 3. Scheme of the reaction-range (RR*) concept showing the interaction of heredity and environment. (From *Handbook of Mental Deficiency,* edited by N. Ellis. Copyright © 1963 McGraw-Hill, Inc. Used by permission of McGraw-Hill Book Company)

example Down's syndrome (Mongolism), phenylketonuria, and Huntington's chorea, would produce individuals of normal intellect only in unusual environments, if at all. Such genotypes are associated with autosomal chromosomal aberrations, a pair of recessive genes, and a dominant gene, respectively (Penrose, 1963). Curve Type A with a natural habitat mean IQ less than 40 is intended to represent roughly these classes of individuals who cannot be accounted for by the polygenic model (Gottesman, 1963*b*; Roberts, 1952).[3] The IQ distribution of very large and unselected samples of school children shows a "bump" at the low end; the severely retarded are overrepresented. Curve A individuals are in this bump. Much more frequent, and thus of more importance to the current discussion, are Curves B and C. An infinite number of such curves could be drawn to represent the continuous gradation of genetic potential for intelligence within the continuous range of IQs—50 to 150. Notice that a major difference between A and the other curves is a wider reaction range (*RR*) for the latter; that is, the innate intellectual potential is

[3] The taxonomy of mental retardation is intimately tied to IQ testing of white children and adults. Generalizations to other races or to whites from atypical backgrounds are unwarranted without great caution. Generally, persons with tested IQs under 70 are labeled retarded, and those under 50 as severe or low-grade retarded. IQs under 40 are almost always associated with pathogenic simple dominant or recessive genes, chromosomal errors, and traumatic or infectious brain injury.

more susceptible to upward or downward changes. Another difference is that Curves B, C, and D rise with increasing rates with enriched environments. The first difference is inferred from human and animal data, but the second is largely a speculation. From the overlap in reaction ranges it should be apparent that with no other information than an individual's IQ score, you could not tell whether he was of Genotype B, C, or D. Similarly three individuals with IQs of 80, 100, and 120 could theoretically all be of Genotype C. These two examples are merely a concrete way of saying again that the same phenotype may have different genotypes, and different phenotypes may have the same genotype.

Within the broad range of continuous variation in measured IQ, two aspects of the environment, *favorableness* and *commonness,* are important to the concept of reaction range. By this we mean to imply that each genotype has its own more or less natural habitat, at least in a society that fosters social mobility using ability as the sole criterion. In the light of what has been said in the introduction to this book and the literature on the effects of stimulation in early infancy (Casler, 1961; Riesen, 1961; Thompson and Schaefer, 1961), there is every reason to doubt that a typical Negro infant is reared in a typical white infant's natural habitat. In regard to the character intelligence, a natural habitat would include a normal delivery and freedom from organic impairment, an adequate diet, home rearing by both parents or adequate surrogates, exposure to adequate sensory stimulation, and exposure to an adequate system of compulsory education. One of the assumptions underlying the reaction-range concept is that marked deviation from the natural habitat occurs with a low probability. It is only when two individuals or two groups come from equally favorable environments (the horizontal axis in Fig. 3) that a difference in measured IQ can be interpreted to indicate a difference in genetic potential.

Studies on identical twins reared apart, as mentioned earlier, afford us some insight into the effects of differing environments on the same genotype. This information can permit a rough estimate of the reaction range for average individuals under natural conditions. It is probably not more than 12 IQ points in either direction and most probably less; that is, the vertical distance in the middle part of RR*C in our Fig. 3 covers 24 points. Thus, IQs from 88 to 112 indicate the phenotype of equivalent genotypes under the conditions specified. The data from *MZ* twins reared apart (Shields, 1962) do not correspond to environmental differences much more extreme than those indicated by upper and lower limits of natural habitat in the reaction range scheme. Only fourteen of Shields' forty-four *MZ* pairs reared apart were brought up in unrelated families, and in seven of these fourteen pairs one of the twins was reared by a relative.

Despite the length of this article, it still constitutes only an introduction to the dialectics of heredity and environment. Hopefully the ideas presented have introduced enough information to facilitate a valid perspective on the controversial issues.

GENETIC ASPECTS
OF SOCIAL-CLASS DIFFERENCES

. . . In the prehistory of man, a class system probably evolved after food gathering had been replaced by food producing. An efficient agriculture then elicited the need for labor organization which involved a stratification into leaders and laborers. Sir Cyril Burt, an eminent English psychologist, has made an intensive analysis and a spirited defense of the idea that class differences in intelligence are largely due to genetic variation (1959; 1961). Much stronger views on the subject are advanced by Darlington (1963). It should be possible to examine the merits and degrees of validity of such positions without subscribing to social Darwinism or to the sickness of race and class prejudice (Gottesman, 1963a; 1965).

Support for the view that the structure of modern societies is at least in part dependent on biological phenomena rests on the demonstration that stratification is based on ability and, further, that individual differences in ability are partially genetically conditioned. In a truly democratic system an open-class society (Lerner, 1957) permits the formation of differentiated social classes and, most importantly, fosters class change and mobility. Thus a migration from one class to another based on presence or absence of ability is the final essential requirement for a biologically based model of social structure.

Burt (1959, pp. 23–24) said,

> Roughly speaking . . . the formation of an elite or upper class is determined, in the course of a nation's evolution, chiefly by physical force at the outset, then by blood-relationship, and later by property or wealth, and finally by mental efficiency. Most of the time no doubt each of these factors is operative simultaneously though in varying proportions, and at every stage mental efficiency must have played *some* part; but its importance must have steadily increased until at the present time it now preponderates over the others.

Some degree of class mobility has gone on for the past nine hundred years or so in Great Britain. Wherever class differences in intelligence, as measured by IQ tests, have been examined, a spread between the means of the highest and lowest class has been found. It is very important to specify whether the means are obtained from children classified on the basis of their fathers' occupations or from the adult members of a social class. And if the latter, whether they are the parents of children and thus a group selected for higher intelligence than the childless or unmarried adults in a stratum of the occupational hierarchy (Reed and Reed, 1965).

Data collected by Burt (1961) on intelligence in some 40,000 adults and their children as a function of occupational status are presented in Tables 1 and 2. The information was collected in the Greater London area during the

Table 1   Distribution of Intelligence According to Occupational Class: Adults
(from Burt, 1961)

IQ	Professional Higher I	Professional Lower II	Clerical III	Skilled IV	Semi-skilled V	Unskilled VI	Total
50–60						1	1
60–70					5	18	23
70–80				2	15	52	69
80–90			1	11	31	117	160
90–100			8	51	135	53	247
100–110			16	101	120	11	248
110–120		2	56	78	17	9	162
120–130		13	38	14	2		67
130–140	2	15	3	1			21
140+	1	1					2
Total	3	31	122	258	325	261	1000
Mean IQ	139.7	130.6	115.9	108.2	97.8	84.9	100

period 1913 to 1960. Sample sizes have been made proportional to a base of 1000; the N of 3 (per 1000) for Higher Professionals represents 120 fathers. The row totals reflect the estimated proportions for the total population, for example, only 3 per 1000 adults are actually employed in the Higher Professional category.

Notice that the mean IQs for adults (Table 1) range from 139.7 for Class I to 84.9 for Class VI. Those for the children of these adults (Table 2) show the expected regressions toward the population mean and only range from 120.8 to 92.6. In the United States, military testing in the 1940's of adults classified by occupation showed a range of mean IQs from 120 for Class I to 95 for the lowest class. Mean IQs for the white children used in the 1937 standardization of the Stanford-Binet, classified by their fathers' occupation, ranged from 116 to 96 (Johnson, 1948). The definitions of the occupation classes differ somewhat in the two countries, and Burt's subjects were largely urban.

Tables 1 and 2 provide a great deal of food for thought. It is apparent that the mean IQ of the children in each class is closer to the population mean of 100 than their fathers', and the IQs of the children vary much more than their fathers'. Within the occupational classes the standard deviation for adults is 9.6 contrasted with 14 for their children. The value of the standard deviation is 15 in the total population. Evidence now available shows a constant gradient of high to low IQ for the occupational distribution of IQs from one generation to the next. Thus it must follow that if the children of Table 2 are to have the same distribution of IQs when they grow up as the adults of Table 1, a large number will have to change to a social class different from their fathers'. It should be noted in passing that the intelligent offspring of the dull parents and the dull children of the bright parents are phenomena difficult to account for on an environmental hypothesis of the origin of individual

Table 2 Distribution of Intelligence According to Father's Occupational Class: Children (from Burt, 1961)

IQ	Professional		Clerical	Skilled	Semi-skilled	Unskilled	Total
	Higher I	Lower II	III	IV	V	VI	
50–60					1	1	2
60–70				1	6	15	22
70–80			3	12	23	32	70
80–90		1	8	33	55	62	159
90–100		2	21	53	99	75	250
100–110	1	6	31	70	85	54	247
110–120		12	35	59	38	16	160
120–130	1	8	18	22	13	6	68
130–140	1	2	6	7	5		21
140+				1			1
Total	3	31	122	258	325	261	1000
Mean IQ	120.8	114.7	107.8	104.6	98.9	92.6	100

Table 3 Adults: Percentage in Each Group Whose Intelligence Is Below, Above, or Equivalent to that of Their Occupational Class (from Burt, 1961)

	Below	Equivalent	Above	Number
Class I–III	46.2	45.5	8.3	156
Class IV–V	26.6	50.1	23.3	583
Class VI		73.2	26.8	261
Total population	22.7	55.4	21.9	1000

differences in intelligence. Such findings are, however, completely predictable from the polygenic theory of intelligence (Gottesman, 1963b).

If, for purposes of illustration, we may assume that vocational adaptation depends exclusively on intelligence as measured by tests, many adults in Table 1 have too much or too little intelligence for their roles. In terms of IQ, the borderlines between the occupational classes could be set at 141, 127, 115, 103, and 90. Burt calculated that only 55 percent of the adults were "correctly" placed; 23 percent were above their level and 22 percent were too low. Be that as it may, the great variation among the children of a social-class stratum would make for even greater mismatching if there were no mobility Tables 3 and 4 regroup the adults and children in terms of this "matching." In order to estimate the extent of social mobility for this British population, the task becomes one of estimating the compensating change to bring the frequency distributions for the children of Table 4 in line with that of the adults in Table 3. Burt (1961, p. 17) carried out the task.

Let us look first at the lowest occupational class of all—the unskilled workers (class VI). Among the children, it will be remembered, as many as 57 per cent have an intelligence above what is required for work of this type as against 27 per cent of the adults. . . . Hence (57 — 27) = 30 per cent of the children will presumably move up to a higher occupational class as they grow up. Similarly (75 — 46) = 29 per cent of the upper group—that comprising classes I, II, and III—will move down. In the intermediate group—classes IV and V—the changes both upward and downward will be smaller. Thus, as a comparison of the last lines of the two tables [our Tables 3 and 4] suggests, the over-all mobility will be at least (55 — 33) = 22 per cent. This figure I regard as indicating the minimum amount of mobility—the amount that is required to maintain what (if I may borrow a phrase from the astronomers) might be called a "steady state." It constitutes what may be termed "basic mobility."

Allowing for currently greater permeability of class boundaries through greater availability of higher education, Burt goes on to estimate that the amount of intergenerational mobility must be nearer 30 percent than the derived one of 22 percent.

In comparison to the social structure of Great Britain, the "open class" aspects of democratic society are much more pronounced in the United States. In the mid-1960's more than 40 percent of secondary-school graduates are enrolling in college. It seems logical to expect that intergenerational mobility in our country is greater than 30 percent and is moving toward the theoretical maximum of 66.5 percent suggested by the bottom line of Table 4, at least for our white population.

It is possible to approach this topic from a slightly different point of view, one closer to home. In a society which provides for social mobility, the varieties of genotypes migrate to different strata or social ecological niches by social selection. In this schema the strata are ordered by the single major variable—money-reward. Tryon (1957), a pioneer in American behavior genetics research, outlined the workings of the model:

Individuals receiving the same money-reward but for different kinds of ability tend to gravitate to the same social area. The hierarchy of social strata is determined by the hierarchy of money-reward characteristic of all occupations. The abilities requisite for performance in the different occupations depend upon different sensory-motor components, which are in turn determined by different independent polygenic combinations. Most matings occur within strata so that a correlation among abilities is developed not [only] because there is one general factor underlying achievement in all fields, but because of the selective influence of the common denominator, money-reward, which collects comparable levels of various abilities within the same social strata. [Assortative mating for intelligence averages about an r of 0.50 in many studies. Tryon has found an r of about 0.60 between the social area ratings, i.e., neighborhood status, of spouses even when reared in different cities.] . . . The picture being drawn is a statistical one. It does not assert that all of the genetically controlled constitutional factors responsible for high achievement are confined to the highest social stratum or that all of the factors responsible for low achievement are to be found in the lowest stratum. All factors are to be found in all strata. The strata are believed to differ, however, with respect to the relative frequency with which the factors occur (Hirsch, 1958, pp. 2–3).

Table 4   Children: Percentage in Each Group Whose Intelligence Is Below, Above, or Equivalent to that of Their Father's Occupational Class (from Burt, 1961)

	Below	Equivalent	Above	Number
Class I–III	75.5	16.8	7.7	156
Class IV–V	34.8	34.3	30.9	583
Class VI		42.9	57.1	261
Total population	32.1	33.5	34.4	1000

. . . It would appear that social classes can be profitably construed as Mendelian populations that have diverged genetically and are continuing to do so. The existence of class barriers, however permeable, fosters relative reproductive isolation; yet social mobility permits a constant winnowing for achievement and learning ability. Migration to an appropriate social ecological niche follows. The net result of an open class system with equality of opportunity and assortative mating is to make genetic factors no less important for an understanding of human society than they are for other mammalian species. "Organic diversity is the adaptive response of living matter to the challenge of the diversity of environments" (Dobzhansky, 1962, p. 221).

SIMULTANEOUS CONSIDERATION OF RACE AND CLASS DIFFERENCES

Is it inconsistent to attribute race differences in intelligence to environmental differences but social-class differences to genetic factors? It must be remembered that we are dealing with differences between populations, not between individuals, and that the differences are quantitative, not qualitative.

If we estimate that our species Homo sapiens has been on the face of the earth for the past 500,000 years, detailed knowledge about our existence covers a period of little more than 1 percent of the total time. It was only after the introduction of agriculture and domestic animals in the Neolithic era some 10,000 years ago that two distinctive niches became available. It requires two or more niches, each with its own rate of selection pressure, for a trait such as intelligence to show eventually a divergence in trait frequencies. Only a little more than three hundred generations have passed since the introduction of agriculture. I would posit that the essential ingredients of what we call general intelligence are learning ability and problem solving, and that the two niches, or habitats, did not exert differential selection pressure for intelligence. Some evolutionists (for example, Mayr, 1963) maintain that man has not improved biologically for the past 30,000 years.

For some traits three hundred generations have been sufficient to lead to significant differences. Post (1962a, b; 1964) has examined the literature for population differences in color and acuity deficiencies in vision and for hearing acuity. He found evidence to support the hypothesis that contemporary hunting and gathering cultures have a much lower prevalence of vision and hearing deficiencies than populations removed in time and habitat. In support of the ideas advanced in this chapter, the observed differences were not accounted for by race per se, but by adaptation to a habitat followed by selection. For example, the Chinese, long removed from hunting and gathering, had poor color vision but the American Indian did not, and the Brahmin caste had a higher prevalence of defect than other tested castes.

For general intelligence, then, the selection pressures from one geographical race to another have either not been sufficiently different or have not yet been in effect long enough to lead to significant differences in the genetic basis for this character. However, intelligence can be partitioned into many components. Guilford (1959), a psychological authority on the character of intelligence, suggested that there may be as many as 120 factors or relatively independent components to general intelligence. It is not possible to rule out the possibility that races may differ in the trait (and gene) frequencies for any number of the *factors* of general intelligence. The possibility has yet to be explored and the appropriate tests have yet to be developed.

Within a race or other Mendelian population that has occupational diversity and provides for social mobility, large differences in general intelligence between noncontiguous strata (such as I and III, or II and VI in Table 1) may have an appreciable genetic component. The continuous gene migration together with fairly high degrees of assortative mating yield results somewhat analogous to the high *artificial* selection pressures seen in the improvement of crops and domestic animals. Perhaps the reader will agree that these speculations about the structure of human society are based on a not unreasonable interpretation of the available data.

In summary, it is again relevant to invoke the concept of the reaction range. Given uniformity of trait-relevant environment, almost all the observed phenotypical variance in general intelligence is associated with genotypic differences. Given equivalent genotypes for a particular trait, almost all the observed phenotypical variance must be attributed to environmental differences. Given both genetic and environmental heterogeneity as is most frequent for human populations, trait variability must be attributed to some combination of genetic and environmental differences.

FERTILITY, FITNESS, AND THE FUTURE

Concern over the quality of human populations has been expressed by most scientists who are aware of differential reproduction. By this is meant the observation that all individuals do not contribute the same number of offspring to the next generation. Differential reproduction is the heart of the modern concept of natural selection and hence evolution (Simpson, 1958). Fitness is actually a technical term and is defined completely by the number of offspring left by an individual (or specified group) who survive to the age of reproduction. The value is expressed as a proportion of the population average. Natural selection favors reproductive success without necessarily a regard for general adaptedness (Mayr, 1963). It is for this reason that many scientists have suggested that man take a more active role in controlling his own evolution. Of the many topics that might be discussed in this section, only the relationship between intelligence and family size will be treated, and that only in an introductory fashion. More complete coverage can be found in Anastasi (1956; 1959), Burt (1952), and Spuhler (1963).

Differential fertility was recorded in Europe for urban versus rural and rich versus poor strata of society as early as the 1600's. With the advent of intelligence testing and the construction of valid instruments, surveys relating a child's IQ to the number of his siblings became feasible. It was not until the second Scottish survey of 1947 that such research was done on a truly large scale (see Maxwell, 1954, for references). The results from testing almost every eleven-year-old child in all of Scotland confirmed earlier findings. The more brothers and sisters a child had, the lower was his IQ. The correlation between family size and IQ in various studies clusters around a value of —0.30. From these kinds of evidence, many scientists predicted a gradual decline in the intellectual level of the population of from 2 to 4 IQ points per generation. If true, it meant that the total forces of selection were favoring lower intelligence.

From a comparison of the 1932 Scottish survey with the one done in 1947, it was apparent that not only had the mean IQ not declined, it had undergone a small improvement (for the group test only, not on the Stanford-Binet). Similar findings were reported by Cattell (1951) for English children. A paradox existed and efforts towards its solution finally paid off in the work of Higgins et al. (1962).

Direct studies of the relationship between IQ and fertility had been impossible because early IQ tests were designed for children, and no tested children had been followed to the completion of their reproductive lives. Other commentators had objected to the conclusions about the decline in IQ because a survey of children excludes the unmarried and infertile adults from the data. Other objections were reviewed by Anastasi (1959) but they turn out not to be crucial to the solution of the paradox. Penrose (1948) and Willoughby and Goodrie (1927) entertained models which may have anticipated the data provided by Higgins et al.

The Minnesota geneticists in their monumental study of mental retardation (Reed and Reed, 1965) covering six generations of 289 index families (82,217 persons) directed their attention to fertility and intelligence. They reasoned that if the average intelligence of those who failed to reproduce in each generation was appreciably lower than those who did reproduce, the negative r between family size and IQ could not be valid. Among their total population they had IQ values recorded for 1016 families in which both parents and at least one child had been tested. The parents had been tested when they were schoolchildren. In addition, the investigators had IQ-test data for 884 married siblings of the parents as well as for 66 unmarried and childless siblings of the parental generation.

Table 5   Intelligence of Children and Family Size (after Reed and Reed, 1965)

Family Size	Mean IQ of Children	S.D.[a]	Number of Children
1	106	16	141
2	110	13	583
3	107	14	606
4	109	13	320
5	106	16	191
6	99	20	82
7	93	21	39
8	84	20	25
9	90	18	37
10	62	28	15

[a] S.D., standard deviation.

It should be noted that most of the individuals in this large subsample were unrelated to the original 289 retarded subjects except by marriage. The IQ distribution for the 2032 parents was essentially normal with the mothers' mean equal to 103, and the fathers', equal to 101. The relationship between the IQs and size of family for the 2039 children of the parental sample is shown in Table 5. The results are quite in line with the earlier Scottish and English surveys. Up to a sibship of five, no marked difference exists in the mean IQs of the children. For the entire sample of children, the r between family size and IQ was —0.30.

A direct test of the relationship between IQ of parents and children was then made. The usual correlation of about +0.5 was obtained. The larger families with the lower IQ children were being produced by the lower IQ parents. It is easy to see the relationship between the IQ of parents and the average number of their children (that is, their fertility) in Table 6. Each of the 2032 parents is taken individually and grouped according to IQ ranges that correspond to standard deviations in the normal distribution. The mentally retarded parents, as defined by IQ 70 and below, had an average of 3.81 children. The latter average was by far the highest of any of the parent groups. Does this mean that the dire predictions about the decline of intelligence are indeed coming true? Not quite. At this point the geneticists proceeded to use their unique data on the other siblings in the parental generation.

First the spouses who married into the sibships under study were removed from the analysis. To the remaining parents were added their married brothers and sisters to form a sample of 1900 married siblings. Again the form of distribution of Table 6 was found. Persons under IQ 55 averaged 3.64 children; those from 56 to 70 averaged 2.84; and parents with IQs above 130 averaged 2.96. The key to the mystery must then be associated with the 66 unmarried siblings in the parental generation. When they are added to the 1900 married siblings the distribution of fertility as a function of intelligence

Table 6   Intelligence of Parents and Reproductive Rate (from Reed and Reed, 1965)

IQ of Parent	Number of Parents	Average Number of Children
70 and below	73	3.81 ± 0.32
71–85	180	2.98 ± 0.14
86–100	597	2.65 ± 0.05
101–115	860	2.68 ± 0.04
116–130	287	2.70 ± 0.08
131 and up	35	2.94 ± 0.25
Totals	2032	2.75

changes markedly. Table 7 shows that when *all* the siblings are followed up, the lowest IQ range produced the fewest children and the highest, the most. The average number of children ranged from 1.38 to 2.96. Previously obtained negative correlations of —0.30 between the size of the family and the intelligence of the children disappear when the single siblings are included.

It would thus appear that the net direction of selective forces for intelligence is in a favorable direction for the species. One of the means by which this comes about is for the persons with low IQ to remain unmarried. Reed and Reed (1965) found that only 38 percent of their total sibling group with IQs 55 and below married. Between IQs 56 and 70 the proportion married jumped to 86 percent, still below the remainder of the sample which ranged from 97 percent to 100 percent married. The latter figure of 100 percent married was for the brightest group with IQs 131 and above. The mean IQ for the unmarried siblings was 80, althought it was 100 for the total sample of married siblings.

Other recent work supports the suggestion that the direction of selection for intelligence is not dysgenic. Carter (1962) reports a study by Quensel in Sweden of the fertility and marriage of a large sample of IQ-tested recruits born in 1924. Although none of the men had completed their reproduction at age 29 (when the data were collected), trends were already evident. The

Table 7   Intelligence of All Siblings and Reproductive Rate (from Reed and Reed, 1965)

IQ of Siblings	Number of Siblings	Average Number of Children
55 and below	29	1.38 ± 0.54
56–70	74	2.46 ± 0.31
71–85	208	2.39 ± 0.13
86–100	583	2.16 ± 0.06
101–115	778	2.26 ± 0.05
116–130	269	2.45 ± 0.09
131 and above	25	2.96 ± 0.34
Totals	1966	2.27

dullest group had the highest fertility within marriage, but the lowest proportion married, that is, 57 percent. In a study by Bajema (1963) in a Michigan
city, the completed fertility of all native white subjects (Ss) born in 1916 and
1917 who had reached the beginning of the seventh year of schooling was
examined. The adults had been tested at an average age of 11.6 years. Although the Bajema sample was smaller than that of Higgins et al., the results
are quite close. For IQ-range greater than 130 the average number of children
was 3.00; it dropped to 2.05 for the range 71 to 85 (the 3 subjects under IQ
70 did not reproduce). Relative fitness is defined as the ratio of population
growth rate per individual of a specific IQ group to the same rate for the
optimum phenotype (IQ 120 and above) in the Bajema study. Thus the relative fitness value for the IQ 120 and above group was 1.0; for the IQ-range
69 to 79 it was only 0.58. An intriguing bimodal distribution for IQ and
fertility was found by both the Reeds and Bajema. It should serve as a challenge to other researchers.

 While this brief review of some recent findings on the direction of selection for intelligence may quiet the fears that society is headed for a chaos in
which the dull would inherit the earth, it should not lull us into complacency
about the quality of the species. Five million of the six million retarded persons in the United States are the offspring of a retarded parent or a normal
parent who has a retarded sibling (Reed and Reed, 1965).

A SUMMING UP

 . . . Man is continuing to evolve both culturally and biologically. At the
present time Negro and while differences in general intelligence in the United
States appear to be primarily associated with differences in environmental
advantages. Social-class differences in general intelligence in stratified, open-
class societies appear to be moving in a direction where such differences will
have an appreciable genetic component. Fears about a decline in the population potential for intelligent behavior as a result of differential fertility are
not warranted in the light of recent research. So long as persons at the lower
end of the IQ distribution are at a reproductive disadvantage, that is, less fit,
there will be positive selection for this prized human trait. Evolution should
continue in an adaptive direction.

REFERENCES

Allen, G. Intellectual potential and heredity. Science, 1961, 133, 378–379.
Allison, A. C. Protection afforded by sickle-cell trait against subterian malarial infec-
    tion. British Medical Journal, 1954, 1, 290–292.
Anastasi, Anne. Intelligence and family size. Psychological Bulletin, 1956, 53, 187–209.
Anastasi, Anne. Differential psychology. Ed. 3. New York: Macmillan, 1958a.
Anastasi, Anne. Heredity, environment and the question "how"? Psychological Review,
    1958b, 65, 197–208.

Anastasi, Anne. Differentiating effects of intelligence and social status. *Eugenics Quarterly*, 1959, 6, 84–91.

Bajema, C. Estimation of the direction and intensity of natural selection in relation to human intelligence by means of the intrinsic rate of natural increase. *Eugenics Quarterly*, 1963, 10, 175–187.

Baker, P. T. Racial differences in heat tolerance. *American Journal of Physical Anthropology*, 1958, 16, 287–305.

Barnicot, N. A. Climatic factors in the evolution of human populations. *Cold Spring Harbor Symposia on Quantitative Biology*, 1959, 24, 115–129.

Boyd, W. *Genetics and the races of man*. Boston: Little, Brown, 1950.

Brackbill, Yvonne (ed.). *Research in infant behavior: A cross indexed bibliography*. Baltimore: Williams & Wilkins, 1964.

Burt, C. *Intelligence and fertility: The effect of the differential birth rate on inborn mental characteristics*. London: The Eugenics Society and Cassell & Company, Ltd., 1952.

Burt, C. Class differences in general intelligence: III. *British Journal of Statistical Psychology*, 1959, 12, 15–33.

Burt, C. Intelligence and social mobility. *British Journal of Statistical Psychology*, 1961, 14, 3–24.

Carter, C. O. *Human heredity*. Baltimore: Penguin, 1962.

Casler, L. Maternal deprivation: A critical review of the literature. *Monographs of the Society for Research in Child Development*, 1961, 26, No. 2.

Cattell, R. B. The fate of national intelligence: Test of a thirteen-year prediction. *Eugenics Review*, 1951, 42, 136–148.

Conway, J. Class differences in general intelligence: II. A reply to Dr. Halsey. *British Journal of Statistical Psychology*, 1959, 12, 5–14.

Coon, C. S., S. M. Garn, and J. B. Birdsell. *Races*. Springfield, Ill.: C. C. Thomas, 1950.

Cooper, R., and J. Zubek. Effects of enriched and restricted early environments on the learning ability of bright and dull rats. *Canadian Journal of Psychology*, 1958, 12, 159–164.

Darlington, C. D. "The genetics of society." In A. V. Gregor (ed.), *A symposium on race: An interdisciplinary approach*. Honolulu: Hawaii University Press, 1963.

Dobzhansky, T. *Evolution, genetics, and man*. New York: Wiley, 1955.

Dobzhansky, T. *Mankind evolving*. New Haven, Conn.: Yale University Press, 1962.

Dobzhansky, T., and O. Pavlovsky. An experimental study of interaction between genetic drift and natural selection. *Evolution*, 1957, 11, 311–319.

Donnan, E. Documents illustrative of the history of the slave trade to America. Carnegie Institute Publications, No. 409, Vol. IV, 1935.

Freedman, D. Constitutional and environmental interactions in rearing of four breeds of dogs. *Science*, 1958, 127, 585–586.

Fuller, J. L. *Nature and nurture: A modern synthesis*. New York: Doubleday, 1954.

Fuller, J. L. Comparative studies in behavioral genetics. *Acta Genetica Statistica Medica*, 1957, 7, 403–407.

Fuller, J. L. and W. R. Thompson. *Behavior genetics*. New York: Wiley, 1960.

Garn, S. M. (ed.). *Readings on race*. Springfield, Ill.: C. C. Thomas, 1960.

Garn, S. M. *Human races*. Springfield, Ill.: C. C. Thomas, 1961.

Glass, B. On the unlikelihood of significant admixture of genes from the North American Indians in the present composition of the Negroes of the United States. *American Journal of Human Genetics*, 1955, 7, 368–385.

Glass, B., and C. C. Li. The dynamics of racial intermixture—An analysis based on the American Negro. *American Journal of Human Genetics*, 1953, 5, 1–20.

Gottesman, I. I. Science or propaganda. *Contemporary Psychology,* 1963a, *8,* 381–382.

Gottesman, I. I. "Genetic aspects of intelligent behavior." In N. Ellis (ed.), *Handbook of mental deficiency: Psychological theory and research.* New York: McGraw-Hill, 1963b, 253–296.

Gottesman, I. I. "Personality and natural selection." In S. G. Vandenberg (ed.), *Methods and goals in human behavior genetics.* New York: Academic Press, 1965, 63–80.

Guilford, J. P. Three faces of intellect. *American Psychologist,* 1959, *14,* 469–479.

Hebb, D. *The organization of behavior.* New York: Wiley, 1949.

Herskovits, M. J. *The anthropometry of the American Negro.* New York: Columbia University Press, 1930.

Herskovits, M. J. *The myth of the Negro past.* New York: Harper & Row, 1941.

Higgins, C., and C. H. Sivers. A comparison of Stanford-Binet and Colored Ravens Progressive Matrices IQs for children with low socio-economic status. *Journal of Consulting Psychology,* 1958, *20,* 465–468.

Higgins, J., Elizabeth W. Reed, and S. Reed. Intelligence and family size: A paradox resolved. *Eugenics Quarterly,* 1962, *9,* 84–90.

Hirsch, J. Recent developments in behavior genetics and differential psychology. *Diseases of the Nervous System,* 1958, *19,* No. 7 (Monograph supplement).

Hirsch, J. Individual differences in behavior and their genetic basis. In E. Bliss (ed.), *Roots of behavior.* New York: Harper & Row, 1962, 3–23.

Hunt, E. E. Anthropometry, genetics, and racial history. *American Anthropologist,* 1959, *61,* 64–87.

Hunt, J. M. *Intelligence and experience.* New York: Ronald Press, 1961.

Johnson, D. M. Applications of the standard-score IQ to social statistics. *Journal of Social Psychology,* 1948, *27,* 217–227.

Kennedy, W., V. Van Deriet, and J. White. A normative sample of intelligence and achievement of Negro elementary school children in the southeastern United States. *Monographs of the Society for Research in Child Development,* 1963, *28,* No. 6 (Whole No. 90).

Lerner, M. *America as a civilization.* New York: Simon & Schuster, 1957.

Liverant, S. Intelligence: A concept in need of re-examination. *Journal of Consulting Psychology,* 1960, *24,* 101–110.

Louttit, C. M. *Clinical psychology of exceptional children.* Ed. 3. New York: Harper & Row, 1957.

Maher, B. A. "Intelligence and brain damage." In N. Ellis (ed.), *Handbook of mental deficiency: Psychological theory and research.* New York: McGraw-Hill, 1963, 224–252.

Maxwell, J. Intelligence, fertility and the future. *Eugenics Quarterly,* 1954, *1,* 244–274.

Mayr, E. *Animal species and evolution.* Cambridge, Mass.: Harvard University Press, 1963.

McClearn, G. E. "Genetics and behavior development." In M. L. and Lois W. Hoffman eds.), *Review of child development research.* New York: Russell Sage, 1964, *I,* 433–480.

McNemar, Q. Note on Wellman's reanalysis of IQ changes of orphanage preschool children. *Journal of Genetic Psychology,* 1945, *67,* 215–219.

Meehl, P., and A. Rosen. Antecedent probability and the efficiency of psychometric signs, patterns, or cutting scores. *Psychological Bulletin,* 1955, *52,* 194–216.

Mourant, A. R. *The distribution of the human blood groups.* Oxford, Eng.: Blackwell, 1954.

Mourant, A. R., and I. M. Watkin. Blood groups, anthropology, and language in Wales and the western counties. *Heredity,* 1952, *6,* 13–36.

Neel, J. V. The inheritance of sickle-cell anemia. *Science,* 1949, *110,* 64.

Newman, H., F. Freeman, and K. Holzinger. *Twins: A study of heredity and environment.* Chicago: University of Chicago Press, 1937.

Newman, M. T. Adaptation of man to cold climates. *Evolution,* 1956, *10,* 101–105.

Penrose, L. J. The supposed threat of declining intelligence. *American Journal of Mental Deficiency,* 1948, *53,* 114–118.

Penrose, L. J. *The biology of mental defect.* Ed. 3. New York: Grune & Stratton, 1963.

Pettigrew, T. *A profile of the Negro American.* Princeton, N. J.: Van Nostrand, 1964.

Pollitzer, W. S. The Negroes of Charleston (S. C.): A study of hemoglobin types, serology, and morphology. *American Journal of Physical Anthropology,* 1958, *16,* 241–263.

Pollitzer, W. S., R. C. Hartmann, H. Moore, R. E. Rosenfield, H. Smith, S. Hakim, P. J. Schmidt, and W. C. Leyshon. Blood types of the Cherokee Indians. *American Journal of Physical Anthropology,* 1962, *20,* 33–43.

Post, R. H. Population differences in red and green color vision deficiency: A review and a query on selection relaxation. *Eugenics Quarterly,* 1962a, *9,* 131–146.

Post, R. H. Population differences in vision acuity. *Eugenics Quarterly,* 1962b, *9,* 189–212.

Post, R. H. Hearing acuity variation among Negroes and whites. *Eugenics Quarterly,* 1964, *11,* 65–81.

Reed, Elizabeth W., and S. C. Reed, *Mental retardation: A family study.* Philadelphia: Saunders, 1965.

Riesen, A. H. "Stimulation as a requirement for growth and function in behavioral development." In D. W. Fiske and S. R. Maddi (eds.), *Functions of Varied Experience.* Homewood, Ill.: Dorsey, 1961, 57–80.

Roberts, D. F. The dynamics of racial intermixture in the American Negro—Some anthropological considerations. *American Journal of Human Genetics,* 1955, *7,* 361–367.

Roberts, J. A. F. The genetics of mental deficiency. *Eugenics Review,* 1952, *44,* 71–83.

Shields, J. *Monozygotic twins brought up apart and brought up together.* London: Oxford University Press, 1962.

Shields, J., and I. I. Gottesman. Age at separation and IQ differences in identical twins reared apart. Unpublished manuscript, 1965.

Simpson, G. G. "The study of evolution: Methods and present status of theory." In Anne Roe and G. G. Simpson (eds.), *Behavior and evolution.* New Haven: Yale University Press, 1958, 7–26.

Sinnott, E. W., L. C. Dunn, and T. Dobzhansky. *Principles of genetics.* Ed. 5. New York: McGraw-Hill, 1958.

Spuhler, J. N. "The scope for natural selection in man." In W. J. Schull (ed.), *Genetic selection in man.* Ann Arbor: University of Michigan Press, 1963, 1–111.

Thompson, W. R. Traits, factors, and genes. *Eugenics Quarterly,* 1957, *4,* 8–16.

Thompson, W. R., and T. Schaefer. "Early environmental stimulation." In D. W. Fiske and S. R. Maddi (eds.), *Functions of varied experience.* Homewood, Ill.: Dorsey, 1961, 81–105.

Tryon, R. Behavior genetics in social psychology. *American Psychologist,* 1957, *12,* 453. (Abstract.)

Tyler, Leona E. *The psychology of human differences.* Ed. 3. New York: Appleton-Century-Crofts, 1965.

Waddington, C. H. *The strategy of the genes.* New York: Macmillan, 1957.

Willoughby, R. R., and Mirandi Goodrie. Neglected factors in the differential birth rate problem. *Journal of Genetic Psychology,* 1927, *34,* 373–393.

Workman, P. L., B. S. Blumberg, and A. J. Cooper. Selection, gene migration and polymorphic stability in a U.S. white and Negro population. *American Journal of Human Genetics*, 1963, *15*, 429–437.

GLOSSARY

Admixture—see Gene flow.

Allele—one of two or more alternative forms of a gene, occupying the same locus of paired chromosomes.

Assortative mating—the tendency for like to marry like evidenced by a correlation between mates for some traits, for example, IQ and skin color.

Autosome—chromosomes other than sex-chromosomes; humans have 44 autosomes.

Balanced polymorphism—two or more distinct types of individuals coexisting in the same breeding population. The balance is maintained by the selective advantage of the heterozygote over either homozygote.

Differential reproduction—see also Fitness, Darwinian or biological. Reproduction in which different genotypes do not contribute to the next generation in proportion to their numbers.

Dominance—the expression of a gene even when present in single dose.

Dysgenic—term applied to a trend which may be harmful in the genetic make-up of a population.

Ecological niche—the configuration of environmental factors into which a species or subgroup of humans fits.

Fitness, Darwinian or biological—the number of offspring, left by an individual, who reach the age of reproduction.

Gene flow—also called (gene) migration. The spread of genes from one population to the next as a result of migration of people; it can lead to rapid changes in gene frequency.

Gene frequency—in a population in which two or more alleles of a particular gene occur, the relative proportion of each in the gene pool.

Gene pool—the sum total of genes of a given breeding population at a given time.

Genetic drift—the occurrence of changes in gene frequency not due to selection, mutation, or immigration but to chance; especially noticeable in small isolates.

Genotype—the genetic make-up of an individual; this may refer to one, several, or all loci.

Heterozygote—an individual with different alleles at one or more corresponding loci of the two parental chromosomes.

Homozygote—an individual with identical alleles at one or more loci.

Isolating mechanisms—properties of individuals or niches that prevent or reduce successful interbreeding between members of different populations.

Locus (*pl.* loci)—the position of a particular gene on a chromosome.

Phenotype—the sum total of all observable characteristics of an individual (biochemical, anatomical, physiological, psychological, and so on). It is the result of the interaction of the genotype with the effective environment. Also used to refer to a trait associated with one or many genes.

Polygenic inheritance—inheritance of a trait measured phenotypically in quantitative, as opposed to qualitative, fashion. Many genes (three or more) act independently to produce their effect in a cumulative manner.

Polymorphism—the coexistence of several discontinuous phenotypes or alleles in a breeding population; even the rarest type is more frequent than can be accounted for by mutation.

Polytypic—generally, a species composed of several geographic races or subspecies.

Recessiveness—the failure of a gene to express itself phenotypically when present in single dose; only homozygous individuals show the trait.

Sickle-cell anemia—an anemia due to a hemoglobin mutation and usually lethal to homozygotes. Heterozygotes for the recessive allele have the "sickling trait."

Transient polymorphism—temporary polymorphism observed when one adaptive type is in the process of being replaced by a more adaptive one.

Factors Associated with Impairment of the Early Development of Prematures

M. D. S. Braine, C. B. Heimer,
H. Wortis, and A. M. Freedman

UNIVERSITY OF CALIFORNIA, SANTA BARBARA
AND NEW YORK MEDICAL COLLEGE

INTRODUCTION

This report is based on a longitudinal study of the development of a group of prematurely born infants during the first 15 months of their lives. It provides information on the extent to which impairment of development was related to a number of independent variables, many of which have been suspected of being sources of paranatal brain injury.

· · ·

It is widely rcognized that premature infants are exposed to hazards that are absent or less frequent in full-term infants. Many of these hazards can

Reprinted from *Monograph Society Research Child Development,* copyright © 1966 by The Society for Research in Child Development, Inc., *31,* 1, 5–6, 24–25, 37–38. By permission.

reasonably be anticipated to cause brain damage, but little reliable evidence can be found of precisely which hazards are associated with injury in survivors and how much developmental impairment results.

The study was anterospective. All Negro single births admitted during a certain time period to the premature nursery at Kings County Hospital, Brooklyn, New York, automatically became subjects if they fulfilled certain requirements. A randomly selected reference group of term babies born at the same hospital was also followed but was re-examined less frequently. The original impetus to the study was the desire to evaluate the sequelae of elevated neonatal bilirubin levels in a group of infants in whom the hyperbilirubinemia was not confounded with erythroblastosis. However, it was quickly realized that to achieve this goal the sequelae of other complications that are probably confounded with hyperbilirubinemia (e.g., hypoxia associated with respiratory distress) would also have to be investigated. Information on other variables (e.g., maternal complications) proved to be readily accessible in other hospital departments and permitted the effects of these variables to be investigated at little or no extra cost. The study thus developed into a general exploration of possible sources of impairment of the development of premature infants.

The independent variables were of three types: general (sex and birth weight), insult, and sociocultural. Sex and birth weight require little discussion. Since sex differences have been reported by others (Thurston, Graham, Ernhart, Eichman, & Craft, 1960) and were suggested at an early stage in this study, data are generally presented for each sex individually. Birth weight was used as an index of degree of prematurity, and the amount of correlation between birth weight and scores on standardized developmental tests is reported.

THE SUBJECTS

Definition of the Premature and Term Samples

The prematures.   Between October 1956 and June 1958, all Negro single births admitted to Kings County Hospital Premature Nursery who weighed 2100 grams or less at birth, were automatically followed if they survived 24 hours and if a Coombs test and a test for ABO incompatibility provided no evidence of blood-group sensitization.[1] Between October 1958 and June 1959, only Negro single births weighing 1250 grams or less were followed (again, if they survived 24 hours and if there was no evidence of sensitization). This group was added to increase the number of infants of very low birth weight.

The group defined by the above conditions comprised 406 infants. Of

---

[1] White single births and twins were also followed but are not reported here. The Negro single births constituted a large socioculturally fairly homogeneous group, whereas the white infants were many fewer in number and had a wide range of social-class backgrounds. Analysis of data on the twins posed special problems because the degree of prematurity is less predictable from the birth weight.

these, 55 died in the premature nursery. A further five acquired a neurological disease after discharge from the nursery and are omitted from all statistics presented. The remaining 346 infants, 157 males and 189 females, constituted the premature sample; 331 were still alive at the end of the testing period.

The term infants. The term infants were full-term Negro single births born at Kings County Hospital. The selection was random, although requirements were set that each infant weigh more than 2500 grams, be the product of a normal labor and delivery, not require resuscitation or show clinical signs of respiratory distress, and show no serologic evidence of sensitization because of blood-group incompatibility. The term sample comprised 50 infants with birth weights ranging from 2500 to 4700 grams. None died during the period covered by this report.

Social Background of the Subjects

Kings County Hospital in Brooklyn serves the medically indigent of an area that includes sections with a large Negro population, and with lower median incomes and higher population densities than those prevalent in Brooklyn. The rates of prematurity and infant mortality in Bedford, the area where the majority of the subjects lived, are the highest in the borough (Community Council of Greater New York, 1959).

Of the mothers, 70 per cent were born outside New York State, usually in the rural South, and over 40 per cent had lived in New York City for less than 10 years. No prenatal care at all was received by 20 per cent, and a further 30 per cent did not start prenatal care until the third trimester of pregnancy. In general, the social characteristics of the families were those of a low social-class group. Less than 30 per cent of the mothers had graduated from high school. More than one-third were not married to the infant's father, and 25 per cent had never been married. Less than 60 per cent lived in a husband-wife family, over 30 per cent living in families with a female head, usually the mother herself. Nearly 40 per cent lived in households in which the crowding index was more than 1.5 persons per room. About half the mothers had worked during their pregnancy, almost always as factory or domestic workers. The median family income, less than $4,000 in 1957, was close to that prevalent in Bedford. Public Assistance supported 19 per cent of the families at the time of the infants' births. At the time of their first birthdays, 88 per cent of the infants were living with their mothers, and 12 per cent lived elsewhere. Often several persons had been responsible at different times for the infant's daily care, only 60 per cent having been cared for by the mother continuously. The social backgrounds of the subjects are discussed in more detail elsewhere (Wortis, Bardach, Cutler, Rue, & Freedman, 1963; Wortis, Heimer, Braine, Redlo, & Rue, 1963).

No evidence was found of a difference between the premature and term samples in social-background characteristics. Specific evidence of similarity is presented later.

• • •

THE DEPENDENT VARIABLES

Schedule of Examinations

Of the five developmental examinations designed, all were scheduled for the premature sample but only two for the full-term infants (the "4-day" and the "13½-month" examinations). At each examination, children were seen as close to a specified "target" age as was administratively possible, and several different measures were obtained. These measures constitute the dependent variables.

The staff members performing the examinations rarely knew whether a particular paranatal complication had been present. The peak neonatal serum bilirubin level was always unknown; the other complications were known only to pediatric staff members who examined the child before his discharge from the Premature Center.

The schedule was as follows:

1. The 4-day examination. On the third, fourth, or fifth day of life, gross motor behavior was examined, and measures were obtained of the strength of the grasp reflex and the completeness and normality of the Moro reflex. Anthropometric measures and physical and neurological assessments were also made, but these data are not presented here. Both premature and term babies were examined.

2. The 6-week examination. The prematures were examined at this age so that the average corrected chronological age (CCA) for the group would be about 40 weeks after conception. The examination covered the same areas of development as the 4-day examination. Some of the examinations were done in the nursery, others in the well-baby clinic; 93 per cent of the subjects tested were between five and seven weeks of age.

3. The 4-month examination. In addition to assessments of gross motor development, grasp reflex, and Moro, obtained as in the earlier examinations, a test of the adequacy of visual fixation and following was administered. The examinations were conducted in the well-baby clinic. Ninety per cent of the subjects examined were between 15 and 19 weeks of age.

4. The 7½-month examination. Gross motor development was again assessed, and the Cattell Infant Intelligence Scale was administered. The subjects were examined in the well-baby clinic; 93 per cent of those examined were between 30 and 35 weeks of age.

5. The 13½-month examination. A "target" age of 13½ months was chosen so that the average CCA for the prematures would be about one year. The examination comprised a further assessment of gross motor development and the administration of the Cattell Infant Scale. Both the premature and term babies were examined. A special effort was made to see every infant possible by special appointment, either in a testing room set aside for the purpose or, if necessary, at home. Of the subjects examined, 92 per cent were between 12 and 15 months old. The term babies were examined somewhat closer to their first birthday than were the prematures.

Measures of Behavior Obtained
General characteristics. The tests may be divided into two classes: *(a)* standardized tests and *(b)* measures devised for this study. For the standardized tests, there already existed a scoring system and general norms, but for the devised measures it was necessary to work out a scoring system and a method of making adjustments to take account of variations in CCA.

The tests fell into three general content areas: *(a)* assessments of the grasp and Moro reflexes (devised for the study); *(b)* measures of gross motor development (devised tests were given at the first four examinations, and a standardized test was given at the 13½-month examination); *(c)* measures of cognitive and mental functions—a test of visual fixation and following, devised for use at the 4-month examination, and a standardized infant "intelligence" test, used at 7½ and 13 months.

• • •

RESULTS: DEVELOPMENTS IN RELATION TO BIRTH WEIGHT, SEX, AND SOCIAL VARIABLES

Impairment Correlated with Prematurity
Because of the nature of the deviation scores in the tests devised for the study, the relation of developmental status to birth weight can be reported only for the standardized tests, that is, for the gross motor DQ at 13½ months and for the Cattell scale DQ's at 7½ and 13½ months. The premature and term groups can be directly compared only on the test at 13½ months, since these were the only standardized tests received by both groups.

The relation of motor and mental development at 13½ months to birth weight in each sex is shown in Fig. 1. Within the male premature group at this age, a significant correlation was found between birth weight and both motor ($r = .30$, $N = 84$, $p < .01$) and mental ($r = .26$, $N = 103$, $p < .01$) development. In the female premature group, there was a moderate but significant relation between birth weight and motor development ($r = .31$, $N = 122$, $p < .001$), but the correlation with mental development ($r = .14$, $N = 145$, $p < .05$) was surprisingly low, although just significant. (Significance levels are for one-tailed tests.)

Comparisons between the full-term and premature groups of each sex revealed significant differences between the mean quotients of the male prematures, taken as a group, and the full-term infants for both motor (17.3 DQ points, $p < .01$) and mental (12.1 DQ points, $p < .01$) development, favoring the full-term infants. For the female groups, the full-term infants were significantly superior to the prematures in motor development (14.8 DQ points, $p < .001$), but the difference in mental development (6.5 DQ points,

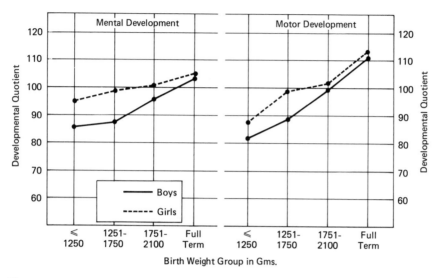

Fig. 1. Mean quotients for mental and motor development at 13½ months of age. Computations of DQ are based on corrected age to remove effects merely due to differences in chronological maturity. From left to right, the mental DQ's are based on 13, 36, 54, and 19 boys, and 26, 39, 80, and 21 girls; and the motor DQ's on 11, 28, 45, and 19 boys, and 24, 31, 67, and 22 girls.

in favor of the term infants) was not significant. When the mean Cattell scale DQ's of the female weight groups were compared with each other, no significant differences were found between the term infants and either the high (1751–2100 grams) or middle (1251–1750 grams) weight premature groups; however, the mean DQ of the low-weight female group (under 1250 grams) was lower than that for both the term infants and the high-weight premature group ($p < .01$, in both cases).

Thus it appears that in the male prematures both motor and mental development at 13½ months were impaired relative to the full-term infants, with the average degree of impairment for the group proportional to the degree of prematurity (or inversely proportional to the birth weight). In the female prematures, there was a similar impairment proportional to the degree of prematurity in gross motor development, but the relation of prematurity to mental development was weaker—only the lowest weight group appeared to be impaired relative to the term infants.

The relation of the Cattell scale DQ at 7½ months to birth weight is shown in Fig. 2.[2] The correlations of this measure with birth weight ($r = .29$

[2] The fact that data are not available for a term Negro group makes the absolute values of the scores not readily interpretable. That the less impaired groups scored above 100 is consistent with other evidences that culturally deprived groups, for example, U. S. accelerated early development and fall behind later.
Negro (Gilliland, 1949) and underprivileged Russian (Dubnoff, 1938), may show a slightly

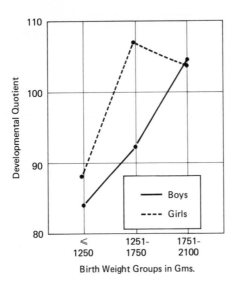

Fig. 2. Mean Cattell scale DQ's at 7½ months of age. Computations are based on corrected age. The points (from left to right) are based on 6, 12, and 18 boys, and 13, 12, and 22 girls.

in both sexes, $p < .05$, one-tailed tests) were based on many fewer subjects (36 males and 47 females) than for the 13½-month test, so that higher values were required for statistical significance. It can be seen from Fig. 2 that the pattern of the relation of DQ to birth weight at 7½ months was similar to that found for the same test at 13½ months: an impairment proportional to the degree of prematurity in the males, and in the females, a deficit demonstrable only in the extreme prematures.

Figures 1 and 2 indicate that the average amount of impairment associated with prematurity was substantial. In gross motor development, the mean difference between the extreme prematures (under 1250 grams) and the term infants amounted to 29.5 and 25.9 DQ points in the males and females, respectively. On the Cattell scale at 13½ months, the analogous differences were 17.4 and 10.7 points. On the Cattell scale at 7½ months, the average differences between the low- and high-weight premature groups were 20.7 and 15.0 points, respectively.

Figures 3 and 4 show the DQ distributions at 13½ months with the numerically small low- and middle-weight premature groups combined. Notwithstanding the decrements in the lower-weight groups, the distributions indicate considerable variability among the children, with many high-weight infants doing poorly and low-weight infants doing well. The distributions have a fairly similar shape in all groups, although motor development was significantly more variable (by F test on the variances for each of the premature sex groups) and perhaps more skewed than mental development.

The distribution for the most premature groups (under 1750 grams.) tended as a whole to be shifted somewhat to the left of that for the high-weight premature group, which in turn was usually displaced slightly to the left of the term group. There was also a small number of very low-scoring

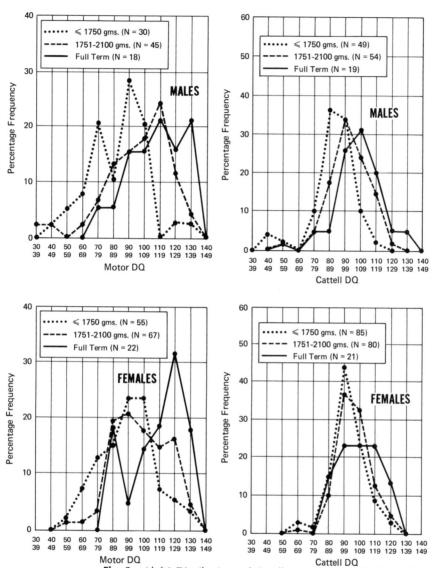

Fig. 3. (left) Distributions of Gesell gross motor DQ's from the 13½-month examination for various birth-weight groups.

Fig. 4. (right) Distributions of Cattell scale DQ's from the 13½-month examination for various birth-weight groups.

subjects at the lower end of the scales. The tendency for the distributions to shift downward with increasing prematurity was somewhat clearer in the males than in the females, and for motor than for mental development. The figures clearly indicate that the poorer average scores of the children of lower birth weight not only resulted from the presence of a few greatly impaired subjects in an other wise intact group, but, also, from a small downward shift of the group as a whole. The impairment correlated with low birth weight appears, therefore, not to be an all-or-none phenomenon.

In the absence of alternative interpretations, the described differences among the groups are attributed to the presence of brain damage among the prematures and of more injury among the prematures of low than of high birth weight. Social variables did not distinguish the term from the premature infants and did not correlate with birth weight in the prematures; therefore, any relations between social variables and test scores does not change the interpretation.

Impairment Correlated with Socio-Environmental Variables

In principle, an environmental effect may act either prenatally through the uterine environment or postnatally. Since a child must presumably live in an environment for some time in order to experience its influence, a postnatal effect would be more likely to appear only at the later examinations. The effects of some forms of brain damage may also be delayed.

In the prematures, the correlations of the two socio-environmental variables with the measures of motor and cognitive development are not shown because most of the coefficients were close to zero. As expected, no evidence of a relation between these variables and developmental scores appeared for the early examinations (4 days, 6 weeks, and 4 months). Further, the correlations provided no evidence for a relation between socio-environmental variables and developmental scores in the girls at any examination. However, in the boys at the 7½- and 13½-month examinations, all eight correlations of the two environmental variables with the two motor and the two cognitive tests were positive (varying from .01 to .32), and the correlation between mother's education and the 13½-month Cattell scale score ($r = .29$) was significant at the .01 level (two-tailed test). Table 1 shows the average DQ's at 13½ months for the various levels of the social variables in the males. Although the correlations between the environmental variables and motor development in the males did not reach significance, Table 1 suggests that both environmental variables were related to motor as well as to mental development.

Sex Differences in the Amount of Impairment

Figures 1 and 2 show that the males rather consistently obtained poorer scores than the females. In the case of the middle- and low-weight premature groups particularly, the differences were relatively large. To test the significance of sex difference in the prematures, an analysis of covariance was performed, partialling out birth weight that covaried with DQ. The F ratios obtained were statistically significant for motor development ($p < .05$) and

Table 1 Average Test Scores at 13½ Months of Age for the Premature Male Infants as a Function of the Environmental Variables

Environmental Rating	Motor Development		Mental Development	
	N	DQ	N	DQ
Mother's education:				
Six years or less	7	82.9	7	79.0
7–8 years	13	90.3	15	86.4
Some high school	36	95.0	44	93.6
High school graduate	16	96.7	23	94.1
Some college	5	98.6	7	95.7
Social status:				
Rating 0	7	86.3	7	86.3
Rating 1	18	89.8	19	89.8
Rating 2	36	95.0	46	92.9
Rating 3	17	98.2	21	91.7
Rating 4	5	99.4	6	91.8

Note: Five group means will fall in an anticipated order from lowest to highest only once in 120 times by chance.

the Cattell scale at 13½ months ($p < .001$) but did not reach significance for the Cattell scale at 7½ months. Thus the male prematures obtained, weight for weight, significantly lower scores than the females in both mental and motor development tests at the 13½-month examination. In the term infants, the differences between the boys and girls were very small and not significant, although the differences that did exist were in favor of the females. No one, to the writers' knowledge, has ever reported significant sex differences in motor and cognitive functions in normal children at this age for either white or Negro groups.

The sex difference was thus negligible in the term infants, and, in the prematures, for whom the difference was statistically significant, it appeared to be greater in the middle- and low-weight groups than in the high-weight group, that is, the sex difference was greatest in those groups with the most impairment of functioning. . . .

One of the original hypotheses was that a poor environment may be selectively handicapping to children with some degree of cerebral injury. This hypothesis implies that the environmental variables affect development only, or primarily, in groups of infants in whom there is reason to suspect a substantial amount of brain injury, that is, the 13½-month test scores should be more affected by the poorer environments in the low- and middle-weight male infants than in the high-weight male infants. In the females, the only group in which there was evidence of much impairment was the low-weight group; for them, therefore, relations between the environmental variables and the test scores should be comparable to those in the low- and middle-weight male groups, whereas relations should be small or absent in the middle- and high-weight female groups that appeared to be relatively intact.

To make a satisfactory test of this pattern of relations, it was desirable to find an environmental variable that would relate more linearly and strongly to development than either of the present variables. A new scale was constructed that combined social status and educational ratings in such a way that heavy numerical weight would be given to the extremes of poverty and poor education. The scale measured only the extent to which families were below average on either or both of the original environmental variables.

The new measure was constructed as follows: Any child who rated average or above on both variables (i.e., whose mother entered high school, or whose family obtained a social-status rating of 2 or over) was given a rating of 4 on the new measure; the rating of 4 was reduced by 1 point if the social-status rating had been 1 and by 2 points if it had been 0; 1 point was also subtracted if the mother had not entered high school, and 2 points if she had failed to complete the elementary grades. Since the group as a whole was an underprivileged one, all families with less than the maximum rating on the new measure were considered underprivileged, even by the standards of the Brooklyn slums. For this reason, the measure was called the "Extreme Underprivilege Index." Since most families had been average or above average on each of the original variables, the distribution of ratings on the new index was J-shaped as a little more than half the subjects obtained the highest ratings. Ratings on the new index were not significantly correlated with birth weight in either sex, nor with any of the insult variables, except for a somewhat increased frequency of toxemia of pregnancy among the mothers of the boys ($r = -.23, p < .05$).

Since the construction of the Extreme Underprivilege Index was based on the information in Table 1, a high correlation between the index and motor and mental development in the males is guaranteed and, therefore, has no logical significance. However, nothing in the construction of the scale would lead to a higher relation for low rather than high birth weight in the males, or to any such expectation for the females. The correlations between the index and the 13½-month developmental measures are shown for the various sex and birth-weight groupings in Table 2. It can be seen that, for both sexes, poorer scores tended to be correlated with extreme underprivilege in just those groups for which there was good evidence of neurological damage.

Since the index was not associated with birth weight, the pattern of correlations in Table 2 indicates some effect of the environment on the more premature children: Low birth weight and social factors in some way interacted in the production of deficits. Since the results were predicted from the hypothesis that a poor environment is selectively handicapping to the brain-injured child, they provide support for this explanation of the environmental effect. However, there are other possible explanations: The results themselves do not specify when the environmental effect took place, and conceivably it took place *in utero*, that is, extreme underprivilege may have been associated with more brain injury in susceptible groups, rather than with a negative influence on development. Thus, poor nutrition, lack of

Table 2 Degree of Correlation of Extreme Underprivilege with Motor and Mental Development at 13½ Months in Various Sex and Birth-Weight Groups

Birth-Weight Group (gms.)	Motor Development			Mental Development		
	N	r	p	N	r	p
≤ 1250:						
M	11	.49	.06	12	.43	.08
F	20	.31	.09	22	.32	.07
M and F	31	.42	< .05	34	.45	< .01
1251–1750:						
M	24	.20	. . .	30	.58	< .001
F	31	.02	. . .	36	.10	. . .
1751–2100:						
M	42	.14	. . .	53	.11	. . .
F	64	− .01	. . .	76	.02	. . .
Term: M and F	40	− .08	. . .	39	.08	. . .

Note: Significance levels are for two-tailed tests.

prenatal care, or other factors associated with extreme poverty and poor education may have led to making an infant more vulnerable to the hazards of extreme prematurity. It is also possible that the environment acted, at least in part, to increase the incidence of maternal toxemia. A low, but significant, correlation between extreme underprivilege and toxemia was noted in the mothers of the boys, and evidence is presented later for some correlation between maternal toxemia and injury to the infant, at least in the lower-weight male infants.

DISCUSSION

The findings of developmental differences between the term and premature infants, and of significant relations in the prematures between birth weight or degree of prematurity and later developmental status, are consistent with the results of a number of previous studies that were reviewed. They reported mental retardation and a variety of deficits in prematures as compared with term infants; some, like the present study, found significant linear relations between the amount of impairment and the degree of prematurity.

The distributions of the scores found in our study indicate that the impairment associated with low birth weight is not an all-or-none phenomenon: There appears to be a continuum, rather than serious injury and overwhelming impairment to a few children with the remainder intact. This result is consistent with the concept of a continuum of reproductive casualty (Knobloch, Pasamanick, Harper, & Rider, 1959). The findings may be compared with those reported recently by Graham et al. (1962) for anoxia in the newborn. They found that anoxia was associated with a slight reduction in 3-year intelligence in most subjects, rather than with deficits that were severe but confined to a few children.

The quite large sex difference in the degree of impairment associated with prematurity has not been directly reported by other authors. It is not clear, however, how seriously previous data have been examined from this point of view, since in reports of average performances of different weight groups the sexes were combined prior to computing the average. Asher and Roberts (1949) reported four times as many children of low birth weight among mentally subnormal as among mentally normal children; since "low birth weight" was defined by them as 1247 grams for girls and 1474 grams for boys, the differential impairment rate for the sexes is implicit.

The sex difference in amount of impairment associated with prematurity is consistent with the well known fact that neonatal mortality is substantially greater among male than female prematures. These mortality differences cannot readily be explained by assuming that male infants are less mature (at least chronologically), since evidence presented earlier indicates little difference in gestation periods. It seems, therefore, that, weight for weight, more male than female prematures fail to survive and that those that do show evidence of more neurological damage later. The data on the incidence of the nursery and maternal complications presented earlier indicate that among survivors there were no significant differences between the sexes in either the incidence or average severity of any of the complications. If it may be assumed that the insult variables chosen for study were the relevant ones, and that the measures were adequate, then the males were not more exposed to paranatal insult than the females. The sex difference in amount of impairment appears, therefore, to indicate a greater vulnerability to insult, rather than an increased exposure, in the males. Greater impairment in males than females has been shown to occur following risks other than prematurity: It has been demonstrated for erythroblastosis fetalis by Allen and Diamond (1954), and more recently by Thurston et al. (1960) as the sequel to a variety of paranatal complications. Whether the apparently greater vulnerability of the males holds for all insults or only for some is discussed later.

The data for the social variables suggest that within this low socio-economic class, a poorer environment contributed to the impairment shown by the prematures, but its effects were conditional on other variables. No effects were found in the term infants or in the more intact high-birth-weight prematures. An association was found only in the lowest weight groups and in the male middle-weight group, the groups in which some degree of damage appeared to be fairly widespread. In these groups, only scores on the later examinations were affected. It is not clear from the data whether the poor environment acted by potentiating the effects of brain injury, that is, by selectively handicapping the development of children who already had some cerebral damage, or whether it acted prenatally by actually increasing the amount of brain injury (or, of course, in both ways). The fact that relations appeared only on the later examinations may seem to favor the first interpretation, but it is also possible that the effects of some brain injuries do not manifest themselves on early developmental examinations. Whatever the nature of the environmental effect, extreme levels of underprivilege appear to have been required to produce it.

REFERENCES

Allen, F. R., Jr., & Diamond, L. K. Prevention of kernicterus: management of erythroblastosis fetalis according to current knowledge. *Journal of the American Medical Association*, 1954, *155*, 1209–1213.

Alm, I. *The long term prognosis for prematurely born children.* Uppsala: Almquist & Wiksell's Bocktryckeri Ab., 1953.

Apgar, J., Girdany, B. R., McIntosh, R., & Taylor, H. C., Jr. Neonatal anoxia. I. A study of the relation of oxygenation at birth to intellectual development. *Pediatrics*, 1955, *15*, 653–68.

Asher, C., & Roberts, J. A. F. A study of birthweight and intelligence. *British Journal of Social Medicine*, 1949, *3*, 56–68.

Baird, D. The influence of social and economic factors on still-births and neonatal deaths. *Journal of Obstetrics and Gynaecology of the British Empire*, 1945, *52*, 217–234.

Bauman, W. A. Early feeding of dextrose and saline solution to premature infants. *Pediatrics*, 1960, *26*, 756–761.

Bauman, W. A., & Nadelhaft, J. Chest radiography of prematures. *Pediatrics*, 1958, *21*, 813–824.

Bayley, N. On the growth of intelligence. *American Psychologist*, 1955, *10*, 805–818.

Bayley, N., & Jones, H. E. Environmental correlates of mental and motor development: a cumulative study from infancy to six years. *Child Development*, 1937, *8*, 329–341.

Benton, A. Mental development of prematurely born children. *American Journal of Orthopsychiatry*, 1940, *10*, 719–745.

Billing, B. H., & Lathe, G. H. The excretion of bilirubin as ester glucuronide giving the direct van der Bergh reaction. *Biochemical Journal*, 1956, *63*, 6–9.

Blegen, S. D. The premature child. The incidence, etiology, mortality and the fate of the survivors. *Acta Paediatrica*, 1953, *42*, Suppl. 88.

Bound, J. P., & Telfer, T. F. Effect of vitamin K dosage on plasma—bilirubin levels in premature infants. *Lancet*, 1956, *270*, 720–722.

Braine, M. D. S. The ontogeny of certain logical operations; Piaget's formulation examined by nonverbal methods. *Psychological Monographs*, 1959, *73*, No. 5 (Whole No. 475).

Brown, A. K., & Zuelzer, W. W. Studies in hyperbilirubinemia. I. Hyperbilirubinemia of the newborn unrelated to isoimmunization. *American Journal of Diseases of Childhood*, 1957, *93*, 263–273.

Cattell, P. *The measurement of intelligence of infants and young children.* New York: Psychological Corp., 1940.

Community Council of Greater N. Y. *Brooklyn communities, population characteristics and neighborhood social resources.* New York: The Council, 1959, Vol. 1.

Cutler, R., Heimer, C. B., Wortis, H., & Freedman, A. M. The effects of prenatal and neonatal complications on the development of premature children at age ½ years. *Journal of Genetic Psychology*, in press.

Dann, M., Levine, S. Z., & New, E. The development of prematurely born children with birth weights or minimal postnatal weights of 1,000 grams or less. *Pediatrics*, 1958, *22*, 1037–1053.

Darke, R. A. Late effects of severe asphyxia neonatorum: preliminary report. *Journal of Pediatrics*, 1944, *24*, 148–158.

Day, R. L. Inhibition of brain respiration in vitro by bilirubin: reversal of inhibition by various means. *Proceedings of the Society of Experimental Biology and Medicine,* 1954, *85,* 261–264.

Day, R. L. Kernicterus, *Pediatrics,* 1956, *17,* 925–928.

Day, R. L., & Johnson, L. Kernicterus. In L. M. Tocantins (Ed.), *Progress in hematology.* Vol. 2. New York: Grune & Stratton, 1959.

Deaver, G. C. Etiological factors in cerebral palsy. *Bulletin of the New York Academy of Medicine,* 1952, *28,* 532–536.

Dine, M. S. Hyperbilirubinemia in the new born premature infant. *American Journal of Diseases of Childhood,* 1954, *88,* 810–811.

Douglas, J. W. B. Some factors associated with prematurity. The results of a national survey. *Journal of Obstetrics and Gynaecology of the British Empire,* 1950, *57,* 143–170.

Douglas, J. W. B. Mental ability and school achievement of premature children at 8 years of age. *British Medical Journal,* 1956, *1,* 1210–1214.

Douglas, J. W. B., & Mogford, C. Health of premature children from birth to four years. *British Medical Journal,* 1953, *1,* 748–754.

Drillien, C. M. Growth and development in a group of children of very low birth weight. *Archives of Diseases of Childhood,* 1958, *33,* 10–18.

Drillien, C. M. A longitudinal study of the growth and development of prematurely and maturely born children. III. Mental development. *Archives of Diseases of Childhood,* 1959, *34,* 37–45. (a)

Drillien, C. M. A longitudinal study of the growth and development of prematurely and maturely born children. IV. Morbidity. *Archives of Diseases of Childhood,* 1959, *35,* 210–217. (b)

Dubnoff, B. A comparative study of mental development in infancy. *Journal of Genetic Psychology,* 1938, *53,* 67–73.

Eastman, N. J. Prematurity from the viewpoint of the obstetrician. *American Practitioner,* 1947, *1,* 343–352.

Ernster, L., Herlin, L., & Zetterstrom, R. Experimental studies on the pathogenesis of kernicterus. *Pediatrics,* 1957, *20,* 647–652.

Evans, P. R. Antecedents of infantile cerebral palsy. *Archives of Diseases of Childhood,* 1948, *23,* 213–219.

Fraser, N. S., & Wilks, J. The residual effects of neonatal asphyxia. *Journal of Obstetrics and Gynaecology of the British Empire,* 1959, *66,* 748–752.

Gesell, A., & Amatruda, C. S. *Developmental diagnosis.* New York: Hoeber, 1947.

Gilliland, A. R. Environmental influences on infant intelligence test scores. *Harvard Educational Review,* 1949, *19,* 142–146.

Gluck, L., & Silverman, W. A. Phagocytosis in premature infants. *Pediatrics,* 1957, *20,* 951–957.

Gorten, M. K., Shear, S., Hodson, M., & Bessman, S. P. Complications of hyperbilirubinemia in the newborn—possible relation to the metabolism of ammonia. *Pediatrics,* 1958, *21,* 27–39.

Graham, F. K., Ernhard, C. B., Thurston, D., & Craft, M. Development three years after perinatal anoxia and other potentially damaging newborn experiences. *Psychological Monographs,* 1962, *76,* No. 3 (Whole No. 522).

Graham, F. K., Pennoyer, M. M., Caldwell, B. M., Greenman, M., & Hartmann, A. F. Relationship between clinical status and behavior test performance in a newborn group with histories suggesting anoxia. *Journal of Pediatrics,* 1957, *50,* 177–189.

Greenspan, L., & Deaver, G. C. The clinical approach to the etiology of cerebral palsy. *Archives of Physical Medicine,* 1953, *34,* 478–485.

Hansman, C. F., & Maresh, M. M. A longitudinal study of skeletal maturation. *American Journal of Diseases of Childhood,* 1961, *101,* 305–319.

Harris, R. C., Lucey, J. F., & MacLean, J. R. Kernicterus in premature infants associated with low concentration of bilirubin in the plasma. *Pediatrics,* 1958, *21,* 875–884.

Heimer, C. B., Cutler, R., & Freedman, A. M. The neurologic sequelae of premature birth. *American Journal of Diseases of Childhood,* 1964, *108,* 122–133.

Holman, G. H. Studies on physiologic hyperbilirubinemia of Negro and white premature infants. *Pediatrics,* 1958, *22,* 1115–1133.

Hugh-Jones, K., Slack, J., Simpson, E., Grossman, A., & Hsia, D. Y-Y. Clinical course of hyperbilirubinemia in premature infants. A premiliary report. *New England Journal of Medicine,* 1960, *263,* 1223–1229.

Ingram, T. T. S., & Russell, E. M. The reproductive histories of mothers of patients suffering from congenital diplegia. *Archives of Diseases of Childhood,* 1961, *36,* 34–41.

James, J. A. The later health of premature infants: a field for further study. *Pediatrics,* 1958, *22,* 154–160.

Johnson, L. N., Figueroa, E., Garcia, M. L., & Newmark, H. The effect of certain substances on bilirubin levels and occurrence of kernicterus in jaundiced rats. *American Journal of Diseases of Childhood,* 1959, *98,* 602–603.

Johnson, L., Garcia, M. L., Figueroa, E., & Sarmiento, F. Kernicterus in rats lacking glucuronyl transferase. *American Journal of Diseases of Childhood,* 1961, *101,* 322–349.

Jones, H. E. The environment and mental development. In L. Carmichael (Ed.), *Manual of Child Psychology.* New York: Wiley, 1954.

Knobloch, H., Pasamanick, B., Harper, P. A., & Rider, R. V. The effect of prematurity on health and growth. *American Journal of Public Health,* 1959, *49,* 1164–1173.

Knobloch, H., Rider, R., Harper, P., & Pasamanick, B. Neuropsychiatric sequelae of prematurity. *Journal of the American Medical Association,* 1956, *161,* 679.

Lucey, J. F. Hyperbilirubinemia of prematurity. *Pediatrics,* 1960, *25,* 690–710.

McGraw, M. B. *The neuromuscular maturation of the human infant.* New York: Columbia University Press, 1943.

Malloy, H. T., & Evelyn, K. A. The determination of bilirubin with the photo-electric colorimeter. *Journal of Biological Chemistry,* 1937, *119,* 481–490.

Meyer, T. C. A study of serum bilirubin levels in relation to kernicterus and prematurity. *Archives of Diseases of Childhood,* 1956, *31,* 75–80.

Miller, C. A., & Reed, H. R. The relation of serum concentrations of bilirubin to respiratory function of premature infants. *Pediatrics,* 1958, *21,* 362–369.

Mohr, G. J., & Bartelme, P. Mental and physical development of children prematurely born. *American Journal of Diseases of Childhood,* 1930, *40,* 1000–1015.

Odell, G. B. Studies in kernicterus. I. The protein binding of bilirubin. *Journal of Clinical Investigations,* 1959, *38,* 823–833.

Pincus, J. B., Gittleman, I. F., Saito, M., & Nobel, A. E. A study of plasma levels of Na, K, Cl, CO_2 (p CO_2), sugar, urea and the protein base binding power, pH and hematocrit in premature infants on the first day of life. *Pediatrics,* 1956, *18,* 39–49.

Pomerance, W., & Steiner, M. D. Studies on prematurity. III. The influence of toxemia of pregnancy on fatality rate. *American Journal of Obstetrics and Gynaecology,* 1951, *61,* 436–439.

Rider, M., Tabac, M., & Knobloch, H. Association between premature birth and socio-economic status. *American Journal of Public Health,* 1955, *45,* 1022–1029.

Saito, M., Gittleman, I. F., Pincus, J. B., & Sobel, A. E. Plasma protein patterns in premature infants of varying weights on the first day of life. *Pediatrics,* 1956, *17,* 657–662.

Schacter, F. F., & Apgar, V. Perinatal asphyxia and psychologic signs of brain damage in childhood. *Pediatrics,* 1959, *24,* 1016–1025.

Schmid, R. Direct-reacting bilirubin, bilirubin glucuronide, in serum, bile and urine. *Science,* 1956, *124,* 76–77.

Silverman, W. A. *Dunham's Premature Infants.* New York: Hoeber, 1961.

Silverman, W. A., & Anderson, D. H. A controlled clinical trial of effects of water mist on obstructive respiratory signs, death rate and necropsy findings among premature infants. *Pediatrics,* 1956, *17,* 1–10.

Thurston, D., Graham, F. K., Ernhart, C. B., Eichman, F. L., & Craft, N. Neurologic status of 3-year-old children originally studied at birth. *Neurology,* 1960, *10,* 680–690.

Trolle, D. Discussion on the advisability of performing exchange transfusion in neonatal jaundice of unknown aetiology. *Acta Pediatrica,* 1961, *50,* 392–398.

Walker, H. M., & Lev, J. *Statistical inference.* New York: Holt, Rinehart & Winston, 1953.

Waters, W. J., & Bowen, W. R. Bilirubin encephalopathy: studies related to cellular respiration. *American Journal of Diseases of Childhood,* 1955, *90,* 603. (Abstract)

Wegman, M. C. Weight at birth and survival of the newborn. *Pediatrics,* 1954, *14,* 396–400.

Wortis, H., Bardach, J. L., Cutler, R., Rue, R., & Freedman, A. M. Child-rearing practices in a low socio-economic group. *Pediatrics,* 1963, *32,* 298–307.

Wortis, H., Heimer, C. B., Braine, M. D. S., Redlo, M., & Rue, R. Growing up in Brooklyn: the early history of the premature child. *American Journal of Orthopsychiatry,* 1963, *33,* 535–539.

Zetterstrom, R., & Ernster, L. Bilirubin, an uncoupler of oxidative phosphorylation in isolated mitochondria. *Nature,* 1956, *178,* 1335–1337.

Zuelzer, W. W., & Brown, A. K. Neonatal jaundice. A review. *American Journal of Diseases of Childhood,* 1961, *101,* 113–153.

Experimental Studies of Appetitional Behavior in Human Newborns and Infants

Hanuš Papoušek

INSTITUTE FOR CARE OF MOTHER AND CHILD
PRAGUE, CZECHOSLOVAKIA

Probably every parent has a similar experience when seeing his newborn baby's behavior for the first time: The monotonous crying that is the only vocal manifestation and the diffuse mass activity that is often elicited by inadequate stimuli are so strikingly different from the behavior of adults that they seem to be completely incomprehensible. Yet most parents are soon able to find clues for understanding the basic meaning of the neonate's behavior and to learn to detect even the very early manifestations of developing integrated patterns of voluntary activity.

Reprinted from H. W. Stevenson, E. H. Hess, H. L. Rheingold (Eds.), *Early behavior: comparative and developmental approaches*. New York: Wiley, 1967, pp. 249–278. By permission.

The author wishes to thank his research assistants Jarmila Melicharova and Svatava Sýkorova, as well as the staff of the research unit, for their devoted and skillful assistance in both nursing care and research investigation. Thanks are due also to our statistical consultant, Dr. J. Vondraček, Institute of Mathematics, Czechoslovak Academy of Sciences, Prague, for his suggestions.

49

The author of this report sought to find a pattern of behavior that under experimental control might be used to study the learning abilities of newborns, and that would represent a model for the analysis of the development of intentional behavior. The motor components of appetitional behavior seemed particularly advantageous for this purpose because the need for food is a factor that is both effective and controllable. Inborn responses associated with feeding have therefore been repeatedly applied in studies of such basic learning processes as conditioning or conditioned discrimination.

Conditioning methods were first used for the systematic study of higher nervous functions in immature human subjects soon after Pavlov's basic experiments in dogs (Krasnogorskii, 1907). But until the last two decades the studies of infants dealt more often with the problems of the onset of conditioning or with the capacity for sensory perception than with the development of learning processes. Recent surveys by Rheingold and Stanley (1963) and by Lipsitt (1963) have called attention to the fact that most studies of learning in infants have merely described the occurrence of the phenomenon; and the authors suggest that there is a need for additional studies of the processes underlying infant learning.

In the comparative physiology of infrahuman infants, attempts to analyze the development of the conditioning process have already appeared. Comparative data recently summarized by Sedláček (1963) indicated that the form and adaptive significance of temporary connections depended on the development of the CNS in individual species, and that the three main types of connections—the summation reflex (Wedenskii in 1881), the dominant center reflex (Ukhtomskii in 1911), and Pavlov's conditioned reflex—can be considered different evolutionary degrees of the same general process of synthesis in the CNS. Orbeli (1949) explained the ontogenetic development of central nervous functions by means of a similar evolutionary view. He hypothesized a genetic relation between inherited, unconditioned responses and acquired, conditioned responses, with an intermediate continuum of various transitory forms. Sedláček (1962; 1964) made a serious attempt to prove this hypothesis through studies of prenatal conditioning in relatively mature newborns, such as chickens and guinea pigs.

In man, prenatal conditioning has been studied either directly in the human fetus during pregnancy (Ray, 1932; Sontag & Wallace, 1934; Spelt, 1938; 1948), or in premature infants (Kasatkin, 1951; Irzhanskaia & Felberbaum, 1954). These studies have shown evidence of conditioned responses before the expected date of birth, but were not concerned with the mechanisms of temporary connections or with their development.

The lack of information about the earliest development of higher nervous functions in human infants stimulated the team to which the present author belongs to undertake a developmental study of individual differences in conditioning abilities. Unlike similar studies in the Pavlovian literature on typological differences in children (Ivanov-Smolenskii, 1953; Krasnogorskii, 1958) and infants (Volokhov, 1959), individual differences were defined by us in a much broader sense than the limits imposed by typological parameters. In order to maximize the generalizability of our conclusions, the same infants were exposed to several different conditioning methods—aversive, appetitional, and orientational—and to the analysis of sleep and waking, emotional and social behaviors, and EEG patterns.

Here we shall be concerned mainly with the data on learned appetitional responses and with the models for complex patterns of intentional behavior. Although the classical conditioning method of salivary response has been used with children, it is not appropriate for infants (Krasnogorskii, 1958). Therefore the analysis of conditioned sucking movements that was recommended by Bekhterev and Stshelovanov (1925) has been preferred by most authors. The first natural conditioned sucking was reported during the third week of life by Denisova and Figurin (1929), and Ripin and Hetzer (1930). The conditioning of sucking in infants to acoustic stimuli during the second or third month and to visual stimuli during the third or fourth month was reported by Kasatkin and Levikova (1935). Conditioned discrimination with vestibular stimulation was first reported by Nemanova (1935) in her study of infants 2 to 4 months old. Marquis (1931) reported much earlier conditionability; in 8 of 10 newborns she obtained conditioned oral responses to a buzzer at the age of 4 or 5 days, but her study lacked necessary controls for pseudoconditioning. On the other hand, Wenger (1936) could not establish conditioned responses before the tenth day of age with either appetitional or aversive techniques.

The problems of early conditioning continued to engage the attention of later investigators who used newer techniques and larger samples of infants (Kasatkin, 1964). Lipsitt and Kaye (1964) confirmed appetitional conditionability in 3- to 4-day-old newborns. Sucking movements were also used for testing the influence of hunger on conditioning (Kantrow, 1937), for detecting neonatal brain injuries (Dashkovskaia, 1953), and for studying premature infants (Polikanina, 1955; Polikanina & Probatova, 1957).

Until recent years, methods using other motor components of appetitional behavior were not employed adequately; Irwin (1930) discussed general motor activity, and Kriuchkova and Ostrovskaia mentioned head-turning (1957).

For the purposes of our studies, the sucking method appeared inconvenient, particularly because of the regressive changes in sucking movements that are in contrast to the progressive development of higher nervous functions (Papoušek, 1960). With increasing age, anticipatory sucking movements gradually disappear, perhaps because they are nonfunctional or nonadaptive.

Head-turning, therefore, was chosen by the author as another conditionable motor component of infantile appetitional behavior. As an inborn response, head-turning has been studied by many neurophysiologists since the first observations published by Darwin (1886) and Preyer (1895). According to Minkowski (1928), head movements appear in the human fetus by the third postconceptional month and are fully functional at birth. They can be elicited by various stimuli and during periods of hunger, occur without any discernible stimulation (Prechtl, 1953). According to Babkin (1953), an inborn rooting reflex, probably coordinated in the diencephalon, should be differentiated from the purposive movements that develop gradually, probably under cortical control, into various learned behavioral patterns such as orientational, aversive, or appetitional movements.

Natural conditioning of head movements to a visual (bottle) stimulus by the first month of life was described by Peiper (1958). After satiation, both conditioned and unconditioned food-seeking activity was suppressed.

For several reasons, head-turning seemed advantageous for conditioning studies. The movement matures earlier than do movements of the extremities, and its intensity and latency can be more easily quantified. It can be used with different kinds of reinforcement: appetitional or aversive, incidental or intentional. Thus it is suitable for molding a simple inborn reflex movement into a complex purposive or voluntary response. Finally, because head-turning involves bilateral response, and differential reinforcement can be applied for responses to the left or right, it can be used for the simultaneous study of two symmetrical responses in a single subject.

A method was devised for appetitional conditioning with milk reinforcement (Papoušek, 1959, 1961a, 1961b). For orientation conditioning with visual reinforcement the method was modified by another member of our team (Koch, 1962) and, within an operant framework, has been successfully explored by Siqueland (1964) and Siqueland and Lipsitt (in press).

METHOD

Subjects

For our investigations infants up to 6 months of age were reared in a special unit under relatively standard conditions. As far as possible, we tried to keep their life conditions comparable, at the same time meeting the demands of individual infants. Between 1956 and 1965, more than 130 infants were observed. They were healthy, full term, and without any evidence of pathology in the mothers' pregnancies or deliveries. The infants were cared for by their mothers and by specially trained nurses who could substitute for the mothers if necessary. Our team included a pediatrician who watched over the infants' health, nutrition, and somatic development, and a psychologist who was concerned with their mental development and educational care. If an occasional break in experimentation exceeded five days, the procedure being investigated during the period was eliminated from consideration.

The infants were also used by other members of the team for other experimental conditioning studies, such as conditioned eye-blinking (Janoš, 1965) and orientational head-turning (Koch, 1962).

Stimuli and Apparatus

The sounds of an electric bell (CS_1) or a buzzer (CS_2) were the conditioning stimuli. The unconditioned reinforcement (UCS) was milk presented from one side or the other through a rubber nipple connected to a thermos bottle.

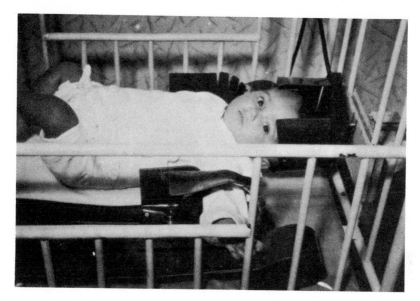

Fig. 1. The stabilimeter crib.

Electronic equipment enabled the experimenter to program the kind and duration of both conditioning and reinforcing stimuli and to operate them and the timing mechanisms by a single button, thus freeing the experimenter to make detailed observations of the infant's behavior.

A seven-channel polygraph recorded the presentation of the stimuli and the infant's head-turning, breathing, and general motor activity. On a protocol, the experimenter recorded, by means of codes, intensity and latency of head-turning, changes in general behavior, and vocal, facial, and oral responses.

The infant lay in a stabilimeter crib, partially immobilized, in order to eliminate any disturbing activity of his upper extremities (Fig. 1). An elastic pad oscillated with the infant's movements; the oscillation was transmitted to the polygraph through a pneumatic system. This system also included a special calibrator allowing actograms of infants of different body weights to be compared. Breathing movements were recorded by means of a pneumatic pick-up.

The infant's head was placed in a plastic head cradle lined with plastic foam. The cradle's rotations on a horizontal axis changed the potential in a two-potentiometer circuit, and these changes were recorded as reflections from the baseline on the polygraph (Fig. 2). The attachment of the head cradle to the axis could be shifted vertically to balance the cradle and eliminate the influence of head weight, enabling even a newborn to turn his head or keep it in a central position without difficulty.

Thus information was gathered not only on the specific response—

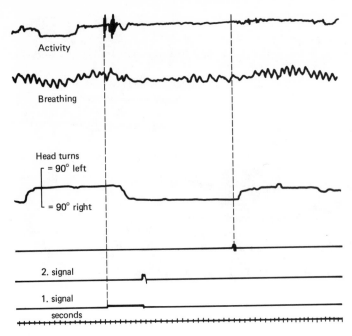

Fig. 2. Polygraph recordings from an experimental session.

head-turning—but also on concomitant changes in general activity (decrease or increase in general motor activity), vocalization, facial responses, eye movements, and breathing. Records of such changes were essential for estimating the general state of wakefulness during the experiment and the inhibitory or excitatory effects of the experimental stimuli.

Procedure and Measures

Infants were tested in the late morning, approximately 10 minutes after their regular sleep in the fresh air. The routine schedule of feeding and sleep in the sequence of sleep, feeding, and waking enable us to examine the subjcts in comparable states of hunger and wakefulness.

First, a baseline measure of head-turning prior to experimental stimulation was recorded. Then, all Ss received five pre-experimental trials of CS_1 and CS_2 without reinforcement. The source of the stimuli was in the midline behind the infant's head so that the sounds by themselves did not elicit head-turning. The first presentation of milk occurred prior to the conditioning trials and from the midline so that Ss might adapt to the experimental situation. Interruptions in feeding did not result in problems, particularly if the interruptions followed spontaneous breaks in the infant's sucking.

The development of the conditioned reflex to the bell (CR) was then initiated with the milk (UCS) being presented from the left side. The UCS was presented by the assistant, who sat screened behind S's head. If S re-

sponded to the bell and turned to the left, milk was offered to him immediately. The bell continued ringing until S started sucking the milk. If S did
not respond to the presentation of the CS within 10 seconds, the assistant
(nurse) tried eliciting the head turn by tactile stimulation, touching the left
corner of his mouth with the nipple. If this stimulation was ineffective, she
turned his head to the left and placed the nipple in his mouth. At the end
of reinforcement the nurse turned his head back to the middle, leading it
with the nipple, and then took the nipple from his mouth.

Ten such trials occurred during one session, which covered one normal
feeding period of 10 to 15 minutes. The intertrial interval was one minute,
on the average, but was intentionally changed to avoid temporal conditioning. A head turn of 30° or more from the central position was considered a
positive response. The criterion of conditioning was five consecutive positive
responses in the 10 trials of one daily session.

There was, therefore, considerable biological significance to head-turning
under this procedure. The hungry infant had to rotate his head to obtain
milk, and the sooner he did so, the sooner he was fed. Under these conditions, the gradual shortening of the latency of response could be considered
a parameter of the process of conditioning.

Extinction was the next procedure. CS_1 was presented without the UCS
for 10 seconds; as in the conditioning procedure, 10 trials were given in
one session. After the criterion of five consecutive negative responses was
reached, reconditioning took place. The process was the same as the first
conditioning procedure.

Next, the Ss were trained to discriminate between the two stimuli; CS_1
(bell) was reinforced from the left and CS_2 (buzzer), from the right. In any
one session, five CS_1 and five CS_2 were presented in random order. Six consecutive correct responses (three bell and three buzzer CR's in random order)
represented the criterion of learning for this phase of the procedure. After
reaching criterion, the signals were reversed: CS_1 was reinforced from the
right, CS_2 from the left. The criterion for concluding this portion of the procedure was analogous to that employed in the trials for the first discrimination.

In addition to these basic procedures, other experiments were designed
for the analysis of stimulus influence and for the shaping of more complex
forms of learned behavior, such as the conditioned emotional behavior or
the development of intentional behavior. These experiments are discussed
later.

STUDIES OF BASIC LEARNING ABILITIES

The data given first demonstrate the early development of learning abilities in infants, their age peculiarities, and the individual differences among
them. These data were gathered from the basic six conditioning procedures
that were studied with three independent groups of Ss: newborns (A),
3-month-old infants (B), and 5-month-old infants (C). The variability of initial

Table 1   Means and Standard Deviations of Responses of Three Groups of Infants to the Six Basic Conditioning Procedures

Groups of Infants	N	Initial Age in Days		Trials to Criterion		Latency in Seconds			
						CR 1		CR 2	
		Mean	S.D.	Mean	S.D.	Mean	S.D.	Mean	S.D.
Conditioning:									
A	14	3.42	1.01	177.14	93.40	4.95	0.74		
B	14	85.78	1.76	42.28	18.38	3.92	1.08		
C	16	142.50	2.63	27.75	13.70	3.55	1.29		
Extinction:									
A	12	31.83	13.89	26.83	12.90	5.49	1.01		
B	14	94.14	4.58	25.07	10.39	3.70	0.94		
C	16	149.06	4.07	27.31	15.29	3.25	0.99		
Reconditioning:									
A	12	37.25	13.34	42.83	29.88	4.90	0.93		
B	14	100.35	1.45	31.64	19.84	2.73	0.65		
C	16	153.93	3.43	22.37	11.88	3.28	0.85		
Discrimination:									
A	11	43.90	15.68	223.54	99.23	4.00	0.58	3.90	0.63
B	13	105.92	6.48	176.23	82.52	2.62	0.66	3.03	0.71
C	14	159.92	5.46	68.14	28.72	2.10	0.77	2.66	0.87
Reversal 1:									
A	11	76.36	18.68	195.18	86.85	3.43	0.65	3.47	0.81
B	12	135.58	11.57	120.00	66.01	2.58	0.66	2.48	0.60
C	10	170.00	4.81	79.40	79.83	2.83	1.01	2.56	0.83
Reversal 2:									
A	11	107.54	23.81	94.63	35.51	3.29	0.91	2.91	0.74
B	12	155.41	19.08	82.41	37.74	2.34	0.91	2.15	0.74
C	10	182.80	13.50	77.60	63.60	2.29	0.97	2.72	0.97

A = newborns.
B = 3-month infants.
C = 5-month infants.

age within each group was reduced to a minimum. The results for the 44 infants in the three groups are summarized in Table 1. In this table are presented the means and standard deviations for initial age, rapidity of learning as measured by the number of trials necessary to achieve criterion, and latency of CRs.

In addition to the analysis of these data, attention was also paid to the appearance of typical phases in the course of learning and to the various concomitant patterns of behavior. In these observations the group of newborns deserve more attention, particularly in comparison with group B, because a marked qualitative change in the development of higher nervous functions occurs during the first three months of life (Janoš, Papoušek, & Dittrichová, 1963).

Conditioning in Newborns

In newborns we had a rare opportunity to study experimental motor learning before spontaneous natural learning substantially inferred. Slow conditioning permitted an easier analysis of its phases that in older infants often passed too quickly and could be interpreted as accidental deviations.

In newborns the baseline before conditioning usually showed no head movements. Even tactile stimulation with the nipple elicited head-turning only in three of the 14 newborns on the first reinforcement, whereas three to 22 trials were necessary for the remaining 11 Ss (mean = 6.57). In group B the tactile stimulation itself elicited head-turning more quickly, usually after one or two trials (mean = 1.23). This difference was highly significant ($p <$ 0.001).[1]

The rate of conditioning, as shown in Table 1, was very slow in newborns. On the average, 32.21 trials preceded the first conditioned head turn in group A, whereas only 9.43 trials were necessary in group B. Such a significant decrease ($p < 0.001$) indicates a rapid development of conditionability during the first three months of life. A similar decrease of the mean number of trials to criterion also supported this conclusion; the difference between groups A and B was highly significant ($p < 0.001$), whereas the difference between groups B and C was significant at the .05 level. The mean number of 177 trials for group A represented approximately three weeks of conditioning, and shows that during the 28 days of the neonatal period most newborns can achieve even a relatively severe criterion of conditioning. But wide individual differences in the newborns were apparent; the fastest conditioners needed only 7, 10, 11, or 12 days, the slowest ones, more than a month.

The latency of the CR is here considered in the behavioral sense, rather than in the physiological. Latency was defined as the interval between the onset of CS and a head turn of 30° or more. It depended, therefore, not only on the interval preceding the onset of CR, but also on the rate at which the head was turned. An analysis of variance showed significant age differences for the three groups ($p < 0.005$), indicating that newborns carry out the CRs more slowly than older infants. For newborns, there was also a significant correlation during conditioning between latency and speed of conditioning, indicating longer reaction times in slower conditioners ($r = 0.68$, $p < 0.01$).

Several different stages could be distinguished during the course of conditioning. To a certain degree they were comparable to the four stages of conditioned sucking described by Kasatkin (1948): indifference to the CS, inhibition of general activity, unstable CR, and, finally, a stable CR.

During the first phase the CS usually elicited nonspecific orientational behavior (wider opening of the eyes, inhibition of other activities, changes in

---

[1] The following statistical procedures were employed, depending on the particular data being analyzed: the Mann-Whitney U test; the Kruskal-Wallis one-way analysis of variance for k-sample cases; for large samples, the Snedecor F test with logarithmic transformation of scores and, if necessary, with Scheffé's (1959) method of multiple comparison; and Spearman rank-order correlation coefficients.

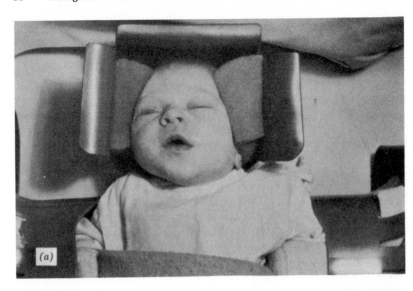

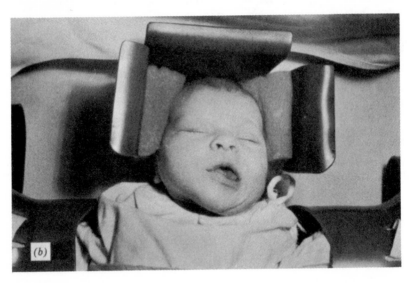

Fig. 3. Head-turning and unilateral mouthing.

breathing) that was quickly extinguished. After a period of indifference to the CS, this phase was succeeded by one during which partial responses and later the first CRs were manifested. In newborns this phase was relatively long and had several features that should be noted. Its main features were gradual coordination of individual components of CR, such as head-turning and unilateral mounting or eye turning (Fig. 3), increased general motor ac-

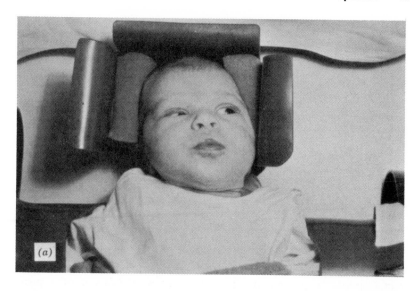

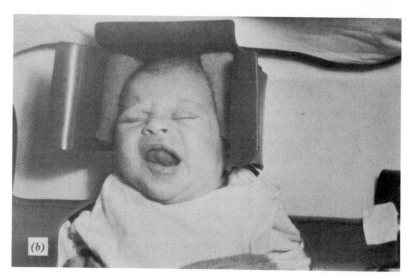

Fig. 4. Facial signs of distress.

tivity, and concomitant vocal and facial responses that are generally accepted as signs of distress (Fig. 4). Before a good coordination developed, the newborn could be seen to be upset, fussing, and grimacing, turning his eyes and contracting his mouth to the left, but not yet turning his head. Marked signs of such an insufficient coordination were present in 50% of the Ss in group A, but only in .7% of the Ss in group B.

Table 2 Grouping of Conditioned Responses of Three Groups of Infants, in Percentages

			The First 10 Positive Conditioned Responses	
Group of Infants	N	Isolated	in Groups	
			2	3 or More
		%	%	%
A	14	60.7	32.9	6.4
B	14	34.9	17.2	47.9
C	16	18.7	20.6	60.6
		A:B $p < 0.001$	A:B $p < 0.01$	A:B $p < 0.001$
		B:C $p < 0.025$	B:C $p > 0.05$	B:C $p > 0.05$

A = newborns.
B = 3-month infants.
C = 5-month infants.

The next phase was that of unstable conditioning. The frequency of correct responses increased, but the responses were isolated or appeared in small groups with fluctuating intensity and latency. Insufficient coordination was still evident in two characteristic features: (a) a generalized form of CR (the S responds with the whole body), and (b) an increased frequency of unilateral or bilateral intertrial head turning. The first feature, considered a sign of increased irradiation of central nervous processes in immature organisms, was more frequent in group A. The second feature, indicating central dominance, usually appeared only in the unilateral form in group A and was less frequent (50%) than in group B (71%).

The gradual consolidation of the CR, that is, the increasing ability to carry out more CRs consecutively, also appears to be a function of age. The analysis of the first 10 CRs (Table 2) showed that in group A, 60.7% of the responses were isolated, whereas in group C, 60.6% appeared consecutively in groups of three or more. It is evident that the main development of this ability again occurs during the first three months of life.

Three main types of cumulative curves appeared to characterize the course of conditioning in the infants: (a) relatively constant increase of percentage in CRs, (b) increase of percentage with several gross waves, and (c) increase of percentage after a retarded onset. The second type may indicate a functional lability of the CNS, typical of immature organisms, and the third, a phasic maturation of the CNS (Janoš, 1965). It can be seen in Table 3 that the relative frequency of the three types differed in the three age groups, and that the last two types were more characteristic of the newborns.

The final phase is that of stable conditioning. The frequency of CRs approaches 100%, and the CRs are stronger, faster, well coordinated, and carried out economically with shorter and more regular latencies. They were no longer accompanied by emotional signs of distress; on the contrary, the

Table 3   Frequency of Different Types of Conditioning Curves in Individual Age Groups

Types of Acquisition Curves	Age Groups		
	A	B	C
Relatively constant			
percentage increase	6	12	16
Several gross waves	6	2	—
Retarded onset	2	—	—
Total	14	14	16

older infants often showed vocal or facial patterns of pleasure (Fig. 5). In this phase the Ss reached the criterion of 5 successive correct CRs and, at the same time, the average number of CRs in three successive days usually exceeded 50% (see p. 62).

Even in this phase, the stability of conditioning was only relative, particularly in the younger groups in which a sudden decrease sometimes appeared after a period of consistent responses. Alternation between increased excitation and inhibition seems typical for newborns and probably caused the limited occurrence of consecutive CRs. Polygraphic records of breathing and general motor activity provided more sensitive indications of increased excitation or inhibition than the apparent state of wakefulness.

No relation was found in newborns between the occurrence of the first CR and the number of trials to criterion, but there was a significant correlation between the occurrence of the first group of two CRs and the criterion ($r = 0.71$, $p < 0.01$) or between the first group of three consecutive CRs and the criterion ($r = 0.86$, $p < 0.01$).

All these indices of age characteristics in the higher nervous functions of newborns confirm the hypothesis that the immaturity of the CNS manifests itself in the functional lability of higher centers and in the weakness of the basic central nervous system processes of excitation and inhibition. A similar conclusion was drawn from the analysis of developmental changes of sleeping and waking states in these infants (Dittrichová, 1962; Dittrichová, Janoš & Papoušek, 1962). Even under conditions involving relative immaturity of the CNS, it is apparent that a basic pyramidal response can be learned which, in later weeks and months, develops into a more complicated pattern of behavior. Our data suggest, in fact, that learning does occur in humans within the first days of life.

Further Development of Conditioning Capacity

In the older infants, as compared with the newborns, developmental changes were observed of both a quantitative and a qualitative nature. The significant increase with age in the speed of conditioning was discussed in the preceding section on newborns. This finding is important for developmental studies since experimental evidence, in spite of many ontogenetic

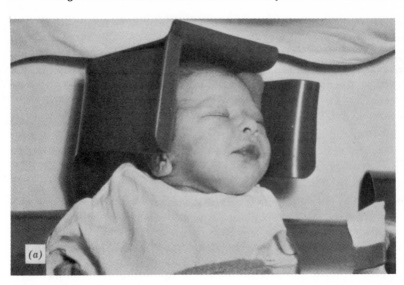

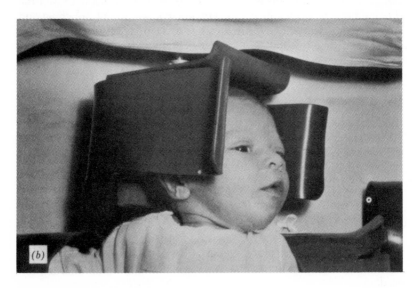

Fig. 5. Facial signs of pleasure.

studies, is still equivocal. As shown recently (Janoš et al., 1963), during the first half-year of infancy an age difference of one month may produce significant differences in both aversive and appetitional conditioning.

With increased speed of conditioning, the individual phases in the conditioning process that are characteristic of newborns become shorter, and often such phases are detected only fleetingly, particularly in fast conditioners. Nevertheless, several qualitative differences could still be observed in groups B and C. Incoordination of partial components of the CR, associated with the appearance of the first CRs in newborns, was absent or appeared in a slight form only in a few trials. The generalization of the CR, observed in the phase of unstable conditioning, was also different. In newborns the CR was preceded or accompanied by increased movements of the whole trunk and extremities, and by changes in breathing and vasomotor responses, etc. These changes can be considered the result of nonspecific diffuse irradiation of the central excitatory process. It was observed that older infants showed more specific generalization, which was expressed in the specific vocal or facial signs of emotional arousal frequently shown by older children or adults in solving difficult problems.

An increase in the number of head turns during the intertrial intervals was more frequently found in older infants during the phase of unstable conditioning, and, unlike what is found in newborns, here the bilateral form of the intertrial head turns prevailed. It is difficult to estimate the proportion of maturation and extraexperimental learning in the qualitative differences found between newborns and older infants.

Extinction and Reconditioning

The main purpose of our extinction and reconditioning procedures was to confirm the critical feature of the CR—its temporary character—and thus to differentiate it from pseudoconditioning. According to previous experience (Papousek, 1961a, 1961b) and to analogous findings in aversive conditioning (Janoš, 1965), we did not expect to gain as much information about the development of learning abilities from the study of extinction and reconditioning as we found in the use of other procedures.

Table 1 shows that extinction occurs more quickly than conditioning but no significant difference in the speed of extinction was found among the three groups. This finding is difficult to explain. The experiments dealing with extinction may have involved an age span different from that in which the main development of extinction ability occurs; or the role of age may have been obliterated by the level of conditioning necessary to achieve the relatively severe criterion of conditioning employed. It is interesting that in group A, a negative correlation between trials to conditioning and trials to extinction was found ($r = -0.66$, $p < 0.05$), indicating faster extinguishing in slower conditioners. Moreover, the newborns had a significantly longer latency of the CR ($p < 0.001$) than did groups B and C.

To a certain extent, the course of extinction is a mirror image of conditioning. The CRs gradually cease to be made and their latencies become longer. The negative responses appear first as isolated events and later in consecutively larger numbers. The individual components of the CR do not extinguish simultaneously, particularly in younger Ss. For example, in response to the CS_1, the S may stop turning his head to the left but may continue to turn his eyes to the left or contract the left corner of his mouth for some time. A negative response to the CS still does not mean that the CS is totally indifferent to the S. Particularly during the phase of unstable extinction, the CS obviously exerts an inhibitory influence upon the S's behavior, sometimes to such an extent that it can elicit a catatonic-like state in the S for several seconds.

Reconditioning may be considered a repetition of the first conditioning process. Here, however, the differences between individual age groups were at the limit of significance, according to a Kruskal-Wallis analysis of variance ($p > 0.05$).

Only in younger groups is reconditioning significantly faster than conditioning. The difference in speed between conditioning and reconditioning can be the effect of either maturation or relearning. The first seems more plausible since the difference was highly significant in group A ($p < 0.001$), in which the Ss were 34 days older during reconditioning than they were during conditioning, but was at the limit of significance in group B ($p < 0.05$), and nonsignificant in group C ($p < 0.05$), in which the Ss were only 15 and 11 days older. Within the total sample (but not within individual age groups), the correlation between trials to conditioning and trials to reconditioning was significant ($r = 0.38, p < 0.01$).

Discrimination

There is a lack of data in the literature on the development of discriminative abilities in man. It was not the goal of this study to answer the question of the age at which human infants begin to discriminate different acoustic stimuli. The Ss had to proceed through several other procedures before the discrimination tests were begun. But even under these conditions evidence was found that in the fastest conditioners the ability to discriminate was functional as early as the second month of life. In group A, the mean age at which the Ss reached the criterion of discrimination between bell and buzzer was 2½ months.

During the following months of the first half year of life the ability to discriminate improves substantially and the speed of differentiation increases. An analysis of variance among groups A, B, and C, showed significant differences dependent on age ($p < 0.005$). Furthermore, the latencies of response to both CS_1 and CS_2 were significantly lower ($p < 0.005$) for group A than for groups B and C.

Individual variability in the speed of acquisition of prior procedures results in a gradual increase of the variability in the age at which Ss begin subsequent procedures. Ranking according to age is in this case identical with ranking in order of decreasing speed in the preceding procedures; within individual groups the slower the Ss were in preceding tests the older they were in succeeding tests. Therefore, the correlation between age and speed of discrimination or its reversals was not significant within individual groups, although in some procedures the span of the initial age exceeded one month. It has been reported by Janoš et al. (1963) that such an age difference may be associated with significant differences in the speed of conditioning.

Several main phases may be distinguished in the course of discrimination and particularly in the reversal of discrimination. There is first a disintegration of the previously learned ability that is followed by a gradual adaptation leading to successful acquisition of the new discrimination. Secondary phases were also present, such as alternating dominance of left or right CRs in Ss' responses to both kinds of CSs. The frequency, sequence, and expressiveness of these secondary phases were, however, less constant.

Developmental differences were evident in the course of discrimination. In group A, a marked decline in both CRs was observed in 6 of the 11 Ss soon after CS_2 was introduced. After the period of decline, a gradual increase in both CRs occurred simultaneously, with gross waves as the dominant type of acquisition curve. In groups B and C, such a general decline was never observed. A gradual increase in responses to CS_2 usually occurred with a stable or only a transitory decrease in the level of responses to CS_1. The periods of alternating dominance of left or right responses were less frequent in groups B and C. In all groups the stability of discrimination was only relative even after reaching criterion; a marked decline could be easily produced by various interfering factors.

Reversals of Discrimination

In the last two procedures included in Table 1, the variability of the age at which the procedures were introduced increased to such an extent that the group limits overlapped, but the differences between mean ages still remained highly significant.

The speed of learning significantly increased from discrimination to the second reversal in groups A and B, but not in group C. It appears that by 6 months of age further improvement based upon age alone was not in evidence. For the first reversal, a one-way analysis of variance showed a reliable age trend reflecting a decrease in the number of trials to criterion ($p < 0.005$). In the second reversal, however, this trend was no longer significant. Similar relations were observed in the latency data. Within individual age groups there was no significant correlation between age and speed of the reversals. A possible interpretation was discussed in the previous section on discrimination. The speed with which the first reversal was acquired was positively related to the speed of discrimination ($r = 0.37$, $p < 0.025$).

The first reversal was established, on the average, in group A by the third month of life, and the second reversal by $3\frac{1}{2}$ months. We may conclude, therefore, that during the first trimester there has developed not only the capacity to discriminate but also the capacity to reverse a discrimination.

DETERMINANTS OF INDIVIDUAL DIFFERENCES

Individual differences in addition to those based upon age were found in all groups and in all of the quantitative and qualitative indices. The literature contains different opinions on the detectability of differences in higher nervous function during early infancy. Chesnokova (1951) and Krasuskii (1953)

Group A
(Newborn)

Group B
(3-Month Infants)

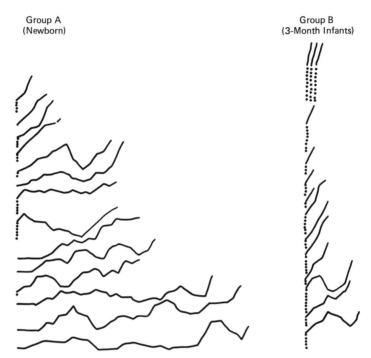

Fig. 6. Acquisition curves of conditioning for groups A and B.

assumed that differences in higher nervous activity continued to develop until adulthood and could not be assessed definitely at earlier ages. Troshikhin (1952) and Volokhov (1953), on the other hand, recommended that they be studied as early as possible. Kriuchkova and Ostrovskaia (1957) and, in a project similar to ours, Kaplan (1963) reported stable individual differences in higher nervous function from the first months of life through later infancy.

In the present study, marked individual differences were found to be present in newborns according to all indices. As an illustrative example, acquisition curves of conditioning for groups A and B are presented in Fig. 6. Whether or not the observed differences represent permanent characteristics of individual Ss cannot be answered because our studies have not yet been oriented toward this problem. It should be noted, however, that studies on aversive conditioning in the same infants have also shown marked individual differences in learning abilities at early ages (Janoš, 1965).

In Table 1, the standard deviations for the trials-to-criterion measures of conditioning and discrimination decreased from group A to group C, indicating a developmental change in the variability of these functions. The F tests comparing groups A and C indicated that the decrease in variability was significant in both instances ($p < 0.001$).

Other determinants of the individual differences found in learning abilities were also investigated, for example, sex differences, nutrition, somatic differences, seasonal influences, etc. A preliminary analysis of our data showed no significant sex differences in any procedure between 19 girls and 25 boys of the present sample. Seasonal difference was not significant either when performances were compared for the first and the second halves of the calendar year, or for the spring through the summer with the autumn through the winter.

It did not appear that the individual differences in learning ability that were found could be attributable to somatic or constitutional factors studied, such as birth weight and birth length, head and chest circumference, or gain in weight or length during the first trimester. Only in newborns did some parameters of learning abilities seem to be related to some of the mentioned determinants. A significant correlation was found, for example, between the CR latency and chest circumference ($r = -0.67$, $p < 0.05$), indicating that a conditioned head turn was carried out more quickly in stouter newborns.

Since appetitional behavior can be substantially influenced by nutritional factors, the mean calorie quotient (daily intake in calories per kilogram of body weight) was calculated during each experimental procedure and was correlated with the conditioning parameters. In groups A and B, significant correlations of .59 ($p < 0.05$) and .63 ($p < 0.02$), respectively, indicated that conditioning proceeded more quickly in infants with a lower daily intake of milk, that is, they indicated an excitatory effect of a mild degree of hunger that can appear in younger infants during, for example, the period of additional feeding when a supplementary formula is kept slightly reduced in order to maintain adequate sucking at the mother's breast.

Similarly, a breast-to-cow-milk ratio was calculated during conditioning to test the influence of breast feeding and, indirectly, also of mother's presence, since mothers usually stayed at our unit as long as they could nurse. No significant correlation was evident between this ratio and the parameters of conditioning. It was the practice, however, to compensate for the mother's absence by providing substitute mothering and adequate emotional stimulation.

Thus, in general, we can conclude that this preliminary analysis of the potential determinants of individual differences in performance during the procedures employed did not contradict the hypothesis that with the conditioning procedures considered here, we were testing differences in higher nervous functions.

ROLE OF ENVIRONMENTAL STIMULATION

In the preceding sections it has been shown that various indifferent external stimuli may play an important role if they become conditioned stimuli, particularly in connection with a significant form of reinforcement such as that used in these studies of appetitional conditioning. Acoustic signals can elicit striking changes in general motor activity, in the general state of excita-

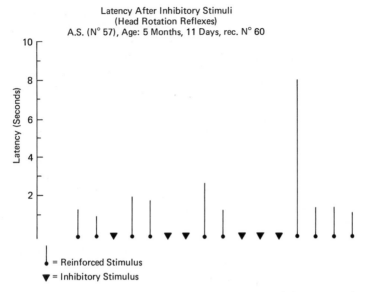

Fig. 7. Latencies of responses after presentation of inhibitory stimuli.

tion or inhibition, and in emotional and other forms of behavior. Although the effect sometimes can be too slight to be observed in general behavior, it can still be detected during the process of conditioning.

Such an example is illustrated in Fig. 7. In a 5-month-old infant with an established discrimination between the bell, reinforced with milk from the left, and the buzzer, reinforced from the right, the reinforcement associated with the buzzer was stopped in order to reverse the buzzer to an inhibitory stimulus. After a period of training, the buzzer ceased to elicit the CR, but an inhibitory after-effect appeared in an increased latency in succeeding CRs to the bell. The more inhibitory stimuli were applied consecutively, the greater was the increase in latency.

In infants of the second trimester, further observation illustrated the effectiveness of the CSs, and, in addition, an interesting interrelation between learned and unlearned behavior. For instance, in several Ss, after completing a normal conditioning session with 10 trials and after a normal amount of milk had been presented as reinforcement, another 10 or 20 CSs were applied to test the influence of satiation upon the emission of CRs. Under these conditions the Ss did not stop responding to the CSs, even when they were fully satiated. At every sound of the bell they turned to the left, even though they refused the milk presented. Any attempt to feed them elicited avoiding head turns.

Other experimental situations for studying the interrelation between learned and nonlearned behavior were undertaken by using different tasting fluids. These situations used 15 Ss, aged 88 to 201 days, in whom a left-right discrimination in head-turning had already been established. For instance, sweet milk was used as the UCS presented from the left in CS_1 and a weak solution of the quinine tincture was presented from the right in CS_2. Soon the concomitant emotional responses appropriate to the kind of UCS became differentiated, so that the Ss responded to the CS_1 with quiet sucking and head-turning, but to the CS_2 with arousal, grimacing, increased salivation, and aversive tongue movements. When in this situation the discrimination was reversed, the Ss sucked the bitter solution from the left with CS_1 without any signs of displeasure, and refused the sweet milk from the right with CS_2. For some period, this maladaptive behavior indicated that the effectiveness of conditioning stimuli was stronger than the effects of unconditioned reinforcement. Finally, a readaptation appeared and led to a new, adequate differentiation. These studies indicate that even emotional behavior, like other kinds of behavior, can be conditioned and thus put under experimental control.

Natural conditioning procedures, similar to those described above, can normally occur in the infant's life. Various environmental stimuli can in this way become conditioned stimuli of great effectiveness. It is not difficult to realize that under unfavorable conditions, for example, in various frustration situations in which many CSs remain unreinforced and become inhibitory stimuli, a cumulative inhibitory influence can produce undesirable effects in the infant's behavior.

MODELS OF VOLUNTARY BEHAVIOR

We attempted to mold a simple example of voluntary behavior in 12 infants of whom four were newborns aged 4.5 days on the average, and eight were in the second trimester, with an average age of 130.1 days. The Ss were trained in a discrimination and one or two reversals of it with only one kind of CS. The CS was reinforced with either sweetened milk from the left or unsweetened milk from the right. If he did not carry out a head turn himself, tactile stimulation with a rubber nipple was applied with the restriction that equal numbers of tactile stimulations were applied to both sides. Otherwise, the S was allowed to choose the kind of milk himself.

An exact quantitative analysis was not possible since different kinds of stimulation were used, but several general conclusions seem warranted. All Ss preferred the sweetened milk, and this preference gradually developed in a manner similar to the discrimination described in the basic conditioning procedures. The criterion of five consecutive CRs to the same side was reached in an average of 290 trials (ranging from 246 to 390) in the newborns and in 38 trials (9 to 109) in the older infants.

After achieving the criterion, the UCSs were reversed—the sweetened milk was presented from the right side and the unsweetened milk from the left. A gradual reversal in CRs occurred, consequently, and its course was analogous to that of the reversal described earlier. During the disintegration phase

Z.C. (no. 51), Age: 5 Months 22 Days, rec. no. 1-8

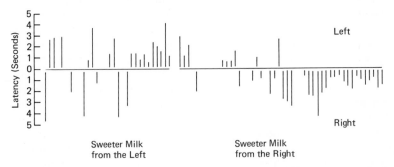

Fig. 8. Latencies of responses in initial learning and following reversal of the UCSs.

of a previously learned ability, accidental head turns to the side of sweetened milk helped the Ss to find the source of the preferred UCS. Concomitant emotional responses, gradual grouping of CRs to the preferred side, and other signs indicated that this simple model of voluntary behavior was learned in the same way as in the basic conditioning procedures. In the younger infants 108 trials (15 to 185) were necessary for achieving the criterion, whereas only 70 (10 to 162) were necessary in the older infants. In a schematic form, one typical case is illustrated in Fig. 8.

When I speak of voluntary behavior in infants of prelingual age, I do not assume that I am thereby simplifying a difficult problem. I wish only to emphasize that the chosen pyramidal movement, brought under experimental control at a very early stage of postnatal development, can be molded to patterns resembling voluntary behavior. Perhaps it would be better to say that through conditioning processes, the organism can be brought to the beginning of a long and complicated pathway of structuring, at the end of which there are patterns of behavior as highly coordinated as those generally designated as voluntary behavior.

SUMMARY

Head movements were chosen as a conditionable motor complex of infantile appetitional behavior to study the early development of learning abilities and the molding of a simple response to a pattern of intentional behavior.

A method was developed for appetitional conditioning with milk reinforcement in newborns and infants. The basic conditioning procedures—conditioning, extinction, reconditioning, discrimination and is double reversal—were studied as early forms of learning in three independent age groups of healthy full-term infants (newborns, 3-month infants, and 5-month infants).

Quantitative and qualitative differences among these groups were analyzed with particular attention to the peculiarities of the learning processes in newborns, and evidence was found that learning occurs during the first days of life. In the course of investigating various procedures in the study of conditioning in newborns, different phases of learning became apparent. The immaturity of the central nervous system manifests itself in the functional lability and in the infirmity of the basic central nervous processes of excitation and inhibition. The evidence for this appears in the slow grouping of consecutive CRs, gross waves in the acquisition curves, and instability in the percentage, intensity and latency of CRs.

In several indices the comparison among individual groups indicated that major developmental changes occur during the first three months of life. During this period there develops not only the capacity to discriminate between various acoustic stimuli but also the capacity to reverse such a discrimination.

Marked individual differences are present from the neonatal period on in all parameters of conditioning employed. An analysis of the correlation between these differences and various potential determinants such as sex, somatic development, nutrition, mother-infant interaction, or seasonal influence support the hypothesis of independent variability in higher nervous function as a cause of the observed individual differences.

Further studies helped to elucidate the interrelation between learned and nonlearned behavior, indicating increasing effectiveness of conditioning stimuli in comparison to unconditioned ones. A left-right differentiation of head-turning reinforced by two as different and as emotionally effective taste stimuli as sweet and bitter solutions indicated that even emotional behavior can be put under experimental control and can be conditioned in young infants.

Finally, there is reported the attempt to design experimental conditions under which the learned response can be considered as the earliest precursor of later intentional or voluntary behavior. Here, head-turning was conditioned to one CS, and that CS was reinforced either with sweetened or unsweetened milk, depending on the side to which S turned his head. All Ss appeared to prefer the sweetened milk and to be able to find its source on the opposite side when the two variants of UCS were reversed. Learning of such a response proceeded on the same principles as conditioned discrimination or its reversal.

REFERENCES

Babkin, P. S. (1953). Head-turning reflexes in infants. (Rus.) *Zh. Nevropat. Psikhiat.* 53, 692–696.

Bekhterev, V. M., & Stshelovanov, N. M. (1925). The principles of genetic reflexology, (Rus.) In *Novoie refleksologii i fiziologii nervnoi sistemy.* USSR: Leningrad-Moscow.

Chesnokova, A. P. (1951). Dynamism of higher nervous activity in puppies during their individual development. (Rus.) *Zh. vys. nerv. Deiat.* 1, 555–565.

Darwin, C. (1886). Biographische Skizze eines kleinen Kindes. (Germ.) *Kleinere Schriften* (Leipzig) 2.B., 134.

Dashkovskaia, V. S. (1953). The first conditioned responses in newborns under normal and pathologic conditions. (Rus.) *Zh. vys. nerv. Deiat. 3,* 247–259.

Denisova, M. P., & Figurin, N. L. (1929). The question of the first associated appetitional reflexes in infants. (Rus.) *Vopr. genet. Refleksol. Pedol.* Mladen. *1,* 81–88.

Dittrichová J. (1962). Nature of sleep in young infants, *J. appl. Physiol. 17,* 543–546.

Dittrichová, J., Janoš, O., & Papoušek, H. (1962). Characteristics of higher nervous activity in newborns. (Czech.) *Sb. čsl. lékař. kongresu.* Prague. Pp. 254–255.

Irwin, O. C. (1930). The amount and nature of activities of newborn infants under constant external stimulating conditions during the first ten days of life. *Genet. Psychol. Monogr. 8,* 1–92.

Irzhanskaia, K. N., & Felberbaum, R. A. (1954). Some data on conditioned activity in premature infants. (Rus.) *Fiziol. Zh. SSSR 40,* 668–672.

Ivanov-Smolenskii, A. G. (1953). Studies on the types of higher nervous activity in animals and in man. (Rus.) *Zh. vys. nerv. Deiat. 3,* 36–54.

Janoš, O. (1965). (Czech.) *Age and individual differences in higher nervous activity in infants.* Prague: SzdN.

Janoš O., Papoušek, H., & Dittrichová, J. (1963). The influence of age upon various aspects of higher nervous activity in the first months of life. (Czech.) *Activ. nerv. super. 4,* 407–410.

Kantrow, R. W. (1937). Studies in infant behavior. IV. An investigation of conditioned feeding responses and concomitant adaptive behavior in young infants. *Univer. Iowa Stud. Child Welf. 13,* No. 3, 1–64.

Kaplan, L. I. (1963). To the question of the development of individual typologic differences of higher nervous activity in infants. (Rus.) *Mater. 6th scient. conf. devel. morphol., physiol., biochem.* Moscow: Izd. APN. P. 354.

Kasatkin, N. I. (1948). (Rus.) *Early conditioned reflexes in the ontogenesis of man.* Moscow: Medgiz.

Kasatkin, N. I. (1951). (Rus.) *An outline of the development of the higher nervous activity during early infancy.* Moscow: Medgiz.

Kasatkin, N. I. (Ed.) (1964). (Rus.) *From the simple to the complex.* Moscow-Leningrad: Izd. Nauka.

Kasatkin, N. I., & Levikova, A. M. (1935). On the development of early conditioned reflexes and differentation of auditory stimuli in infants. *J. exp. Psychol. 18,* 1–9.

Koch, J. (1962). Die Veränderung des Exzitations Prozesses nach der Nahrungseinnahme und nach dem Schlafe bei Säuglingen in Alter von 5 Monaten. (Germ.) *Z. arztl. Forb. 55,* 219–223.

Krasnogorskii, N. I. (1907). An experience with establishing experimental conditioned reflexes in infants. (Rus.) *Russkii vrach 36.* In (Rus.) *Studies in the research of higher nervous activity in man and animals.* (1954) Moscow: Medgiz.

Krasnogorskii, N. I. (1958). (Rus.) *The higher nervous activity in the child.* Leningrad: Medgiz.

Krasuskii, V. K. (1953). Methods of studying the types of nervous system in animals. (Rus.) *Trudy Inst. Fiziol. Pavlov 2,* 111–119.

Kriuchkova, A. P., & Ostrovskaia, I. M. (1957). Developmental and individual differences of higher nervous activity in infants. (Rus.) *Zh. vys. nerv. Deiat. 7,* 63–74.

Lipsitt, L. P. (1963). Learning in the first year of life. In L. P. Lipsitt & C. C. Spiker (Eds.), *Advances in child development and behavior,* Vol. 1. New York: Academic Press, Pp. 147–195.

Lipsitt, L. P., De Kaye, H. (1964) Conditioned sucking in the human newborn. *Psychon. Sci. 1*, 29–30.

Marquis, D. P. (1931). Can conditioned responses be established in the newborn infant? *J. genet. Psychol. 39*, 479–492.

Minkowski, H. (1928). Neurobiologische Studien an menschlichen Fruchten. *Abderhalden's Handb. biolog. Arbeitsmeth* (Berlin) 5, 5b, 511–618.

Nemanova, C. P. (1935). The earliest positive and negative aversive and nutritive conditioned responses to vestibular stimuli in infants. (Rus.) *Vopr. Pediat. Okhran. 7, 278.*

Orbeli, L. A. (1949). On the mechanism of the development of cerebrospinal coordinations. (Rus.) In *The problems of higher nervous activity.* Moscow-Leningrad: Izd. AN SSSR. Pp. 7–20.

Papoušek, H. (1959). A method of studying conditioned food reflexes in young children up to the age of six months. (Rus.) *Zh. vys. nerv. Deiat. 9,* 136–140.

Papoušek, H. (1960). Conditioned motor alimentary reflexes in infants. I. Experimental conditioned sucking reflexes. (Czech.) *Cesk. Pediat. 15,* 861–872.

Papoušek, H. (1961). Conditioned head rotation reflexes in infants in the first months of life. *Acta Paediatr. 50,* 565–576. (a)

Papoušek, H. (1961). (Czech.) *Conditioned motor nutritive reflexes in infants.* Thomayer, Sb., Prague: SrdN. P. 409. (b)

Peiper, A. (1958). Unbedingte und bedingte Reflexe der Nahrungsaufnahme. (Germ.) *Kinderäerzt. Prax. 26,* 507–515.

Polikanina, R. I. (1955). Origin and development of a nutritive conditioned response to sound in premature infants. (Rus.) *Zh. vys. nerv. Deiat. 5,* 237–246.

Polikanina, R. I., & Probatova, L. J. (1957). Development of an orienting response and a conditioned motor nutritive response to color in premature infants. (Rus.) *Zh. vys. nerv. Deiat, 7,* 673–682.

Prechtl, H. F. R. (1953). Die Kletterbewegungen beim Saugling. (Germ.) *Mnschr. Kinderhk. 101,* 519–521.

Preyer, W. (1895). *Die Seele des Kindes.* (4th ed.) (Germ.) Leipzig.

Ray, W. S. (1932). A preliminary report on a study of fetal conditioning. *Child Developm. 3,* 175–177.

Rheingold, Harriet L., & Stanley, W. C. (1963). Developmental psychology. *Ann. Rev. Psychol. 14,* 1–28.

Ripin, R., & Hetzer, H. (1930). Frühestes Lernen des Sauglings in der Ernährungssituation. (Germ.) *Z. Psychol. 118,* 82–127.

Scheffé, H. (1959). *The analysis of variance.* New York: Wiley.

Sedláček, J. (1962). Functional characteristics of the center of the unconditioned reflex in elaboration of a temporary connection in chick embryos. (Czech.) *Physiol. Bohemoslov. 11,* 313–318.

Sedláček, J. (1963). Problems of the ontogenetic formation of the mechanism of temporary connections. (Rus.) *Acta Univer. Carol. Medica 4,* 265–317.

Sedláček, J., Hlaváčkova, V., & Svenlová, M. (1964) New findings on the formation of the temporary connections in the prenatal and perinatal period in the guinea pig. (Czech.)

Siqueland, E. R. (1964). Operant conditioning of head turning in four-month infants. *Psychom. Sci. 1,* 223–224.

Siqueland, E. R., & Lipsitt, L. P. Conditioned head-turning behavior in newborns. *J. exp. child Psychol.* (In press.)

Sontag, L. W., & Wallace, R. F. (1934). Study of fetal activity. (Preliminary report on the Fels Fund). *Amer. J. Dis. Child. 49,* 1050.

Spelt, D. K. (1938). Conditioned responses in the human fetus in utero. *Psychol. Bull. 35,* 712–713.

Spelt. D. K. (1948). The conditioning of the human fetus in utero. *J. exp. Psychol. 38,* 338–346.

Troshikhin, V. A. (1952). Some tasks in the research of higher nervous activity in onto-genesis. (Rus.) *Zh. vys. nerv. Deiat.* 2, 561–571.

Ukhtomskii, A. A. (1952). The principle of dominant center. (Rus.) In I. M. Sechenov, I. P. Pavlov, & N. E. Wedenskii (Eds.), *Physiology of the nervous system.* Vol. 1. (3rd ed.) Moscow: Medgiz. Pp. 262–266.

Volokhov, A. A. (1953). Typologic differences of nervous system in infants. (Rus.) *Med. Rabot, 16,* 2–3.

Volokhov, A. A. (1959). Typologic differences in higher nervous activity in infants and their reflection in some autonomic functions. (Rus.) *Mater. 7th Congr. Soviet. Pediat.* 77–80.

Wedenskii, N. E. (1952). Relationship between rhythmical processes and functional activity of an excited neuromuscular apparatus. (Rus.) In I. M. Sechenov, I. P. Pavlov, & N.E. Wedenskii (Eds.), *Physiology of the nervous system.* Vol. 2. (3rd ed.) Moscow: Medgiz.

Wenger, M. A. (1936). An investigation of conditioned responses in human infants. *Univer. Iowa Stud. Child Welf. 12,* 9–90.

Pattern Preferences and Perceptual-Cognitive Development in Early Infancy

Robert L. Fantz and Sonia Nevis

WESTERN RESERVE UNIVERSITY

From birth the infant is receptive and responsive to environmental stimulation. This is a fact for which evidence has been accumulating at an accelerating rate during the past decade. But the implications of this fact for theories and practices of infant development are largely unknown. Presumably the young infant has the opportunity for experiencing and learning about objects and places in his surroundings. But to what extent can he use this opportunity to prepare for later adaptive responses to those objects and places? And how

Reprinted from *Merrill-Palmer Quarterly of Behavior and Development* 1967, *13,* No. 1, 77, 88–108. By permission.

Presented at The Merrill-Palmer Institute Conference on Research and Teaching of Infant Development, February 10–12, 1966, directed by Irving E. Sigel, chairman of research. The conference was financially supported in part by the National Institute of Child Health and Human Development. The research reported in this paper was supported by Grant HD 00314 from the National Institute of Child Health and Human Development, USPHS. The authors wish to acknowledge the assistance of Mrs. Mary Parker in the gathering and analysis of the data.

can we make use of our knowledge in this area to facilitate the psychological development of the infant, as well as to assess the progress of that development? Questions such as these need to be answered before the significance of the recent findings can be evaluated.

Recent data on the infant, obtained by a variety of methods, concern auditory and other modalities as well as vision. But this paper will be restricted to information on visual perception obtained by the visual preference method, with emphasis on some findings of an intensive longitudinal study, just completed and presented here for the first time.

It has long been known that the newborn infant can respond to light stimulation and probably to color. But it is patterned visual stimulation for which the vertebrate eye evolved, and from which derives almost all of the useful information taken in through the eye. Spatial orientation, object recognition, and social responsiveness in the child and adult are based largely on the perception of subtle variations in form and texture. Without pattern vision a person is blind for most practical purposes, even though light and color are received. Pattern vision is therefore of critical importance in studying perceptual development in the infant.

The traditional theory was that pattern vision and form perception were acquired through an associational process, acting upon the "primary sensory elements" of brightness and color. But it is now proven that even in the early weeks the young infant can resolve and discriminate patterns and other configurational aspects; also, that the young infant spends most of his time looking at these behaviorally important parts of the environment. The selectivity for patterns is just as important as the discrimination of patterns. The infant or adult who concentrated his attention on uniformly colored surfaces or spaces could make little use of his pattern-vision capacities. The behavioral evidence illustrated below is well supported by neurological evidence showing that the vertebrate visual system from retina to cortex is, predominantly and inherently, receptive and responsive to patterned input, rather than to unpatterned light (e.g., Hubel and Wiesel, 1963; Sackett, 1963).

· · ·

DETERMINING SIGNIFICANCE OF PREFERENCE CHANGES

This experiment represented a departure from the previous aims of pinning down the relevant stimulus variables for, and the effects of experience on, visual preferences. Here the primary aim was to determine whether the various changes in visual preferences that had appeared previously were indicative of basic perceptual-cognitive development. If this could be demonstrated, then the age-of-occurrence of these changes might be useful for the purposes for which the various developmental scales or "baby tests" had been devised but have failed to serve satisfactorily (Bayley, 1955). The failure of such tests to predict later behavior or intelligence might be due to the absence during the early months or years of individual differences correlated with later differences. But the failure might also be due to the fact that those tests primarily measured motor development, sensory-motor coordination, and other overt performances, rather than more strictly perceptual-cognitive functions such as discrimination and selectivity. If so, this gap might be filled in part by measures of the early development of pattern discrimination and selection.

The success of the present project in obtaining some clear-cut results may be attributed to the selection of subjects, stimulus targets, and testing procedures. In order to avoid waiting five years or so to see if infant visual preferences were predictive of later performance, the traditional representative-sample paradigm of longitudinal studies was reversed. Two samples were selected which could be expected to represent the upper and lower reaches of the intellectual continuum, to the degree that this might be possible on the basis of parentage and environmental beginnings. During the course of the study ten infants of the university faculty, reared in private homes, were compared with ten foundlings, reared in an institution. All of the institution-reared infants were presumably of Caucasian parents and all were healthy; the Apgar scores available for eight of them were all in the normal range (either 9 or 10).

The stimulus pairs were selected partly on the basis of early data indicating a change in preference during the first 6 months, partly on the basis of results of a pilot study of a wide variety of stimulus variations, and partly on "experimental intuition." The final 18 pairs (Fig. 1) all had some promise of bringing out developmental changes in selective attention, and thereby revealing individual or group differences in rate of development (see p. 78).

Such a large battery of visual-preference tests required more effective techniques for obtaining the undivided attention of the subjects than had been used in the past. Such techniques were perfected in the pilot study, after being initially tried out on any available captive subject (this being, on most occasions, the senior author's infant daughter). The improved testing procedure (Fig. 2) was designed to keep the subject both comfortable and alert. The infant was held in a semi-reclining orientation in an adjustable canvas "baby seat" on the lap of an assistant seated in a rocking chair. Exposures were limited to 20 seconds and the contiguous presentations of the same pair of targets limited to two (with reversed positions of the pair). The infant was allowed to look at an interesting pattern during the between-exposure periods, which were made as brief as possible by an event recorder (to eliminate the manual recording of responses from timers), by a simple movable stage for exposing targets and by an electric-plug arrangement for quickly attaching and removing stimulus targets. Any stratagems were allowed (rocking, talking, moving the arms, etc.) between exposures for arousing or quieting the infant as needed. Finally, and probably most essentially, the assistant was allowed to administer *ad libitum* a pacifier.

Such manipulations of the subject's state did not constitute lack of experimental control. To the contrary, they tended to maintain, as much as

Fig. 1. The pairs of stimulus targets used in the longitudinal study, numbered according to order of presentation during each weekly test. In each pair, the target on the left is the one for which percentages were calculated in graphs of the results (except for familiarization tests). All of the targets were attached to blue felt plaques which matched the chamber lining. With the exception of eight of the pairs, the targets were made from cardboard or non-glossy photographic prints glued to the felt and were either white, black-and-white, or a shade of gray. The eight other pairs were as follows: Pair 2, brightly colored plastic fruit vs. red, blue, and white nursery light-switch plaque; Pair 4, boards covered with colored patterned plastic, one board slanting out and the other vertical; Pair 6, solid model of a head and flat outline of the same head; Pair 7, wire-mesh attached to wood with holes, partly painted white, vs. fluorescent red-and-yellow disc, rotating at 4 r.p.m.; Pair 9, fluorescent red checks and square; Pair 10, sphere and disc, each covered with pebble-textured white paint; Pair 15, solid head model with achromatic painted features vs. photograph of the same; Pair 16, an Egyptian art reproduction vs. translucent globe with a 40-watt orange light, flashing 48 times a minute.

was possible, a constant state of alertness for the successive stimulus pairs and for different subjects and ages. Moreover, the response measured was was the direction of gaze, not the degree of arousal or other intensive aspects of attention. If there was any bias in the control of alertness between groups, it favored the institutionalized infants, who were more readily available for starting or for finishing the testing later in the day or on another day at a more auspicious time.

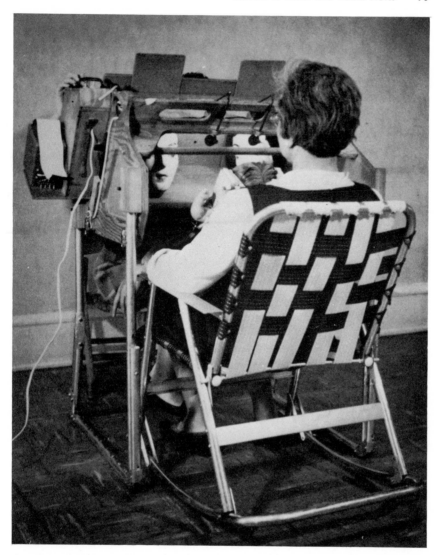

Fig. 2. Visual-preference testing apparatus in operation. Assistant (back toward camera) supports the infant on her lap in a canvas baby-seat with foam head-holder. Observer, barely visible behind the apparatus, looks through the peephole between the two targets and records fixations by pressing switch levers (upper left) to cause marks on the moving tape. The plaques to which the targets are attached extend up past the top of the stage.

A final essential ingredient in the experiment was the fortitude and perseverance shown by the investigator, Mrs. Nevis, and her assistant, Mrs. Parker. It often fell to their lot, after carrying a station wagon full of equipment through sleet and snow or up several flights of stairs to the residence of each subject for the weekly test, to politely concur when the subject decided the test had been scheduled at the wrong time or on the wrong day, pacifier or no, and however interesting the show!

The results are presented in detail elsewhere (Nevis and Fantz, in prep.). As an indication of the overall consistency of the results, a significant visual preference (.05 level, two-tailed sign test) was shown among the 20 infants on more than half of the 19 testing sessions (given weekly from 2 to 16 weeks and then biweekly through 24 weeks) for ten of the stimulus pairs. In one case (Pair 11), the bull's eye pattern was looked at longer than the stripes by each of the 20 infants on seven of the testing weeks. Only two of the stimulus pairs (16 and 17)—showing a significant differential on only two or three testing weeks—failed to meet the criterion for significance of a series of related results. Definite age changes in the direction of the preference—either from one to the other target, or from no preference to a consistent preference (or the reverse)—were shown by both groups for all but Pairs 13 and 18. A preference change of 40% or more was shown for Pairs 3, 6, 7, 8, and 11. This does not imply necessarily that such strong differential visual responses and such marked age changes are frequent among everyday objects of the infant's environment (an interesting question requiring a different manner of choosing targets), but only that we succeeded in choosing stimulus pairs revealing of early developmental changes.

The questions of most interest here are the differences in development for the two highly selected samples of infants, and the type of stimulus variables showing the most change and the most difference between samples.

GROUP DIFFERENCES IN PREFERENCE DEVELOPMENT

Starting with the fixation time for 40-second exposure of each pair (with reversed positions after 20 seconds), the percentage for a particular target of the pair (the one pictured on the left in Fig. 1) was obtained for each testing week. Successive percentage scores for a single infant were sometimes quite variable. To reduce the random part of the variation and accentuate any developmental changes, the individual response curves were smoothed by making a running average (one-half of a given point combined with one-quarter of the preceding and following points), rather than by averaging several weeks and thereby losing the advantage of the weekly tests. The resulting curves were averaged for each sample. To fill in the age gap prior to the first test at 2 weeks, 20 unselected infants from a hospital newborn ward, less than one week of age, were tested with 12 of the stimulus pairs. The average scores for these infants are indicated on the same graphs.

The most consistent difference between samples was for Pair 3—linear vs. circular line arrangements—as shown in Fig. 3. The two curves are almost identical, except that the home curve is shifted about 2 weeks to the left, as if a basic developmental process was involved but was speeded up slightly for the home sample.

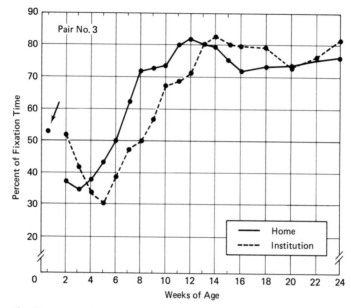

Fig. 3. Age-preference curves for the circular over the linear arrangement of line segments, for two samples of 10 infants on successive
weeks of age. Initial point (indicated by arrow) is for 20 unselected
newborn infants.

To determine the statistical significance of such a difference, the preference scores for the two groups were compared at each week of age by a one-
tailed Mann-Whitney U test (.05 level) of ranked percentages. The hypothesis
was for higher percentages to be shown by the home sample for each of the
pairs—except for Pairs 8, 17, and 18, where the change was downward and
lower percentages were thus expected. For Pair 3 the hypothesized difference
was shown at 7, 8, 9, and 11 weeks of age.

To determine the developmental significance of the between-sample
difference, visual-preference results were related to results from a traditional
type of infant performance test, in which was determined the age of first
occurrence of postural, locomotor, sensory-motor, vocal, social, or other
responses. For this purpose, we used the Griffiths Mental Development Scale
(Griffiths, 1954) but omitted those items which seemed to be ambiguous in
preliminary trials with infants of varying ages, or which may have been biased
against institution-reared infants—e.g., those based on the mother's report,
those involving reactions to the mother, or those requiring experiences or
training more likely present in a private home. This performance scale was
given weekly, usually following the preference testing. The average scores
for the two samples (Fig. 4) showed increasing differentiation during the 6
months, but the difference was not significant until 15 weeks of age and

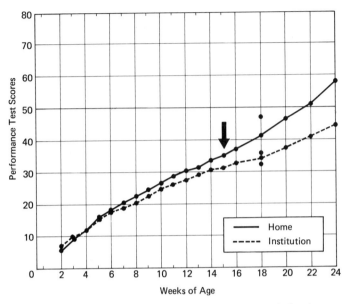

Fig. 4. Number of items passed on an infant mental development scale (performance test) at successive weeks of age. The heavy arrow indicates the first significant difference between the two samples. The separate points at 18 weeks of age are the average scores for the top-5-home, middle-10, and bottom-5-institution subsamples.

thereafter. This in itself provided substantiation for the expected difference between the two samples in rate of behavior development, even though it was not until the fourth month of age. To gain further information, the 20 infants were redivided into three subsamples based on performance scores at 18 weeks, the last test for which all the institution infants were still available. These three subsamples consisted of the top 5 of the home sample (which were above any of the institution sample), the bottom 5 of the institution sample (which overlapped the home sample), and the remaining 10 (which clustered closely together).

The visual-preference results for the three subsamples were then compared. The rationale was this: if the visual-preference changes were related to and predictive of the later rate of psychological development (as measured by the performance test), then the top-home and bottom-institution subsamples might show a wider separation in preference curves than the original home and institution samples. This was the case for Pair 3 (Fig. 5), showing about a 5-week difference between the "top 5" and the "bottom 5" curves in the age of development of a strong preference for the circular pattern.

The hypothesized group difference was supported by the overall results for the 17 pairs (this excluded Pair 2; see below, p. 93). Considering all tests during the first three months of life—the period of development of most

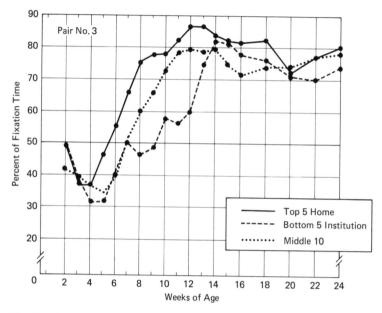

Fig. 5. Age-preference curves for the circular over the linear line-arrangements, for subsamples based on performance test scores (compare with Fig. 6).

of the preferences—21 significant differences favored the home sample, while 4 favored the institution sample. Pairs 1, 3, 4, 5, 7, 13, and 17 favored the home sample on two or more of the testing weeks. For all of these except Pair 13, more difference was shown between the top and bottom subsample curves than between the total home and institution samples. Pairs 6 and 9 alone showed differences favoring the institution sample on two of the testing weeks, and for both pairs less difference was shown between the subsamples.

Furthermore, the findings were clearly related to the stimulus variables. Three of the seven pairs that brought out a significant earlier or more marked preference change for the home sample consisted of two complex, flat, unfamiliar, achromatic patterns. In addition, Pair 14, which showed increased differentiation for the subsamples, was in this stimulus category. The only pair which could be placed in this category and which did not show a group difference was Pair 11, the only patterns with simple, unbroken contours. This and the other four pairs of patterns all brought out a marked change in preference during the second month of life, followed by a consistent differential response to one of the patterns through the remainder of the first six months.

The results for two of the five pairs of patterns (Pairs 3 and 11) have been given. For pair 5 (Fig. 6), the checkerboard arrangement was preferred to the lattice arrangement a week or so sooner for the home sample (reliably so); and the top-home subsample was a little earlier in this development

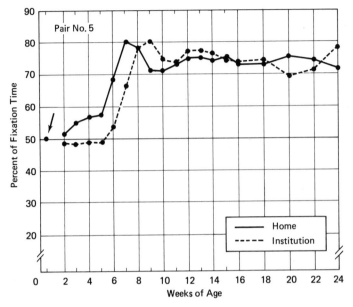

Fig. 6. Age-preference curves for the checkerboard over the lattice arrangement of white squares. Initial point (indicated by arrow) is for the unselected newborn infants.

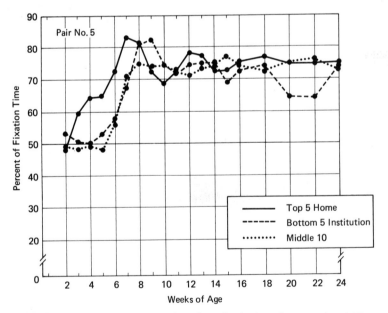

Fig. 7. Age-preference curves for the checkerboard over the lattice arrangement of squares, for the performance test subsamples (compare with Fig. 9).

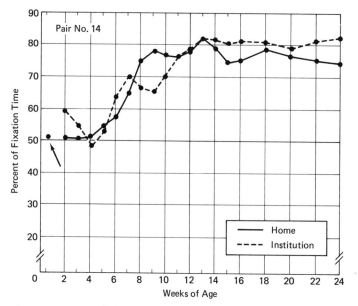

Fig. 8. Age-preference curves for the random over the lattice arrangement of black squares on white background. Initial point (indicated by arrow) is for unselected newborn infants.

(Fig. 7). For Pair 14 (Fig. 8), the suggested difference in the development of preference for a random over a regular arrangement of squares was not reliable; however, the curves for the top-home and bottom-institution sub-samples were separated much further (Fig. 9). For Pair 1 (Fig. 10), there was a change in predominant visual attention from the irregular, angular pattern to the "polka dot" pattern; the change occurred earlier and more markedly for the home infants (the difference being reliable between samples and given some support by the subsample results). This pair differed in more stimulus dimensions than the other four. It had been included in the study not as a variation in intrinsic pattern properties, but to bring out the effect of repeated exposures of one of two patterns of expected equal initial attention value (see below). It is interesting that this pair nevertheless elicited preference changes and group differences comparable to those of the other pairs of abstract patterns.

Three other pairs were similar in that they included unfamiliar patterns or objects, but the physical stimulus difference was much greater. A strong preference for red checks over a red square (Pair 9) developed during the first two months; a small but significant developmental difference between the two samples favored the institution sample. For Pair 7 there was a shift in predominant attention during the first 3 months from a bright red spot rotating slowly on a bright yellow field to a dull, complex, stationary object. More advanced development was suggested for the home than for the

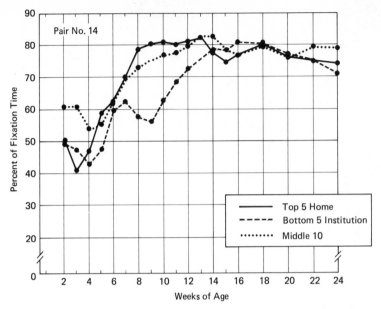

Fig. 9. Age-preference curves for the random over the lattice arrangements, for the performance test subsamples (compare with Fig. 11).

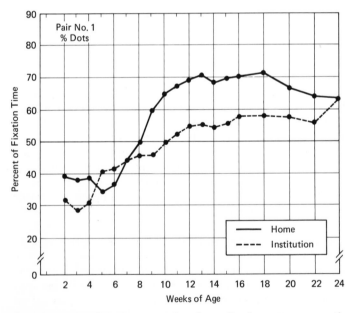

Fig. 10. Age-preference curves for the polka-dot pattern over the irregular-angular pattern on first presentation of this pair, before familiarization exposures.

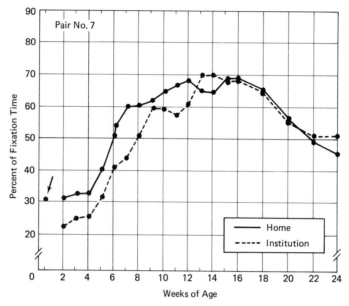

Fig. 11. Age-preference curves for the complex wire-mesh and wood object over the rotating bright red spot. Initial point (indicated by arrow) is for the unselected newborn infants.

institution sample (Fig. 11). This was supported by the subsample curves, showing little initial preference for the bright-colored moving object by the top-home subsample. Pair 16 presented perhaps the grossest stimulus varia-tions of all, but was one of the few pairs which did *not* bring out a reliable preference throughout the testing! In spite of the high variability in direction of preference, the trend was from an early low preference for the flashing orange light to a stronger preference for Egyptian art during the third month, then back to equal response. The home sample appeared to be a little ahead in this development. On balance, these three pairs suggest a higher prefer-ence for highly complex targets over plain, brightly colored, and moving or flashing targets by the home-reared infants. But this high degree of stimulus difference elicited less differential attention and less group differentiation than some relatively subtle differences between patterns.

The remaining stimulus variations are for the most part similar to those used in the earlier attempts (see above) to determine the effects of experi-ence. A number of pairs were representations of social stimuli, with varia-tion in the degree of resemblance to a face. The most easily interpreted result was for Pair 17: an early preference for a life-size schematic face pattern over the same pattern reduced in size dropped to the chance level during the third month (Fig. 12). This change occurred earlier for the home sample (reaching statistical significance) and still earlier for the top-home subsample. Since the change was in the wrong direction to be an experiential preference

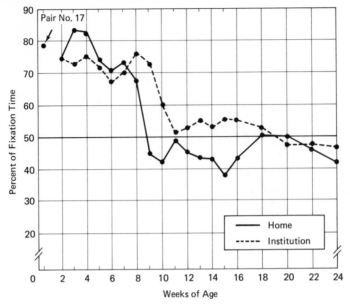

Fig. 12. Age-preference curves for the natural-size over the small schematic face. Initial point (indicated by arrow) is for the un-selected newborn infants.

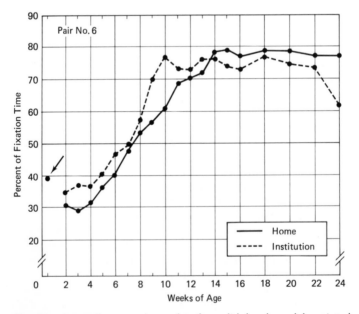

Fig. 13. Age-preference curves for the solid head model, painted white, over the while outline form. Initial point (indicated by arrow) is for the unselected newborn infants.

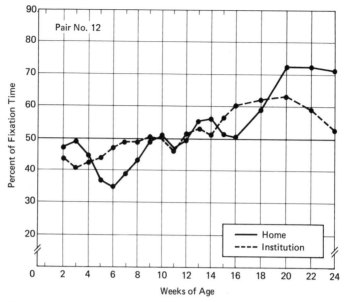

Fig. 14. Age-preference curves for the schematic face over the scrambled pattern.

for the more realistic facelike stimulus, it must instead be attributed to a decrease in the intrinsic attention value of size—at least, the size of an interesting pattern (other results have indicated a continuing size preference with unpatterned targets). That the change is earlier for the home infants is in keeping with their earlier or more marked attention to configurational differences.

Another significant group difference relative to face-like targets was for Pair 6 (Fig. 13), showing an earlier development by the institution sample of preference for a solid model of a head (without painted features). It is not at all clear that this was a "social preference" rather than a "solidity preference," since a solidity preference appeared at about the same age for two other target pairs. Nor is the meaning of the group difference clear, since one of the other solid-versus-flat pairs (Pair 4) favored the home sample significantly, while the other (Pair 10) showed little difference. To further confuse the matter, for another pair varying in both solidity and facial resemblance (Pair 15), a head model with painted features was not reliably preferred to a photograph of the model until 20 weeks of age, and even then the degree of differential was not great.

The correct location of "eye spots" on an oval (Pair 13) was slightly preferred throughout the age range by the home infants, but not until after 2 months of age by the institution infants. The latter result is in fair accord with earlier studies (see Fantz, 1966, table 3). But the correct arrangement of schematic features (Pair 12) was not reliably preferred over the scrambled face

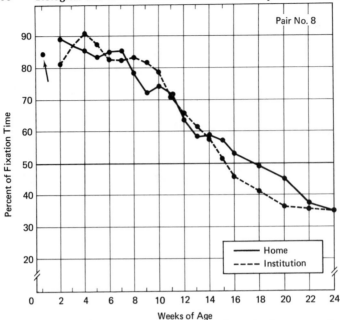

Fig. 15. Age-preference curves for the schematic face over the photographic reproduction of an actual face. Initial point (indicated by arrow) is for the unselected newborn infants.

by either group until late in the first 6 months of age (Fig. 14), and the scrambled pattern was preferred on several early testing weeks. This is in contrast to the earlier studies which had varying results but, taken together, showed the most consistent preference between 2 and 3 months of age. Aside from this discrepancy, which we cannot account for, all results from these two pairs have agreed in the high variability and low degree of differential attention, in contrast to the frequent strong and consistent preferences found for pairs varying in intrinsic stimulus properties. Similarly, it would appear that the strongest preference elicited by a pair of face-like stimuli in this study (Pair 8, Fig. 15) can be accounted for only by attraction to intrinsic stimulus properties, since the schematic face pattern, with high contrast and low complexity, was initially preferred to the more realistic face photograph.

One class of stimulus variation remains: experimental variation in visual exposure, either on a long-term or short-term basis. Long-term exposure was provided by hanging one of the toys of Pair 2 above the home crib of each infant from the third week of age until the end of the experiment. The results (Fig. 16) were the biggest disappointment of the study. We expected attachment and increased attention to the familiar object from the familiar environment, and were encouraged in this by repeated reports from mothers and attendants of high attraction to the mobile from an early age. As it turned out, this was one of the pairs giving least evidence of a consistent differential

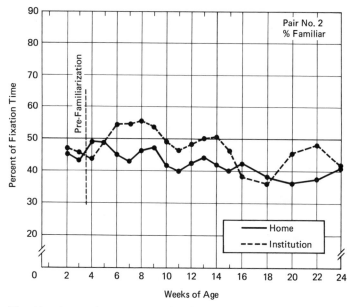

Fig. 16. Age-preference curves for the single toy taken from Pair 2, which was hung continually over the home crib of each infant from the third week to the end of the experiment.

response or of a consistent age change. Moreover, the slight change suggested was towards the novel, *not* towards the familiar object. The difference between groups suggested by the curves did not reach significance. One explanation—supported by the consistent choice by many infants for the "fruit" object (familiar or not) throughout the testing—is that intrinsic visual preferences were of more effect on the visual responsiveness than familiarity. Results from another laboratory have also been inconclusive on visual responsiveness to a familiar mobile, and have shown interference from preferences among the objects used (Greenberg, Hunt, and Uzgiris, in MS.; Uzgiris and Hunt, 1965).

Initial preferences were better controlled for the short-term variation in exposure by changing the familiarization pattern every other testing week, and by comparing the responsiveness to the particular pattern before and aften the familiarization exposures. These exposures were given by attaching a duplicate of one of the test patterns (Pair 1) on the underside of the movable "stage" so that it was visible to the infant between each of the following test exposures until Pair 1 was again tested (usually following Pair 12). The results indicate decreasing relative fixation of the repeatedly exposed pattern with increasing age (Fig. 17). The choice of the novel object was significant for both groups after 3 months of age; the suggested difference between groups, favoring the home sample, was not quite significant. Again it is ap-

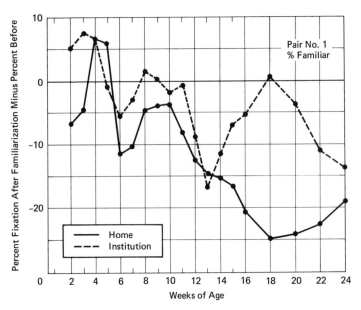

Fig. 17. Relative attention to that pattern of Pair 1 which was repeatedly exposed during the particular test session, compared with response to the same pattern at the beginning of each session.

parent, from the consistent pattern preferences elicited by this pair (see Fig. 10) that effects of previous experience on visual preferences are more difficult to bring out *by the present methods* than the effects of variations in the patterns themselves.

DISCUSSION

Several findings stand out forcibly from the mass of data obtained from young infants by the visual-preference method. First, the relative amount of time spent in looking at various targets is very largely a function of the stimulus properties of the target rather than determined by previous exposure history or similarity to familiar objects. This is, of course, limited to the experimental conditions—including the exposure of certain types of artificial or laboratory-specific stimuli in a reduced and unfamiliar stimulus situation for short periods of time, with no active contact or feedback from the stimuli—conditions which favor free visual exploration of the environment. It is likely that there are other conditions (e.g., a fear-producing situation or the home crib) in which specific past experiences would have more effect on visual preferences.

The determining stimulus variables are numerous and interrelated even under these restricted conditions. But certainly prominent—and more basic than color, reflectance, or size—are variations in *pattern*. And two important types of variation are the degree of the patterning (complexity) and the form of the patterning (configuration). It is not possible to state the relative importance of complexity and form in general, or even to make a clear distinction between the two in many cases. Yet many aspects of the results point to a special significance of configurational variations. This is the finding upon which the further interpretations will be based.

Configurational differences (form of contours, arrangement or orientation of pattern elements) elicited some of the strongest and most consistent preferences, even when the targets were quite similar overall. Configurational differences brought out some of the earliest, most abrupt and most consistent age changes in preference. Infants can and do discriminate configurational differences at least by the second month of life (significant differentials shown at 5, 7, and 6 weeks for Pairs, 3, 5, and 11, respectively). It is not clear whether the newborn infant can discriminate patterns of similar complexity or not; the age changes may represent the development of this ability (or this selectivity). The direction of the change is often towards circular or random configurations over linear or regular ones. Nevertheless, this generalization was reversed in once case (Fig. 10) and does not adequately describe the stimulus variation in other cases. Perhaps form is multidimensional for the infant as well as for the adult.

Configurational differences also brought out the most consistent differences in the age of preference-change between the two highly selected samples of infants. This fact, with wide implications, must be interpreted carefully. That the two groups differed in rate of development of pattern preferences is quite clear from the data, but the meaning is less certain. We cannot differentiate among the various possible sources of difference, including genetic makeup, prenatal and postnatal care and nutrition, and early environment. Regarding the nature of the difference brought about by any or all of these factors, there is some basis for speculation.

The rough correlation between the pattern preference scores and the scores on a "mental development scale" both supports the group difference and suggests that it involves basic aspects of psychological development, which are revealed earlier by pattern preference changes than by the appearance of various active, coordinated behaviors. The group difference was not related to sensory-motor development; the institution infants were actually a bit ahead in passing visual fixation and pursuit items. The preference changes most revealing of developmental differences involved selection and discrimination among similar forms or patterns—comparable to many items of intelligence tests given to children or adults (at least more so than the development of motor coordination or social responsiveness).

There is some basis for a tentative conclusion that the development of selective visual attention to configurational variables represents an early stage of basic perceptual-cognitive development—a stage which may be not only predictive of later stages in this development, but also may facilitate further development by making visual exploration of the environment a more effective learning process. At first glance, the latter possibility does not seem to be in accord with the various results failing to show an effect of experience on the attention value of stimuli, or even showing the opposite of the expected increased responsiveness to the familiar object or pattern. But these results most likely indicate, not that learning through early visual explorations is absent, but that we are looking for the wrong effects of this learning. The primary effects of early visual experience are probably in the reception, organization, differentiation, and accumulation of information from the visual input, rather than in an increased or decreased tendency to fixate a familiar target, or in any other change in response frequency or duration.

The latter kind of change may give little information about the former kind. Thus a change in duration of fixation of a target from one occasion to another in itself tells us nothing about what information was received and assimilated in the course of fixating the target on either occasion. But a change in the *relative* attention to several stimulus targets may do so. The development of a preference for one of several pattern arrangements, for example, indicates that certain configurational variations can now be discriminated and tend to be selected for attention. This has an effect comparable to putting the infant in a more enriched or variegated environment, and thus of giving increased and more selective opportunities for perceptual learning. For the development of such a pattern preference to occur earlier for a given infant may or may not have been the result of a prior stimulus-rich environment and more variegated experience. In either case the infant thereby has a head start in the opportunity to discriminate, become familiar with, and take in information from configurational parts of his surroundings. This analysis assumes a perceptual learning process such as that described by Gibson and Gibson (1955), progressing towards increasing stimulus differentiation. It also postulates an important role of selectivity, at both the peripheral and central level, in the learning process.

In other words, we are proposing that what goes on during the long hours the young infant spends in visual exploration and examination of his surroundings is not to be discovered in altered responsiveness to specific objects from reinforcement or repetition, since the primary changes are to be found in finer differentiations, better integrations, and more selective examinations of the total visual input. These cumulative, non-specific effects of experience are difficult to study directly. Some indirect information is given from changes in the stimulus variations which are selected and discriminated at successive points in development, and which can then affect what is subsequently learned through visual exploration.

Whether a difference of several weeks in the development of certain pattern preferences can be of any practical use in the prediction of future mental development or in the study of effects of varying early environmental circumstances remains to be determined. The possibilities might be summed up in this way: Could it be that the infant's future prospects, as well as his past experiences and present interests, are reflected in his eyes? With that bit of crystal-ball gazing, we rest our case.

REFERENCES

Baley, Nancy. On the growth of intelligence. *Amer. Psychologist,* 1955, *10,* 805–818.

Berlyne, D. E. The influence of albedo and complexity of stimuli on visual fixation in the human infant. *Brit. J. Psychol.,* 1958, *49,* 315–318.

Bower, T. G. R. Stimulus variables determining space perception in infants. *Science,* 1965, *149,* 80–89.

Brennan, W. M., Ames, E. W., & Moore, R. W. Age differences in infants' attention to patterns of different complexities. *Science,* 1966, *150,* 354–356.

Fantz, R. L. A method for studying early visual development. *Percept. mot. Skills,* 1956, *6,* 13–15.

Fantz, R. L. Visual discrimination in a neonate chimpanzee. *Percept. mot. Skills,* 1958, *8,* 59–66. (a)

Fantz, R. L. Pattern vision in young infants. *Psychol. Rec.,* 1958, *8,* 43–47. (b)

Fantz, R. L. The origin of form perception. *Scient. American,* 1961, *204,* 66–72.

Fantz, R. L. Visual experience in infants: decreased attention to familiar patterns relative to novel ones. *Science,* 1964, *146,* 668–670.

Fantz, R. L. Visual perception from birth as shown by pattern selectivity. In H. E. Whipple (Ed.), New issues in infant development. *Ann. N.Y. Acad. Sci.,* 1965, *118,* 793–814. (a)

Fantz, R. L. Ontogeny of perception. In A. M. Schrier, H. F. Harlow, & F. Stollintz (Eds.), *Behavior of nonhuman primates. I.* New York: Academic Press, 1965. Pp. 365–403. (b)

Fantz, R. L. Pattern discrimination and selective attention as determinants of perceptual development from birth. In Aline H. Kidd & J. L. Rivoire (Eds.), *Perceptual development in children.* New York: Internat. Univer. Press, 1966.

Fantz, R. L. Visual perception and experience in early infancy: a look at the hidden side of behavior development. In H. W. Stevenson, E. H. Hess, & Harriet Rheingold (Eds.), *Early behavior: comparative and developmental approaches.* New York: Wiley, 1967.

Fantz, J. L., Ordy, J. M., & Udelf, M. S. Maturation of pattern vision in infants during the first six months. *J. comp. physiol. Psychol.,* 1962, *55,* 907–917.

Graefe, O. Versuche uber visuelle Formwahrnehmung im Saugglingsalter. *Psychol. Forsch.,* 1963, *27,* 177–224.

Greenberg, D. L., Hunt, J. McV., & Uzgiris, I. C. Infants' preference for visual stimuli: the role of complexity and familiarity. Unpublished paper.

Griffiths, R. *The abilities of babies.* New York: McGraw-Hill, 1964.

Haith, M. M. The response of the human newborn to visual movement. *J. exp. Child Psychol.,* 1966, *3,* 235–243.

Hayek, F. *The sensory order.* Chicago: Univer. Chicago Press, 1952.

Gibson, J. J., & Gibson, Eleanor J. Perceptual learning: differentiation or enrichment? *Psychol. Rev.,* 1955, *62,* 32.

Haynes, H., White, B. L., & Held, R. Visual accommodation in human infants. *Science,* 1965, *148,* 528–530.

Hershenson, M. Visual discrimination in the human infant. *J. comp. physiol. Psychol.,* 1964, *58,* 270.

Hershenson, M., Munsinger, H., & Kessen, W. Preference for shapes of intermediate variability in the newborn human. *Science,* 1965, *147,* 630–631.

Hubel, D. H. & Wiesel, T. N. Receptive fields of cells in striate cortex of very young, visually inexperienced kittens. *J. Neurophysiol.,* 1963, *26,* 994–1002.

Kagan, J., & Lewis, M. Studies of attention in the human infant. *Merrill-Palmer Quart.,* 1965, *11,* 95–127.

Lewis, M., Meyers, W., Kagan, J., & Grossberg, R. Attention to visual patterns in infants. *Amer. Psychologist,* 1963, *18,* 357.

Nevis, Sonia, & Fantz, R. L. Visual preference and psychological development: a longitudinal comparison of two selected samples. In J. Hellmuth (Ed.), *The exceptional infant.* Special Child Publications, in preparation.

Saayman, G., Ames, E. W., & Moffett, A. Response to novelty as an indicator of visual discrimination in the human infant. *J. exp. Child Psychol.,* 1964, *1,* 189–198.

Sackett, G. P. A neural mechanism underlying unlearned, critical period, and developmental aspects of visually controlled behavior. *Psychol. Rev.,* 1963, *70,* 40–50.

Spears, W. Assessment of visual preference and discrimination in the four-month-old infant. *J. comp. physiol. Psychol.,* 1964, *57,* 381–386.

Stechler, G. The effect of medication during labor on newborn infants. *Science,* 1964, *144,* 315–317.

Stechler, G., Bradford, S., & Levy, H. Attention in the newborn: effect on motility and skin potential. *Science,* 1966, *151,* 1246–1248.

Stirnimann, F. Uber das Forbenempfinden Neugeborener. *Ann. Paedia.,* 1944, *163,* 1–25.

Thomas, H. Visual fixation responses in infants to stimuli of varying complexity. *Child Develpm.,* 1965, *36,* 629–638.

Uzgiris, I. C., & Hunt, J. McV. A longitudinal study of recognition learning. Paper presented at Soc. Res. Child Developm., Minneapolis, March, 1965.

Wolff, P. H. Observations on the early development of smiling. In B. M. Foss (Ed.), *Determinants of infant behavior: II.* New York: Wiley, 1963. Pp. 113–114.

Child Development Research: An Edifice Without a Foundation

Burton L. White

HARVARD UNIVERSITY

THE GOALS OF RESEARCH IN HUMAN INFANCY

What are our individual and collective aims as students of infant development? There is, of course, the simple urge to know which though not fundable is still legitimate. In addition, it seems fair to assume that solid knowledge about infants would make it possible for parents to get a good deal

Reprinted from *Merrill-Palmer Quarterly of Behavior and Development*, 1969, *15*, No. 1, 47–78. By permission. This paper is excerpted from a longer paper in which a discussion of the theoretical foundations of developmental psychology is elaborated.

Presented at The Merrill-Palmer Institute Conference on Research and Teaching of Infant Development, February 15–17, 1968.

At various stages, extending over the last six years, the research for this paper has received support from Grant M–3657 from the National Institute of Mental Health; Grant 61–234 from the Foundation's Fund for Research in Psychiatry; Grants HD–00761 and HD–02054 from the National Institutes of Health, the Optometric Extension Program;

more satisfaction out of experiences with their infants and in turn make infancy more pleasurable for their offspring. Of course our highest priority goals are usually thought to be the compilation of the knowledge necessary to guide child-rearing practices so as to prevent harmful experiences and to maximize the likelihood of optimal development for each infant. Finally, I should mention the potential usefulness of infant research to shed light on problems of general animal behavior; adult human and infra-human.

• • •

I believe the work that comes closest to a proper scientific approach to infant behavior is Piaget's work on early intellectual development (1952). I do not claim that his work embodies a complete scientific plan. It does not. On the other hand, it starts at the beginning as few other infant studies have. By the beginning I do not refer only to the age of his subjects but rather to the logical "beginning" of a scientific inquiry.

ORIENTING THE INQUIRY

Piaget started with an interest in a piece of the general problem of infant development which was, compared to most modern studies, very large and of obvious psychological meaning. His topic was the ontogenesis of intelligence. Most modern studies refer briefly to similarly large problems, such as socialization, learning, or language development, but from this very early point on, Piaget's approach differs radically from that of most investigators. His next step was to determine what to observe *in the field*. He apparently assumed that gathering specimens of the phenomenon under study was the proper next step. He had to delineate what for Americans would be termed the dependent variables in the age range under study. But notice where he looked for his dependent variables, at the behavior of intact infants. Where do we find ours? In addition, since he brought to his work a general theoretical bias towards an interactionist position based on the biological concept of dynamic adaptation of organism to environment, he had to include within his focus some consideration of relevant environmental and experiential factors (or in our terms the independent variables). The concept of "aliment" refers to the former, and the processes of assimilation and accommodation refer to the latter. He therefore went into the field, like many a naturalist before him, and started collecting examples of what he

Grant NSG–496 from the National Aeronautics and Space Administration; Grant AF–AFOSR354–63 from the Office of Scientific Research, United States Air Force; the Rockefeller Foundation; and contract number OE5–10–239 from the Office of Education. The research was conducted at the Tewksbury Hospital, Tewksbury, Massachusetts. I am very grateful for the assistance of Dr. Richard Held, Mr. Peter Castle, Mrs. Kitty Clark, Mr. Richard Light, and Mrs. Cherry Collins, and for the consideration and aid given by Drs. John Lu, Solomon J. Fleischman, Peter Wolff, and Lois Crowell and head nurses Helen Efstathiou, Frances Craig, and Virginia Donovan.

was interested in. In this procedure he differed radically from most students of infant development.

CHARTING THE COURSE OF DEVELOPMENT
OF AN ABILITY AND ITS RELEVANT
ECOLOGICAL CONDITIONS

Piaget's six stages of sensorimotor intelligence summarize in a coherent way, what he learned about intelligent behavior in infancy. In building the case for his particular view of the developmental process, he described the precursors of intelligent behavior, the emergence of intelligent or purposeful, means-ends behavior and its progressive forms which culminate in behaviors which point clearly to the emergence of representational intelligence at the end of the second year of life.

Piaget not only went beyond unfocused naturalistic observation by observing systematically, he also introduced numerous ingenious test situations to pin down his preliminary judgments. An excellent example of such a test is the object permanence test which is now being standardized by Uzgiris and Hunt among others.

In gathering his data Piaget restricted his efforts to his own children. Certainly our discipline requires study of considerably larger numbers of subjects and rearing conditions. Further, his approach could and should be improved by the utilization, *at the proper time,* of objective means of data collection, standardized tests, and sophisticated statistical analyses. In addition, *all* major developmental processes should be studied this way. The resultant body of data on intelligence and the other major developmental processes would constitute a legitimate foundation for a science of infant development. It is just such information which is missing in our field even after seventy years of activity. I maintain that it is not only necessary but patently obvious that such data must be accumulated at the beginning of any scientific inquiry into infant development and certainly should precede elaborate theorizing. After all, the basic function of a theory is to bring form and coherence into an array of facts. Granted, theory at some level should guide observations and compilations of factual data. The rate of progression of theory-building, however, must be linked to the volume of available empirical data. Without such coordination theory degenerates into easy speculation and vulgarity. It is my belief that this is our current status.

THEORIZING—A COMBINATION
OF DEDUCTIVE AND INDUCTIVE MODES

Inductive theorizing should start from observational data. Provided that the data base is extensive enough, it is often rather easy in its early stages. As Wright points out (1960), nature provides innumerable leads to theory in the countless arrangements of circumstances and individuals that exist. It only waits for the tireless investigator to go out and look with disciplined unbiased eyes. I am not advocating a purely inductive approach; but, I would feel so relieved if instead of relying almost exclusively on deduction our language theorists, for example, would go out and gather some data. For all the brilliant thoughts on how humans acquire language, almost no one has bothered to examine the process during late infancy when presumably some remarkable language learning often takes place. In a recent editorial (1967) Alberta Siegel points out that not a single study concentrating on toddlers (1 to 3 years of age) appeared in *Child Development* in 1965 or 1966. For that matter only 15 of the 152 papers on human subjects published concentrated on infants six days to one year of age. We will never come of age as a field as long as we let easy availability of subjects and the herd instinct determine who and what we will study.

EXPERIMENTAL STUDIES ON THE ROLE OF EXPERIENCE IN INFANT DEVELOPMENT

As far as I can tell, and I do not pretend to be an expert, scientific method in 1968 is insufficiently advanced for guiding an airtight program of experimental-longitudinal research in human infancy. Many of the reasons that make evaluation of compensatory pre-school education a methodological nightmare exist in the investigation of early experience. There is a vast difference between a laboratory-based, 20-minute long experiment and an attempt at isolating causes in the acquisition of language over for example, a six-month period. In the area of intellectual development, the problem is probably even more complicated.

My recommendations to cope with this dilemma will not bring joy to the heart of the methodological purist, but I know of no feasible alternatives. I would propose that we attempt a clean grasp on our dependent variables via systematic observational studies, then a deliberately global handling of independent variables. The problem of which achievements we want to enhance is far simpler than the determination of causes. If one goal might be the early acquisition of instrumental behavior for example, I am confident we can devise ways of dependably assessing an infant's status in this regard. The emergence of such an ability, however, will probably be determined by factors considerably more complex than whether he is fed pablum or cream of wheat. It is the perverse nature of human infants to be so complicated that not only will physical factors such as diet contribute to this development, but no doubt so will parental behaviors, crib materials and other ingredients as well. The unravelling of the staggering number of interactions and contingencies as they cumulate over time in the ongoing life of an infant is a scientific problem we are nowhere near prepared to tackle. Like our colleagues in other complicated areas of research such as cancer and heart disease, we have to be lucky to separate relevant items from the mass; and, we must recognize that to the degree that the acquisitions we seek to understand are not traceable to a small number of discrete causal events, our problem becomes even more difficult.

I propose then, that rather than keep all but one or two independent variables constant or randomize them while manipulating one or two, that we look instead for "clusters of experience" which prevail more often in the experiential histories of precocious infants and manipulate rearing conditions so as to maximize such exposure for our experimental subjects. By focusing on a global analysis of experiential histories of precocious versus slow infants, I believe we can capture relevant causal factors in a rather large net at first. Subsequent studies will sift the experiential clusters through finer and finer screens until we have a reasonably sure handle on what the significant experiential factors are. I am advocating a kind of "bracketing" or successive approximation technique. Rather than continue at this abstract level, I would like to use my own program of research in infancy to clarify these ideas.

· · ·

As I have already mentioned, I'm not an advocate of elaborate theorizing in the field of infancy at this stage of development. I am impressed by Piaget's general biological view of development as a continuing process of adaptation. I am also impressed by his concepts of assimilation and accommodation, among others. But, Piaget's theory does not deal with the mechanisms of development in the moment to moment experiences of the child. For example, Held claims that information is processed and the infant develops only when he performs certain motor acts within certain kinds of sensory surrounds. Hunt argues that the infant's motor involvement can be restricted to the ocular and extraocular muscles in the first month and that more extensive motor involvement only becomes necessary later. Such discussion of mechanisms speaks to a very practical level of experimental design in contrast to the concepts of assimilation and accommodation which are fairly high-level abstractions. There are other theoretical views of this problem but I prefer to gather a more comprehensive data base and perhaps save the wasted effort of premature theorizing. I have found so often in the last few years that theoretical notions about infancy, espoused by many leading figures simply do not stand up to the facts.

We did one handling study because there was a weight of evidence from several sources which was consistent with what we had learned about infants in the first weeks of life. Mainly, however, I prefer to assume that active involvement by the infant is the general prerequisite for development and then to concentrate on the quality of that involvement. Major clues to the types of experience to sponsor come from what we discover about emerging abilities and interests of infants. An additional assumption therefore is that "feeding" newly emerging abilities is the clue to designing the optimal

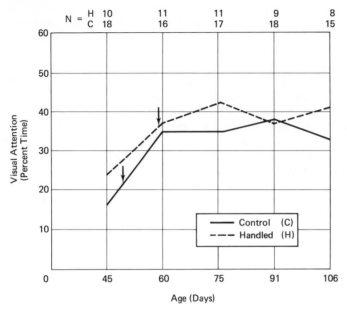

Fig. 1.

"match" between infant and environment. Beyond this point, I am not ready to go.

LONGITUDINAL EXPERIMENTAL STUDIES—FIRST MODIFICATION OF REARING CONDITIONS

Handling Study

Many recent studies have reported the remarkable effects of postnatal handling on the subsequent development of laboratory-reared animals (Denenberg & Karas, 1959; Levine, 1957; Meier, 1961). Mice, kittens, and dogs given small amounts of extra handling grew up to be better animals as measured by a wide variety of tests—they were superior in many physical and adaptive respects. Recent surveys of maternal deprivation studies by Yarrow (1961) and Casler (1961) suggest that early handling appears necessary for adequate human development. Sylvia Brody in her *Patterns of Mothering* (1951) noted that infants who received moderate handling were consistently more visually attentive than those receiving minimal handling. Would extra handling of our subjects, who normally receive minimal amounts, result in accelerated visual-motor development?

From day 6 through day 36, nurses administered 20 minutes of extra handling each day to each of ten infants. Measures of overall development,

Table 1 Summary of Visual Attention Data

Group and Period Observed	N Subjects[a]	N Scores[a]	Mean Percentage of Time Attending
37–112 days			
Control	45	113	32.1
Handled	11	102	36.8
Massive enrichment	13	118	32.8
Modified enrichment	14	146	40.1
Total	83	479	
37–75 days			
Control	34	59	29.9
Handled	10	58	34.2
Massive enrichment	13	68	26.3
Modified enrichment	14	78	36.7
Total	71	263	
76–112 days			
Control	16	43	33.5
Handled	8	37	41.4
Massive enrichment	9	43	46.9
Modified enrichment	13	70	42.5
Total	46	193	

[a] Number of subjects and observations varies because subjects, though overlapping, were not identical for the three periods.

physical growth, general health, development of reaching, and visual attention, were taken at weekly intervals between days 37 and 152 (White & Castle, 1964).

No changes were found in any developmental process except the growth of visual attention. The handled group was more visually attentive than controls. Note that the shapes of the curves in Fig. 1 are quite similar.[1] Sustained hand regard appeared somewhat later in the handled group (day 60) than in controls (day 49). Upon relocation in large, open-sided cribs the handled group, like the control group, exhibited a sharp increase in visual attentiveness (see Tables 1 and 2).

This study suggested that innocuous environmental modifications might alter the development of important visual-motor functions such as exploratory behavior. No evidence for comparable plasticity in other visual-motor developments was found following the extra handling. It is possible that further exploration of the effects of early handling would produce still greater increases in visual exploratory behavior.

[1] In a previous report (White & Castle, 1964), we indicated that this increase in visual attention was statistically significant. In fact, the analysis used was somewhat inappropriate. In addition, we have added data from one new subject. Subsequent analysis (see Table 2) indicates a strong trend that fails to reach significance at the .05 level.

Table 2   Significance of Differences Between Mean Visual Attention Scores for Experimental and Control Groups Observed at Age 37–75 Days and/or 76–112 Days

Group Means Compared[a]	t	df	p[b]
37–112 Days Old			
C (32.1) vs. H (36.8)	1.72	213	< .05
C (32.1) vs. ME (32.8)			NS
C (32.1) vs. MOD E (40.1)	3.10	257	< .005
H (36.8) vs. ME (32.8)			NS
H (36.8) vs. MOD E (40.1)			NS
ME (32.8) vs. MOD E (40.1)	2.96	262	< .005
MOD E (40.1) vs.			
C + H + ME (33.8)	3.50	477	< .0005
37–75 Days Old			
C (29.9) vs. H (34.2)			NS
C (29.9) vs. ME (26.3)			NS
C (29.9) vs. MOD E (40.1)	3.21	135	< .005
H (34.2) vs. ME (26.3)	2.42	124	< .01
H (34.2) vs. MOD E (40.1)	1.87	134	< .05
ME (26.3) vs. MOD E (40.1)	4.56	144	< .0005
ME (26.3) vs.			
C + H + MOD E (33.9)	2.97	262	< .01
76–112 Days Old			
C (33.5) vs. H (41.4)	1.73	78	< .05
C (33.5) vs. ME (46.9)	3.06	84	< .005
C (33.5) vs. MOD E (42.5)	2.29	111	< .025
H (41.4) vs. ME (46.9)			NS
H (41.4) vs. MOD E (42.5)			NS
ME (46.9) vs. MOD E (42.5)			NS

[a] C = Control Group; H = Handled Group; ME = Massive Enrichment Group; MOD E = Modified Enrichment Group.

[b] Because six significance figures are being calculated in each group, a conservative position would increase the required level of significance to $10/K(K - 1)$, where K = Number of Groups. In this case, $K = 4$, and the more stringent level required would be .0083 (Ferguson, 1959, p. 238).

Second Modification of Rearing Conditions—
the Massive Enrichment Study

Several studies seem to indicate that visual-motor performance depends to a significant extent on experience of some kind for its development. Riesen's (1958) work demonstrated that chimpanzees required exposure to patterned environment is also required for adequate development (Riesen, 1958). Held and his collaborators (Held & Bossom, 1961; Held, 1961; Mikaelian & Held, 1964) have repeatedly demonstrated the importance of self-induced movement in dependably structured environments for adaptation to rearranged sensory inputs in human adults. More recently, their study of neonatal kittens showed the applicability of these findings to developmental

processes (Held & Hein, 1963). The results of this study indicated that movement per se in the presence of dependable surroundings was insufficient for
normal visual-motor development. Kittens whose movements were externally-
produced rather than self-induced did not develop normally. Self-induced
movement in dependable surroundings was found necessary for adequate
development as well as for maintenance of stable visual-motor behavior.

Our subjects were usually reared under conditions that are obviously less
than optimal with respect to the kinds of experience discussed above. Motility was limited by soft mattresses with depressions in them as well as by
the supine posture in which these infants were kept. The visual surroundings
were poorly figured. Consequently, according to our hypothesis, heightened
motility in enriched surroundings should produce accelerated visual-motor
development.

As a first test we enriched the environment of a group of nineteen infants in as many respects as feasible (White, 1967): (a) Increased tactual-
vestibular stimulation. Each infant received 20 minutes of extra handling each
day from day 6 through day 36. (b) Increased motility. Infants were placed in
the prone posture for 15 minutes after the 6 A.M., 10 A.M., and 2 P.M., feeding each day from day 37 through day 124. At these times, the crib liners were
removed, making the ward activities visible to the child. Movements of the
head and trunk in the presence of figured visual surroundings resulted from
the normal tendency of infants to rear their heads under such circumstances.
The crib mattresses were flattened, thereby facilitating head, arm, and trunk
motility. (c) Enriched visual surroundings. A special stabile featuring highly
contrasting colors and numerous forms against a dull white background was
suspended over these infants from days 37 through 124 (see Fig. 2). In addition, printed multicolored sheets and bumpers were substituted for the
standard white ones. These changes were designed to reproduce heightened
visual interest and increased hand movement because of the normal tendency
of infants to swipe at visible objects nearby.

Weekly measures of prehensory responses and visual attention were
made. The rates of development of spontaneous behaviors related to visual-
motor function such as hand regard, hands touching at the midline, mutual
fingering, and turning of the torso were assessed from the records of the
three-hour observation periods. Performance on the Gesell tests was recorded
at biweekly intervals to determine general developmental progress. Also,
records of rate of weight gain and general health were kept.

RESULTS

Hand regard and swiping. Hand regard as such was much less frequently shown by this group than by controls. Instead the hands were generally first observed as they contacted portions of the experimental stabile.
We called this pattern monitored stabile play and considered it together
with monitored bumper play as forms of hand regard. By these criteria the

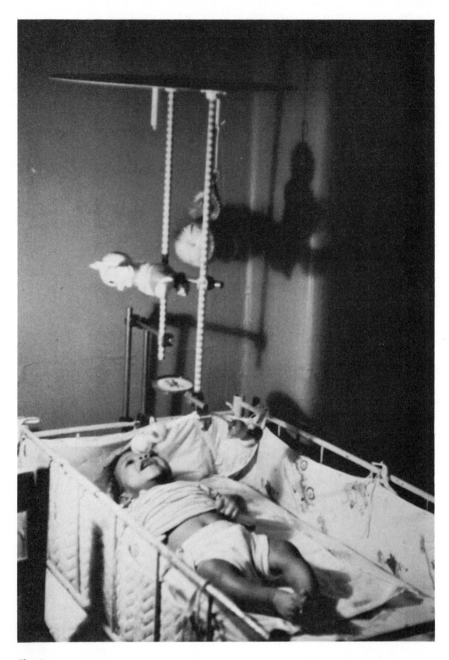

Fig. 2.

Table 3 Significance of Differences Between Experimental and Control Groups in Age at Onset of Sustained Hand Regard[a]

Condition (N of Ss; Mdn Age in Days at Onset)	Handled (N = 10; Mdn = 60)	Massive Enrichment (N = 14; Mdn = 61)	Modified Enrichment (N = 15; Mdn = 44)
Control (N = 16; Mdn = 49)	.1469, NS	.0571, NS	.1867, NS
Handled (N = 10; Mdn = 60)		.4168, NS	.0136
Massive Enrichment (N = 14; Mdn = 61)			.0016

[a] Table entries are significance levels based on Mann-Whitney U (1-tailed) tests. In order to conclude that the groups compared come from signficantly different (.05 level) parent populations, compensation must be made for the fact that a number of pairs have been sampled. In this case, six pairs are sampled, and the significance level must reach .008 before it can be concluded that the two groups differ. This value was derived from the following formula: $p = (1 - \alpha^n$, where $p = .05$, n = number of pairs compared, and α = the level of significance which must be found for any single pair in order to conclude that there is more than one parent population involved.

onset of hand regard was delayed for some twelve days in our experimental group (NS; see Table 3). The onset of swiping was also set back, but only by some five days (NS; Mann-Whitney U Test). Figure 3 illustrates the responses to the test object leading to reaching for this group.

Prehension.   The median age for the first appearance of top-level reaching was 98 days for the experimental group, an advance of some 45 days over the control group ($p < .001$; Mann-Whitney U Test). Some kinds of preliminary responses reported for our control group did not occur before the onset of top-level reaching.

Visual attention. The course of development of visual attention was also altered dramatically in our experimental group (see Fig. 4). Concurrent with the unexpected delay in the onset of hand regard was a decrease in visual exploratory behavior for the first portion of the test period. On the other hand, once the group began to engage in prehensory contacts with the stabile and the figured bumpers, visual attention increased sharply.

Clearly, the results of this study demonstrated the plasticity of several visual-motor developments. That the onset of hand regard is in part a function of environmental factors is not novel. Hand regard is a behavior for day 84 on the Gesell scale. Our control infants, with virtually nothing else to look at, discovered their hands before 50 days of age. Piaget (1952) noted that the onset of this behavior varied by as much as 30 days among his own children as a function of differing environmental circumstances. Therefore, the fact that infants provided with enriched surroundings were late in discovering their hands as compared with controls was not totally unexpected.

We were surprised that the group exhibited less visual attention during the first five weeks in the enriched visible surroundings. In fact, not only did they tend to ignore the stabile and bumpers, but it is our impression that they

Response	Observed in	Total N
Swipes at Object	11	14
Unilateral Hand Raising	12	13
Both Hands Raised	12	13
Alternating Glances (Hand and Object)	10	11
Hands to Midline and Clasp	7	10
One Hand Raised with Alternating Glances, Other Hand to Midline Clutching Dress	5	9
Torso Oriented Towards Object	4	9
Hands to Midline and Clasp and Oriented Towards Object	3	9
Piaget-Type Reach	6	9
Top Level Reach	9	9

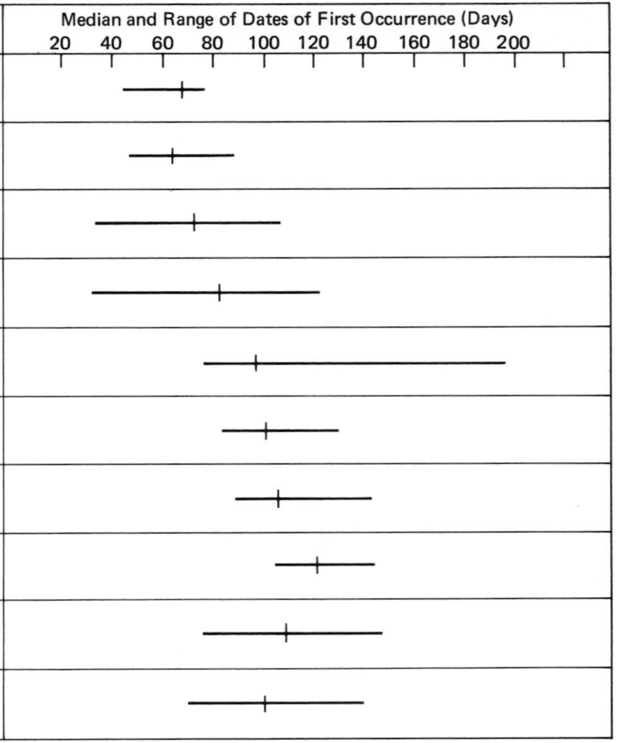
Median and Range of Dates of First Occurrence (Days)
20 40 60 80 100 120 140 160 180 200

Fig. 3. The development of visually directed reaching. Study B–massive enrichment.

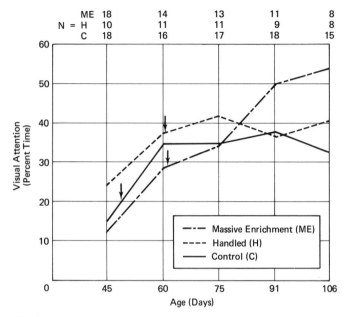

Fig. 4.

engaged in much more crying than did the control group during the same period. Starting at about 72 days of age this group began to engage in a great deal of stabile play. As we had suspected, the rattles were repeatedly swiped at, thereby producing far more monitored hand and arm movements than would normally have occurred. Subsequently, in less than one month, the integration of the grasp with approach movements had been completed. Control infants had required almost three months for this transition.

Earlier we had noted that the course of development of visual exploratory behavior seemed to reflect the availability of interesting things to look at. We had seen that in control and handled groups the slope of the curve of visual attention increased sharply when the hands were discovered and then decreased during the next six weeks. In this experimental group it appears that for about a month, starting at day 37, the enrichment was actually ineffective and perhaps even unpleasant. However, once positive responses to the surroundings began to occur, visual attention increased sharply, in striking contrast with the previous groups; the dip seen at 3½ months in both previous groups was absent.

Third Modification of the Environment

Until day 37 procedures for the third study were the same as in the second study, but instead of enrichment by prone placement, the stabile, and printed sheets and bumpers, there was only one modification from days 37 to

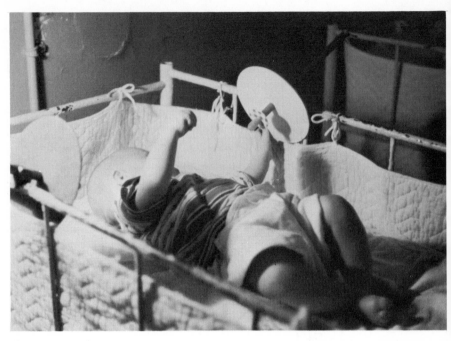

Fig. 5.

68 (White, 1967). Two pacifiers were mounted on the crib rails, and were made to stand out visually by appending to them a red and white pattern against a flat white background (Fig. 5). The objects were 6 to 7 inches away from the corneal surfaces of the infant's eyes. They were positioned so as to elicit maximum attention from six- to ten-week-old infants, whose eyes normally accommodate at about 8 to 10 inches. It was assumed that the pacifiers might have the effect of orienting the infant toward the discovery of his own hands. It was further assumed that these objects might provide appropriate anchor points in space intermediate between the locus of spontaneous fixation and the ordinary path of motion of the hand extended in the tonic neck reflex posture.

At 68 days, the infant was placed in a crib with a stabile similar to the one used in the previous study until he was 124 days of age. We hypothesized that these infants would be more consistently precocious in the attainment of visually directed reaching. We also expected consistently higher visual attention from this group.

RESULTS

Hand regard and swiping. In the control group the onset of sustained hand regard occurred at day 49, and infants in the handling study were be-

Response	Observed in	Total N	Median and Range of Dates of First Occurrence (Days)
Swipes at Object	13 11 14	13 14 16	
Unilateral Hand Raising	15 12 13	15 13 16	
Both Hands Raised	16 12 13	18 13 16	
Alternating Glances (Hand and Object)	18 10 12	19 10 14	
Hands to Midline and Clasp	15 7 10	15 10 14	
One Hand Raised with Alternating Glances, Other Hand to Midline Clutching Dress	11 5 7	19 9 14	
Torso Oriented Towards Object	15 4 5	18 9 12	
Hands to Midline and Clasp and Oriented Towards Object	14 3 4	19 9 12	
Piaget-Type Reach	12 6 8	18 9 13	
Top Level Reach	14 9 13	14 9 13	

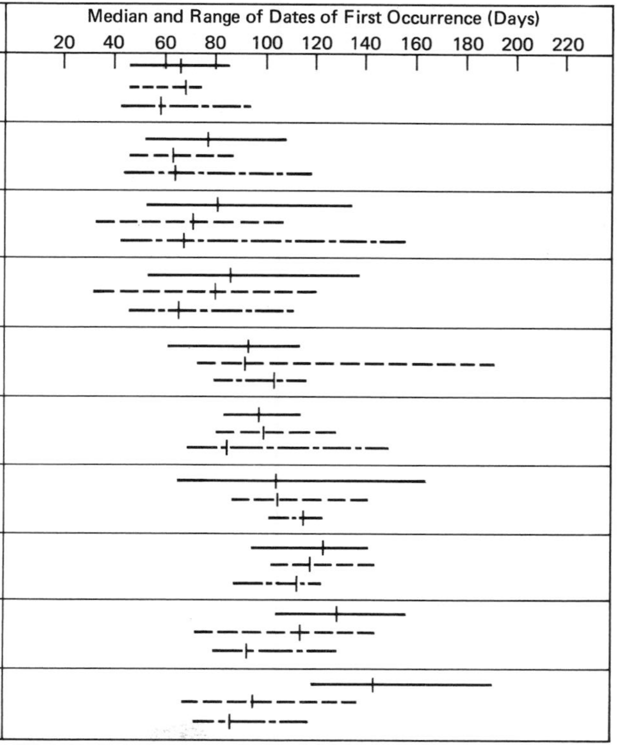

Scale: 20 40 60 80 100 120 140 160 180 200 220

———— Control and Handled
– – – – Massive Enrichment
–·–·– Modified Enrichment

Fig. 6. Comparison of prehensory responses among all groups.

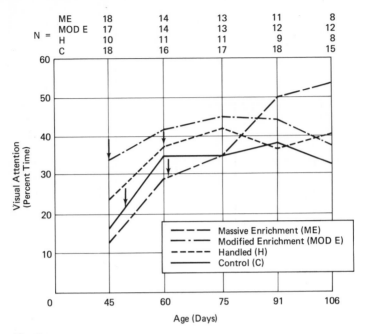

Fig. 7.

hind (day 60). Infants in the second study were even later in this respect (day 61), supporting the idea that the discovery of the hand is, in part, a function of the availability of interesting visible objects. The modified enrichment of this study seemed more appropriate for the infant during the second month of life; infants exhibited sustained hand regard at day 44 (see Table 3). It should be noted that control infants reared in bland surroundings are about as advanced in hand regard at this age. The onset of swiping responses followed the same general pattern with infants in the third study exhibiting this behavior earlier than all other groups (day 58; see Fig. 6).

   Prehension.   Apparently, the modified or paced enrichment of the third study was the most successful match of external circumstances to internally developing structures. This indicated the acquisition of top-level reaching at less than three months of age (day 89—significantly earlier than controls at [$p < .001$; Mann-Whitney U Test]).

   Visual attention.   Figure 7 shows visual attention data for the subjects of the four groups. The depression of visual interest shown by the infants in the second study from day 37 to 74 has been eliminated, and the Modified Enrichment group consistently is more attentive ($p < .0005$) throughout the test period (see Table 2). Curiously, although the third group was more consistently attentive than the others, the reduction of such behavior at 3½ months appeared as it had in the control and the first groups. It would appear that some uncontrolled variable is interacting with our various attempts at modifying the function.

WE ARE PLEASED TO SEND YOU A COPY OF:
1 0447029 READINGS CHILD DEV & PER 2ND MUSSEN

WITH THE COMPLIMENTS OF RONALD RIER

FOR YOUR EXAMINATION AND CONSIDERATION AS TEXTS IN YOUR
CLASSES. WE SHALL BE PLEASED TO HAVE ANY COMMENTS YOU
MAY CARE TO MAKE.

181

HARPER & ROW, PUBLISHERS

HARPER & ROW, PUBLISHERS
49 EAST 33RD STREET
NEW YORK, N. Y. - 10016

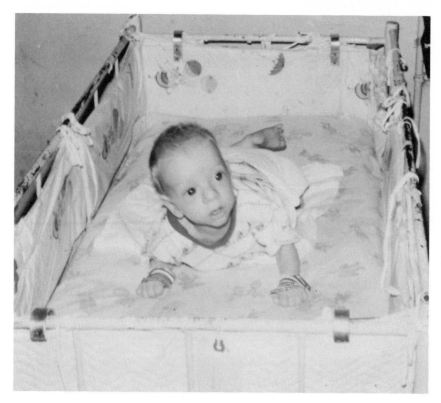

Fig. 8.

Fourth Modification of Rearing Conditions—
the Mitt Study

The three major clusters of experience that seemed appropriate for manipulation during the first three months of life are hand regard, nonspecific visual attention while supine, and visual attention while prone and with head elevated. The purposes of this latest study were to induce earlier acquisition of flexible accommodation and whatever perceptual mechanisms underlie the blink response to approaching visible targets.

The following alterations of rearing conditions were instituted from 21 to 105 days of age. Red and white striped golfer's mitts were worn by experimental subjects (Fig. 8). Their plain white sheets and bumpers were replaced with others featuring various colors and forms. Finally, experimental subjects were placed in the prone position for 15 minutes after the 6:00 A.M., 10:00 A.M., and 2:00 P.M. feedings. These procedures were designed to hasten the visual discovery of the hands and to provide a more easily perceivable and informative interesting visible surround. Whether passive visual scanning or scanning while moving head, torso, and hands is more effective in early development is an open question. We hoped to address the more primitive

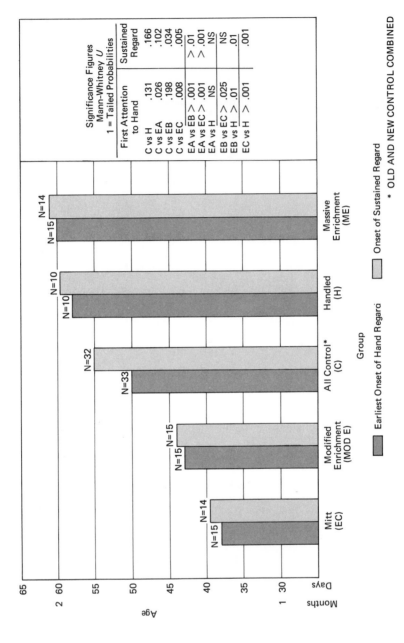

Fig. 9. Comparative hand regard data. Medium date of onset of brief glances and sustained regard.

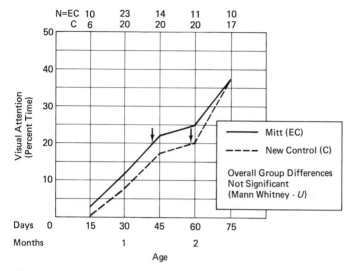

Fig. 10. Comparative visual attention data.

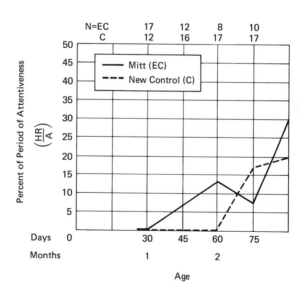

Fig. 11. Comparative hand regard data. Development of proportion of visual attention devoted to sustained hand regard.

general question of the plasticity of the behaviors in question by increasing both kinds of learning opportunities.

RESULTS

Hand regard. The onset of sustained hand regard was markedly enhanced (Fig. 9).

Visual attention. The total amount of visual attention was unchanged but the disposition of attention while alert was altered considerably (Figs. 10 and 11). Hand regard occurred in the experimental group as a common activity during most of the second month of life whereas virtually none was seen in the new control group.

•   •   •

CONCLUDING REMARKS

I do not intend to insult your intelligence by ending this paper by tying a figurative blue ribbon and neatly snipping the ends. I do not claim to have a perfectly clear vision of how to handle the many facets of the extremely complicated problem of infant development. I have attempted to present an evaluation of our current state, a gloomy prognosis and a partial prescription for a cure. I have also tried to marshal some empirical support for my recommendations.

Bibliography

Brody, S. *Patterns of mothering.* New York: International Universities Press, 1951.

Casler, L. Maternal deprivation: a critical review of the literature. *Monographs of the Society for Research in Child Development,* 1961, *26,* 1–64.

Denenberg, V. H., & Karas, G. G. Effects of differential infantile handling upon weight gain and mortality in the rat and mouse. *Science,* 1959, *130,* 629–630.

Eisenberg, R. B. The development of hearing in man: an assessment of current status. Report to: National Advisory Neurological Disease and Blindness Council, September 7, 1966.

Gesell, A., & Amatruda, C. *Developmental diagnosis.* New York: Hoeber-Harper, 1941.

Gesell, A., & Ilg, F. *Infant and child in the culture of today.* New York and London: Harper Brothers, 1943.

Haynes, H., White, B. L., & Held, R. M. Visual accommodation in human infants. *Science,* 1965, *148,* No. 3669, 528–530.

Held, R. M. Exposure-history as a factor in maintaining stability of perception and coordination. *Journal of Nervous and Mental Diseases,* 1961, *132,* 26–32.

Held, R. M., & Bossom, J. Neonatal deprivation and adult rearrangement: complementary techniques for analyzing plastic sensory-motor coordinations. *Journal of Comparative and Physiological Psychology,* 1961, *54,* 33–37.

Held, R. M., & Hein, A. V. Movement-produced stimulation in the development of visually-guided behavior. *Journal of Comparative and Physiological Psychology,* 1963, *56,* 872-876.

Levine, S. Infantile experience and resistance to physiological stress. *Science,* 1957, *126,* 405.

Meier, G. W. Infantile handling and development in Siamese kittens. *Journal of Comparative and Physiological Psychology,* 1961, *54,* 284–286.

Mikaelian, H., & Held, R. M. Two types of adaptation to an optically-rotated visual field. *American Journal of Psychology,* 1964, *77,* 257–263.

Piaget, J. *The origins of intelligence in children,* 2nd ed. New York: International Universities Press, 1952.

Pratt, K. The neonate. In L. Carmichael (Ed.), *Manual of child psychology,* 2nd ed. New York: Wiley, 1954, pp. 215–292.

Riesen, A. H. Plasticity of behavior: psychological series. In H. F. Harlow and C. N. Woolsey (Eds.), *Biological and biochemical bases of behavior.* Madison: University of Wisconsin Press, 1958, pp. 425–450.

Seigel, A. E. Editorial. *Child Development,* 1967, *38,* No. 4, p. 901.

White, B. L. An experimental approach to the effects of experience on early human behavior. In J. P. Hill (Ed.), *Minnesota symposium on child psychology.* Minneapolis, Minn.: University of Minnesota Press, 1967, *1,* 201–225.

White, B. L., Castle, P., & Held, R. M. Observations on the development of visually-directed reaching. *Child Development,* 1964, *35,* 349–364.

White, B. L., & Castle, P. Visual exploratory behavior following postnatal handling of human infants. *Perceptual and Motor Skills,* 1964, *18,* 497–502.

Wolff, P. H. Observations on newborn infants. *Psychosomatic Medicine,* 1959, *21,* 110–118.

Wright, H. F. Observational child study. In P. Mussen (Ed.), *Handbook of research methods in child development.* New York: Wiley, 1960, pp. 71–139.

Yarrow, L. J. Maternal deprivation: toward an empirical and conceptual re-evaluation. *Psychological Bulletin,* 1961, *58,* 459–490.

Learning
to Love

Harry F. Harlow and Margaret Harlow
UNIVERSITY OF WISCONSIN

It is our firm belief that in the primate order there are five relatively separable affectional systems. In the present paper, we shall discuss only three of the affectional systems: the maternal or mother-infant affectional system; the infant-mother affectional system, which is in many ways both behaviorally and probably neurophysiogically a reciprocal affectional system; and the age-mate or peer affectional system, which is intimately associated with the first two affectional systems from the developmental point of view although it is apparently quite discrete in terms of the stimuli which elicit its response patterns and probably quite discrete in terms of its underlying neurophysiological mechanisms.

Reprinted from *American Scientist* (1966), *54*, No. 3, 244–272. By permission.
Learning to Love—A Sigma Xi-RESA National Lecture, 1965–1966 Series.
This research was supported by USPHS grants MH-11894 and FR-0167 from the National Institutes of Health to the University of Wisconsin Primate Laboratory and Regional Primate Research Center, respectively.

MATERNAL AFFECTIONAL SYSTEM

The maternal affectional system in the rhesus macaque, and presumably in all the *Anthropoidea*—monkeys, apes, and men—goes through at least three basic developmental stages: (1) the stage of maternal attachment and protection; (2) the transitional or ambivalence stage, which might also be described as the disattachment stage; and (3) the stage of maternal separation or rejection. These stages proceed about twice as rapidly in monkeys as in anthropoid apes and about twice as rapidly in anthropoid apes as in human beings. However, the nature of the stages and their sequential development in all higher primates show striking analogies if one allows for the intellectual differences between the various *Anthropoidea*, the differences in cultural complexity, and the fact that each species within the primate order has certain species-specific social signaling systems. Classical examples are the smiling response in man and the infant-retrieval responses of the macaque mother (see Harlow, Harlow, and Hansen, 1963, pp. 261–263).

The development of these stages is seen more clearly in monkeys than in men because of the greater simplicity and invariance of their expression in monkeys. Furthermore, with monkey subjects we can experimentally distort or disrupt any or all of the normal developmental stages. Thus, we can create adequate and inadequate monkey mothers at will and specify the early-experience conditions which will produce these dichotomous maternal types. We do not believe that monkey research will give us total understanding of human behavior, but at the least we can achieve idealized models in which salient developmental variables may be brought into clear relief.

Maternal Attachment and Protection Stage

During the first maternal stage, the stage of attachment and protection, the behavior of the normal, "good" primate mother is characterized by total, tender, loving care. She either does not punish her infant or at most punishes it with complete gentility. During this initial period the female has three primary functions: (1) handling the baby's nutritional, temperature, and eliminative needs, (2) providing the baby with physical support and intimate physical contact comfort, which seem to be important in the development of childhood security, and (3) protecting the infant from external threats whether these are occasioned by intraspecies or extraspecies offenders or by the dangers to which the unknowledgeable infant inadvertently exposes itself as it begins to explore the physical world that surrounds it. In the monkey this stage is maintained for at least three or four months, and presumably this temporal span is at least doubled for the anthropoid apes and at least quadrupled in the case of the human being. The outstanding quality of the good primate mother's behavior during this time is total or near total acceptance of her infant—the infant can do no wrong—and she anxiously supervises its beginning sallies beyond her arm's reach. But as we shall see, the role of the

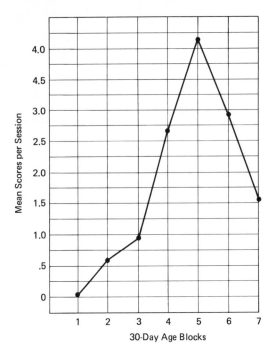

Fig. 1. Punitive and rejecting responses of rhesus mothers toward their infants per 30-min. observation session in the play-pen. Negative responses decrease after 5 months, reflecting increased skill of the infants in avoiding punishment and reduced contact with their mothers during play sessions.

good primate mother gradually changes as the initial maternal stage wanes and the second stage develops.

The Transitional or Ambivalence Stage

In the second maternal stage, that of transition or ambivalence, the mother remains attentive and protective, but she progressively relaxes physical restraint of the exploratory responses of her infant and with increasing frequency disciplines it, forcefully but not brutally. The developmental course of the rejective and punitive responses in the rhesus mother is shown in Fig. 1. We believe that these negative responses of the mother assist the infant in gradually breaking its dependency relationship to her, a necessary step in the socialization process of all mammals, and consequently represent good mothering for this period of the infant's development. All our macaque data indicate that the tie to the mother is so strong that the infant has difficulty in effectively emancipating itself. Left to its own devices, the tendency of the infant is to prolong the period of dependency and to cling to the mother for comfort and security. Faced with occasional rejections by its mother, the infant gains external support for its emerging exploratory responses, the responses that bring it into contact with the enlarged physical and social environment. Thus, the mother's negative responses to her infant serve to facilitate its development as an independent social being with increasing competence to meet the problems of its larger world.

The transition between the first two maternal stages is not sudden, and the timing, the severity of the rejection behavior, and the progression of the transition are influenced by diurnal factors, by the previous experiences of the mother, and probably by her status in the group. It is likely, too, that personality variables in the mother and behavioral characteristics of the infant also affect the course of this second stage. While we have stressed the addition of negative responses to maternal behavior, it should be noted that throughout the maternal transitional stage the infant remains in close physical proximity to the mother during the evening, night, early morning periods, and much of the day and is within sight or call of the mother the remainder of the time. The mother maintains an attitude of watchful vigilance and is fiercely protective if her infant is threatened by any external danger.

The Maternal Separation Stage

The third normal maternal stage is that of separation or rejection of the infant, and in many monkey species this appears with relatively dramatic suddenness upon the advent of a new baby. The appearance of the new baby re-elicits in the mother the first maternal stage, with the neonate as its object, and thus the older baby is often totally physically displaced from the mother and the degree of psychological emancipation may be dramatic. Indeed, field studies report monkey infants during this period showing true symptoms of separation anxiety; these symptoms may be so intense that in some monkey societies and some monkey species, including at least some groups of *Macaca fuscata, Cercopithecus ascanius, M. speciosa, M. irus, Papio ursinus,* and *P. anubis,* large adult males will actually physically adopt these displaced monkey juveniles and hold them in their arms or carry them about on their backs, treating them for a considerable period of time in a maternal manner within the physiological limitations inherent in the primate male (Fig. 2 on p. 122).

There is also evidence in at least one monkey species—the rhesus (*M. mulatta*)—and among those apes which have been studied in the field that the separation process may be far less precipitous for many primate juveniles. Although the youngster no longer suckles, it may remain physically and psychologically close to its mother for many years, including the adult period if it is a female and through much of the juvenile period if it is a male. It is likely that long-term field studies will increasingly reveal the lasting quality of maternal ties in many subhuman primates, and such data have already been reported by Imanishi (1963) and Koford (1965) for semiwild groups. The problem to date has been the brevity of the studies and the difficulty, in other than semiwild colonies, of identifying the blood relationships of animals displaying affectional ties.

THE INFANT-MOTHER AFFECTIONAL SYSTEM

The infant-mother affectional system proceeds through a series of developmental stages that complement, in a reciprocal manner, the maternal

Fig. 2. Male bonnet macaque holding young juvenile he has adopted.

stages. The interactions of infant and mother have cumulative effects on the progression of the stages in both affectional systems, and in the infant-mother system as in the mother-infant system there is a fixed sequence in the development of successive stages in the infant's affectional ties to the mother. It is in the timing of the stages and the intensity of the behaviors that individual variations appear. The stages in the infant-mother system are: (1) the reflex stage; (2) the stage of comfort and attachment; (3) the security stage; and (4) the separation stage.

The Reflex Stage

Although the newborn monkey is far more mature than the human neonate, many or most of the monkey neonate's behaviors are of a forced, reflex nature. These include orienting the head up, hand and foot grasping, clasping, "climbing" and rooting, sucking, righting, and contactual following. The course of the appearance and waning of many of these early responses in the rhesus neonate has been traced by Mowbray and Cadell (1962), revealing that generally the reflex behaviors are supplanted after 10 to 20 days of age by partially, then totally, voluntary responses. Thus, the reflex period of the infant's relationship to the mother is a brief one in the developmental span, but it serves to guarantee survival by assuring proper orientation to and contact with the mother's body, nourishment, and physical support when the infant is unable to control its own movements. Socialization begins during this period when the baby's tie to the mother is involuntary. The neonate may learn to identify its own mother, it starts to imitate her behaviors, and it develops visual following responses. Primarily, however, it is a stage of physical adjustment rather than socialization.

Comfort and Attachment Stage

It is during this second stage—the stage of comfort and attachment— which begins in the latter half of the first month of life, that true affectional bonds between offspring and mother are formed and basic social relationships are established. The infant's responses are now under semivoluntary or totally voluntary control. As in the first stage, however, it maintains close physical contact with the mother through mechanisms associated with nursing, mechanisms associated with intimate bodily contact, and mechanisms which enable the infant to follow and to imitate appropriate maternal behaviors.

Homologous basic mechanisms binding the human infant to the mother have been described by Bowlby (1958) as primary object sucking, primary object clinging, and primary object following. The position we have presented (see Harlow, 1959) for the monkey is similar to Bowlby's and differs principally in that we assign relatively more importance to clinging than to nursing whereas Bowlby stresses nursing over clinging.

We hypothesize that the neonatal and infantile nursing and clinging responses may be two components of a single attachment pattern. When the macaque infant attaches to its mother, it attaches to her body with its arms and legs and to her nipple with its mouth. This oral attachment by the infant is far more frequently a nonnutritional attachment without nursing than an attachment associated with suckling, and the proportional frequency of non-nutritional to nutritional attachment to the nipple increases with age. Even if the two responses are similarly linked in the human primate, the infant has limited opportunity to display the full pattern, at least in western cultures, because child rearing practices limit nipple attachment opportunities to the nursing situation; if the infant mouths or sucks supplementarily, it does so on its own body or on inanimate objects.

The developmental course of primary object following has not been traced and analyzed in either monkeys or man as intensively as has the development of sucking and clinging. In both primates, however, there is evidence of visual fixation and following from the early days of life and, in the

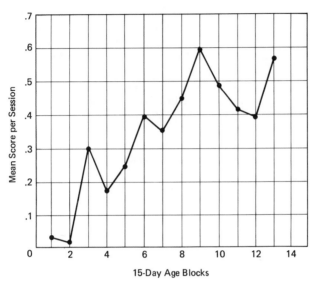

Fig. 3. Infant imitations of mother's behavior per 30-min. session in the playpen.

monkey, there is locomotor following as well. Infantile following is doubtless the basis for the infant's imitation of maternal behaviors. We have traced the development of infant-mother imitative responses in the macaque (see Fig. 3), and the progressive increase in frequency attests to the importance of following-imitation as a socializing force in this primate. The rhesus infant follows maternal behavior and within the limits of its capabilities matches the mother's action. The infant follows the mother's peregrinations: when the mother explores a physical object, so does the infant; when the mother mouths and ingests a food substance, so does the infant; when the mother is startled or frightened, the infant clings to the mother's body and observes. Such primitive imitation has been described by Miller and Dollard (1941) as matched-dependent behaviors. These behaviors enable the infant to profit from maternal experience so that its own exploratory behavior is not blind and the dangers inherent in untutored exploration are minimized. Furthermore, we believe that these maternal associations, reinforced by maternal bodily contact during moments of doubt, abet the development of the infant security stage.

Out of the maternal stage of attachment and protection and the reciprocal infantile stage of comfort and attachment, the monkey (and doubtless the human) infant develops strong feelings of safety and security in the mother's presence. All the mother-infant interactions related to nursing, bodily contact, and following-imitation contribute to security, although there is evidence that sheer bodily contact-comfort is the dominant variable in the rhesus monkey.

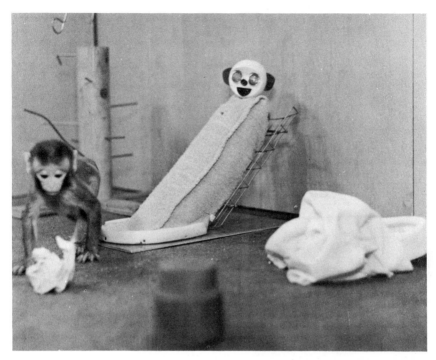

Fig. 4. Rhesus infant raised with a cloth surrogate mother displaying security and exploratory behavior in a strange situation in the mother's presence.

Security Stage

The third infant-mother affectional stage is that of security. We discovered some years ago that macaque infants achieve a great sense of personal security when raised by inanimate cloth surrogate mothers. Certainly monkey and human infants achieve an even stronger and far more socially useful sense of security when raised by real monkey mothers and by real human mothers. During this period the infant, in the presence of the mother, surrogate or real, shows a growing tendency to go out and explore the inanimate and animate world about it, returning from time to time to the mother's body for comfort and reassurance. Thus, the presence of the surrogate mother in a strange situation greatly facilitates the infant's exploration, as shown in Fig. 4. In contrast, a baby raised by a cloth mother demonstrates abject terror in the identical test situation when the surrogate mother is absent (see Fig. 5). Although this stage of security is important in supporting the infant's exploration of the physical world, it is even more important in the self-assurance it provides the infant in its exploration of the animate world, particularly the animate world of the infant's own age-mates or peers. Gradually as the stage progresses, the infant decreases the frequency and

Fig. 5. Rhesus infant raised with a cloth surrogate mother displaying fear in a strange situation in absence of the mother.

duration of its maternal contacts during play sessions, probably deriving a sense of security from the sight of its mother, as well as touch, and acquiring self-confidence in its new social interactions, thereby preparing it for the final stage in its relationship with its mother.

Separation Stage

The development of security during the third stage greatly facilitates the development of the fourth and longest infant-mother affectional stage, which we call the separation stage, recognizing that the separation process is very gradual and that final mother-infant separation is achieved more by maternal behaviors than by infant behaviors. The separation stage complements the maternal transitional or ambivalence stage and, somewhat later, the maternal separation stage. It is, perhaps, best characterized as a period during which age-mate associations are slowly gaining preeminence over infant-maternal relationships. Maternal security is one of the important variables making possible the infant-separation stage, and a second, possibly more important, variable is the mechanism of curiosity. From an early age the monkey is attracted to the novel in its environs but its exploratory tendencies are held somewhat in check, first by the mother, subsequently by its own fears. The

Fig. 6. Rhesus infants in ventral-ventral clasp typical for infants raised as pairs without mothers.

sense of security gained from the maternal relationship, the reinforcements from positive exploratory experiences, the motor and intellectual increments with maturing and learning, and the growing rejection responses of the mother must all play a role in reducing the conflict between remaining in the safety and comfort of the mother's reach and exploring the attractions beyond. As positive social experiences cumulate, the age-mates become more and more rewarding companions and the mother loses her status as the sole affectional object of the maturing infant. Before separation is achieved, the third primate affectional system is well advanced—the age-mate or peer affectional system. The peer affectional ties by no means supplant the maternal affectional ties but, rather, become additional ties which satisfy the needs now dominant in the older infant and young juvenile.

AGE-MATE OR PEER AFFECTIONAL SYSTEM

As with the other affectional systems, the peer system progresses through an orderly series of developmental stages. It differs from the systems just described, however, in that the first two stages are probably artifacts of the laboratory situation, whereas all the stages of the infant-mother and mother-

Fig. 7. Rhesus infants showing typical "choo-choo" pattern of monkeys raised in groups without mothers.

infant affectional systems are clearly discernible both in the laboratory and in the field. The initial stages of the peer system are the reflex stage and the manipulation stage. These stages are followed by interactive play, which is well defined both in the laboratory and in the naturalistic setting, and by a mature interactional stage in which play is minimal but affectional ties are manifested through physical proximity, friendly interchanges, and cooperative behavior.

Reflex Stage

This first stage in the peer affectional system is apparent in the early weeks of life if neonatal monkeys are given the opportunity to make contact. During this period of motor incoordination and domination by reflexes infants fixate each other visually and make approach attempts. If they succeed in contacting each other, they cling reflexly as they do to their mothers and follow each other between episodes of clinging and clasping. When two infants are together, the clinging typically assumes a ventral-ventral clasp (Fig. 6), and when more than two are together, the pattern tends to be a "choo-choo" formation—a chain of infants, one in the lead and one at end and with intermediate infants clinging to the back of the infant in front of it (Fig. 7). In keeping with the motor limitations of the monkeys at the stage of development, there is little activity other than clinging and following. If the animals remain together in a cage without interference, the clinging is interrupted by only brief respites and then resumes. The pattern appears to be that of utilizing the partner or partners for bodily contact, and this behavior tend to become fixated and to persist long after the clinging reflex disappears if the infants are kept together continuously from early infancy. This clinging fixation is comparable to that observed in infant monkeys raised with cloth surrogates. It cannot occur in live-mother-raised infants because the mother actively prevents continuous clinging. She forces the infant to readjust its position by her own movements and by herself adjusting the infant's position frequently, sometimes for her own comfort and at other times to groom the infant, nuzzle it, and care for its physical needs. Similarly, under natural conditions the infant would have no opportunity to display reflex clinging to another infant because mothers prevent their babies from venturing beyond arm's reach during this early period of life. Thus, the appearance of the reflex stage of peer relations depends upon the absence of a live mother to exercise restraint on the infant's movements, and the nature of the behavior when restraint is lacking merely reflects the primary need and the limited behavioral repertoire of the neonatal monkey.

Manipulation Stage

Toward the end of the first month of life, when reflex domination of behavior has given way to semivoluntary and voluntary control, rhesus infants respond to each other in the laboratory as they would to novel physical objects. They explore each other with eyes, hands, mouth, and body, and they alternate manipulation of age-mates with manipulation of the physical environment. This, like the preceding stage, is a presocial period in peer relationships, and the exploratory activity that characterizes it persists into the stage of interactive play. The simplicity of the behavior reflects the social, intellectual, and motor immaturity of the infants at one to two months of age. Nonetheless, in the laboratory situation throughout the period, they spend steadily increasing time in proximity to each other and make progressively increasing numbers of physical contacts. Gradually they come to respond to each other as social objects instead of physical objects, and social play emerges from the matrix of manipulatory play.

In the wild, opportunities for infant monkeys and apes to show a manipulation stage in interactions with peers are limited because most mothers still keep their infants close to them in this period of development and retrieve them if they escape. The same behavior is, however, manifested toward

Fig. 8.   Infants engaging in rough-and-tumble play in the playroom situation.

the mother and physical objects. Monkey, ape, and human infants, as they gain in coordination of their eye movements, hands, and large muscles, intensively explore their mother's body and everything in the environment within reach.

Interactive Play

The third stage in the age-mate or peer affectional system is interactive play, and it marks the start of true social interactions among peers. It overlaps with manipulatory play, at the start being interspersed with many sequences of physical exploration. Moreover, it probably appears a little earlier in laboratory-raised monkeys with early peer experience than in monkeys raised without prior peer contacts. With or without earlier peer experience, however, infant monkeys in the laboratory show the same sequence of play behaviors from two or three months of age as do feral monkeys, and infant apes in the field show the same patterns when they meet their peers at four to six months or later. Human infants probably display a similar sequence when they reach a comparable state of maturity in the second year of life and thereafter. Where age-mates are not available, primate infants—monkey, ape, and human—universally direct their play toward younger or older members of the species, including adults. Apparently, the underlying mechanisms re-

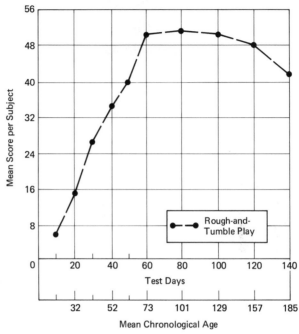

Fig. 9. Developmental course of rough-and-tumble play in the playroom situation.

sponsible for play are similar throughout the Primate Order and find expression in social interactions if responsive partners are available.

The stage of interactive play can be broken down into developmental components. We believe that the first stage is that of rough-and-tumble play, illustrated in Fig. 8, and its course is traced in Fig. 9 for groups of four animals allowed to interact in our playroom situation (Fig. 10) or playpen situation (Fig. 11). This behavior pattern is one of wrestling, sham-biting, and close body contact. A more complex type of interactive play gradually develops, and we have described this pattern as approach-withdrawal or noncontact play, as illustrated in Fig. 12. In this type of interaction there is pursuit and retreat, often with the subjects alternating roles in quick succession without actually touching each other. This second type of play does not supplant rough-and-tumble play but appears as an additional pattern. As is shown in Fig. 13, the developmental courses of rough-and-tumble and approach-withdrawal play are very similar, and they are not clearly separated in time. When the infantile developmental period ends and the juvenile period begins at about one year of age, the tempo of play markedly increases and there appears an intermixing of rough-and-tumble and approach-withdrawal play without intervening pauses, so that the two patterns flow smoothly from one to the other. We have tentatively described this as a third

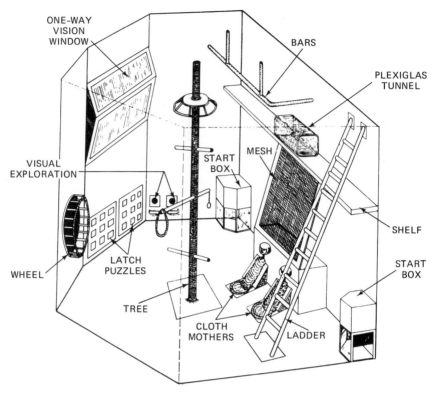

Fig. 10. Schematic drawing of the social playroom. The room is 8 foot high and has approximately 46 square feet of floor space.

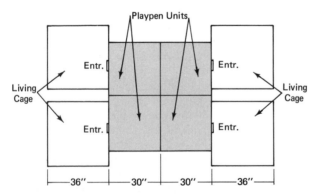

Fig. 11. Diagram of the playpen situation showing living cages and adjoining playpens. Mothers are confined to the living cages but infants have access to playpen areas.

Fig. 12. Approach-withdrawal play in the playpen situation.

interactive play stage, the stage of integrated play, but an equally tenable position is that integrated play is but the initiation of a truly new play stage, that of aggressive play.

This final play stage, which we prefer now to term aggressive play, is chiefly characterized by a new quality in the interactions of the play group. Whereas previously infants have engaged in wrestling, rolling, and sham-biting behaviors without inflicting injury, they now begin to hurt and to be hurt in close body contact, usually by biting. The contests take on a progres-sively increasing aggressive quality while the individuals struggle for position within the group, and a dominance-ordering gradually emerges. Overt aggres-sion then diminishes and threats are sufficient to maintain the order between challenges of the group structure. During periods of status contention, how-ever, fighting increases until the order is again stabilized or a new order is

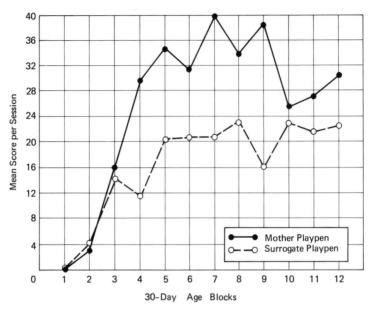

Fig. 13. Developmental course of approach-withdrawal play for mother-raised and surrogate-raised infants in the playpen situation (compare with Fig. 9).

established. Thus, this last play stage involves no new kind of play. It is the increased speed and power of the movements, the improved motor skills displayed, the underlying motivation, and the emotional quality of the interactions that differentiate the monkeys' play from that prevalent in the first year of life.

It should not be assumed that aggression replaces affection in the juvenile period. The evidence is to the contrary: aggression is simply an additional social mechanism operating in peer interactions. Indeed, if the juveniles have long known each other and thus have already established affectional relationships, the injuries that come during aggressive play are trivial; in spite of the dominance hierarchies, basic, strong intragroup affectional relationships persist. This is strikingly illustrated when separately raised groups of juveniles are brought together. The in-group coheres in defense against out-groups, and while friendships eventually develop between members of different groups, the older in-group ties come into evidence whenever a member is threatened.

Long before aggressive play appears there is a strong, progressive tendency for sexual separation within the play groups, with males coming to prefer masculine playmates and females, feminine playmates. When aggressive play develops, this sexual separation process becomes exaggerated even though within a particular social group masculine-feminine juvenile affectional relationships persist. Again, existence of friendships is evident in the behavior of separately reared groups of juveniles brought together in a playroom. A dominance ordering for the total group evolves rather quickly, and the emergent top male protects his female friends from aggression of any out-group male. In fact, he may protect them so successfully that they enjoy through his association enormous dominance over out-group males that are obviously physically stronger and could otherwise dominate them. Field studies indicate that in adult life the female friends of dominant males enjoy similar social dominance, and this endowed or conferred dominance may even carry over to the female's infant.

Mature Interaction Stage

Primates differ markedly in their over-all playfulness from species to species, and there are age differences as well in playfulness in all species. In this area we must rely on field studies for our data, and it is only in very recent years that play has been observed at all in a planned manner. The data that are available indicate that play in monkeys, apes, and man is predominantly an infantile and juvenile behavior that persists in weaker degree into adolescence and tends to drop off markedly in adult life. Across species, however, differences may be so great that adults of one species are more playful than adolescents or possibly juveniles of another species. Thus, of the primates observed to date, chimpanzees would appear to be the most playful of all, playing even in adulthood (Goodall, 1963), while mountain gorillas appear to be outstanding in the paucity of their play. Infant and juvenile gorillas play, but the amount of this play as reported by Schaller (1963) seems far less than that of chimpanzees, langurs, baboons, and rhesus of comparable developmental stages. During adolescence, gorillas apparently show almost no play while the other species, particularly as represented by their male members, continue to show some social play.

Although play appears to decrease in all species during adolescence and adult life, there are ample indicators of the continuance of affectional ties among members, both like-sexed and opposite-sexed. Thus, while original peer ties develop in play, these ties may continue to function after play no longer is an important social behavior. Morever, once peer affection develops, new affectional ties to peers can develop without play. Propinquity in periods of rest and feeding may show stability over periods of time and reflect companionship preferences. Mutual grooming is an activity that is probably confined to pairs or groups with strong attachments and may serve as a test of trust and intimacy. Indeed, when unacquainted rhesus adolescents were placed together on an island in the Madison zoo, it was observed that grooming appeared subsequent to the beginnings of friendship groupings and then gradually increased in frequency. Still another indicator of affectional ties is the cooperative efforts of pairs or groups against the threat or attack of one of the members by another individual of the larger group. Perhaps the strongest test of a female's peer attachments is sharing her infant with other females. Species differ in the generosity of females in permitting others to touch, groom, or hold their young, but in all species the young are a source of attraction for females of the group. Northern Indian langurs are the most

Fig. 14. Living situation of infants being raised in semi-isolation in the nursery.

generous of the species thus far studied, tending to allow the young infant to be passed from hand to hand (Jay, 1963). Other primate species appear to be much more selective in this behavior, with the female's particular friends being permitted closest and earliest scrutiny of the baby. Wherever primates have been observed in group-living situations, whether in the wild or in captivity, groupings have been found indicating companion preferences. There is every reason to believe that affectional relationships among mature individuals are an important aspect of primate social life within and between sexes.

EFFECTS OF SOCIAL DEPRIVATION

During the last five years we have conducted a series of studies on the effects of social deprivation in early life. From birth onward for predetermined periods of time, monkeys have been denied both mothering and contact with peers. These deprivation studies have taken two forms: In the one form, partial social deprivation, monkeys are housed in individual bare wire cages where they can see and hear other monkeys but make no physical

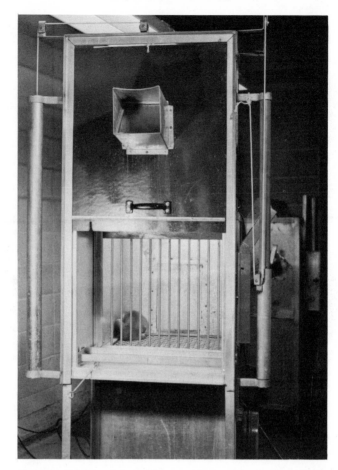

Fig. 15. Total social isolation cabinet with front wall in raised position at the termination of the period of confinement. Light and sound stimulation are provided throughout isolation, but the subject is fed and cared for without ever seeing a monkey or human during the isolation period.

contact with them, as shown in Fig. 14. We have also subjected monkeys to total social deprivation in the apparatus shown in Fig. 15. In this situation the subjects see no animal of any kind for the predetermined period even though sensory deprivation is held to a minimum. As would be expected, total social deprivation produces more dramatic and pervasive effects than partial social deprivation although we now know, somewhat to our surprise, that the differences between these two forms of social deprivation are not nearly as great as we would have predicted, primarily because partial social deprivation is more damaging than we had anticipated.

Fig. 16. Rhesus monkey viewed immediately after raising the wall of the isolation chamber where it was confined from birth to 12 months of age. The monkeys typically retreat to a back corner of the box and display a crouching posture which includes some form of self-clutching and shielding of the eyes. Such postures are also common during confinement and continue after the animals are housed in wire-mesh cages in the nursery.

Two studies show that release of the animals after three months of essentially total social deprivation leaves them in a state of emotional shock. Their initial responses are characterized by self-clutching and crouching, as illustrated in Fig. 16, which resembles a postural expression of human autistic children. If, however, the monkeys can survive the immediate emotional trauma of release from total social deprivation and are then allowed to interact with control age-mates 30 minutes a day in our playroom situation, they very rapidly establish effective social relationships with their peers, as is illustrated in Fig. 17. Such long-term studies as we have to date point to essentially complete social recovery, normal learning, and normal sexual adjustment in adolescence. We can find no indication in these same animals of any intellectual loss (Fig. 18) and we doubt that any will be uncovered on laboratory learning problems (see p. 140).

We have limited data showing that six months of partial social deprivation greatly impairs the ability of infant monkeys to interact socially with

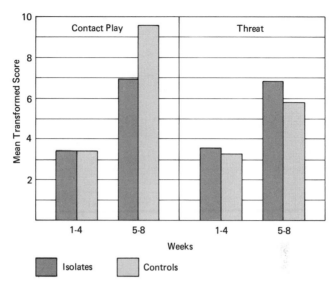

Fig. 17. Two measures of social behavior in the playroom for four monkeys subjected to 3 months of social isolation and four control monkeys. Interactions are for 8 weeks beginning in the subjects' fourth month of life.

control age-mates, and we have data which seem to indicate that these social inadequacies persist over periods of years even when the animals are subsequently given some opportunity to associate continuously with age-mates over long periods of time.

We have much more definitive data on the effects of 6 and 12 months of total social isolation. The results clearly indicate that even 6 months of total social isolation leaves the monkeys unable to interact socially with age-mates when pairs of them are placed with pairs of controls raised in partial social deprivation and tested in our playroom situation. One comparison of 6-month isolates and their controls in the 2 months following isolation is given in Fig. 19, and a comparable difference exists for all the social measures. Moreover, the effects persist throughout the period of social coexistence as illustrated for social threat (Fig. 20). Nonetheless, the isolates do show a small gain in social interactions with each other, but not with the controls, in the course of 6 to 7 months of social testing. Twelve months of total social deprivation, compared with 6 months, produces even more socially devastating results. The 12-month isolates display essentially no social interaction with each other or with controls, as illustrated for the simplest form of play— activity play (Fig. 21). Indeed, in this experiment we had to conclude the social tests after 10 weeks because the control animals were increasingly abusing the social isolates, and we were convinced that the isolates would have been killed if testing had continued (see pp. 141–142).

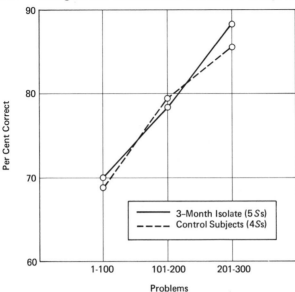

Problems

Fig. 18. Performance of 3-month social isolates and control subjects of the same age on 300 discrimination learning set problems administered in the second year of life. Performance is percentage of correct responses on trials 2-6 of each problem. Trial 1 is a blind trail that provides the subject information on the correct stimulus. Differences between the groups are not significant ($p > 0.05$).

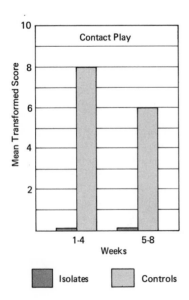

Fig. 19. Contact play in the playroom for 6-month social isolates and controls during the were released from isolation. As is apparent, there was essentially no contact play exhibited first 8 weeks after the experimental subjects by isolates.

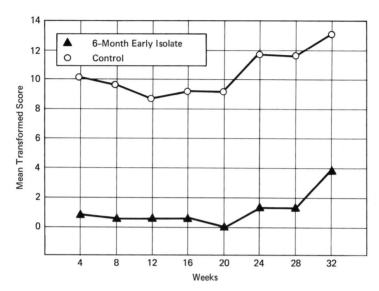

Fig. 20. Social threats in the playroom by 6-month social isolates and control subjects during the course of 32 weeks of interactions in the playroom. Threats exhibited by isolates were entirely directed to other isolates.

Despite the social ineptitude of both the 6- and 12-month social isolates, their intellectual abilities appear to have been spared (Fig. 22). Like the 3-month isolates (cf. Fig. 18), the 6- and 12-month isolates were tested on discrimination learning set problems in the second year of life. They performed at a level not statistically different from that of control subjects of the same age. Discrimination learning set performance has been a consistently successful test in differentiating intellectual functioning among rhesus monkeys of different ages, among various genera of primates, and between primates and lower mammals (Warren, 1965).

We now have a long-term follow-up of animals subjected to 6 and 12 months of total social isolation. As preadolescents and adolescents, they were individually paired in separate tests with a single normal adult, a normal age-mate, and a normal young juvenile. The total social isolates showed fear of adults, age-mates, and even juveniles, but while showing fear, the 6-month isolates—not the 12-month isolates—also demonstrated, completely to our surprise, violent and abnormal aggressive behaviors. These included aggression against juveniles, a pattern of response seldom or never seen in normal adolescent monkeys, particularly normal adolescent female monkeys, and brief outbursts of suicidal aggression against adults—aggressions which they

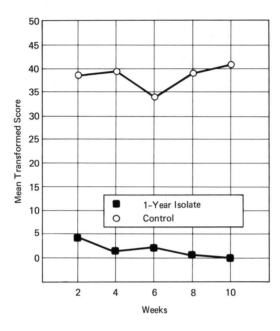

Fig. 21. Activity play, a non-social form of play, exhibited by 12-month social isolates and control subjects in 10 weeks of exposure to the playroom. Decreasing frequency of the play in the experimental subjects doubtless reflects their increasing fear of the control subjects.

never displayed more than once, since the bursts of aggression were always unsuccessful; these isolates learned the social facts of life the hard and bloody way. The 12-month isolates, on the other hand, showed no aggression, apparently because fear inhibited its external expression in these animals.

We have a number of studies in which we have raised baby monkeys with cloth surrogate mothers, with brutal abnormal mothers—our so-called "motherless mothers"—or with no mothers whatsoever. In these situations the infants were given opportunities to form age-mate or peer affectional relationships, and the data made it appear on first sight that perhaps normal mothering is dispensable as a social variable. We now have some reservations about the earlier conclusion.

Baby monkeys raised with cloth surrogate mothers as compared with real monkey mothers were somewhat slow in forming adequate play patterns with their peers, but by the end of a year they were interacting effectively, and they have made normal heterosexual adjustments with age-mates as juveniles and preadolescents. Babies raised with motherless mothers but allowed to interact socially in our playpen situation showed an initial lag in adjusting to their age-mates, but this difficulty rapidly ended and there was even precocious heterosexual adjustment.

The babies which we raised with no mothers whatsoever but allowed to interact with age-mates form what we have previously called our "together-together" monkeys, and the group which has been studied most intensively is a group of four, one male and three females. These infants showed greatly depressed patterns of play in our play room situation and showed exaggerated

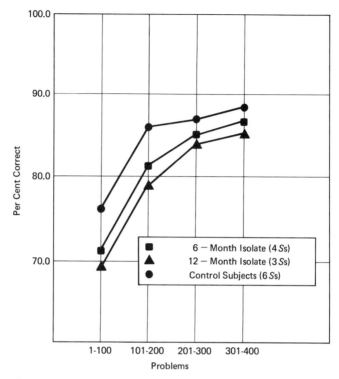

Fig. 22. Discrimination learning set performance of 6-month and 12-month social isolates and control subjects of comparable age during the second year of life. Performance is measured by percentage of correct trial 2-6 responses during successive blocks of 6-trial problems (compare with Fig. 18).

tendencies toward partner clinging even though these clinging responses tended to ameliorate with time. Again, it appeared that heterosexual behavior was normal, even precocious. The first of the females has become a mother and she is a perfectly normal mother, and we hopefully predict that when the other females achieve maternity, they will treat their infants in a kind, tender, and loving manner.

Thus, the three diverse kinds of peer-experienced but mother-deprived groups have made adequate social adjustments though delayed in each case and continuously depressed in the instance of the play of together-together animals. Heterosexual behavior has been adequate or precocious. Maternal behavior will be studied as the females reproduce, with only one of these animals having so far been observed, but the expectation is that mothering will be normal. There is, however, one question that the studies leave unanswered: Could unmothered or inadequately mothered infants with peer experience adjust normally to mothered infants with peer experience? We suspect that during the first year of life, particularly the first six months, un-mothered or inadequately mothered animals would be disadvantaged in inter-actions with mothered animals and would likely develop subnormally or abnormally. Their inferiority might well carry over into adolescence and maturity under these conditions. The later the admixture of the mother-deprived and mother-reared infants, however, the less would be the expected differences. There is evidence that, at 18 months of age, surrogate-mothered monkeys raised with each other in the playpen can adjust adequately to monkeys of the same age raised by their natural mothers and with equivalent playpen peer experience. The question of dispensability of mothers, then, hinges on testing the adequacy of mother-deprived infants in interactions in infancy with mothered infants, and the best guess at the present time is that the mother-deprived infants would have marked difficulties. Normal mother-ing, we believe, confers early social advantages upon the recipients, and these advantages would be expected to facilitate early peer adjustments. Early success might well confer an additional advantage that could be main-tained indefinitely, similar to the advantages which seem to accrue to infants whose mothers are favored by dominant males (Imanishi, 1963).

During the last year an interesting study has been completed by Alexan-der in which he raised babies with their mothers for periods of two weeks (control group), four months, and eight months while depriving them of any opportunity to form age-mate or peer affectional relationships. We call these infants our "mother-only" or "mother-captive" infants. After ½, 4, or 8 months of maternal captivity, these infants were permitted daily contacts with their age-mates, and the rapidity of their play development was inversely related to their age at the time peer experience began. All three groups de-veloped play and social behavior, but the four-month group showed greater wariness of close contact and greater aggressiveness than the control group, and the eight-month group showed both characteristics in far greater degree. Cautiousness and hyperaggression in the experimental groups may have re-sulted from their inability to escape from maternal punishment as the mothers went into the transitional, or ambivalent, maternal stage. These characteristics could have been bolstered by the absence of peer affectional ties when fear matured and the weakness of such ties when social aggression matured. It is possible that these traits might be a social advantage in contention with animals having earlier peer experience, although this has not been tested to date. Be this as it may, it is perfectly obvious that monkey mothers can be infant substitutes or "infant surrogates" for their babies throughout a large part of the first critical year of life, and one would predict that this role would be even more adequately played by the human mother since she has an interest and a capability in playing with her infant that totally transcend those of the rhesus macaque. The implication, we believe, is that mothering is important not only as a source of social security, but also as a very powerful agent in the social training of infants, and we are happy to state that we now believe that real mothering, monkey or human, is a very important social factor and that real mothering is here to stay!

In designing our original studies we tended to contrast the relative importance of mother-infant relationships as opposed to infant-infant affectional relationships in the socialization process. We are now convinced that this is the wrong way to look at these social forces. Both normal mothering and normal infant-infant affectional development are extremely important variables in the socialization of rhesus monkeys and presumably of the higher primates. These variables are interactive, and they interact in a totally orderly sequential manner. Interference with either variable may not of necessity socially destroy an infant monkey if it is subsequently allowed to lead a normal or more or less normal life, but there can be no doubt that the easier and safer way to become a normal monkey is to learn to love and live with both mothers and age-mates.

REFERENCES

Bowlby, J. The nature of the child's tie to his mother. *Int. J. Psycho-anal.,* 1958, *39,* 1–24.

Goodall, J. My life among wild chimpanzees. *Nat. Geographic,* 1963, *124,* 272–308.

Harlow, H. F. Love in infant monkeys. *Sci. Amer.,* 1959, *200,* 68–74.

Harlow, H. F., and Harlow, M. K. The affectional systems. In A. M. Schrier, H. F. Harlow, and F. Stollnitz (Eds.), *Behavior of nonhuman primates,* Vol. 2. New York: Academic Press, 1965, pp. 287–334

Harlow, H. F., Harlow, M. K., and Hansen, E. W. The maternal affectional system of rhesus monkeys. In H. L. Rheingold (Ed.), *Maternal behavior in mammals.* New York: Wiley, 1963, pp. 254–281.

Imanishi, K. Social behavior in Japanese monkeys, *Macaca fuscata.* In C. H. Southwick (Ed.), *Primate social behavior.* Princeton, N. J.: Van Nostrand, 1963, pp. 68–81.

Jay, P. Mother-infant relations in langurs. In H. L. Rheingold (Ed.), *Maternal behavior in mammals.* New York: Wiley, 1963, pp. 282–304.

Koford, C. B. Population dynamics of rhesus monkeys on Cayo Santiago. In I. DeVore (Ed.), *Primate behavior.* New York: Holt, 1965, pp. 160–174.

Miller, N. E., and Dollard, J. *Social learning and imitation.* New Haven: Yale University Press, 1941.

Mowbray, J. B., and Cadell, T. E. Early behavior patterns in rhesus monkeys. *J. comp. physiol. Psychol.,* 1962, *55,* 350–357.

Schaller, G. B. *The mountain gorilla: Ecology and behavior.* Chicago: University of Chicago Press, 1963.

Warren, J. M. Primate learning in comparative perspective. In A. M. Schrier, H. F. Harlow, and F. Stollnitz (Eds.), *Behavior of nonhuman primates,* Vol. 1. New York: Academic Press, 1965, pp. 249–281.

The Course
of Infant Smiling
in Four Child-Rearing
Environments
in Israel

J. L. Gewirtz

NATIONAL INSTITUTES OF HEALTH

INTRODUCTION

Smiling may be assumed to be a key human response system, since it mediates, and thus could index efficiently, much of initial social development and learning. A preliminary report is herein presented of an attempt to chart the course of the smile response, in the first eighteen months of life, in groups of infants rared in diverse child-rearing environments in Israel. These environments appear to offer different contexts for early development and learning.

. . . Israel provides a unique variety of child-rearing environments which constitute differential behavior contexts. These could facilitate an understanding of the bases of early human smiling. It is thought that many of the pe-

Reprinted from B. M. Foss (Ed.), *Determinants of infant behaviour:* III. London: Methuen (New York: Wiley), 1965, pp. 205–260. By permission.

culiarly human qualities of the adaptive infant are acquired through the opportunities, particularly for learning, provided in interaction with his care-taking environment. Hence, apparent differences among these Israeli child-rearing contexts are most interesting theoretically, for they can be taken to represent various levels of availability of selected classes of stimulus condi-tions, which would index differences of opportunity, including those for a variety of learnings. As antecedents, these differences would imply dissimilar consequences in the social behavior patterns, including smiling, exhibited by the children reared in those settings. Infants from hospital-like residential institutions and day nurseries, who could provide a developmental picture of the early course of smiling under relatively limited conditions of environ-mental stimulation, are compared under standard conditions of observation to those from kibbutzim (collective settlements) and middle-class town fami-lies. Thus, the age course of smiling is contrasted in infants coming from widely differing child-rearing settings, having, it is assumed, different back-grounds of experience.

•   •   •

The Course of the Smile Response in the First Year

Observations of the course of the human smile response in the first year are dependent on many factors, including the stimuli employed, the response measures taken, and the samples used. A brief summary of findings follows:

"Spontaneous" or *"reflex"* smiling: the first phase.   This earliest phase of human smiling is thought to be relatively brief; smiles occur in the ab-sence of readily identifiable stimuli (e.g., "gastric smiles") as well as to a variety of kinesthetic, tactual or contact stimuli (e.g., stroking lips or cheeks). The early developmental form of the smile elicited in the first days of life may not involve the entire configurational pattern of the face which is taken to define the smile response at later months, when it usually occurs to iden-tifiable social stimuli. Koehler (1954) and Wolff (1959) have reported such "reflex" smiles in the first twenty-four hours.

"Social" smiling: the second phase.   The second smiling phase begins somewhere between 2 and 8 weeks (Jones, 1926; Bühler, 1933; Shirley, 1933; Gesell & Thompson, 1934; Söderling, 1959; Bayley, 1961). Here it appears that the smile is evoked by a variety of stimuli, many apparently visual in character and social in origin, in addition to some of those operating in the first phase. In typical infant environments, the most prominent stimuli for smiling seem provided by the human face (sometimes paired with a voiced sound); hence, the term "social" smiling (Watson, 1925). As the infant's capacities develop, the critical properties of the human face which evoke smiling may change (Ahrens, 1954). At least two theories have been advanced for infant social responsiveness and smiling to social stimuli in earliest life: the first has assumed they are already conditioned, emphasizing the concepts of classical conditioning and its variants (Darwin, 1872; Watson, 1925; Dennis, 1935; Gesell & Thompson, 1934; Spitz & Wolf, 1946); the second has pro-

posed they are initially unlearned (Bühler, 1933; Piaget, 1952; Bowlby, 1958; Rheingold, 1961).

"Selective" social smiling: the third phase.   The beginning of the third phase of smiling is placed before 20 weeks, when it is assumed to be at peak level to familiar and stranger adult faces (Washburn, 1929; Dennis, 1935; Spitz & Wolf, 1946; Ahrens, 1954; Ambrose, 1961). Whereas in the second phase the infant's smile appears to occur indiscriminately to social stimuli, in this phase only selected social stimuli are thought to continue to bring out the smile. In so far as infant smiles continue to be evoked by human faces, the rate is thought to remain unchanged or to rise to "familiar" adult faces, but to decline, even disappear, to "unfamiliar" (stranger) faces. It has been noted also that concomitant with this decline in smiling, the infant might sober, even withdraw or cry, at the sight of a stranger's face, however responsive it might be.

RATIONALE OF THE PRESENT STUDY

Even while some studies have been qualitative, and on institution Ss, several represent steps in the direction of providing a basis for understanding the developmental age course of the smile in the first year. Kaila (1932), Spitz & Wolf (1946) and Ahrens (1954) have concentrated on identifying dimensions of stimuli evoking smiles at different age points. Spitz and Wolf also have attempted a preliminary charting of smiling through the first year under more or less constant stimulus conditions. And Ambrose (1961) has used a standard condition of minimal social stimulation and quantitative response indices to chart the course of smiling during the first half-year. Still, the stimuli which control the response, both initially and subsequently through learning, remain obscure. In part, this may be because the tendency has been to attribute apparent declines in smile rates around 6 months not simply to a change in the discriminative stimuli for smiling and the correlated decline in smile response strength to the earlier controlling stimuli, but to the sudden onset of a "fear of strangers" process conceived to be incompatible with smiling.

This study was mounted to chart the course of the smile response through the first eighteen months. It was thought the learning-experience basis of smile response strength could be clarified by examining differences in its age course in what appear to be heterogeneous child-rearing environments. Quantitative response indices were devised, as was a standard stimulus setting selected to focus attention on the shifts in smiling from apparently unconditioned to conditioned stimulus control, and from gross social to selective social stimulus control, under conditions in which the smile response would be relatively unconfounded by incompatible responses or processes (e.g., "fear," "curiosity" and "exploration," and those generated by internal or external discomfort as might be brought on by fatigue, hunger, illness, or soiled diapers). Observers were to follow a brief standard procedure for approaching infants when they appeared to be at their peak of comfort and alertness, for presenting themselves to these infants, and occasionally for responding briefly and making initiations to a small portion of them, prior to but not immediately preceding the observation proper. In this way, the likelihood that a zero smile score would index the operation of a process incompatible with smiling was lowered; and the study became oriented towards getting from every infant a score for a single measure, smile frequency, which would reflect mainly smile response strength. Even so, other measures of overall responsiveness of the infants to the observer and to the experimental setting were obtained, at the same time as was the measure for the frequency of smiling, to provide a broader context for understanding the implications of the use of this relatively unencumbered smile measure. The light shed on the smile scores by these ancillary measures will be considered in a subsequent report.

METHOD

Sample

Institution. Subjects (Ss) received complete care in one of six residential institutions for infants in Israel. Many Ss were from lower socio-economic backgrounds, but few were orphaned. Most never received visits from parents. In general, caretaking routines in institutions at the time of observation followed this pattern: five or six infants of the same age in a living-room might be in the care of a female caretaker, usually professionally trained. In institutions which had training programs for children's nurses, a trainee might be in charge of a group for several months, until rotated. If the group contained more than six infants, the major caretaker might have help. During days off, holidays and illnesses of caretakers, substitutes would serve. Caretakers and/or their assistants might rotate in and out of groups. Relief caretakers might come into a group during the day, to diaper, to give medications, sometimes to feed.

Day nursery. Infants would spend some eight or nine hours per day, six days per week, in the custody of caretakers, some of whom might be professionally trained. Most Ss would receive all meals in the day nursery. Mothers of day-nursery infants generally represent lower socio-economic strata, have lived in Israel for only a few years, have several other children at home, and are day workers. Some day-nursery infants are from "broken" homes. The ratio of caretakers to children in the day nurseries sampled is low, there being typically more infants per caretaker than in the residential institutions. The care given is for the most part routine, and the environment seems less differentiated than that of the residential institution.

Family. Ss were from families dwelling in Jerusalem apartments. Their values and style of life would be termed "middle class" in Israel. Infants were sometimes housed in their parents' bedrooms, but often their cribs were situated in separate rooms which they sometimes shared with older siblings.

Typically the mother was at home during the day. Apart from the hot period around noon, these Ss would spend much of the day during warm seasons out-of-doors on terraces. They were typically taken on walks at least once daily, by their mother or substitute caretaker, and sometimes by their father late in the afternoon and on Sabbaths. Usually free at those times, fathers might spend much time then with their infants.

Kibbutz. The kibbutz or collective settlement in Israel is a small, typically rural, for the most part agricultural, self-contained social and economic unit. Educationally above average, kibbutz memberships represent voluntary highly select groups made up of persons ideologically committed to living out their lives on collective settlements, to owning little personal property, and to having their children raised collectively. Members of a kibbutz would devote much thought and effort to the care, socialization and education of the children of their collective. Children's needs would be paramount for them, transcending many economic and practical considerations. Usually from birth onward, a kibbutz infant is reared in a separate children's house, in the continuing care of a particular female kibbutz member, trained as a caretaker ("metapelet") and herself usually a parent. The interweaving of all spheres of kibbutz life makes of the children's house not only a place of "work" for the caretaker, but also a "home" in which her own children might be reared. A kibbutz caretaker is therefore highly committed to her four or five children. Caretaking would be supervised by an active kibbutz education committee.

Typically nursed and fed in the children's house for much of the first year by their mothers, young infants receive frequent visits from their parents, about whose room they would spend several hours during the latter part of each day, in addition to much time Sabbaths and holidays. A portion of each visit is spent in the parents' room (apartment), in which the ambulatory child has a "corner" which is his alone, and which becomes one of the two foci of his life. The children's house provides the other focus. Each focal place will involve different patterns of duties and privileges, with different sets of stimuli provided and different classes of responses that are appropriate. Yet in the first year of life there is considerable overlap between the two focal environments, for the parents also attend to the infant during the day in the children's house. Further, infants would often interact with adults who visit neighboring infants, and who would have become familiar. The kibbutz provides infants with a differentiated environment, in terms of the frequency, variety and complexity of available stimuli. This environment is quite different from those of even the better Institution, the nuclear Family, and the Day Nursery.

Number of Ss from each environment. These numbers of normal infants were observed in the various settings: in Institutions, in the 1- through 18-month range, 228 Ss were approached at least once and 226 of those not eliminated for crying, fussing, or sleeping were observed for two full minutes; in Day Nurseries, where only Ss between 8 and 18 months were observed, 107 were approached and 105 were observed for two full minutes; in Families, where only infants between 2 and 18 months were observed, 91 were

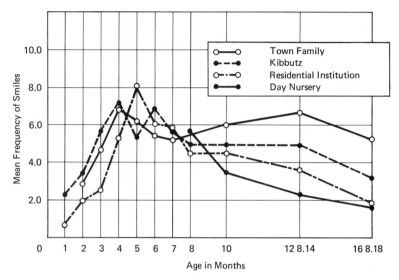

Fig. 1. Age curves for mean frequency of smiles in 2 minutes for infants from four Israeli child-rearing environments, in the 1- through 18-lunar-month range. Indexes in all figures are based on smiles to a woman's unresponsive face in the first approach of 2 minutes during which the infant exhibited less than a defined minimum of crying or fussing, and during which he did not appear sleepy. Note that Day Nursery and Family Ss are not represented at every monthly point.

approached and 91 were observed for two full minutes; and in Kibbutzim, 236 infants were approached and 235 were observed for two full minutes. The two-minute score was generally gotten on the first approach to each S. In keeping with the custom set in the smiling literature (e.g., Spitz & Wolf, Ahrens, Ambrose), in the preliminary analysis being reported here the simplifying assumption is made that there are no sex differences.

. . .

RESULTS

The Age Course of Smiling in the Four Environments in the First 18 Months

Mean frequency of smiles. The basic group index of smile response strength is the *mean frequency* of all smiles emitted by Ss in given age-groups to O's unresponsive face. These cross-sectional data are available for comparison of Ss in the Institution and Kibbutz environments from 1 through 18 months, in the Family from 2 through 18 months, and in the Day Nursery from 8 through 18 months. Mean frequency age curves are shown in Fig. 1.

It is seen there that the stimulus of the "unresponsive" face of a relatively unfamiliar woman O has evoked some smiling in the two groups represented at the first month, Institution and Kibbutz. From initially lower levels, it appears that the age curves for the three environments represented in the early months all display rapid increases in mean smile rate, after the second month in the Kibbutz and Family curves to peaks at 4 months, and after three months in the Institution curve to a peak at 5 months. Thereafter, no decline from its peak is seen in the Family curve, and a moderate decline is seen in the Kibbutz curve. (This decline relative to the Family curve is discounted for the reasons detailed in the preceding section.) The Institution curve declines from its peak (and the Nursery curve parallels it after 8 months) in a gradual and most orderly manner, to the terminal point at 18 months. At no age point after its peak month does any environmental mean curve decline to a zero level; and where a decline in smiling is seen after 16 or 20 weeks, it is nowhere abrupt.

· · ·

DISCUSSION

Age Curve Differences Among Environments in Level of Smiling

In this section there will be attempted heuristic analyses of the possible bases of the differences between the Family-Kibbutz and the Institution-Nursery age curve patterns of smiling to the standard stimulus of the woman's unresponsive face. This speculative analysis has two independent foci: the first involves the possible bases for different rates of smiling in the early months, where the Family and Kibbutz curves were higher and rose to an earlier peak than did the Institution curve; and the second involves the possible bases for the difference in level in the mean smile age curves in the post-peak portion of the age range, where the Kibbutz and Family curves were higher generally than were the Institution and Nursery curves, and where they declined less.

Possible Bases for Environmental Curve Differences in Rise to Peak Smile Rate

There have been identified what seem to be differences in the age course of smiling among groups from diverse environments, which could provide differential opportunities for the occurrence of smiling and for its conditioning. Hence, it seems appropriate to attempt to identify those differences among the environments which might be bases of the pattern of results. Even for this heuristic purpose, it will here be possible only to list in a loose, schematic way, but not to identify definitively, how the child-rearing environments studied potentially could differ, according to some of our current conceptions of processes through which stimulus conditions could have systematic, long-term, impacts on behavior, to account for the pattern of obtained results. Several theoretical cases for learning processes are outlined in the following sections. However, due to the gross nature of our two independent variables, "age" and "environmental group," there would be no conclusive way of selecting from among the possibilities listed there the cases which best order the results we are here attempting to explain. For the psychological analysis required, it would be necessary to coordinate these independent variables with events at the level of stimuli and responses. This analysis would consider the identities and frequencies of stimuli provided, their pairing and timing relations with smiles, whether preceding or following, and the opportunities for the classical and operant conditioning of smiles which the patterns of these variables differentially could constitute. A companion study (J. L. & H. B. Gewirtz) is in progress in three of the same environments. Its formal observations should ultimately provide information at the required level of analysis on antecedent and contemporaneous determinants of the smile response, and of other key behaviors, as well as on the learning processes which, to different degrees and at different times, may be involved to determine the results we are here attempting to order.

With these cautions in mind, we may now turn to an heuristic analysis of the possible bases for the apparent differences in the age curves for smiling to the standard stimulus of the woman's unresponsive face in the *early* months between Kibbutz-Family and Institution groups. This analysis will take into account some conceptions found in the literature of the bases of human smiling as well as the data from which these conceptions have evolved. The heuristic attempt is made to consider which of the available conceptions most plausibly could represent the relationships evident in the literature between smiling and its determinants, environmental and organismic, as well as the relationships presented in this paper. The present section will concentrate on conceptions which, while they stress the importance of different kinds of learning in the developmental course of the smile response, are entirely open to the operation of "innate" processes. This conceptual analysis of possible differences among the environments that might account for differences in early smiling will have two complementary themes throughout. The first theme is the relative "richness" of the environment, in the sense of the simple *availability of stimuli* for smiling (and other behaviors). The second theme is the differential *opportunities for learning* of various types involving smiles (and other interaction behaviors) in the environments, which would depend on the sequential and temporal relationships holding between available stimuli and smiles. Both themes overlap, and are involved in every one of the conceptions that follow.

Differential availability of stimuli (for smiles). Pertinent to the dimension of the relative availability of stimuli would be such attributes of the stimuli provided as their type, frequency, range, variety, novelty, and complexity. Such stimuli could elicit or evoke smiles and/or could reinforce them. In the context of the availability or provision of particular relevant stimuli, the infant's smiles (like many of his earliest behaviors) may be viewed initially as unconditioned responses (URs), either (a) *elicited* by (e.g. "releasing," "sign") stimuli which could increase the rate of a specific reflex, or *(b) evoked* by stimulus events which could increase non-specifically the likelihood of occurrence of various occurring behaviors, including smiling among others. On the *elicitation* point, *a,* we have noted that early smiling to stimulation has been conceived by some as being essentially *unlearned* (e.g., Bühler, Piaget, Bowlby, Rheingold); and it is possible, to the extent that eliciting or evoking unconditioned stimuli continue to control occurrences of smiles, that these stimuli might change in strength with developmental level. On the *evocation* point, *b,* we note that recent studies (e.g., Berlyne, 1958) have shown that infants tend to respond by attending, approaching, exploring, and/or smiling to complex or novel stimuli presented in their environments. The critical feature of this first conceptual focus then is, if a variety of stimuli were simply available, that Ss might: *first,* habituate disagreeable stimuli and hence become less encumbered in approaching and smiling to these and to stimuli generally; *second,* respond to instances of effective positive stimuli within classes and ranges, and, hence, as one consequence, acquire the *capacity to discriminate* along diverse dimensions of stimulus difference; and *third,* employ responses which could be *conditioned* (on a classical or operant basis) in circumstances conducive to learning (the second theme which follows). These circumstances would depend on the sequential and temporal relationships between stimuli and responses. On this last point also, in addition to evoking such responses as smiles, complex or novel stimuli and those permitted to recover from satiation might also operate more effectively (relative to simple or familiar stimuli) to *reinforce* such behaviors if made contingent upon them, as under the operant conditioning case detailed below.

On this basis, then, the apparent difference between child-rearing environments in the first 4 months might be due primarily to the fact that Institutions provided fewer stimulus possibilities for smiling to occur than did Kibbutz and Family environments, perhaps at an early point when the organism had the capacities required and was relatively unencumbered by the results of past learnings. (Some might term this a "critical" age range.) Further, the environments may differ on the complexity and novelty of stimuli they provide, and hence in the potency of potential evoking stimuli for smiling (as well as for attending, approaching and exploring). Environments might differ also in the reinforcing potency that stimuli with these attributes (relative to simple or familiar stimuli) might have differentially for such behaviors if made contingent on them, as under the operant conditioning case detailed below.

Lastly, the differential effect of environment could be based on the conception that the smile response might acquire strength in the early months as a function simply of the opportunities to emit smiles, i.e., of *practice.* In an analysis of gross independent variables such as ours here it would be difficult to separate a practice from a learning basis of smiles, for learning as conventionally conceived also involves the passage of time and practice. Moreover, even if a valid residual concept of practice could plausibly be defined, it would be most difficult to rule out the role of learned components of smile response strength. Even so, it seems worth while maintaining this distinction for our heuristic purpose here.

Differential opportunities for smile learning.   Several conceptions of the smile as a learned response may be advanced also. Not incompatible in principle, smile learning may be taking place concurrently under several of these cases. One basis for smiling may be *classical* (Pavlovian) conditioning (Darwin, 1872; Watson, 1925). There are some difficulties in applying this basic paradigm to the early acquisition of smile response strength. First, the term "reflex" typically has been reserved for cases in which a *specific* unconditioned stimulus (US) or those within a quite narrow stimulus range, upon *discrete* presentation, exhibits the capacity repeatedly to elicit a *specific* narrowly defined unconditioned response (UR), which UR usually involves directly elements of the autonomic nervous system (e.g., pupil constriction brought on by an intense light US). The conditions under which smiling is typically evoked in the early months seem to differ considerably from these: *First,* it appears that USs in a wide range, rather than in an exceedingly narrow one, may be capable of eliciting smiling. These USs would include visual, auditory, kinesthetic, and tactual stimuli (provided, e.g., through jogging, lifting, tickling, caressing, throwing or dropping the infant through space, or by distant or disjunctive sights and sounds). *Second,* rather gross stimuli, in particular the human face, when presented not discretely but continuously and which are apparently unchanging, seem capable for periods of evoking smiles repeatedly. *Third,* the to-be-conditioned stimulus (CS) complex, the most likely one for infant social smiling being some discriminable aspect of the caretaker's appearance or face, must (a) have no initial US value for smiling, and (b) permit discrete presentation for effective pairing, on both of which counts the caretaker's appearance-face may not qualify. For these reasons, it would be difficult to specify with confidence whether and exactly how the smile would be conditioned classically.

Even while it is difficult easily to assume that these three requirements hold for the case of infant smiling, it would be instructive to follow through how the classical conditioning model might apply. It would emphasize that the smile could come rapidly under the control of CSs through their regular association with the US. For this case, a variety of USs might operate, like those earlier listed. Assuming that it is not a continuous and unchanging event, that it could be presented on discrete occasions (trials), and that it has no US value for smiling, the caretaker's appearance-face could function as the to-be-CS complex. On the assumption, then, that it would systematically precede USs on a sufficient number of occasions with proper timing relationships, the caretaker's appearance-face would soon come to function as the CS class for the infant's smiles. Thereafter, the caretaker's appearance-face would elicit smiles from the infant, assuming the continuation of maintenance pairings between CS and US. Thus, from the viewpoint of learning opportunity, one way in which environments could differ in the early months is in the pattern of stimuli they provide, specifically in the sequence and timing relationships between those stimuli and smiling which would constitute opportunities for the Pavlovian conditioning of smiling. To explain our findings, relative to the Institution, Kibbutz and Family environments might earlier provide more instances of readily discriminable to-be-CSs, which precede uniformly, in effective timing relationships, the occurrence of USs for smiling.

Dennis (1935) has suggested that smiling could become a classical CR to any stimulus which brings about a cessation of fretting, unrest and crying, and that it is *not* elicited by an US. Gesell & Thompson (1934) and Spitz & Wolf (1946) in a not too dissimilar vein have assumed that the smile as CR somehow comes to be produced by the "satisfaction" inherent in "need-gratification," and that somehow it then could become an *anticipatory* response to that "satisfaction," for which the caretaker's face becomes the CS. In so far as classical conditioning is the actual or implied model, the implicit assumptions of these conceptions would be even more tenuous than those required for the straightforward application to smiling of the Pavlovian conditioning paradigm. In this section, we have noted the difficulties involved in a straightforward application of the classical paradigm to smile learning. As will be detailed in the following section, many of the phenomena these theorists have attempted to explain may be ordered readily with the conception of the S-R chain, i.e., operant conditioning and the conditioned discriminative stimulus (cue). The stimulus of the appearance-face would signal, as it were, that a smile response could lead to a reinforcing consequence (e.g., food, water, being held). Hence, appearance would come to control (evoke) smiling.

The second potential learning basis for smiling is that of *instrumental* or *operant* conditioning. This conception may be applied to the case of smile learning with far fewer reservations than that of Pavlovian conditioning just considered. For this paradigm, aspects of freely occurring responses of the infant are differentiated out ("shaped") and conditioned by those immediate environmental consequences which function as "reinforcing" stimuli (cf. Gewirtz, 1959). Any stimulus event which follows a free response (e.g., smile) of the infant and which systematically increases some index of that response, would be termed a (positive) reinforcing stimulus. Accordingly, smiling as an operant response could become conditioned to occur more frequently in the context in which it has been followed by reinforcing stimuli, of which a great variety is provided in most caretaking environments. Reinforcing stimuli might be provided through the potential USs listed for the classical conditioning case, through the provision of relatively more complex and novel stimuli, and through such responses as talking to the infant and picking him up as was demonstrated by Brackbill (1958) with 3-4 month Ss. [For other examples, see Gewirtz (1961).] Indeed, due to the great value placed on infant smiles by most caretaking communities, it would be most unusual for smiles to remain long unanswered (unreinforced) by the responses of witnessing caretakers who are not encumbered or occupied. As was indicated in the preceding paragraph, a minor extension of this operant paradigm would be one in which a discriminative (cue) stimulus occurred to signal that a response, if

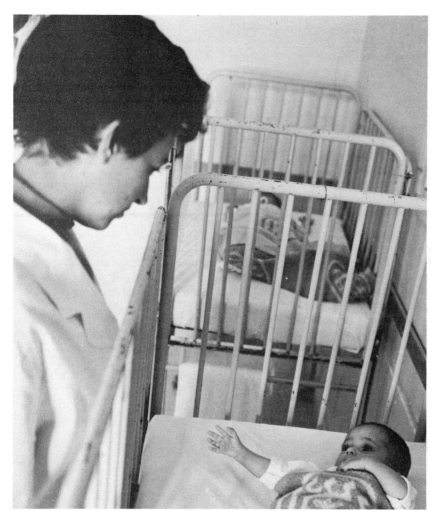

Fig. 2. Observer presenting unresponsive face 3 feet from face of supine Institution infant to evoke smiling. (Distance was 2 feet in formal observations). Photo
by Dr. J. L. Gewirtz.

emitted, could be followed by a reinforcing stimulus. For example, the caretaker's appearance or face could provide the cue to the infant that he might
be reinforced (e.g., by his being picked up) if he would smile; hence, he
might smile to the appearance of the face.

Therefore, another possible way in which environments might differ is
in the opportunities they provide for the operant conditioning of smiling.
As in the Pavlovian case above, it is axiomatic for this case also that stimuli
be available to the child, particularly those which could function to reinforce

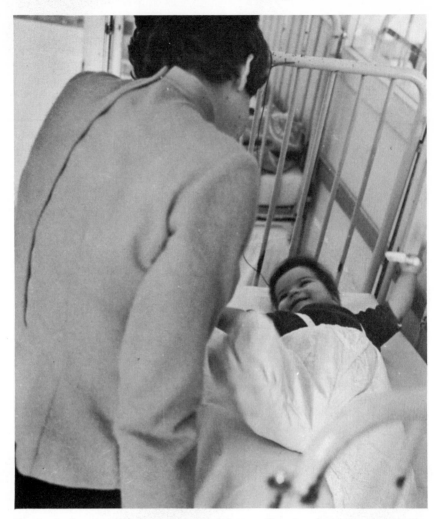

Fig. 3. Supine 6-month-old Institution infant smiling to observer's unresponsive face. (Bed-side would remain up during formal observations.) Photo by Dr. J. L. Gewirtz.

behaviors if made immediately contingent on them. Specifically, if occurrences of smiles would be followed as consequences closely and frequently by any of a variety of stimulus events which function as reinforcers, the incidence of smiling in that setting would increase; i.e., the smile would become conditioned. To explain the differences in results among environments, it would be assumed that caretakers in Institutions might have relatively less time for each infant in their care. Further, even when in the infant's vicinity, they would often be busy with neighboring infants. Hence, it is thought that

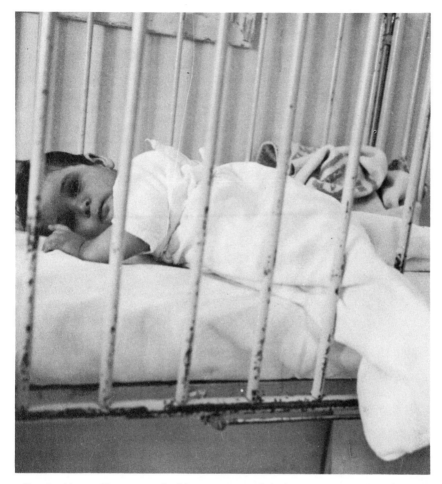

Fig. 4. Non-smiling 7-month-old Institution infant fixating seated observer's un-responsive face (out of picture). Photo by Dr. J. L. Gewirtz.

relative to Kibbutz and Family caretakers, Institution caretakers might respond to the infant's smiles (and other behaviors) relatively less often and less quickly (it is recalled that the most effective reinforcement follows imme-diately the response), perhaps also providing potential reinforcing stimuli in a narrower range and of less complexity or novelty, and in fewer settings.

Lastly, we emphasize two additional ways in which environments may differ, deriving from or extensions of the two preceding conditioning para-digms. We have seen that the operant paradigm may be extended to where an environment would provide stimuli so that the smile as operant is rein-forced only on occasions when it is emitted in the presence of (or when it is preceded by) a particular stimulus (e.g., a woman's face), which then would

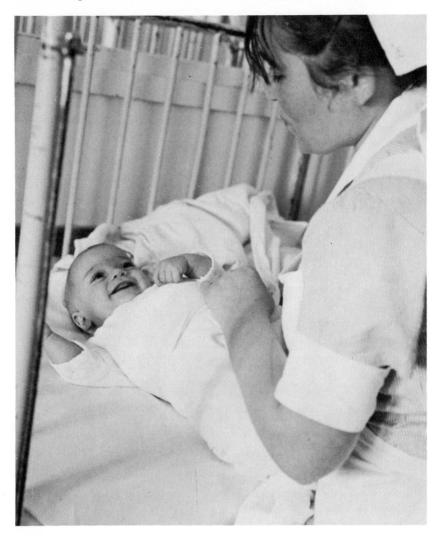

Fig. 5. Four-month-old Institution infant smiling to caretaker while being dressed. Photo by Dr. J. L. Gewirtz.

become a *discriminative* (or cue) stimulus for smiling. This paradigm may be relevant to the test procedure of this study. In the Institution environment this learning might occur rather later than it might in the other environments, either because the stimuli are not presented as often or because effective contingencies between stimuli and the smile response do not occur until much later there. Finally, the environments may differ in that they provide stimuli in contingencies with the smile to make it possible for elements of the Pavlovian and operant paradigms to occur in sequence. In essence, once elicited by an US or CS, or evoked, some elements of the smile functioning not unlike a free operant might be in a position to be reinforced by stimulus consequences. The same environment patterns would hold as were earlier detailed separately under the classical and operant cases.

It is perhaps important to point out once again that the preceding analysis of possible differences in smiling between the Institution and the Family-Kibbutz environments was an heuristic one. Several theoretical ways in which stimuli might have been provided differentially by those environments in connection with smiling were detailed. The observation study surveying stimulus conditions and their relations to behaviors (including smiles) in the early months in the same three environments, just concluded by Dr. Hava Gewirtz and the writer, should provide pertinent information for evaluating the role of each of the possible bases outlined for the pattern of differences in smile curves found in the earliest months between the Institution and the Kibbutz and Family environments.

Possible Bases for Environmental Curve Differences
in Post-Peak Smile Rate

Our method deviated from the modal procedure found in the smile literature, which has involved the approach to Ss of a complete stranger. Instead, our O employed a brief preliminary habituation-familiarization phase on first approaching S, before the formal observation but not immediately preceding it. This habituation phase was established to limit responses incompatible with smiling, for the purpose of making it possible to study that response system when relatively unencumbered. Hence, the smile curve patterns found and the difference in level between the two curve patterns (neither of which reflect a sudden onset and continuing state of a hypothesized "fear of strangers" response pattern) do not bear directly on the issue of whether there is a decline in smiling to strangers with a concomitant rise in fear around 6 months. When the post-peak segments of the relatively homogenerous mean frequency and proportion smile age curve patterns were examined, a fairly constant level of smiling was noted through that upper age range for the Kibbutz and Family curves, while a systematic decline with age was noted for the Institution and Nursery curves.

A statistical test has indicated that the peak levels of mean smiling reached at 4 or 5 months by the three environmental groups were homogeneous, at an age before it could be assumed that various discriminative stimuli acquire much differential control over the smile response. Hence, it would appear that the levels of smiling found in the upper portions of the age range are not simple reflections of overall smile response strength. Rather it is thought one plausible explanation of the differences in level among the environmental age-group curves is that the pattern found is due to differences among the environments in the discriminative stimulus conditions that control infant smiles. These differences would be reflected in differences in the discriminative value or meaning of the standard stimulus for smiling that was used for Ss in each of these environments, namely O's unresponsive face. Thus, it is thought likely that the different mean curve levels reflect mainly the technical difference between the stimuli controlling caretaker behaviors and infant smiling in each environment *and* our test condition under which smiling could be evoked by O's unresponsive face. For example, in Kibbutz and Family environments, more than in the Institution or Day Nursery, the near presence or distant sight of a caretaker or other adult, even with an unresponsive face, might cue S that some initiation (for instance, a smile) would be likely to lead to a reply by that person (e.g., a change in her face, like a smile). The caretaker's response might have reinforcer value sufficient to terminate the initiation, or it might imply that the interaction chain thus begun could culminate in a reinforcing consequence. On this assumed basis, there should be greater (stimulus) generalization from adults generally in the environment to O; and the two-minute presentation of O's appearance-face (standing as discriminate for reinforcing consequences) should evoke higher smile rates from Kibbutz and Family Ss than from Institution and Nursery Ss, through the post-peak age range. We are drawn to this more or less *ad hoc* explanation as a plausible and parsimonious basis for the pattern of differences found between environmental group smile curves in the upper portion of the range studied.

Smiling, Social Responsiveness, "Satisfaction" and "Joy"

It would not seem parsimonious to think of the incidence of group smiling as having special implications for "satisfaction with life" or "happiness," and on this basis alone to conclude that some of the child-rearing settings studied are more wholesome or adequate than others. The point has been made that, before the discriminative stimulus control of smiling is reached, overall smile rate would reflect mainly conditioning history. Further, by 5–6 months, smile rate very likely has begun to come under close conditioned discriminative stimulus control and, thus, may reflect in social settings primarily the degree of an infant's involvement in social interaction sequences appropriate to those settings. (As a key response in those interaction sequences, the smile would be functioning in an instrumental or "communicative" role there, with the appearance characteristics of persons functioning as the basic discriminative stimuli.) Infants for whom the appearance and behaviors of persons are not discriminative for reinforcement (i.e., those who are not "dependent" upon others, or who do not "relate" to persons) should exhibit to O relatively fewer smiles and other responses. Thus, we might expect fewer smiles to persons by Ss in environments characterized by low child-caretaker ratios and high personnel turnover; and it is on the basis of this limited responsiveness to persons displayed by those Ss that such environments might be evaluated as inadequate.

The smile has been thought also by some to reflect "satisfaction" or "joy," during reveries or after becoming anticipatory for the attainment of some reinforcing event, thus functioning in an "expressive" role. (We have noted earlier that the infant's smile might communicate information to the person who could provide reinforcers, and also that it might function as a reinforcing stimulus for that person's behaviors.) Prior to conditioning, however, the infant's smile in the early social phase would seem to have minimal communicative meaning, and only in a limited sense to have expressive meaning. On the expressive point, aside from indexing smile threshold, the infant's smile could indicate that he was alert and fixating a stimulus, that he was not crying or fussing, and hence that he was not preoccupied with strong "internal" stimuli (e.g., due to "gas," hunger, fatigue, illness, or discomfort due to wet or soiled diapers). This pattern could provide information to an observer who might assume that an uncomfortable or bothered infant would not be likely to smile or even effectively to fixate stimuli. Outside the implication that smiling could index the absence of behaviors reflecting "discomfort," there would seem to be no independent index of "satisfaction" which might be related to the smile in the early months. The notion of the smile as "expressive" may also reflect Pavlovian conditioning. Thus, if the discriminate appearance of a CS face is systematically followed by such activities as lifting or tickling (the US) which produce smiling or laughter, subsequent appearances of the face could elicit the smile response. These classically conditioned smiles or laughs might be thought by some to be expressions of the infant's "joy," as e.g., at the approach of his father.

REFERENCES

Ahrens, R. (1954). Beitrag zur Entwicklung der Physiognomie und Mimikerkennens, Zeit für exp. und ang. Psychol., 2(3), 414–454; and 2(4), 599–633.

Ainsworth, M. (1963). The development of infant-mother interaction among the Ganda. In B. M. Foss (Ed.), Determinants of infant behaviour II. London: Methuen, pp. 67–104.

Altmann, S. A. (1962). A field study of the sociobiology of rhesus monkeys, Macaca mulatta, New York Acad. Sci., 102, 338–435.

Ambrose, J. A. (1960). The smiling and related responses in early human infancy: an experimental and theoretical study of their course and significance. Ph.D. thesis, London University

Ambrose, J. A. (1961). The development of the smiling response in early infancy. In B. M. Foss (Ed.), Determinants of infant behaviour. London: Methuen, pp. 179–201.

Arsenian, J. M. (1943). Young children in an insecure situation, J. abn. soc. Psychol., 38, 225–49.

Baer, D. M. & Sherman, J. A. Quoted in L. P. Lipsitt & C. C. Spiker (Eds.), Advances in Child Development and Behaviour. New York; Academic Press, 1963, pp. 221–6.

Auble, D. (1953). Extended tables for the Mann-Whitney statistic, Bull. Dist. Educ. Res. Bloomington: Indiana Univer.

Bandura, A. & Walters, R. H. (1963). Social learning and personality development. New York: Holt, Rinehart and Winston.

Barabash-Nikiforov, I. I. (1962). The sea otter. Jerusalem: Israel Program for Scientific Translations (available from the Office of Technical Services, U.S. Dept. of Commerce, Washington, D.C.).

Bartholomew, G. A. (1959). Mother-young relations and the maturation of pup behaviour in the Alaskan fur seal, *Animal Behav., 7*, 163–71.

Bayley, N. (1961). Personal communication.

Beach, F. A. (1939). Maternal behavior of the pouchless marsupial *Marmosa cinerea*, *J. Mammal., 20*, 315–22.

Beach, F. A. & Jaynes, J. (1956a). Studies of maternal retrieving in rats. I: Recognition of young, *J. Mammal., 37*, 177–80.

Beach, F. A. & Jaynes, J. (1956b). Studies of maternal retrieving in rats. II: Sensory cues involved in the lactating female's response to her young, *Behaviour, 10*, 104–25.

Beach, F. A. & Wilson, J. R. (1963). Effects of prolactin, progesterone and estrogen on maternal reactions of nonpregnant rats to foster young, *Psychol. Rep., 13*, 231–9.

Beniest-Noirot, E. (1958). Analyse du comportement dit maternal chez la souris, *Monog. Françaises de Psychol., 1*. Paris: Centre National de la Recherche Scientifique.

Berlyne, D. (1958). The influence of the albedo and complexity of stimuli on visual fixation in the human infant, *Brit. J. Psychol., 49*, 315–18.

Birch, H. G. (1945). The relation of previous experience to insightful problem-solving, *J. comp. Psychol., 38*, 367–83.

Birch, H. G. (1956). Sources of order in the maternal behavior of animals, *Amer. J. Orthopsychiat., 26*, 279–84.

Bobbitt, R. A., Jensen, G. D. & Kuehn, R. E. (1964). Development and application of an observational method: a pilot study of the mother-infant relationship in pigtail monkeys, *J. genet. Psychol., 105*, 257–74.

Bourlière, F. (1954). *The natural history of mammals*. New York: Knopf.

Bowlby, J. (1958). The nature of the child's tie to his mother. *Int. J. of Psychoanal., 39*, 350–73.

Brackbill, Y. (1958). Extinction of the smiling response in infants as a function of reinforcement schedule, *Child. Devel., 29*, 115–24.

Bruce, H. M. (1961). Observations on the suckling stimulus and lactation in the rat, *J. Reprod. Fertil., 2*, 17–34.

Buchsbaum, R. (1948). *Animals without backbones*. Chicago: Univer. Chicago Press.

Bühler, C. (1939). The social behaviour of children. In C. A. Murchison (Ed.), *Handbook of child psychology*, 2nd ed., revised. Worcester, Mass.: Clark Univer. Press.

Burton, M. (1957). Nature's wonderland, No. 8, *Illustrated London News*, March 2, 1957, 356–7.

Butler, R. A. (1953). Discrimination by Rhesus monkeys to visual exploration motivation, *J. comp. physiol. Psychol., 46*, 95–8.

Calhoun, J. B. (1953). The ecology and sociology of the Norway rat, *U.S. Public Health Service Publ.*, no. 1008, 1–288.

Causey, D. & Waters, R. H. (1963). Parental care in mammals with especial reference to the carrying of young by the albino rat, *J. comp. Psychol., 22*, 241–54.

Cloudsley-Thompson, J. L. (1960). *Animal behaviour*. London: Oliver and Boyd.

Cockrum, E. L. (1962). *Introduction to mammalogy*. New York: Ronald Press.

Comfort. (1961) *Darwin and the naked lady*. London: Routledge.

Coolidge, H. J., Jr. (1933). Notes on a family of breeding gibbons, *Human Biology, 5*, 288–94.

Cornwell, A. C. & Fuller, J. L. (1961). Conditioned responses in young puppies, *J. comp. physiol. Psychol., 54*, 13–15.

Cowie, A. T. & Folley, S. J. (1961). The mammary gland and lactation. In W. C. Young

(Ed.), *Sex and internal secretions*, 3rd ed. Baltimore: Williams and Wilkins, pp. 590–642.

Crawford, M. P. & Spence, K. W. (1939). Observational learning of discrimination problems by chimpanzees, *J. comp. Psychol., 27*, 133–47.

Curio, E. (1955). Der Jungentransport einer Gelbhalsmaus (*Apodemus f. flavicollis Melch.*), *Z. Tierpsychol. 12*, 459–62.

Darling, F. F. (1937). *A herd of red deer*. Oxford: University Press.

Darwin, C. (1872). *The expression of emotion in man and animals*. London: Murray. New York: Philosophical Library, 1955.

David, M. & Appell, G. (1961). A study of nursing care and nurse-infant interaction. In B. M. Foss (Ed.), *Determinants of infant behaviour*. London: Methuen.

Davis, R. B., Herreid, C. F. II & Short, H. L. (1962). Mexican freetailed bats in Texas, *Ecol. Monogr., 32*, 311–46.

Dennis, W. (1935). An experimental test of two theories of social smiling in infants, *J. Soc. Psychol., 6*, 214–23.

Devore, I. (1963). Mother-infant relations in free-ranging baboons. In H. L. Rheingold (Ed.), *Maternal behavior in mammals*. New York: John Wiley, pp. 305–35.

Eibl-Eibesfeldt, I. (1955). Angeborenes und Erworbenes in Nestbauverhalten der Wanderratte, *Naturwissenschaften, 42*, 633–4.

Eibl-Eibesfeldt, I. (1958). Das Verhalten der Nagetiere. In J. G. Helmcke, H. v. Lengerken and D. Starck (Eds.), *Handbuch der Zoologie*, Vol. 8, Lief. 12. Berlin: Walter de Gryter.

Everett, J. W. (1961). The mammalian female reproductive cycle and its controlling mechanisms. In W. C. Young (Ed.), *Sex and internal secretions*, 3rd ed. Baltimore: Williams and Wilkins, pp. 497–555.

Fisher, E. M. (1940). Early life of a sea otter pup, *J. Mammal., 21*, 132–7.

Foss, B. M. (1964). Mimicry in mynas (*Gracula religiosa*): a test of Mowrer's theory, *Brit. J. Psychol., 55*, 85–8.

Freedman, D. G. (1961). The infant's fear of strangers and the flight response, *J. child Psychol. Psychiat., 4*, 242–8.

Freedman, D. G. (1963). 16-mm. sound film: *Development of the smile and fear of strangers*. PCR-2140, Penn. Psychol. Cinema Reg., University Park, Penna.

Freedman, D. G. & Keller, B. (1963). Inheritance of behavior in infants, *Science, 140*, 196–8.

Freud, S. (1922). *Introductory lectures on psycho-analysis*. London: Allen and Unwin.

Fuller, J. L. & Du Buis, E. M. (1962). The behaviour of dogs. In E. S. E. Hafez (Ed.), *The behaviour of domestic animals*. London: Baillière, Tyndall and Cox, pp. 415–52.

Gesell, A. & Thompson, H. (1934). *Infant behavior: its genesis and growth*. New York: McGraw-Hill.

Gewirtz, J. L. (1959). Discussion of the use of operant conditioning techniques with children. In S. Fisher (Ed.), *Child research in psychopharmacology*. Springfield, Ill.: Chas. C Thomas, pp. 127–36.

Gewirtz, J. L. (1961). A learning analysis of the effects of normal stimulation, privation and deprivation on the acquisition of social motivation and attachment. In B. M. Foss (Ed.), *Determinants of infant behaviour*. London: Methuen, pp. 213–99.

Gewirtz, J. L. (1965). The course of smiling by groups of Israeli infants in the first 18 months of life. In *Studies in psychology: Scripta Hierosolymitana, 14*, Jerusalem: Hebrew University Press.

Goldstein, K. (1957). The smiling of the infant and the problem of understanding the "other," *J. Psychol., 44*, 175–91.

Goodpaster, W. W. & Hoffmeister, D. F. (1954). Life history of the golden mouse, *Peromyscus muttalli*, in Kentucky, *J. Mammal., 35,* 16–27.

Guiford, J. P. (1954). *Psychometric methods,* 2nd ed. New York: McGraw-Hill.

Hansen, E. W. (1962). The development of infant and maternal behavior in the rhesus monkey. Ph.D. thesis. University of Wisconsin.

Harlow, H. F. (1958). The nature of love, *Amer. Psychologist, 13,* 673–85.

Harlow, H. F. (1961). The development of affectional patterns in infant monkeys. In B. M. Foss (Ed.), *Determinants of infant behaviour.* London: Methuen, pp. 75–88.

Harlow, H. F. (1962). Development of the second and third affectional systems in macaque monkeys. In T. T. Tourlentes, S. L. Pollack and H. F. Himwick (Eds.), *Research aproaches to psychiatric problems: a symposium.* New York: Grune and Stratton, pp. 209–29.

Harlow, H. F. (1963). The maternal affectional system. In B. M. Foss (Ed.), *Determinants of infant behaviour: II.* London: Methuen.

Harlow, H. F., Harlow, M. K. & Hansen, E. W. (1963). The maternal affectional system of rhesus monkeys. In H. L. Rheingold (Ed.), *Maternal behavior in mammals.* New York: Wiley, pp. 254–81.

Hatt, R. T. (1927). A gray squirrel carries its young, *J. Mammal., 8,* 244–5.

Hayes, K. J. & Hayes, C. (1952). Imitation in a home raised chimpanzee, *J. comp. physiol. Psychol., 46,* 99–104.

Hediger, H. (1955). *Studies of the psychology and behaviour of captive animals in zoos and circuses* (Trans. by G. Sircom). New York: Criterion Books.

Hinde, R. A. (1962). Sensitive periods and the development of behaviour. *Lessons from animal behaviour for the clinician, Little club clinic in developmental medicine, 7,* 25–36.

Hinde, R. A. & Rowell, T. E. (1962). Communication in postures and facial expressions in the rhesus monkey (*Macaca mulatta*), *Proc. zool. Soc. Lond. 138,* 1–21.

Hinde, R. A., Rowell, T. E. & Spencer-Booth, Y. (1964). Behaviour of ·socially living rhesus monkeys in their first six months, *Proc. zool. Soc. Lond., 143,* 609–49.

Horner, B. R. (1947). Parental care of young mice of the genus *Peromyseus, J. Mammal., 28,* 31–36.

Howell, A. B. & Little, L. (1924). Additional notes on California bats; with observations upon the young of *Eumops, J. Mammal., 5,* 261–3.

Huestis, R. R. (1933). Maternal behavior in the deer mouse, *J. Mammal., 14,* 47–9.

Humphrey, G. (1921). Imitation and the conditioned reflex, *Ped. Sem., 28,* 1–21.

Itani, J. (1959). Paternal care in the wild Japanese monkey, *Macaca fuscata fuscata, Primates: J. Primatology, 2,* 61–93.

James, M. (1960). Premature ego development: some observations upon disturbances in the first three months of life, *Int. J. Psychoanal., 41.*

Jay, P. (1962). Aspects of maternal behavior in langurs, *Proc. N.Y. Acad. Sci., 102,* 468–76.

Jay, P. (1963). Mother-infant relations in langurs. In H. L. Rheingold (Ed.), *Maternal behavior in mammals.* New York: John Wiley, pp. 282–304.

Jensen, G. D. (1961). The development of prehension in a Macaque, *J. comp. physiol. Psychol., 54,* 11–12.

Jensen, G. D. & Tolman, C. W. (1962a). Aspects of the mother-child tie in the monkey: the effect of brief separation and mother specificity, *J. comp. physiol. Psychol., 55,* 131.

Jensen, G. D. & Tolman, C. W. (1962b). Activity level of the mother monkey, *Macaca nemestrina*, as affected by various conditions of sensory access to the infant following separation, *Animal Behaviour, 10,* 228–30.

Jones, M. C. (1926). The development of early behavior patterns in young children, *Ped. Sem. J. Genet. Psychol., 33,* 537–85.

Kaila, E. (1943). Die Reaktionen des Säuglings auf das manschliche Gesicht, *Annales Universit. Aboensis* Series B, 17, 1–114.

Kinder, E. F. (1927). A study of the nest-building activity of the albino rat, *J. exp. Zool., 47,* 117–61.

King, J. A. (1958). Maternal behavior and behavioral development in two subspecies of *Peromyscus maniculatus, J. Mammal., 39,* 117–90.

Klopfer, P. H. (1959). Social interactions in discrimination learning with special reference to feeding behaviour in birds, *Behaviour, 14,* 282–99.

Klopfer, P. H. (1960). Observational learning in birds: the establishment of behavioural modes, *Behaviour, 15,* 71–9.

Koehler, O. (1954). Das Lächeln als angeborene Ausdrucksbewegung, *Zeit. f. Menschliche Vererbung u. Konstit., 32,* 390–8.

Kris, E. (1962). Decline and recovery in the life of a three-year-old: or—data in psycho-analytic perspective on the mother-child relationship, *Psychoanal. study Child,* 17.

Labriola, J. (1953). Effects of caesarean delivery upon maternal behavior in rats, *Proc. soc. exp. Biol. N.Y., 83,* 556–7.

Lang, H. (1925). How squirrels and other rodents carry their young, *J. Mammal., 6,* 18–24.

Lehrman, D. S. (1961). Hormonal regulation of parental behavior in birds and infrahuman mammals. In W. C. Young (Ed.), *Sex and internal secretions,* 3rd ed. Baltimore: Williams and Wilkins, pp. 1268–1382.

Leyhausen, P. (1956). Verhaltensstudien an Katzen, *Z. Tierpsychol.* Beiheft 2.

Lott, D. F. (1962). The role of progesterone in the maternal behavior of rodents, *J. comp. physiol. Psychol., 55,* 610–13.

Lott, D. F. & Fuchs, S. S. (1962). Failure to induce retrieving by sensitization or the injection of prolactin, *J. comp. physiol. Psychol., 55,* 1111–13.

Lundin, R. W. (1961). *Personality: an experimental approach.* New York: Macmillan.

McGraw, M. B. (1945). *The neuromuscular maturation of the human infant.* New York: Columbia Univer. Press.

Miller, G. A., Galanter, E. & Pribram, K. H. (1960). *Plans and the structure of behavior.* New York: Henry Holt.

Miller, N. E. & Dollard, J. (1941). *Social learning and imitation,* New Haven: Yale Univer. Press.

Mirsky, J. A., Miller, R. E. & Murphy, J. U. (1958). The communication of affect in rhesus monkeys. I. An experimental method. *J. Am. Psychoanalyt. A, 6,* 933.

Moore, J. C. (1957). Newborn young of a captive manatee, *J. Mammal., 38,* 137–8.

Mowrer, O. H. (1950). *Learning theory and personality dynamics.* New York: The Ronald Press.

Mowrer, O. H. (1960). *Learning theory and the symbolic process.* New York: John Wiley.

Nemtsova, O. L., Morachevskaia, E. V. & Andreyeva, E. I. (1958). Changes in the conditioned reflex activity of animals during pregnancy, *Pavlov J. Higher Nerv. Activity, 8,* 223–33.

Newson, J. & Newson, E. (1963). *Infant care in an urban community.* London: Allen and Unwin.

Nicoll, C. S. & Meites, J. (1959). Prolongation of lactation in the rat by litter replacement, *Proc. Soc. exp. Biol. N.Y.*, *101*, 81–2.

Orr, L. W. (1930). An unusual chipmunk nest, *J. Mammal.*, *11*, 315.

Pearson, O. P., Koford, M. R. & Pearson, A. K. (1952). Reproduction of the lump-nosed bat (*Corynorhinus rafinesquei*) in California, *J. Mammal.*, *33*, 273–320.

Piaget, J. (1952). *The origins of intelligence in children.* New York: International Univers. Press.

Pournelle, G. H. (1952). Reproduction and early post-natal development of the cotton mouse, *Peromyscus gossypinus gossypinus*, *J. Mammal.*, *33*, 1–20.

Prechtl, H. F. R. (1963). The mother-child interaction in babies with minimal brain damage. In B. M. Foss (Ed.), *Determinants of infant behaviour: II*. London: Methuen, pp. 53–9.

Price, B. (1950). Primary biases in twin studies, *Amer. J. Hum. Genet.*, *2*, 293–352.

Rheingold, H. L. (1961). The effect of environmental stimulation upon social and exploratory behaviour in the human infant. In B. M. Foss (Ed.), *Determinants of infant behaviour*. London: Methuen, pp. 143–77.

Rheingold, H. L. (1963a). Controlling the infant's exploratory behaviour. In B. M. Foss (Ed.), *Determinants of infant behaviour: II*. London: Methuen, pp. 171–5.

Rheingold, H. L. (1963b). Maternal behavior in the dog. In H. L. Rheingold (Ed.), *Maternal behavior in mammals*. New York: John Wiley, pp. 169–202.

Richardson, W. B. (1943). Wood rats (*Neotoma albigula*): their growth and development, *J. Mammal.*, *24*, 130–43.

Riddle, O., Lahr, E. L. & Bates, R. W. (1942). The role of hormones in the initiation of maternal behavior in rats, *Amer. J. Physiol.*, *137*, 299–317.

Riess, B. F. (1950). The isolation of factors of learning and native behavior in field and laboratory studies, *Ann. N.Y. Acad. Sci.*, *51*, 1093–1102.

Riess, B. F. (1954). The effect of altered environments and age in mother-young relationships among animals, *Ann. N.Y. Acad. Sci.*, *57*, 606–10.

Riopelle, A. J. (1960). Complex processes. Chapter 8 in R. H. Waters, D. A. Rethlingshafer and W. E. Caldwell (Eds.), *Principles of comparative psychology*. New York: McGraw-Hill.

Robertson, Joyce (1962). Mothering as an influence on early development, *Psychoanal. study Child*, *17*.

Rosenblatt, J. S., Turkewitz, G. & Schneirla, T. C. (1961). Early socialization in the domestic cat as based on feeding and other relationships between female and young. In B. M. Foss (Ed.), *Determinants of infant behaviour*. London: Methuen, pp. 51–74.

Rosenblatt, J. S. & Lehrman, D. S. (1963). Maternal behavior of the laboratory rat. In H. L. Rheingold (Ed.), *Maternal behavior in mammals*. New York: John Wiley, pp. 8–57.

Ross, S., Denenberg, V. H. Frommer, G. P. & Sawin, P. B. (1959). Genetic, physiological, and behavioral background of reproduction in the rabbit. V. Nonretrieving of neonates, *J. Mammal.*, *40*, 91–6.

Roth, L. L. & Rosenblatt, J. S. (1964). Pregnancy changes in the self-licking patterns of rats. Paper presented at meetings of the American Psychological Association in Los Angeles.

Rothchild, I. (1969). The corpus luteum–pituitary relationship, *Endocrinology*, *67*, 9–14.

Rowell, T. E. (1960). On the retrieving of young and other behaviour in lactating golden hamsters, *Proc. Zool. Soc. London*, *135*, 265–82.

Rowell, T. E. & Hinde, R. A. (1962). Vocal communication by the rhesus monkey (*Macaca mulatta*), *Proc. Zool. Soc. London, 138*, 279–94.

Rowell, T. E., Hinde, R. A. & Spencer-Booth, Y. (1964). "Aunt"-infant interaction in captive rhesus monkeys, *Anim. Behav. 12*, 219–26.

Salk, L. (1960). The effects of the normal heartbeat sound on the behavior of the new-born infant: implications for mental health, *World ment. Health, 12*, 1–8.

Sander, L. W. (1962). Issues in early mother-child interaction, *J. child Psychiat. 1*, 1.

Schaller, G. B. (1963). *The mountain gorilla, ecology and behavior.* Chicago: Univer. Chicago Press.

Scheffer, V. B. (1945). Growth and behavior of young sea lions, *J. Mammal. 26*, 390–2.

Schiff, W., Caviness, J. A. & Gibson, J. J. (1962). Persistent fear responses in rhesus monkeys to the optical stimulus of "looming," *Science, 136*, 982–3.

Schneirla, T. C. & Rosenblatt, J. S. (1961). Behavioral organization and genesis of the social bond in insects and mammals, *Amer. J. Orthopsychiat., 31*, 223–53.

Schneirla, T. C. & Rosenblatt, J. S. (1963). "Critical" periods in the development of behavior, *Science, 139*, 1110–15.

Schneirla, T. C., Rosenblatt, J. S, & Tobach, E. (1963). Maternal behavior in the cat. In H. L. Rheingold (Ed.), *Maternal behavior in mammals.* New York: John Wiley, pp. 122–68.

Scott, J. P. (1958). Critical periods in the development of social behavior in puppies, *Psychosomat. Med., 20*, 42–54.

Scott, J. P. (1962). Critical periods in behavioral development, *Science, 138*, 949–58.

Shirley, M. M. (1933). *The first two years: a study of twenty-five babies: Vol. II. Intellectual development.* Minneapolis: Univer. of Minnesota Press.

Silver, I. A. (1956). Vascular changes in the mammary gland during engorgement with milk, *J. Physiol., 133*, 65p–66p.

Söderling, B. (1959). The first smile: a developmental study, *Acta Paediatrica, 48*, supplement 117, 78–82.

Spitz, R. A. (1955). A note on the extrapolation of ethological findings, *Int. J. Psychoanal., 36*, 162–5.

Spitz, R. A. & Wolf, K. M. (1946). The smiling response: a contribution to the ontogenesis of social relations, *Genet. Psychol. Monogr., 34*, 57–125.

Stanley W. C., Cornwell, A. C., Poggiani, C. & Trattner, A. (1963). Conditioning in the neonatal puppy, *J. comp. physiol. Psychol., 56*, 211–14.

Stellar, E. (1960). The marmoset as a laboratory animal: maintenance, general observations of behavior, and simple learning *J. comp. physiol. Psychol., 53*, 1–10.

Sturman-Hulbe, M. & Stone, C. P. (1929). Maternal behavior in the albino rat, *J. comp. Psychol., 9*, 203–37.

Svihla, R. D. (1930). A family of flying squirrels, *J. Mammal., 11*, 211–13.

Svihla, A. & Svihla, R. D. (1930). How a chipmunk carried her young, *J. Mammal., 11*, 314–15.

Tevis, L., Jr. (1950). Summer behavior of a family of beavers in New York State, *J. Mammal., 31*, 40–65.

Thorpe, W. H. (1950). *Learning and instinct in animals.* London: Methuen.

Thorpe, W. H. (1961). *Bird-song: the biology of vocal communication and expression in birds.* Cambridge Monographs in Experimental Biology, 12. Cambridge: University Press.

Tinkelpaugh, O. L. & Hartman, C. G. (1932). Behavior and maternal care of the new-born monkey (*Macaca mulatta*—"*M. rhesus*"), *Ped. Sem. & J. genet. Psychol., 40*, 257–85.

Tomilin, M. I. & Yerkes, R. M. (1935). Chimpanzee twins: behavioral relations and development, *Ped. Sem. & J. genet. Psychol., 46,* 239–63.

Van Hooff, J. A. R. A. M. (1962). Facial expressions in higher primates, *Symp. zool. Soc. Lond., 8,* 97–125.

Wade, O. (1927). Breeding habits and early life of the thirteen-striped ground squirrel, *Citellus tridecemlineatus* (Mitchill), *J. Mammal. 8,* 269–76.

Wagman, W. E., Christoferson, E. & Friedlich, O. (1964). Self-licking and the maternal behavior of laboratory rats. Paper presented at the Eastern Psychological Association Meetings, Philadelphia, Penna.

Warren, E. R. (1924). A muskrat moves its young, *J. Mammal., 5,* 202–3.

Washburn, R. W. (1929). A study of the smiling and laughing of infants in the first year of life, *Genet. Psychol. Monogr. 6,* 397–535.

Watson, J. B. (1925). *Behaviorism* New York: Norton (Revised ed. 1930).

Weiskrantz, L. & Cowey, A. (1963). The aetiology of food reward in monkeys, *Anim. Behav., 11,* 225–34.

Wharton, C. H. (1950). Notes on the life history of the flying lemur, *J. Mammal., 31,* 269–73.

Wiesner, B. P. & Sheard, N. M. (1933). *Maternal behaviour in the rat.* Edinburgh: Oliver and Boyd.

Wolf, K. M. (1953). Observations on individual tendencies in the first year of life. In M. J. E. Senn (Ed.), *Problems of infancy and childhood.* New York: Josiah Macy, Jr. Foundation, p. 114.

Wolff, P. H. (1959). Observations on newborn infants, *Psychosomat. Med., 21,* 110–18.

Wolff, P. H. (1963). Observations on the early development of smiling. In B. M. Foss (Ed.), *Determinants of infant behaviour: II.* London: Methuen, pp. 113–34.

Young, S. P. & Goldman, E. A. (1944). *The wolves of North America.* Washington, D.C.: Amer. Wildlife Inst.

Young, W. C. (1961). The mammalian ovary. In W. C. Young (Ed.), *Sex and internal secretions,* 3rd ed. Baltimore: Williams and Wilkins, pp. 449–96.

Zarrow, M. X., Sawin, P. B., Ross, S. & Denenberg, V. H. (1962). Maternal behavior and its endocrine basis in the rabbit. In E. L. Bliss (Ed.), *Roots of behavior.* New York: Hoeber-Harper, pp. 187–97.

Sex, Age, and State as Determinants of Mother-Infant Interaction

Howard A. Moss

NATIONAL INSTITUTE OF MENTAL HEALTH

A major reason for conducting research on human infants is derived from the popular assumption that adult behavior, to a considerable degree, is influenced by early experience. A corollary of this assumption is that if we can precisely conceptualize and measure significant aspects of infant experience and behavior we will be able to predict more sensitively and better understand adult functioning. The basis for this convention concerning the enduring effects of early experience varies considerably according to the developmental

Reprinted from *Merrill-Palmer Quarterly of Behavior and Development*, 1967, *13*, No. 1, 19–36. By permission.

Presented at The Merrill-Palmer Institute Conference on Research and Teaching of Infant Development, February 10–12, 1966, directed by Irving E. Sigel, chairman of research. The conference was financially supported in part by the National Institute of Child Health and Human Development. The author wishes to express his appreciation to Mrs. Helene McVey and Miss Betty Reinecke for their assistance in preparing and analyzing the data presented in this paper.

model that is employed. Yet there remains considerable consensus as to the long term and pervasive influence of the infant's experience.

Bloom (1964) contends that characteristics become increasingly resistant to change as the mature status of the characteristic is achieved and that environmental effects are most influential during periods of most rapid growth. This is essentially a refinement of the critical period hypothesis which argues in favor of the enduring and irreversible effects of many infant experiences. Certainly the studies on imprinting and the effects of controlled sensory input are impressive in this respect (Hess, 1959; White and Held, 1963). Learning theory also lends itself to support the potency of early experience. Since the occurrence of variable interval and variable ratio reinforcement schedules are highly probable in infancy (as they are in many other situations), the learnings associated with these schedules will be highly resistant to extinction. Also, the pre-verbal learning that characterizes infancy should be more difficult to extinguish since these responses are less available to linguistic control which later serves to mediate and regulate many important stimulus-response and reinforcement relationships. Psychoanalytic theory and behavioristic psychology probably have been the most influential forces in emphasizing the long-range consequences of infant experience. These theories, as well as others, stress the importance of the mother-infant relationship. In light of the widespread acceptance of the importance of early development, it is paradoxical that there is such a dearth of direct observational data concerning the functioning of infants, in their natural environment, and in relation to their primary caretakers.

Observational studies of the infant are necessary in order to test existing theoretical propositions and to generate new propositions based on empirical evidence. In addition, the infant is an ideally suitable subject for investigating many aspects of behavior because of the relatively simple and inchoate status of the human organism at this early stage in life. Such phenomena as temperament, reactions to stimulation, efficacy of different learning contingencies, perceptual functioning, and social attachment can be investigated while they are still in rudimentary form and not yet entwined in the immensely complex behavioral configurations that progressively emerge.

The research to be reported in this paper involves descriptive-normative data of maternal and infant behaviors in the naturalistic setting of the home. These data are viewed in terms of how the infant's experience structures potential learning patterns. Although the learning process itself is of primary eventual importance, it is necessary initially to identify the organizational factors, in situ, that structure learning opportunities and shape response systems.

A sample of 30 first-born children and their mothers were studied by means of direct observations over the first 3 months of life. Two periods were studied during this 3-month interval. Period one included a cluster of three observations made at weekly intervals during the first month of life in order to evaluate the initial adaptation of mother and infant to one another. Period two consisted of another cluster of three observations, made around 3 months of age when relatively stable patterns of behavior were likely to have been established. Each cluster included two 3-hour observations and one 8-hour observation. The 3-hour observations were made with the use of a keyboard that operates in conjunction with a 20-channel Esterline-Angus Event Recorder. Each of 30 keys represents a maternal or infant behavior, and when a key is depressed it activates one or a combination of pens on the recorder, leaving a trace that shows the total duration of the observed behavior. This technique allows for a continuous record showing the total time and the sequence of behavior. For the 8-hour observation the same behaviors were studied but with the use of a modified time-sampling technique. The time-sampled units were one minute in length and the observer, using a stenciled form, placed a number opposite the appropriate behaviors to indicate their respective order of occurrence. Since each variable can be coded only once for each observational unit, a score of 480 is the maximum that can be received. The data to be presented in this paper are limited to the two-hour observations. The data obtained with the use of the keyboard will be dealt with elsewhere in terms of the sequencing of events.

The mothers who participated in these observations were told that this was a normative study of infant functioning under natural living conditions. It was stressed that they proceed with their normal routines and care of the infant as they would if the observer were not present. This structure was presented to the mothers during a brief introductory visit prior to the first observation. In addition, in order to reduce the mother's self-consciousness and facilitate her behaving in relatively typical fashion, the observer emphasized that it was the infant who was being studied and that her actions would be noted only in relation to what was happening to the infant. This approach seemed to be effective, since a number of mothers commented after the observations were completed that they were relieved that they were not the ones being studied. The extensiveness of the observations and the frequent use of informal conversation between the observer and mother seemed to contribute further to the naturalness of her behavior.

The observational variables, mean scores and sample sizes are presented in Table 1. These data are presented separately for the 3-week and the 3-month observations. The inter-rater reliabilities for these variables range from .74 to 1.00 with a median reliability of .97. Much of the data in this paper are presented for males and females separately, since by describing and comparing these two groups we are able to work from an established context that helps to clarify the theoretical meaning of the results. Also, the importance of sex differences is heavily emphasized in contemporary developmental theory and it is felt that infant data concerning these differences would provide a worthwhile addition to the literature that already exists on this matter for older subjects.

The variables selected for study are those which would seem to influence or reflect aspects of maternal contact. An additional, but related consideration in the selection of variables was that they have an apparent bearing on the organization of the infant's experience. Peter Wolff (1959), Janet

Table 1   Mean Frequency of Maternal and Infant Behavior at 3 Weeks and 3 Months

	3-Week Observation		3-Month Observation[a]	
Behavior	Males[b] (N = 14)	Females (N = 15)	Males[b] (N = 13)	Females (N = 12)
Maternal variables				
Holds infant close	121.4	99.2	77.4	58.6
Holds infant distant	32.2	18.3	26.7	27.2
Total holds	131.3	105.5	86.9	73.4
Attends infant	61.7	44.2	93.0	81.8
Maternal contact				
(holds and attends)	171.1	134.5	158.8	133.8
Feeds infant	60.8	60.7	46.6	41.4
Stimulates feeding	10.1	14.0	1.6	3.6
Burps infant	39.0	25.9	20.9	15.3
Affectionate contact	19.9	15.9	32.8	22.7
Rocks infant	35.1	20.7	20.0	23.9
Stresses musculature	11.7	3.3	25.8	16.6
Stimulates/arouses infant	23.1	10.6	38.9	26.1
Imitates infant	1.9	2.9	5.3	7.6
Looks at infant	182.8	148.1	179.5	161.9
Talks to infant	104.1	82.2	117.5	116.1
Smiles at infant	23.2	18.6	45.9	46.4
Infant variables				
Cry	43.6	30.2	28.5	16.9
Fuss	65.7	44.0	59.0	36.0
Irritable (cry and fuss)	78.7	56.8	67.3	42.9
Awake active	79.6	55.1	115.8	85.6
Awake passive	190.0	138.6	257.8	241.1
Drowsy	74.3	74.7	27.8	11.1
Sleep	261.7	322.1	194.3	235.6
Supine	133.7	59.3	152.7	134.8
Eyes on mother	72.3	49.0	91.0	90.6
Vocalizes	152.3	179.3	207.2	207.4
Infant smiles	11.1	11.7	32.1	35.3
Mouths	36.8	30.6	61.2	116.2

[a] Four of the subjects were unable to participate in the 3-month observation. Two moved out of the area, one mother became seriously ill, and another mother chose not to participate in all the observations.

[b] One subject who had had an extremely difficult delivery was omitted from the descriptive data but is included in the findings concerning mother-infant interaction.

Brown (1964), and Sibylle Escalona (1962) have described qualitative variations in infant state or activity level and others have shown that the response patterns of the infant are highly influenced by the state he is in (Bridger, 1965). Moreover, Levy (1958) has demonstrated that maternal behavior varies as a function of the state of activity level of the infant. Consequently, we have given particular attention to the variables concerning state (cry, fuss, awake active, awake passive, and sleep) because of the extent to which these behaviors seem to shape the infant's experience. Most of the variables listed in Table 1 are quite descriptive of what was observed. Those which might not be as clear are as follows: *attends infant*—denotes standing close or leaning over infant, usually while in the process of caretaking activities; *stimulates feeding*—stroking the infant's cheek and manipulating the nipple so as to induce sucking responses; *affectionate contact*—kissing and caressing infant; *stresses musculature*—holding the infant in either a sitting or standing position so that he is required to support his own weight; *stimulates/arouses infant*—mother provides tactile and visual stimulation for the infant or attempts to arouse him to a higher activity level; and *imitates infant*—mother repeats a behavior, usually a vocalization, immediately after it is observed in the infant.

The sex differences and shifts in behavior from 3 weeks to 3 months are in many instances pronounced. For example, at 3 weeks of age mothers held male infants about 27 minutes more per 8 hours than they held females, and at 3 months males were held 14 minutes longer. By the time they were 3 months of age there was a decrease of over 30% for both sexes in the total time they were held by their mothers. Sleep time also showed marked sex differences and changes over time. For the earlier observations females slept about an hour longer than males, and this difference tended to be maintained by 3 months with the female infants sleeping about 41 minutes longer. Again, there was a substantial reduction with age in this behavior for both sexes; a decrease of 67 and 86 minutes in sleep time for males and females, respectively. What is particularly striking is the variability for these infant and maternal variables. The range for sleep time is 137–391 minutes at 3 weeks and 120–344 minutes at 3 months, and the range for mother holding is 38–218 minutes at 3 weeks and 26–168 minutes for the 3-month observation. The extent of the individual differences, reflected by these ranges seems to have important implications. For instance, if an infant spends more time at a higher level of consciousness this should increase his experience and contact with the mother, and through greater learning opportunities, facilitate the perceptual discriminations he makes, and affect the quality of his cognitive organization. The finding that some of the infants in our sample slept a little over 2 hours, or about 25% of the observation time and others around 6 hours or 75% of the time, is a fact that has implications for important developmental processes. The sum crying and fussing, what we term irritability level of the infant, is another potentially important variable. The range of scores for this behavior was from 5–136 minutes at 3 weeks and 7–98 at 3 months. The fact that infants are capable through their behavior of shaping maternal treatment is a point that has gained increasing recognition. The cry is a signal for the mother to respond and variation among infants in this behavior could lead to differential experiences with the mother

Table 2 presents *t* values showing changes in the maternal and infant behaviors from the 3-week to the 3-month observation. In this case, the

Table 2 Changes in Behavior Between 3 Weeks and 3 Months ($N = 26$)

Maternal Variables	t-Values	Infant Variables	t-Values
Higher at 3 weeks:		*Higher at 3 weeks:*	
Holds infant close	4.43^d	Cry	2.84^c
Holds infant distant	.56	Fuss	1.33
Total holds	4.00^d	Irritable (cry and fuss)	1.73^a
Maternal contact		Drowsy	9.02^d
(holds and attends)	.74	Sleep	4.51^d
Feeds infant	3.49^c		
Stimulates feeding	3.42^c		
Burps infant	3.28^c		
Rocks infant	1.08		
Higher at 3 months:		*Higher at 3 months:*	
Attends infant	5.15^d	Awake active	2.47^b
Affectionate contact	2.50^b	Awake passive	5.22^d
Stresses musculature	3.42^c	Supine	1.75^a
Stimulates/arouses infant	2.63^b	Eyes on mother	3.21^c
Imitates infant	4.26^d	Vocalizes	3.56^c
Looks at infant	.38	Infant smiles	6.84^d
Talks to infant	2.67^b	Mouths	3.69^c
Smiles at infant	4.79^d		

$^a p < .10.$
$^b p < .05.$
$^c p < .01.$
$^d p < .001.$

data from the males and females are combined since the trends, in most instances, are the same for both sexes. It is not surprising that there are a number of marked shifts in behavior from 3 weeks to 3 months, since the early months of life are characterized by enormous growth and change. The maternal variables that show the greatest decrement are those involving feeding behaviors and close physical contact. It is of interest that the decrease in close contact is paralleled by an equally pronounced increase in attending behavior, so that the net amount of maternal contact remains similar for the 3-week and 3-month observations. The main difference was that the mothers, for the later observation, tended to hold their infants less but spent considerably more time near them, in what usually was a vis-à-vis posture, while interacting and ministering to their needs. Along with this shift, the mothers showed a marked increase in affectionate behavior towards the older infant, positioned him more so that he was required to make active use of his muscles, presented him with a greater amount of stimulation and finally, she exhibited more social behavior (imitated, smiled, and talked) toward the older child.

The changes in maternal behavior from 3 weeks to 3 months probably are largely a function of the maturation of various characteristics of the infant. However, the increased confidence of the mother, her greater fa-

Table 3 Correlations Between Observations at 3 Weeks and at 3 Months $(N = 26)$

Maternal Variables	$r =$	Infant Variables	$r =$
Holds infant close	.23	Cry	.28
Holds infant distant	.04	Fuss	.42[b]
Total holds	.18	Irritable (cry and fuss)	.37[a]
Attends infant	.36[a]	Awake active	.25
Maternal contact		Awake passive	.26
(holds and attends)	.25	Drowsy	.44[b]
Feeds infant	.21	Sleep	.24
Stimulates feeding	.37[a]	Supine	.29
Burps infant	.20	Eyes on mother	− .12
Affectionate contact	.64[d]	Vocalizes	.41[b]
Rocks infant	.29	Infant smiles	.32
Stresses musculature	.06	Mouths	− .17
Stimulates/arouses infant	.23		
Imitates infant	.45[b]		
Lookas at infant	.37[a]		
Talks to infant	.58[c]		
Smiles at infant	.66[d]		

[a] $p < .10$.
[b] $p < .05$.
[c] $p < .01$.
[d] $p < .001$.

miliarity with her infant, and her developing attachment toward him will also account for some of the changes that occurred over this period of time.

By 3 months of age the infant is crying less and awake more. Moreover, he is becoming an interesting and responsive person. There are substantial increases in the total time spent by him in smiling, vocalizing, and looking at the mother's face, so that the greater amount of social-type behavior he manifested at three months parallels the increments shown in the mothers' social responsiveness toward him over this same period. The increase with age in the time the infant is kept in a supine position also should facilitate his participation in vis-à-vis interactions with the mother as well as provide him with greater opportunity for varied visual experiences.

Table 3 presents the correlations between the 3-week and the 3-month observations for the maternal and infant behaviors we studied. These findings further reflect the relative instability of the mother-infant system over the first few months of life. Moderate correlation coefficients were obtained only for the class of maternal variables concerning affectionate-social responses. It thus may be that these behaviors are more sensitive indicators of enduring maternal attitudes than the absolute amount of time the mother devoted to such activities as feeding and physical contact. The few infant variables that show some stability are, with the exception of vocalizing, those concerning

Table 4   Sex Differences in Frequency of Maternal and Infant Behaviors at 3 Weeks and 3 Months

Maternal Variables	t-Values		Infant Variables	t-Values	
	3 Weeks	3 Months		3 Weeks	3 Months
Male higher:			Male higher:		
Holds infant close	1.42	1.52	Cry	1.68	1.11
Holds infant distant	2.64[b]		Fuss	2.48[b]	3.47[c]
Total holds	1.65	1.12	Irritable (cry		
Attends infant	2.66[b]	1.10	and fuss)	2.23[b]	2.68[b]
Maternal contact			Awake active	1.66	.57
(holds and attends)	2.09[b]	1.57	Awake passive	2.94[c]	1.77[a]
Feeds infant	.06	.27	Drowsy		.41
Burps infant	1.67	.69	Supine	2.30[b]	1.07
Affectionate contact	.90	1.00	Eyes on mother	1.99[a]	.75
Rocks infant	1.21		Mouths	.64	
Stresses musculature	2.48[b]	1.67			
Stimulates/arouses					
infant	2.20[b]	1.53			
Looks at infant	1.97[a]	1.36			
Talks to infant	1.02	.79			
Smiles at infant	.57				
Female higher:			Female higher:		
Holds infant distant		.05	Drowsy	.03	
Stimulates feeding	.62	1.47	Sleep	3.15[c]	2.87[c]
Rocks infant		.82	Vocalizes	1.34	.23
Imitates infant	.80	1.76[a]	Infant smiles	.02	.08
Smiles at infant		.44	Mouths		2.57[b]

[a] $p < .10$.
[b] $p < .05$.
[c] $p < .01$.

the state of the organism. Even though some of the behaviors are moderately stable from three weeks to three months, the overall magnitude of the correlations reported in Table 3 seem quite low considering that they represent repeated measures of the same individual over a relatively short period.

Table 4 presents t-values based on comparisons between the sexes for the 3-week and 3-month observations. A number of statistically significant differences were obtained with, in most instances, the boys having higher mean scores than the girls. The sex differences are most pronounced at 3 weeks for both maternal and infant variables. By 3 months the boys and girls are no longer as clearly differentiated on the maternal variables although the trend persists for the males to tend to have higher mean scores. On the other hand, the findings for the infant variables concerning state remain relatively similar at 3 weeks and 3 months. Thus, the sex differences are relatively

Table 5 Sex Differences After Controlling for Irritability and Sleep Time through Analysis of Covariance*

Maternal or Infant Behaviors	Sleep Time Controlled for		Sex with Higher Mean Score	Irritability Controlled for		Sex with Higher Mean Score
	3 Weeks	3 Months		3 Weeks	3 Months	
Variables	t	t		t	t	
Holds infant close	.30	1.22		.64	1.70	
Holds infant distant	.59	− .20		.92	− .20	
Totals holds	.43	.88		.86	1.08	Males
Attends infant	1.12	1.36		1.91^a	.94	
Maternal contact (holds and attends)	.62	1.04		1.20	1.12	
Stimulates feeding	.55	− 1.12		− .09	− 1.06	
Affectionate contact	− .46	.91		.56	1.27	
Rocks	.35	− .70		.44	− 1.44	
Stresses musculature	1.84^a	.71	Males	1.97^a	1.40	
Stimulates/arouses infant	2.09^b	1.82^a	Males	2.43^b	2.31^b	Males
Imitates infant	− .91	− 2.73^a	Females	− .63	− 2.14^b	Females
Looks at infant	.58	1.35		1.17	1.02	
Talks to infant	− .48	.24		.70	.59	
Infant supine	.82	− .03		1.36	.69	
Eyes on mother	.37	.58		1.76^a	− .37	Males

^{a} $p < .10$.
^{b} $p < .05$.
* A positive t-value indicates that males had the higher mean score, and a negative t-value indicates a higher mean score for females.

stable for the two observations even though the stability coefficients for the total sample are low (in terms of our variables).

In general, these results indicate that much more was happening with the male infants than with the female infants. Males slept less and cried more during both observations and these behaviors probably contributed to the more extensive and stimulating interaction the boys experienced with the mother, particularly for the 3-week observation. In order to determine the effect of state we selected the 15 variables, excluding those dealing with state, where the sex differences were most marked and did an analysis of covariance with these variables, controlling for irritability and another analysis of covariance controlling for sleep. These results are presented in Table 5. When the state of the infant was controlled for, most of the sex differences were no longer statistically significant. The exceptions were that the t-values were greater, after controlling for state, for the variables "mother stimulates/arouses infant" and "mother imitates infant." The higher score for "stimulates/arouse" was obtained for the males and the higher score for the "imitates" by the females. The variable "imitates" involves repeating vocalizations made by the child, and it is interesting that mothers exhibited more of this behavior with the girls. This response could be viewed as the reinforcement of verbal behavior, and the evidence presented here suggests that the mothers differentially reinforce this behavior on the basis of the sex of the child.

In order to further clarify the relation between infant state and maternal treatment, product-moment correlations were computed relating the infant irratability score with the degree of maternal contact. The maternal contact variable is based on the sum of the holding and attending scores with the time devoted to feeding behaviors subtracted out. These correlations were computed for the 3-week and 3-month observations for the male and female samples combined and separate. At 3 weeks a correlation of .52 ($p < .01$) was obtained between irritability and maternal contact for the total sample. However, for the female subsample this correlation was .68 ($p < .02$) and for males only .20 (non. sig.). Furthermore, a somewhat similar pattern occurred for the correlations between maternal contact and infant irritability for the 3-month observation. At this age the correlation is .37 ($p < .10$ level) for the combined sample and .54 ($p < .05$ level) for females and $-.47$ ($p < .10$ level) for males. A statistically significant difference was obtained ($t = 2.40$, $p < .05$ level) in a test comparing the difference between the female and male correlations for the 3-month observation. In other words maternal contact and irritability positively covaried for females at both ages; whereas for males, there was no relationship at 3 weeks, and by 3 months the mothers tended to spend less time with the more irritable male babies. It should be emphasized that these correlations reflect within group patterns, and that when we combine the female and male samples positive correlations still emerge for both ages. Since the males had substantially higher scores for irritability and maternal contact than the females, the correlation for the male subjects does not strongly attentuate the correlations derived for the total sample, even when the males within group covariation seems random or negative. That is, in terms of the total sample, the patterning of the male scores is still consistent with a positive relationship between irritability and maternal contact.

From these findings it is difficult to posit a causal relationship. However, it seems most plausible that it is the infant's cry that is determining the maternal behavior. Mothers describe the cry as a signal that the infant needs attention and they often report their nurturant actions in response to the cry. Furthermore, the cry is a noxious and often painful stimulus that probably has biological utility for the infant, propelling the mother into action for her own comfort as well as out of concern for the infant. Ethological reports confirm the proposition that the cry functions as a "releaser" of maternal behavior (Bowlby, 1958; Hinde et al., 1964; Hoffman et al., 1966). Bowlby (1958) states:

> It is my belief that both of them (crying and smiling), act as social releasers of instinctual responses in mothers. As regards crying, there is plentiful evidence from the animal world that this is so: probably in all cases the mother responds

promptly and unfailingly to her infant's bleat, call or cry. It seems to me clear that similar impulses are also evoked in the human mother. . . .

Thus, we are adopting the hypothesis that the correlations we have obtained reflect a causal sequence whereby the cry acts to instigate maternal intervention. Certainly there are other important determinants of maternal contact, and it is evident that mothers exhibit considerable variability concerning how responsive they are to the stimulus signal of the cry. Yet it seems that the effect of the cry is sufficient to account at least partially for the structure of the mother-infant relationship. We further maintain the thesis that the infant's cry shapes maternal behavior even for the instance where the negative correlation was noted at 3 months for the males. The effect is still present, but in this case the more irritable infants were responded to *less* by the mothers. Our speculation for explaining this relationship and the fact that, conversely, a positive correlation was obtained for the female infants is that the mothers probably were negatively reinforced for responding to a number of the boys but tended to be positively reinforced for their responses toward the girls. That is, mothers of the more irritable boys may have learned that they could not be successful in quieting boys whereas the girls were more uniformly responsive (quieted by) to maternal handling. There is not much present in our data to bear out this contention, with the exception that the males were significantly more irritable than the girls for both observations. However, evidence that suggests males are more subject to inconsolable states comes from studies (Serr and Ismajovich, 1963; McDonald, Gynther, and Christakos, 1963; Stechler, 1964) which indicate that males have less well organized physiological reactions and are more vulnerable to adverse conditions than females. The relatively more efficient functioning of the female organism should thus contribute to their responding more favorably to maternal intervention.

In summary, we propose that maternal behavior initially tends to be under the control of the stimulus and reinforcing conditions provided by the young infant. As the infant gets older, the mother, if she behaved contingently toward his signals, gradually acquires reinforcement value which in turn increases her efficacy in regulating infant behaviors. Concurrently, the earlier control asserted by the infant becomes less functional and diminishes. In a sense, the point where the infant's control over the mother declines and the mother's reinforcement value emerges could be regarded as the first manifestation of socialization, or at least represents the initial conditions favoring social learning. Thus, at first the mother is shaped by the infant and this later facilitates her shaping the behavior of the infant. We would therefore say that the infant, through his own temperament or signal system, contributes to establishing the stimulus and reinforcement value eventually associated with the mother. According to this reasoning, the more irritable infants (who can be soothed) whose mothers respond in a contingent manner to their signals should become most amenable to the effects of social reinforcement and manifest a higher degree of attachment behavior. The fact that the mothers responded more contingently toward the female infants should maximize the ease with which females learn social responses.

This statement is consistent with data on older children which indicate that girls learn social responses earlier and with greater facility than boys (Becker, 1964). Previously we argued that the mothers learned to be more contingent toward the girls because they probably were more responsive to maternal intervention. An alternative explanation is that mothers respond contingently to the girls and not to the boys as a form of differential reinforcement, whereby, in keeping with cultural expectations, the mother is initiating a pattern that contributes to males being more aggressive or assertive, and less responsive to socialization. Indeed, these two explanations are not inconsistent with one another since the mother who is unable to soothe an upset male may eventually come to classify this intractable irritability as an expression of "maleness."

There are certain environmental settings where noncontingent caretaking is more likely and these situations should impede social learning and result in weaker attachment responses. Lenneberg (1965) found that deaf parents tended not to respond to the infant's cry. One would have to assume that it was more than the inability to hear the infant that influenced their behavior, since even when they observed their crying infants these parents tended not to make any effort to quiet them. The function of the cry as a noxious stimulus or "releaser" of maternal behavior did not pertain under these unusual circumstances. Infants in institutions also are more likely to be cared for in terms of some arbitrary schedule with little opportunity for them to shape caretakers in accordance with their own behavioral vicissitudes.

Although we have shown that there is a covariation between maternal contact and infant irritability and have attempted to develop some theoretical implications concerning this relationship, considerable variability remains as to how responsive different mothers are to their infants's crying behavior. This variability probably reflects differences in maternal attitudes. Women who express positive feelings about babies and who consider the well-being of the infant to be of essential importance should tend to be more responsive to signals of distress from the infant than women who exhibit negative maternal attitudes. In order to test this assumption, we first derived a score for measuring maternal responsiveness. This score was obtained through a regression analysis where we determined the amount of maternal contact that would be expected for each mother by controlling for her infant's irritability score. The expected maternal contact score was then subtracted from the mother's actual contact score and this difference was used as the measure of maternal responsivity. The maternal responsivity scores were obtained separately for the 3-week and the 3-month observations. The parents of 23 of the infants in our sample were interviewed for a project investigating marital careers, approximately 2 years prior to the birth of their child, and these interviews provided us with the unusual opportunity of having antecedent data relevant to prospective parental functioning. A number of variables from this material were rated and two of them, "acceptance of nurturant role," and the "degree that the baby is seen in a positive sense" were corre-lated with the scores on the maternal responsivity measures[1] Annotated definitions of these interview variables are as follows:

> "Acceptance of nurturant role" concerns the degree to which the subject is invested in caring for others and in acquiring domestic and homemaking skills such as cooking, sewing, and cleaning house. Evidence for a high rating would be describing the care of infants and children with much pleasure and satisfac-tion even when this involves subordinating her own needs.
>
> The interview variable concerning the "degree that the baby is seen in a posi-tive sense" assesses the extent to which the subject views a baby as gratifying, pleasant and non-burdensome. In discussing what she imagines infants to be like she stresses the warmer, more personal, and rewarding aspects of the baby and anticipates these qualities as primary.

Correlations of .40 ($p < .10$ level) and .48 ($p < .05$ level) were obtained between the ratings on "acceptance of nurturant role" and the maternal responsivity scores for the 3-week and 3-month observations, respectively. The "degree that the baby is seen in a positive sense" correlated .38 ($p < .10$ level) and .44 ($p < .05$ level) with maternal responsivity for the two ages. However, the two interview variables were so highly intercorrelated ($r = .93$) that they clearly involve the same dimension. Thus, the psycho-logical status of the mother, assessed substantially before the birth of her infant, as well as the infant's state, are predictive of her maternal behavior. Schaffer and Emerson (1964) found that maternal responsiveness to the cry was associated with the attachment behavior of infants. Extrapolating from our findings, we now have some basis for assuming that the early attitudes of the mother represent antecedent conditions for facilitating the attachment behavior observed by Schaffer and Emerson.

The discussion to this point has focused on some of the conditions that seemingly affect the structure of the mother-infant relationship and influ-ence the reinforcement and stimulus values associated with the mother. Next we would like to consider, in a more speculative vein, one particular class of maternal behaviors that has important reinforcing properties for the infant. This discussion will be more general and depart from a direct consideration of the data. There has been mounting evidence in the psychological literature that the organism has a "need for stimulation" and that variations in the quantity and quality of stimulation received can have a significant effect on many aspects of development (Moss, 1965; Murphy et al., 1962; White and Held, 1963). Additional reports indicate that, not only does the infant require stimulation, but that excessive or chaotic dosages of stimulation can be highly disruptive of normal functioning (Murphy et al., 1962). Furthermore, there appear to be substantial individual differences in the stimulation that is needed or in the extremes that can be tolerated. As the infant gets older he becomes somewhat capable of regulating the stimulation that is assimilated.

---

[1] Dr. Kenneth Robson collaborated in developing these variables and made the ratings.

However, the very young infant is completely dependent on the caretaking environment to provide and modulate the stimulation he experiences. It is in this regard that the mother has a vital role.

The main points emphasized in the literature are that stimulation serves to modulate the state or arousal level of the infant, organize and direct attentional processes, and facilitate normal growth and development. Bridger (1965) has shown that stimulation tends to have either an arousing or quieting effect, depending on the existing state of the infant. Infants who are quiet tend to be aroused, whereas aroused infants tend to be quieted by moderate stimulation. Moreover, according to data collected by Birns (1965), these effects occur for several stimulus modalities and with stable individual differences in responsivity. (We found that mothers made greater use of techniques involving stimulation—"stresses musculature" and "stimulates/arouses"—with the males who as a group were more irritable than the females.)

The capacity for stimulus configurations to direct attention, once the infant is in an optimally receptive state, also has been demonstrated by a number of studies. Young infants have been observed to orient toward many stimuli (Razran, 1961; Fantz, 1963), and certain stimuli are so compelling that they tend to "capture" the infant in a fixed orientation (Stechler, 1965). Other studies have demonstrated that infants show clear preferences for gazing at more complex visual patterns (Fantz, 1963). Thus, stimulation can influence the set of the infant to respond by modifying the state of the organism as well as structure learning possibilities through directing the infant's attention. White (1959) has systematically described how stimulation contributes to the learning process in infants. He points out that the infant is provided with the opportunity to activate behavioral potentials in attempting to cope with control stimulation. Motor and perceptual skills eventually become refined and sharpened in the process of responding to stimulus configurations and it is this pattern of learning which White calls "effective behavior."

Not all levels of stimulation are equally effective in producing a condition whereby the infant is optimally alert and attentive. Excessive stimulation has a disruptive effect and according to drive reduction theorists the organism behaves in ways aimed at reducing stimulation that exceeds certain limits. Leuba (1955), in an attempt to establish rapprochement between the drive reduction view and the research evidence that shows that there is a need for stimulation, states that there is an optimal level of stimulation that is required, and that the organism acts either to reduce or to increase stimulation, so as to stay within this optimal range.

The mother is necessarily highly instrumental in mediating much of the stimulation that is experienced by the infant. Her very presence in moving about and caring for the infant provides a constant source of visual, auditory, tactile, kinesthetic and proprioceptive stimulation. In addition to the incidental stimulation she provides, the mother deliberately uses stimulation to regulate the arousal level or state of the infant and to evoke specific responses from him. However, once the infant learns, through conditioning, that the mother is a source of stimulation he can in turn employ existing responses that are instrumental in eliciting stimulation from her. Certain infant behaviors, such as the cry, are so compelling that they readily evoke many forms of stimulation from the mother. It is common knowledge that mothers, in attempting to quiet upset infants, often resort to such tactics as using rocking motion, waving bright objects or rattles, or holding the infant close and thus provide warmth and physical contact. The specific function of stimulation in placating the crying infant can be somewhat obscured because of the possibility of confounding conditions. In our discussion so far we have indicated that stimulation inherently has a quieting effect irrespective of learning but that crying also can become a learned instrumental behavior which terminates once the reinforcement of stimulation is presented. However, it is often difficult to distinguish the unlearned from the learned patterns of functioning, since the infant behavior (crying) and the outcome (quieting) are highly similar in both instances. Perhaps the best means for determining whether learning has occurred would be if we could demonstrate that the infant makes anticipatory responses, such as the reduction in crying behavior to cues, prior to the actual occurrence of stimulation. In addition to the cry, the smile and the vocalization of the infant can become highly effective, and consequently well-learned conditioned responses for evoking stimulation from adult caretakers. Rheingold (1956) has shown that when institutional children are given more caretaking by an adult they show an increase in their smiling rate to that caretaker as well as to other adults. Moreover, for a few weeks after the intensive caretaking stopped there were further substantial increments in the smiling rate, which suggests that the infant after experiencing relative deprivation worked harder in attempting to restore the stimulation level experienced earlier.

It seems plausible that much of the early social behavior seen in infants and children consists of attempts to elicit responses from others. We mentioned earlier that it has been stressed in recent psychological literature that individuals have a basic need for stimulation. Since the mother, and eventually others, are highly instrumental in providing and monitoring the stimulation that is experienced by the infant, it seems likely that the child acquires expectancies for having this need satisfied through social interactions and that stimulation comes to serve as a basis for relating to others. Indeed, Schaffer and Emerson (1964) have shown that the amount of stimulation provided by adults is one of the major determinants of infants' attachment behavior. Strange as well as familiar adults who have been temporarily separated from an infant often attempt to gain rapport with the infant through acts of stimulation. It is quite common for the father, upon returning home from work, to initiate actions aimed at stimulating the child, and these actions are usually responded to with clear pleasure. Because of the expectancies that are built up some of the provocative behaviors seen in children, particularly when confronted with a non-responsive adult, could be interpreted as attempts to elicit socially mediated stimulation.

The learning we have discussed is largely social since the infant is dependent on others, particularly the mother, for reinforcements. This dependency on others is what constitutes attachment behavior, and the specific makeup of the attachment is determined by the class of reinforcements that are involved. The strength of these learned attachment behaviors is maximized through stimulation, since the mother is often the embodiment of this reinforcement as well as the agent for delivering it. The social aspect of this learning is further enhanced because of the reciprocal dependence of the mother on the infant for reinforcement. That is, the mother learns certain conditioned responses, often involving acts of stimulation, that are aimed at evoking desired states or responses from the infant.

In conclusion, what we did was study and analyze some of the factors which structure the mother-infant relationship. A central point is that the state of the infant affects the quantity and quality of maternal behavior, and this in turn would seem to influence the course of future social learning. Furthermore, through controlling for the state of the infant, we were able to demonstrate the effects of pre-parental attitudes on one aspect of maternal behavior, namely, the mother's responsiveness toward her infant. Many investigators, in conducting controlled laboratory studies, have stressed that the state of the infant is crucial in determining the nature of his responses to different stimuli. This concern is certainly high relevant to our data, collected under naturalistic conditions.

REFERENCES

Becker, W. C. Consequences of different kinds of parental discipline. In M. L. Hoffman & Lois W. Hoffman (Eds.), *Review of child development research: I.* New York: Russell Sage Found., 1964. Pp. 169–208.

Birns, B. Individual differences in human neonates' responses to stimulation. *Child Develpm.*, 1965, 36, 249–256.

Bloom, B. S. *Stability and change in human characteristics.* New York: Wiley, 1964.

Bowley, J. The nature of a child's tie to his mother. *Internat. J. Psychoanal.*, 1958, 39, 350–373.

Bridger, W. H. Psychophysiological measurement of the roles of state in the human neonate. Paper presented at Soc. Res. Child Develpm., Minneapolis, April, 1965.

Brown, Janet L. States in newborn infants. *Merrill-Palmer Quart.*, 1964, 10, 313–327.

Escalona, Sibylle K. The study of individual differences and the problem of state. *J. Child Psychiat.*, 1962, 1, 11–37.

Fantz, R. Pattern vision in newborn infants. *Science*, 1963, 140, 296–297.

Hess, E. H. Imprinting. *Science*, 1959, 130, 133–141.

Hinde, R. A., Rowell, T. E., & Spencer-Booth, Y. Behavior of living rhesus monkeys in their first six months. *Proc. Zool. Soc., London*, 1964, 143, 609–649.

Hoffman, H., *et al.* Enhanced distress vocalization through selective reinforcement. *Science*, 1966, 151, 354–356.

Lennenberg, E. H., Rebelsky, Freda G., & Nichols, I. A. The vocalizations of infants born to deaf and to hearing parents. *Vita Humana*, 1965, 8, 23–37.

Leuba, C. Toward some integration of learning theories: The concept of optimal stimulation. *Psychol. Rep.*, 1955, 1, 27–33.

Levy, D. M. *Behavioral analysis.* Springfield, Ill.: Charles C Thomas, 1958.

McDonald, R. L., Gynther, M. D., & Christakos, A. C. Relations between maternal anxiety and obstetric complications. *Psychosom. Med.,* 1963, *25,* 357–362.

Moss, H. A. Coping behavior, the need for stimulation, and normal development. *Merrill-Palmer Quart., 1965, 11,* 171–179.

Murphy, Lois B., et al. *The widening world of childhood.* New York: Basic Books, 1962.

Noirot, Eliane. Changes in responsiveness to young in the adult mouse: the effect of external stimuli. *J. comp. physiol. Psychol.,* 1964, *57,* 97–99.

Razran, G. The observable unconscious and the inferable conscious in current Soviet psychophysiology: Interoceptive conditioning, semantic conditioning, and the orienting reflex. *Psychol. Rev.,* 1961, *68,* 81–146.

Rheingold, Harriet L. The modification of social responsiveness in institutional babies. *Monogr. Soc. Res. Child Develpm.,* 1956, *21,* No. 2 (Serial No. 23).

Schaffer, H. R. & Emerson, Peggy E. The development of social attachments in infancy. *Monogr. Soc. Res. Child Develpm.,* 1964, *29,* No. 3 (Serial No. 94).

Serr, D. M. & Ismajovich, B. Determination of the primary sex ratio from human abortions. *Amer. J. Obstet. Gyncol.,* 1963, *87,* 63–65.

Stechler, G. A longitudinal follow-up of neonatal apnea. *Child Develpm.,* 1964, *35,* 333–348.

Stechler, G. Paper presented at Soc. Res. Child Develpm., Minneapolis, April, 1965.

White, B. L. & Held, R. Plasticity in perceptual development during the first six months of life. Paper presented at Amer. Ass. Advncmnt. Sci., Cleveland, December, 1963.

White, R. W. Motivation reconsidered: the concept of competence. *Psychol. Rev.,* 1959, *66,* 297–323.

Wolff, P. H. Observations on newborn infants. *Psychosom. Med.,* 1959, *21,* 110–118.

Patterns
of Response
to Physical Contact
in Early
Human Development

H. R. Schaffer and Peggy E. Emerson

UNIVERSITY OF STRATHCLYDE, GLASGOW

INTRODUCTION

It has long been assumed that physical contact plays an important part in early human development and that all normal infants actively seek and enjoy this mode of interaction with their social environment. To be rocked, fondled, held, stroked and cuddled is to writers such as Ribble (1944) an essential precondition to psychological growth, and not to achieve close contact with the body of the mother is regarded by them as a form of deprivation with possibly serious consequences. This view has been reinforced by the findings of Harlow and his co-workers (1958, 1959), which have demonstrated the importance of contact comfort in the establishment of the young monkey's social attachments. For human infants experimental proof is, of course,

Reprinted from *Journal of Child Psychology and Psychiatry,* 1964, *5,* No. 1, 1–13. Published by Pergamon Press. By permission.

difficult to obtain, and as even systematic field observations are as yet lacking, our conclusions about the role of physical contact in the development of the young child are still largely of a speculative and controversial nature. Rheingold (1961), for instance, has reminded us of the inability of the infant in the early months to cling, and has put forward her belief that visual, not physical, contact is at the basis of human sociability; yet writers such as Casler (1961) continue to maintain that the effects of tactile and kinaesthetic stimulation received through handling are essential to proper developmental progress.

Some material bearing on this problem arose in the course of a longitudinal investigation concerned with the formation of social attachments in infancy (Schaffer, 1963, Schaffer and Emerson, 1964). While carrying out this study it was noted that not all infants eagerly seek physical contact in the way that the literature might lead one to expect—indeed that a considerable proportion of the subjects actively resisted and protested at certain types of such interaction. It had not originally been one of the aims of the project to study contact behavior, but as spontaneous reports from the mothers of the infants repeatedly forced our attention in this direction, it was decided that a more systematic analysis of this aspect was called for.

PROCEDURE

The sample from which data concerning reactions to physical contact were obtained comprised 37 infants, mostly from working-class families, living in their own homes and of normal developmental status. Contact with the families was, in the first place, made through a Child Welfare Clinic in the early weeks of the infant's first year. Once the mother's agreement to participate in the project had been obtained, all subsequent interviews took place in the family's home. Interviews were spaced at four-weekly intervals throughout the first twelve months, after which one more interview at eighteen months took place. The main purpose of the interviews was to obtain data regarding the development of social attachments: this material and the relevant methodology will be described in the appropriate section below when the attachment data will be treated as dependent variables.

While casual observations and reports concerning the infants' reactions to various forms of physical contact had been gathered throughout the follow-up period, the data to be presented here are based on the mothers' answers to an interview schedule specifically concerned with this aspect. The schedule was administered at two points: at the end of the infant's first year (in order to obtain information about the whole of the first twelve months) and again at eighteen months (to cover behavior in the preceding six months). The questions in the schedule dealt with the following aspects:

(a) the infant's behavior in a number of commonly occurring contact situations, such as being cuddled, carried, held on lap, stroked, kissed, fed on knee, and swung or bounced;

(b) the consistency of these reactions with age, person offering the contact, and the infant's internal condition (i.e., the effect of pain, illness, fatigue or fear);

(c) evidence for contact-seeking in relation to inanimate objects or the self;

(d) the mother's behavior in contact situations and her reactions to any contact avoidance on the infant's part.

Though guided by the schedule, interviews assumed a largely unstructured form, the mothers being encouraged to give as free and full a description of the infant's reactions in the relevant situation as possible. These descriptions were frequently illustrated by spontaneous demonstrations which the mothers enacted with the infant before the interviewer.

THE CONTACT GROUPS: DESCRIPTIVE DATA

The maternal reports made it evident that considerable and consistent individual differences could be found in response to certain forms of physical contact. This applied in particular to those situations where the contact involved a close and direct form of interaction, being most clearly in evidence in the cuddling situation. Thus a number of mothers found that from an early age their infants unfailingly protested at, resisted and avoided, this form of interaction, whatever the circumstances and whatever the condition of the child. A group of 9 such "Non-Cuddlers" was isolated by using as our criteria of classification (1) the consistency with age throughout the entire period of eighteen months with which the infant responded negatively to cuddling, and (2) the failure to modify this behavior at any time when tired, frightened, ill, or in pain. In the rest of the sample acceptance of cuddling was reported, yet here too some variation occurred. A group of 19 infants were said to accept, enjoy, and (once their motor development enabled them to do so) actively seek physical contact in all forms, under all circumstances, and at all ages. We shall refer henceforth to these infants as the "Cuddlers." The remaining 9 infants may be said to form an intermediate group, in that acceptance of cuddling was reported but with certain reservations, e.g., only when the infant was tired, ill, etc., or only within a limited age range. For the sake of clarity of presentation we shall only be concerned here with the "pure" cases, i.e., the "Cuddlers" and the "Non-Cuddlers," and describe our findings in terms of the contrast between these two groups. Their sex and birth order distribution are given in Table 1.

To illustrate the difference between the two groups, the following phrases may be quoted from the reports given by the mothers of the Non-Cuddlers regarding the infant's reaction to cuddling, i.e., that form of physical contact where the baby is picked up, held with both arms in an upright position on the adult's lap, pressed against her shoulder and usually given some skin-to-skin contact such as kissing or cheek stroking.

Table 1 Sex and Birth Order Distribution Among Contact Groups

| | Sex | | Birth Order | |
	Male	Female	First Born	Others
"Cuddlers"	8	11	7	12
"Non-Cuddlers"	6	3	4	5
p^a		N.S.		N.S.

[a] Fisher exact test, two-tailed (Latscha, 1953).

"Gets restless when cuddled, turns face away and begins to struggle."
"Will not allow it, fights to get away."
"Has never liked this since able to struggle, squirms and whimpers."
"Gets restless, pushes you away."
"Wriggles and arches back, and only stops when put down again."
"Restless and whiny until allowed back in cot."
"Will kick and thrash with his arms, and if you persist will begin to cry."

These phrases may be contrasted with the following from the mothers of the Cuddlers:

"Cuddles you back."
"Snuggles into you."
"Holds quite still and puts on a soppy face."
"Loves it."
"Laps it up."
"Would let me cuddle him for hours on end."

The two groups are similarly differentiated by their behavior when the mother merely held the infant quietly on her lap, i.e., cradling or supporting him with her arms while having him lie or sit on her knee:

"Not fond of being held, cries until put down."
"Never has liked sitting on knee, it is easier to play with him by sitting beside him on the floor."
"When on your knee will fight to get down again."
"Arches back and slides off."
"Asks to be lifted, yet the moment you hold him on your lap he pushes against you till he is down again."
"Won't sleep in your arms, has to be put down in cot."

Again the Cuddlers provide a striking contrast:

"Will sit on your knee for ages and play."
"Loves being handled, is always asking to be really close to you."
"Has to be nursed in your arms for half an hour before going to bed, else cries."
"Would be up on my lap all day if I let her."
"I have to rock him in my arms every night till he falls asleep."

All Non-Cuddlers were said to have shown their peculiarities from the early weeks—initially through restlessness and subsequently through more purposive struggling. At 9 or 10 m*, when such locomotor skills as crawling and walking first appeared, opening up a much wider environmental range for exploration, resistance to handling became still more pronounced.

At times of distress, while the Cuddlers found relief in close contact, the Non-Cuddlers needed different forms of comfort:

> "You can't calm him by picking him up even when he is teething—wheeling him round in his pram is much more effective."
> "Stops crying most quickly if put back on floor and diverted."
> "Even when poorly will settle much better in her cot."
> "Most easily comforted by walking him round and showing him things."
> "Holding her up on her feet is the best way of calming her."

In general, diversion techniques such as walking or carrying the child around, playing with him, or giving him a biscuit or a bottle were found to be the most effective means of dealing with the Non-Cuddlers when ill or in pain. This does not mean that this group of infants showed a lack of orientation towards the mother: she was still regarded as a "haven of safety" and when frightened (as, for instance, by the approach of a stranger) the Non-Cuddlers too sought her proximity. Their means of establishing proximity was, however, different, for instead of the close physical contact which the other infants sought for reassurance, the Non-Cuddlers either made visual contact with the mother by looking away from the frightening object and turning towards her, or established a much less close physical contact such as holding on to the mother's skirt or hiding their face against her knee.

Feeding on the mother's lap did not produce the same clear-cut differentiation. Two of the Non-Cuddlers were said to protest even then, and to accept food only when sitting in a high chair or standing next to the mother's knee. This, however, applied only from the age of 6 or 7 m on, and no cases of propped bottles due to the infant's resistance to handling were reported for the first half-year.

From the above descriptions it can be seen that, while marked differences exist between the Cuddlers and the Non-Cuddlers, the latter do not by many means resist all forms of physical contact. Their protests, it appears, are elicited only by those types of interaction which involve a close physical contact, as seen at its clearest in the cuddling situation. Skin contact alone, such as occurs when the child is kissed or has his face stroked without being picked up, when he is tickled, or when "skin games" are played with him, failed to differentiate the two groups, for none of the infants was reported as avoiding or protesting at these forms of interaction. Handling also does not appear to be the crucial factor: the Non-Cuddlers not only tolerated but actively enjoyed being swung, bounced, danced around or romped with, in any way which involved contact but not restraint. As soon as restraint

* Editor's note: throughout, m = months.

was applied, however, i.e., the infant was not merely supported but also had his movements actively restricted, struggling and resistance occurred.

We must conclude, therefore, that it is not contact per se that is avoided by the Non-Cuddlers but only the restriction of movement that is involved in certain of the contact situations. However, because of their resistance in situations in which contact tends to be most commonly offered, the total amount of physical contact obtained by the Non-Cuddlers is likely to be considerably reduced in comparison with the Cuddlers. We will proceed to ask, in the first place, whether this reduction is associated with differences in the manner in which the first social attachments were formed by the two groups and, in the second place, whether any aetiological factors can be isolated to account for the phenomena described.

THE FORMATION OF SOCIAL ATTACHMENTS BY THE TWO CONTACT GROUPS

The attachment function (defined as the tendency of the young to seek the proximity of certain other members of the species) may be described in terms of three parameters:

(a) age at onset, i.e., the age when the capacity to form attachments to specific individuals is first manifested;

(b) its intensity at any given age point;

(c) its breadth at these various points, i.e., the number of objects towards whom it is directed.

In infancy it may be most suitably assessed by the reaction to the object's withdrawal in any of the separation situations which tend to occur in the everyday life of all infants. The following 7 such situations were examined in this project: left alone in a room; left with other people; put down in cot at night; passed by while in cot or chair; put down after being on adult's knee; left in pram outside house; and left in pram outside shops. From maternal reports the infant's amount of protest in each situation as it occurred in the preceding four-weekly period was ascertained at every interview and rated on a four-point scale: (0) no protest reported; (1) protests occur, but there are qualifications in respect of *both* their intensity and their regularity; (2) protests occur, but there are qualifications in respect of *either* intensity or regularity; (3) protests occur and there are no qualifications as to intensity or regularity. The combined ratings for all 7 situations yielded, for any given age point investigated, a quantitative measure of the intensity of each infant's attachment function. The identity of the individuals towards whom protests were directed was also ascertained for each situation, breadth being defined as the total number of objects reported for any given age point. Age at onset was defined as the point midway between the interview which first yielded information as to the establishment of attachments to specific individuals and the previous interview.

It has been shown (Schaffer and Emerson, 1964) that the majority of in-

Table 2   Age at Onset and Intensity Score or Specific Attachments Related
to Contact Group

	Age at Onset		Intensity Scores up to 12 m		Intensity Scores at 18 m	
	Mean (Weeks)	Range (Weeks)	Mean	Range	Mean	Range
"Cuddlers"	33.63	22–50	5.19	1.15–9.00	6.68	3.00–15.40
"Non-Cuddlers"	44.77	26–65	2.33	1.33–5.83	4.31	2.30– 9.30
p^a	N.S.		<0.02		N.S.	

^{a} *Based* on Mann-Whitney U-test. A non-parametic technique was used as, for age at
onset, a significantly different variance was found for the two groups and, in the case
of the intensity scores, the assumption of equal scale intervals was avoided.

fants first provide evidence of a need for the proximity of certain specific
individuals (rather than an indiscriminate need for company and attention in
general sometime during the third quarter of the first year. Investigating the
influence of contact group on age at onset (see Table 2), the Non-Cuddlers
are found to reach this developmental milestone somewhat later than the
Cuddlers. Due to the very much greater variance among the Non-Cuddlers,
however, the difference fails to reach statistical significance and gives no
basis for rejecting the null hypothesis.

As to the intensity with which specific attachments are manifested, comparison may be made at two points, namely for the first year (taking the
mean of all intensity scores obtained by each infant up to 12 m) and at 18
m. For the former, the Non-Cuddlers are found to show specific attachments
to a significantly less intense degree than the Cuddlers (Table 2). The tie to
particular individuals, when first established, is thus weaker in those infants
who experienced reduced physical contact with other people. At 18 m, however, although the Non-Cuddlers are still showing less intense specific attachments than either of the other two groups, they appear to have made up
a considerable part of the leeway and no longer differ to a significant degree
from the Cuddlers in this respect.

For the third parameter of the attachment function investigated here,
namely, breadth, no differences were found between the two groups, in
that all showed attachments to a similar number of objects both in the first
year and at 18 m.

Reduced physical contact is thus associated to only a minor degree with
the manner in which social attachments are established. The association is
seen most clearly in the earliest stages of attachment formation to specific
individuals, but there is no indication that the Non-Cuddlers are in any way
severely or more than temporarily affected.

AETIOLOGICAL CONSIDERATIONS

In seeking an explanation for the observed differences in reactions to
physical contact, two alternative hypotheses may be examined. According

Table 3 Association of Maternal Handling Type with Contact Group

| | Maternal Types | |
	Handlers	Non-Handlers
"Cuddlers"	9	10
"Non-Cuddlers"	2	7

$p > 0.10$, Fisher exact test.

to the first, a need for physical contact is potentially present in all infants, but in certain cases environmental conditions (with particular reference to early maternal handling) do not permit the full expression of this need which therefore becomes blocked and frustrated. According to the second hypothesis, congenital rather than environmental forces provide the crucial explanation, there being a factor in the infant's inherent make-up which impels some subjects to seek close physical contact while preventing others from doing so. We shall, as far as the data permit, investigate each of these two hypotheses in turn.

For the most likely environmental force responsible for blocking the contact need we may look to the mother-infant relationship. Observing the sensuous way in which mothers often interact with their infants, one is struck by the fact that it is not only infants but also adults who can have such a need. There are, however, some who prefer not to handle their infant more than is necessary and who will, whenever possible, interact with him through means other than physical contact. On the basis partly of observations of casual interaction sequences between mother and child taking place during interviews, and partly of reports from the mothers as to the method of dealing with the child's demands for attention, each mother was allocated by two judges, who had read through all the relevant material gathered in the course of the project, according to her *preferred* mode of interaction with the infant to one of three categories: personal-handling (interaction takes place mainly through physical contact), personal non-handling (stimulation is provided by the mother mainly through visual and auditory means), and impersonal (toys, food, etc., are used to "divert" the child's demands for attention away from the mother herself). Combining the last two categories as representing Non-Handlers and comparing them with the first category, the Handlers, the distribution for the two contact groups is as given in Table 3. These figures provide no support for the hypothesis that contact type is a direct function of the mother's customary mode of handling: though most of the Non-Cuddlers had mothers who preferred other than physical means of interaction, the prevalence of non-handling mothers amongst the Cuddlers suggests that this variable cannot, in itself, be regarded as the crucial aetiological condition.

Table 3 does, however, raise the interesting problem of non-matching couples. Pursuing this point in interview, it was found that the Cuddlers with non-handling mothers obtained the desired contact comfort either from other members of the family or occasionally from the mother herself, in that the latter found that she just had to give way to the infant's demands from time

Table 4 Association of Siblings' Reactions to Physical Contact with Contact Group

| | Siblings' Reactions | |
	Accepted	Resisted
"Cuddlers"	14	4
"Non-Cuddlers"	0	5
p^a	0.05	

[a] Fisher exact test. The figures in this table refer to number of siblings, not to number of subjects.

to time. Complete rigidity and utter failure to bring about mutual adjustment was therefore not observed in this group. The same applies to the two Non-Cuddlers with handling mothers: although this situation might well be the first step in the development of a pathological relationship, in this sample the mothers were able to adjust to the infant's peculiarities and relate to him by using alternate modes of interaction. The mothers' comments on the child's dislike of cuddling varied: some expressed considerable surprise, while others had encountered it before in other children; some regretted it, others asserted that they did not mind as it was "less bother" for them. None of the mothers regarded it as a form of rejection, as all felt that the child was able to show his affection in other ways. One or two interpreted this phenomenon as showing "independence of mind," "self-will," or an indication that "he is not soft." Their explanations also varied: the mothers with non-cuddling sons mostly believed that this was a characteristic of boys generally, whereas the same explanation with regard to girls was heard from the mother of a non-cuddling daughter. Heredity was also invoked as a cause, mainly on the basis of similar reactions having been observed in other members of the family (one might include here the somewhat wistful comment from one mother: "He is just like his father—not one for a bit of love!").

One of our questions referred to the reactions of older siblings to close physical contact in infancy. Insofar as this involved retrospective data, we were only able to distinguish two categories: those who had accepted and those who had resisted this type of stimulation. As Table 4 shows, a close similarity in reaction is found between siblings, with none of the older children in the families of Non-Cuddlers being reported as having been Cuddlers.

However, neither these nor any of the other findings quoted above can provide conclusive evidence as to the influence of maternal handling practices. Similarity in reaction of older siblings, for instance, may be as much due to innate factors as to identical modes of child-rearing. The possibility that early learning produced through "contagion" (Escalona's [1953] term for the process whereby maternal feelings are transmitted to the infant through physical interaction) is responsible for the child's resistance to cuddling can only be confirmed or denied by an observational approach applied very much more intensively and earlier than had been the case in this study. The cruder indices which we used to describe early maternal practices failed to differ-

Table 5   Use of "Cuddly Toys" and Incidence of Autoerotic Activities Related to Contact Group

| | Use of "Cuddly Toys" | | Autoerotic Activities | |
	Reported	Not Reported	Reported	Not Reported
"Cuddlers"	10	9	9	10
"Non-Cuddlers"	1	8	0	9
p^a	0.10		0.10	

[a] Fisher exact test.

entiate between the contact groups: method of feeding, for instance, was very similar, in that all infants except one Cuddler were bottle- rather than breast-fed after the first month; rigidity of feeding schedule, which might produce associations of tension with handling, also did not differentiate between the groups; and the same applies to the degree of maternal responsiveness to the infant's crying for attention, in that Non-Cuddlers were not left to cry any longer than Cuddlers.

There is, however, another, though more indirect, means of investigating the frustration hypothesis. If some maternal force were indeed blocking the Non-Cuddler's inherent contact need, one might expect to observe some sign of the frustrated need seeking other outlets. There are three main ways in which this could take place, involving respectively people other than the mother, inanimate objects, or the self.

As to the other people, it was reported by all mothers of the Non-Cuddlers that the infant behaved similarly with everybody. While we have no way of confirming the veracity of this statement, casual observations during interviews produced no contradictory evidence. Some of the mothers indeed mentioned their embarrassment when doting relatives and other visitors would attempt to cuddle an otherwise friendly child and be confronted with a violently negative reaction on his part. It may also be recalled in this connection that the two contact groups did not differ with regard to number of attachment objects, suggesting that the Non-Cuddlers did not seek satisfaction from a wide range of other figures in the environment.

Soft toys and other contact-providing objects are another source to which a frustrated child might be expected to turn. The number of infants in each group who, up to the age of 18 m, had at any time in the first 18 m made use of "favorite cuddlies" (most often bits of sheet or blanket which were taken to bed or resorted to at times of pain and illness) is given in Table 5. The trend revealed there goes in the opposite direction to that predicted by the frustration hypothesis.

The same table also gives the incidence in the sample of those autoerotic activities which, according to the mothers, had become established habits at any time during the first 18 m. None of our infants was a confirmed rocker, rubber, or masturbator, and the autoerotic activities refer therefore mainly to oral habits such as thumb-sucking. Once again the distribution gives no evidence of a frustrated need seeking other outlets—on the contrary, the in-

Table 6   Reactions of Contact Groups in Two Restraint Situations—Dressed and Tucked into Bed

	Dressed		Tucked into Bed	
	Protest	No Protest	Protest	No Protest
"Cuddlers"	3	16	2	17
"Non-Cuddlers"	6	3	5	4
p^a		0.05		0.05

[a] Fisher exact test.

teresting conclusion is indicated that the more contact a child receives the more is he likely to show other sensual responses too.

We turn now to the second hypothesis concerning aetiology, namely that an infant's reactions to close physical contact is a function of certain inherent characteristics present in the child from the beginning. In attempting to isolate such a characteristic, one may begin with a theme which recurs constantly in the reports of the Non-Cuddlers' behavior, namely the restlessness which these infants generally display over a wide range of situations. The following are some of the descriptions taken from the mothers' reports of the child's behavior on their knees:

> "Not content just to sit on your lap, likes to move around."
> "Loves being bounced up and down, but otherwise just would not sit still on your knee."
> "Enjoys being swung in your arms but not to sit still."
> "Will only sit for a couple of seconds on your lap, then struggles to get down."
> "Wriggles constantly on knee, likes movement."
> "Won't keep still on your knee, walks up you or rocks backwards and forwards."

The Cuddlers, on the other hand, emerge on the whole as far more placid, quiet and content. Activity ratings on a five-point scale, based on observations of the infant's behavior during all the interviews held in the course of the study, give quantitative form to this impression. The mean ratings for the Cuddlers and Non-Cuddlers were, respectively, 3.11 and 3.75, indicating a difference only just short of statistical significance ($t = 1.83$, $p < 0.10$).

It is possible, therefore, that the two contact groups may be differentiated on some such basis as the congenital activity types described by Fries (1953). Hyperactive, restless infants would be more likely to resist those forms of physical contact which involve restraint of their movements, and it is this element which, as we have seen, appears to be the crucial one in calling forth their protests in the cuddling situation. We attempted further to pinpoint this difference in reaction to restraint by asking about the infants' behavior in relation to two other situations also involving motor restraint: being dressed and being tucked into bed (see Table 6). In both instances a clear difference is shown between the contact groups when mothers were asked whether or not the child had consistently protested in the relevant situation from the age of at least 6 months on: thus the Non-Cuddlers are far more often reported as showing dislike of being wrapped, changed, or having their clothes put on than the Cuddlers, and the same difference also emerges for behavior in bed in that struggling when tucked into bed, kicking off blankets, and general restlessness when actually asleep were characteristics found to a significantly greater extent amongst the Non-Cuddlers than the Cuddlers. Even the actual amount of sleep differentiates the two groups: when asked to detail the number of hours which the infants spent asleep per 24 hr (the infants being 9–10 m old at the time this information was sought), the mothers of the Non-Cuddlers reported a mean value of 11.89 hr as compared with the 13.16 hr reported by the mothers of the Cuddlers ($t = 4.12$, $p < 0.001$).

The restlessness of the Non-Cuddlers appears to have one further consequence which is illustrated in Table 7. In their motor development these infants appear to be well ahead of the Cuddlers, reaching such milestones as the ability to sit unsupported, to stand holding on, and to crawl, considerably sooner than the Cuddlers (the failure to obtain a significant difference with regard to the onset of walking may well be due to the fact that in many cases the relevant information was not obtained until the 18 m visit, i.e., 6 m after the last interview compared with the four-weekly intervals between intervals in the first year, and consequently many mothers tended to give the vague answer "at about a year" to our question about onset). The Cattell Infant Scale (Cattell, 1940) was administered to all infants around the age of 6 m and here too a significant difference was obtained between Cuddlers and Non-Cuddlers. As the items composing the test around this age are mainly concerned with motor, particularly manipulative, functioning, further confirmation is given to the association between contact type and early locomotor development. The Non-Cuddlers' restlessness thus appears to provide a drive to motor functioning which results in increased achievement in this sphere when compared with the more placid infants of the Cuddler group.

We may conclude that the Non-Cuddlers' avoidance of close physical contact is concerned with a phenomenon that is not peculiar to the relationship with the mother or indeed to social relationships in general. These children, it appears, were distinguished by a general behavioral characteristic affecting a wide range of functions and apparent in non-social as well as social situations. In the absence of any positive evidence that the mothers of the two contact groups could be clearly distinguished according to a criterion aetiologically associated with the infants' reaction to contact, and in view of our failure to find signs of a frustrated need seeking other outlets, we are inclined to regard the congenital explanation as the more likely of the two hypotheses considered. Only further investigation will, however, provide a conclusive answer.

Table 7 Age at Onset of Motor Skills and Developmental Quotients in the Two Contact Groups

	Sitting		Standing		Crawling		Walking		D.Q.	
	Mean (Wks)	S.D. (Wks)	Mean (Wks)	S.D. (Wks)	Mean (Wks)	S.D. (Wks)	Mean (Wks)	S.D. (Wks)	Mean	S.D.
"Cuddlers"	30.11	2.91	37.18	5.01	43.43	5.17	55.08	7.02	110.36	9.76
"Non-Cuddlers"	27.80	4.85	31.33	4.35	36.83	3.89	51.72	4.66	122.50	12.74
t	1.82		2.26		2.12		1.15		2.43	
p	<0.10		<0.05		<0.05		N.S.		<0.05	

DISCUSSION

For some infants, it appears, contact is not comforting. Certain forms of it may be sought for the sake of obtaining extra stimulation ("rough play," carrying around, etc.), but the closer, more intimate kind of physical contact which is so satisfying to some infants is resisted and actively avoided by others. As a result, the total amount of handling received by the latter will be very much less than that received by more cuddly infants and, furthermore, the nature of their interaction with the mother will tend to assume a less direct form.

Comparison with recent animal studies on the role of contact comfort cannot easily be made. Due to the non-experimental nature of the study, with its lack of direct control over the independent variable, the difference between the groups in terms of the amount of contact received was not as extreme as one would like for a crucial test, for the Non-Cuddlers did not by any means experience a total lack of handling and in the feeding situation, for instance, could not be distinguished at all from the rest of the sample. Moreover, the initiative for the reduction of contact came from the infants themselves, not from an experimenter. It is quite possible that externally imposed deprivation of this type of stimulation could have more serious consequences for some infants than for others, and that the Cuddlers in particular require physical contact for satisfactory developmental progress. Yet, despite these qualifications, it is apparent that, in the case of human infants in general, caution is needed before one can ascribe to contact comfort the overwhelming importance that this variable has been found to assume in certain lower species. Our examination of the development of social attachments bears out this conclusion: reduced physical contact is associated with less intense attachments, but the difference between Cuddlers and Non-Cuddlers appears to be only a temporary one found in the initial stages of attachment formation. The reason, we may assume, lies in the greater flexibility of the human being in comparison with lower animals: prevented from obtaining the usual amount of close physical contact, both mother and child are able to use alternative ways of relating to one another. Rough play, carrying or walking around, and interaction through toys and other material objects were the most frequent examples quoted to us by the mothers of the Non-Cuddlers. Insofar as some of these modes of relating involved interaction through other objects, rather than direct interaction as occurs in cuddling, the initially less intense degree of attachment of the Non-Cuddlers becomes readily understandable. Support is thus given to the notion that what appears to matter in the establishment of primary social bonds is the type of more general mechanism of social arousal advocated by Scott (1962), rather than one particular mode of achieving such arousal. The aim of the attachment function is to obtain the proximity of the object, but such an aim can be attained in many ways, and if one way is blocked (as happens, for instance, in blind babies), other means are still possible. It is thus unlikely than in *all* human infants a great deal of physical contact is a *sine qua non* for early social development.

Aetiologically, we have not been able to produce conclusive evidence for either of the two hypotheses advanced, though, despite our inability to discount totally the effects of certain subtle interaction processes occurring early on between mother and child, a congenital origin appears to us the more likely explanation. Of particular significance here is the suggestion that resistance to close physical contact is not primarily a social phenomenon at all but an expression of a more primitive and more general aspect of the infant's personality, to be observed above all in the level of his activity drive. Schaefer and Bayley (1963) have recently reported evidence pointing to the genetic origin of an individual's activity level and have indicated the need to find out more about its behavioral correlates and consequences. The data presented here suggest that one of these consequences refers to the manner in which the infant's interpersonal behavior is shaped. Thus the avoidance of close physical contact may be interpreted as stemming from a pervasive innate response tendency which will affect the initial development of social behavior and which may, in some cases, even be responsible for imposing a considerable strain on the mother-child relationship. From a clinical point of view, however, it seems unlikely that the non-cuddling pattern is per se a bad sign prognostically. In only those instances where a mother is too rigid to use alternate ways of relating, or where she interprets the infant's behavior as "rejection," may one be confronted with the first step in the development of a pathological relationship.

SUMMARY

In the course of a longitudinal investigation covering the first eighteen months of life, data regarding the infants' reactions to naturally occurring physical contact situations were systematically obtained through maternal reports. On the basis of their behavior two groups of infants were isolated: those who accepted close physical contact under all conditions and those who actively resisted it at all times. Descriptive data, highlighting the behavioral differences between the two groups, are presented, comparisons are made with regard to the manner in which each group forms the first social attachments, and some aetiological considerations to account for the differences between the groups are put forward.

REFERENCES

Casler, L. (1961). Maternal deprivation. *Monogr. Soc. Res. Child Develpm.*, 26, No. 2 (Serial No. 80).

Cattell, P. (1940). *The measurement of intelligence of infants and young children.* New York: The Psychological Corporation.

Escalona, S. (1953). Emotional development in the first year of life. In M. J. E. Senn (Ed.), *Problems of infancy and childhood: transactions of the sixth Josiah Macy Conference.* New York: Macy.

Fries, M. E., and Woolf, P. J. (1953). Some hypotheses on the role of the congenital activity type in personality development. *Psychoanal. Stud. Child, 8,* 48–62.

Harlow, H. F. (1958). The nature of love. *Amer. Psychol., 13,* 673–685.

Harlow, H. F., and Zimmerman, R. R. (1959). Affectional responses in the infant monkey. *Science, 130,* 421–432.

Latscha, R. (1953). Tests of significance in a 2 × 2 contingency table: extension of Finney's table. *Biometrika, 40,* 74–86.

Rheingold, H. L. (1961). The effect of environmental stimulation upon social and exploratory behavior in the human infant. In B. M. Foss (Ed.), *Determinants of Infant Behaviour.* London: Methuen.

Ribble, M. A. (1944). Infantile experiences in relation to personality development. In J. McV. Hunt (Ed.), *Personality and the behaviour disorders.* New York: Ronald Press.

Schaefer, E. S., and Bayley, N. (1963). Maternal behaviour, child behaviour and their intercorrelation from infancy through adolescence. *Monogr. Soc. Res. Child Develpm., 28,* 3 (Serial No. 87).

Schaffer, H. R. (1963). Some issues for research in the study of attachment behavior. In B. M. Foss (Ed.), *Determinants of Infant Behaviour: II:* London: Methuen.

Schaffer, H. R., and Emerson, P. E. (1964). The development of social attachments in infancy. *Monogr. Soc. Res. Child Develpm., 29,* 3 (Serial No. 94).

Scott, J. P. (1962). Critical periods in behavioural development. *Science, 138,* 949–958.

part II
Early Language and Cognitive Development

During the preschool period, the child's perceptions become more accurate and differentiated, and his language abilities rapidly undergo extensive and profound changes. Vocabulary grows by leaps and bounds, complex grammatical (syntactic) rules are acquired, and the use of language becomes more efficient, precise, and subtle. These changes have profound, pervasive effects, for the use and understanding of language and symbolic representation appear to be of central importance for all aspects of cognitive development. Progress in language is generally antecedent to improvements in the processes of thinking, perceiving, abstraction, reasoning, imagining, categorizing, learning, problem-solving, and concept formation.

Children acquire the basic rules of grammar (syntax) very early—although, of course, they can't state them—and at a rate that defies explanation in terms of traditional learning principles, rewarded responses, or imitation. Some kinds of complex, active cognitive processes, such as concept formation and induction, must be involved in the acquisition of syntax. Longitudinal observations of mother-child verbal interactions by Roger Brown and Ursula Bellugi provide some excellent insights into the development of grammar. In the first paper in this part, these investigators show that the child's syntactic competence cannot be accounted for simply by imitation and expansion (the mother's responding to the child's speech by adding something to what the child says or expanding it). Induction or discovery of latent structure is the most important process involved, and this requires the child's active processing of the speech he hears, searching for regularities, so as to induce the rules.

It has been clearly established that the child's early linguistic environment strongly affects his rate of cognitive and linguistic development. Compared with middle-class children, those from culturally disadvantaged backgrounds are generally deficient in all aspects of language development, largely because of the lack of language stimulation in their homes. The most significant and stimulating research on this problem is that of Basil Bernstein, an English educational sociologist. His comparisons of the language of middle- and lower- (disadvantaged) class mothers, showed that the latter use a "restricted" linguistic code in their interactions with their children, talking less, avoiding difficult questions and conceptualizations and using short grammatically simple sentences.

In the second paper, Professor Bernstein and his colleague, Dorothy Henderson, summarize some earlier findings which show that middle-class mothers use language primarily in socializing their children in interpersonal relations and by teaching them in such a way that the child learns operations, principles, and a sense of autonomy in skill acquisition. The working-class mother, on the other hand, uses language more in teaching basic skills and her child learns operations rather than principles. Moreover, he is encouraged to be passive and dependent in the learning process, so that he may be at a considerable disadvantage in the kind of learning situation he encounters in school.

With improved comprehension and use of language, the child can begin to use verbal mediators and mediated generalizations—for example, applying labels to objects and events—which may enhance thinking and problem solution considerably. The experiments of Tracy Kendler and her colleagues provide impressive evidence of the importance of verbal mediators in tasks involving concept formation and inference. Her work, summarized in the third study of this part, shows that the child who uses verbal mediators can solve reversal-shift problems (learning to switch responses to do the opposite of what he has previously done in the same situation) and integrate independently acquired responses in making inferences. Younger children who do not use verbal mediators cannot solve these problems adequately.

A child may be able to understand, and use a word correctly but not use it spontaneously as a mediator. In the fourth paper, John Flavell, David Beach, and Jack Chinsky show that kindergarten children who can name depicted objects are much less likely than older children to verbalize these names (i.e., to use verbal mediators) in a serial learning task. The tendency to generate and use verbal mediators actively and spontaneously in learning and in solving problems tends to increase continuously with age between kindergarten and grade 5.

Is it possible, by means of special training, to compensate for linguistic and cognitive deficiencies such as those of the disadvantaged child that apparently have their roots in lack of adequate early verbal stimulation at home? Recent research provides a basis for at least a moderately optimistic answer. An example of successful compensatory preschool education is found in the work of Marion Blank and Frances Solomon summarized in the fifth paper in this part. These investigators worked intensively with nursery school children, individually, for 15 to 20 minutes a day for a period of four months. In the training sessions, the child was actively engaged in tasks requiring language comprehension, thought, abstraction, cognitive organization, and problem solution. The program was impressively successful in raising IQ's and in bringing about beneficial changes in the behavior of the children who participated.

No one has had more influence or contributed more, theoretically and substantively, to our understanding of cognitive development than Jean Piaget of the University of Geneva. Piaget's theory traces the development of cognition from its roots in the earliest primitive reflexes of the infant to the complex formal logical thinking of the adult. The four major stages of cognitive development—sensorimotor, preoperational, concrete operations, formal operations—form an invariant sequence. Each of these stages is defined and described briefly in the concluding paper, which also provides some explanations of such fundamental Piagetian concepts as schemata, conservation, and equilibration.

Three Processes in the Child's Acquisition of Syntax

Roger Brown and Ursula Bellugi

Some time in the second six months of life most children say a first intelligible word. A few months later most children are saying many words and some children go about the house all day long naming things *(table, doggie, ball,* etc.) and actions *(play, see, drop,* etc.) and an occasional quality *(blue, broke, bad,* etc.). At about eighteen months children are likely to begin constructing two-word utterances, such a one, for instance, as *Push car.*

A construction such as *Push car* is not just two single-word utterances spoken in a certain order. As single word utterances (they are sometimes called holophrases) both *push* and *car* would have primary stresses and terminal intonation contours. When they are two words programmed as a single utterance the primary stress would fall on *car* and so would the highest level

Reprinted from *Harvard Educational Review,* Spring, 1964, *34,* No. 2, pp. 133–151. By permission.

This investigation was supported in whole by Public Health Service Research Grant MH7088 from the National Institute of Mental Health.

of pitch. *Push* would be subordinated to *car* by a lesser stress and a lower pitch; the unity of the whole would appear in the absence of a terminal contour between words and the presence of such a contour at the end of the full sequence.

By the age of thirty-six months some children are so advanced in the construction process as to produce all of the major varieties of English simple sentences up to a length of ten or eleven words. For several years we have been studying the development of English syntax, of the sentence-constructing process, in children between eighteen and thirty-six months of age. Most recently we have made a longitudinal study of a boy and girl whom we shall call Adam and Eve. We began work with Adam and Eve in October of 1962 when Adam was twenty-seven months old and Eve eighteen months old. The two children were selected from some thirty whom we considered. They were selected primarily because their speech was exceptionally intelligible and because they talked a lot. We wanted to make it as easy as possible to transcribe accurately large quantities of child speech. Adam and Eve are the children of highly educated parents, the fathers were graduate students at Harvard and the mothers are both college graduates. Both Adam and Eve were single children when we began the study. These facts must be remembered in generalizing the outcomes of the research.

While Adam is nine months older than Eve, his speech was only a little more advanced in October of 1962. The best single index of the level of speech development is the average length of utterance and in October, 1962, Adam's average was 1.84 morphemes and Eve's was 1.40 morphemes. The two children stayed fairly close together in the year that followed; in the records for the thirty-eighth week Adam's average was 3.55 and Eve's, 3.27. The processes we shall describe appeared in both children.

Every second week we visited each child for at least two hours and made a tape recording of everything said by the child as well as of everything said to the child. The mother was always present and most of the speech to the child is hers. Both mother and child became very accustomed to our presence and learned to continue their usual routine with us as the observers.

One of us always made a written transcription, on the scene, of the speech of mother and child with notes about important actions and objects of attention. From this transcription and the tape a final transcription was made and these transcriptions constitute the primary data of the study. For many purposes we require a "distributional analysis" of the speech of the child. To this end the child's utterances in a given transcription were cross classified and relisted under such headings as: "A + noun"; "Noun + verb"; "Verbs in the past"; "Utterances containing the pronoun *it*," etc. The categorized utterances expose the syntactic regularities of the child's speech.

Each week we met as a research seminar, with students of the psychology of language,[1] to discuss the state of the construction process in one of the

[1] We are grateful for intellectual stimulation and lighthearted companionship to Dr. Jean Berko Gleason, Mr. Samuel Anderson, Mr. Colin Fraser, Dr. David McNeill, and Dr. Daniel Slobin.

Table 1 A Section from Adam's First Record

Adam	Mother
See truck, Mommy.	
See truck.	
	Did you see the truck?
No I see truck.	
	No, you didn't see it?
	There goes one.
There go one.	
	Yes, there goes one.
See a truck.	
See truck, Mommy.	
See truck.	
Truck.	
Put truck, Mommy.	
	Put the truck where?
Put truck window.	
	I think that one's too large to go in the window.

two children as of that date. In these discussions small experiments were often suggested, experiments that had to be done within a few days if they were to be informative. At one time, for instance, we were uncertain whether Adam understood the semantic difference between putting a noun in subject position and putting it in object position. Consequently one of us paid an extra visit to Adam equipped with some toys. "Adam," we said, "show us the duck pushing the boat." And, when he had done so: "Now show us the boat pushing the duck."

Another week we noticed that Adam would sometimes pluralize nouns when they should have been pluralized and sometimes would not. We wondered if he could make grammatical judgments about the plural, if he could distinguish a correct form from an incorrect form. "Adam," we asked, "which is right, 'two shoes' or 'two shoe'?" His answer on that occasion, produced with explosive enthusiasm, was "Pop goes the weasel!" The two-year-old child does not make a perfectly docile experimental subject.

The dialogue between mother and child does not read like a transcribed dialogue between two adults. Table 1 offers a sample section from an early transcribed record. It has some interesting properties. The conversation is, in the first place, very much in the here and now. From the child there is no speech of the sort that Bloomfield called "displaced," speech about other times and other places. Adam's utterances in the early months were largely a coding of contemporaneous events and impulses. The mother's speech differs from the speech that adults use to one another in many ways. Her sentences are short and simple; for the most part they are the kinds of sentences that Adam will produce a year later.

Perhaps because they are short, the sentences of the mother are perfectly grammatical. The sentences adults use to one another, perhaps because they are longer and more complex, are very often not grammatical, not well formed. Here for instance is a rather representative example produced at a conference of psychologists and linguists: "As fas as I know, no one yet has done the in a way obvious now and interesting problem of doing a in a sense a structural frequency study of the alternative syntactical in a given language, say, like English, the alternative possible structures, and how what their hierarchical probability of occurrence structure is."[2] It seems unlikely that a child could learn the patterns of English syntax from such speech. His introduction to English ordinarily comes in the form of a simplified, repetitive, and idealized dialect. It may be that such an introduction is necessary for the acquisition of syntax to be possible but we do not know that.

In the course of the brief interchange of Table 1 Adam imitates his mother in saying: "There go one" immediately after she says "There goes one." The imitation is not perfect; Adam omits the inflection on the verb. His imitation is a reduction in that it omits something from the original. This kind of imitation with reduction is extremely common in the records of Adam and Eve and it is the first process we shall discuss.

IMITATION AND REDUCTION

Table 2 presents some model sentences spoken by the mothers and the imitations produced by Adam and Eve. These were selected from hundreds in the records in order to illustrate some general propositions. The first thing to notice is that the imitations preserve the word order of the model sentences. To be sure, words in the model are often missing from the imitation but the words preserved are in the order of the original. This is a fact that is so familiar and somehow reasonable that we did not at once recognize it as an empirical outcome rather than as a natural necessity. But of course it is not a necessity, the outcome could have been otherwise. For example, words could have been said back in the reverse of their original order, the most recent first. The preservation of order suggests that the model sentence is processed by the child as a total construction rather than as a list of words.

In English the order of words in a sentence is an important grammatical signal. Order is used to distinguish among subject, direct object, and indirect object and it is one of the marks of imperative and interrogative constructions. The fact that the child's first sentences preserve the word order of their models partially accounts for the ability of an adult to "understand" these sentences and so to feel that he is in communication with the child. It is conceivable that the child "intends" the meanings coded by his word orders and that, when he preserves the order of an adult sentence, he does so because he wants to say what the order says. It is also possible that he preserves word order just because his brain works that way and that he has no

[2] H. Maclay and C. E. Osgood, "Hesitation phenomena in spontaneous English speech," *Word*, XV (1959), 19–44.

Table 2   Some Imitations Produced by Adam and Eve

Model Utterance	Child's Imitation
Tank car	Tank car
Wait a minute	Wait a minute
Daddy's brief case	Daddy brief case
Fraser will be unhappy	Fraser unhappy
He's going out	He go out
That's an old time train	Old time train
It's not the same dog as Pepper	Dog Pepper
No, you can't write on Mr. Cromer's shoe	Write Cromer shoe

comprehension of the semantic contrasts involved. In some languages word order is not an important grammatical signal. In Latin, for instance, "Agricola amat puellam" has the same meaning as "Puellam amat agricola" and subject-object relations are signalled by case endings. We would be interested to know whether children who are exposed to languages that do not utilize word order as a major syntactic signal, preserve order as reliably as do children exposed to English.

The second thing to notice in Table 2 is the fact that when the models increase in length there is not a corresponding increase in the imitation. The imitations stay in the range of two to four morphemes which was the range characteristic of the children at this time. The children were operating under some constraint of length or span. This is not a limitation of vocabulary; the children knew hundreds of words. Neither is it a constraint of immediate memory. We infer this from the fact that the average length of utterances produced spontaneously, where immediate memory is not involved, is about the same as the average length of utterances produced as immediate imitations. The constraint is a limitation on the length of utterance the children are able to program or plan.[3] This kind of narrow span limitation in children is characteristic of most or all of their intellectual operations. The limitation grows less restrictive with age as a consequence, probably, of both neurological growth and of practice, but of course it is never lifted altogether.

A constraint on length compels the imitating child to omit some words or morphemes from the mother's longer sentences. Which forms are retained and which omitted? The selection is not random but highly systematic. Forms retained in the examples of Table 2 include: Daddy, Fraser, Pepper, and Cromer; tank car, minute, briefcase, train, dog and shoe; wait, go, and write; unhappy and old time. For the most part they are nouns, verbs, and adjectives, though there are exceptions, as witness the initial pronoun He and the preposition out and the indefinite article a. Forms omitted in the samples of Table 2 include: the possessive inflection —s, the modal auxiliary will, the

[3] Additional evidence of the constraint on sentence length may be found in R. Brown and C. Fraser, "The acquisition of syntax," C. N. Cofer and Barbara Musgrave, eds., Verbal behavior and learning (New York: McGraw-Hill, 1963).

contraction of the auxiliary verb *is,* the progressive inflection *—ing,* the preposition *on,* the articles *the* and *an,* and the modal auxiliary *can.* It is possible to make a general characterization of the forms likely to be retained that distinguishes them as a total class from the forms likely to be omitted.

Forms likely to be retained are nouns and verbs and, less often, adjectives, and these are the three large and "open" parts-of-speech in English. The number of forms in any one of these parts-of-speech is extremely large and always growing. Words belonging to these classes are sometimes called "contentives" because they have semantic content. Forms likely to be omitted are inflections, auxiliary verbs, articles, prepositions, and conjunctions. These forms belong to syntactic classes that are small and closed. Any one class has few members and new members are not readily added. The omitted forms are the ones that linguists sometimes call "functors," their grammatical *functions* being more obvious than their semantic content.

Why should young children omit functors and retain contentives? There is more than one plausible answer. Nouns, verbs, and adjectives are words that make reference. One can conceive of teaching the meanings of these words by speaking them, one at a time, and pointing at things or actions or qualities. And of course parents do exactly that. These are the kinds of words that children have been encouraged to practice speaking one at a time. The child arrives at the age of sentence construction with a stock of well practiced nouns, verbs, and adjectives. Is it not likely then that this prior practice causes him to retain the contentives from model sentences too long to be reproduced in full, that the child imitates those forms in the speech he hears which are already well developed in him as individual habits? There is probably some truth in this explanation but it is not the only determinant since children will often select for retention contentives that are relatively unfamiliar to them.

We adults sometimes operate under a constraint on length and the curious fact is that the English we produce in these circumstances bears a formal resemblance to the English produced by two-year-old children. When words cost money there is a premium on brevity or to put it otherwise, a constraint on length. The result is "telegraphic" English and telegraphic English is an English of nouns, verbs, and adjectives. One does not send a cable reading: "My car has broken down and I have lost my wallet; send money to me at the American Express in Paris" but rather "Car broken down; wallet lost; send money American Express Paris." The telegram omits: *my, has, and, I, have, my, to, me, at, the, in.* All of these are functors. We make the same kind of telegraphic reduction when time or fatigue constrain us to be brief, as witness any set of notes taken at a fast-moving lecture.

A telegraphic transformation of English generally communicates very well. It does so because it retains the high-information words and drops the low-information words. We are here using "information" in the sense of the mathematical theory of communication. The information carried by a word is inversely related to the chances of guessing it from context. From a given string of content words, missing functors can often be guessed but the message "my has and I have my to me at the in" will not serve to get money to Paris. Perhaps children are able to make a communication analysis of adult speech and so adapt in an optimal way to their limitation of span. There is, however, another way in which the adaptive outcome might be achieved.

If you say aloud the model sentences of Table 2 you will find that you place the heavier stresses, the primary and secondary stresses in the sentences, on contentives rather than on functors. In fact the heavier stresses fall, for the most part, on the words the child retains. We first realized that this was the case when we found that in transcribing tapes, the words of the mother that we could hear most clearly were usually the words that the child reproduced. We had trouble hearing the weakly stressed functors and, of course, the child usually failed to reproduce them. Differential stress may then be the cause of the child's differential retention. The outcome is a maximally informative reduction but the cause of this outcome need not be the making of an information analysis. The outcome may be an incidental consequence of the fact that English is a well-designed language that places its heavier stresses where they are needed, on contentives that cannot easily be guessed from context.

We are fairly sure that differential stress is one of the determinants of the child's telegraphic productions. For one thing, stress will also account for the way in which children reproduce polysyllabic words when the total is too much for them. Adam, for instance, gave us 'pression for expression and Eve gave us 'raff for giraffe; the more heavily stressed syllables were the ones retained. In addition we have tried the effect of placing heavy stresses on functors which do not ordinarily receive such stresses. To Adam we said: "You say what I say" and then, speaking in a normal way at first: "The doggie will bite." Adam gave back: "Doggie bite." Then we stressed the auxiliary: "The doggie will bite" and, after a few trials, Adam made attempts at reproducing that auxiliary. A science fiction experiment comes to mind. If there were parents who stressed functors rather than contentives would they have children whose speech was a kind of "reciprocal telegraphic" made up of articles, prepositions, conjunctions, auxiliaries, and the like? Such children would be out of touch with the community as real children are not.

It may be that all the factors we have mentioned play some part in determining the child's selective imitations; the reference-making function of contentives, the fact that they are practiced as single words, the fact that they cannot be guessed from context, and the heavy stresses they receive. There are also other possible factors: for example, the left-to-right, earlier-to-later position of words in a sentence, but these make too long a story to tell here.[4] Whatever the causes, the first utterances produced as imitations of adult sentences are highly systematic reductions of their models. Furthermore, the telegraphic properties of these imitations appear also in the child's spontaneously produced utterances. When his speech is not modeled on an immediately prior adult sentence, it observes the same limitation on length and the same

[4] Brown and Fraser, ibid.

predilection for contentives as when it is modeled on an immediately prior sentence.

IMITATION WITH EXPANSION

In the course of the brief conversation set down in Table 1, Adam's mother at one point imitates Adam. The boy says: "There go one" and mother responds: "Yes, there goes one." She does not exactly reproduce the model sentence of the child but instead adds something to it or expands it. What she adds is a functor, the inflection for third-person on the verb, the very form that Adam had omitted when he imitated his mother.

One of the first things we noticed when we began to study child speech several years ago was the frequency with which adults imitated children. Indeed they seemed to imitate more often than did the children themselves. We later came to realize that adult imitations are seldom exact reproductions; they are usually expansions. The mothers of Adam and Eve responded to the speech of their children with expansions about thirty per cent of the time. We did it ourselves when we talked with the children. Indeed we found it very difficult to withhold expansions. A reduced or incomplete English sentence seems to constrain the English-speaking adult to expand it into the nearest properly formed complete sentence. Table 3 lists a few sample expansions from the hundreds in the records.

The first thing worthy of attention in the expansions of Table 3 is the fact that the words spoken by the mother preserve the order of the words in the child's sentences. To be sure, words and inflections are added but they are fitted in—before, and after and between the words the child used; they are not generally permitted to disturb the order of the child's words. It is as if these latter were taken as constants by the mother, constants to which some sentence had to be fitted. She acts as if she were assuming that the child means everything he says, all the words and also their order, but as if he might also mean more than he says. From the mother's point of view an expansion is a kind of communication check; it says in effect: "Is this what you mean?"

The second thing to notice about Table 3 is the character of the forms added to the child's utterances. They include the auxiliaries *is* and *will*; the prepositions, *in, on, to,* and *up*; the verb forms *is, have, had,* and *having*; the articles *a* and *the*; the pronouns *her, he,* and *it*. For the most part, the words added are functors and functors are of course the words that the child omits in his reductions.

The interaction between mother and child is, much of the time, a cycle of reductions and expansions. There are two transformations involved. The reduction transformation has an almost completely specifiable and so mechanical character. One could program a machine to do it with the following instructions: "Retain contentives (or stressed forms) in the order given up to some limit of length." The expansion accomplished by Adam's mother when she added the third-person inflection to the verb and said "There goes one"

Table 3 Expansions of Child Speech Produced by Mothers

Child	Mother
Baby highchair	*Baby is in the highchair*
Mommy eggnog	*Mommy had her eggnog*
Eve lunch	*Eve is having lunch*
Mommy sandwich	*Mommy'll have a sandwich*
Sat wall	*He sat on the wall*
Throw Daddy	*Throw it to Daddy*
Pick glove	*Pick the glove up*

is also a completely specificable transformation. The instructions would read: "Retain the forms given in the order given and supply obligatory grammatical forms." To be sure this mother-machine would have to be supplied with the obligatory rules of English grammar but that could be done. However, the sentence "There goes one" is atypical in that it only adds a compulsory and redundant inflection. The expansions of Table 3 all add forms that are not grammatically compulsory or redundant and these expansions cannot be mechanically generated by grammatical rules alone.

In Table 3 the topmost four utterances produced by the child are all of the same grammatical type; all four consist of a proper noun followed by a common noun. However, the four are expanded in quite different ways. In particular the form of the verb changes: it is in the first case in the simple present tense; in the second case the simple past; in the third case the present progressive; in the last case the simple future. All of thse are perfectly grammatical but they are different. The second set of child utterances is formally uniform in that each one consists of a verb followed by a noun. The expansions are again all grammatical but quite unlike, especially with regard to the preposition supplied. In general, then, there are radical changes in the mother's expansions when there are no changes in the formal character of the utterances expanded. It follows that the expansions cannot be produced simply by making grammatically compulsory additions to the child's utterances.

How does a mother decide on the correct expansion of one of her child's utterances? Consider the utterance "Eve lunch." So far as grammar is concerned this utterance could be appropriately expanded in any of a number of ways: "Eve is having lunch"; "Eve had lunch"; "Eve will have lunch"; "Eve's lunch," etc. On the occasion when Eve produced the utterance, however, one expansion seemed more appropriate than any other. It was then the noon hour, Eve was sitting at the table with a plate of food before her, and her spoon and fingers were busy. In these circumstances "Eve lunch" had to mean "Eve is having lunch." A little later when the plate had been stacked in the sink and Eve was getting down from her chair the utterance "Eve lunch" would have suggested the expansion "Eve has had her lunch." Most expansions are not only responsive to the child's words but also to the circumstances attending their utterance.

What kind of instructions will generate the mother's expansions? The following are approximately correct: "Retain the words given in the order given and add those functors that will result in a well-formed simple sentence that is appropriate to the circumstances." These are not instructions that any machine could follow. A machine could act on the instructions only if it were provided with detailed specifications for judging appropriateness and no such specifications can, at present, be written. They exist, however, in implicit form in the brains of mothers and in the brains of all English-speaking adults and so judgments of appropriateness can be made by such adults.

The expansion encodes aspects of reality that are not coded by the child's telegraphic utterance. Functors have meaning but it is meaning that accrues to them in context rather than in isolation. The meanings that are added by functors seem to be nothing less than the basic terms in which we construe reality: the time of an action, whether it is ongoing or completed, whether it is presently relevant or not; the concept of possession and such relational concepts as are coded by *in, on, up, down,* and the like; the difference between a particular instance of a class ("Has anybody seen *the* paper?") and any instance of a class ("Has anybody seen *a* paper?"); the difference between extended substances given shape and size by an "accidental" container (*sand, water, syrup,* etc.) and countable "things" having a characteristic fixed shape and size (a *cup,* a *man,* a *tree,* etc.). It seems to us that a mother in expanding speech may be teaching more than grammar; she may be teaching something like a world-view.

As yet it has not been demonstrated that expansions are *necessary* for learning either grammar or a construction of reality. It has not even been demonstrated that expansions contribute to such learning. All we know is that some parents do expand and their children do learn. It is perfectly possible, however, that children can and do learn simply from hearing their parents or others make well-formed sentences in connection with various nonverbal circumstances. It may not be necessary or even helpful for these sentences to be expansions of utterances of the child. Only experiments contrasting expansion training with simple exposure to English will settle the matter. We hope to do such experiments.

There are, of course, reasons for expecting the expansion transformation to be an effective tutorial technique. By adding something to the words the child has just produced one confirms his response insofar as it is appropriate. In addition one takes him somewhat beyond that response but not greatly beyond it. One encodes additional meanings at a moment when he is most likely to be attending to the cues that can teach that meaning.

INDUCTION OF THE LATENT STRUCTURE

Adam, in the course of the conversation with his mother set down in Table 1, produced one utterance for which no adult is likely ever to have provided an exact model: "No I see truck." His mother elects to expand it as "No, you didn't see it" and this expansion suggests that the child might have created the utterance by reducing an adult model containing the form

Table 4 Utterances Not Likely To Be Imitations

My Cromer suitcase	*You naughty are*
Two foot	*Why it can't turn off?*
A bags	*Put on it*
A scissor	*Cowboy did fighting me*
A this truck	*Put a gas in*

didn't. However, the mother's expansion in this case does some violence to Adam's original version. He did not say *no* as his mother said it, with primary stress and final contour; Adam's *no* had secondary stress and no final contour. It is not easy to imagine an adult model for this utterance. It seems more likely that the utterance was created by Adam as part of a continuing effort to discover the general rules for constructing English negatives.

In Table 4 we have listed some utterances produced by Adam or Eve for which it is difficult to imagine any adult model. It is unlikely that any adult said any of these to Adam or Eve since they are very simple utterances and yet definitely ungrammatical. In addition it is difficult, by adding functors alone, to build any of them up to simple grammatical sentences. Consequently it does not seem likely that these utterances are reductions of adult originals. It is more likely that they are mistakes which externalize the child's search for the regularities of English syntax.

We have long realized that the occurrence of certain kinds of errors on the level of morphology (or word construction) reveals the child's effort to induce regularities from speech. So long as a child speaks correctly, or at any rate so long as he speaks as correctly as the adults he hears, there is no way to tell whether he is simply repeating what he has heard or whether he is actually constructing. However, when he says something like "I digged a hole" we can often be sure that he is constructing. We can be sure because it is unlikely that he would have heard *digged* from anyone and because we can see how, in processing words he has heard, he might have come by *digged.* It looks like an overgeneralization of the regular past inflection. The inductive operations of the child's mind are externalized in such a creation. Overgeneralizations on the level of syntax (or sentence construction) are more difficult to identify because there are so many ways of adding functors so as to build up conceivable models. But this is difficult to do for the examples of Table 4 and for several hundred other utterances in our records.

The processes of imitation and expansion are not sufficient to account for the degree of linguistic competence that children regularly acquire. These processes alone cannot teach more than the sum total of sentences that speakers of English have either modeled for a child to imitate or built up from a child's reductions. However, a child's linguistic competence extends far beyond this sum total of sentences. All children are able to understand and construct sentences they have never heard but which are nevertheless well-formed, well-formed in terms of general rules that are implicit in the sentences the child has heard. Somehow, then, every child processes the speech to which he is exposed so as to induce from it a latent structure. This

Table 5 Noun Phrases in Isolation and Rule for Generating Noun Phrases at Time 1

A coat	More coffee
A celery[a]	More nut[a]
A Becky[a]	Two sock[a]
A hands[a]	Two shoes
The top	Two tinker-toy[a]
My Mommy	Big boot
That Adam	Poor man
My stool	Little top
That knee	Dirty knee

$$N P \rightarrow M + N$$

M → a, big, dirty, little, more, my, poor, that, the, two.
N → Adam, Becky, boot, coat, coffee, knee, man, Mommy, nut, sock, stool, tinker-toy, top, and very many others.

[a] Ungrammatical for an adult.

latent rule structure is so general that a child can spin out its implications all his life long. It is both semantic and syntactic. The discovery of latent structure is the greatest of the processes involved in language acquisition and the most difficult to understand. We will provide an example of how the analysis can proceed by discussing the evolution in child speech of noun phrases.

A noun phrase in adult English includes a noun but also more than a noun. One variety consists of a noun with assorted modifiers: *The girl; The pretty girl; That pretty girl; My girl,* etc. All of these are constructions which have the same syntactic privileges as do nouns alone. One can use a noun phrase in isolation to name or request something; one can use it in sentences, in subject position or in object position or in predicate nominative position. All of these are slots that nouns alone can also fill. A larger construction having the same syntactic privileges as its "head" word is called in linguistics an "endocentric" construction and noun phrases are endocentric constructions.

For both Adam and Eve, in the early records, noun phrases usually occur as total independent utterances rather than as components of sentences. Table 5 presents an assortment of such utterances at Time 1. They consist in each case of some sort of modifier, just one, preceding a noun. The modifiers, or as they are sometimes called the "pivot" words, are a much smaller class than the noun class. Three students of child speech have independently discovered thtat this kind of construction is extremely common when children first begin to combine words.[5, 6, 7]

It is possible to generalize the cases of Table 5 into a simple implicit

[5] M. D. S. Braine, "The ontogeny of English phrase structure: the first phrase," *Language,* XXXIX (1963), 1–13.
[6] W. Miller and Susan Ervin, "The development of grammar in child language," Ursula Bellugi and R. Brown, eds., *The Acquisition of Language, Child Developm. Monogr.* (1964).
[7] Brown and Fraser, *op. cit.*

rule. The rule symbolized in Table 5 reads: "In order to form a noun phrase of this type, select first one word from the small class of modifiers and select, second, one word from the large class of nouns." This is a "generative" rule by which we mean it is a program that would actually serve to build constructions of the type in question. It is offered as a model of the mental mechanism by which Adam and Eve generated such utterances. Furthermore, judging from our work with other children and from the reports of Braine and of Miller and Ervin, the model describes a mechanism present in many children when their average utterance is approximately two morphemes long.

We have found that even in our earliest records the M + N construction is sometimes used as a component of larger constructions. For instance, Eve said: "Fix a Lassie" and "Turn the page" and "A horsie stuck" and Adam even said: "Adam wear a shirt." There are, at first, only a handful of these larger constructions but there are very many constructions in which single nouns occur in subject or in object position.

Let us look again at the utterances of Table 5 and the rule generalizing them. The class M does not correspond with any syntactic class of adult English. In the class M are articles, a possessive pronoun, a cardinal number, a demonstrative adjective or pronoun, a quantifier, and some descriptive adjectives—a mixed bag indeed. For adult English these words cannot belong to the same syntactic class because they have very different privileges of occurrence in sentences. For the children the words do seem to function as one class having the common privilege of occurrence before nouns.

If the initial words of the utterances in Table 5 are treated as one class M then many utterances are generated which an adult speaker would judge to be ungrammatical. Consider the indefinite article a. Adults use it only to modify common count nouns in the singular such as coat, dog, cup, etc. We would not say a celery, or a cereal, or a dirt; celery, cereal, and dirt are mass nouns. We would not say a Becky or a Jimmy; Becky and Jimmy are proper nouns. We would not say a hands or a shoes; hands and shoes are plural nouns. Adam and Eve, at first, did form ungrammatical combinations such as these.

The numeral two we use only with count nouns in the plural. We would not say two sock since sock is singular, nor two water since water is a mass noun. The word more we use before count nouns in the plural (more nuts) or mass nouns in the singular (more coffee). Adam and Eve made a number of combinations involving two or more that we would not make.

Given the initial very undiscriminating use of words in the class M it follows that one dimension of development must be a progressive differentiation of privileges, which means the division of M into smaller classes. There must also be subdivision of the noun class (N) for the reason that the privileges of occurrence of various kinds of modifiers must be described in terms of such sub-varieties of N as the common noun and proper noun, the count noun and mass noun. There must eventually emerge a distinction between nouns singular and nouns plural since this distinction figures in the privileges of occurrence of the several sorts of modifiers.

Sixteen weeks after our first records from Adam and Eve (Time 2), the

Table 6 Subdivision of the Modifier Class

(A) PRIVILEGES PECULIAR TO ARTICLES	
Obtained	Not Obtained
A blue flower	*Blue a flower*
A nice nap	*Nice a nap*
A your car	*Your a car*
A my pencil	*My a pencil*

(B) PRIVILEGES PECULIAR TO DEMONSTRATIVE PRONOUNS	
Obtained	Not Obtained
That my cup	*My that cup*
That a horse	*A that horse*
That a blue flower	*A that blue flower*
	Blue a that flower

differentiation process had begun. By this time there were distributional reasons for separating out articles (*a, the*) from demonstrative pronouns (*this, that*) and both of these from the residual class of modifiers. Some of the evidence for this conclusion appears in Table 6. In general one syntactic class is distinguished from another when the members of one class have combinational privileges not enjoyed by the members of the other. Consider, for example, the reasons for distinguishing articles (Art) from modifiers in general (M). Both articles and modifiers appeared in front of nouns in two-word utterances. However, in three-word utterances that were made up from the total pool of words and that had a noun in final position, the privileges of *a* and *the* were different from the privileges of all other modifiers. The articles occurred in initial position followed by a member of class M other than an article. No other modifier occurred in this first position; notice the "Not obtained" examples of Table 6A. If the children had produced utterances like those (for example, *blue a flower, your a car*) there would have been no difference in the privileges of occurrence of articles and modifiers and therefore no reason to separate out articles.

The record of Adam is especially instructive. He created such notably ungrammatical combinations as "a your car" and "a my pencil." It is very unlikely that adults provided models for these. They argue strongly that Adam regarded all the words in the residual M class as syntactic equivalents and so generated these very odd utterances in which possessive pronouns appear where descriptive adjectives would be more acceptable.

Table 6 also presents some of the evidence for distinguishing demonstrative pronouns (Dem) from articles and modifiers (Table 6B). The pronouns occurred first and ahead of articles in three-and-four-word utterances —a position that neither articles nor modifiers ever filled. The sentences with demonstrative pronouns are recognizable as reductions which omit the copular verb *is*. Such sentences are not noun phrases in adult English and ultimately they will not function as noun phrases in the speech of the children,

Table 7   Rules for Generating Noun Phrases at Time 2

$NP_1 \rightarrow Dem + Art + M + N$	$NP \rightarrow (Dem) + (Art) + (M) + N$
$NP_2 \rightarrow Art + M + N$	
$NP_3 \rightarrow Dem + M + N$	
$NP_4 \rightarrow Art + N$	( ) means class within
$NP_5 \rightarrow M + N$	parentheses is optional
$NP_6 \rightarrow Dem + N$	
$NP_7 \rightarrow Dem + Art + N$	

but for the present they are not distinguishable distributionally from noun phrases.

Recall now the generative formula of Table 5 which constructs noun phrases by simply placing a modifier (M) before a noun (N). The differentiation of privileges illustrated in Table 6, and the syntactic classes this evidence motivates us to create, complicate the formula for generating noun phrases. In Table 7 we have written a single general formula for producing all noun phrases at Time 2 $[NP \rightarrow (Dem) + (Art) + (M) + N]$ and also the numerous more specific rules which are summarized by the general formula.

By the time of the thirteenth transcription, twenty-six weeks after we began our study, privileges of occurrence were much more finely differentiated and syntactic classes were consequently more numerous. From the distributional evidence we judged that Adam had made five classes of his original class M: articles, descriptive adjectives, possessive pronouns, demonstrative pronouns, and a residual class of modifiers. The generative rules of Table 7 had become inadequate; there were no longer, for instance, any combinations like "A your car." Eve had the same set except that she used two residual classes of modifiers. In addition nouns had begun to subdivide for both children. The usage of proper nouns had become clearly distinct from the usage of count nouns. For Eve the evidence justified separating count nouns from mass nouns, but for Adam it still did not. Both children by this time were frequently pluralizing nouns but as yet their syntactic control of the singular-plural distinction was imperfect.

In summary, one major aspect of the development of general structure in child speech is a progressive differentiation in the usage of words and therefore a progressive differentiation of syntactic classes. At the same time, however, there is an integrative process at work. From the first, an occasional noun phrase occurred as a component of some larger construction. At first these noun phrases were just two words long and the range of positions in which they could occur was small. With time the noun phrases grew longer, were more frequently used, and were used in a greater range of positions. The noun phrase structure as a whole, in all the permissible combinations of modifiers and nouns, was assuming the combinational privileges enjoyed by nouns in isolation.

In Table 8 we have set down some of the sentence positions in which both nouns and noun phrases occurred in the speech of Adam and Eve. It is

Table 8 Some Privileges of the Noun Phrase

Noun Positions	Noun Phrase Positions
That (flower)	*That (a blue flower)*
Where (ball) go?	*Where (the puzzle) go?*
Adam write (penguin)	*Doggie eat (the breakfast)*
(Horsie) stop	*(A horsie) crying*
Put (hat) on	*Put (the red hat) on*

the close match between the positions of nouns alone and of nouns with modifiers in the speech of Adam and Eve that justifies us in calling the longer constructions noun phrases. These longer constructions are, as they should be, endocentric; the head word alone has the same syntactic privileges as the head word with its modifiers. The continuing failure to find in noun phrase positions whole constructions of the type "That a blue flower" signals the fact that these constructions are telegraphic versions of predicate nominative sentences omitting the verb form *is*. Examples of the kind of construction not obtained are: "That (that a blue flower)"; "Where (that a blue flower)?"

For adults the noun phrase is a subwhole of the sentence, what linguists call an "immediate constituent." The noun phrase has a kind of psychological unity. There are signs that the noun phrase was also an immediate constituent for Adam and Eve. Consider the sentence using the separable verb *put on*. The noun phrase in "Put the red hat on" is, as a whole, fitted in between the verb and the particle even as is the noun alone in "Put hat on." What is more, however, the location of pauses in the longer sentence, on several occasions, suggested the psychological organization: "Put . . . the red hat . . . on" rather than "Put the red . . . hat on" or "Put the . . . red hat on." In addition to this evidence the use of pronouns suggests that the noun phrase is a psychological unit.

The unity of noun phrases in adult English is evidenced, in the first place, by the syntactic equivalence between such phrases and nouns alone. It is evidenced, in the second place, by the fact that pronouns are able to substitute for total noun phrases. In our immediately preceding sentence the pronoun "It" stands for the rather involved construction from the first sentence of this paragraph: "The unity of noun phrases in adult English." The words called "pronouns" in English would more aptly be called "pro-noun-phrases" since it is the phrase rather than the noun which they usually replace. One does not replace "unity" with "it" and say "The *it* of noun phrases in adult English." In the speech of Adam and Eve, too, the pronoun came to function as a replacement for the noun phrase. Some of the clearer cases appear in Table 9.

Adam characteristically externalizes more of his learning than does Eve and his record is especially instructive in connection with the learning of pronouns. In his first eight records, the first sixteen weeks of the study, Adam quite often produced sentences containing both the pronoun and the noun or noun phrase that the pronoun should have replaced. One can here see the

Table 9 Pronouns Replacing Nouns or Noun Phrases and Pronouns Produced Together with Nouns or Noun Phrases

Noun Phrases Replaced by Pronouns	Pronouns and Noun Phrases in Same Utterances
Hit ball	*Mommy get it ladder*
Get it	*Mommy get it my ladder*
Ball go?	*Saw it ball*
Go get it	*Miss it garage*
Made it	*I miss it cowboy boot*
Made a ship	*I Adam drive that*
Fix a tricycle	*I Adam drive*
Fix it	*I Adam don't*

equivalence in the process of establishment. First the substitute is produced and then, as if in explication, the form or forms that will eventually be replaced by the substitute. Adam spoke out his pronoun antecedents as chronological consequents. This is additional evidence of the unity of the noun phrase since the noun phrases *my ladder* and *cowboy boot* are linked with *it* in Adam's speech in just the same way as the nouns *ladder* and *ball*.

We have described three processes involved in the child's acquisition of syntax. It is clear that the last of these, the induction of latent structure, is by far the most complex. It looks as if this last process will put a serious strain on any learning theory thus far conceived by psychology. The very intricate simultaneous differentiation and integration that constitutes the evolution of the noun phrase is more reminiscent of the biological development of an embryo than it is of the acquisition of a conditional reflex.

Social Class Differences in the Relevance of Language to Socialization

Basil Bernstein and Dorothy Henderson
UNIVERSITY OF LONDON INSTITUTE OF EDUCATION

SUMMARY

This paper reports social class differences in the emphasis placed upon the use of language in two areas of the socialization of the child: interperson relationships and the acquisition of basic skills. The sample of 100 mothers is a sub-sample of 120 mothers who live in a middle-class area and 192 mothers who live in a working-class area. (The correlation between area and the social class position of the family is 0.74.) The results obtained from the

Reprinted from *Sociology*, 1969, 3, No. 1. By permission of the authors and Clarendon Press, Oxford. A brief section on methodological criticisms has been omitted.

The work reported in this paper was supported by grants from the Department of Education and Science and the Ford Foundation to whom, gratefully, acknowledgment is made. Thanks are also given to the local education authorities for their close help and cooperation in the research.

228

use of a closed schedule show that the middle-class mothers, relative to the working-class mothers, place a much greater emphasis upon the use of language in the person area; whereas the working-class mothers, relative to the middle-class mothers, place a greater emphasis upon the use of language in the transmission of basic skills. The results are consonant with the prediction derived from the theory of restricted and elaborated linguistic codes which has also been used to generate a model for the understanding of social learning and forms of cultural discontinuity between the home and the school.

INTRODUCTION

Perhaps one of the most important movements in the sciences since the war is the convergence of interest upon the study of basic processes of communication and their regulative functions. The one discipline which appears so far least affected is sociology. However, from different quarters there are now signs of growing interest (Grimshaw, 1967; Fishman, 1966; Cicourel, 1964; Garfinkle, 1967; Hymes, 1968). The study of the educationally disadvantaged has also led to a concentration of research into the process of language acquisition, into the relationships between language and cognition and into the social antecedents and regulative consequences of forms of language use.

The Sociological Research Unit at the University of London is engaged upon an exploratory study of forms of familial socialization which affect orientations towards the use of language. We shall present here the results of a closed schedule designed to reveal the relative emphasis which members of social class groups place upon the use of language in different areas of the socialization of the preschool child. Although this report is confined to a study only of the mothers' *orientation* towards the relevance of language, as this group of mothers have been interviewed twice within a three-year period and because two speech samples have been collected from their children when aged five years and seven years, it should prove to be possible to obtain some measure of both the reliability and validity of the mothers' reports.

This report is the first step in the analysis of the section of the second questionnaire given to the mothers which enquired into the orientation of the mother towards various uses of language. As the other sections were concerned with the decision-making process within the family, its kinship and community relationships, the procedures of control and role definition, the relationships between home and school, we can relate the orientation towards various uses of language to a range of variables.

In the discussion section of the paper we present a model which gives a sociological explanation of social learning in terms of the mediation of the linguistic process in socialization.

HYPOTHESES

The following hypotheses (derived from Bernstein 1966 and 1968) are to be tested:

(1) Both middle-class and working-class would place greater emphasis upon the use of language in interpersonal aspects of socialization than the emphasis placed upon language in the socialization into basic skills.

(2) The shift in emphasis in the use of language from the skill to the person area would be much greater for the middle-class group.

(3) Within the skill area the middle-class group would place a greater emphasis upon language in the transmission of principles.

DESCRIPTION OF THE SAMPLE

The total sample consists of 311 mothers drawn from two areas, one a working-class area and the other a middle-class area. The r between area and social class of the parents is 0.74. The index of social class was constructed by W. Brandis of the Sociological Research Unit and is based upon the terminal education and occupation of husband and wife. A full description of the Index will be found in W. Brandis and D. Henderson (1968). Social class in measured on a ten-point scale, 0–9. The sample used in this paper consists of 50 mothers randomly selected from the middle-class area and 50 mothers randomly selected from the working-class area. It was necessary to limit the sample size of this study in order that a detailed analysis could be carried out, and to examine possible social class differences in response to the schedule. In terms of the ten-point scale, the mean social class position of the middle-class group is 2.8 and the mean social class position of the working-class group is 6.9.

THE CLOSED SCHEDULE[1]

The closed schedule consisted of a list of eleven statements which covered the major aspects of socialization. As the schedule was presented, the interviewer put to each mother the question which was printed above the list of statements: "If parents could not speak, how much *more* difficult do you think it would be for them to do the following things with young children who had not yet started school?" The mother's attention was then directed to the statements and she was asked to assess the difficulty she thought dumb parents would experience in dealing with each situation. A six-point scale was provided: very much more difficult, much more difficult,

[1] The schedule was designed by Marian Bernstein and Basil Bernstein.

more difficult, not too difficult, fairly easy, easy. The statements are listed below in the order in which they were presented on the schedule:

1. Teaching them everyday tasks like dressing, and using a knife and fork.   (Motor skill)
2. Helping them to make things.   (Constructional skill)
3. Drawing their attention to different shapes.   (Perceptual skill)
4. Playing games with them.   (Dummy)
5. Showing them what is right and wrong.   (Moral principles)
6. Letting them know what you are feeling.   (Mother-oriented affective)
7. Showing them how things work.   (Cognitive)
8. Helping them to work things out for themselves.   (Independent-cognitive)
9. Disciplining them.   (Control)
10. Showing them how pleased you are with their progress.   (Dummy)
11. Dealing with them when they are unhappy.   (Child-oriented affective)

Statements 4 and 10 were deliberately inserted as dummy statements designed to move the mother's responses across to "fairly easy" and "easy" and thus mitigate the emphasis placed on "difficulty" in the initial question. In fact, these statements elicited the responses "fairly easy" or "easy" from 72 percent of the middle-class mothers and from 76 percent of the working-class mothers. No other statements shifted both groups to the "easy" points of the scale to this extent. Four of the statements—1, 2, 3, and 7—were concerned with the transmission of skills. Five of the statements—5, 6, 8, 9, and 11—were concerned with aspects of social control. Statements 1, 2, 3, and 7 will be referred to as the *skill* area of statements, and statements 5, 6, 8, 9, and 11 will be referred to as the *person* area of statements. The points of the scale "very much more difficult," "much more difficult," and "more difficult" will be referred to as the "difficult" points of the scale, whilst "fairly easy" and "easy" will be referred to as the "easy" points of the scale. "Not too difficult" will be referred to as the mid-point of the scale.

It will be remembered that the aim of the schedule was to examine the effect of the social class position of the mothers on their perception of the role of language as a socializing process. In order to obtain such information it was necessary to focus the mother's attention upon the relevance of language across a number of different areas. It was thought that mothers would experience great difficulty if they were simply asked to what extent they relied upon language when dealing with their children. We constructed a general situation such that each mother was faced with a problem of comparison. She also had to access the difficulty of transmitting skills and dealing with inter-personal processes without language. This focused her attention upon the relevance of the linguistic component of the interaction. At the same time, it was necessary to ensure, as far as possible, that the mother should not feel that the problem was a challenge to her own extra-verbal ingenuity with her child, and so the problem was presented with the general referents *parents* and *young children*. It was equally necessary to preclude the possible use of other linguistic alternatives and therefore we stated the problem in terms of young children who had *not yet started school* and were thus unlikely to be able to read written instructions or explanations.

METHOD

The analysis was carried out in three stages. In the first stage we examined the population scores, in the second stage we examined the responses of individual mothers within each social class to each statement, and in the third stage analyses of variance were carried out in order to examine the interaction between the social class position of the mothers and their responses within and between the *skill* and *person* areas of statements.

First Stage
The population scores enabled us:

(A) to examine the distribution of maternal responses across the scale for each statement (Table 1).

(B) to examine the total number of responses across the scale within each area of statements (Table 2).

(C) to compare the total population scores within each area of statements in terms of "difficult" and "easy" responses (Table 3).

We were then in a position to compare differences in patterns of response in relation to the statements.

Second Stage
The difference between the number of "difficult" responses and the number of "easy" responses to each statement was examined in terms of the social class of the mothers. This procedure also enabled us to compare the "difficult" to "easy" responses for each statement with reference to social class (Table 4).

Third Stage
(A)   A 2 × 2 analysis of variance on repeated measures was carried out. This type of analysis enabled us to control for within-person variance as well as for between-people variance and residual variance. Each point on the scale was assigned a score as follows:

Very much more difficult	+3
Much more difficult	+2
More difficult	+1
Not too difficult	0
Fairly easy	−1
Easy	−2

The basic unit of the analysis here was the individual mother's mean response score to the four *skill* statements. This was compared to the mother's mean response score to the five *person* statements. The analysis enabled us to test

Table 1 Distributions of Population Responses to Statements

	The Scale[a]	Skill Statements				Person Statements				
		1	2	3	7	5	6	8	9	11
	0	0	1	1	3	12	12	13	19	11
	1	0	4	5	9	12	12	12	8	11
Middle-class	2	7	12	11	13	19	12	18	14	15
responses	3	20	21	16	17	5	11	4	8	9
	4	15	7	12	7	2	2	3	0	2
	5	8	5	5	1	0	1	0	1	2
	0	9	4	4	4	4	10	11	11	10
	1	5	5	5	6	13	4	9	7	4
Working-class	2	3	7	6	8	11	12	14	13	11
responses	3	23	23	27	20	14	10	11	8	10
	4	5	7	6	10	4	8	4	9	8
	5	5	4	2	2	4	6	1	2	7

[a] Note: 0 = Very much more difficult
1 = Much more difficult
2 = More difficult
3 = Not too difficult
4 = Fairly easy
5 = Easy

for significance the differential emphasis upon difficulty in response to each area of statements and its relationship with social class.

(B) A 2 × 5 analysis of variance on repeated measures was carried out on the maternal responses to each of the statements within the *person* area, in order to find out whether there was a significant interaction effect between the social class of the mothers and the individual statements.

(C) For the same reason a 2 × 4 analysis was carried out on the maternal responses to the individual statements within the *skill* area.

RESULTS

First, we will deal briefly with the results which were found when the population scores were examined. It must be emphasized that the main justification for this stage of the analysis was to discover whether differences between the responses to the statements, as well as differences between the social class groups, were sufficiently large to justify carrying out a more sensitive analysis on the data. We will then deal at greater length with the results of the second and third stages of the analysis.

The Population Responses

The distribution of the population responses across the scale shows that the patterns of distributions differ markedly between the *person* statements and the *skill* statements (Table 1). The responses cluster at the "different"

Table 2 Summed Population Responses for the Person Area
and the Skill Area

	Scale:	0	1	2	3	4	5	Total
Person statements	M.C.	67	55	78	37	9	4	250
	W.C.	46	37	61	53	33	20	250
Skill statements	M.C.	5	18	43	74	41	19	200
	W.C.	21	21	24	93	28	13	200

points of the scale in response to the *person* statements, whereas the distribution is normal, with "not too difficult" operating as the mid-point, in response to the *skill* statements. Since the two areas of statements were clearly eliciting quite different patterns of response, we decided to compare the summed scores across all the statements within each area for each point of the scale. We then found that although both middle-class and working-class mothers showed a marked move to "difficult" responses within the *person* area in comparison with their responses within the skill *area*, the relative shift was greater in the case of the middle-class responses (Table 2). In order to make a more stringent comparison the responses "very much more difficult" and "much more difficult" were summed within each social class and compared with the summed responses "fairly easy" and "easy." We found that the social class differences in response within each area of statements were very great. In particular, the shift of middle-class responses from the *skill* area to the *person* area in terms of the emphasis upon difficulty was just over 5 to 1, whereas the shift of working-class responses from the *skill* area to the *person* area was just under 2 to 1 (Table 3).

Individual Responses to Statements

In the next stage of the analysis we examined the *individual* responses within each social class to each statement, in terms of the ratios of "difficult" to "easy" responses. Again we found that both middle-class and working-class mothers had shifted to the "difficult" points of the scale in response to the *person* statements. But *within* the *person* area, middle-class mothers placed greater emphasis upon difficulty than did working-class mothers (Table 4).

Table 3 Summed Difficult/Easy Population Responses in Each Area

		Difficult (0, 1)	Easy (4, 5)
Person statements	M.C.	122	13
	W.C.	83	53
		Difficult (0, 1)	Easy (4, 5)
Sikll statements	M.C.	23	60
	W.C.	42	41

Table 4 Number of Mothers Giving Difficult/Easy Responses
             to Individual Statements

		Skill Statements				Person Statements				
		1	2	3	7	5	6	8	9	11
Number of mothers giving "difficult" (0, 1) responses	Middle Class:	7	17	17	25	43	36	43	41	37
	Working Class:	17	16	15	18	28	26	34	31	25
Number of mothers giving "easy" (4, 5) responses	Middle Class:	23	12	17	8	2	3	3	1	4
	Working Class:	10	11	8	12	8	14	5	11	15

Within the *skill* area we found a reversal in the pattern of response on the part of middle-class mothers. Middle-class mothers were less likely to give an "easy" response to the statement "Showing them how things work" than the working-class mothers. Table 4 also shows that more working-class mothers than middle-class mothers gave a "difficult" response to the statement "Teaching them everyday tasks like dressing, and using a knife and fork."

The Analysis of Variance

(A) The results of the 2 × 2 analysis of variance on repeated measures show that the differential emphasis on difficulty between the two areas is highly significant ($F_{1, 98} = 294.53$, $p > .001$). Very much greater emphasis was placed upon difficulty within the *person* area of statements than within the *skill* area of statements. However, the analysis also showed that, although greater emphasis was placed on the difficulty of dealing with the situations described in the *person* area by *all* the mothers, the difference between the responses of the middle-class mothers in relation to the two areas of statements was significantly greater than the difference between the responses of the working-class mothers ($F_{1, 98} = 73.60$, $p > .001$). Middle-class mothers placed much *greater* emphasis upon the difficulty of doing the things described in the *person* area than the working-class mothers, but they placed much *less* emphasis upon the difficulty of doing the things described in the *skill* area than the working-class mothers. This highly significant interaction effect illustrates the polarisation of the responses of middle-class mothers in relation to the two areas of statements.

We will now turn to the results of the analyses of maternal responses *within* each area.

(B) Within the *skill* area the results show that middle-class mothers placed very much less emphasis on language than working-class mothers on the difficulty of doing the things described in these statements, and that this difference in response was highly significant ($F_{1, 98} = 228.78$, $p > .001$). This

Table 5 2 x 2 Analysis of Mothers' Responses in Each of the Two Areas

Source of Variation	S.S.	d.f.	M.S.	F	Sign Level
Between subjects	104.66	99	1.05	—	N.S.
Social class	2.31	1	2.31	—	N.S.
Subjects within groups	102.35	98	1.04		
Within subjects	70.65	100	0.70	—	N.S.
Statements	44.18	1	44.18	294.53	.001
Social class x statements	11.04	1	11.04	73.60	.001
Statements x subjects within groups	15.43	98	0.15		

Summary Table of Mean Scores

	Statements		
	Skill Area	Person Area	Total $\bar{x}$
$\bar{x}$ Middle Class	.07	1.48	.78
$\bar{x}$ Working Class	.33	.80	.56
$\bar{x}$ Total	.20	1.04	

Table 6 2 x 4 Analysis of Mothers' Responses to the Skill Statements

Source of Variation	S.S.	d.f.	N.S.	F	Sign Level
Between subjects	155.25	99	1.56	—	N.S.
Social class	272.25	1	272.25	228.78	.001
Subjects within groups	−117.00	98	−1.19		
Within subjects	84.50	300	0.28	—	N.S.
Statements	3.76	3	1.25	—	N.S.
Statements x social class	−258.38	3	−86.12	74.88	.001
Statements x subjects within groups	339.12	294	1.15		

Summary Table of Mean Scores

	Skill Statements				
	1	2	3	7	Total x
$\bar{x}$ Middle Class	−.48	.12	.04	.62	.30
$\bar{x}$ Working Class	.48	.28	.36	.36	1.50
$\bar{x}$ Total	.01	.20	.20	.49	

Table 7   2 x 5 Analysis of Mothers' Responses to the Person Statements

Source of Variation	S.S.	d.f.	M.S.	F	Sign Level
Between subjects	466.44	99	4.71	—	N.S.
Social class	59.17	1	59.17	14.25	.001
Subjects within groups	407.27	98	4.15		
Within subjects	265.20	400	0.66	—	N.S.
Statements	16.38	4	4.09	6.49	.001
Statements x social class	3.01	4	0.75	—	N.S.
Statements x subjects within groups	245.81	392	0.63		

Summary Table of Mean Scores

	Person Statements					
	5	6	8	9	11	Total $\bar{x}$
$\bar{x}$ Middle Class	1.54	1.36	1.56	1.70	1.28	7.44
$\bar{x}$ Working Class	.74	.60	1.18	.94	.54	4.00
$\bar{x}$ Total	1.14	.98	1.37	1.32	.91	

finding replicates the result found by the previous analysis. However, a highly significant interaction effect between the social class of the mothers and responses to individual *skill* statements was revealed by this analysis. Working-class mothers placed significantly greater emphasis on difficulty in response to the statement "Teaching them everyday tasks like dressing and using a knife and fork," than did middle-class mothers; middle-class mothers, on the other hand, placed significantly greater emphasis on difficulty in response to the statement "Showing them how things work" than did working-class mothers ($F_{3, 294} = 74.88$, $p > .001$).

(C) The 2 × 5 analysis of maternal responses to the five *person* statements shows that middle-class mothers considered that these situations would be more difficult to deal with without language than did working-class mothers. This differential emphasis on difficulty in relation to the *person* statements is highly significant ($F_{1, 98} = 14.25$, $p > .001$). A highly significant main order effect, *irrespective* of the social class position of the mothers, arose out of differences in response to individual statements ($F_{4, 392} = 6.49$, $p > .001$).

This result shows that individual statements within the *person* area had elicited very different responses from both middle-class and working-class mothers. We were therefore interested to know how the responses differed *between* the *person* statements. In other words, how were the *person* statements *ranked* in difficulty? In order to clarify this result we used the Newman-Keuls procedure which tests for significance of the differences between all possible pairs of means. Sample means were used because the analysis did not reveal a significant interaction effect between social class and individual

Table 7A Test on Means Using Newman-Keuls Procedure[a]

		11	6	5	9	8
Person Statements						
Ordered means		.91	.98	1.14	1.32	1.37
		11	6	5	9	8
Differences between						
pairs	11		.07	.23	.41	.46
	6			.16	.34	.39
	5				.18	.23
	9					.05
$SB = .002$		$r =$	2	3	4	5
q, 99 $(r, 392)$			3.64	4.12	4.40	4.60
$SB\ q$, 99 $(r, 392)$			.07	.08	.09	.09
		11	6	5	9	8
	11			a	a	a
	6			a	a	a
	5			a	a	a
	9					

[a] Winer (1962).

statements. The Newman-Keuls test shows that the responses of the mothers, irrespective of social class, are subject to a significant three-way split in relation to particular *person* statements.

This distinction between the statements is significant at the .01 level. The ranking of statements in terms of difficulty is shown below.

Person Statements	Scale of Difficulty
8. Helping them to work things out for themselves. ⎫ 9. Disciplining them. ⎬	Most difficult
5. Showing them what is right and wrong.	Less difficult
6. Letting them know what you are feeling. ⎫ 11. Dealing with them when they are unhappy. ⎬	Least difficult

There was no significant difference in response between statements 8 and 9, or between statements 6 and 11.

SUMMARY OF RESULTS

Differences in response were shown to be due to (a) the statements within each area, (b) the social class of the mothers, and (c) the interaction between social class and individual statements. We find that middle-class mothers consider language less relevant to the situations described by the *skill* statements than do working-class mothers. There is one exception. Middle-class mothers considered that "Showing them how things work," would be *more* difficult to deal with without language than working-class mothers. Conversely, middle-class mothers place greater emphasis upon language than working-class mothers in response to the *person* statements. However, *all* the mothers considered the *person* situations more difficult to cope with than the *skill* situations. Within the *person* area all mothers assign the greatest difficulty to statements 8 and 9, less difficulty to statement 5, and least difficulty to statements 6 and 11: this finding strongly suggests that the mothers were discriminating between the "difficult" points of the scale and that this discrimination applied irrespective of the social class of the mothers.

• • •

DISCUSSION

The results show that the middle class, relative to the working class, places a greater emphasis upon the use of language in dealing with situations within the person area. The working class, relative to the middle class, places a greater emphasis upon the use of language in the transmission of various skills. However, within the skill area the middle class places a greater emphasis upon the use of language in their response to the statement, "Showing them how things work," whereas within the same area the working class places a greater emphasis upon the use of language in response to the statement, "Teaching them every day tasks like dressing, and using a knife and fork."

Can these differences in emphasis be accounted for in terms of differences in the relevance of these two *areas* for the social classes? In other words, does the move to language simply reflect the relevance of the area? Or is it the case that both areas respectively have equal relevance to the social classes but their verbal realization is different? It is unlikely that the middle class relative to the working class value basic skills less and yet it is this group which places a reduced emphasis upon language in the skill area. It would be just as difficult to maintain that socialization into relationships between persons is not of *equal* relevance to every sub-cultural group, although the *form* of that socialization may well vary. On the other hand, the very marked shift by *both* groups towards language in the person area and away from language in the skill area may well reflect the greater importance of control over persons rather than control over the development of skills in the socialization of the very young child. It is therefore unlikely that the shifts in emphasis placed upon the use of language in each of the two areas respectively, by the two social class groups can be explained in terms of the difference in the relevance of the skill area and the person area. It might be that middle-class mothers can conceive of a variety of ways, other than linguistic, for the acquisition of skills and for this reason these mothers place less emphasis upon language, whereas the working-class mothers can conceive of fewer alternatives to language for the acquisition of skills. This might seem to be a plausible explanation, but we think that it by no means accounts for the differences between the social classes.

We shall argue that the explanation is to be found in the nature of the social relationship when skills and person relationships are transmitted. If it is the case that in the working-class knowledge is transmitted through a social relationship in which the receiver is relatively passive and if, in the middle class, knowledge is transmitted through a social relationship in which the receiver is active, then we might expect the distribution of responses which have been revealed. It may be that motor, perceptual, and manipulative skills are acquired by the child in the middle class by his exposure to varied and attractive stimuli which the child explores on his *own* terms. In other words, in the acquisition of motor, perceptual, and manipulative skills, the child regulates his own learning in a carefully controlled environment. It is of significance that despite the relatively greater emphasis placed upon language in the skill area by the working-class group, the middle class place greater emphasis upon language in response to the statement, "Showing them how things work." It is likely that this statement, for the middle class, raises questions of the transmission of principles, whereas the other three statements within the same area do *not*. If this is the case, then the situation for the middle-class child is particularly fortunate. For, on the one hand, he is socialized into elementary skill learning through role relationships which emphasize autonomy *and* he has access to principles.

In the working-class group, the concept of learning may well be different and, therefore, the form the social relationship takes when skills are acquired would be of a different order. The concept of learning here seems to be less one of self-regulated learning in an arranged environment and more a concept of a didactive theory of learning implying a passive receiver, in which a mother has little alternative but to tell or instruct a child. Although the emphasis in the working-class group, relative to the middle class, is upon language, presumably upon *telling* or instructing, the child is much less likely to receive explanations of principles. Thus it may be that the working-class child learns skills in terms only of an understanding of the operations they entail, whereas the middle-class child learns both the operations and principles.

Other work of the Sociological Research Unit can be referred to here in support of these hypotheses. Two years prior to the interview in which the present schedule was administered, a sample of 351 middle-class and working-class mothers (of which the sample used in this paper is a sub-sample) were given a questionnaire in which the mothers were invited to give their views upon a range of experiences relevant to their child's behavior in the infant school. We found that when middle-class mothers were asked to rank in order of importance six possible uses of toys, they ranked more highly than did the working-class mothers "To find out about things" (Bernstein & Young, 1967). Further, middle-class mothers saw the role of the infant school child as an active role, whereas the working-class mothers tended to see this role as a passive one (Jones, 1966). Middle-class mothers, relative to working-class mothers, indicated that "play" in the infant school had educational significance (Bernstein, 1967).

It would appear then that the difference in the response of middle-class and working-class mothers to the relevance of language in the acquisition of various skills is more likely to arise out of differences in the concept of learning than out of differences between the social classes in terms of the value placed upon the learning of such skills. The socialization of the middle-class child into the acquisition of skills is into both operations and principles which are learned in a social context which emphasises *autonomy*. In the case of the working-class child, his socialization into skills emphasizes operations rather than principles learned in a social context where the child is accorded *reduced autonomy*.

We will now turn to discuss the differences between the social classes in their emphasis upon the use of language in interpersonal contexts. The results are very clear. Where the context is interpersonal, the middle-class, relative to the working class, move markedly towards the use of language. Further, the shift in the emphasis upon language from the skill area to the person area is very much greater in the middle class than in the working class. Thus, the verbal realization of affects, moral principles and their application to behavior, and independence in cognitive functioning, is much more likely to be linguistically elaborated in the middle class than in the working class. This is *not* to say that these aspects of socialization do not have the same significance in the working class, only that (according to the mothers' responses) language is of less relevance in the form of the socialization. Indeed, Table 7A shows that *both* classes rank the statements (in the person area) in the same order of difficulty.

It is not possible to infer from the mothers' responses what they actually would say to the child, but again we can refer to evidence obtained from the first interview with the mothers two years earlier. This evidence strongly suggests that:

(1) the middle-class mothers are more likely than working-class mothers to take up the child's attempts to interact verbally with the mother in a range of contexts.

(2) the middle-class mothers are less likely to avoid or evade answering difficult questions put to them by their children.

(3) the middle-class mothers are less likely to use coercive methods of control.

(4) the middle-class mothers are more likely to explain to the child why they want a change in his behavior (Bernstein and Brandis, 1968).

Thus, we have good reason for believing that not only is there a difference between the social classes in their emphasis upon language in contexts of interpersonal control, but there is a difference in the meanings which are verbally realized. It would seem that the internalizing of the principles of the moral order, the relating of this order to the specifics of the child's behavior, the communication of feeling, are realized far more through language in the middle class than in the working class. The *social* is made explicit in one group, whereas the social is rendered less explicit in the other. Where the social is made explicit through language then that which is internalized can itself become an object (Mead, 1934). Perhaps here we can begin to see that the form of control over persons in the middle class induces a reflexive relation to the social order, whereas, in the working class, the form of control over persons induces a relatively less reflexive relation to the social order (see Note B).

The question of the relatively greater emphasis upon the use of language in the interpersonal area raises fundamental questions about the nature of middle-class forms of socialization which would take us beyond the confines of an empirical research report. In Bernstein (1966 and particularly 1968) there is an extensive discussion of the social antecedents of forms of language use and socialization. The view taken in these and other papers is that linguistic codes are realizations of social structure, and both shape the contents of social roles and the process by which they are learned. In short, it has been suggested that the use of elaborated codes renders the implicit explicit, whereas the use of restricted codes reduces the possibility of such explicitness. Thus the codes and their variants regulate the cultural meanings which are rendered both explicit and individuated through the use of language. While there is no evidence in this paper that middle-class mothers use forms of an elaborated code and working-class mothers use forms of a restricted code, Robinson and Rackstraw's analysis (1967) of the answering behavior of mothers in the main sample indicates grounds for believing that these coding orientations are likely to be found. Further, the works of Bernstein and Brandis (1968) and Cook (1968) show that the forms of control used by the middle class and the working class are consonant with the predictions derived from the socio-linguistic theory. We will have further evidence when Miss Cook's analysis of the speech of the mothers is completed.

We have suggested that in the middle class skills are acquired in such a way that the child has access both to operations and principles. He tends to regulate his own learning in an arranged environment which encourages autonomy in skill acquisition. For this reason the middle-class mothers place less emphasis upon the use of language in the statements within the skill area. In the case of the working-class child, we have argued that he is socialized more into the acquisition of operations than into principles through a social relationship which encourages passivity in the learner and so reduces autonomy in skill acquisition. Thus the working-class mothers, relative to middle-class mothers, place greater emphasis upon the use of language when responding to the statements in the skill area. In the case of control over persons, we have suggested that the forms of such control in the middle class arise out of a social structure which is realized through the use of elaborated codes, whereas the forms of control in the sub-group of the working class under examination arise out of a social structure which is realized through forms of a restricted code. As a result, the form of control in the middle class induces a reflexive relation upon the part of the child towards the social order, whereas in the working class the forms of control induce a much less reflexive relation to the social order.

We should point out that a developed reflexive relation to the social order does not necessarily imply role distancing behavior. In the same way, reduced reflexiveness to a particularistic social order does not necessarily imply that role distancing behavior will *not* occur in relation to members of a society holding universalistic status.

We can best summarize our interpretations of the results of this analysis, and the more general explanation given in this paper, by the use of the following model:

		Social Structure	
		↓	
		Emphasis on Language	
Orientation	*Role/Self-concept*	M.C.	W.C.
Persons	Reflexiveness: →	High	Low
Skills	Autonomy: →	Low	High
		Self-regulating	Didactic

IMPLICIT THEORY OF LEARNING

The model should be read *horizontally* in relation to the areas of orientation and consequent emphasis on language, and *vertically* in relation to implicit theories of learning and emphasis upon language. For example, if there is a *high* emphasis upon the use of language in terms of orientation to persons then this will tend to generate high *reflexiveness* of the self-concept; if the emphasis on the use of language is *low* then this will generate *reduced reflexiveness* of the self-concept. In terms of the orientation to *skills,* a *low* emphasis on language will generate *autonomy* in the self-concept, while a *high* emphasis on language in this area will *reduce* autonomy in the self-concept. At the same time, the relative emphasis upon the use of language in these two areas perhaps implies different implicit theories of learning. Where the emphasis upon the use of language is *high* in terms of orientation to persons or *low* in terms of orientation to skills, then the implicit theory of learning is *self-regulating.* Where the emphasis on the use of language is *low* in terms of orientation to persons or *high* in terms of orientation to skills, then the implicit theory of learning is *didactic.*[2] It is important to add that, in this paper, because of the small sample, we have treated the middle class and working class as homogeneous groups. When the total sample is analyzed it may be possible to show that there are sub-groups within each social class group who respond differently in relation to these two areas. It is quite possible that differential emphasis upon the use of language in terms of the acquisition of skills or interpersonal control is related to differences in the form of the social relationships. A sub-culture may give rise to an implicit theory of learning which is self-regulating in terms of orientation to persons and didactic in terms of orientation to skills,

---

[2] On implicit theories of learning, see J. Klein. *Samples of British culture,* Vol. II. Routledge & Kegan Paul, 1965; G. Trasler (Ed.). *The formative years.* B.B.C. Publication, 1968; R. D. Hess & V. C. Shipman. Early experience and the socialization of cognitive modes in children, *Child Development.* 1965, 36, No. 4, 869–886.

or *vice versa* (see Note A). The relationship between culture, linguistic codes, implicit theories of learning, and differential emphasis upon the use of language is a matter of investigation. An extensive discussion in Bernstein (1968) deals with the relationship between social structure, forms of social relationship, linguistic codes, and different orders of meaning. The hypotheses on which our model is based are derived from this paper.

We can now develop our discussion in regard to possible discontinuities between implicit theories of learning in the home and explicit theories of learning in the school. It is suggested that there may be, for the working-class child in the primary school, two sources of discontinuity; one in the area of skill acquisition and the other in the area of interpersonal relations. If, for example, the school emphasizes autonomy in the acquisition of skills but the implicit concept of learning in the home is didactic in relation to skills, this will be a major source of discontinuity. Similarly, if the school is concerned with the development of reflexive relations in the area of interpersonal relations but the implicit concept of social learning in the home operates to reduce reflexiveness in this area, then this will be another source of discontinuity. It may be unreasonable to expect children exposed to such discontinuities to respond initially to forms of control which presuppose a culture and socialization very different from their own.

Earlier in this discussion we referred to the fortunate situation of the middle-class child in terms of the results of our analysis. His role relationships emphasize autonomy in the acquisition of skills and reflexiveness in the area of interpersonal relations. He is accorded discretion to *achieve* his social role. On the other hand, the role relationships of the working-class child, in terms of our analysis, reduce his autonomy in the skill area and reduce reflexiveness in the interpersonal area. He has much less discretion—his social role is *assigned*.

In this paper we have shown that maternal definitions of the role of language as a socializing process are dependent upon the area of orientation, and that this differential emphasis on the use of language is related to different forms of social relationship within the social structure. Further, we have argued that the differential emphasis on the use of language in relation to certain areas of orientation may reflect different implicit theories of learning which affect the self-concept of the child. We have suggested that these different implicit theories of learning in the home may conflict with the theories of learning in the school, and in this way give rise to major sources of discontinuity between the home and the school.

This analysis has enabled us to construct a model which gives a sociological explanation of social learning through the mediation of the linguistic process of socialization.

CONCLUSION

We must emphasize that our data consist of mothers' reports not of their actual behavior, and that these reports have been obtained through the

use of a closed schedule. The analysis of the degree and type of discrimina-
iton on the part of the middle-class and working-class mothers gives us
reasonable grounds for believing that the scaling procedures and the statements were appropriate. We also believe that the situation constructed was
such that the "right" or conventional response was not obvious to the
mothers. We have shown that both groups ranked the statements in the
person area according to the same gradient of difficulty. However, we cannot
present at the moment an analysis of possible differences between the social
classes in their interpretation of the statements. We may be able to throw
some light on social class differences in the interpretation of the statements
when the responses of the mothers to the closed schedule is related to their
responses to the other schedules within the language section of the second
questionnaire *and* to the results of the analysis of the initial questionnaire.

The findings presented here indicate very clear differences between the
social class groups in their relative emphasis upon language. We hope to be
able to utilize the model offered in the conclusion of the discussion to show,
when the total sample is analyzed, *intraclass* differences in the orientation to
the use of language in these two areas of socialization. Perhaps the most
important conclusion of this paper is to stress the need for small-scale naturalistic and experimental studies of the channels, codes, and contexts which
control the process of socialization.

In conclusion, it is the case that the three hypotheses given in the introduction have been confirmed. The findings have also revealed that working-
class mothers relative to middle-class mothers place a greater emphasis
upon language in the acquisition of basic skills. The inferential structure
developed in the discussion makes explicit the relationships between macro
aspects of social structure and micro aspects of socialization.

NOTE A

The diagram should be read as follows. The vertical and horizontal axes
are scaled in terms of the emphasis upon language. The vertical axis refers
to degrees of reflexiveness in socialization into relationships with persons
and the horizontal axis refers to degrees of autonomy in the acquisition of
skills. The four quadrants contain similiarities and differences between implicit
theories of learning. These control the forms of the socialization into the two
basic areas of socialization. While quadrants "B" and "D" would apply to sections of the middle class and working class respectively, the model indicates
the probability of intraclass variance both at one point of time and over
time.

The model only permits statements about the emphasis upon language:
no inferences can be drawn which refer to the nature of the information.
In order to examine the latter it would be necessary to know the dominant
linguistic code used in each area of socialization. While it is unlikely that
individuals limited to restricted codes would hold self-regulating theories of
learning (except embryonically) didactic theories of learning may well be

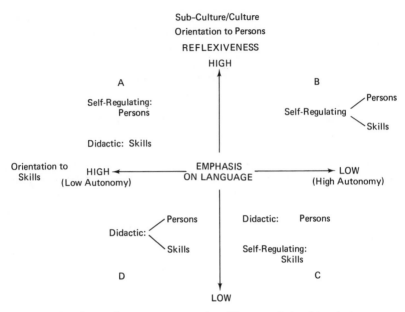

Fig. 1. The above diagram sets out the different relationships between re-flexiveness and autonomy which may arise as a result of the cultural meanings realized through language.

held by users of both elaborated and restricted codes. The hypothetical relationships between social structure, family role systems, linguistic codes, and person and object verbally realized meanings are set out in Bernstein (1968).

NOTE B

The Concept of Reflexiveness[3]

It is useful to distinguish between two aspects of reflexiveness: a role and an ideational aspect.

Ideational aspects.   Reflexiveness here refers to the degree to which an individual is able to make explicit verbally the principles underlying object and person relationships. Thus we could have high or low reflexiveness towards objects and/or persons.

Role aspects within role.   Reflexiveness here refers to the range of alternatives or options which are accorded to any given role. Thus we could have high or low reflexiveness in terms of the range of alternatives made available.

Between role.   Reflexiveness here would refer to the degree of insulation among the *meanings* made available through role relationships. Roles

---

[3] We are very grateful to Michael Young, Lecturer in the Sociology of Education, University of London, Institute of Education, for his comments upon this formulation.

may be more or less insulated from each other and so may the meanings to which the roles give access. Where the meanings made available through different roles are highly insulated we could say that there is low reflexiveness; where the meanings made available through different roles *reverberate* against each other (low insulation) we could say there is high reflexiveness.

This formulation indicates that the relationship between language and reflexiveness and the cultural and the institutional order is indeed complex.

Bibliography

Bernstein, B. (1965). A sociolinguistic approach to social learning. In J. Gould (Ed.), *Social science survey*. Penguin.

Bernstein, B. (1967). Play and the infant school, *Where,* Supplement 11, *Toys,* Christmas, 1967.

Bernstein, B. (1968). A socio-linguistic approach to socialisation. In J. Gumperz & D. Hymes (Eds.), *Directions in socio-linguistics.* Holt, Rinehart and Winston (in press). Also in *Human Context,* Dec., 1968, *1.*

Bernstein, B., & Young, D. (1967). Social class differences in conceptions of the uses of toys. *Sociology,* May, 1967 *1,* No. 2.

Bernstein, B., & Brandis, W. (1968). Social class differences in communication and control. In W. Brandis & D. Henderson (Eds.), *Primary socialisation, language and education.* Vol. I: *Social class, language and communication.* University of London, Institute of Education, Sociological Research Unit Monograph Series directed by Basil Bernstein, Routledge & Kegan Paul (in press).

Cicourel, A. V. (1964). *Method and measurement in sociology.* The Free Press of Glencoe.

Cook, J. (1969). Familial processes of communication and control. University of London, Institute of Education, Sociological Research Unit Monograph Series directed by Basil Bernstein, Routledge & Kegan Paul (in press).

Fishman, J. (1966). *Language loyalty in the United States.* Mouton & Co.

Garfinkle, H. (1967). *Studies in ethnomethodology.* Prentice-Hall, Inc.

Grimshaw, A. D. (1968). Socio-linguistics. In W. Schramm, I. Pool, N. Maccoby, E. Parker, & L. Fein (Eds.), *Handbook of communication.* Rand McNally & Co. (in press).

Hymes, D. (1967). On communicative competence. This paper is revised from the one presented at the *Research Planning Conference on Language Development Among Disadvantaged Children,* held under the sponsorship of the Department of Educational Psychology and Guidance, Ferkauf Graduate School, Yeshiva University, 1966. The paper is available from Department of Social Anthropology, University of Pennsylvania, Philadelphia.

Jones, J. (1966). Social class and the under-fives. *New Society,* Dec., 1966.

Loevinger, J. (1959). Patterns of parenthood as theories of learning. *J. Social & Abnormal Psychol., 59,* pp. 148–150.

Mead, G. H. (1934). *Mind, self and society.* University of Chicago Press.

Robinson, W. P. & Rackstraw, S. J. (1967). Variations in mothers' answers to children's questions, as a function of social class, verbal intelligence test scores and sex. *Sociology, I,* No. 3.

Winer, B. J. (1962). Statistical principles in experimental design. McGraw-Hill, chs. 4 and 8.

Development
of Mediating
Responses
in Children

Tracy S. Kendler

UNIVERSITY OF CALIFORNIA,
SANTA BARBARA

Learning theory and general behavior theory have, for the most part, shown little concern with developmental research. This is not to be taken as reflecting a lack of interest in children. There is an honorable, but spotty, tradition of experimental studies that used children as subjects dating back to Watson and his famous Albert. But the use of children does not automatically make the research developmental, especially if the emphasis is on the generality of behavior principles across species or across age levels within any one species.

Perhaps this indifference arises because developmental research appears

Reprinted from J. C. Wright & J. Kagan (Eds.), *Basic cognitive processes in children*, *Monogr. Soc. Res. Child Develpm.*, copyright © 1963 by The Society for Research in Child Development, *28*, No. 2, pp. 33–52. By permission.

The research described in this paper is supported by a grant from the National Science Foundation.

to be more concerned with finding *differences* between age groups than in finding general laws of behavior applicable to all age groups. Learning theory, on the other hand, commits the investigator to studying general processes that relate the organism to its environment through its past history. "The organism," which may range from amoeba to *Homo sapiens,* is often either a white rat or a pigeon. The use of these animals is not due to any particular interest in the species but rather to some very important advantages they provide to the researcher. For example, their past histories and motivational states can be manipulated or controlled at will and there are few ethical limitations imposed on the tasks they may be required to perform. Though he may restrict his research to some convenient laboratory organism, the behavior theorist implicitly assumes that at least some aspects of his findings are common to a wide range of organisms, usually including mankind. Within this tradition investigators who use human beings as subjects, and are explicit about the species, are often more interested in demonstrating the universality of the behavioral laws derived from animal experiments than in obtaining differences that might appear to reduce their generality.

If a discipline like comparative or developmental psychology is as much interested in differences as in similarities, then its findings may supply the ammunition for an attack on the vital assumption of the generality of behavioral laws. This is possible, but it is not necessarily so. If the principles generated by research with laboratory animals are applicable to higher level human behavior, then research directed at understanding the changes that take place with increasing maturity can extend the range and the vitality of behavior theory. If some of the knowledge derived from learning experiments can give direction to developmental research and can help to explain and organize its findings, behavior theorists may yet convert a potential enemy into a valuable ally.

It will come as no surprise to the reader that the developmental research to be described, which was conducted jointly with Howard H. Kendler and our colleagues, derives from an S-R learning theory pretheoretical framework. Among the reasons for this choice (besides the fact that we were trained in this discipline) are the substantial body of relevant knowledge and the well developed experimental techniques that can be adapted to the study of higher mental processes. Moreover, learning theory possesses a rigor that may help to tighten a field where the temptation to be vague is great.

The mediated response is one of the mechanisms most often used to find a common theme between simple and complex behavior within this theoretical framework. The mediator is a response, or series of responses, which intercede between the external stimulus and the overt response to provide stimulation that influences the eventual course of behavior. These responses may be overt, but they are usually presumed to be covert. The mediated response is not an original idea. All theories of thinking, motor or central, behaviorist or phenomenological, dealing in the second-signal system or using computer models, postulate internal processes that intervene between the presentation of the problem and its solution, between the input and output, or between the stimulus and the response. The differences arise in the model used to generate hypotheses about the nature of this internal process and in the methods used to validate these hypotheses. Watson, who coordinated thinking with subvocal talking, used conditioning as his model and sought verification by direct measurement of the muscles of speech. The contemporary behaviorist approach allows for a wider range of mediating responses and for the possibility of treating them as theoretical constructs rather than as directly observable behavior. The scheme is exemplified in the research to be described in this paper.

The research started with a general interest in the mediating process and has become more and more concerned with how the process develops in children. This development has been studied in two interrelated ways. One way is primarily comparative. It consists of presenting a similar experimental situation to different species and to different age levels to study the uncontrolled changes that occur as a function of the differences among subjects. The other way employs the experimental method to discover and manipulate the variables that appear to be related to these "natural" developmental changes in order to determine how they come about and consequently render them subject to experimental control.

We have experimented in two areas that are generally conceded to be part of that area variously called cognitive process, thinking, or problem solution. One of the areas is *concept formation* or *abstraction*. The other is *inference,* defined as the spontaneous integration of discretely acquired habits to solve a problem. These processes have been reduced to some very simple operations in order to study them at their inception in young children. The operations are so simple that there may be some disagreement about their continuity with the high level process that they presume to study. The prepared reply to such potential objection is that there is no known way of reliably determining, on an a priori basis, the proper level of analysis for scientific research. It is only by its fruits that we shall know it.

CONCEPT FORMATION

The experimental paradigm used in the investigation of concept formation is based on procedures developed by Buss (1953) and Kendler and D'Amato (1955). It consists essentially of studying mediation by means of the transfer demonstrated from an initial to a subsequent discrimination. The initial discrimination presents stimuli that differ simultaneously on at least two dimensions, only one of which is relevant. After criterion is reached, another discrimination is presented that utilizes the same or similar stimuli but requires a shift in response. One type of shift, called a *reversal shift,* requires the subject to continue to respond to the previously relevant dimension but in an opposite way. In another type of shift, called a *nonreversal shift* the subject is required to respond to the previously irrelevant dimension. For example, if a subject is initially trained on stimuli that differ simultaneously in brightness (black vs. white) and size (large vs. small) by being rewarded for responses to black regardless of size, a reversal shift would consist of learning to respond to white, and a nonreversal shift would consist of learning to respond to small. Comparisons between these two types of shifts are of particular interest because theories based on single-unit versus mediated S-R connections yield opposed predictions about their relative efficiency. A single-unit theory assumes a direct association between the external stimulus and the overt response and would predict a reversal shift to be more difficult than a nonreversal shift. This is because reversal shift requires the replacement of a response that has previously been consistently reinforced with a response that has previously been consistently extinguished. In a nonreversal shift previous training has reinforced responses to the newly positive and negative stimuli equally often. Strengthening one of these associations does not require as much extinction of its competitor as in a reversal shift and should, therefore, be acquired more easily. Kelleher (1956) confirmed the prediction that, for rats, a reversal shift was more difficult than a nonreversal shift.

A theory that includes a mediating link (or links) between the external stimulus and the overt response leads to a different prediction. The mediating link is conceived of as a perceptual or verbal response, often covert, to the relevant dimension, which produces cues that elicit the overt response. In a reversal shift, the initial dimension maintains its relevance, hence, so does the mediated response. Only the overt response needs to be changed, and since the experimental situation provides only one alternative overt response, the problem presents no great difficulty. In a nonreversal shift the previously acquired mediation is no longer relevant, consequently both the mediating and the overt response must be replaced, making the task more difficult than a reversal shift. It is therefore to be expected that for subjects who mediate, a reversal shift will be acquired more easily than a nonreversal shift. Experiments by Buss (1953), Kendler and D'Amato (1955), and Harrow and Friedman (1958), using a more complex variation of the reversal-nonreversal technique with college students, confirmed the prediction of the mediational analysis. Unlike rats, college students learn a reversal shift more easily than a nonreversal shift.

This discontinuity between rats and adult humans led to two investigations with young children to determine whether their behavior, in this type of situation, was more consistent with the single-unit or the mediational formulation. The results suggested that children between 3 and 4 years of age respond predominantly in the single unit manner (Kendler, Kendler, and Wells [1960]) and that children between 5 and 7 years of age divide about evenly, with half mediating and half not (Kendler and Kendler [1959]). What seemed to be implied was a developmental process in which very young children's behavior is governed by a relatively primitive, single-unit S-R process. Increasing maturity leads to increases in the proportion of children whose performance is determined by some mediating system of responses.

A recent investigation of the shift behavior of children from five age levels (3, 4, 6, 8, and 10 years) provided a direct test of these developmental implications (Kendler *et al.* [1962]). Previous procedures were modified to allow each subject to choose whether or not he would behave mediationally. This was accomplished in the following way. For their initial discrimination (series I) the children were presented, in random alternation, with two pairs of stimulus cards. One pair consisted of a large black square (LB) and a small white square (SW). The other pair consisted of a large white square (LW) and a small black square (SB). Each concept (L, B, S, W) was correct for one fourth of the subjects.

For the purpose of illustration let us take a child for whom black was the correct concept and size was irrelevant. For him all responses to SB or LB were rewarded with a marble. If he responded to SW or LW, he had to return a marble to the experimenter. After he reached the criterion of nine out of ten successive correct responses, a second discrimination (series II) was presented that involved only one of the stimulus pairs, e.g., LB and SW, and the reward pattern was reversed. Now only responses to SW were rewarded, and he was again run to a criterion of nine out of ten successive correct responses. The child could reach criterion in this series by responding to the whiteness, in which case he was categorized as a *reversal* subject since he was responding in a reverse way to the original concept. Such a child is, by virtue of the previous analysis, presumed to have made relevant mediating responses in the first discrimination which either led to other relevant mediators or continued to be relevant in the second discrimination, thus requiring a shift only in the overt response.

A child could also reach criterion in series II by responding to the smallness of SW. Such a choice would be expected from nonmediators since during series I responses to small were rewarded half of the time, while responses to whiteness were never rewarded. Such a child would, therefore, respond more readily to a stimulus from the previously irrelevant dimension (S) than to the incorrect stimulus of the previously relevant dimension (W) and would consequently be categorized as a nonreversal subject.

The last possibility is that the child learned to respond to both the smallness and the whiteness. A single-unit analysis would predict this result for nonmediating children who take a relatively long time to learn series II since each reinforcement should increase the habit strength of both stimulus components. As the trials increase, the difference in the excitatory strengths of white and small should decrease and ultimately disappear. Such children, for reasons that will soon be clear, were categorized as *inconsistent*.

In order to determine on which of the three possible bases series II was learned, it was followed immediately by a third series. During this last series both pairs of stimuli were again shown in random alternation. The pair that had not been used in series II, which is LW and SB in our illustration, served as the test pair. With this pair the child could respond either to the whiteness or to the smallness but not to both simultaneously. The test pair was presented ten times and either choice was rewarded. On the basis of his choices to this pair the child was classified as one of the three categories just described.

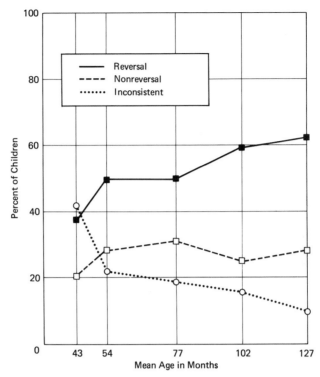

Fig. 1. Percentage of children in each choice category as a function of chronological age.

The function of the other pair, which maintained its previous reinforcement pattern, was to keep the child responding as he did in series II.

The results for each category are presented in Fig. 1. The prediction, based on theoretical analysis and previous results, was that the percentage of children who reversed (mediated) would be below 50 between the ages of 3 and 4 (Kendler, Kendler, and Wells [1960]), rise to about 50 between 5 and 7 (Kendler and Kendler [1959]), and then continue to increase with increasing age until some relatively high asymptote was reached. The results, which are in good agreement with the prediction, serve to confirm the general developmental implications of previous studies.

It was expected, of course, that the percentage of nonmediators would decrease with age. There seemed no a priori reason for making a discrimination between the nonreversal and inconsistent children, and so the decrease was expected in both categories. The results show a sharp and steady decrease for the inconsistent category. There was, however, no perceptible trend in the nonreversal group.

Despite the need for explanation of the performance of the nonreversal

Table 1   Percentage of Subjects Giving Various Descriptions as a Function
of Their Choices in Series III

Kind of Choice	Verbalized Correct Dimension	Verbalized Incorrect Dimension	No Relevant Verbalization
Reversal	84.8	7.6	7.6
Nonreversal	66.7	25.6	7.7
Inconsistent		57.7[a]	42.3

[a] If the behavior was categorized as inconsistent neither dimension could be considered correct. Therefore, mentions of either dimension were combined and placed between the two columns to indicate their special character.

group, to which we shall return presently, it seems reasonable to conclude that the results of this experiment bear out the implication that there is a transition in the course of human development from unmediated, single-unit behavior to mediated behavior, at least with reference to size and brightness concepts. They also suggest that the proportion of children who have made this transition increases in a gradual and lawful manner. It remains for further research to determine whether the same or similar relationships will obtain with other concepts.

In addition to these results there were some *ad hoc* observations about the verbal behavior of the children that provide interesting suggestions about the nature of the mediation process and its development. These verbalizations should not be regarded as demonstrative of confirmed relationships. They should be regarded as empirically derived suggestions that require further experimental verification.

After the children had completed series III, they were shown the stimulus pair used in series II and asked a series of questions to find out whether they could or would give a correct verbal report of what they had been doing and whether there would be any relationship between this after-the-act verbal behavior and mediated choices in series III. Table 1 presents these results arranged in three categories that are illustrated as follows. If a child had been responding to brightness in the test pair and described the "winner" as white (or black), he was grouped with those who *verbalized the correct dimension*. If he said "the square one" or "that one," or merely pointed without saying anything at all, he was placed with the *no relevant verbalization* group.

Despite the pressure on the child to respond generated by *E's* persistent questions, with the stimulus cards in full view, 42 per cent of the inconsistent children failed to produce any relevant verbalization. If verbalization is important for the mediating process, then it would follow that nonmediators would be relatively inarticulate. By the same token, mediating (reversal) children should produce a relatively large proportion of verbal comment that was relevant to their previous performance. The data in Table 1 support this expectation. If the pattern is clear for the reversal and inconsistent children, the nonreversal children present more complications. Two statements may be made about this group. First, an overwhelming proportion produced descriptions of the stimuli in terms of at least one of the manipulation dimensions. The proportion for the nonreversal group was just as large as that for the reversal group, suggesting that, under pressure to do so, the non-mediators could verbally describe the stimuli as well as the mediators. However, the verbalizations of nonreversal children were less frequently relevant to their previous behavior than were those of reversal children.

One tentative way to tie these observations together, and simultaneously throw further light on the fact that the proportion of nonreversal children did not decrease with age, is to propose that reversal, nonreversal, and inconsistent choice behavior represent a three-stage hierarchy of development. Reversal choice reflects the highest level where covert verbal responses occur during training and mediate choice behavior. Nonreversal choice constitutes an intermediate level, at which covert verbal responses can occur and sometimes do, but either occur rather late in the learning or they do not necessarily or readily mediate choice behavior. The most primitive level is characterized by little or no covert response and is manifested in inconsistent choice behavior. With increasing CA more and more children reach the highest level (i.e., reversal) and fewer and fewer are left at the lowest level (i.e., inconsistent), but at each age tested the proportion in transition between the two extreme levels (i.e., nonreversals) tends to be constant.

Such an analysis would lead to the expectation that the proportion of children who verbalized correctly would increase with age; the proportion of children whose verbalizations were absent or irrelevant would decrease with age; and the incorrect dimension category would not change. Fig. 2 presents the verbalization data in terms of chronological age. The data demonstrate considerable correspondence between expectation and results and show a striking similarity to the choice behavior presented in Fig. 1, a similarity that occurs despite the fact that the children who comprise each set of parallel developmental trends are not identical. For example, the "verbalized-correct-dimensions" results of Fig. 2, which parallel the "reversal-choice" trend of Fig. 1, included 67 per cent of the nonreversal children as well as 85 per cent of the reversal children. Thus, although these results do not point to a perfect relationship between verbal and choice behavior, the similarity of trends certainly suggests that the development of the mediational process is intimately related to the development of the ability to relate words to actions.

There is one more suggestive result yielded by the verbalization data that may help to explain (a) the high proportion of nonreversal children who verbalized correctly, (b) why the reversal results approached such a low asymptote, and (c) the lack of a decrease in the nonreversal category even at the ripe old age of 10. Some children described the "winner" accurately by mentioning both dimensions, e.g., "The big, white one." When this tendency was sorted out by age, it was found that the percentage of children who accurately described *both dimensions* was zero at age 3 and increased gradually to 25 at age 10, implying, reasonably enough, that there is a develop-

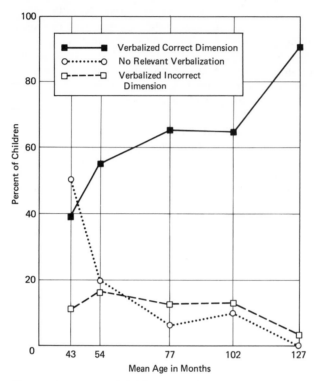

Fig. 2. Percentage of children in each verbalization category as a function of chronological age.

mental aspect to the number of simultaneous mediating responses a child can handle. It also implies that at the upper age levels a nonreversal response to situations as simple as series II may not necessarily denote a primitive process. Instead it may represent the ability to integrate more than one mediating response. This is another way of saying that the task may have been too easy for the older children and that consequently they complicated it for themselves. It may be that the failure of the reversal curve to rise above 62 per cent and the nonreversal curve to drop below 28 per cent at age 10 is due to a perennial difficulty in developmental research: devising one task that is easy enough for the lower end of the scale and yet difficult enough to pose the proper challenge at the upper end. Although in the present instance the task was clearly capable of differentiating among the various age levels tested, it may be that the differences at the upper age levels were attenuated.

Thus far, the data derived from a comparative type of analysis show a measurable transition from a lower to a higher level behavioral process as a function of increasing chronological age. They also suggest that this development is somehow related to language. The relationship is probably not simple. Even the youngest children had a vocabulary sufficient for describing the simple concepts used. Moreover, one of the early experiments had demonstrated that with simple instructions all of the children could interpose relevant verbal comment between the presentation of the stimuli and their overt choice. It is clear that, if the overt behavior of the younger children is not influenced by mediating verbal discriminators, it is not because they are incapable of making these responses. This leaves two alternatives. One is that, although they are capable of doing so, they nevertheless do not, in the ordinary course of events, make such responses. The other is that they do make some verbal responses, but these responses, for some reason, do not serve as mediators. In order to explore some of these issues another experiment was performed which manipulated overt verbal mediation to ascertain its effect on the reversal shift behavior of 4- and 7-year-old children. Note that, while this study has developmental implications, it is more experimental in nature.

The same stimuli were used as in the study previously described, but they were presented differently. The initial discrimination used only one pair of discriminanda, thus rendering both stimulus dimensions relevant. Under these circumstances a child could be required to describe the correct stimulus according to either one of its two components. For example, if LB was correct, the child could be instructed to use either "large" or "black" to describe the correct stimulus. In the second discrimination both pair of stimuli were presented and all children learned a reversal shift. Only one dimension was relevant. For some children the reversal was on the size dimension, and for some it was on the brightness dimension. In this way the verbalization during the initial discrimination was rendered relevant or irrelevant according to the experimental group to which the child had been randomly assigned. For example, if the child had learned to describe the correct stimulus (LB) as "large," he would be rewarded in the second discrimination for response to SB and SW (small) if he was in the relevant group. If he was in the irrelevant group, he was rewarded for responses to SW and LW (white). A control group with no verbalization completed the design.

The first question to be asked is whether such overt verbalization, intervening between stimulus and response, affects the acquisition of the reversal shift. The answer is clear: it does. For both age groups relevant verbalization produced significantly faster shifts than irrelevant verbalization. These results add credence to the mediating response model used to explain reversal-nonreversal shift behavior. They also provide a technique for exploring the interaction between verbal and other developmental variables.

Another question this research was designed to answer was whether the utilization of verbal mediators differs with age as has been suggested by Luria (1957). That is, will the difference between the reversal shift behavior of younger and older children be reduced or eliminated when both are provided with the same verbal response, or is there another ingredient, associated

Table 2   Mean Number of Trials to Criterion on Reversal Shift for Each
Verbalization Condition at Two Age Levels

	Verbalization Condition		
	Relevant	Irrelevant	None
4 years	16.1	30.4	22.2
7 years	8.3	35.6	8.8

with development, which is necessary before words exercise control over overt behavior?

Table 2 presents the results analyzed separately for each age group. It can be seen that the effects were somewhat different for the two age levels. As expected, when there was no verbalization the 4-year-olds took significantly more trials to reverse than the 7-year-olds. Relevant verbalization did not facilitate the shift for the older chidren, presumably because they did not require instruction about verbalization to supply relevant mediation. They were able to supply it themselves. The responsiveness of the older children to verbal labels is seen, however, in the sharp increase in learning difficulty produced by irrelevant verbalization.

The 4-year-olds, on the other hand, profited from relevant verbalization and, like the older children, were hindered by irrelevant verbalization. This suggests that, although they are not likely to supply their own mediators, they can use their own words in this capacity when language responses are required. Although the results suggest an interesting interaction between verbalization and age, the implied interaction, as assessed by analysis of variance, fell short of statistical significance ($.10 > p > .05$). The definitive study of such interaction remains to be done.

Although it is clear that we have much to learn, some general conclusions can be drawn from these several studies. In this simple situation, which straddles the boundary between discrimination learning and concept formation, it seems that the single-unit S-R model adequately explains the behavior of the majority of children below 5 or 6 years of age. It does not explain the behavior of the majority of the older children. Invoking the theoretical construct of the mediating response can account for the more mature behavior within the S-R framework. This approach has the advantage of providing for continuity between the laws governing the behavior of younger and older children, since it attributes the observed developmental changes to a new and important system of responses, probably bound up with the development of language, rather than to a different set of behavioral laws. It is not sufficient, however, to point to an explanatory mechanism. After recognizing its potential it becomes necessary to show when and how it functions. The study of mediating responses in children can provide information about the nature and development of mediating processes at their source. Such information can serve to enlarge the scope of behavior theory until it can encompass human problem solving.

INFERENCE

Although it cannot be attributed to any preliminary strategy, our research on inference falls into a logical format resembling that of the research on concept formation. The phenomenon we have called *inference* bears considerable resemblance to Kohler's "insight" (1925) and Maier's "reasoning" (1929). Initially we sought to convert an experimental paradigm into a research vehicle for studying problem solving in very young children. The paradigm was adapted from that of Hull (1935, 1952) in his analysis of the behavior of Maier's reasoning rats. Subjects are trained on three separate behavior segments, each of which presents a distinctive stimulus, requires a different response, and yields a different reward. Two of these segments, designated as A-B and X-Y, lead to subgoals. The third segment, B-G, leads to the major goal. After being trained on each of these segments individually, the subject is presented with a test trial in which only the A-B and X-Y segments are available to him and he is motivated to get the major goal. The solution to this problem is to link the behavior segments by responding to A to acquire B and then use B to get G. The X-Y segment serves as a control against which to assess the inferential behavior. For example, in our most recent study we used an apparatus with three horizontally arranged panels, one for each segment. For some children, the A-B segment consisted of pressing a button on the right hand panel to obtain a glass marble. The X-Y segment consisted of pressing a button on the left hand panel to obtain a steel ballbearing. The B-G segment consisted of dropping a marble into a hole in the center panel which yielded a fairy tale charm. During the preliminary training on B-G, the subject was provided with a marble and a ballbearing, but only the marble would work. In the test situation neither was provided; instead all of the panels were opened and the child was told that if he did what he was supposed to he could get the charm. Solution consisted of pressing A to get the marble and then dropping the marble into B to get the charm. For half of the children the A-B segment was on the right, and for half it was on the left. Similarly, for half of the children the marble was the B subgoal, and for half it was the ballbearing (in which case only the ballbearing would operate the B-G segment).

In a somewhat comparable but more loosely controlled experimental situation, Maier found that rats were capable of inference (1929). As far back as 1935, Hull, who accepted this datum, was so impressed with the necessity for a behavior theory to explain such a phenomenon that he set out to provide his own explanation. Hull suggested that during the acquisition of each segment of behavior, not only was the overt S-R connection strengthened, but the subject also acquired an anticipatory goal response (r_g) appropriate to the goal object. This r_g worked backward until stimuli that marked the beginning of the segment became capable of evoking it. The stimulus properties associated with the distinctive r_g for the major goal thus became connected with the A-B segment; they did not become associated with the X-Y segment. Since more connections have been associated with the response to A, and since these response tendencies summate, the subject should, when presented with a choice between A and X, while motivated for G, choose the former. Once A is responded to, it produces B, which in turn leads to the response necessary to produce G, by virtue of previous training. Thus, the habit segments were supposed to become linked to produce inferential behavior.

It is characteristic of Hull's explanations that they generate many deductions, several of which he made explicit. There was one readily testable and fundamental implication that he did not enumerate: inference should occur more readily when the order of training consists of presenting B-G before A-B, since this order maximizes the conditions for the associations between A and the r_g of the major goal.

The assembly of habit segments can also be viewed as an exercise in chaining. Skinner's formulation (1938) points out that in setting up a chain of behavior it is usually most efficient to start with the last link, in this case B-G. In that way the discriminative stimulus (B), through its association with the goal stimulus (G), acquires secondary reinforcing powers, which can serve to strengthen the A-B link. Since Y acquires no such additional secondary reinforcing capacity, the X-Y link should not be able to compete successfully with the A-B link. This analysis should engender the same prediction as was derived from Hull, namely that the optimum order would be that in which B-G precedes A-B.

Notice that both of these explanations are developed to account for the presumably demonstrated capacity of the rat to infer and consequently contain no response mechanism not available to that species.

Our initial interest in inferential behavior was to test the prediction about order using children as subjects. Before this could be done it was necessary to devise suitable experimental techniques. In the course of this search it was found that, given sufficiently simple segments, some nursery school children could infer (Kendler and Kendler [1956]) and this kind of inference. was, like simple associative learning, influenced by reinforcement and motivation variables (Kendler et al. [1958]). More recently a study was completed that expressly tested the effect of order of presentation of the several segments on inferential behavior in preschool children (35 to 65 months) (Kendler and Kendler [1961]). The findings showed that there was *no order effect.* This study used a somewhat more complex procedure than the earlier ones and drew its sample from a lower socioeconomic level. Under these conditions, there was very little inferential behavior, and the little there was did not seem to be readily accounted for by the associative principles proposed by Hull.

The data were somewhat difficult to reconcile with the theoretical superstructure underlying the Hullian account and with Maier's data about the rat's capacity in this area. But after the study had been completed, an article by Koronakos (1959) appeared in the literature. He used the Hullian paradigm to study inferential behavior in rats. What he found began to help us see our results as part of a familiar pattern. After initial training when the rats were presented with the A or X choice, they chose one as often as the other. There was no evidence that rats could, in this carefully controlled situation, combine the habit segments spontaneously to attain the major goal.

It is now beginning to look as though inference, like reversal shift, may be a process that is not readily available to lower phylogenetic species and perhaps not to young children. Inference may be another developmental process with ontogenetic as well as phylogenetic implications. The last study to be described undertook to explore this possibility. All of the results have not yet been analyzed, and no statistical significances have yet been computed; nevertheless, some of the findings are sufficiently cogent to warrant presentation now.

This study compared the behavior of 64 kindergarten children (5 to 6 years old) with 64 third grade children (8 to 10 years old) on the inference task. When confronted with the test situation, only 50 per cent of the younger children as compared with 72 per cent of the older children chose to respond to A (the inferential choice). Furthermore, of the children who made the initial A choice only 12 per cent of the younger children and 67 per cent of the older children went on to complete the inferential sequence to obtain the major goal with no unnecessary steps.

This seems to be rather clear evidence that, in this situation, the capacity to combine independently acquired habit segments is present in very few youngsters below about 6 years of age. But among the third graders there were many more who plainly displayed such integrative capacity. Moreover, there is indication from other aspects of this experiment that the response of the two age levels to the connecting stimulus (B) is quite different. For the younger children it is necessary to have B in order to make the integrative response. For a substantial proportion of the older children the final integration is *more* dependent on self-produced cues than on the external stimulus B. Apparently the occurrence of inference, like the occurrence of reversal shift, is dependent on a system of covert mediating responses which occurs more readily in older than younger children. It seems that the experimental study of inferential behavior in children may provide another useful vehicle for examining the development of the covert response system underlying the higher mental processes.

CONCLUSION

Some interesting developmental changes occurring between early and middle childhood have emerged from applying an S-R learning theory approach to problem solving in children. Analyses of these changes in terms of a very broad conception of behavior theory has shown that the behavior of very young children is dependent on environmental cues, with which relatively simple S-R connections are formed and to which the laws of learning derived from simpler species are applicable. Older children's behavior, if it is to be dealt with in an S-R framework, must be conceptualized in terms of chains of responses in which some of the links are or become covert. It is proposed that a combined developmental-experimental approach can provide an understanding of how this transition occurs by studying it at its inception.

REFERENCES

Buss, A. H. Rigidity as a function of reversal and nonreversal shifts in the learning of successive descriminations. *J. exp. Psychol.*, 1953, *45*, 75–81.

Harrow, M., & Friedman, G. B. Comparing reversal and nonreversal shifts in concept formation with partial reinforcement controlled. *J. exp. Psychol.*, 1958, *55*, 592–597.

Hull, C. L. The mechanism of the assembly of behavior segments in novel combinations suitable for problem solution. *Psychol. Rev.*, 1935, *42*, 219–245.

Hull, C. L. *A behavior system.* Yale Univer. Press, 1952.

Kelleher, R. T. Discrimination learning as a function of reversal and nonreversal shifts. *J. exp. Psychol.*, 1956, *51*, 379–384.

Kendler, H. H., & D'Amato, M. F. A comparison of reversal shifts and nonreversal shifts in human concept formation behavior. *J. exp. Psychol.*, 1955, *49*, 165–174.

Kendler, H. H., & Kendler, T. S. Inferential behavior in preschool children. *J. exp. Psychol.*, 1956, *51*, 311–314.

Kendler, H. H., Kendler, T. S., Plisskoff, S. S., & D'Amato, M. F. Inferential behavior in children: I. The influence of reinforcement and incentive motivation. *J. exp. Psychol.*, 1958, *55*, 207–212.

Kendler, T. S., & Kendler, H. H. Reversal and nonreversal shifts in kindergarten children. *J. exp. Psychol.*, 1959, *58*, 56–60.

Kendler, T. S., & Kendler, H. H. Inferential behavior in children: II. The influence of order of presentation. *J. exp. Psychol.*, 1961, *61*, 442–448.

Kendler, T. S., Kendler, H. H., & Learnard, B. Mediated responses to size and brightness as a function of age. *Amer. J. Psychol.*, 1962, *75*, 571–586.

Kendler, T. S., Kendler, H. H., & Wells, D. Reversal and nonreversal shifts in nursery school children. *J. comp. physiol. Psychol.*, 1960, *53*, 83–87.

Kohler, W. *The mentality of apes.* Harcourt, Brace, 1925.

Koronakos, C. Inferential learning in rats: the problem-solving assembly of behavior segments. *J. comp. physiol. Psychol.*, 1959, *52*, 231–235.

Luria, A. R. The role of language in the formation of temporary connections. In B. Simon (Ed.), *Psychology in the Soviet Union.* Stanford Univer. Press, 1957.

Maier, N. R. F. Reasoning in white rats. *Comp. Psychol. Monogr.*, 1929, No. 9.

Skinner, B. F. *The behavior of organisms.* Appleton-Century, 1938.

Spontaneous Verbal Rehearsal in a Memory Task as a Function of Age

John H. Flavell, David R. Beach, and Jack M. Chinsky

UNIVERSITY OF MINNESOTA
STATE UNIVERSITY OF NEW YORK AT BUFFALO
UNIVERSITY OF CONNECTICUT

There is considerable research attention currently being given to the possibility that the relation between the child's linguistic and nonlinguistic behavior undergoes important developmental changes during the preschool and early school years (e.g., Kendler, 1963; Luria, 1961; Reese, 1963; Weir & Stevenson, 1959). Reese (1962) has reviewed much of this literature and has also given a name to the principal developmental hypothesis which has animated it. According to this, the "mediational-deficiency hypothesis," there is a stage in ontogenesis during which the child tends not to mediate or

Reprinted from *Child Development*, copyright © 1966 by The Society for Research in Child Development, Inc., 37, No. 2, 283–299. By permission.

The writers are indebted to Mr. Lawrence W. Utter, principal at Rochester Public School 49, and his staff for their excellent cooperation in providing Ss and testing facilities for this study. They wish also to thank Drs. Ralph N. Haber, James R. Ison, Emory L. Cowen, and Dean H. Obrecht, and Miss Frances C. Wynns for their advice and assistance during the design and pilot-testing phases.

regulate his overt behavior verbally, despite the fact that he is able to understand and correctly use the words in question; subsequently, this discrepancy between linguistic and mediational capacities gets reduced, that is, mediational deficiency tends to disappear with age.

Maccoby (1964) has recently called attention to an apparent ambiguity in the meaning of this hypothesis: "The question is, then, whether they [i.e., these young children] simply fail to use the verbal labels which are presumably available to them, or whether they do use them, but for some reason the words do not serve to mediate the response" (p. 213). It appears that there are really two distinct and separate developmental hypotheses which ought to be entertained here, distinct and separate in the sense that the truth or falsity of one is not logically dependent on the truth or falsity of the other. One of these hypotheses would assert that the younger child does indeed spontaneously produce the potential verbal mediators at the appropriate point in the task situation, just as the older child does, but that these verbalizations for one reason or another fail to have their expected mediational effects on his overt behavior; in brief, they occur when they ought but do not mediate as they ought. The second hypothesis would simply predict that the younger child tends not to produce the relevant words in the first place, and this suffices to explain the apparent nonmediated character of his overt task behavior. It is stipulated that he "knows" the relevant words and that he can and does produce them in some situations; his deficiency here consists solely in the fact that this particular task (or perhaps tasklike situations in general) fails to elicit them.

It is suggested that the expression "mediational deficiency" be restricted henceforth to the first of these two hypotheses, since it is that hypothesis alone which predicts that the young child's operant verbalizations tend to be deficient in mediational power. A new modifier, "production deficiency," is proposed for the second hypothesis, implying as it does that the child's difficulty may not lie in an inability to use the words which he produces in a mediational fashion, but rather a lack of ability or disposition to produce or emit them on appropriate occasions.

What are the ideal experimental conditions for testing each of these hypotheses? In the case of the mediational-deficiency hypothesis, there appear to be four:

Elicitation.   The task situation used ought to be such that most mature human *S*s would more or less naturally follow a verbal-mediational approach in trying to cope with it. That is, one should employ a task which is likely to exert considerable verbal mediational "pull" for *S*s who are deficient in neither production nor mediational skills.

Mediation.   *E* should be able to distinguish mediated (i.e., verbally mediated) from nonmediated overt responses on this task. Ideally, he ought to be able to make this discrimination for each individual response, rather than simply for the overall pattern of responses, for example, faster versus slower learning, as measured by number of trials to criterion.

Production.   *E* should have some procedure for establishing whether

S actually produced any potentially mediating verbalization at each of the various points in the task sequence where such verbalization would have a reasonable chance of mediating something, that is, in at least rough temporal contiguity with the overt task responses just mentioned. The *E* might insure such production for all *S*s by instructing them to make the appropriate verbalization, but if he does, he should also make sure that they are instructed to do so at the appropriate times.

Competence.   *E* has of course to be sure that his younger *S*s have about the same receptive and productive command of the words in question that his older *S*s do. That is, he should be able to provide evidence that all the children in his sample can use and interpret these words in approximately the same way.

If these four conditions are satisfied, the mediational-deficiency hypothesis can be tested by examining only those task responses for which there was in fact relevant and temporarily contiguous verbal production. The hypothesis is then confirmed if older *S*s show more responses judged to be mediated than younger *S*s do. Only the Elicitatation, Production, and Competence conditions need be satisfied when testing the production-deficiency hypothesis. As regards the Production condition, however, there obviously can be no instructions to verbalize, since spontaneous production versus nonproduction constitutes the dependent variable. The hypothesis is supported if older *S*s simply verbalize on a greater number of the appropriate occasions than do younger *S*s.

A review of existing research would show little unequivocal evidence for or against either of these two hypotheses.[1] This is of course partly a consequence of the fact that the developmental problem here has not been analyzed in terms of a clear distinction between production and mediational sources of variance. More than that, however, the tasks and methodology which have characterized the typical study in this area appear not even to approach the experimental conditions outlined above. To be sure, these conditions are ideal standards, severe and restrictive, and perhaps there is no feasible experimental study which can do better than approximate them. They may, nonetheless, serve the heuristic function of making us rethink our traditional methods of seeking research answers in this area, just as the production-mediation distinction has done with respect to the research questions. Our own rethinking has so far centered on the production- rather than mediational-deficiency hypothesis and has led us to the conclusion that a credible test of it might be made if only one could find a way to assess *S*'s

---

[1] Some of Luria's research (e.g., 1961) comes quite close to satisfying the conditions for a test of the mediational-deficiency hypothesis. He claims to have shown that there is an early childhood phase during which *S*'s own self-commands fail to regulate—indeed, may interfere with—his motor actions, followed by a phase when such commands facilitate organized motor responding. Although we shall not review his procedure in detail here, suffice it to say that it does appear to meet at least the Mediation, Production, and Competence conditions fairly well. There remains the problem, however, of whether to trust his reported findings: a recent, very careful replication study by Jarvis (1963) failed to turn up even a hint of any such deficiency in young American children.

spontaneous verbal production directly, that is, by actually observing it as it happens rather than having to infer its occurrence from task performance or other data. The experiment reported here was thus designed to approximate the requisite Elicitation, Production, and Competence conditions, with particular emphasis on realizing the Production condition through direct observation of S's uninstructed, task-related verbalization.

METHOD

Research Strategy

The initial research step was to find a task which would accord with the Elicitation condition. Such a task ought itself to be wholly nonverbal in character but, at the same time, should tend to elicit a considerable amount of spontaneous verbalization in older Ss. The work of Glanzer & Clark (1963), Ranken (1963), and others suggested that some sort of serial recall task might have such properties. Spiker (1956) observed, moreover, that young children sometimes spontaneously rehearsed stimulus names aloud during the delay period of his delayed-reaction task. A memory task might thus have the further advantage of constituting an experimental setting in which whatever mediating speech is produced would tend to be more overt than in other settings, thereby enhancing opportunities for direct observation. The task finally selected was the following: S sees seven pictures, each depicting a single object, spread out randomly before him. E then slowly points to, say, some randomly chosen three of these pictures in succession. Either immediately or after a 15-second delay, S is presented with a duplicate set of pictures (set out in a different random arrangement, so that spatial position cannot serve as a memory aid), and his task is to point to the same three pictures and in the same sequence that E had pointed to them previously. It was expected that a relatively mature S would try to cope with this task verbally: name to himself each object as it was pointed to, rehearse the resulting list of names (perhaps a number of times if there is a delay period), and then work directly from the list when it came time for him to reproduce the sequence gesturally.

The stimuli to be recalled and the conditions under which their recall was tested were designed with the Competence and Production conditions in mind. The objects shown in the pictures were intended to be familiar ones which even the youngest Ss tested would find easy to label (an attempt was subsequently made to verify this empirically). The names of most of these objects had the further property of entailing rather large and conspicuous mouth movements when pronounced—words like "pipe," "flag," etc. Furthermore, these mouth-movement patterns were relatively distinctive and discriminable, one name from another. Prior to the experiment, one of us (Beach) trained himself to become as expert as he could at lip-reading this specially selected seven-word "language." And finally, S was semiblindfolded during the delay period of all delayed-recall trials, both to give him some sense of being alone and undisturbed (a condition which might facilitate semiovert verbalization) and also to permit *E* to stare fixedly at his mouth throughout this period without causing embarrassment or discomfort. It was never supposed that these particular procedures would necessarily yield the largest possible fraction of observable speech to total speech produced. One could, for example, imagine testing *S* in true rather than partial isolation; one could likewise imagine utilizing sensitive throat microphones, and so on. It was hoped, however, that the yield from the present method would be sufficient to make a convincing test of the production-deficiency hypothesis.

Subjects

The *S*s were 60 public school children, 10 boys and 10 girls at each of grades K, 2, and 5. The group mean ages were 69, 93, and 129 months, respectively. The *S*s were drawn from their classrooms on an essentially random basis, with no attempt to match groups on variables other than grade and sex.

Procedure

The *S*s were tested individually, all three authors serving as *E*s. A testing session lasted 20–25 minutes and was composed of the following sequence of events.

Introduction. The child was told that he would play some games for which he might win little prizes and that we would actually begin things by giving him one of these prizes. He was thereupon offered a choice of two prizes, drawn from a collection of plastic rings, key chains bearing charms, balloons, and toy money. He was then assured that if he tried hard and did his best in the games, he would get some more prizes.

Pretraining on "same order." *S* was instructed to point to each of a series of wooden blocks (a two-block series was used first, then a four-block series) in the same order that *E* had just pointed to them, regardless of intervening changes in spatial arrangement. The *E* continuously verbalized what he and *S* were doing (e.g., "First I point to this one, and then I point, etc.") and concluded by defining "same order" in terms of *S* pointing first to the same block *E* had pointed to first, *S* pointing second to the same block *E* had pointed to second, etc. This brief pretraining was not expected to teach *S* a new concept, but rather to prime or set him to use one he doubtless already possessed at some level, as well as to familiarize him with the verbal expressions *E* would subsequently employ in instructing him to use it.

Habituation to space helmet. *S* was next presented with a brightly colored toy space helmet and was assisted in placing it on his head. Its adjustable plastic visor was covered with white tape, which effectively prevented him from seeing *E*s or task materials when the visor was in the down position. His visual field was not appreciably darkened, however, both because the tape was essentially translucent and because a considerable amount of light could enter at the top, bottom, and sides of the visor. The *S* was trained to raise and lower the visor himself on *E*'s command, that is, "Visor up!" and

"Visor down!" and was gradually habituated to a visor-down period of 15 seconds. None of the Ss appeared to be particularly disturbed at having to wear the space helmet, lower the visor, etc., although appearances here may of course have been deceiving; some of them were manifestly amused by the whole thing.

Immediate Recall (IR). The Immediate Recall (IR) and Delayed Recall (DR) subtasks constituted the "heart" of the experimental sequence, the ones from which the most important data were expected. Half of the Ss of each grade and sex experienced them in the IR-DR order; the other half in the DR-IR order. The following equipment was used for these two subtasks and for the last, Point and Name (PN) subtask. There were two identical sets of seven colored paintings of objects, each photographically reproduced on a 3 × 4-inch card. The paintings depicted an apple, comb, an American flag, two yellow flowers on a stem, a moon, an owl, and a pipe. There was a 21 × 14 × ¼-inch board covered with a special black felt which tends to adhere to itself. One of the two sets of pictures was backed with the same felt, thus permitting E to place and displace these pictures freely on the board without fear of slippage, even when the board was held in a vertical position. The third major item was a two-tiered wooden rack, 27 inches long and 10 inches high, covered with ordinary green felt. The rack tilted slightly backward, away from S, permitting the second set of pictures to sit securely in a near-upright position on the two tiers. The final item was an ordinary stop watch used to time the 15-second delay period.

Throughout the experiment, S and the three Es sat in small chairs around a small table. One E (Beach), seated directly across the table from S (about 3 feet away), was occupied almost exclusively with recording any speech he could hear or lip read during the three subtasks. Another E (Chinsky) pointed to the pictures and recorded the child's pointing. The particular pictures pointed to, as well as their sequence, were random for each S, subtask, and trial. The third E (Flavell) did the instructing and other verbal interacting with S, randomly rearranged the pictures on the portable board and stationary rack after each recall trial, dispensed the prizes, etc.

The IR procedure on each trial was as follows: E held the portable board upright in front of S in such a position that S could not see the stationary rack sitting on the table just behind it. The second E then pointed to a given number of the pictures on the portable board at the rate of one point per 2 seconds. As soon as he had finished, the portable board was removed from view, and S tried to point to the same pictures in the same order on the rack. The E then rearranged the pictures on both board and rack in preparation for the next trial. The IR subtask began with preliminary instructions followed by two practice trials, each involving sequences of two pictures. The first of these trials was purely demonstrational: one E carefully explained the procedure, repeatedly stressing that S's recall was to be ordered, etc., while the other E did both the original pointing and, simulating S, the recall pointing. The second practice trial was indistinguishable from the subsequent test trials, except that S was corrected if he made an error. A minimum of three test trials followed. These involved sequences of first two, then three, then four pictures for grades K and 2, and first three, then four, then five pictures for grade 5. If S should perform correctly on the third of these trials, he was presented with progressively longer sequences until he failed; only a small minority of Ss recalled well enough to require any additional trials on this or the other two subtasks, however. As soon as the IR trials were completed, S was allowed to choose a second prize, regardless of how well he had performed.

Delayed Recall (DR).   The procedure for this subtask was identical to the preceding one, except that the space helmet visor was pulled down for a 15-second period between E's and S's pointing. As in IR, S was allowed to choose a third prize after the last DR trial.

Inquiry.   S was given a brief break following the third reward (he was encouraged to stand up and stretch if he wished, etc.), during the course of which E casually asked him the following question: "When he pointed to the pictures, you knew you were supposed to try to remember them, so you could point to the same ones afterward. Right? What did you *do* to remember them? I mean, how did you go *about* trying to keep them straight in your head?" Although E sometimes asked additional probing questions on the basis of S's answer, no S was later classified as having reported using a verbal rehearsal strategy unless he had given an unambiguous answer to that effect in response to this initial question.

Picture Naming.   Directly following the inquiry, E directed S's attention to the rack and asked: "By the way, can you tell me what each picture is a picture of? What's this [points], and this . . .?"

Point and Name (PN).   This subtask was identical to the DR subtask, except that S was instructed to name each depicted object aloud as E pointed to it, and again to name each one as he pointed to it during the recall period. The fourth of S's prizes was dispensed immediately afterward, and S returned to his classroom.

HYPOTHESES

The major prediction was that the second-grade Ss would produce significantly more detectable verbal coding and rehearsal of the depicted objects across the IR and DR trials than would the kindergarten Ss. If it turned out that the younger Ss could readily and accurately name the objects when asked to (Picture Naming), the above finding ought to constitute a reasonably adequate confirmation of the production-deficiency hypothesis, at least within the area of functioning represented by this task. A fifth-grade group was included in the sample only to test a minor hypothesis, derived from Vygotsky's (1962) writings on the development of inner speech. While it was of course supposed that fifth graders would be at least as likely to handle our task verbally as would the second graders, it might be predicted that their verbalizations would be relatively more covert and hence that our observer would see or hear a smaller proportion of the total actually produced. Taking both hypotheses together, one would expect something like an inverted U-shaped curve when observed verbal production is plotted against grade. Like the inclusion of the fifth-grade group, the addition of the third (PN) subtask constituted an excursion from the major focus of the study. We simply wondered if induced labeling would affect either S's recall score or his tendency to rehearse during the delay intervals. There are, of course, additional questions which could be put to the verbalization and recall data of this investigation; most of these will be taken up below.

RESULTS

An examination of the Picture-Naming data is a necessary preliminary to any empirical test of the production-deficiency hypothesis. These data strongly suggest that any production deficiency which may characterize our kindergarten group could not be attributed to an inability to name the stimuli. As would be expected, no second- or fifth-grade S mislabeled any of the seven pictures. Five kindergarten Ss made one minor labeling error each (e.g., moon = "sun," flowers = "roses" (they were not), owl = "eagle" or "bird"). Two Ss (including one of these five) were unable to name one picture each. This constitutes a total of only two serious and five minor naming problems out of 140 picture identifications made by these 20 Ss.

As indicated earlier, one of the Es—previously trained to lip read the seven object names—spent each testing session watching and listening for any verbalization he could detect. He was unable to see either set of picturs from where he sat and thus had no knowledge (unless S verbalized) as to exactly which pictures on a given IR or DR trial were being pointed to (he did know during the PN trials, of course, because S overtly labeled each pointing). While some Ss actually verbalized aloud or half-aloud on occasion, most of what E detected was at the level of soft whispering or soundless mouth movements. Anything E observed was immediately coded as belonging to one of three categories. The first category consisted of behavior which was indisputably stimulus labeling: E could either hear a specific word, lip read it with certainty, or both. The second category comprised lip-movement activity which E could with reasonable assurance interpret as labeling, even though he could not positively identify the particular word or words being spoken. An example would be an undecipherable but speechlike-movement pattern which was repeated several times over during a delay period. Lip-movement activity about which E had no such assurance constituted the third category: some of it looked like it definitely did not represent speech activity; some looked like it may have, but E did not feel sufficiently sure to categorize it as such. He occasionally noted other behaviors which may also have attested to covert verbal rehearsal, for example, rhythmic head nodding. However, only observations which could be assigned to the first two categories were treated as speech for data analy-

Table 1 Number of Ss Showing 0, 1–2, and 3+ Verbalization Instances on
Subtasks IR and DR Combined

	Number of Instances		
Grade	0	1–2	3+
K	18	1	1
2	8	7	5
5	3	4	13
Total	29	12	19

sis purposes. As things turned out—happily—the results to be presented
would have been about the same if we had adopted the more conservative
course of accepting only first-category instances as evidence for speech production, since the first and second categories tended to be highly correlated
within Ss. For example, the first column of Table 1 would read 18, 9, 4 instead of 18, 8, 3, if only first-category data were considered.

Within a single recall trial, there were between one and three occasions
when spontaneous speech could occur, these occasions corresponding to
subtask segments. In the case of the DR subtask, speech could occur during
the presentation segments (when E points), during the delay segments, or during the recall segments (when S points). The number of possible occasions is
reduced to two on IR trials (presentation and recall segments), and to one on
PN trials (delay segment). A "verbalization instance" can then be defined as
the occurrence of any detectable speech (first category, second category, or a
mixture of both) on one of the available occasions within one trial of one
subtask. "Any detectable speech" could thus refer to a single word, or it
could refer to the 11 complete rehearsals of a three-picture sequence which
one second-grade boy managed to squeeze into the delay period of a DR
trial.

Table 1 shows the number of Ss at each grade level who produced a
total of 0, 1–2, or 3 or more verbalization instances during the IR and DR
trials combined. As predicted, there is a substantial increase in spontaneous
verbal production from grade K to grade 2 ($\chi^2 = 11.02$; $df = 2$; $p < .01$). Much
to our surprise, however, production continues to increase from grade 2 to
grade 5, and this increase is likewise statistically significant $\chi^2 = 8.10$; $df = 2$;
$p < .02$). As the table shows, much of the change here appears to concern
how much verbalization S does, rather than whether he engages in any. The
fact that the production curve continues to rise between second and fifth
grade seems to render even more improbable any naming-deficiency explanation for a child's failure to verbalize on this task.

Table 2 shows the age distribution of production-nonproduction within
each segment of each subtask, including PN. There seems to be a fairly
regular grade-by-grade increase on all segments of all subtasks (χ^2s for all
columns are statistically reliable), with the exception of the grade 2–grade 5
portion of Presentation-IR. As regards the comparisons among columns, the

Table 2 Number of Ss Showing 1+ Verbalization Instances on Each
Segment of Each Subtask

	Segments and Subtasks					
	Presentation		Delay		Recall	
Grade	IR	DR	DR	PN	IR	DR
K	1	0	2	7	1	1
2	4	7	7	13	5	7
5	11	6	10	16	13	12
Total	16	13	19	36	19	20

IR and DR tasks appear not to have differed much in their capacity for evoking verbalization on comparable, that is, Presentation and Recall, segments. One might have expected that the total for column three would be higher than that of either the first two or the last two columns; for one thing, the sheer time available for verbalization was greater on this segment than on the others. Nonetheless, the probability of S making at least one verbalization seems not to have been significantly higher here than elsewhere. The most interesting comparison in the table is that between Delay-DR and Delay-PN. At all grade levels, the PN total is 5–6 Ss higher; indeed, this is the only subtask segment in which more than one or two kindergarten Ss show any verbalization. Some caution is required in interpreting this finding, however. On the one hand, the PN subtask came last in the experimental sequence (a fact which may have had some influence on the recall scores, at least, as will be shown). On the other hand, the observer always knew which pictures E had pointed to on this subtask, and this may have helped him promote to the first or second category certain lip-movement patterns which would otherwise have been relegated to the third-category. The following fact may or may not reflect such a scoring bias: there were five Ss who were recorded as showing nothing higher than third-category responses on Delay-DR trials but who went on to produce second- or third-category responses on Delay-PN. These caveats notwithstanding, it is hard to avoid believing that the PN procedure really did boost S's disposition to rehearse the stimulus names during the delay period. There were 17 Ss who produced no detectable verbalization during Delay-DR but did produce some during Delay-PN; there were no Ss who showed the opposite pattern.

Table 3 presents the observed verbalization data taken in conjunction with Ss responses to the inquiry question. Reported and observed behavior were consistent for 45 of the 60 Ss and inconsistent for 15. Of the 15, eight showed behavioral evidence of verbalization but did not unambiguously report that they had; they said that they did not know how they had remembered the items, or that they "tried to remember" them, or that they "thought" about them, etc. Interestingly enough, none of these eight produced more than one or two verbalization instances, or to put it differently, no S with three or more instances on IR and DR combined failed to state

Table 3   Number of Ss Showing Various Patterns of Observed and Reported
Verbalization on Subtasks IR and DR Combined

Pattern		Grade			
Observed	Reported	K	2	5	Total
+	+	1	7	15	23
0	0	18	4	0	22
+	0	1	5	2	8
0	+	0	4	3	7

that he had managed the task verbally. What of the seven Ss who said they had verbalized but did not produce any speech overt enough for E to detect? We found their retrospections very convincing. These two second graders were representative: "When he pointed to them, I just sayed them to myself, when he pointed to them." "Well, I kept saying them in my mind. (Like what did you say?) Well, he'd point to the apple and then to the flag, and I'd keep saying 'apple,' 'flag,' 'apple,' 'flag.'" It would be incredible if our gross detection procedure had not failed to identify as verbalizers at least some Ss who actually were. These seven 0+ children were surely among the false negatives, and there were undoubtedly others in the 00 group. It may be noted in passing that if one uses a disjunctive criterion for verbal production on this task—S either shows it or reports it—the number of producers remains at 2 in kindergarten but rises from 12 to 16 in second grade and from 17 to a unanimous 20 in fifth grade.

While this study was obviously not designed with mediation as opposed to production issues in mind, it would naturally be of interest to see if some of its data turned out to be relevant to these issues. There are two questions here for which one might look for tentative answers. First, does verbalization of the picture names actually assist the ordered recall of the pictures for either older or younger Ss? We had chosen this particular task in the first place on the hunch that Ss beyond a certain level of development would tend to handle it verbally (in an attempt to meet the Elicitation condition), and the evidence just presented suggests that this hunch was probably correct. We had further supposed that a verbal mediational strategy would attain this popularity precisely because it is a useful way of managing this sort of task, but this supposition may have been wrong. The second question is the familiar mediational-deficiency one: if verbalization is in fact a useful strategy here, is it less useful to younger children than to older children?

The recall scores obtained under the PN versus the IR and DR task conditions might give evidence relevant to the first question. If recall under PN turned out to be significantly superior to that under the other two conditions and if this superiority could not be attributed to subtask order effects, it would suggest that verbalization was facilitative. The S was given a recall score for each of the three subtasks. This score was simply the number of objects contained in the longest object series (test trials only) which he re-

Table 4 Group Mean Recall Scores by Subtask and Subtask Order

Grade	Subtask		Subtask Order		
	IR	DR	First	Second	Third (PN)
K	1.75	1.40	1.30	1.85	2.20
2	2.50	2.90	2.55	2.85	3.50
5	3.95	3.70	3.60	4.05	3.95
All Ss	2.73	2.67	2.48	2.92	3.22

called correctly. For example, a kindergarten or second-grade child who pointed to the correct objects in correct sequence on his second trial but not on his first and third would receive a score of 3. Any S who failed all three test trials was arbitrarily assigned a score of 1. Table 4 presents the mean recall scores for IR and DR (order counterbalanced within each group), and also for the first subtask administered (IR or DR), the second (IR or DR), and the third (PN for all Ss). There is no suggestion in the table that the IR and DR conditions per se led to differences in recall. On the other hand, it does appear that subtask order was a variable, S tending to improve in recall with each successive subtask, regardless of which subtasks occupied the first and second position in the sequence. The analysis of variance shown in Table 5 confirms this impression: subtask order is a significant main effect. It is therefore apparent that no conclusions about verbal facilitation can be drawn from this segment of the data.

Another way to test for verbal facilitation might be to divide each group of Ss into two approximately equal-sized subgroups, based upon how much spontaneous verbalization they apparently engaged in, and then compare subgroup recall scores. This obviously cannot be done with the kindergarten group, since there were only two Ss who showed any detectable verbalization. Neither can it be done with the fifth graders for the opposite reason: all of

Table 5 Summary of Analysis of Variance of Recall Scores

Source	df	MS	F	p
Between Ss:	59			
Grade (A)	2	65.51	52.82	< .01
Sex (B)	1	1.61	1.29	. . .
A × B	2	1.57	1.27	. . .
Error (b)	54	1.24	. . .	. . .
Within Ss:	120			
Subtask order (C)	2	8.16	11.79	< .01
A × C	4	0.90	1.30	. . .
B × C	2	3.76	5.43	< .01
A × B × C	4	0.80	1.15	. . .
Error (w)	108	0.69	. . .	. . .

Note: For all other Fs, p > .25.

Table 6 Mean Recall Scores of Second-Grade Ss Reporting (N = 11) and Not Reporting (N = 9) Verbalization

| | Subtask | | |
Verbalization	IR	DR	PN
Reported	2.82	3.27	3.45
Not reported	2.11	2.44	3.45

them either reported that they had verbalized, produced detectable verbalization, or both. The data on the second graders appear more promising in this respect, but there is the question of exactly what basis to use for dividing the group. The division ought to be a plausible one, and it also ought to yield two subgroups of roughly equal Ns. The division which appears to come closest to satisfying these two criteria is that which separates these 20 Ss into those who reported having verbalized during the recall trials ($N = 11$) and those who did not ($N = 9$); one might assume that the former subgroup did more verbalizing, at least, than the latter did. Table 6 shows the subgroup recall scores. The 11 recalled better than the 9 on both IR and DR, significantly so in the latter case ($t = 2.59$; $df = 18$; $p < .02$). Had these subgroup differences been simply a matter of differential recall skills, unrelated to the use of verbalization, one would have expected a similar difference on the PN subtask; as the table shows, however, the mean recall scores are identical there. Although this finding is suggestive, it must be regarded as rather slender evidence for the hypothesis.

A mediational-deficiency hypothesis would receive support in our study if either of the following were shown to be true: (1) the PN condition does not facilitate recall as much for kindergarten nonproducers as it does for second-grade non-producers, or (2) differences in recall scores (on IR and DR) between producers and nonproducers of the same grade should be smaller in the kindergarten than in the second-grade group. Since there really is no good evidence as yet that PN facilitates anyone's recall, and since the comparison suggested in (2) above is impossible in the case of the kindergarten Ss, it is obvious that our data can provide no sort of test for this hypothesis. It would certainly be interesting to establish that verbalization does in fact assist memory on this type of task, and even more interesting to prove that this assistance is less marked in younger versus older children. The present study was manifestly not intended to accomplish either of these things and, not surprisingly, did not succeed in doing so by chance.

DISCUSSION

The results of this study confirm the existence of something akin to a verbal production deficiency in young children, at least within the experimental setting we used to test for it. They do not, however, shed any light whatever on the precise nature and meaning of this deficiency or on the mechanisms responsible for its apparent decline during the elementary school years. Why, exactly, did most of the kindergarten Ss seemingly fail to use naming and rehearsal as a cognitive "trick" to aid their recall? Perhaps for either or both of two reasons.

The failure might have reflected an immaturity that was specifically linguistic in nature, performance on Picture Naming notwithstanding. According to this line of explanation, there is more to language development than just a gradual mastery of its phonology, morphology, and syntax. The child who "has" a language, in the sense of having acquired such mastery, may still not know exactly when and where to use what he has, in rather the same way that an individual may "have" a concept or cognitive rule and yet not think to apply it on every appropriate occasion. While the 5-year-old has learned to translate linguistic competence into verbal utterance in a number of contexts where an adult would do the same—in communicative ones, notably—he may well not have learned to do this in all appropriate contexts. Thus, the genesis of language in its broadest sense may partly entail a progressive "linguification" of more and more situations. Initially, only a limited number of behavioral contexts call forth speech activity, but this number gradually increases as development proceeds. To borrow an expression from Wittgenstein (1958), the number and variety of "language games" the child knows how to "play" is a function of his developmental level, and most kindergarten children have simply not yet acquired the one demanded by our task.

When the present study had been completed, the senior author reported the findings to the school principal and the three teachers whose children had served as Ss. Hoping to get some leads for future research, he brought along two lists of second graders: the five most verbally productive Ss among the seven who showed the + + pattern (see Table 3), and the four who showed the 00 pattern. The second-grade teacher was asked to guess which group had used verbal rehearsal in our task. She identified the correct list without a moment's hesitation, and when asked how she knew, she replied to the effect that those were the ones who perpetually talked in class. It may be that these particular children have simply learned to "linguify" a great variety of stimulus situations, situations which do not obviously call for verbal responding (such as our task) as well as those which do.

A second line of explanation would stress a more general cognitive immaturity, one which could make for a deficiency in verbal and nonverbal production alike, depending upon which kind of behavior the task demanded. Verbal coding and rehearsal on a task such as ours could be construed as reflecting or embodying certain intellectual competencies which have nothing intrinsically verbal about them. An S who codes and rehearses is, first of all, responding to the task in an intellectually active fashion. Not content simply to track the picture sequence in a purely—and passively—sensory fashion, he "goes beyond the information given" to transform this perceived sequence into an isomorphic sequence of vocal responses in accordance with what looks like a self-generated cognitive strategy. Second, in continuously rehearsing the stimulus names during the delay period, S is demonstrating a capacity for sustained attentional focusing in the absence of both perceptual and social (i.e., instructional) supports for doing so. Third, coding and rehearsal represents a systematic plan for coping effectively with the task requirements; it is, as such, a kind of problem-solving "algorithm" of S's own devising. And finally, it represents a time-binding, goal-directed effort on his part. He codes for the future when the stimuli are first presented, and he also keeps the past alive by carrying that code forward into the recall period. Viewed in this way, our kindergarten Ss may have failed to talk to themselves for reasons having nothing whatever to do with their level of linguistic development. That is, they may simply have been too young to engage in the kinds of intellectual activities which assume the guise, in this particular task, of verbal coding and rehearsal. The work of Piaget and others on this age group would support such a view.

As indicated earlier, the continuing increase in detectable verbalization from second to fifth grade came as a surprise, and appears inconsistent with Vygotsky's (1962) speculations about the progressive internalization of nonsocial speech during early childhood. A recent study by Klein (1963) also provides evidence relevant to Vygotsky's internalization hypothesis. He looked and listened for any detachable speech which 3–7-year-old children produced when left alone in an observation room with cut-out puzzles and drawing materials. He found a significant decrease with age in the ratio of "audible-comprehensible" speech (that which could be clearly understood on tape playback) to total speech (audible-comprehensible plus incomprehensible muttering, soundless lip movements, etc.). There was, however, no such decrease with age in the number of Ss on whom those ratios could be calculated, that is, within that subset of children (about half the total group) who produced any detectable verbalization at all. What both Klein's findings and our own signify for the internalization hypothesis seems to depend upon one's interpretation of "internalized," that is, upon just how far the alleged internalization is thought to proceed in the course of maturation. If soundless or near-soundless lip-movement activity is accepted as "internalized," that is, considered a likely ontogenetic end point, then Klein's first result supports the hypothesis. Our data, in turn, could probably be dismissed as either irrelevant to it or consistent with it: our youngest verbalizers (second graders, largely) were the same age as Klein's oldest and, together with the still older fifth graders, mostly talked at this critical, barely detectable level when rehearsing. If, on the other hand, "internalized" is taken literally to mean *really covert*—well below what either we or Klein could hope to detect with our gross procedures—the data must be construed differently. Klein's second finding now becomes the relevant one and provides no support for the hypothesis across the 3–7 year span. Our data complement his for the 7–10-year span and likewise fail to show any developmental movement toward complete internalization. One pays his money and takes his choice.

We are presently inclined to guess that there is something to Vygotsky's hypothesis, actually, but that it needs a more complicated restatement. The restated version is that in most or all cases where the intensity level of non-social speech changes with age, that change will in fact be in the direction of lesser intensity. However, what the initial level is; how much, if any, developmental reduction will occur (and hence, what the final level will be); what the rate of reduction will be across childhood, and when asymptote will be reached—all of these will vary in as yet unknown ways both with the individual and with the context or setting in which the speech occurs. For example, rehearsal in a memory task may show little if any reduction in level as a function of age, but may vary with what has to be remembered and how much difficulty S has in trying to remember it, and surely will vary among individuals at a given age level (recall Table 3). The import of Vygotsky's hypothesis, or any restatement of it, really amounts to this: an adequate account of the noncommunicative uses of language will eventually have to deal with two major questions. First and foremost, in what contexts do individuals tend to engage in nonsocial speech and to what effect? This is an oversimplified statement of what is usually referred to as the "language-thought" question, the question of the precise role and significance of language in cognitive and other activities. Second, in those situations where speech is produced, what governs its intensity level? This second question has seldom been broached, let alone answered. It may be important to ask and answer it, however, because doing so may provide us with valuable insights concerning the first, ultimately more interesting questions.

REFERENCES

Glanzer, M., & Clark, W. H. The verbal loop hypothesis: binary numbers. *J. verb. Learn. verb. Behav.*, 1963, *2*, 301–309.

Jarvis, P. E. The effect of self-administered verbal instructions on simple sensory-motor performance in children. Unpublished doctoral dissertation, Univer. of Rochester, 1963.

Kendler, Tracy S. Development of mediating responses in children. In J. C. Wright, & J. Kagan (Eds.), Basic cognitive processes in children. *Monogr. Soc. Res. Child Develpm.*, 1963, *28* (2), 33–52.

Klein, W. An investigation of the spontaneous speech of children during problem-solving. Unpublished doctoral dissertation, Univer. of Rochester, 1963.

Luria, A. R. The genesis of voluntary movements. In N. O'Connor (Ed.), *Recent Soviet psychology*. New York: Pergamon, 1961. Pp. 165–185.

Maccoby, Eleanor E. Developmental psychology. *Ann. Rev. Psychol.*, 1964, *15*, 203–250.

Ranken, H. B. Language and thinking: positive and negative effects of learning. *Science*, 1963, *141*, 48–50.

Reese, H. W. Verbal mediation as a function of age level. *Psychol. Bull.*, 1962, *59*, 502–509.

Reese, H. W. "Perceptual set" in young children. *Child Develpm.*, 1963, *34*, 151–159.

Spiker, C. C. Stimulus pretraining and subsequent performance in the delayed reaction experiment. *J. exp. Psychol.*, 1956, *52*, 107–111.

Vygotsky, L. S. *Thought and language.* Trans. Eugenia Hanfmann and Gertrude Vakar. Cambridge, Mass. and New York: M.I.T. Press and Wiley, 1962.

Weir, M. W., & Stevenson, H. W. The effect of verbalization in children's learning as a function of chronological age. *Child Develpm.,* 1959, *30,* 143–149.

Wittgenstein, L. *Preliminary studies for the "philosophical investigations," generally known as the blue and brown books.* Oxford: Blackwell, 1958.

A Tutorial Language Program To Develop Abstract Thinking in Socially Disadvantaged Preschool Children

Marion Blank and Frances Solomon

ALBERT EINSTEIN COLLEGE OF MEDICINE, YESHIVA UNIVERSITY

Widespread deficiencies ranging across the cognitive, affective, motivational, and social areas have been found in deprived children. Compensatory programs have therefore aimed at exposing the children to a different and wider range of almost every type of stimulus deemed to be beneficial (e.g., better equipment, parent participation, trips, perceptual training). In essence, this approach assumes that all factors contribute an equal amount to the alleviation of the deficits found in the deprived child.

This paper outlines an approach which offers an alternative to the philo-

Reprinted from *Child Development,* copyright © by The Society for Research in Child Development, Inc., *39,* No. 2, 379–389. By permission.

This research was supported by U.S. Public Health Service grant K3-MH-10,749. The authors wish to thank the Bronx River Day Care Center and Miss E. Johnson for their cooperation and participation in this research. A preliminary version of this paper was presented at the meetings of the Society for Research in Child Development, New York, March, 1967.

sophy of total enrichment. The premise of this approach is that, while total enrichment is not without value, it does not diagnose the key deficits of the deprived child. The usual concept of enrichment is also limited by the idea that exposure to the previously absent stimuli is sufficient for learning.

We feel that exposure to an infinite number of ostensibly enriching stimuli does not necessarily overcome the deficits. Presentation alone does not insure that the child will partake of newly available material. If learning is to occur, the child must involve himself actively with the stimuli so as to comprehend their significance. Active involvement refers, not to motor activity, but rather to the internal mental manipulation of experience. The latter applies to skills involving the ability to organize thoughts, to reflect upon situations, to comprehend the meaning of events, and to structure behavior so as to be able to choose among among alternatives.

These skills coincide with many of the characteristics defining the abstract attitude (Goldstein, 1959). Research by the senior author (Blank & Bridger, 1964, 1966, 1967) has led us to postulate that the failure to develop this abstract attitude represents the most glaring deficiency of deprived children. *Their behavior reflects the lack of a symbolic system by which to organize the plentiful stimulation surrounding them.*

The problem then arises of what is the most effective means for developing abstract thinking. We feel that an internal symbolic system can best be achieved through the development of abstract language (Vygotsky, 1962). Certain types of language, such as labeling clear, circumscribed objects (e.g., bottle, table, ball), can be grasped easily through illustration and/or imitation. Therefore, no great effort is required to learn these words. By contrast, words referring to properties which are not immediately evident require much elaboration for understanding. For example, a word such as "top" is much more abstract than a word such as "book." The word "top" can refer to such physically different things as the "top" of one's head, the "top" of one's desk, and the "top" of a building. The word unites these instances only when there is an understanding that "top" refers to the highest point on anything, regardless of how different the "anythings" look. Other examples requiring a similar level of abstraction are time (before, after), direction (underneath, between), and relative judgments (warmer, heavier). It is here that an articulate person, be it mother, teacher, or sibling, is required to offer the necessary corroboration or negation of the child's emerging ideas.

This type of feedback is readily available in the middle-class home, but it is rare in the lower-class home (see Freeberg & Payne, 1967). We therefore propose that this lack of an ongoing, elaborated dialogue is the major experiential deficit of the deprived child (Bernstein, 1960).

Previous attempts to transmit this aspect of learning to disadvantaged children have relied on using the group situation (Bereiter & Engelmann, 1966; Deutsch, 1964; Gray & Klaus, 1965). A serious question arises of whether early language skills can be fostered in a group situation or whether we must in some way mirror the middle-class one-to-one situation. For example, if given a direction to "place the red block on top of the blue one," a child in the group setting can wait to see what the other children do and simply *imitate* their action. Of course, the child *might* listen to the language and associate it with the key features of the performance he just imitated. However, this method relies on the hope that the child will avail himself of this opportunity to learn. Nothing inherent in the situation requires him either to heed or to understand the language in order to fulfill the demands placed upon him.

In the latter example, the child at least had to make a response; in many classroom situations, no overt response is required. It is assumed that, when the teacher instructs, the child makes the appropriate inner response even though he is not required to answer overtly. If the inner response is lacking, he cannot follow the dialogue, and the teaching, no matter how well organized, is lost. By contrast, the one-to-one situation can be easily designed so that the child is required to use his language skills, and then he cannot function on a level lower than the goals set by the teacher. In addition, since goals set in individual instruction are designed for the child's specific capabilities, they are more likely to be appropriate.

Although most educators acknowledge that ideal teaching would be a one-to-one relation, this has been deemed impractical because of the costs involved. The conclusion of excessive costs is based on the implicit assumption that individual teaching would or should occupy most of the teaching day. Little consideration has been given to the possible effectiveness of short periods of daily individual instruction, even though such instruction is widely and effectively used in the initial teaching of language to other language-deficient groups, such as deaf children (Blank, 1965). In addition, the limited attention spans of young children suggest that relatively brief sessions involving frequent reinforcement of new (language) skills would theoretically be the most effective means of teaching.

In summary, our assumptions were:

1. Deprived preschool children do not have a firm language base for thinking. They will develop one only if they are given consistent guidance. This leads to the further assumption that the most effective teaching is based on individual tutoring.

2. Language acquisition, like any new complex skill, may be met with some resistance. To prevent resistance from becoming established, the child should not be permitted to leave a task unfinished. If necessary, the task can be simplified, but the child should still be required to fulfill the demands set by the teacher. Once these initial difficulties have been conquered, the child is able to experience great pleasure both in using this new tool and in knowing that he has this tool to use.

3. Young children have short attention spans and therefore need relatively brief but frequent reinforcement of new skills (i.e., 5 days a week for 15–20 minutes each day, resulting in a total of about 1½ hours of tutoring per week).

4.   The new command of language will allow the child to cope more

effectively with an otherwise debilitating environment. Therefore, marked improvements in many aspects of maladaptive behavior should occur.

Based on these considerations, an exploratory program was developed which involved brief daily teaching of language skills for abstract thinking. The central hypothesis was that intervention limited to the development of language for reflection would play such a vital role in cognition that it would facilitate not only language but many other aspects of thinking.

METHOD

Teaching Techniques

Even though we are stressing abstract language, we are not deceived into thinking that the young child is capable of the highest level of concept formation. His concepts must still be bound to direct referents because he needs some tangible evidence of the idea being demonstrated. Nevertheless, the young child can be taught to bring to his level of conceptualization the processes of thinking vital to the development of abstraction.

The first goal of the teaching was to have the child recognize that information relevant to his world was not immediately evident but could be and *had* to be sought from his previous experience. Thus he was taught to question, to probe, to investigate. For example, the teacher put on her coat at the end of a session. The child said, "Why are you going home?" The teacher replied, "How do you know I am going home?" to which the child said, "You're not going home?" This response meant that the child had dropped any attempt at reasoning; he had interpreted the teacher's query to mean that he must negate his earlier inference. To encourage the child to pursue the matter, the teacher said "I *am* going home, but what makes you think I am going home? When you get ready to go home, what do you do?" The child said, "I get my coat." A discussion then followed to solidify the significance of these observations. Thus Socratic dialogue was employed instead of didactic teaching.

Various teaching methods were devised to achieve these goals. A common denominator of all the methods was that the child was confronted with situations in which the teacher used no gestures; to accomplish the task correctly, the child had to understand and/or use language. Another consistent factor was that the child was led to produce an independent response relevant to a situation created by the teacher and to extend the situation set forth by her. This extension focused on having the child discuss situations which did not exist in front of him at the moment but which were relevant to the present situations (e.g., past, future, alternative courses of action, giving explanations of events). By structuring the teaching time in this way, the teacher made maximum use of every opportunity to aid the child in developing his budding ability to think and to reflect. Some of the major techniques used are described below. As the work progresses, we hope to expand and refine this list. It should be noted that each technique is specifically geared to overcome a particular deficiency. This is in contrast to the concept of an enriched environment where the aim is to give a massive dosage that will somehow hit the individual deficiencies. Specifically, the method attempted to develop the following:

(a) *Selective attention.*   The young child has few guidelines to assist him in discriminating selectively from the plethora of stimuli which surround him. He tends to be drawn to stimuli which may not be of great cognitive importance but which have potent perceptual qualities (e.g., blast of a horn, a whirling disk). The aim of this technique was to teach the child to recognize essential elements by requiring him to compare objects and make choices among them (e.g., if given a group of different-colored blocks, he was asked to take "two red blocks and one green block"). In this example, the higher-level concept of number helps the child restrain his impulse to respond primitively to the sensory impact of color alone.

(b) *Categories of exclusion.*   When the adult gives specific instructions (e.g., "get a crayon"), the child does not need to reflect upon the characteristics of a particular category; he merely responds to direct commands. When the adult gives no direction, the child works aimlessly. When the child can work within the confines of exclusion, however, it means that he has understood the teacher's frame of reference and can independently make appropriate responses. To develop this skill, the child may be asked to make decisions within the confines set by the teacher. For example, the child may be asked to draw something, and he may draw a circle. To encourage the development of exclusion, he would then be asked to draw something "other than a circle."

(c) *Imagery of future events.*   The young child can easily describe existing objects and situations. Difficulty arises when he must perceive the meaning of this information relevant to a particular context (see John, 1963). To increase this capacity, the child was required to think through the results of realistically possible but not present courses of action. The child might be first asked to locate a doll that was on the table. After the child completed this correctly, the doll would remain on the table, and the child might be asked, "Where would the doll be if it fell from the table?"

(d) *Relevant inner verbalization.*   We have found that many deprived children will use language to direct their problem-solving only when asked to; they will not spontaneously use language when these external requirements are not imposed. Thus it is not a matter of not having the words but rather a matter of not voluntarily using these words without specific demands. This technique attempts to train the children to develop inner verbalization by retaining words as substitutes for objects. In this method, the child must use language silently and then express it upon request. He might be asked to look at a picture, say the name to himself, and then after the picture has been removed tell the name to the teacher.

(e) *Separation of the word from its referent.*   Young children tend to respond to language automatically without fully recognizing that the word exists independently of the object or action represented. If this separation is not achieved, the child will not generalize the meaning of words beyond the particular contexts in which he hears them. To encourage the ability to reflect upon meaning, the child might be given a command which he must repeat aloud *before* acting out the command—for example, "Jump up two times," "Walk to the door and open it."

(f) *Models for cause-and-effect reasonings.* Our research (Blank & Bridger, 1966, 1967) has indicated that the perceptual powers of deprived children are intact; they need help, however, in organizing their observations so as to comprehend their significance. To achieve this comprehension, the child can be led to observe common but not frequently noted phenomena (e.g., "What is the weather outside today?" "Can we go out and play today?"). He can then be asked to draw upon his previous experience to determine the reasons underlying these observations (e.g., "Why can't we go out and play?" "Where is the rain coming from?").

(g) *Ability to categorize.* The place of categorization in thinking has been well documented, and its importance was recognized in this project. To aid the children in this sphere, elementary categories such as food, clothing, transportation, and job functions were taught. Thus, after feeding a doll an imaginary apple, the child was asked to name some other fruits that the doll might eat. Then, utilizing the process of exclusion *(b* above), the child might be asked to name some foods that were *not* fruits.

(h) *Awareness of possessing language.* Frequently young children are only passive recipients of instruction. This deficiency means that they are unaware that they can independently invoke language to help order their world. This weakness can be overcome by techniques such as asking the child to give commands to the teacher. The teacher might say to the child, "What shall I do with these pencils?" "Now *you* ask *me* to draw something," "Now tell me what the doll should do this afternoon."

(i) *Sustained sequential thinking.* Just as musical notes attain their full meaning only when heard within a melody, words attain their full potential only when imbedded in context. This is true even at the elementary level of a simple sentence, and it becomes increasingly important as chains of events extending into time and space must be understood. To be able to see objects, events, and words as located within their appropriate framework, the child has to be taught to maintain concentration and to determine all the possibilities of a course of action. For example, in discussing ways in which material can be altered, the discussion might begin with vegetable dyes (their function, their appearance, etc.). The issue can then be raised as to what can happen to these dyes under various conditions (diluting them with water, leaving them in concentrated form, etc.). In each case, the child is required to apply the necessary change (e.g., add the water) so that he can directly and immediately experience the phenomenon being discussed.

These techniques for achieving higher mental processes are in contrast to the language programs stressing concepts as an end in themselves. In our view, concepts were seen as the necessary preliminary tools for thinking; accordingly, they occupied only a segment of the program. The type of concept taught could not be illustrated by simple direct examples or simple labeling. For example, to call an object a "book" may facilitate communication, but it does not serve to abstract anything more of the object than does a gesture. In addition, the child who can label glibly is often deceptive, since his facile use of words gives the false appearance of understanding. Concepts such as number, speed, direction, temperature, and emotions are suitable for stressing the more abstract functions of language. Techniques for teaching these concepts have been well documented by Bereiter and Englemann (1966).

Common inexpensive objects readily available in the child's environment were the only ones used in the teaching, (e.g., papers, crayons, blocks, toy cars, simple books). The materials were used only as points of departure from which the child could discuss increasingly abstract (nonpresently existing) situations which were relevant to the materials. The same materials, when used alone by the child without supervision, might prove useless in terms of the aims of the study—namely, the avoidance of aimless, scattered, stimulus-bound activity.

Subjects and Procedure

The subjects were selected from a nursery school in a socioeconomically deprived area in New York City. All 22 children from the youngest classes were tested on the Stanford-Binet Intelligence Test (S-B Test) and the Leiter Scale. The children ranged in age from 3 years, 3 months to 4 years, 7 months. Based on these test results, the children were divided into four groups, two tutored and two untutored, matched as closely as possible for IQ, age, and sex. Each child in the first tutored group received individual teaching for 15–20 minutes daily, five times per week; each child in the second tutored group received the same training only three times a week. This tutoring involved taking the child for this short period from his classroom to a familiar room in the school. Each child in one untutored group had daily individual sessions with the same teacher, but no attempt was made to tutor the child. During this time, the child was exposed to the identical materials and was permitted to engage in any activity of his choice. While the teacher was warm and responsive to the child's questions and comments, she did not initiate or extend any cognitive interchange. This group was included to control for the possible role of individual attention alone in facilitating intellectual performance. Another untutored group of seven children remained in the regular nursery school program with no additional attention.

All the tutoring was conducted by a professional nursery school teacher who was trained in the techniques outlined above. The experiment took place over a 4-month period, after which the children were retested. Both the pre- and posttesting were conducted by two research assistants who did not know to which of the groups the children had been assigned and who had had no contact with the children other than at the time of testing.

RESULTS

The pre- and posttest results on the S-B Test are shown in Table 1. Mean IQ increases in tutored groups 1 and 2 were 14.5 and 7.0 points, respectively; in untutored groups 1 and 2, the changes were 2.0 and 1.3 points, respectively. A Kruskal-Wallis analysis of variance indicated that the changes in the four groups were significantly different ($p < .05$). A Mann-Whitney Test indicated that the rise in the tutored groups was significantly greater than the rise in the untutored groups ($p < .02$). Although the difference was not significant, the gain by the group tutored five times a week was greater than that of the group tutored three times a week. This suggests that improvements in performance may be directly correlated to the amount of tutoring per week. The lack of a clear difference in gain between the two untutored groups indicates that the element of individual attention from an adult, without specialized tutoring was not sufficient to achieve the rise in IQ scores.

The results on the Leiter Scale, though somewhat less marked, are in accord with those on the S-B Test. Thus, tutored groups 1 and 2 showed mean increases of 4.5 and 9.5, respectively, while untutored groups 1 and 2 showed 5.0 and 1.9, respectively. The lower overall gains on the Leiter Scale may also be a reflection of the fact that this test does not require verbal abilities, while the teaching techniques emphasized verbal development. The Leiter scores, however, showed erratic variations. For example untutored children who remained in the classroom showed spontaneous losses and gains of up to 20 points. This result leads us to believe that the Leiter performance is not a reliable indicator of functioning at this age range.

These IQ changes must also be evaluated in conjunction with the dramatic behavioral changes that accompanied these rises. For example, three of the children were so excessively withdrawn that they had not uttered any coherent verbalizations during their entire time in school. They also exhibited other severe symptoms, such as drooling, "ramlike" headbutting, and bizarre physical coordination. Within 1 month after the program was started, all three were speaking clearly, coherently, and appropriately, and there was a diminution of all symptomatology. No comparable changes were noted in the two children from the control groups who exhibited similar symptomatology.

Even among the children who were relatively well functioning, striking improvements were found. For example, on the S-B Test the pretest response of one girl in describing a picture was "a lady, a horse"; the posttest response was, "The mother is trying to catch the dog with the clothes, the dog takes the clothes, and the mother was trying to get it." This response illustrates the growth from simple labeling to a coordinated, sequential story construction.

The most striking gains in the program were the apparent joy in learning

Table 1   Pre- and Posttest Stanford-Binet Scores

Sex	Age[a]	Total Hours Tutored	IQ Pre	IQ Post	IQ Change
Tutored group 1 (5 times/ wk.):					
F1	3.8	11	70	98	+28
F2	3.11	11	100	109	+9
F3	3.4	13	104	115	+11
M1	3.3	12	111	127	+16
M2	3.11	14	90	109	+19
M3	3.7	14	111	115	+4
Mean			97.7	112.2	+14.5
Tutored group 2 (3 times/ wk.):					
F4	3.9	8	89	105	+16
F5	4.7	6	86	98	+12
F6	4.5	7	103	103	0
F7	3.3	6	79[b]	96	+17
M4	3.11	9	94	93	−1
M5	4.0	5	107	105	−2
Mean			93.0	100.0	+7.0
Untutored group 1 (5 times/wk.):					
F8	4.1	13	107	111	+4
M6	4.4	10	101	99	−2
M7	4.2	11	80	84	+4
Mean			96.0	98.0	+2.0
Untutored group 2 (classroom):					
F9	4.6	. . .	97	99	+2
F10	3.5	. . .	105	107	+2
F11	3.11	. . .	105	103	−2
F12	4.2	. . .	117	114	−3
M8	4.2	. . .	115	124	+9
M9	4.2	. . .	88	88	0
M10	3.5	. . .	93	94	+1
Mean			102.8	104.1	+1.3

[a] Age at beginning of study.
[b] No basal score was achieved; a basal MA of 2 years was assumed for the calculations, thus overestimating the score.

and the feeling of mastery which the children displayed as the tutoring progressed. The untutored children, even those who received individual attention, showed none of these attitudes. This result is extremely important in that it strongly suggests that exposure to materials, a school-like situation, and an interested adult is not sufficient for learning. Both mastery and enthusiasm for learning will come only when the child can be shown how to become actively involved in the learning process.

DISCUSSION

The program outlined above is offered as a means of teaching those language skills necessary for developing abstract thinking in disadvantaged preschool children. We feel that most enrichment programs, and indeed most nursery school programs, are remiss in this area. It is generally assumed that abstract thinking will evolve naturally by school age from having an enriched environment available in the early years. This expectation is often met in the case of middle-class children, because the skills not taught by the nursery school are learned in the verbally rich home environment. In the case of the lower-class child, these experiences are not available.

Although the disadvantaged child has not been given the necessary tools for thinking, there are implicit expectations when he enters school that he has a well-formulated abstract attitude. For example, multiple-choice questions are common in reading-readiness tests. Aside from the content, this type of question assumes that the child can evaluate a series sequentially, can refocus attention selectively, and can realize that he must make a definitive choice between alternatives. How is this abstract attitude to emerge? Our research indicates that high-level language skills are central to the development of this kind of thinking. Even at the preschool level, there are tasks for which abstract language is the only means of solution (Blank & Bridger, 1964). Therefore, it is risky to hope that the "fallout" from a perceptually enriched environment will encourage the formation of what is the central core of intelligence.

Even where the language deficits of the deprived preschooler are recognized, they are treated through enlarging the vocabulary, since vocabulary is seen as the basic unit of language. Implicit in this approach is that, as in perceptual training, mere exposure to the basic units will "lubricate" the entire language system. It is our thesis that these children do not simply need more and better words; rather, they need to use the language they already have, as well as any new words they learn, to structure and guide their thinking.

Although this approach benefited the children in this study, its full potential needs further exploration. In addition, it is believed that the program would have to be maintained for a considerable period of time, probably for about 2–3 years, for the gain to be maintained independently thereafter by the child. Reasoning is still difficult for these children, and they need continuing guidance for it to become firmly established. However, considering the amount of time (approximately 60–90 minutes per week per child), the low cost of the materials, and the rapid gains in performance, it seems worthwhile to pursue this program as a technique for facilitating cognitive growth in young children from deprived backgrounds.

REFERENCES

Bereiter, C., & Englemann, S. Teaching disadvantaged children in the preschool. Englewood Cliffs, N.J.: Prentice-Hall, 1966.

Bernstein, B. Language and social class. British Journal of Sociology, 1960, 2, 271–276.

Blank, M. Use of the deaf in language studies: a reply to Furth. Psychological Bulletin, 1965, 63, 442–444.

Blank, M., & Bridger, W. H. Cross-modal transfer in nursery school children. Journal of Comparative and Physiological Psychology, 1964, 58, 277–282.

Blank, M., & Bridger, W. H. Deficiencies in verbal labeling in retarded readers. American Journal of Orthopsychiatry, 1966, 36, 840–847.

Blank, M., & Bridger, W. H. Perceptual abilities and conceptual deficiencies in retarded readers. In J. Zubin (Ed.), Psychopathology of Mental Development. New York: Grune & Stratton, 1967, 401–412.

Deutsch, M. Facilitating development in the preschool child: social and psychological perspectives. Merrill-Palmer Quarterly, 1964, 10, 249–263.

Freeburg, N. E., & Payne, D. T. Parental influence on cognitive development in early childhood: a review. Child Development, 1967, 38, 65–87.

Goldstein, K. Functional disturbances in brain damage. In S. Arieti (Ed.), American Handbook of Psychiatry. Vol. 1. New York: Basic Books, 1959, 770–794.

Gray, S. W., & Klaus, R. A. An experimental preschool program for culturally deprived children. Child Development, 1965, 36, 887–898.

John, V. P. The intellectual development of slum children: some preliminary findings. American Journal of Orthopsychiatry, 1963, 33, 813–822.

Vygotsky, L. S. Thought and language. New York: Wiley, 1962.

The Stages
of the Intellectual
Development
of the Child

Jean Piaget

UNIVERSITY OF GENEVA

A consideration of the stages of the development of intelligence should be preceded by asking the question, What is intelligence? Unfortunately, we find ourselves confronted by a great number of definitions. For Claparède, intelligence is an adaptation to new situations. When a situation is new, when there are no reflexes, when there are no habits to rely on, then the subject is obliged to search for something new. That is to say, Claparède defines intelligence as groping, as feeling one's way, trial-and-error behavior. We find this trial-and-error behavior in all levels of intelligence, even at the superior level, in the form of hypothesis testing. As far as I am concerned, this definition is too vague, because trial and error occurs in the formation of habits,

Reprinted from *Bulletin of the Menninger Clinic*, 1962, *26*, No. 3, 120–145. By permission.

The three lectures by Dr. Piaget contained in this issue of the *Bulletin* were presented as a series to the Menninger School of Psychiatry, March 6, 13, and 22, 1961.

and also in the earliest established reflexes: when a newborn baby learns to suck.

Karl Bühler defines intelligence as an act of immediate comprehension; that is to say, an insight. Bühler's definition is also very precise, but it seems to me too narrow. I know that when a mathematician solves a problem, he ends by having an insight, but up to that moment he feels, or gropes for, his way; and to say that the trial-and-error behavior is not intelligent and that intelligence starts only when he finds the solution to the problem, seems a very narrow definition. I would, therefore, propose to define intelligence not by a static criterion, as in previous definitions, but by the direction that intelligence follows in its evolution, and then I would define intelligence as a form of equilibration, or forms of equilibration, toward which all cognitive functions lead.

But I must first define equilibration. Equilibration in my vocabulary is not an exact and automatic balance, as it would be in Gestalt theory; I define equilibration principally as a compensation for an external disturbance.

When there is an external disturbance, the subject succeeds in compensating for this by an activity. The maximum equilibration is thus the maximum of the activity, and not a state of rest. It is a mobile equilibration, and not an immobile one. So equilibration is defined as compensation; compensation is the annulling of a transformation by an inverse transformation. The compensation which intervenes in equilibration implies the fundamental idea of reversibility, and this reversibility is precisely what characterizes the operations of the intelligence. An operation is an internalized action, but it is also a reversible action. But an operation is never isolated; it is always subordinated to other operations; it is part of a more inclusive structure. Consequently, we define intelligence in terms of operations, coordination of operations.

Take, for example, an operation like addition: Addition is a material action, the action of reuniting. On the other hand, it is a reversible action, because addition may be compensated by subtraction. Yet addition leads to a structure of a whole. In the case of numbers, it will be the structure that. the mathematicians call a "group." In the case of addition of classes which intervene in the logical structure it will be a more simple structure that we will call a grouping, and so on.

Consequently, the study of the stages of intelligence is first a study of the formation of operational structures. I shall define every stage by a structure of a whole, with the possibility of its integration into succeeding stages, just as it was prepared by preceding stages. Thus, I shall distinguish four great stages, or four great periods, in the development of intelligence: first, the sensori-motor period before the appearance of language; second, the period from about two to seven years of age, the pre-operational period which precedes real operations; third, the period from seven to 12 years of age, a period of concrete operations (which refers to concrete objects); and finally after 12 years of age, the period of formal operations, or propositional operations.

SENSORI-MOTOR STAGE

Before language develops, there is behavior that we can call intelligent. For example, when a baby of 12 months or more wants an object which is too far from him, but which rests on a carpet or blanket, and he pulls it to get to the object, this behavior is an act of intelligence. The child uses an intermediary, a means to get to his goal. Also, getting to an object by means of pulling a string when the object is tied to the string, or when the child uses a stick to get the object, are acts of intelligence. They demonstrate in the sensori-motor period a certain number of stages, which go from simple reflexes, from the formation of the first habits, up to the coordination of means and goals.

Remarkable in this sensori-motor stage of intelligence is that there are already structures. Sensori-motor intelligence rests mainly on actions, on movements and perceptions without language, but these actions are coordinated in a relatively stable way. They are coordinated under what we may call schemata of action. These schemata can be generalized in actions and are applicable to new situations. For example, pulling a carpet to bring an object within reach constitutes a schema which can be generalized to other situations when another object rests on a support. In other words, a schema supposes an incorporation of new situations into the previous schemata, a sort of continuous assimilation of new objects or new situations to the actions already schematized. For example, I presented to one of my children an object completely new to him—a box of cigarettes, which is not a usual toy for a baby. The child took the object, looked at it, put it in his mouth, shook it, then took it with one hand and hit it with the other hand, then rubbed it on the edge of the crib, then shook it again, and gave the impression of trying to see if there were noise. This behavior is a way of exploring the object, of trying to understand it by assimilating it to schemata already known. The child behaves in this situation as he will later in Binet's famous vocabulary test, when he defines by usage, saying, for instance, that a spoon is for eating, and so on.

But in the presence of a new object, even without knowing how to talk, the child knows how to assimilate, to incorporate this new object into each of his already developed schemata which function as practical concepts. Here is a structuring of intelligence. Most important in this structuring is the base, the point of departure of all subsequent operational constructions. At the sensori-motor level, the child constructs the schema of the permanent object.

The knowledge of the permanent object starts at this point. The child is not convinced at the beginning that when an object disappears from view, he can find it again. One can verify by tests that object permanence is not yet developed at this stage. But there is there the beginning of a subsequent fundamental idea which starts being constructed at the sensori-motor level.

This is also true of the construction of the ideas of space, of time, of causality. What is being done at the sensori-motor level concerning all the foregoing ideas will constitute the substructure of the subsequent, fully achieved ideas of permanent objects, of space, of time, of causality.

In the formation of these substructures at the sensori-motor level, it is very interesting to note the beginning of a *reversibility*, not in thought, since there is not yet representation in thought, but in action itself. For example, the formation of the conception of space at the sensori-motor stage leads to an amazing decentration if one compares the conception of space at the first weeks of the development with that at one and one-half to two years of age. In the beginning there is not one space which contains all the objects, including the child's body itself; there is a multitude of spaces which are not coordinated: there are the buccal space, the tactilokinesthetic space, the visual and auditory spaces; each is separate and each is centered essentially on the body of the subject and on actions. After a few months, however, after a kind of Copernican evolution, there is a total reversal, a decentration such that space becomes homogenous, a one-and-only space that envelops the others. Then space becomes a container that envelops all objects, including the body itself; and after that, space is mainly coordinated in a structure, a coordination of positions and displacements, and these constitute what the geometricians call a "group"; that is to say, precisely a reversible system. One may move from A to B, and may come back from B to A; there is the possibility of returning, of reversibility. There is also the possibility of making detours and combinations which give a clue to what the subsequent operations will be when thought will supersede the action itself.

PRE-OPERATIONAL STAGE

From one and one-half to two years of age, a fundamental transformation in the evolution of intelligence takes place in the appearance of symbolic functions. Every action of intelligence consists in manipulating significations (or meanings) and whenever (or wherever) there is significations, there are on the one hand the "significants" and on the other the "significates." This is true in the sensori-motor level, but the only significants that intervene there are perceptual signs or signals (as in conditioning) which are undifferentiated in regard to the significate; for example, a perceptual cue, like distance, which will be a cue for the size of the distant object, or the apparent size of an object, which will be the cue for the distance of the object. There, perhaps, both indices are different aspects of the same reality, but they are not yet differentiated significants. At the age of one and one-half to two years a new class of significants arises, and these significants are differentiated in regard to their significates. These differentiations can be called symbolic function. The appearance of symbols in a children's game is an example of the appearance of new significants. At the sensori-motor level the games are nothing but exercises; now they become symbolic play, a play of fiction;

these games consist in representing something by means of something else. Another example is the beginning of delayed imitation, an imitation that takes place not in the presence of the original object but in its absence, and which consequently constitutes a kind of symbolization or mental image.

At the same time that symbols appear, the child acquires language; that is to say, there is the acquisition of another phase of differentiated significants, verbal signals, or collective signals. This symbolic function then brings great flexibility into the field of intelligence. Intelligence up to this point refers to the immediate space which surrounds the child and to the present perceptual situation; thanks to language, and to the symbolic functions, it becomes possible to invoke objects which are not present perceptually, to reconstruct the past, or to make projects, plans for the future, to think of objects not present but very distant in space—in short, to span spatio-temporal distances much greater than before.

But this new stage, the stage of representation of thought which is superimposed on the sensori-motor stage, is not a simple extension of what was referred to at the previous level. Before being able to prolong, one must in fact reconstruct, because behavior in words is a different thing from representing something in thought. When a child knows how to move around in his house or garden by following the different successive cues around him, it does not mean that he is capable of representing or reproducing the total configuration of his house or his garden. To be able to represent, to reproduce something, one must be capable of reconstructing this group of displacements, but at a new level, that of the representation of the thought.

I recently made an amusing test with Nel Szeminska. We took children of four to five years of age who went to school by themselves and came back home by themselves, and asked them if they could trace the way to school and back for us, not in design, which would be too difficult, but like a construction game, with concrete objects. We found that they were not capable of representation; there was a kind of motor-memory, but it was not yet a representation of a whole—the group of displacements had not yet been reconstructed on the plan of the representation of thought. In other words, the operations were not yet formed. There are representations which are internalized actions; but actions still centered on the body itself, on the activity itself. These representations do not allow the objective combinations, the decentrated combinations that the operations would. The actions are centered on the body. I used to call this egocentrism; but it is better thought of as lack of reversibility of action.

At this level, the most certain sign of the absence of operations which appear at the next stage is the absence of the knowledge of conservation. In fact, an operation refers to the transformation of reality. The transformation is not of the whole, however; something constant is always untransformed. If you pour a liquid from one glass to another there is transformation; the liquid changes form, but its liquid property stays constant. So at the preoperational level, it is significant from the point of view of the operations of intelligence that the child has not yet a knowledge of conservation. For example, in the case of liquid, when the child pours it from one bottle to the other, he thinks that the quantity of the liquid has changed. When the level of the liquid changes, the child thinks the quantity has changed—there is more or less in the second glass than in the first. And if you ask the child where the larger quantity came from, he does not answer this question. What is important for the child is that perceptually it is not the same thing any more. We find this absence of conservation in all object properties, in the length, surface, quantity, and weight of things.

This absence of conservation indicates essentially that at this stage the child reasons from the configuration. Confronted with a transformation, he does not reason from the transformation itself; he starts from the initial configuration, then sees the final configuration, compares the two but forgets the transformation, because he does not know how to reason about it. At this stage the child is still reasoning on the basis of what he sees because there is no conservation. He is able to master this problem only when the operations are formed and these operations, which we have already sensed at the sensori-motor level, are not formed until around seven to eight years of age. At that age the elementary problems of conservation are solved, because the child reasons on the basis of the transformation per se, and this requires a manipulation of the operation. The ability to pass from one stage to the other and be able to come back to the point of departure, to manipulate the reversible operations, which appears around seven to eight years of age, is limited when compared with the operations of the superior level only in the sense that they are concrete. That is to say, the child can manipulate the operations only when he manipulates the object concretely.

STAGE OF CONCRETE OPERATIONS

The first operations of the manipulation of objects, the concrete operations, deal with logical classes and with logical relations, or the number. But these operations do not deal yet with propositions, or hypotheses, which do not appear until the last stage.

Let me exemplify these concrete operations: the simplest operation is concerned with classifying objects according to their similarity and their difference. This is accomplished by including the subclasses within larger and more general classes, a process that implies inclusion. This classification, which seems very simple at first, is not acquired until around seven to eight years of age. Before that, at the pre-operational level, we do not find logical inclusion. For example, if you show a child at the pre-operational level a bouquet of flowers of which one half is daisies and the other half other flowers and you ask him if in this bouquet there are more flowers or more daisies, you are confronted with this answer, which seems extraordinary until it is analyzed: The child cannot tell you whether there are more flowers than daisies; either he reasons on the basis of the whole or of the part. He cannot understand that the part is complementary to the rest, and he says there are more daisies than flowers, or as many daisies as flowers, without understanding this inclusion of the subclass, the daisies, in the class of flowers. It is only around seven to eight years of age that a child is capable of solving a problem of inclusion.

Another system of operation that appears around seven to eight years of age is the operation of serializing; that is, to arrange objects according to their size, or their progressive weight. It is also a structure of the whole, like the classification which rests on concrete operations, since it consists of manipulating concrete objects. At this level there is also the construction of numbers, which is, too, a synthesis of classification and seriation. In numbers, as in classes, we have inclusion, and also a serial order, as in serializing. These elementary operations constitute structures of wholes. There is no class without classification; there is no symmetric relation without serialization; there is not a number independent of the series of numbers. But the structures of these wholes are simple structures, groupings in the case of classes and relations, which are already groups in the case of numbers, but very elementary structures compared to subsequent structures.

STAGE OF FORMAL OPERATIONS

The last stage of development of intelligence is the stage of formal operations or propositional operations. At about eleven to twelve years of age we see great progress; the child becomes capable of reasoning not only on the basis of objects, but also on the basis of hypotheses, or of propositions.

An example which neatly shows the difference between reasoning on the basis of propositions and reasoning on the basis of concrete objects comes from Burt's tests. Burt asked children of different ages to compare the colors of the hair of three girls: Edith is fairer than Susan, Edith is darker than Lilly; who is the darkest of the three? In this question there is seriation, not of concrete objects, but of verbal statements which supposes a more complicated mental manipulation. This problem is rarely solved before the age of 12.

Here a new class of operations appears which is superimposed on the operations of logical class and number, and these operations are the propositional operations. Here, compared to the previous stage, are fundamental changes. It is not simply that these operations refer to language, and then to operations with concrete objects, but that these operations have much richer structures.

The first novelty is a combinative structure; like mathematical structures, it is a structure of a system which is superimposed on the structure of simple classifications or seriations which are not themselves systems, because they do not involve a combinative system. A combinative system permits the grouping in flexible combinations of each element of the system with any other element of that system. The logic of propositions supposes such a combinative system. If children of different ages are shown a number of colored disks and asked to combine each color with each other two by two, or three by three, we find these combinative operations are not accessible to the child at the stage of concrete operations. The child is capable of some combination, but not of all the possible combinations. After the age of 12, the child can find a method to make all the possible combinations. At the same time he acquires both the logic of mathematics and the logic of propositions, which also supposes a method of combining.

A second novelty in the operations of propositions is the appearance of a structure which constitutes a group of four transformations. Hitherto there were two reversibilities: reversibility by inversion, which consists of annulling, or canceling; and reversibility which we call reciprocity, leading not to cancellation, but to another combination. Reciprocity is what we find in the field of a relation. If A equals B, by reciprocity B equals A. If A is smaller than B, by reciprocity B is larger than A. At the level of propositional operations a new system envelops these two forms of reversibility. Here the structure combines inversion and reversibility in one single but larger and more complicated structure. It allows the acquisition of a series of fundamental operational schemata for the development of intelligence, which schemata are not possible before the constitution of this structure.

It is around the age of 12 that the child, for example, starts to understand in mathematics the knowledge of proportions, and becomes capable of reasoning by using two systems of reference at the same time. For example, if you advance the position of a board and a car moving in opposite directions, in order to understand the movement of the board in relation to the movement of the car and to other movement, you need a system of four transformations. The same is true in regard to proportions, to problems in mathematics or physics, or to other logical problems.

The four principal stages of the development of intelligence of the child progress from one stage to the other by the construction of new operational structures, and these structures constitute the fundamental instrument of the intelligence of the adult.

part III
Familial Influences on Socialization and Personality Development

Socialization—the process of acquiring behavior patterns and characteristics appropriate to one's own sex, family, social class, ethnic, and religious groups —begins very early. The child's first learning experiences, stemming from interactions with members of his family, particularly his mother, may have immediate or enduring impacts on the development of his personal characteristics, motivations, social behavior, and emotional adjustment. Socialization is accomplished, in part, by means of direct rewards or reinforcements by parents and others, for appropriate acceptable responses, and punishment for inappropriate or disapproved behavior.

In studying parental patterns of reward and punishment, many investigators have focused on the consequents of experiencing different kinds of home atmosphere (e.g., permissive or strict, warm or cold, democratic or authoritarian). For example, in democratic homes, children learn to express their opinions freely and to assert themselves and these behaviors generalize to situations outside the home.

It is often assumed that the mother and father consistently reinforce behavior that will be appropriate for the social role the child will fulfill. In the first paper of this part, Mary Rothbart and Eleanor Maccoby show that this assumption is not always valid, for, in many matters, parental behavior toward the child varies as a function of the sex of the child and of the parent. In general, mothers tend to be more permissive and more attentive toward their sons and fathers toward their daughters. This applies even to aggression and dependency, generally considered sex-typed characteristics. Apparently consistent reinforcement of sex-typed behavior by both parents is not the rule; a parent may treat his child in a way consistent with his sex role in one area of behavior but not in another.

Not all aspects of the child's socialization and personality development can be explained as functions of simple reward learning or imitation. Many complex behavior patterns, personality characteristics, motivations, ideals, and attitudes are acquired by means of *identification* with parents or other models. A child is said to be identified with the model when he feels similar to the model and this feeling of similarity may be increased through the child's adoption of the model's attributes. Since the child's models are generally carriers and examplars of culturally approved behavior patterns, identification contributes enormously to the process of socialization.

In the second study Jerome Kagan hypothesizes that the child is motivated to identify with his parent because he perceives many important differences between his own and his parent's abilities, powers, and privileges. Through identification the child begins to feel he shares his parent's mastery of the environment.

The third paper by Paul Henry Mussen and his collaborator, Ann Parker, presents data showing that a mother's general warmth and nurturance foster her daughter's tendency to identify with the mother and to imitate her incidental behavior (behavior not oriented toward the task) in a novel problem-solving task. Daughters of relatively nonnurturant, aloof mothers are less likely to imitate their mother's responses in this situation.

In the fourth paper of this part, E. Mavis Hetherington and her coworker, Gary Frankie, summarize several hypotheses about the motivations underlying identification and delineate the impacts of both parental power (dominance) and nurturance. Maternal warmth fosters the girl's imitation of her mother, while the father's domination is more important as an antecedent of the son's father-identification.

In the final paper, Kenneth Purcell illustrates the complex interactions between biological factors and parent-child relationships in the development and amelioration of asthmatic symptoms, generally considered to be of psychosomatic origin. Some asthmatic children become and remain symptom free as soon as they are separated from their parents; others retain their symptoms. Asthmatic attacks of rapidly remitting children were more likely to be precipitated by fear, anger, and anxiety at home, and they were more likely to have authoritarian and punitive parents. Asthmatic children with low allergic potential (as determined by medical tests) give relatively little evidence of neurotic conflict and disturbed relationships with parents.

Parents' Differential Reactions to Sons and Daughters

Mary K. Rothbart and Eleanor E. Maccoby

STANFORD UNIVERSITY

The existence of sex differences in psychological functioning has been repeatedly documented in psychological literature. Often the differences have been unexpected and have taken complex forms (Oetzel, 1966). Any theory of sex typing that attempts to understand the sources of these differences must consider the possible effects of differential parent pressures occurring as a function of the sex of the child. Few studies have as yet explored the nature of differential parent behaviors toward boys and girls, and any complete study of this kind would have to consider sex of parents as another

Reprinted from *Journal of Personality and Social Psychology*, 1966, *4*, No. 3, 237–243. Published by the American Psychological Association. By permission.

The authors would like to express their gratitude to Clarene Dong, Carol Spielman, and Paul Wick, who assisted in the development and administration of the initial pilot study, and to Aimée Leifer, who worked on all phases of the final study. This research was financed in part by Public Health Service Predoctoral Fellowship No. 5 F1 MH-20, 971-02, National Institute of Mental Health.

important source of variation. The present study therefore attempts to examine parent behavior toward a child as a function of (a) sex of the parent, and (b) sex of the child.

Previous studies of mother-father differences in treatment of boys and girls have been of two major types. The first involves children's perceptions of their parents' behavior; the second involves parents' perceptions of their own behavior and attitudes toward their children. Numerous studies of children's perceptions of their parents have been carried out, and the literature is summarized and briefly criticized by Droppleman and Schaeffer (1963). Considering only studies with preadolescent children, a common finding has been that both boys and girls "prefer" the mother to the father and find her friendlier and easier to get along with (Hawkes, Burchinal, & Gardner, 1957; Kagan, 1956; Simpson, 1935).

Cross-sex findings suggesting an interaction between sex of parent and sex of child have also been reported. When Simpson (1935) questioned children ranging in ages from 5 to 9, the boys said they were punished (spanked) more by their fathers than their mothers. Girls said mothers spanked them more, but the inference from their projective responses was that the father punished more. Kagan and Lemkin (1960) interviewed children ages 3–8 and found few sex differences in reports of parent practices. Both boys and girls reported that the opposite-sex parent "kissed the most." Girls saw the father as more punitive and affectionate than the mother, while boys saw him only as more punitive. Kagan (1956) interviewed first-, second-, and third-grade children on four issues: Who (the mother or the father) would be on the child's side in an argument; who punishes; who is the boss of the house; who is more feared. With children of all ages combined, there was little cross-sex difference in response. When the younger and older children were treated separately, the older children showed a consistent tendency to see the same-sex parent as less benevolent and more frustrating.

In studies involving parents rather than children, Aberle and Naegele (1952) and Tasch (1952) used only fathers as subjects. Fathers reported different expectations for sons and daughters and said that they participated in different activities with their sons than with their daughters. Sears, Maccoby, and Levin (1957) used only mothers as subjects, interviewing at length mothers of nursery school children. Mothers reported that they permit more aggressiveness from boys when it is directed toward parents and children outside the family, no difference in permissiveness of aggression against siblings. No differences in severity of punishment for aggression nor in permissiveness for dependency were found. Mothers reported they did most of the disciplining of both sexes, but that the father took a larger role in disciplining his son when both parents were at home. In a study with both parents, Goodenough (1957) found that mothers were less concerned about their child's appropriate sex typing than were fathers. Fathers also reported they were actively involved in implementing sex typing of their children, while mothers reported they did not consciously attempt to influence sex typing.

Emmerich (1962) gave questionnaires for assessing nurturance and restrictiveness to parents of children ages 6–10, defining nurturance as reward for positive behavior and dependency, and restrictiveness as punishment for negative behavior. The two scales were combined as a measure of power. Mothers were found to be more nurturant and less restrictive toward children of both sexes. A marked trend was also found for fathers to exert more power toward their sons than their daughters, and a similar but less powerful trend for mothers to exert more power toward their daughters than toward their sons. Emmerich's data are suggestive of differences between mothers and fathers in their treatment of boys and girls, but only on a very general dimension. The questions asked of parents were also quite amorphous, for example, rating the extent to which he compliments his daughter "when she does what she knows she should do," or gives her "something at the time she wants it."

The present experiment is an attempt to study parents' reactions to specific child behaviors, including some regarded as sex typed, for example, dependency and aggression.

We are also interested in a test of a hypothesis proposed by social learning theorists to account for sex differences in behavior. Mischel (in press) suggests:

> The greater incidence of dependent behaviors for girls than boys, and the reverse situation with respect to physically aggressive behavior, seems directly explicable in social learning terms. Dependent behaviors are less rewarded for males, physically aggressive behaviors are less rewarded for females in our culture, and, consequently there are mean differences between the sexes in the frequency of such behaviors after the first few years of life.

Assuming that the family constitutes the major "culture" to which the preschool child is exposed, we might predict from this learning-theory interpretation that both parents would consistently reinforce dependency more strongly in girls and aggression more strongly in boys. The present study is designed to test this prediction.

Parents were put in a hypothetical situation with a child and were asked to record their immediate reactions to what the child said and did. To avoid the additional variables that would compound an adult's reaction to an actual boy or girl, the recorded voice of a single child constituted the stimulus material. The voices of a number of 4-year-olds were recorded, and one was chosen which judges could not readily identify as to sex. Some of the parents were informed that it was a boy's voice, some that it was a girl's voice, and differences in their responses were examined. A questionnaire was also used to measure the extent to which a parent differentiates between the sexes by either (a) feeling boys and girls are different on selected characteristics, or (b) feeling boys and girls *should* differ on these characteristics. It was hypothesized that parents showing high differentiation between boys and girls would show greater differences in reaction to the boy's voice compared with the girl's voice than would parents who differentiated little between the sexes.

METHOD

This study was preceded by an initial individual testing of 58 mothers. A small pilot group of both mothers and fathers was then tested in a group-administered procedure, and the coding categories and questionnaire were revised. The final testing involved both fathers and mothers in a group administration.

Selection of the Stimulus Voice

The child speaker was chosen by recording nine nursery school children reciting a prepared script. Six adult judges rated the sex of each child after hearing the tape recordings. The voice selected (that of a boy) was judged to be a boy by half the judges and a girl by the other half. In the actual study, none of the parent subjects questioned the sex attributed to the voice they heard.

The statements comprising the script were adaptations of actual statements of 3- and 4-year-old children recorded in the same locality approximately a year before the final study. An attempt was made to make the script as realistic as possible, and a number of mothers in the individually administered pretest remarked that the recorded child sounded very much like their own nursery school child.

Subjects

Subjects were 98 mothers and 32 fathers of children enrolled in a parent-education nursery school. These parents came from a range of socioeconomic status levels, with a concentration of upper-middle-class families.

Of these parents, 60 mothers and 21 fathers were told that the voice was a girl's, 38 mothers and 11 fathers that it was a boy's. The reason for a larger number of parents hearing the girl's than the boy's voice was that only the number of parents expected to attend had been matched acccording to sex and age of the nursery school child and assigned to the two groups. More parents attended than had been anticipated, and the extra parents all heard the girl's voice.

The group hearing the boy's voice and the group hearing the girl's voice proved to be matched according to sex of nursery school age child, but it was later found that the two groups were not well matched with respect to whether the parent had children of only one or of both sexes. Our sample was divided according to this variable, and no differences in a direction that would influence our results were found.

Presentation of the Stimulus Voice

Parents were tested in four separate groups (fathers-girl's voice, fathers-boy's voice, mothers-girl's voice, mothers-boy's voice), with female experimenters. Each experimenter introduced the parents to the situation represented by the tape-recorded voice. The subject was asked to imagine that he (or she) was at home reading, with his 4-year-old boy, Johnny (or girl, Susan), playing with a puzzle in an adjacent room. With the child is the 1-year-old baby. Subjects were asked to give their immediate reactions to the 4-year-old's statements by writing down what they would say or do in response to each statement. The child's statements were as follows. (Due to some lack of clarity in the tape, each statement of the child was repeated by the experimenter to assure that it was understood by all subjects.)

1. Daddy (or Mommy), come look at my puzzle.
2. Daddy, help me.
3. Does this piece go here?
4. Baby, you can't play with me. You're too little.
5. Tell him he can't play with my puzzle—it's mine!
6. Leave my puzzle alone or I'll hit you in the head!
7. I don't like this game—I'm gonna break it!
8. I don't like this game. It's a stupid game. You're stupid, Daddy.
9. Ow! Baby stepped on my hand!
10. Daddy—it hurts.
11. Daddy, get me another puzzle.
12. It's not raining now—I'm going across the street and play.

After each statement, the experimenter stopped the tape while subjects recorded their reactions.

Parents' responses were coded for each item, and items were grouped according to 7 different scales: Help Seeking (Items 1, 2, 3, 11), Comfort Seeking (9, 10), Dependency (Help and Comfort Seeking scales combined), Aggression (6a, 7a, 8a), Allowing Child to Stop Game (7, 8), Siding with Child versus Baby (4, 5, 6), and Autonomy (12). Scores on all scales ranged generally from permissiveness for the child (low score) to nonpermissiveness for the child's actions (high score). For example, in response to the child's statement 9 ("Ow! Baby stepped on my hand!"), a rating of high comfort was given to the response, "Here, Mommy will kiss it," while a rating of low comfort was given to the response, "Keep your hand away from the baby's foot." In response to Statement 5 ("Tell him he can't play with my puzzle—it's mine!"), a parent who said, "That's right. Let's find the baby something else," was rated as siding with the child. A response of "Johnny, let your brother help you" was rated as siding with the baby. All protocols were coded by one rater, and 25 were coded independently by a second rater. Reliabilities ranged from .83 to 1.00, with a mean scale correlation of .90.

Questionnaire

The parent questionnaire, administered immediately after the tape-recorded script, measured two aspects of parents' attitudes about sex differences. Part 1 asked parents' opinions about differences they felt actually existed between boys and girls. The items included were taken from statements given by mothers to open-ended interview questions about sex differences from the files of the Sears et al. (1957) study. The format for the questionnaire was adapted from Sherriffs and Jarrett (1953). A sample from the 40-item list is as follows:

More likely to be obedient are: ___ ___ ___.
G   B   X

Here, G represents girls, B boys, and X no sex differences. The measure of sex-role differentiation for this part of the scale was the total number of X responses, with a large number of X responses indicating low sex-role differentiation.

Part 2 of the questionnaire measured what differences parents felt *should* exist between boys and girls. Boys and girls were rated separately on how important it was to the parent that his child be described by each characteristic. A sample item is:

Very impor- tant *not* to	Fairly impor- tant *not* to	Unimportant to	Fairly impor- tant to	Very impor- tant to	
					be obedient.

As a measure of sex-role differentiation for Part 2 of the questionnaire, absolute differences between ratings of an item's importance for girls and importance for boys were summed. The higher this difference (D) score, the higher the sex-role differentiation that was indicated.

RESULTS

Parents' Response to the Child's Voice

When the direction of differences for all scales are considered, a general trend emerges. Mothers tend to be more permissive for the boy's voice and fathers more permissive for the girl's voice (see Table 1). While only one main effect was significant (Scale 7—fathers allowed more autonomy than mothers, $p < .05$), interactions were significant for Scale 2 (Comfort Seeking, $p < .05$), Scale 3 (Dependency, $.05 < p < .10$), Scale 5 (Allowing Child to Stop Game, $.05 < p < .10$), and Scale 6 (Siding with Child Versus Baby, $p < .01$) as shown in Table 2. On all of these scales, the interaction was in the direction of mothers showing more permissiveness and positive attention to their sons than to their daughters, fathers showing more permissiveness and positive attention to their daughters than to their sons.

Our failure to find a significant interaction for the Aggression scale was somewhat surprising, since in the initial pilot study we had found a strong tendency for mothers to allow more aggression from their sons than from their daughters. In the pilot study, our measure of aggression had been composed chiefly of aggression directed against the parent. For this reason, item

Table 1 Mothers' and Fathers' Reactions to Boy's Versus Girl's Voice

	Help Seeking (High score-refuses help)		Comfort Seeking (High score-refuses)		Dependency (High score-refuses)		Aggression (High score-does not permit)	
Voice	Mothers	Fathers	Mothers	Fathers	Mothers	Fathers	Mothers	Fathers
Boy's								
M	8.71	8.45	4.24	5.82	12.95	14.18	4.95	5.64
SD	1.71	1.51	1.73	2.18	2.32	2.92	1.29	2.16
N	38	11	38	11	38	11	37	11
Girl's								
M	9.15	8.39	5.02	4.84	14.17	13.12	4.91	4.86
SD	1.93	1.61	1.86	1.56	3.05	2.55	1.32	1.62
N	59	18	59	19	59	17	56	21

	Allowing Child to Stop Game (High score-does not)		Siding with Child Versus Baby (High score-sides with baby)		Autonomy (High score-does not permit)		Aggression Toward Parent (High score-does not permit)	
	Mothers	Fathers	Mothers	Fathers	Mothers	Fathers	Mothers	Fathers
Boy's								
M	3.62	4.18	6.13	7.64	1.97	2.27	1.59	2.27
SD	1.09	1.17	1.43	1.43	.64	.64	1.76	1.01
N	37	11	37	11	37	11	38	11
Girl's								
M	4.00	3.62	6.76	6.20	2.10	2.40	1.75	1.67
SD	1.09	1.16	1.47	1.61	.47	.60	1.16	1.11
N	57	21	59	19	60	20	60	21

Note: Mean scores.

Table 2 Summary of Analyses of Variance Interaction Tests Between Sex of
Parent and Sex of Child's Voice

Variable	Interaction (MS)	Error (MS)	F
Help Seeking	1.81	3.24	.56
Comfort Seeking	16.29	3.28	4.97[b]
Dependency	27.06	7.67	3.53[a]
Aggression	3.13	2.11	1.48
Allowing Child to Stop Game	5.54	1.31	3.70[a]
Siding with Child Versus Baby	24.94	2.16	11.55[c]
Autonomy	.04	.32	.12
Aggression Toward Parent	4.02	1.02	3.94[b]

[a] $p < .10$, $df = 1/121, 1/122$.
[b] $p < .05$, $df = 1/123, 1/125$.
[c] $p < .05$, $df = 1/123$.

8a (Aggression Toward Parent) was examined separately from the rest of the Aggression scale. Item 8a showed a significant interaction ($p < .05$), with fathers allowing more aggression from their daughters than from their sons and mothers allowing more aggression from their sons than from their daughters.

Questionnaire

Parents' X scores on the questionnaire (extent to which parent felt differences *do* exist between boys and girls) were correlated with parents' D scores (extent to which parent felt differences *should* exist between boys and girls). The correlation between X and D scores for mothers was −.53; the correlation for fathers was −.40. Since a high D score and a low X score both represent high sex-role differentiation, these findings indicate a positive correlation between the two measures.

There were no significant differences between mothers' and fathers' sex-role differentiation scores, but parents who had heard the girl's voice tended to have higher sex-role differentiation scores than parents who had heard the boy's voice. This trend appeared in mothers' X and D scores and in fathers' D scores, but was significant only for mothers' D scores ($p < .05$). This finding is difficult to explain, and it suggests that questionnaire scores may be influenced by situational variables.

Finally, parents with high sex-role differentiation scores were separated from parents with low sex-role differentiation scores. Both X and D scores for mothers and fathers were standardized, and divided approximately at the median for the high- and low-differentiation groups. Since not all parents received the questionnaire, Ns for the fathers' group were quite small. Parents' responses to the child's voice were then compared, with the expectation that high-differentiation parents would show larger differences between their treatment of boys and girls than would low-differentiation parents. It was

Table 3 Mean Standard Scores Representing Degree of Overall Permissiveness for High- and Low-Differentiation Parents

	Mothers		Fathers	
	High diff.	Low diff.	High diff.	Low diff.
Voice	Groups Assigned According to D Scores			
Boy's				
M	48.74	47.72	56.75	50.92
SD	4.90	2.15	2.40	4.74
N	15	12	5	6
Girl's				
M	53.05	49.23	47.63	50.48
SD	5.45	4.09	4.49	4.57
N	10	11	8	9
	Groups Assigned According to X Scores			
Boy's				
M	48.62	48.52	55.15	53.05
SD	4.53	3.95	2.78	4.67
N	14	15	7	4
Girl's				
M	53.26	47.60	49.93	49.90
SD	4.81	5.12	3.85	4.52
N	11	9	9	10

Note: High scores = nonpermissiveness.

also expected that these differences would be in the direction of promoting sex-typed behavior. The first part of this prediction received some support in this study; the second part did not. When scores for all scales were standardized and summed for each subject, giving a general permissiveness score toward the child, high-differentiation parents tended to show greater permissiveness to the opposite-sex child (see Table 3). High sex-role differentiation parents showed larger differences between treatment of boys and girls than did low-differentiation parents for fathers separated on the basis of D scores $(p < .02)$ and for mothers separated on the basis of X scores $(p < .05)$. The differences were in the same direction but not significant for mothers separated according to D scores and fathers separated according to X scores.

In testing the hypothesis that differences would run in a sex-stereotyped direction, parents' responses on the Dependency and Aggression scales were more closely examined. On the basis of all parents' responses to the D questionnaire, it was expected that high-differentiation parents would act to promote dependency in girls and assertiveness in boys. When these scales are examined, however, the differences seem rather to be for high-differentiation parents to show greater relative permissiveness to the opposite-sex child than low-differentiation parents. These differences were significant only in Scales 1 and 3 for mothers separated according to D scores (high-differentiation mothers more permissive of dependency in boys, $p < .05$ for both scales), and Scale 3 for fathers separated according to X scores (high-differentiation fathers more permissive of dependency in girls, $p < .05$). The direction of these results suggests that high-differentiation parents do not necessarily promote sex-role stereotypes; they rather show an intensification of the kinds of differences found for parents as a whole. When the scores of all high-differentiation parents (regardless of which voice they heard) were compared with those of low-differentiation parents, there was an additional tendency for low-differentiation parents to show more general permissiveness than high-differentiation parents, but in no case was this difference significant.

DISCUSSION

Although previous studies have found clear differences between the behavior of mothers and fathers independent of the sex of the child, the present study found only one difference (permissiveness for autonomy) to be independent of the child's sex. A source of this discrepancy may be that earlier studies relied on verbal reports of children and parents; these reports might be expected to be influenced by the cultural stereotypes of the mother and the father. The present study differed from the earlier ones in that a measure more closely approaching the behavior of a parent in an actual situation was used. Also, the fact that the fathers in this study were attending a meeting concerning their children indicates an involvement with the child that may not be found in the father population as a whole.

Another interesting discrepancy exists between some of the current findings and the predictions expected on the basis of common-sense notions of sex typing. For example, the mothers in this study were more likely to allow aggression toward themselves from their boys, as expected in sex-role stereotypes, but they were also more acceptant of comfort seeking in their sons than in their daughters, an entirely unexpected finding. Fathers, on the other hand, were more acceptant of their daughters' comfort seeking, but also allowed more aggression to be directed toward themselves from their daughters than from their sons. In short, the sex of parent seems to be a better predictor of his differential response to boys and girls than does a sex-role stereotype.

This finding presents some difficulties for the social learning theory interpretation of sex differences outlined at the beginning of this paper (Mischel, in press). Rather than consistent reinforcement of sex-typed behavior by both parents, inconsistency between parents seems to be the rule, and while a parent may treat his child in a manner consistent with the cultural stereotype in one area of behavior, in another he may not.

It is, of course, possible that the only reinforcement counter to the cultural stereotype comes from the child's parents, and that reinforcement from other sources serves to counteract inconsistent parental pressures. It is also possible that parents shift their reinforcing behaviors as their children become older. These possibilities might apply to sex differences in dependency, which seem to emerge late enough to be affected by influences outside the home or later shifts in parental behavior. However, sex differences in aggression have been observed early, while the family is still the primary influence, and our findings fail to support the interpretation that differential reinforcement from both parents is of a kind to promote these differences at this early age level. Perhaps there is a biological component in these sex differences which is of importance either in its own right or in interaction with socialization practices.

There are several possible sources of the cross-sex interaction. In instances of permissiveness for the child's dependent behavior, the parent may be simply responding to the young child as a member of the opposite sex, reacting more favorably to the actions of the child who most resembles his marital partner. Or, reflecting the other side of the Oedipal coin, the parent may react less favorably to the same-sex child because of feelings of rivalry with this child. Another hypothesis, this one concerned with parents' differential responses to negative behavior in the child, suggests that parents may tend to punish the expression of impulses that they do not allow in themselves. As a child, the parent has been punished for certain actions and thoughts, and he may react negatively when he sees expression of these actions and thoughts in his child. When the child is of the same sex as himself, the parent may be more strongly reminded of the situation in which he had been punished, and more negative feelings are evoked. The parent is therefore more likely to punish the same-sex child for negative actions than the opposite-sex child.

This list of possibilities suggests that family interaction springs from multiple motivations, and that any tendency parents may have to reinforce culturally stereotypic behavior in their children may be outweighed by other determinants of their behavior. Parent behavior, then, may not always be consistent with preparing children for the social roles they will fill. Indeed, the child may acquire some aspects of his appropriate role behavior in spite of, rather than because of, what at least one of his parents does as a reinforcing agent.

Although the questionnaire results are by no means conclusive, they suggest a pattern of differences for high-differentiation parents that is simply a stronger statement of the general findings of the study. Perhaps parents with high-differentiation scores are more aware of the differences that distinguish their sons and daughters, but tend to react in a sex-specific way to these sex differences rather than actively promoting sex-typed behavior in their children.

Parents taking the questionnaire for the most part had fairly low sex-role differentiation scores. If this study were replicated with a lower-class sample of parents, we would expect a wider range of sex-role differentiation scores and even stronger interaction effects than were found in this study.

REFERENCES

Aberle, D. F., & Naegele, K. D. Middle class fathers' occupational role and attitudes toward children. *American Journal of Orthopsychiatry*, 1952, *22*, 366–378.

Droppleman, L. F., & Schaeffer, E. S. Boys' and girls' reports of maternal and paternal behavior. *Journal of Abnormal and Social Psychology*, 1963, *67*, 648–654.

Emmerich, W. Variations in the parent role as a function of the parent's sex and the child's sex and age. *Merrill-Palmer Quarterly*, 1962, *8*, 3–11.

Goodenough, E. W. Interest in persons as an aspect of sex differences in the early years. *Genetic Psychology Monographs*, 1957, *55*, 287–323.

Hawkes, G. R., Burchinal, L. G., & Gardner, B. Pre-adolescents' views of some of their relations with their parents. *Child Development*, 1957, *28*, 393–399.

Kagan, J. The child's perception of the parent. *Journal of Abnormal and Social Psychology*, 1956, *53*, 257–258.

Kagan, J., & Lemkin, I. The child's differential perception of parental attributes. *Journal of Abnormal and Social Psychology*, 1960, *61*, 440–447.

Mischel, W. A social learning view of sex differences in behavior. In E. E. Maccoby (Ed.), *The development of sex differences*. Stanford: Stanford University Press, 1966.

Oetzel, R. M. Selected bibliography on sex differences. In E. E. Maccoby (Ed.), *The development of sex differences*. Stanford: Stanford University Press, 1966.

Sears, R. R., Maccoby, E. E., & Levin, H. *Patterns of child rearing*. Evanston, Ill.: Row, Peterson, 1957.

Sherriffs, A. C., & Jarrett, R. F. Sex differences in attitudes about sex differences. *Journal of Psychology*, 1953, *35*, 161–168.

Simpson, M. Parent preferences of young children. *Teachers College of Columbia University Contributions to Education*, 1935, No. 652.

Tasch, R. G. The role of the father in the family. *Journal of Experimental Education*, 1952, *20*, 319–361.

The Concept
of Identification

Jerome Kagan

HARVARD UNIVERSITY

Several years ago Sanford (20) presented an analysis of the concept of identification. In brief, Sanford suggested that the term be applied to situations in which "an individual may be observed to respond to the behavior of other people or objects by initiating in fantasy or reality the same behavior himself . . . the individual strives to behave in a way that is exactly like that of the object" (20, p. 109). Sanford further suggested that the motive for this imitative behavior was a threat to the person's self-esteem. By limiting the

Reprinted from *Psychological Review,* 1958, *65,* No. 5, 296–305. Published by the American Psychological Association. By permission.

This research was supported, in part, by a research grant (M-1260) from the National Institute of Mental Health of the National Institutes of Health, United States Public Health Service. The views of Wesley Allinsmith, Vaughn J. Crandell, Leonard M. Lansky, and Howard A. Moss are especially acknowledged. A major stimulus for the present essay was a workshop in parent-child relations supported by USPHS Grant 1649 and held at the Merrill-Palmer School, Detroit, Michigan, July 14–27, 1957.

term "identification" to those imitative behavioral sequences in which the motivation for the act was anxiety over self-esteem, Sanford emphasized two points: (a) mere similarity in overt behavior between a subject and a model was not necessarily a measure of identification, and (b) the motive for the imitative behavior was one of the defining characteristics of an identificatory response.

The various behavioral phenomena which have been labeled "identification" differ in their manifest properties and motivations. The following four classes of behavior have been described as related to the process of identification because they all can lead to similarities in behavior between a subject and a model.

IMITATION LEARNING

This term refers to the initiation and practice of certain responses (gestures, attitudes, speech patterns, dress, etc.) which are not subject to prohibition by the social environment and which are assumed to be the result of an attempt to imitate a model. The behavior has been labeled either "matched-dependent behavior" or "copying" by Miller and Dollard (17). Miller and Dollard posit that initially the imitative act occurs by chance and the act can only be reinforced if some drive is reduced following the execution of the response. According to this view only direct reward from the social environment, like praise or affection, can strengthen the person's tendency to imitate a model. Mowrer (18) distinguishes between developmental and defensive identification. In the former process, the person imitates or reproduces the behavior of a model in order to "reproduce bits of the beloved and longed-for parent" (18, p. 615). Mowrer suggests that most imitation of a model is the result of the desire to reproduce responses which have acquired secondary reward value through association with a nurturant and affectionate model. Thus, Mowrer emphasizes the self-rewarding aspect of certain imitative acts as opposed to Miller and Dollard's emphasis on direct reward from the social environment.

PROHIBITION LEARNING

This term refers to the adoption and practice of the prohibitions of the parents and parent substitutes. The acquisition of these prohibitions bears some relation to the process of superego development as described by psychoanalytic theory (2, 3, 4, 11). Several investigators have suggested that a major motivation for the acquisition of some prohibition is anxiety over anticipated loss of love (10, 11, 18, 20, 23). Sanford labeled this process "introjection" and suggested that the learning and maintenance of this class of behavior might be explained without use of the concept of identification.

IDENTIFICATION WITH THE AGGRESSOR

This phrase refers to the adoption of behaviors which are similar to those of an aggressive or threatening model. The motivation for this "imitation" is assumed to be anxiety over anticipated aggression or domination by the threatening model. It is difficult to explain this behavior as a product of either prohibition or imitation learning, since the motive and reinforcement do not seem related to anxiety over anticipated loss of love or desire for a direct, social reward like praise or affection. Anna Freud (2) has labeled this phenomenon "identification with the aggressor," Mowrer has called this process "defensive identification" (as distinct from developmental identification), and Sanford has suggested that the term "identification proper" be restricted to this class of behavior.

VICARIOUS, AFFECTIVE EXPERIENCE

This phrase refers to the experience of positive or negative affect on the part of a person as a result of an event which has occurred to a model. Salient examples of this phenomenon are (a) a child's elation or depression at learning that his parent is a success or failure, or (b) a mother's elation following the success of her child in school. This phenomenon of vicarious, affective experience has been attributed to a person's identification with a model, but this affective response has been difficult to explain and often neglected by psychologists investigating the identification process. These four phenomena (imitation learning, prohibition learning, identification with the aggressor, and vicarious, affective experience) appear to be mediated by different motives and rewards, and an analysis of each of them is one purpose of this paper.[1]

In different contexts, social scientists have used the term "identification" to refer to three different sets of variables: (a) the process of identification; (b) individual differences in the content of the behaviors, motives, and attitudes acquired as a result of the identification process; and (c) the differential effect of various models that are used during the identification process (3, 4, 5, 7, 9, 11, 13, 15, 16, 25, 26). This paper recognizes the relevance of the model and content dimensions but is primarily concerned with the process of identification, and will attempt to analyze this process in behavioral terms. It is suggested that the process remains the same regardless of the models

[1] In an unpublished paper presented at a symposium at Harvard University in 1957, Bronfenbrenner described three types of identification: (a) anaclitic identification, (b) identification with a source of power, and (c) identification through reinforcement of a role model. These three terms are similar in meaning to the present phrases of prohibition learning, identification with the aggressor, and imitation learning, respectively.

used or the specific behavioral content that is acquired as a result of an identification.

DEFINITIONS OF IDENTIFICATION

The concept of identification originated in psychoanalytic theory, and Freud made a distinction between primary and secondary identification (3, 4, 5). Primary identification referred to the initial, undifferentiated perception of the infant in which an external object was perceived as part of the self, while secondary identification began after the child had discriminated a world of objects separate from the self. Freud implied in his later writings that the process of secondary identification was motivated primarily by the motives and anxieties created by the Oedipal situation. In order to reduce the anxiety over anticipated aggression or rejection from the same-sex parent and obtain vicariously the affection of the opposite-sex parent, the child identified with the former. Identification was described by Freud as "the endeavor to mould a person's own ego after the fashion of one that has been taken as a model" (5, p. 63).

Mowrer's concept of "defensive identification," Sanford's definition of "identification proper," and Anna Freud's description of "identification with the aggressor" are all related to the earlier psychoanalytic hypothesis that the threat value of the same-sex parent motivated the child to identify with him in order to reduce the anxiety associated with this threat. However, it is suggested that an individual may identify with a model not only to reduce anxiety over anticipated aggression from a model but also to experience or obtain positive goal states which he perceives that the model commands. The thesis of this paper is that the motivation to command or experience desired goal states of a model is salient in the development and maintenance of an identification.[2] It will be suggested later that two major goal states involved in identification behavior are (a) mastery of the environment and (b) love and affection. However, it is not implied that these are the only goals which an individual desires to command.

Definition

Identification is defined as an acquired, cognitive response within a person (S). The content of this response is that some of the attributes, motives, characteristics, and affective states of a model (M) are part of S's psychological organization. The major implication of this definition is that the S may react to events occurring to M as if they occurred to him.

---

[2] It is assumed that anticipation of a positive goal state is associated with the anticipation of a change in affect, and thus the phrase "experience goal states of the model" will be used synonymously with the phrase "experience affective states of the model." This assumption agrees with McClelland's definition of a motive as an "anticipation of a change in affective state" (14, p. 466).

The Acquisition and Maintenance of an Identification

Although identification has been defined as a cognitive response, it is not implied that the content of the response is available to consciousness or easily verbalized. Thus the terms "cognitive response," "belief," "wish," or "assumption" will be used in this text to include cognitive processes not always available through verbal report. Identification is not viewed as an all-or-none process. Identification is a response that can vary in strength and there will be differences in the degree to which an S believes that the characteristics of a model, whether assets or liabilities, belong to him. In addition, the S may become identified, to differing degrees, with a variety of models. The motives and reinforcements that are involved in the acquisition and maintenance of this cognitive response are elaborated in the following assumptions.

Assumption 1.   Initially the S perceives that the M possesses or commands goals and satisfactions that the S desires. This perception leads to a wish to possess these desired goal states.

Assumption 2.   This wish to command the goal states of the M leads to the desire to possess the characteristics of the M because S believes that if he were similar to the M he would command the desired goals. That is, the S assumes that the more similarity there is between the S and M the more likely S is to possess or command the desired goal states of the M.

To illustrate, let the S be a child and the M a mother, although S and M could be an adolescent boy and the leader of a group, or a girl and her older sister. The child perceives that the mother can feed the child, restrict the child, obtain articles out of the child's reach, punish the child, etc. Thus, to the S, the M appears to command desired skills and goal states. The discrepancy between the child's perception of his inability to obtain these desired goals and his perception of the more adequate adult elicits the wish to possess or control those goals which he perceives that M commands. The perceptions of the child are subject to distortion, and the child may exaggerate the degree to which M commands desired goals. It was assumed (Assumption 2) that the wish to command these goal states led to the expectation that if S possessed M's characteristics he would also command these desired goals. There often is direct reinforcement of the belief that to "be similar to" a model is equivalent to possessing his positive attributes. Often, the social environment tells the child directly that he is similar to a parent in certain characteristics, and this communication may be contiguous in time with statements related to some of the model's desired goal states. For example, parents and relatives may tell the child, "You have your father's eyes," and often add, "You'll grow up to be big and strong just like Daddy." It is suggested that these statements which associate similarities in external attributes with command of desired goal states have an important effect on the child's learning about himself, and lead the child to the expectation that to be similar to the model is equivalent to possessing his positive and desirable attributes.

Assumption 3. The identification response (i.e., "some of the character-istics of the model are mine") is reinforced each time S perceives or is told that he is similar to the M. One type of reinforcement for the identification response occurs when an S is told directly that he and the M are similar in temperament or appearance. It is suggested that a second type of reinforce-ment for this cognitive response is S's own perception of similarity to the M. Once again, consider the case of the small child and his parent. Although the child may perceive marked differences in size, strength, and skills between himself and the M, he may perceive a similarity in affective states, such as joy, anger, or sadness. The importance of the perception of similarities in affective states between the S and M is stressed because a major motive for identification is a desire to experience positive affective states of the model. Thus, perception of similarity in affect is assumed to have saliency as a rein-forcement. If the parent becomes angry, sad, or happy and communicates these affects to the child, the child has the opportunity to perceive that he and the M experience similar feelings. This perception reinforces the belief that there is similarity between the S and M. In addition to similarity in affec-tive states, perception of similarities in external characteristics will reinforce the identification response. With specific reference to the child-parent rela-tion, it is assumed that perception of similarities in sexual anatomy, dress, amount and distribution of hair, and other external attributes are potential reinforcements of the identification. Thus, while the identification response is being learned, the major reinforcements for the response are perceptions of similarity between the S and M.[3] Freud suggested that perceptions of simi-larity strengthen an identification, for he wrote,

> Identification . . . may arise with every new perception of a common quality shared with some other person who is not an object of the sexual instinct. The more important this common quality is, the more successful may this partial identification become, and it may thus represent the beginning of a new tie (5, p. 65).

Assumption 4. In order for the identification belief to be maintained, the S must not only perceive similarity between the S and M but he also must experience some of the desired, affective goal states of the M. Thus, if the M were successful or happy and S believed that M was experiencing positive affect, the S would also feel positive affect appropriate to the success, and this experience would reinforce his identification. The S also may experience affect appropriate to events occurring to M as a result of the expectation that the social environment will respond to him the same way it responds to the

---

[3] It is suggested that the concept of identification has not yielded to a behavioral analysis because the notion of social reinforcement has been viewed as a specific action directed at an individual by a reinforcing agent. There has been a tendency to overlook the possibility that a perception, fantasy, or thought may be a potential reinforcement of a response. A recent experimental finding by Estes and Johns (1) supports the hypothesis that a person's perception of a situation, even though objectively inaccurate, can reinforce his subsequent behavior.

M. That is, when the S has developed some degree of identification with the M he may anticipate that when the social environment praises or rewards the M, it will behave similarly to him. If, on the other hand, the M were sad or criticized, S might experience negative affect because of the identification belief that he and the M were similar and the expectation that the environment might react to him as it did to M. However, if no vicarious command of desired goals or positive affect were experienced as a result of the identification, then the response should extinguish just as any other habit does in the absence of positive reinforcement.[4] That is, some degree of identification should be maintained as long as S perceives that the M commands desired goals. When the S no longer perceives the M in this fashion, then both the motivation for the identification and the intensity of the positive reinforcement should decrease.

THE ACQUISITION OF BEHAVIOR SIMILAR TO A MODEL: THE MOTIVES FOR IMITATION, IDENTIFICATION, AND PROHIBITION LEARNING

Since perceptions of similarity between the S and M reinforce the identification response, the S may imitate the M during the acquisition phase of an identification in order to increase the degree of similarity. It is acknowledged that the social environment rewards imitative behaviors with affection and praise, and these direct, social reinforcements may strengthen the tendency to imitate adults independently of any identification motives. However, it is suggested, along with Sears et al. (23), that direct, social reinforcement of imitative behavior cannot account for all of the imitative responses that the S initiates. A 4-year-old child may simulate adult behaviors when the child is alone or in situations where the parents discourage or punish the imitative response. However, despite the punishment or absence of social reward for some imitative behaviors, the behavior continues to be practiced. Sears et al. call this behavior "role practice" and assume that it is motivated by the "desire to reproduce pleasant experiences" (23, p. 370). Consider the 3-year-old girl who plays the role of mother alone in her room. It is hypothesized that a potential reinforcement for this behavior is the creation, in fantasy, of perceptual similarity, between the behaviors of the S and M. This perception strengthens S's identification with the M and allows S to share vicariously some of the positive goal states which M commands.

A somewhat different phenomenon is the behavior called "identification

---

[4] This view of identification suggests a measurement operation which differs from the usual practice of assessing similarities in behavior between an S and an M. One measure of degree of identification would be the degree to which an S's affective state or behavior was influenced as a result of events that occurred to an M. That is, praise or criticism of an M in S's presence should lead to corresponding changes in the affective state of an S who was identified with the M.

with the aggressor" by Anna Freud or "defensive identification" by Mowrer. Anna Freud describes a girl who was afraid of ghosts and suddenly began to make peculiar gestures as she ran in the dark. She told her brother, "there is no need to be afraid, you just have to pretend that you're the ghost who might meet you" (2, p. 119). The present theory assumes that the child desired the threatening power of the feared object and this motive elicited the imitative behavior. The fantasied perception of similarity to the feared model gave S a vicarious feeling of power and reduced her anxiety over attack. It is suggested that "identification with the aggressor" does not differ from other identification responses with respect to the basic mechanism of acquisition but does involve a specific motive and goal state. Identification with the aggressor involves a specific relationship between the S and M in which S fears the M. Thus, S desires the aggressive power or threat value of the M in order to reduce his own anxiety over anticipated attack. It may be misleading to classify "identification with the aggressor" as qualitatively different from other identificatory behavior merely because the motive and goal differ from those involved in other identifications.

A third motive which can lead to behavioral similarity between an S and M is anxiety over anticipated loss of love or nurturance. It is suggested that many social prohibitions which the M practices are learned by the S in situations in which this anxiety motivates the acquisition and maintenance of the response. The reinforcement for the learned prohibition is continued acceptance and a consequent reduction in anxiety over rejection. The research of Sears et al. (23) suggests a relationship between "high conscience" in a child and a pattern in which the mother is nurturant and uses withdrawal of love as a disciplinary technique. In summary, any one response which is imitative of a model may be mediated by three different motive-reinforcement sequences, and in many instances all three may be involved in producing behavioral similarity between S and M.[5] Thus, "eating neatly," "getting good grades," or "being nonaggressive" could be motivated by the desire for praise as in imitation learning, by anxiety over loss of love as in prohibition learning, or by the desire to create perceptual similarity between the S and M as in identification. Thus, mere similarity in overt behavior between an S and M may not be the most sensitive measure of degree of identification.

At a more speculative level, it is suggested that the behaviors which have been called "self actualizing" (6) could be motivated and reinforced by a desire for perceptual similarity to an M and be an indication of early identification tendencies. Even the most orthodox supporters of the importance of simple imitation learning find it difficult to explain the child's initial imitations of a model. Once the child has begun to imitate a model it is likely that praise and recognition from adults could maintain this behavior. However, why does the child suddenly want to dress himself, sit on the toilet alone, or put

[5] In a manuscript being prepared for publication, H. Kelman suggests that the response of conformity to the attitudes of another person can be mediated by three different motives. His analysis of conformity parallels the present discussion of imitative behavior.

on Daddy's shoes? It is difficult to account for the initial display of this imitative behavior, and the term "self actualization" implies that the child has some biological drive to use his potentialities. This hypothesis seems no more parsimonious than the suggestion that the initiation of these "self actualizing" behaviors is motivated by S's desire to create perceptual similarity between himself and a model.

TWO GOALS MOTIVATING IDENTIFICATION: MASTERY AND LOVE

It has been assumed that S's desire to command certain goal states motivates his identification with a model. It is suggested, for the child especially, that two important goal states that the S desires to command are (a) a feeling of power or mastery over the environment and (b) love and affection. Attainment of these goals should lead to diminution in anxiety over helplessness or loneliness. The young child perceives that he is not able to gratify all of his needs while the parental model is perceived as more capable of dealing with the environment. This discrepancy between the S's perception of his own relative helplessness and the power that he perceives M to possess motivates the wish to have M's power and the search for perceptions of similarity between himself and the M.

Unfortunately, there are no empirical studies which directly test these hypotheses because most of the research on identification has used similarities in behavior between an S and M as the measure of identification. However, there are some results which are at least consistent with the view that the child identifies with the more powerful parent and the one who is perceived to command important sources of gratification. Payne and Mussen (19) reported that adolescent boys who perceived the father as rewarding on projective tests were more highly identified with the father (based on similar answers to a personality inventory) than boys who pictured their fathers as nonrewarding. In addition, boys with dominant and "masculine" mothers tended to be poorly identified with the father. P. S. Sears (22) reported a finding that is more difficult to explain without use of the concept of identification. She found, in a doll-play situation, that kindergarten girls used the mother doll as agent significantly more often than the father doll, while boys used both mother and father dolls with more nearly equal frequency. Since the mother is initially the major controller of gratifications for both sexes, one might expect an initial identification with her for both boys and girls. P. S. Sears (22) also reports that the kindergarten boys who used the mother doll most often had mothers who were (a) more nurturant than the father, (b) more critical of the father, and (c) more restrictive of the child's mobility outside the home. This result is consistent with the hypothesis that the child is predisposed to identify with the parental model who is perceived as controlling important goal states.

A study of Maccoby and Wilson (15) furnishes more direct support for the present hypotheses. The authors showed movies to seventh grade boys and girls and then determined the protagonist with whom the child identified. The most significant result was that a "boy's choice of screen character (the one with whom he was presumed to identify) is more closely related to the social class level *to which he aspires* than to the level his family currently occupies" *(15,* p. 79). This result suggests that the child identified with models who commanded desired goals.

A second goal state which may motivate identification is the desire for nurturance and affection. In addition to Freud's classical hypothesis that the child identified with the same-sex parent in order to receive vicariously the affection of the opposite-sex parent, there are situations in which nonparental models command sources of affection. The relation between siblings is such a situation, and the younger child may identify with an older sibling if the former perceives that the latter commands parental affection. The research of Helen Koch *(12)* indirectly supports this hypothesis. She reported that school-age boys with older sisters tended to develop more feminine attributes than boys with older brothers. On the other hand, girls with older brothers tend to be more masculine than girls with older sisters. In the experiment of Maccoby and Wilson, described earlier, the authors reported that girls were more likely than boys to recall movie content involving boy-girl interaction while boys were superior on recall of aggressive acts by the hero. If one assumes that the need for affection is stronger for girls than for boys, and that the recalled content is influenced by the model chosen for identification, then these results suggest that the specific goal states desired by the S determine the models chosen for identification.

FACTORS INFLUENCING THE STRENGTH OF IDENTIFICATION

The strength of the identification habit, following a basic behavioral law, should be a function of the strength of the motive and the quality and frequency of the reinforcement *(8)*. It would be predicted, therefore, that the most intense identification would occur when the S had strong needs for love and power, felt incapable of gratifying these motives through his own skills, and perceived similarity between himself and an M who commanded these goals. Utilizing this hypothesis, two generalized predictions can be made concerning the strength of identification for different ages and models.

1. The strength of identification tendencies should decrease with age because, in general, the individual's ability to gratify his needs for mastery and love through his own behavior, rather than through a vicarious mechanism, should increase with development. Thus, the identifications of a young child should be more intense than the identifications of older individuals.

2. An identification with an M with whom S was in direct contact should be stronger than with an M with whom S was not in contact, assuming that the motivation for identification was constant and the models were perceived as equally potent. This statement is based on the assumption that the rein-

forcements of perceived similarity are stronger when S perceives the affects and attributes of the M directly as opposed to instances in which he is merely told that he is similar to the M. Thus, degree of identification with a father with whom S was in contact should be greater than with an imagined fantasy father whom S had never seen. Only very indirect evidence is available to support this prediction. However, reports by P. S. Sears (21) and Sears et al. (24) suggest that absence of the father from the home tends to decrease the degree of "masculine" doll play in preschool boys while this experience has little effect on the doll play of girls. The results are open to alternative interpretations but are not inconsistent with the present hypothesis.

SUMMARY

This paper has attempted to analyze the concept of identification and place the concept within a learning-theory framework. Identification was defined as an acquired, cognitive response. The content of this response was that some of the characteristics of a model belonged to the individual and the individual behaved as if some of the characteristics and affective states of the model belonged to him. Identification was not viewed as an all-or-none process. An identification can vary in strength and the individual can identify, to differing degrees, with a variety of models. The motive for the acquisition and maintenance of the identification response was a desire for the positive goal states commanded by the model, and mastery of the environment and love-nurturance were suggested as two important goals. The reinforcement for the acquisition of the identification was perceived similarity in attributes between the person and the model. Thus, the person may strive to imitate aspects of the model's behavior in order to create perceptual similarity between himself and the model. Once the identification was established, the individual behaved as if the goal states of the model belonged to him and the positive affect derived from this vicarious sharing of desired goal states helped to maintain the identification.

It was suggested that the usual emphasis on similarities in overt behavior between an individual and a model is not the best measure of identification, since the motives and reinforcements involved in imitation and prohibition learning could also explain similarities in behavior between two people. A differentiation of imitative behavior based on imitation learning, prohibition learning, and identification was attempted.

REFERENCES

1. Estes, W. K., & Johns, Marcia D. Probability learning with ambiguity in the reinforcing stimulus. *Amer. J. Psychol.*, 1958, *71*, 219–228.
2. Freud, Anna. *The ego and the mechanisms of defense.* London: Hogarth, 1937.
3. Freud, S. *New introductory lectures in psychoanalysis.* New York: Norton, 1933.
4. Freud, S. *The ego and the id.* London: Hogarth, 1935.

5. Freud, S. *Group psychology and the analysis of the ego.* London: Hogarth, 1949.
6. Goldstein, K. *The organism.* New York: American Book, 1939.
7. Gray, Susan W., & Klaus, R. The assessment of parental identification. *Genet. Psychol. Monogr.,* 1956, *54,* 87–114.
8. Hull, C. L. *Principles of behavior.* New York: Appleton-Century-Crofts, 1943.
9. Kagan, J. The child's perception of the parent. *J. abnorm. soc. Psychol.,* 1956, *53,* 257–258.
10. Kagan, J. Socialization of aggression and the perception of parents in fantasy. *Child Develpm.,* 1958, *29,* 311–320.
11. Knight, R. P. Introjection, projection and identification. *Psychoanal. Quart.,* 1940, *9,* 334–341.
12. Koch, Helen L. Attitudes of young children toward their peers as related to certain characteristics of their siblings. *Psychol. Monogr.,* 1956, *70,* No. 19 (Whole No. 426).
13. Lazowick, L. M. On the nature of identification. *J. abnorm. soc. Psychol.,* 1955, *51,* 175–183.
14. McClelland, D. C. *Personality.* New York: Sloane, 1951.
15. Maccoby, Eleanor E., & Wilson, W. C. Identification and observational learning from films. *J. abnorm. soc. Psychol.,* 1957, *55,* 76–87.
16. Martin, W. E. Learning theory and identification: III. The development of value in children. *J. genet. Psychol.,* 1954, *84,* 211–217.
17. Miller, N. E., & Dollard, J. *Social learning and imitation.* New Haven: Yale Univer. Press, 1941.
18. Mowrer, O. H. *Learning theory and personality dynamics.* New York: Ronald, 1950.
19. Payne, D. E., & Mussen, P. H. Parent-child relations and father identification among adolescent boys. *J. abnorm. soc. Psychol.,* 1956, *52,* 358–362.
20. Sanford, R. N. The dynamics of identification. *Psychol. Rev.,* 1955, *62,* 106–118.
21. Sears, Pauline S. Doll play aggression in normal young children: influence of sex, age, sibling status, father's absence. *Psychol. Monogr.,* 1951, *65,* No. 6 (Whole No. 323).
22. Sears, Pauline S. Child rearing factors related to playing sex-typed roles. *Amer. Psychologist,* 1953, *8,* 431. (Abstract)
23. Sears, R. R., Maccoby, Eleanor E., & Levin, H. *Patterns of child rearing.* New York: Harper & Row, 1957.
24. Sears, R. R., Pintler, Margaret H., & Sears, Pauline S. Effect of father separation on pre-school children's doll play aggression. *Child Develpm.,* 1946, *17,* 219–243.
25. Seward, J. P. Learning theory and identification: II. The role of punishment. *J. genet. Psychol.,* 1954, *84,* 201–210.
26. Stoke, S. M. An inquiry into the concept of identification. *J. genet. Psychol.,* 1950, *76,* 163–189.

Mother Nurturance and Girls' Incidental Imitative Learning

Paul Henry Mussen and Ann L. Parker

UNIVERSITY OF CALIFORNIA, BERKELEY
AND GEORGETOWN UNIVERSITY MEDICAL SCHOOL

It has been demonstrated experimentally that the child's incidental imitative learning of a model's behavior increases immediately after nurturant interaction between the model and the child. There is also considerable evidence from correlational studies that a high degree of nurturance toward the child by the same-sex parent is conducive to the child's acquisition of appropriately sex-typed interests and attitudes (Mussen & Distler, 1959; Mussen & Rutherford, 1963). In these studies, it is assumed that the appropriate sex typing is a consequence of identification with the parent of the same sex, or in behavioral terms, the result of incidental imitative learning of that parent's behavior. If this assumption is correct, it follows that parents who are gener-

Reprinted from *Journal of Personality and Social Psychology,* 1965, 2, No. 1, 94–97. Published by the American Psychological Association. By permission.

This study was supported by the National Institute of Mental Health, United States Public Health Service, under Research Grant M-3217, and the University of California Institute of Social Science.

ally warm and nurturant will have a facilitating effect on their children's imitation of parental behavior, even in the absence of specific instruction or of reward for such imitation.

The research reported in this paper was designed to test this hypothesis directly. Mothers served as the experimenter-models, paired with their own daughters, the subjects, in a problem-solving situation involving imitation.

METHOD

Subjects

The subjects were 30 girls between 5 and 6 years of age enrolled in two kindergarten classes of a predominantly middle-class school. Their mothers had volunteered their daughters' and their own participation in the study. Each mother was interviewed and each child was seen for two sessions, one with one of the investigators (ALP) and, for the second session, with this investigator and the mother.

During the first session, the procedure was essentially like Rosenblith's (1959, 1961). After being seated in the room with the investigator, the child was told that she would play a paper and crayon game, and she could choose any crayon she wanted to draw with from the four (red, orange, green, and blue) in front of her. The Porteus Maze Test (Porteus, 1950) was then administered, slightly modified in instructions and procedure to render them more suitable to the age of the children. The test consists of a series of mazes, one maze for each year from ages 3 to 12, two trials being allowed for each maze. Testing is discontinued when the subject fails two consecutive age levels.

Between 3 and 4 weeks after the first session, the child was again called from her classroom by the investigator, who explained that they would "have a second turn at the game." Before entering the room where the testing was conducted, the child was told, "Today we have someone else here to play our games with us." Upon entering the room, the child met her mother and was asked to sit next to her at the table. The mother and child each had her own set of crayons, arranged in identical order on the table, and they were given identical sets of mazes.

Before she met with the subject in the experimental room, the mother had been given explicit instructions about the procedure to be followed. She had been carefully coached to draw slowly and to hesitate at the choice points, to make certain comments before each trial ("hm, hm, let's see now," and upon starting the maze, "here we go") and to make some irrelevant marks while tracing the maze (a loop at any point in her tracing and, a definite final mark such as ⊗).

After instructions were given to the pair, the mother began by "casually" picking up a crayon of the color least frequently selected by the child in the first session, using this crayon to trace the first maze correctly at a deliberately slow pace. The child watched and then was given her own turn on her copy of the same maze. The same procedure was followed for each of the 10 mazes, two trials being allowed for each maze.

Any improvement in maze-test performance between the first and second sessions presumably resulted from direct imitation of the mother's responses, and thus could be used as a measure of the child's tendency to imitate the mother's task-relevant performance. The major hypothesis of the study involved another type of imitation, however—incidental imitation learning, that is, duplication of the model's responses that were not relevant to solving the problem. This type of imitation was scored in terms of the number of times the child picked up a crayon of the same color as the one her mother picked, repeated the mother's irrelevant utterances, and made loops or final marks like the mother's in tracing the maze.

Interviews

Testing the hypothesis required some basic data on child-rearing practices, and more specifically, on the degree of the mother's nurturance of the child. It was also essential to determine the extent of maternal fostering of dependent behavior in the child, for, according to some theories of identification, dependency itself facilitates imitative learning (Sears, Maccoby, & Levin, 1957). These data were obtained from maternal interviews conducted at the mothers' homes between the children's first and second sessions. The interviews consisted of 15 open-ended questions taken from the Sears et al. interview schedule. The questions were related to maternal warmth and hostility, fostering of dependency, restrictions and demands on the child, permissiveness, democracy in the home, and child centeredness of the home. The interviews were tape recorded. Overall ratings of both nurturance and dependence were made on the basis of the analysis of these interview protocols. These ratings were made by the junior author after she had been trained in rating comparable interviews and had achieved 85% agreement with an experienced rater.

The distribution of the rating on nurturance was dichotomized as nearly as possible to the median, and the mothers above the median were considered nurturant ($N = 17$), while those below were considered nonnurturant ($N = 13$).

It should be noted that the ratings of the mother's interaction with the child were made before there was any knowledge of whether, or how much, the child would imitate the mother in the second session. Thus, there was no contamination of maternal rating and the child's tendency to imitate.

Teacher Ratings

Further assessment of the children's dependency came from teacher ratings of the children on four scales: frequency of attention-getting behavior, tendency to cling to the teacher, need for praise and approval, seeking help with tasks child is capable of doing. A rating of 1 on each scale represented the lowest degree of dependency, and a rating of 4, the highest. The child's dependency score was the sum of his ratings on all four scales.

It will be recalled that the subjects were in two kindergarten classes and had different teachers. Each teacher rated only her own pupils, of course, and, since the teachers probably had different standards of evaluating the children, their ratings had to be handled separately. One teacher rated 20 girls (10 in each group), while the other rated 10 girls (7 daughters of nurturant mothers and 3 others).

RESULTS AND DISCUSSION

The major hypothesis was tested by comparing the imitation scores of two groups of girls, those with nurturant and those with nonnurturant mothers. The groups did not differ from each other in average age, ordinal position, number of siblings, or socioeconomic status. Since they did not differ significantly in their first session maze-test performance, it may be inferred that there were no significant intellectual differences between the two groups.

Since maternal nurturance may foster dependency in the child, and this in turn may promote imitative behavior, it was important to establish that maternal nurturance and child dependency were not closely correlated variables in this population. Analysis of the interview data revealed that the highly nurturant mothers in this study did *not* encourage dependency in their daughters. On the contrary, interview ratings of nurturance and encouragement of dependency were slightly, though significantly, negatively correlated ($r = -.33, p = .05$). Apparently in this group, maternal nurturance was accompanied by some encouragement of independence in the child.

There is also some evidence that this encouragement of independence was, in fact, associated with a relatively low level of overt expression of dependency. According to teachers' ratings, the daughters of nurturant mothers were significantly less dependent than the other girls. The average dependency score, based on the teachers' ratings, of the 10 subjects with nurturant mothers was 8.2, the average for the other 10 was 10.1 ($t = 2.2$, $p < .05$). In the other class, the 7 subjects with nurturant mothers had an average dependency score of 10.5; the other 3 averaged 12.0 ($t = 1.6$, $p = .10-.15$).

Table 1 shows the mean scores of the two groups on two types of imitation —imitation of goal-related responses and incidental imitation learning. Since the number of subjects in each group was small, and distributions of the scores were nonnormal, U tests were used to compare rank transformation scores on all these measures of subjects in the two groups. The results of these tests and their significance are summarized in Table 1.

The table shows that the two groups did not differ significantly in imitation of behavior directly related to achievement of the goal in the maze test. The finding is analogous to the findings of Bandura and Huston (1961) that the experimenter-model's nurturance did not significantly affect the children's tendency to imitate his choice (the correct and rewarded box) in a discrimination learning task. Children imitate the model's operant responses that lead to the solution of problems, regardless of the degree of the model's nurturance. Perhaps this is attributable to the power of the direct rewards involved,

Table 1   Mean Imitation Scores of Girls with Highly Nurturant and
Nonnurturant Mothers

Variable	Highly Nurturant Group (N = 17)	Non- Nurturant Group (N = 13)	U
Imitation of goal-related responses (improvement in maze test performance)	5.2	6.4	54.5[a]
Incidental imitation	17.8	12.9	65[b]

[a] In calculating U for this variable, we eliminated the scores of six girls who scored 16 or more (highest possible score = 20) in the first testing.
[b] $p < .05$.

extrinsic (e.g., a prize for learning a discrimination task), intrinsic (such as the feeling of satisfaction derived from successful maze tracing), or both.

As Table 1 shows, the major hypothesis was confirmed. Maternal nurturance was found to be related to the child's incidental imitation learning, that is, to her tendency to match or imitate the mother's behavior that was incidental or irrelevant to solving the problem or achieving the goal. These results are clearly consistent with the conclusions of Bandura and Huston (1961) that

> children display a good deal of social learning of an incidental imitative sort, and that nurturance is one condition facilitating such imitative learning [p. 316].

Either an immediately preceding nurturant interaction between the model and the child or a long-standing nurturant relationship between the two may have this facilitating effect. Thus, if the parent is generally nurturant toward the child, there is an increased tendency for the child to imitate aspects of that parent's behavior spontaneously, that is, in the absence of an immediately preceding experience of nurturance or of direct tuition or specific rewards for this imitation.

It may be inferred that the child's assumption of certain aspects of his parent's behavior may be explained in terms of the principles underlying imitation of a model's incidental behavior, the model's (or parent's) secondary reward value, and the self-rewards that consequently arise from this imitation. The child's acquisition of appropriate sex-typed behavior, which is related to nurturance by the same-sex parent (Mussen & Distler, 1959; Mussen & Rutherford, 1963) may be considered a result of this kind of imitation that occurs without teaching or direct, immediate rewards. In short, it may be concluded that the data support the notion that

> the process subsumed under the term "identification" may be accounted for in terms of incidental learning, that is, learning that apparently takes place in the absence of an induced set or intent to learn the specific behaviors or activities question . . . [Bandura & Huston, 1961, p. 311].

REFERENCES

Bandura, A., & Huston, Aletha C. Identification as a process of incidental learning. *Journal of Abnormal and Social Psychology*, 1961, *63*, 311–318.

Kagan, J., & Mussen, P. H. Dependency theme on the TAT and group conformity. *Journal of Consulting Psychology*, 1956, *20*, 29–32.

Miller, N. E., & Dollard, J. *Social learning and imitation*. New Haven: Yale Univer. Press, 1941.

Mowrer, O. H. *Learning theory and personality dynamics*. New York: Ronald Press, 1950.

Mussen, P. H., & Distler, L. Masculinity identification and father-son relationships. *Journal of Abnormal and Social Psychology*, 1959, *59*, 350–356.

Mussen, P. H., & Rutherford, E. Parent-child relations and parental personality in relation to young children's sex-role preferences. *Child Development*, 1963, *34*, 589–607.

Porteus, S. D. *The Porteus Maze Test and intelligence*. Palo Alto, Calif.: Pacific Books, 1950.

Rosenblith, Judy F. Learning by imitation in kindergarten children. *Child Development,* 1959, *30*, 69–80.

Rosenblith, Judy F. Imitative color choices in kindergarten children. *Child Development*, 1961, *32*, 211–223.

Sears, R. R., Maccoby, Eleanor E., & Levin, H. *Patterns of child rearing*. Evanston, Ill.: Row, Peterson, 1957.

Effects
of Parental Dominance,
Warmth, and Conflict
on Imitation
in Children

E. Mavis Hetherington and Gary Frankie
UNIVERSITY OF WISCONSIN

Most theories of identification agree that identification is based on a process or processes whereby the child, through imitation, modeling, or introjection acquires traits, characteristics, and values similar to the parents. Although there is agreement in the defining characteristics of identification, the various theories diverge in their emphases on the relative importance of different motivational and learning conditions leading to identification. Three variables have frequently been hypothesized by the different theories as affecting identification; namely, parental power, parental warmth, and parental aggression.

Parsons (1955) has emphasized the importance of total parental power in

Reprinted from *Journal of Personality and Social Psychology,* 1967, 6, No. 2, 119–125. Published by the American Psychological Association. By permission.

This study was supported by the Research Committee of the Graduate School of the University of Wisconsin with funds provided by the Wisconsin Alumni Research Foundation.

333

the development of identification. According to Parsons, the child identifies with the parent because he determines or mediates both the rewards and punishments the child receives. Several studies (Hetherington, 1965a; Mussen & Distler, 1959, 1960) do indeed suggest that parental power or dominance influences sex typing in boys. The Hetherington (1965a) study also indicated that parental dominance had little effect on sex typing in girls, although paternal dominance increased father-daughter similarity on non sex-typed traits without interfering with mother-daughter similarity.

Learning theorists focus on anaclitic identification and the effects of warmth and nurturance in the development of identification. Considerable evidence has been accumulated indicating that identification and appropriate sex-role typing are facilitated for both-sex children by warmth in the same-sex parent (Helper, 1955; Mussen & Distler, 1959, 1960; Mussen & Rutherford, 1963; Payne & Mussen, 1956; Sears, 1953).

Psychoanalytic theorists have emphasized the role of fear of punishment and defensive identification with a threatening model. Most of the support for this position has been in clinical case studies, anecdotal evidence, or naturalistic observations such as the German concentration camp studies (Bettelheim, 1943). The Mussen and Distler (1959, 1960) studies did offer some evidence that highly masculine boys perceived their fathers as more punitive as well as more nurturant than feminine boys. No relationship was found between punitiveness and sex typing in girls in a subsequent study by Mussen and Rutherford (1963).

Bandura (1962) has suggested that identification and imitation are synonymous since both encompass the tendency for a person to match the behavior, attitudes, or emotional reactions exhibited by models. If this is true, then the same variables thought to be significant in identification should be salient in the child's imitation of the parent. Experimental studies have found that children imitate a powerful model (Bandura, Ross, & Ross, 1963) or a nurturant model (Bandura & Huston, 1961). Two studies using parents as models have also found that both boys and girls imitate the dominant parent (Hetherington, 1965a), and that maternal nurturance increases imitation by daughters (Mussen & Parker, 1965). Although there is evidence that children imitate aggressive behavior in others, there is only limited evidence that they emulate the behavior of an aggressive model when the aggression is directed toward themselves. A recent study by Mischel and Grusec (1966) has found that children rehearsed aggressive behaviors directed at them more when the model was high in control, and transmitted the aversive behaviors more when the model was high in rewardingness.

Perhaps one reason why evidence for identification with the aggressor is at best suggestive is that it can only be found in certain restricted circumstances. Sarnoff (1951) has suggested that three conditions are essential in producing defensive identification: a hostile individual who directs his aggression toward another person, a victim who is dependent upon the aggressor, and a situation involving stresses and limitations which prevent the victim from escaping the hostile behavior of the aggressor. On the basis of clinical and sociological observations, and Sarnoff's criteria for identification with the aggressor, defensive identification with a hostile dominant parent seems most likely to occur in a stressful home in which both parents are lacking in warmth. Such a home situation would offer the child no escape by seeking a closer relationship with a warm nondominant parent. A stressful, conflictual family relationship should add to the child's feeling of helplessness and increase his tendency toward defensive identification. The present study attempted to test this hypothesis.

A second purpose of the present study was to investigate further the effects of the different variables postulated to affect identification. There seems to be ample evidence that warmth and power do affect identification; a necessary step would appear to be to investigate the interactions of these variables and to find if there are situations under which warmth or dominance are particularly influential. For example, there has been some suggestion in the literature that parental power is more important in the identification of boys than of girls and that warmth is more salient for girls (Hetherington, 1965b; Mussen & Rutherford, 1963).

To test these hypotheses the present study investigated the effects of parental warmth, dominance, and conflict on imitation of parents by boys and girls.

METHOD

Subjects

Subjects were 80 male and 80 female nursery-school and kindergarten children and their parents randomly selected from a large pool of 310 families in which the parents had already taken the Structured Family Interaction Task. These families lived in small Wisconsin towns and most would probably be classified as lower middle class. The ages of the children ranged from 4 years, 4 months to 6 years, 5 months. Half of the subjects were from high-conflict homes and half were from low-conflict homes. Within each conflict group half of the subjects were from mother-dominant homes and half from father-dominant homes. Groups were further subdivided on the basis of all possible mother-father warmth combinations. Thus within each conflict-dominance group there were four warmth combinations: mother high–father low, mother low–father high, mother high–father high, and mother low–father low.

The measures of dominance, conflict, and maternal and paternal warmth were not significantly correlated, although there was an insignificant trend for parental warmth to be associated with low conflict. The number of subjects within each cell in the total populations sampled was approximately equal. These ranged from $N = 13$ in the father-dominant, low-conflict, both-parents-warm, boys group to $N = 9$ in the father-dominant, high-conflict, both-parents-warm, girls group.

Experimental Design

The study utilized a $2 \times 2 \times 2 \times 2 \times 4$ mixed factorial design involving parental dominance, conflict, sex of subject, parent imitated, and parental warmth combination. Each individual subject had two scores, one for imitation of his mother and one for imitation of his father.

Parental Measures

The parental measures of warmth, hostility, conflict, and dominance were obtained from a structured family-interaction task adapted from a procedure developed by Farina (1960). Each parent was seen individually in a quiet room in his own home. He was read 12 hypothetical problem situations involving child behavior and asked how he would handle them when he was by himself. The instructions were as follows:

> We are interested in knowing how a father/mother handles situations that come up when his wife/husband is not around. I'm going to read some situations that _____ might or might not really have been involved in. Imagine that this situation has arisen and that your wife/husband is not around and you must handle the problem yourself.

Both parents were then brought together and asked to arrive at a compatible solution on handling these children's problems.

The instructions for the joint interaction sessions were as follows:

> You have talked about how you would handle these various situations if you were alone; now I would like to go through these situations again, and have you discuss them and come to some agreement as to how you would handle the problem if you were both there. Imagine the situation arising, you are both at home and must deal with the situation. I want you to continue the discussion until you can come to some agreement on how you would handle the problem if you were together, then say "Agreed" and we will go on to the next situation.

The discussion of each problem continued until both parents said the terminating signal, "agreed." The experimenter participated only minimally in the discussion in order to clarify scoring responses. All interviews were tape-recorded and scored later.

In the previous studies, for which the interaction task was initially run (Hetherington, 1965a, 1965b), the results of all 12 situations were used; however, since many parents complained of fatigue and became restless during the last part of the joint interaction sessions only the responses on the first 7 situations were utilized in this study.

The seven situations were as follows:

> 1. Your son/daughter loses his/her temper while playing with a toy and intentionally breaks it.
> 2. You have friends over in the evening. Your son/daughter keeps getting out of bed to see what's going on.

3. Your son/daughter has a friend over to play. The friend wants to play with one of _____'s favorite toys but _____ won't let him.

4. A neighbor calls up and complains that your son/daughter has been throwing rocks at her child.

5. You have gone out of your way to buy something nice for your child and then he/she throws it aside and says he/she doesn't like it.

6. Your child has been asked several times to tidy up his/her room. You find his/her room still a mess and him/her watching TV.

7. You have taken your son/daughter out to dinner in a restaurant as a special treat. He/she is behaving in a generally noisy, ill-mannered way although you have warned him/her to quiet down.

Parental dominance measure.   The index for parental dominance was comprised of five of the measures previously used by Farina (1960), which were: speaks first, speaks last, passive acceptance of spouse's solution, percent of total speaking time, and the amount of yielding from original individual solution to the joint solution. Total scores on each of these measures were used to classify the index as indicating mother or father dominance. If three or more indexes indicated paternal dominance, the family was classified as father dominant; if three or more indicated maternal dominance, the family was classified as mother dominant.

Parental conflict measure.   The parental conflict measures were the same as those used by Farina (1960): total time spoken, disagreements and aggressions, interruptions, frequency of simultaneous speech, and failure to agree. Total time spoken was included as a measure of parental conflict, since it was assumed that the greater the conflict and disagreement the longer it would take to resolve differences and come to a mutually acceptable solution on handling problems. These scores were converted to z scores and combined into a single conflict index. Families which scored above the group mean in conflict were classified as high-conflict homes; those below the mean were classified as low-conflict homes.

Warmth-hostility measure.   The mother and father were separately rated on a 6-point warmth-hostility scale ranging from 1—extremely warm, nurturant, and affectionate; clearly proud of the child, concerned with and enjoys the child as a person; understanding and emphatic—to 6—marked hostility, anger, and punitiveness toward the child; little sympathy or attempt to understand the child's behavior; always interprets the child's behavior in the worst light. Ratings of parental warmth were done on the basis of both the individual sessions and the joint interaction session. A parent scoring below the group mean for his sex was classified as high in warmth; those above the mean were classified as low in warmth.

All the measures on the Structured Family Interaction Task which had previously exhibited any unreliability were rated by two judges. These included the yielding measure of the dominance scale, the warmth-hostility scale, and the conflict measures. Interjudge reliability was .94 for the yielding measure, .81 for the warmth-hostility ratings, and mean interjudge reliability on the conflict measures was .86.

Imitation Task

Each child was run on an imitation task where he watched each parent alternately perform for four trials in a free-play situation. Each parent was preinstructed, given a practice session without the child present, and given a small inconspicuous card to carry summarizing his role in the imitation task. Following the second, fourth, sixth, and eighth trials the child was given a 5-minute session in the playroom. The parental behaviors involved postural, motor, and verbal responses associated with playing with a group of toys and games previously determined to be of equal interest to male and female children. An attempt was made to use activities and behaviors which were appropriate for adults rather than some of the bizarre behaviors used in previous studies. Thus the activities involved were some in which an adult might participate without appearing too ludicrous, such as golf putting, shooting rubber darts at a target, a game of ball throwing at a target which automatically ejected the ball, etc. The parental behaviors involved such things as making predetermined distinctive comments following success or failure, always selecting a toy of a given color and saying, "———— is my lucky color," squatting and lining up golf shots, pulling up a chair, sitting sideways and shooting with two hands in the dart game, and so on.[1] The set of imitative responses assigned to a given parent and the parent performing first were randomly determined. Parents were always absent from the room during the child's test series.

A male and female observer checked the imitative responses on a response check list; perfect interrater agreement was found in the scoring of 95% of the specific imitative responses. The imitation scores were obtained by summing the frequency of responses the child made which were similar to those of a given parent.

RESULTS AND DISCUSSION

The basic analysis of variance for the imitation scores is presented in Table 1. The significant main effect of parent imitation and the significant Sex of Subject × Parent Imitation interaction indicate that although mothers were imitated more than fathers, boys imitated the father more than the mother ($M = 16.82, 15.22$, respectively, $p < .10$),[2] while girls imitated the mother more than the father ($M = 19.65, 12.06$, respectively, $p < .05$). The significant Dominance × Parent Imitation and Warmth × Parent Imitation interactions support the previous findings that parental warmth and dominance are important factors in identification. The means for the Dominance × Parent Imitation interaction show that the dominant parent was imitated

---

[1] Complete details on the imitation procedures may be obtained by writing to the senior author.

[2] Probability values are based on two-tailed t tests, unless otherwise noted.

Table 1   Analysis of Variance of the Imitation Scores

Source	df	MS	F
Conflict (C)	1	116.40	2.85[a]
Dominance (D)	1	1.95	<1.00
Sex of S (S)	1	2.28	<1.00
Warmth (W)	3	600.03	14.71[c]
C × D	1	14.03	<1.00
C × S	1	3.00	<1.00
C × W	3	10.61	<1.00
D × S	1	114.00	2.80[a]
D × W	3	32.19	<1.00
S × W	3	59.91	1.47
C × D × S	1	.03	<1.00
C × D × W	3	2.80	<1.00
C × S × W	3	3.55	<1.00
D × S × W	3	40.35	<1.00
C × D × S × W	3	13.83	<1.00
Error (a)	128	40.78	
Parent imitation (P)	1	717.00	19.77[c]
C × P	1	3.83	<1.00
D × P	1	4096.95	112.99[c]
S × P	1	1688.20	46.56[c]
W × P	3	1048.75	28.92[c]
C × D × P	1	141.79	3.91[a]
C × S × P	1	8.78	<1.00
C × W × P	3	4.56	<1.00
D × S × P	1	1762.51	48.61[c]
D × W × P	3	11.79	<1.00
S × W × P	3	61.64	1.70
C × D × S × P	1	2.27	<1.00
C × S × W × P	3	7.56	<1.00
C × D × W × P	3	53.06	1.46
D × S × W × P	3	45.35	1.25
C × D × S	3	16.41	<1.00
D × P × W			
Error (b)	128	36.26	

[a] $p < .10$.
[c] $p < .01$.

more; in a mother-dominant home the means for imitation of the mother and father were 20.94 and 10.78, respectively ($p < .05$), and in a father-dominant home means for imitation of the mother and father were 13.94 and 18.10, respectively ($p < .05$). In looking at the means for the Warmth × Parent Imitation interaction, it is obvious that a parent high in warmth is imitated more than a parent low in warmth. Mean imitation of the mother under the various warmth conditions was as follows: mother high–father high, 21.25; mother low–father high, 12.85; mother high–father low, 23.27; and mother

Table 2   Means for the Dominance × Sex × Parent Imitated Interaction

Parent Imitated	Mother Dominant		Father Dominant	
	Boys	Girls	Boys	Girls
Mother	20.47	21.40	9.98	17.90
Father	10.22	11.35	23.42	12.78

Note: Critical difference (2-tailed t test, $p < .05$) = 2.67 for comparison of mother versus father imitation within a column, and 2.73 for comparisons across columns.

low–father low, 12.40 (critical difference = 2.73, $p < .05$). It can be seen that a mother high in warmth was imitated more than one low in warmth, regardless of the level of paternal warmth. The same type of results were also obtained for mean imitation of the father under the various warmth conditions: father high–mother high, 16.72; father low–mother high, 10.92; father high–mother low, 17.35; and father low–mother low, 12.77 (critical difference = 2.73, $p < .05$). Also significant ($p < .05$) is the difference between imitation of a highly warm mother and a highly warm father (i.e., comparing imitation of the mother in the warmth conditions of mother high–father high, and mother high–father low versus imitation of the father in the conditions of father high–mother high and father high–mother low). This finding suggests that maternal warmth facilitates imitation of the mother more than paternal warmth facilitates imitation of the father.

However, these general findings must be qualified when we look at the means for the significant Dominance × Sex × Parent Imitated interaction presented in Table 2. Under mother dominance both boys and girls imitated the mothers more. Under father dominance, however, boys imitated the father more while girls continued to imitate the mother. This suggests that parental dominance has a more important effect on the identification of boys than of girls. The age range of the subjects in this study, 3–5, is considered a particularly important transition period in identification for boys where identification must shift from the mother to the father. Paternal dominance may play an extremely salient role in facilitating this shift for boys. It might also be suggested that a dominant father offers a more appropriate role model for boys than does a nondominant father.

For the girls, who do not need to shift their identification, maternal

Table 3   Analysis of Variance for Sex of Subject × Warmth Effects Interactions

Source	df	MS	F
S × Warmth	3		
S × MW	1	161.03	3.95[b]
S × FW	1	1.13	<1.00
S × MW × FW	1	17.58	<1.00

Note: S = sex, MW = mother warmth, FW = father warmth.
[b] $p < .05$.

Table 4   Means for the Significant Sex of Subject × Maternal Warmth Interaction

| | Maternal Warmth | |
Sex	High	Low
Girls	18.66	13.05
Boys	17.41	14.64

warmth seems to be the most salient variable in imitation. When the warmth-combinations variable is broken down into the orthogonal factors of mother and father warmth, the interaction of these factors with sex of subject (presented in Table 3) shows that maternal warmth interacts significantly with sex of subject while paternal warmth facilitates imitation to an equal degree in boys and girls. The means for the significant Maternal Warmth × Sex of Subject interaction are presented in Table 4 and show that maternal warmth affects the girl's imitation more than it does the boy's.

The means for the marginally significant ($p < .06$) Conflict × Dominance × Parent Imitated interaction are presented in Table 5. The pattern of differences in this table suggests that in a stressful home situation having high conflict there is more imitation of the dominant parent than is found in a home having low conflict. This appears to be particularly true if the mother is the dominant parent.

In order to permit clearer evaluation of the interaction of specific variables, and in order to assess the possibility of defensive identification occurring under the previously hypothesized conditions of Sarnoff's (1951) study, the means for all subgroups are presented in Table 6. The means essential for the defensive identification analysis are outlined.

It was assumed that the conditions most likely to lead to identification with the aggressor would be a home in which there is a high conflict and in which both parents were low in warmth. In such a situation there would be no warm supportive parent to whom to turn for succor so that the child might attempt to minimize his insecurity by identifying with a powerful. punitive model. Under the less stressful situation of a low-conflict home or a home in which there is some protection from a warm parent, there should be less tendency to imitate a hostile aggressive parent. Since these assumptions

Table 5   Means for the Conflict × Dominance × Parent Imitated Interaction

| | Mother Dominant | | Father Dominant | |
| | Parent imitated | | Parent imitated | |
Conflict	Mother	Father	Mother	Father
High	22.52	10.82	13.77	19.05
Low	19.35	10.75	14.10	17.15

Note: Critical difference = 2.73, 2-tailed t test, p. $< .05$.

Table 6 Mean Imitation Scores

Homes	Parent Imitated	Mother low–Father low		Mother high–Father low		Mother low–Father high		Mother high–Father high	
		Boys	Girls	Boys	Girls	Boys	Girls	Boys	Girls
Mother dominant High conflict	Mother	20.6	20.2	28.4	27.6	15.0	16.6	25.6	26.2
	Father	8.8	7.8	7.2	9.0	12.4	15.6	12.0	13.8
Low conflict	Mother	13.2	14.2	25.6	27.2	15.0	15.0	20.4	24.2
	Father	10.5	10.0	6.4	8.6	12.0	14.0	12.8	12.0
Father dominant High conflict	Mother	6.8	7.6	13.0	25.4	9.0	11.8	11.2	25.4
	Father	22.5	15.6	19.8	10.4	27.8	14.6	27.8	14.2
Low conflict	Mother	7.0	9.6	13.6	25.4	7.4	13.0	11.8	25.0
	Father	20.6	7.0	16.4	9.6	26.2	16.2	26.6	14.6

Note: Means for evaluating defensive identification under Sarnoff's (1951) criteria are outlined. Critical difference = 6.3, 1-tailed t test, p < .05, for comparing mother imitation versus father imitation at a given level of all other variables. For other comparisons critical difference = 6.5, 1-tailed t, p < .05.

produce directional hypotheses, one-tailed t tests were used in testing the differences in Table 6.

It can be seen that under high conflict, with both parents low in warmth, there is indeed a significant tendency for both boys and girls to imitate the dominant parent regardless of sex of the parent. If either the nondominant parent is warm or conflict is reduced, there is a trend toward less imitation of the aggressive dominant parent, so that the dominant parent is not imitated significantly more than the nondominant one. This trend does not hold in the case of boys with dominant fathers, however. The boy's tendency to imitate a dominant father overrides the effects of variations in conflict and warmth. In contrast, maternal warmth appears to be particularly salient for girls. Even under conditions of high conflict and paternal dominance there is marked imitation of warm mothers by daughters.

In summary, the results seem to be congruent with those of past studies which have found that both parental warmth and power are important in the identification of girls, and paternal dominance is important in the identification of boys. This is in agreement with the earlier findings of Mussen and Rutherford (1963) and Mussen and Distler (1959, 1960). Some support was found for identification with the aggressor under very restricted conditions involving high stress and low warmth in both parents, which might be assumed to result in a sense of extreme helplessness on the part of the child.

REFERENCES

Bandura, A. Social learning through imitation. In M. R. Jones (Ed.), *Nebraska symposium on motivation: 1962.* Lincoln: University of Nebraska Press, 1962. Pp. 211–269.

Bandura, A., & Huston, A. C. Identification as a process of incidental learning. *Journal of Abnormal and Social Psychology,* 1961, *63,* 311–318.

Bandura, A., Ross, D., & Ross, S. A. A comparative test of the status envy, social power, and the secondary-reinforcement theories of identification learning. *Journal of Abnormal and Social Psychology,* 1963, *67,* 527–534.

Bettelheim, B. Individual and mass behavior in extreme situations. *Journal of Abnormal and Social Psychology,* 1943, *38,* 417–452.

Farina, A. Patterns of role dominance and conflict in parents of schizophrenic patients. *Journal of Abnormal and Social Psychology,* 1960, *61,* 31–38.

Helper, M. M. Learning theory and the self-concept. *Journal of Abnormal and Social Psychology,* 1955, *51,* 184–194.

Hetherington, E. M. A developmental study of the effects of sex of the dominant parent on sex-role preference, identification, and imitation in children. *Journal of Personality and Social Psychology,* 1965, *2,* 188–194. (a)

Hetherington, E. M. The effects of parental dominance on imitation of sex typed behaviors. Unpublished manuscript, University of Wisconsin, 1965. (b)

Mischel, W., & Grusec, Joan. Determinants of the rehearsal and transmission of neutral and aversive behaviors. *Journal of Personality and Social Psychology,* 1966, *3,* 197–205.

Mussen, P., & Distler, L. Masculinity, identification and father-son relationships. *Journal of Abnormal and Social Psychology,* 1959, *59,* 350–356.

Mussen, P., & Distler, L. Child rearing antecedents of masculine identification in kindergarten boys. *Child Development,* 1960, *31,* 89–100.

Mussen, P., & Rutherford, E. Parent-child relations and parental personality in relation to young children's sex-role preferences. *Child Development,* 1963, *34,* 589–607.

Mussen, P. H., & Parker, A. L. Mother nurturance and girls' incidental imitative learning. *Journal of Personality and Social Psychology,* 1965, *2,* 94–97.

Parsons, T. Family structure and the socialization of the child. In T. Parsons & R. F. Bales (Eds.), *Family socialization and interaction process.* Glencoe, Ill.: Free Press, 1955. Pp. 35–131.

Payne, D. E., & Mussen, P. H. Parent-child relations and father identification among adolescent boys. *Journal of Abnormal and Social Psychology,* 1956, *52,* 358–362.

Sarnoff, I. Identification with the aggressor: Some personality correlates of anti-semitism among Jews. *Journal of Personality,* 1951, *20,* 199–218.

Sears, P. S. Child-rearing factors related to playing of sex-typed roles. *American Psychologist,* 1953, *8,* 431. (Abstract)

Assessment of Psychological Determinants in Childhood Asthma

Kenneth Purcell

UNIVERSITY OF MASSACHUSETTS

One observation stimulated much of the research story that follows. This was the striking difference noticed among severely asthmatic children who were admitted to the Children's Asthma Research Institute and Hospital (CARIH) in Denver from all parts of the United States. Some of these children (rapid remitters) became nearly symptom free shortly after admission to CARIH and remained that way without regular medication for the 18–24 months of their residence. Others (termed steroid dependents) continued to have symptoms after admission to a degree which required constant maintenance doses of the powerful corticosteroid drugs for adequate control. The central question which arose was, "What are the factors which account for this dramatic difference in symptom response to institutionalization?"

It seemed possible that one of the factors might be of a psychological nature. A number of other psychological investigations of asthma (2, 6), often

By permission of the author.

Much of the research described in this paper was supported by Research Grants MY3269 and HD01529 from the National Institutes of Health.

obtaining negative or inconclusive results, had grouped all asthmatics together, assuming that a fairly distinctive personality pattern or type of conflict was associated with the symptom. If some of these inconclusive results were a function of failure to discriminate important subgroupings within the asthmatic population, then a systematic attempt to classify asthmatics so as to determine the relative importance of allergic, emotional, and infectious stimuli should improve results.

Most of the remainder of this article will describe the evolution of a research program aimed at discriminating between those children for whom psychological determinants play an important role in the maintenance of asthma and those for whom they do not. Studies will be discussed in the chronological sequence in which they occurred so that the thread of the investigation may be more easily followed. Before that, however, it may be helpful to the reader to learn something of the nature of asthma.

DESCRIPTION OF THE SYMPTOM

Asthma is a symptom complex characterized by an increased responsiveness of the airways (trachea, major bronchi, and peripheral bronchioles) to various stimuli. This excessive reactivity is associated with marked narrowing of the airway passages, causing impairment of breathing, primarily in expiration, and wheezing. The airway narrowing may be due to swelling of the walls of the bronchi, increased mucus secretion, spasm of the bronchial muscles, or collapse of the rear walls of the trachea and bronchi during certain types of forced expiration. The significance of these factors may vary from patient to patient and from attack to attack in the same patient. Similarly, the nature of the stimulation, e.g., allergic, infectious, emotional, triggering these physiological processes may vary from patient to patient and attack to attack.

The importance of understanding and effective management of the problem of asthma may be judged from the fact that its incidence in the population has been observed to be between 2.5 and 5 percent depending on the method of estimate. This means that there are a minimum of 5,000,000 persons in this country suffering from asthma. Since past surveys have shown that about 60 percent of the population of asthmatics are below the age of 17, it can be assumed that at least 3,000,000 children now have asthma. Some indication of the socially disabling nature of this symptom is given by the fact that asthma is responsible for nearly one-fourth of the days reported lost from school because of chronic illness conditions in children (18).

SYMPTOM RESPONSE
TO INSTITUTIONALIZATION

As noted earlier, the author and his collaborators (9, 10) have compared subgroups which were defined on the basis of whether or not spontaneous remission of asthmatic symptoms occurred within a short time after admission to the Children's Asthma Research Institute and Hospital. Certain psychological differences between children, particularly between rapidly remitting and steroid dependent groups have been found. For example, in response to a structured interview technique, rapidly remitting children report significantly more often than do steroid dependent children that emotions such as anger, anxiety, and depression triggered their asthma while at home. Furthermore, the results of a questionnaire to assess parental child rearing attitudes indicated that both mothers and fathers of rapidly remitting children show authoritarian and punitive attitudes to a significantly greater degree than the parents of steroid dependent children.

These investigators initially suggested the hypothesis that, among rapidly remitting children, in contrast to steroid dependent children, the symptom of asthma is more often functionally linked with neurotic conflict and affective reactions. The asthmatic symptom of steroid dependent children, on the other hand, was viewed as a response more regularly linked with influences of allergic and infectious factors. These differences between the two groups were regarded as relative rather than absolute.

Another study (12) from the same institute reported a substantial multiple correlation (.61) between two maternal attitude scales ("breaking the will" and "excluding outside influence") and age of onset of asthma in the rapidly remitting group, i.e., the later the age of onset among children classified as rapid remitters, the higher the maternal score on these two variables. Age of onset ranged from birth to 5 years with a mean of 2.1 years. Within the steroid dependent group, the corresponding multiple correlation was −.20, not significantly different from zero. These results were interpreted in two ways. First, and most generally, it was suggested that the finding of a statistically significant relationship between a psychologically defined variable (maternal attitudes) and an asthmatically defined variable (age of onset) in the rapidly remitting group but not in the steroid dependent group was consistent with the hypothesis of psychological determinants having greater relevance for the former than for the latter group. Second, the homogeneity of the rapidly remitting group (with respect to any relationship between psychological variables and asthma) was questioned. The authors reasoned that autocratic and restrictive mothers (mothers of rapidly remitting children as contrasted to mothers of steroid dependent children) pose no special problems for a dependent and confined infant for the first 12–18 months of life. However, with the development of a child's wishes for autonomy and independence, and with a broadening of his social world, autocratic maternal attitudes may make for serious conflicts between mother and child. For example, the period of toilet training often dramatizes the emergent clash of wills between mother and child. Similarly, the growing interest of the developing child in institutions and people outside the home creates particular difficulties for those mothers who feel it important to insulate their child from any outside influence which might lead the child to question his mother's authority. It is during this period of childhood stress that the rapidly remitting child may be highly motivated to learn to use the asthmatic response as a technique of coping with conflict.

If escape from a highly controlling, autocratic maternal relationship has something to do with symptom reduction in those rapid remitters with relatively late age of onset, e.g., 3 to 5 years, then how may one account for improvement among remitters with a very early age of onset? It will be recalled that mothers of this latter group were considerably less autocratic and, therefore, symptom loss must be explained on some other basis. It may be that among these children removal from environmental allergens and/or climate variables are of particular importance. Results of an investigation (13) bearing on this question of further refining the rapidly remitting classification are described later in this paper.

ALLERGIC POTENTIAL CLASSIFICATION

Block and her colleagues (1) challenged the assumption of homogeneity among asthmatic children by assessing a somatic variable. They subdivided asthmatic patients using an Allergic Potential Scale (APS) to evaluate a patient's predisposition to allergic reaction. The APS is based on such items as family history of allergy, skin test reactivity, eosinophile count, ease with which a particular symptom may be diagnosed as related to specific allergens, and total number of different organ systems involved in allergic reactions. Using a thematic analysis of projective tests, these investigators concluded that asthmatic children with low APS (less disposed to allergy but not significantly different from the high APS group on severity of asthma) were more pessimistic, conforming, and had lower frustration tolerance than the high APS children. Mothers and fathers independently described the low APS group more often as nervous, jealous, rebellious, and clinging, than the high APS group. The results of observations of mother-child interaction, quantified by an adjective Q-sort technique, indicated that mothers of low APS children were more intrusive, angry, rejecting, and depriving. Scores on the Parental Attitude Research Instrument substantiated this evidence of undesirable maternal attitudes. Personality assessment of the mothers using the MMPI, TAT, and Rorschach, suggested that, compared with mothers of high APS children, mothers of the low APS children were more fearful, anxious, and self-defeating with more evidence of psychopathology. Interviews and observations of mother-father interaction indicated that the low APS group of parents showed more ambivalent, destructive, and pathological relationships than the high APS group. To sum up, psychopathological factors were observed significantly more often in low APS children and their mothers than in high APS children and their mothers.

APS SCORES AND SYMPTOM RESPONSE
TO INSTITUTIONALIZATION

Finding that steroid dependent and rapidly remitting children did not differ in APS scores, the author and his associates (13) developed an hypothesis as to the interaction between these classificatory variables. They reasoned that children who are institutionalized generally experience a major change in both their physical and psychological environments. Symptom remission following institutionalization may be due to the change in either class of stimuli or both. Those rapid remitters with high APS scores represent children particularly predisposed to react with asthma to allergic stimuli. Therefore, loss of symptoms in such cases may be principally associated with alterations in surrounding allergic stimuli whereas the low APS rapid remitters may be responding more to the alteration in the psychological environment. One may expect to find, then, more evidence of parental psychopathology, and perhaps of child psychopathology, in the low APS remitters as compared to the high APS remitters.

Test data did indeed indicate that low APS remitters were significantly more timid, anxious, depressed, and introverted than high APS remitters. Mothers of low APS remitters appeared significantly more authoritarian, suppressive, and intrusive than mothers of the high APS remitters. There were many more significant differences associated with this breakdown of the subject population than when either high and low APS groups or rapid remitter and steroid dependent groups were compared. Such differences did not occur when low APS steroid dependents were compared with high APS steroid dependents.

These findings are consistent with the suggestion that the remission of asthma symptoms following institutionalization may be a function of two distinctive components—improvement associated with alteration of the total physical environment to which the child is reactive and improvement associated with alteration of the psychological environment. Presumably the low APS remitters, who displayed greater evidence of psychopathology and whose parents gave more indication of undesirable attitudes toward child-rearing, may have responded with substantial changes in their emotional status and in their learned behavior patterns to the massive changes in the psychological environment associated with institutionalization.

Infection is another biological pathway to asthma. In the study already cited (13), two equally severe groups, one scoring high on *both* APS and URI (relevance of upper respiratory infection to asthma) and the other scoring low on APS and URI, were compared psychologically. The parental differences found when children were divided on the basis only of APS were accentuated. In other words, when the contribution of a second biologically defined variable, upper respiratory infection, was added to the APS scores, the indication of greater parental psychopathology in the group with lower biological variable scores (low APS–low URI) was even clearer.

EXPERIMENTAL SEPARATION
OF ASTHMATIC CHILDREN
FROM THEIR FAMILIES

All of the above observations on symptom change associated with institutionalization involve removal of a child from his family home with accompanying changes in surrounding physical *and* psychological stimuli. The evidence implicating physical environmental factors in the perpetuation of asthma in certain children is quite clear. Therefore, if one is to isolate the effects of psychological variables it becomes of central importance to find a way of drastically altering the significant psychological environment with minimum modification of the physical environment.

Toward this end, the author and his collaborators (11) conducted an experiment in which asthmatic children were studied medically and psychologically on a daily basis during periods in which they lived with their families and during an experimental two-week period in which they had no contact with their families but were cared for *in their own homes* by a substitute mother. Every effort was made to maintain an essentially constant physical environment within the limits of normal variation. Children continued their normal daily activities, attended school, ate the same food as usual, etc.

A total of 25 children was evaluated. On the basis of a detailed interview for assessing parental perceptions of the precipitants of asthma attacks, it was predicted that 13 of these children would respond positively to separation while 12 would show no improvement in asthma. For the group of 13 predicted positives, all measures of asthma, including indices of lung function, amount of daily medication required, daily history of asthma, and daily clinical examination by a physician for sounds of wheezing, indicated highly significant improvement occurring during the period of family separation for the group as a whole followed by an increase in symptoms upon the family's return home. For the group of 12 predicted negatives, only the daily history suggested improvement during separation at a borderline level of statistical significance. Without corroboration from other measures the daily history is a highly fallible, subjective indicator since a different adult observer (substitute parent) is involved during the separation as compared to the nonseparation periods.

One of the major pieces of psychological data obtained in this study was a series of tape recorded interviews centered around anticipated and actual reactions to separation from the point of view of the child, parents, and substitute parent. In each case, there were seven interviews with the child, six with the parent, and two with the substitute parent, and two with the substitute parent at standard points in the experimental sequence. The separation produced massive emotional reactions in a number of the mothers. Several of them had frank anxiety attacks in the early days of the separation. One of the mothers crawled onto the roof of her house to peek through a window in order to see her boy without his knowing it. Another, immediately following the end of separation, began to attack the quality of the care given her child by the substitute mother, and then shifted over to marked self-condemnation of her own inadequacy with the emergence of suicidal ideation.

Preliminary findings indicate that parents of predicted positives differ from parents of predicted negatives in their response to experimental separation. Data from the interview given two or three days after separation, shows that both mothers and fathers of predicted positive children displayed more anxiety and concern over their child's welfare, missed the child more, fussed over him more on leave taking, etc., than did the parents of predicted negatives. These findings apply to the only interview thus far thoroughly analyzed —the one taking place two to three days after parents left the child.

One question of prime interest concerns the psychophysiological mechanisms mediating the beneficial effects of separation on the course of asthma. The general topic of psychological influences on asthma and mediating mechanisms is discussed more fully in several review articles (4, 15, 16). In this author's opinion, emotional states, rather than personality types or patterns of interpersonal relationship, represent the most immediately relevant psychophysiological variable to be studied in relation to asthma. First, part of the definition of emotional states refers to processes of physiologic arousal and restraint intimately associated with the endocrine and autonomic nervous systems. As Wolf (20) has noted, the airway obstruction characteristic of asthma may be produced by autonomic nervous system activity stimulating mucus secretion, vascular engorgement, or bronchial contraction. Data on the frequency of occurrence of certain affective states during the course of this experiment are now being processed. Second, emotions have been shown to influence significantly endogenous adrenal steroid output (3), which may, in turn, alter the course of asthma as suggested by Reinberg (17). Third, emotional states are often associated with certain respiratory behaviors, e.g., crying, laughing, coughing, hyperventilation, which may themselves lead to airway narrowing. Children and parents commonly noted such patterns as "she got very upset, cried and then started wheezing." Or "he became angry, red in the face, started to shout and then choked up and then came asthma."

These observations on the role of respiratory activity are consistent with recent evidence described by Simonsson et al. (19) that sensitized cough receptors may be involved in triggering reflex airway constriction in patients with obstructive airway disease. The efferent pathways causing constriction are via the vagus nerves. Crying, laughing, coughing, and hyperventilation may well stimulate the irritant receptors in the airways and initiate a broncho-constrictor reflex. Both parents and substitute parents occasionally reported that children sometimes sought to stop crying or laughing or coughing hard so as not to provoke asthma. The author (9) has previously suggested that the occasionally observed inability of an asthmatic to cry or the silent, suppressed manner of crying, may reflect a learned attempt to avoid initiating the uncomfortable experience of an asthmatic attack rather than any special symbolism associated with crying.

Finally, there exists the possibility that asthma may be maintained in at least some children by a learning process involving parental reinforcement of the symptom. The traditional view has been that psychosomatic symptoms mediated by the autonomic nervous system are subject only to classical conditioning. By contrast, Miller and his associates (5, 6, 7) have produced an impressive series of studies showing that visceral or glandular responses such as heart rate, rate of intestinal contraction, and salivation are subject to instrumental learning. The preliminary differences found in the parental behavior of predicted positives and negatives, e.g., parents of the former group fussing more over the child at the time of separation, showing more concern over the child's welfare, etc., would be consistent with the hypothesis that the asthmatic response is more likely to be reinforced by parents of predicted positives.

CLINICAL IMPLICATIONS
OF THE SUBGROUP HYPOTHESIS

In light of the results described above, how may the clinician approach the evaluation of the relevancy of psychological factors in the particular asthmatic patient with whom he must deal? The tools and cues found most useful clinically are likely to be those which have successfully, albeit imperfectly, discriminated among asthmatic subgroups. There are four classes of information involved: (a) the patient's, or in the case of a child below the age of 8 or 9, his parents', perception of events related to the onset of asthma attacks; (b) the nature of the symptom response to separation from significant figures; (c) biological characteristics of the patient; (d) presence of certain attitudes and/or degree of psychopathology in the parent and child. These will be briefly discussed in sequence.

Information on perceived precipitants of attacks may be obtained from the structured interview which fairly successfully distinguished rapid remitters from steroid dependent children (9), and predicted improvers and nonimprovers in the experimental separation study (11). A practical rule of thumb is to consider psychological variables relevant to the maintenance of asthma when emotions such as anger, anxiety, excitement, or depression are ranked among the first three precipitants of asthma in order of importance by either the patient or his parent and when specific episodes supporting this ranking can be given by the informant.

Changes in symptoms associated with separation from parents or siblings may occur in several different situations. For example, a very prompt response to hospitalization without the use of any potent medication is a frequent report. Some parents have reported a consistent improvement as the child reaches the vicinity of the hospital even before getting to the emergency room. It is useful to inquire closely about the course of asthma during those periods when a child has been separated from one or both of his parents in the normal course of events. For example, husbands may go off on business trips or parents may take vacations for a few days or more at a time leaving their child with a baby sitter. The clinician must always keep in mind that separation from significant persons is frequently accompanied by a change in the physical environment which itself may be associated with alterations in asthmatic symptoms. Often it is not possible to do much more than make an educated guess as to which factors are primarily responsible for a symptom change. When fairly unambiguous data are available on this point, e.g., a child repeatedly improving during separation from his family with any accompanying changes in the physical environment appearing insignificant, it deserves to be heavily weighted in evaluating the role of psychological variables.

Much of the historical information on biological characteristics can be obtained directly by the psychologically oriented clinician. However, some of it must be sought from the physician involved in the case. The strength of constitutional disposition toward allergy varies directly with the degree of positive finding in the APS items mentioned earlier. Unfortunately, quantitative data describing cut-off scores for judging the significance of APS scores are not available.

Indications of highly controlling, autocratic maternal attitudes may point to the operation of psychological variables. It is likely that, when these attitudes are clearly relevant to the maintenance of asthma, one should also find more direct evidence of emotions triggering attacks or of asthma remitting upon separation from such a mother.

Sheer degree of psychopathology in the child is, in the author's judgment, the least valuable cue. For one thing, the evidence on this point is ambiguous. While one study (1) reported differences between asthmatic subgroups in overall degree of psychopathology, another (14) did not. Even more important are data (8) suggesting that behavioral maladjustment among asthmatics is no different than maladjustment found among children suffering from cardiac defects, with both groups differing from the normal. Therefore, even when one finds important indications of emotional disturbance in the child, these may be more the consequences of a chronic illness condition than the antecedents of asthma.

A cautionary note in evaluating all these indices is the fact that asthma is almost always a multiply-triggered symptom. In the individual case, asthma precipitated by physically defined stimuli almost invariably coexists with asthma precipitated by psychologically defined stimuli. Therefore, a seemingly high score on biological characteristics does not preclude the possibility that emotional stimuli are important with the reverse being true as well.

At the least, the results obtained from subgroup studies offer some assistance in making a more informed judgment about whether or not to include some form of psychotherapeutic intervention as part of the treatment program for asthma. The information most useful in guiding clinical decisions at this time is probably that dealing with emotional precipitants of asthma attacks and the effects of separation from family members on the symptoms of asthma.

RESEARCH IMPLICATIONS
OF THE SUBGROUP HYPOTHESIS

Any investigation which fails to discriminate among asthmatics runs the risk of obscuring relationships that may exist only for a portion of the population. For example, using a population of 71 ambulant children with chronic asthma, Dubo and her associates (2) tested the hypothesis of a positive relationship between disturbances in family dynamics and severity of asthma in a child. They failed to find any significant relationships between variables of the family situation and those of the child's asthma. On the other hand, many strong positive relationships were found between extent of family disturbances and behavioral indices of maladjustment in the child, thus confirming the meaningfulness of the family measures. These results led the investigators to question the effect of family variables on asthma itself, as distinguished from the effects on the adjustment of the child with asthma.

The subgroup hypothesis would suggest that the extent of psychological disturbance within a family or a child may be relatively independent of the types of stimulation customarily triggering asthmatic responses. What is hypothesized is an interaction between family variables, severity of asthma, and type of stimulation, i.e., family variables may be positively related or unrelated to severity depending upon the types of stimulation customarily triggering asthmatic attacks. It seems possible, therefore, that appropriate subdivision of children in the Dubo study may have led to somewhat different results than were obtained.

The same indices suggested for clinical evaluation, i.e., symptom response to separation from the family, perceived precipitants of asthma, and APS scores appear to be the most reliable criteria for the research definition of asthmatic subgroups. Finally, the possibility exists and should be explored that careful description of other psychosomatic disorders, e.g., ulcers and hypertension, will lead to equally fruitful subgroup classifications. If experience with asthma represents any guide, then basing the classification on analyses of the specific events which exacerbate or relieve the particular response involved is likely to be more useful than relying on such general descriptions as type of personality constellation, degree of psychopathology, or quality of interpersonal relationships.

REFERENCES

1. Block, Jeanne, Jennings, P. H., Harvey, Elinor, & Simpson, Elaine. Interaction between allergic potential and psychopathology in childhood asthma. *Psychosomatic Medicine*, 1964, 26, 307–320.
2. Dubo, S., McLean, J. A., Ching, A. Y. T., Wright, M. L., Kauffman, P. E., & Sheldon, J. M. A study of relationships between family situations, bronchial asthma, and personal adjustment in children. *Journal of Pediatrics*, 1961, 59, 402–414.
3. Hamburg, D. A. Plasma and corticosteroid plasma levels in naturally occurring psychological stresses. In S. Korey (Ed.), *Ultrastructure and metabolism of the nervous system.* Baltimore: Williams & Wilkins, 1962.
4. Lipton, E., Steinschneider, A., & Richmond, J. B. Psychophysiologic disorders in children. In Lois W. Hoffman & M. L. Hoffman (Eds.), *Review of child development research.* Vol. 2, New York: Russell Sage Foundation, 1966.
5. Miller, N. E. & Banuazizi, A. Instrumental learning by curarized rats of a specific

visceral response, intestinal or cardiac. *Journal of Comparative and Physiological Psychology*, 1968, *65*, 1–7.

6. Miller, N. E. & Carmona, A. Modification of a visceral response, salivation in thirsty dogs, by instrumental training with water reward. *Journal of Comparative and Physiological Psychology*, 1967, *63*, 1–6.

7. Miller, N. E. & DiCara, L. V. Instrumental learning of heart-rate changes in curarized rats: Shaping, and specificity to discriminative stimulus. *Journal of Comparative and Physiological Psychology*, 1967, *63*, 12–19.

8. Neuhaus, E. C. Personality study of asthmatic and cardiac children. *Psychosomatic Medicine*, 1958, *3*, 181–186.

9. Purcell, K. Distinctions between subgroups of asthmatic children: Children's perceptions of events associated with asthma. *Pediatrics*, 1963, *31*, 486–494.

10. Purcell, K., Bernstein, L., & Bukantz, S. C. A preliminary comparison of rapidly remitting and persistently "steroid dependent" asthmatic children. *Psychosomatic Medicine*, 1961, *23*, 305–310.

11. Purcell, K., Brady, K., Chai, H., Muser, J., Molk, L., Gordon, N., & Means, J. Effect of experimental separation from the family on asthma in children. Paper presented at the meeting of the American Psychosomatic Society, Boston, April, 1968.

12. Purcell, K., & Metz, J. R. Distinctions between subgroups of asthmatic children: Some parent attitude variables related to age of onset of asthma. *Journal of Psychosomatic Research*, 1962, *6*, 251–258.

13. Purcell, K., Muser, J., Miklich, D., & Dietiker, K. E. Comparison of psychologic findings in variously defined asthmatic subgroups. *Journal of Psychosomatic Research*, in press.

14. Purcell, K., Turnbull, J. W., & Bernstein, L. Distinctions between subgroups of asthmatic children: Psychological test and behavior rating comparisons. *Journal of Psychosomatic Research*, 1962, *6*, 283–291.

15. Purcell, K., & Weiss, J. Asthma. In C. G. Costello (Ed.), *Symptoms of psychopathology*. New York: Wiley, in press.

16. Purcell, K., Weiss, J., & Hahn, W. Certain psychosomatic disorders. In B. Wolman (Ed.), *Manual of child psychopathology*. New York: McGraw-Hill, in press.

17. Reinberg, A., Chata, D., & Sidi, E. Nocturnal asthma attacks and their relationship to the circadian adrenal cycle. *Journal of Allergy*, 1963, *34*, 323–330.

18. Schiffer, C. G., & Hunt, E. P. Illness among children. *Children's Bureau, U.S. Department of Health & Welfare*, 1963.

19. Simonsson, B. G., Jacobs, F. M., & Nadel, J. A. Role of autonomic nervous system and the cough reflex in the increased responsiveness of airways in patients with obstructive airway disease. *The Journal of Clinical Investigation*, 1967, *46*, 1812–1818.

20. Wolf, S. Life stress and allergy. *American Journal of Medicine*, 1956, *20*, 919–928.

part IV
Extrafamilial Influences on Personality Development

Children are not socialized by parents alone; there are many other agents of socialization. When the child enters nursery school, he encounters many new people who will help socialize him. Nursery school teachers are, to some extent, like parents in reinforcing and thus strengthening some of the child's established patterns of reaction. Through their teaching they may also influence him to modify some of his behavior, personality characteristics, and attitudes. And, as the child becomes more active socially and more highly oriented toward his peers, they inevitably become informal, unselfconscious agents of socialization. Moreover, teachers and peers may present new, attractive models for imitation and identification.

In the first paper in his part, Dr. Walter Emmerich of the Educational Testing Service reports his investigation of the stability of a number of important personality characteristics during the preschool period. Factor analyses of teacher ratings showed marked individual stability in traits such as aggression, dependency, and autonomy throughout the four semesters of nursery school attendance. But nursery school experience produced some interesting changes over time in the structure of these personality factors and important modifications in the behavior of some children. For example, instrumental dependency, manifested by help-seeking, was associated with emotional dependency during the first year of nursery school, but, during the second year, this kind of behavior increasingly became an alternative to autonomy. That is, self-reliance and help-seeking became stable, alternative strategies for solving problems. Boys who were relatively lacking in autonomy at the time they began nursery school were hostile and aggressive, but became less aggressive and more instrumentally dependent later on.

Peers also have enormous potential to influence and modify the behavior of a child in positive ways. This is illustrated in the next two papers. The study by Willard Hartup and Brian Coates indicates that nursery children become more altruistic after they observe a child model behaving in an altruistic way, sharing prizes with another child. The extent to which children imitated the model's altruistic behavior depended on their past experience. Those who had been reinforced frequently by peers imitated rewarding child models, while children who had experienced little reinforcement from peers imitated nonrewarding models more readily.

In the third paper, Albert Bandura and his colleagues at Stanford University report impressive results in reducing children's fear of dogs by showing them a peer model approaching and playing with a dog in a calm, friendly way. The positive, fear-reduction effects were stable and lasting. Children who were initially fearful soon approached a familiar dog and this response generalized to another, unfamiliar one.

The final paper of this part, by K. Eileen Allen and her coworkers at the University of Washington, demonstrates how a nursery school teacher can transform a child's behavior radically by simple and consistent application of behavior principles (behavior therapy). The subject was a 4-year-old nursery school girl who originally isolated herself from peers and interacted only with adults. The nursery school teacher began systematically to reward any interaction she had with another child by giving her a great deal of attention and, at the same time, disregarded her when she interacted with adults. Interactions with other children increased almost immediately and markedly, while interactions with adults decreased. This heightened interest in social relations with peers was maintained throughout the school year.

Continuity
and Stability
in Early
Social Development:
Teacher Ratings

Walter Emmerich

EDUCATIONAL TESTING SERVICE

An earlier study integrated the concepts of behavioral continuity-discontinuity and individual stability-instability into a fourfold scheme for developmental analysis (Emmerich, 1964). This framework was applied to a short-term longitudinal study of early social development, based upon systematic observations of the social behavior of children in the nursery-school setting. The present study extends this approach to a different source of data on the same subjects, that of teacher ratings. First, the dimensionality and continuity of social behavior are examined by means of independent factor analyses of

Reprinted from *Child Development*, copyright © by The Society for Research in Child Development, Inc., 1966, 37, No. 1, 17–27. By permission.

Presented in part at the biennial meeting of the Society for Research in Child Development, Minneapolis, Minnesota, March 27, 1965. The author wishes to express his appreciation to the research and nursery school staffs of the Purdue Longitudinal Study for collecting and making available the data of this report and to Aaron G. Auerbach for his assistance with the analyses.

teacher ratings of the same children in each of four semesters of nursery school. The extent of trait stability is then determined by looking at the correlations among factors having similar structure in all four semesters. Finally, attention is given to changes over time in factor structure and to an accompanying transformation in the behavior of some children.

METHOD

Subjects

The subjects were 53 middle-class children who attended four consecutive semesters of nursery school and participated in the Purdue Longitudinal Study (Emmerich, 1964; Martin, 1964). Since subjects were from four groups entering nursery school in successive years, partial control was achieved over factors associated with calendar year of entry. Because of the small sample sizes, separate factor analyses of the 24 girls and 29 boys were not attempted. The average age was 3.1 years at the beginning of the first semester.

Teacher Ratings

At the end of each semester, the head and assistant teachers independently rated the children on 34 social-behavior scales taken from Beller (1948) with only minor modifications. Ratings were made at any point between 1 (low) and 7 (high) on the scales, but final scores were based upon subsequent groupings of these responses to form 7-point scales. The sequence of presentation of scales was varied among raters and subjects. Interjudge reliabilities were estimated from correlations between the head- and assistant-teachers' ratings. Since the four groups did not necessarily have the same teachers in a particular semester, this procedure led to entry in the same column of ratings by different teachers. The resulting coefficients were therefore conservative estimates of reliability, uncorrected for possible systematic judge differences in scale utilization. Final scores were based upon the sums of the ratings by the two teachers, except for a few instances when only one teacher rated a child in a particular semester, in which case the ratings of the single judge were doubled. In order that the summed ratings contribute reliable individual-difference variance to each factor analysis, a scale was included in the study only if interjudge agreement was significant at the 5 per cent level in *all four* semesters. Twenty-four of the scales met this criterion and are given in Table 1, together with their median and highest reliability coefficients for the four semesters.

Factor Analyses[1]

Scores on the 24 sufficiently reliable scales were intercorrelated (Pearson *r*) within semesters and subjected to independent factor analyses using

[1] The rating scales, unrotated factor loadings, and rotated factor-score intercorrelations have been deposited with the American Documentation Institute. Order Document number 8609 from ADI Auxiliary Publication Project, Photoduplication Service, Library of

Table 1 Rater Reliabilities and Oblique Factor Loadings by Semester[a]

Rating Scales	Semester Reliabilities		Aggression-Dominance				Dependency				Autonomy			
			Semester				Semester				Semester			
	Median	Highest	1	2	3	4	1	2	3	4	1	2	3	4
Threatens children	.55	.70	.88	.89	.90	.93	-.10	-.01	-.04	-.02	-.16	-.13	-.16	-.22
Bosses children	.63	.68	.86	.89	.90	.79	.06	.00	.06	.03	.07	.09	.17	.27
Derogates children	.53	.70	.86	.84	.86	.88	.10	.10	.03	.05	-.10	-.09	-.13	-.05
Directs children	.51	.66	.84	.86	.72	.74	.02	-.13	.12	.04	.13	.25	.47	.46
Dominates children	.51	.55	.80	.68	.69	.60	.04	-.23	.15	.13	.17	.08	.27	.47
Attacks children physically	.62	.85	.68	.83	.84	.83	-.13	-.10	-.08	-.07	-.44	-.31	-.19	-.21
Threatens teacher	.55	.66	.72	.78	.81	.84	.00	.27	.03	.03	-.02	-.01	-.21	-.25
Insists on own ideas	.45	.58	.77	.69	.79	.80	.17	.22	.03	.19	-.08	.02	.02	.05
Destroys property of other children	.57	.76	.59	.72	.79	.79	-.10	-.05	-.01	-.22	-.55	-.33	-.27	-.28
Derogates teacher	.44	.58	.76	.75	.73	.70	-.02	.15	.03	.03	.06	-.10	-.15	-.15
Seeks recognition from children	.29	.45	.53	.71	.58	.33	.41	.10	.27	.51	.06	.16	.35	.28
Submits to children when challenged	.30	.68	-.73	-.83	-.64	-.56	.12	.17	.20	.02	.01	-.09	-.30	-.24
Avoids rough activities	.56	.77	-.57	-.73	-.83	-.67	.20	.35	.24	.22	.18	.14	-.12	-.20
Follows teacher's directions without resistance	.55	.61	-.54	-.65	-.71	-.65	.11	-.07	.11	.12	.38	.52	.38	.45
Seeks to be near teacher	.67	.82	-.23	-.34	-.18	-.39	.90	.83	.85	.75	.03	.09	-.14	-.12
Seeks physical contact with teacher	.62	.75	-.13	-.34	-.20	-.27	.88	.77	.81	.77	.03	-.08	-.02	-.09
Seeks recognition from teacher	.37	.42	.07	.22	.14	.12	.87	.74	.83	.84	.18	.32	-.05	-.02
Seeks attention from teacher	.53	.71	.19	.18	.08	-.01	.77	.89	.85	.81	.00	.12	-.11	-.05
Asks teacher for special privileges	.40	.55	.43	.36	.53	.49	.64	.83	.58	.59	-.21	-.14	-.16	-.08
Asks teacher to do what teacher asks child to do	.29	.59	-.06	.08	.14	.19	.84	.82	.33	.46	-.14	-.09	-.69	-.75
Seeks help from teacher	.43	.53	-.08	-.25	.02	-.12	-.06	.13	-.23	.07	-.35	-.41	-.47	-.67
Completes activities	.47	.69	.66	.68	.56	.47	-.09	-.21	-.16	-.23	.88	.84	.77	.74
Gets intrinsic satisfaction from his work	.46	.55	-.07	-.10	-.13	-.01	.01	.05	-.11	.06	.87	.90	.78	.79
Overcomes obstacles by himself	.44	.66	.02	.11	.11	.03	-.21	-.16	-.05	-.08	.76	.80	.73	.81

[a] Italicized loadings were those used in the computation of factor scores.

Table 2 Factor-Stability Coefficients[a]

Semester	Aggression-Dominance Semester				Dependency Semester				Autonomy Semester			
	1	2	3	4	1	2	3	4	1	2	3	4
1	...	...	...	...	...	...	...	...	...	...	...	...
2	.84	...	...	...	.83	...	...	...	.78	...	...	...
3	.47	.64	...	...	.61	.56	...	...	.44	.63	...	...
4	.47	.66	.81	...	.48	.45	.69	...	.54	.67	.80	...

[a] $p < .001$ for all correlations.

the principal factor method with communalities estimated by the squared multiple-correlation procedure (Harman, 1960). Factors were obliquely rotated by means of Carroll's biquartimin computer program. Initially, six factors were extracted and rotated in each semester, but this procedure resulted in several highly correlated factors within semesters. In order to clarify the developmental analyses of factor continuity and stability, it was first essential to isolate relatively *independent* sources of variance *within* time periods. Therefore, the strategy was adopted of reducing the number of factors to be rotated until the criterion of factor independence within semesters was achieved. This criterion was met by rotation of the first three factors in each semester, accounting for an average among semesters of 82 per cent of the estimated total common variance. Factor scores were derived by selecting the scales having the five highest loadings on a factor, dividing these loadings by their respective standard deviations, and summing the products of these weights by the subject's scores on the five scales.

RESULTS AND DISCUSSION

Continuity and Stability

The same basic factor structures emerged in all four time periods (see Table 1). The first factor, called Aggression-Dominance, accounted for the greatest amount of variance in each semester. The other factors were identified as Dependency and Autonomy. For each factor, six stability coefficients make up the complete longitudinal network (Emmerich, 1964) of relations among the four semesters. All of these stability coefficients were significant (see Table 2). Thus, these three factors exhibited considerable individual stability as well as behavioral continuity throughout this period.

Congress, Washington, D.C. 20541, remitting in advance $1.75 for microfilm, or $2.50 for photocopies. Make checks or money orders payable to: Chief, Photoduplication Service, Library of Congress.

The structural findings replicate in remarkable detail Beller and Turner's (1964) four independent factor analyses of teacher ratings of clinical and non-clinical nursery-school girls and boys, using 14 of the present scales. The great similarity of factor structures in the two studies argues for the generalized salience and unidimensionality of these personality characteristics, at least during this period. Furthermore, the marked individual stability of these dimensions adds to the accumulating evidence for the view that certain attributes of personality become established early in life and tend to be sustained in their original forms (e.g., Emmerich, 1964; Kagan & Moss, 1962; Martin, 1964; Schaefer & Bayley, 1963).

However, several aspects of the present study limit the scope of these conclusions. Factor structures vary according to the range of variables included in them, and alternative factoring procedures could have resulted in different structures.[2] It is also likely that greater discontinuity and instability would occur over longer time spans. And although teachers made their ratings independently, discussions among teachers in carrying out their school responsibilities probably had the effect of increasing consensus with respect to both dimensionality and ratings of individuals. Furthermore, ratings were made in the nursery-school setting only and therefore cannot reveal broad situational variations in trait structure or individual trait scores. Finally, alternative methods of data collection could lead to quite different conclusions. In the case of dependency, for example, there is considerable evidence that systematic observations of child dependency by trained observers do not form a unidimensional trait (Emmerich, 1964; Hartup, 1963; Heathers, 1955b; Sears, 1963). Why ratings should be less complex than observations remains an intriguing problem for investigation. A number of variables would seem to be relevant, including the spatiotemporal scope (molarity) of the unit of observation, the nature of the affective and role relationships between the observer and the observed, and extent of control over halo effects (Hartup, 1963).

Discontinuity and Stability

The above findings do not support a view of marked discontinuity in social behavior during the nursery-school period, at least as reflected by the procedures of this study. However, the detection of less obvious discontinuities requires a closer examination of variations among semesters in the amount of individual-difference variance contributed by each of the three dimensions. Figure 1 portrays the variance contributed by the factors in each semester, based upon the average of the squared loadings on those scales for which the squared loading on the factor in question was .100 or greater in at least one semester. Not surprisingly, Dependency's importance diminished during this period, whereas Autonomy's increased somewhat, although none

---

[2] However, oblique and orthogonal (Varimax) rotations of the first six factors resulted in very similar structures in each semester.

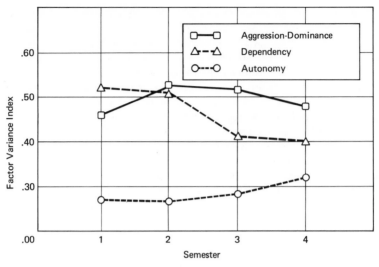

Fig. 1. Factor-variance index by semester.

of the temporal shifts were statistically significant. Inspection of the loadings did reveal interesting qualitative changes, however (see Table 3). The two scales reflecting *instrumental dependency* (Heathers, 1955a) loaded more heavily on Dependency than on Autonomy during the first year, whereas the converse was more frequent during the second year. This structural change bears on the question of the relations among instrumental dependency, emotional dependency, and independence (Beller, 1955; Hartup, 1963; Heathers, 1955a, b). It indicates that instrumental dependency was initially associated with emotional dependency but then increasingly came to signify an *alternative* to autonomy. For several reasons, it is unlikely that this age change was confounded with individual differences among teachers in trait structuring:

Table 3   Prominent Shifts of Factor Loadings over Time

Scale	Dependency Factor				Autonomy Factor			
	Semester				Semester			
	1	2	3	4	1	2	3	4
Seeks help from teacher	.66	.68	.56	.47	−.35	−.41	−.47	−.67
Asks teacher to do what teacher asks child to do	.84	.82	.33	.46	−.14	−.09	−.69	−.75
Destroys property of other children	. . .	. . .	. . .	. . .	−.55	−.33	−.27	−.28
Attacks children physically	. . .	. . .	. . .	. . .	−.44	−.31	−.19	−.21

the four groups did not necessarily have the same teachers within the same semester; the over-all clarity and simplicity of the factor structures indicated that rater similarities greatly outweighed any possible differences; and the structural changes themselves were not of the sporadic sort expected if teacher differences had been marked.

The bipolarity of autonomy and instrumental dependency was not antici- pated, but Crandall and Sinkeldam (1964) report a pattern of intercorrelations among ratings of emotional dependency, instrumental dependency, and achievement in middle-class children ages 6 to 10 that is similar to the structures found in the second year of the present study. Perhaps, then, self- reliance and help-seeking are early formed stable alternative habits or "strategies" used by the child in his goal-directed and problem-solving efforts.

What might be the origins of this bipolarity between autonomy and instrumental dependency? There is evidence that it could arise from differen- tial maternal-reinforcement histories. Crandall, Preston, and Rabson (1960) intercorrelated ratings of child help-seeking, achievement efforts, and mater- nal reinforcements of these behaviors in a middle-class nursery-school group. The relevant findings were that help-seeking and achievement efforts were negatively correlated, as were the maternal rewards for these behaviors, and that the child's achievement efforts were positively correlated with maternal rewards for achievement but negatively (non-significantly) correlated with maternal rewards for help-seeking. On the other hand, a reverse (or mutual) causality explanation is also plausible. Differential maternal reinforcement of autonomy and instrumental dependency could arise from a tendency for mothers to implement the maternal role by supporting whichever of these behaviors happens to be dominant in the child's early repertoire. However, both of these explanations raise the question of why this bipolarity was not present in the first semester, a problem considered later in the discussion.

Another change on the Autonomy factor was a decrease after the first semester in negative loadings on two aggression scales (see Table 3). Taken in conjunction with the above shift of instrumental dependency, this change is evidence for discontinuity in the meaning of autonomy, or more accurately, its bipolar counterpart. The question arises whether this structural shift was accompanied by change in the behavior of the children. In order to evaluate this question, separate scores were computed for both poles of the Autonomy factor in the first and fourth semesters. If the autonomous child remained autonomous while the non-autonomous child's aggression became trans- formed into instrumental dependency, then the autonomy pole of semester 1 should correlate positively with autonomy and negatively with instrumental dependency in semester 4; while the aggression pole of semester 1 should correlate negatively with autonomy, and positively with instrumental depend- ency in semester 4. The results for the combined sexes partially supported these expectations (see Table 4). However, it was noted that the autonomy and aggression poles of semester 1 were clearly bipolar in boys ($r = -.77$, $p < .001$) but not in girls ($r = -.17$, not significant), suggesting that the

Table 4   Intercorrelations Among Autonomy Factor Poles in Semesters 1 and 4

Semester	Factor	Semester 1		Semester 4	
		Autonomy	Aggression	Autonomy	Instrumental Dependency
				Girls	
1	{ Autonomy	−.17			
	{ Aggression				
4	(Autonomy	+.49[b]	+.21		
	{ Instrumental				
	(Dependency	−.28	−.29	−.68[b]	
				Boys	
1	{ Autonomy	−.77[b]			
	{ Aggression				
4	(Autonomy	+.67[b]	−.59[b]		
	{ Instrumental				
	(Dependency	−.56[b]	+.40[a]	−.65[b]	
				Sexes Combined	
1	{ Autonomy	−.58[b]			
	{ Aggression				
4	(Autonomy	+.61[b]	−.30[a]		
	{ Instrumental				
	(Dependency	−.43[b]	+.12	−.65[b]	

[a] $p < .05$.
[b] $p < .01$.

question could be evaluated most meaningfully in boys. As seen in Table 4, this was the case. All the expected correlations were significant in boys, while only the stability coefficient for the autonomy pole was significant in girls.

What brings about this developmental transformation in non-autonomous boys? Since autonomy is positively valued by teachers, the non-autonomous boy's initial failure to meet the teachers' expectations in this respect could result in aggressive attention-seeking outbursts which only gradually become transformed into more acceptable instrumental dependency. This view is supported by the "acting-out" quality of the particular aggression scales that were bipolar to autonomy in the first semester (see Table 3), as contrasted with the more socialized forms of aggression which loaded heavily on the Aggression-Dominance factor (see Table 1). If this transformation includes both a subsiding of frustration-induced hostility and the disinhibition of instrumental dependency, then it could explain why instrumental dependency was subsumed by Dependency rather than being bipolar to Autonomy during the first semester. Also, such a process suggests that the "sleeper effect" (Kagan & Moss, 1962) may involve not only the temporary inhibition

Table 5 Correlations Between IQ and the Autonomy Factor Poles of Semesters 1 and 4

Group	Semester 1		Semester 4	
	Autonomy	Aggression	Autonomy	Instrumental Dependency
Girls	.27	− .28	.43[a]	− .40[a]
Boys	.32[a]	− .33[a]	.34[a]	− .18
Sexes combined	.32[b]	− .33[b]	.39[b]	− .27[a]

[a] $p < .05$.
[b] $p < .01$.

of an earlier- and later-appearing response but also the emergence of an alternative response during the interim.

Perhaps the non-autonomous girl is less likely to go through this process because teachers tolerate more instrumental as well as other forms of dependency in girls (Kagan & Moss, 1962) and/or because girls are generally perceived as more autonomous to begin with. There was empirical support for both these possibilities: girls were higher than boys on the Dependency factor in each semester (all p's $< .01$) and were also more autonomous, but significantly so only in the first semester ($p < .05$).

The present interpretation assumes that socializing agents attempt to bring about greater autonomy in children of this age, especially in those who lack it. But the continued bipolarity of Autonomy throughout the four semesters indicates that such attempts were not very successful. It is of interest that the autonomous child's persistence was also found by Hofstaetter (1954) to be an especially important component of intelligence between 20 and 40 months. There is also evidence that intelligence is a correlate of autonomous-achievement behavior during the elementary-school years (Crandall & Sinkeldam, 1964). Thus, perhaps the less intellectually advanced children were less able to adapt to the autonomy demands made by the teachers. Since all subjects were administered the Stanford Binet (1937 revision) during the first year of nursery school, it was possible to determine whether the autonomy poles were positively related to IQ and, furthermore, whether the bipolar counterparts of autonomy—aggression in semester 1 and instrumental dependency in semester 4—were *negatively* correlated with IQ. The results generally supported this reasoning, although the relationships were not strong (see Table 5). And, of course, this analysis cannot reveal whether reinforcements of autonomy by parents stimulated intelligence (Crandall, 1963), and/or whether such reinforcements were part of a parental-response pattern elicited by rapid intellectual development in the child.

CONCLUSIONS

It can be concluded that Aggression-Dominance, Dependency, and Autonomy are salient personality dimensions having high stability from ages

3 to 5, supporting the view that personality differences arise early in life and are maintained in essentially their original form. However, because of certain methodological limitations, these generalizations should be accepted with caution.

Several factors probably converged in this study to exaggerate the picture of behavioral continuity and individual stability. But despite these masking influences, there was also evidence for structural change over time and for an accompanying behavioral change in non-autonomous boys. Therefore, the results also support the view that development involves significant personality change in certain classes of persons during particular time periods.

Instrumental dependency became increasingly bipolar to autonomy throughout this period. This unexpected finding received post hoc conceptual and empirical support, illustrating how the present methodology can lead to plausible hypotheses about structure and discontinuity in development.

Finally, when the present results for rating are compared with those based upon alternative methods of assessment, it becomes apparent that structural equivalence as well as predictability between data sources cannot be taken for granted. Systematic knowledge is needed on how the "perspective" tied to a particular assessment procedure influences substantive conclusions about personality structure and development.

REFERENCES

Beller, E. K. Dependency and independence in young children. Unpublished doctoral dissertation, State University of Iowa. 1948.

Beller, E. K. Dependency and independence in young children. *J. genet. Psychol.,* 1955, *87,* 23–25.

Beller, E. K., & Turner, J. L. Sex differences: the factorial structure of personality variables in normal and emotionally disturbed preschool children. Paper read at Eastern Psychol. Association, Philadelphia, April, 1964.

Crandall, V. J. Achievement. In H. W. Stevenson (Ed.), *Child psychology: the sixty-second yearbook of the national society for the study of education.* Part I. Chicago: Univer. of Chicago Press, 1963. Pp. 416–459.

Crandall, V. J., Preston, A., & Rabson, A. Maternal reactions and the development of independence and achievement behavior in young children. *Child Develpm.,* 1960, *31,* 243–251.

Crandall, V. J., & Sinkeldam, C. Children's dependent and achievement behaviors in social situations and the perceptual field dependence. *J. Pers.,* 1964, *32,* 1–22.

Emmerich, W. Continuity and stability in early social development. *Child Develpm.,* 1964, *35,* 311–332.

Harman, H. H. *Modern factor analysis.* Chicago: Univer. of Chicago Press, 1960.

Hartup, W. W. Dependence and independence. In H. W. Stevenson (Ed.), *Child psychology: the sixty-second yearbook of the national society for the study of education.* Part I. Chicago: Univer. of Chicago Press, 1963. Pp. 333–363.

Heathers, G. Acquiring dependence and independence: a theoretical orientation. *J. genet. Psychol.,* 1955, *87,* 277–291. (a)

Heathers, G. Emotional dependence and independence in nursery-school play. *J. genet. Psychol.,* 1955, *87,* 37–58. (b)

Hofstaetter, P. R. The changing composition of "intelligence": a study in t-technique. *J. genet. Psychol.*, 1954, *85*, 159–164.

Kagan, J., & Moss, H. A. *Birth to maturity*. New York: Wiley, 1962.

Martin, W. E. Singularity and stability of profiles of social behavior. In C. B. Stendler (Ed.), *Readings in child behavior and development*. New York: Harcourt, Brace & World, 1964. Pp. 448–466.

Schaefer, E. S., and Bayley, N. Maternal behavior, child behavior, and their inter-correlations from infancy through adolescence. *Monogr. Soc. Res. Child Develpm.*, 1963, *28*, No. 87.

Sears, R. R. Dependency motivation. In M. R. Jones (Ed.), *Current theory and research in motivation*. Lincoln: Univer. of Nebraska Press, 1963. Pp. 25–64.

Imitation of a Peer as a Function of Reinforcement from the Peer Group and Rewardingness of the Model

Willard W. Hartup and Brian Coates

UNIVERSITY OF MINNESOTA

Considerable research has been generated by the hypothesis that rewarding models are imitated to a greater extent than nonrewarding models. This hypothesis figures prominently in several general theories of identification, including the theory of anaclitic identification developed by Freud (1914), the secondary reinforcement interpretation of imitation by Mowrer (1950; 1960), and the extension of these theories formulated by Sears (1957) and Sears, Rau, and Alpert (1965).

The formulation developed by Mowrer is particularly specific concerning the mechanisms underlying imitation. Mowrer suggested that rewards given

Reprinted from *Child Development,* copyright © 1967 by The Society for Research in Child Development, Inc., *38,* No. 4, 1003–1016. By permission.

This study was completed with the assistance of a stipend awarded to Brian Coates from grant 5-T01-MHO-6668, National Institute of Mental Health. The authors are particularly grateful to Rosalind Charlesworth for her help and to the collaborating nursery school teachers.

to S by a model increase the secondary reinforcing value (for S) of behaviors manifested by the model. When S reproduces these behaviors, the propriocep-tive feedback from the imitative acts is presumed, as a consequence of stimu-lus generalization, to be secondarily reinforcing. This secondary reinforcement predisposes S to reproduce the behavior of the model. Although Mowrer originally provided this theory as an explanation for the imitation of verbal behavior, the theory has since been extended to account for all imitative acts (Mowrer, 1960; Sears 1957).

Both differential and experimental strategies have been used to test the prediction that rewarding models produce more imitation in children than nonrewarding models. One kind of evidence is provided by studies of the relation between parental affection and nurturance, on the one hand, and identification-related behaviors in children, on the other. Sears (1953) re-ported that boys with warm, affectionate fathers employed the father doll more frequently in doll play than boys of colder, less affectionate fathers. Mussen and Distler (1960) reported that fathers of highly masculine kinder-garten boys were more affectionate than fathers of less musculine subjects, and, in a series of other studies by Mussen and his associates (Mussen & Distler, 1959; Mussen, 1961; Mussen & Rutherford, 1963), highly masculine boys were found to perceive their fathers as more rewarding and nurturant (as well as strong and powerful) than less masculine boys. The results of a recent study by Sears et al. (1965), however, failed to support the hypothesis that warmth and nurturance are related to identification in either girls or boys.

Experimental evidence concerning this hypothesis has been provided by Bandura and Huston (1961), who found that preschool Ss who had received social rewards from the model during two 15-minute play periods repro-duced "incidental" verbal and motor responses displayed by the model to a greater extent than Ss experiencing nonrewarding interaction. These two groups, however, did not differ significantly in duplicating the model's choices in a discrimination task. Next, Bandura, Ross, and Ross (1963) re-ported that nursery school children more frequently imitated models from whom they received social and material rewards than models with whom they competed for such rewards. Mischel and Grusec (1966) found that the rewardingness of the model facilitated imitation, but this effect depended on the type of behavior being modeled ("aversive" or "neutral") and whether imitation was measured in terms of "rehearsal" or "transmission." More recently, Grusec (1966) reported that the model's rewardingness influenced children's imitation of self-criticism, depending on whether the model had previously used withdrawal of love, as opposed to withdrawal of material rewards.

Other evidence pertinent to the secondary reinforcement theory of imitation is provided by Rosenblith (1959), who reported that the attentive-ness of the experimenter-model, as compared to attention withdrawal, en-hanced imitation, but only in girls. Rosenhan and White (1967) reported no effect of the prior relationship existing between S and model on the imita-tion of altruistic behavior, except that boys whose relations with the model were "negative" showed greater continuity in amount of imitation from model-present to model-absent conditions than boys whose relations with the model were positive or boys who had no prior relations with the model.

Stein and Wright (1964) reported that nurturance by an adult model affected imitation in preschool children, depending on the extent of change in the manifestations of dependency by the child during the experimental session. The Ss who responded to withdrawal of nurturance or to isolation with *increased* dependency and Ss who responded to continuous nurturance from E with *decreased* dependency imitated the model to a greater extent than Ss whose changes in dependency were in directions opposite to those mentioned. Lastly, Kobasigawa (1965) reported that adult models who had previously dispensed social rewards and were then observed to undergo a frustration experience elicited no greater emotionality in first-grade boys than models not dispensing social reinforcement.

Many of the findings reviewed above support the secondary reinforcement theory of imitation. Simultaneously, they suggest that situational and individual differences modify the effect of reward from the model on imitation. Sex of S, personality characteristics, and type of response being imitated are examples of such modifiers. But what antecedents are responsible for these interaction effects? What, for example, are the antecedents of sex differences in the impact of rewarding models on imitation? Differences in the socialization history of boys and girls are probably responsible, but which?

The main purpose of this experiment was to study one likely source of variation in the effect of the model's rewardingness on imitation—S's general history of reinforcement from persons resembling the model. The study was based on the hypothesis that the effects of exposure to a rewarding model, as compared to a nonrewarding model, depend on the nature of S's previous experience with people who are like the model. Peers were selected as the class of models to be used. Nursery school children were believed to be appropriate Ss because, even in nursery school groups, the range of reward frequencies exchanged among them is large.

The study was guided by the dimensional prediction stated above. Directional predictions were partially formulated prior to the experiment. For example, it was expected that rewarding peer models would produce more imitation than nonrewarding models for children with a history of frequent reinforcement from their peers. The results for children with histories of infrequent peer reinforcement were more difficult to predict because low frequencies of reinforcement from peers are often characteristic of children who are actively rejected or who are fearful in social situations. Solely on the basis of Mowrer's hypothesis, it would be expected that the rewarding-model effect would be diminished for such Ss. To the extent that such Ss are socially anxious, however, it is possible that nonrewarding peers may exert greater imitative influence than peers who, in the past, have been sources of reassurance and support.

The behaviors modeled in the experiment consisted of an altruistic response plus a group of verbal and motoric actions "incidental" to the altruistic act. Since the study involved peers as models and altruistic behavior as the major dependent variable, it accomplishes two secondary purposes: (a) it contributes to the slowly growing literature concerning the influence of peer models on the socialization of the child (e.g., Bandura & Kupers, 1964; Clark, 1965; Grosser, Polansky, & Lippitt, 1951; Hicks, 1965), and (b) it adds to the sparse evidence concerning imitation as a determinant of altruism (Rosenhan & White, 1967).

METHOD

Subjects

The pool from which Ss were drawn consisted of 64 children enrolled in four groups at the Laboratory Nursery School of the University of Minnesota. This pool included all children enrolled both at the time observations were conducted in the peer group and during a later experimental period. The Ss were 56 children from this pool. Excluded were two children who were receiving psychotherapy, two children who refused to participate, two children whose models failed to carry out the prescribed procedure, and two who were dropped to yield equal cell frequencies. These Ss ranged in age from 3–9 through 5–4, with a mean age of 4–6.

Experimental design. The experimental design consisted of the following groups:

Frequent reinforcement from peers (FR):
  Rewarding peer model (RM) (N = 12)
  Nonrewarding peer model (NRM) (N = 12)
Infrequent reinforcement from peers (IR):
  Rewarding peer model (RM) (N = 12)
  Nonrewarding peer model (NRM) (N = 12)
No model (control) (N = 8)

Assignment of subjects. The initial step in the assignment of Ss was the measurement of reinforcement frequencies occurring in the nursery school peer group. For this purpose, observations were conducted extending over a 5-week period.[1] Briefly, the observations produced 12 3-minute samples of each child's behavior, recorded in running account form by observers stationed in the nursery school. These records contained information concerning the child's activity, persons in his vicinity, and accounts of the interaction occurring between the child and other persons.

The 3-minute protocols were then rated by two judges. The records were screened for instances in which the child dispensed or received "generalized social reinforcers" (Skinner, 1953). Four types of positive social rein-

[1] A detailed description of the observational procedure can be found in Charlesworth & Hartup (1967).

forcers were tabulated: (a) attention and approval (e.g., attending, offering praise, smiling and laughing, offering guidance or suggestions); (b) affection and personal acceptance (both physical and verbal); (c) submission (e.g., passive acceptance of another child's demands, sharing, compromise); (d) tokens (tangible objects).

A total of 161 protocols were rated by both raters. The ratio of agreements concerning the occurrence of social reinforcement divided by agreements plus disagreements was .77.

It was possible to compute the total number of reinforcements dispensed by each child to his peers and the number received. The latter score was assumed to be an index of the total frequency of positive reinforcement the child received from the peer group.[2] It was on the basis of these scores, which ranged from 0 to 55, that the children were divided into two groups: those above the median, for their own nursery school class, in number of reinforcements received (frequent reinforcement group) and those below (infrequent reinforcement group). The mean number of reinforcers received from peers in the FR group was 24.9, while the mean for the IR group was 9.0.

The children in each of the two reinforcement groups were then randomly assigned to model conditions: rewarding peer model (RM) or nonrewarding peer model (NRM). The observational records for each S assigned to group RM were searched for the name of the like-sex peer who had given S the most frequent reinforcement during the observations. This peer was designated as S's model. The RM Ss had received a mean of 5.4 reinforcements from their models during the 36 minutes of observation. Next, a list was prepared for each S in group NRM consisting of all like-sex children in the class who had never been observed to furnish S with reinforcement. One child, randomly selected from this list, was designated as S's model. The mean reinforcements given to the NRM Ss by their models had, of course, been zero.

The final preliminary step consisted of establishing a testing sequence permitting all the available children to serve as Ss. Some children participated only as Ss; others, who were designated as models, participated first as Ss, then were trained and served as models during subsequent sessions (not more than two for any child).

One boy and one girl from each preschool class were required to start the testing by serving as "first" models. These children were randomly selected. If this selection did not make it possible to test all of the children in that preschool class in sequence, substitute first models were picked. Those children designated as first models completed the experimental task prior to being trained as models. This group of eight children (two from each preschool class) thus comprised a no-model control group (C).

[2] The extent to which the total number of positive reinforcements received serves as an index of total interaction is not known. It was possible to compute correlations between receipt of positive and receipt of negative reinforcements for Ss in two of the preschool groups. These correlations were .43 ($p < .10$) and .51 ($p < .05$). Incidents of nonreinforcing contacts among peers were numerous but were not tabulated.

PROCEDURE

No-Model Condition

The S was brought to a laboratory room which contained three hats (maroon, green, and yellow) hung on pegs, three feathers (white, yellow, and orange) placed on a chair, three pencils (black, brown, and green) also hung on pegs, and a table containing a stack of dittoed mazes (simple one-turn puzzles) and three bowls. One bowl, placed in front of the child, was a receptacle for trinkets released by a dispensing device. The other bowls were placed to S's left and right (counterbalanced across Ss); one was designated as belonging to a preschool child (not known to S) whose picture was attached, the other was designated as S's bowl. The following instructions were given:

> We have a game for you today. It is a puzzle game and these are the puzzles. (E displays puzzles.) The way you play this game is to draw a line from one flower to another flower, like this. (E demonstrates.) Now you can do some. (S was helped to complete two or three of the puzzles.) There is one other thing that I want to tell you about the game. Whenever you are doing a good job on the puzzle, some little cats will come out of the machine back there. They will come down this chute and fall into this bowl. Whenever some cats come down the chute I want you to put them in one of these other bowls. Either put them over here in Alec's bowl (Kathy's for female Ss) or over here in your bowl. Alec is another boy in the nursery school. Now remember, whenever you are doing a good job on the puzzle, some little cats will come out of the machine into this bowl here and you are to put them in one of these two bowls, either in Alec's bowl or your bowl, your bowl or Alec's bowl. Do you understand? I have to do some work so I will sit in here.

Nothing further was said concerning whether S could keep the trinkets in his bowl at the conclusion of the session. The E then went into an adjoining room, left the door ajar, and seated himself out of sight. S was told to proceed, and after each maze was completed six trinkets were ejected through the chute. The session consisted of ten mazes, each followed by the dispensing and allocation of six trinkets. If S failed to pick up the trinkets, E urged him to do so by saying, "Put the cats in the bowls; in Alec's bowl or your bowl, your bowl or Alec's bowl."

Model Conditions

Training the model. Each child designated as a model was brought to the laboratory several days after he had participated as S. He was reminded of the earlier session, given an opportunity to complete two mazes, and asked to help E by demonstrating the game for another child from his class. The E stressed that it was necessary to play the game in a particular way. First, M was told that he should go to the hats, pick out the green one (color alternated across Ss) attach the white feather (also alternated) to the hole in the hat, and put the hat on his head. Next, he was told to select the black pencil (color also alternated), to seat himself at the table, and begin work on the puzzles. Then M was instructed to pick up the six trinkets ejected after each maze, place them in a row on the table, and to pick them up one at a time, placing all but the last one in Alec's (or Kathy's) bowl. The M was also instructed to repeat the words "One for Alec" each time a trinket was placed in "Alec's bowl." The E stressed that only the last trinket should be placed in M's own bowl. This procedure was practiced, with E coaching and sometimes demonstrating, until M was able to perform the task with consistent accuracy. The M accompanied E to the nursery school for the purpose of inviting S to play the game.

Experimental session. When the children arrived in the laboratory, E described the game using the instructions given above. He also explained that the children would take turns and that M would be first. The S was seated so as to face M at a 90° angle and was told that he should try not to bother M. The E entered the adjoining room, leaving the door partly open. Then M was told to proceed. If M failed to respond or engaged in distracting behavior, E prompted him from the other room. In no case, however, were mistakes in allocating trinkets corrected. Such mistakes were made by only two Ms whose Ss were subsequently excluded from the experiment.

After ten mazes, the children were told it was time for S to play the game. The M was invited to wait in the adjoining room with E, and the instructions were repeated briefly to S. When everyone had reached his appropriate spot, S was told to begin.

Response Measures

The following information was recorded by E (observing through a small one-way window): (a) whether or not S chose a hat, a feather, and/or a pencil and the colors of these objects; (b) whether or not S lined up the trinkets and whether the trinkets were placed in the bowls one at a time or in groups; (c) frequency with which S reproduced the verbalization of M; and (d) the particular bowl chosen for allocation of each trinket.

The response measures derived from these records included: (a) presence-absence of imitative hat, feather, and pencil choices; (b) presence-absence of "line up" behavior on each trial (ranging from 0 to 10 over entire session); (c) presence-absence of imitative verbalization (ranging from 0 to 6 on each trial); (d) number of trinkets placed in the "other's" bowl (ranging from 0 to 6 on each trial); (e) latency of the first nonaltruistic choice—the number of trinkets placed in "other's" bowl before placement of the first trinket in S's own bowl (ranging from 0 to 7 on each trial).

RESULTS

Intercorrelations among four of the dependent measures are shown in Table 1. All of these measures represent components of the response sequence used in allocating the trinkets. The correlations, which were com-

Table 1   Intercorrelations Among Four Imitation Scores ($N = 48$)

Score	Giving to Other (Total)	Latency of Giving to Self (Total)	Verbali- zation (Total)	Line Up (Total)
Giving to other	...	...	...	...
Latency of giving to self	$.92^b$	...	...	...
Verbalization	$.28^a$	$.32^a$	...	...
Line up	$.32^a$	$.36^a$	$.54^b$	...

$^a p < .05.$
$^b p < .01.$

puted only for S's who observed a model, are all significantly positive, but five are relatively small. It should be noted that the two altruism scores (frequency of "giving to other" and latency of "giving to self") are highly correlated. This relation is artifactual. Consequently, "giving to other" was used alone as the altruism index in the data analysis.

Wherever possible, subsequent analyses were completed with scores divided into two five-trial blocks. Inspection revealed that the treatment effects varied over time.

Effect of Model

To assess the effects of observing a model on altruistic behavior, a one-way analysis of variance was conducted on the data for all five of the groups in the experiment. "Giving to other" scores were analyzed separately for the first and second blocks of five trials. The treatments effect was significant in all instances. For the first trial block, $F = 7.49$, $df = 4/51$, $p < .005$; second trial block, $F = 3.39$, $df = 4/51$, $p < .02$.

Contrasts between the amount of "giving to other" in group C and in each of the model groups (t tests) revealed significant differences for each contrast in both trial blocks. Thus, observation of the model produced significantly more altruism than occurred when no opportunity to observe a model was provided (see Table 2).

Table 2   Mean "Giving to Other" Scores in Blocks of Five Trials by Reinforcement Condition and Type of Peer Model

Group	Trial Block 1	Trial Block 2
Frequent reinforcement:		
Rewarding model	21.00	19.25
Nonrewarding model	13.42	13.83
Infrequent reinforcement:		
Rewarding model	17.50	17.08
Nonrewarding model	22.83	18.58
No model	5.63	3.75

Table 3 Mean Number of "Incidental" Behaviors According to Reinforcement
Condition and Type of Peer Model

Group	Verbalization (Total)	Line-Up Responses (Total)
Frequent reinforcement		
Rewarding model	36.83	4.50
Nonrewarding model	7.58	1.67
Infrequent reinforcement		
Rewarding model	21.08	3.92
Nonrewarding model	18.00	3.92
No model	0.00	0.00

Observing the model also affected the frequency of "incidental" behaviors. Statistical analysis was not performed, but it can be seen in Table 3
that no verbalization or "line up" behavior occurred in group C, although
appreciable amounts were displayed by Ss who had observed a model.

Effects of Peer Reinforcement and Rewardingness of Model
The "giving to other" scores for Ss who observed models were subjected to mixed-design analysis of variance. The between-Ss factors were
reinforcement from peers (FR vs. IR) and type of peer model (RM vs. NRM).
The within-Ss factor consisted of trial blocks (first vs. second five trials).
Mean scores for each subgroup may be seen in Table 2.
The analysis revealed a significant effect of trial blocks ($F = 7.80$,
$df = 1/44$, $p < .01$), indicating that fewer altruistic responses were made
during the second block of five trials than during the first. In addition, the
interaction between reinforcement from peers and type of model was significant ($F = 4.59$, $df = 1/44$, $p < .05$), as was the interaction between reinforcement from peers, type of model, and trial blocks ($F = 7.80$, $df = 1/44$,
$p < .01$). Further analyses revealed that the treatments effects were confined
principally to the first five trials. There was a significant interaction between
reinforcement from peers and type of model in the data for the first five
trials ($F = 8.44$, $df = 1/44$, $p < .01$), but not for the second. During the first
trials, Ss who had received frequent reinforcement from their peers imitated
a rewarding peer model more frequently than a nonrewarding model ($t =
3.17$, $p < .01$). On the other hand, Ss who were observed to receive infre-
quent peer reinforcement imitated a nonrewarding model more frequently
than a rewarding model ($t = 2.61$, $p < .02$). Additional contrasts made on the
data for the first five trials revealed: (a) among Ss who observed a rewarding
model, those with a history of frequent peer reinforcement did not differ
significantly from those with a history of infrequent reinforcement ($t = 1.41$,
$p < .20$); (b) among those who observed a nonrewarding model, Ss who had
received infrequent reinforcement from the peer group imitated significantly
more than those who had received frequent peer reinforcement ($t = 4.88$,
$p < .01$).

Analysis of imitative verbalization scores was conducted as described for the preceding measure. None of the interactions was significant. Rather, a significant main effect of type of model was obtained ($F = 5.39$, $df = 1/44$, $p < .02$). As can be seen from Table 3, Ss who observed a rewarding model reproduced the model's verbal behaviors more frequently than Ss who observed nonrewarding models. This trend is less clear for IR Ss than for FR Ss, and the interaction between reinforcement from peers and type of model approached significance ($F = 3.53$, $df = 1/44$, $p < .10$).

"Line up" scores were collapsed over all ten trials prior to analysis because this score consisted of presence-absence on single trials. None of the main or interaction effects was significant.

The data concerning the child's behavior with the hats, feathers, and pencils were anlyzed by means of X^2. All possible contrasts between pairs of experimental groups were completed. The only significant difference to emerge from these analyses showed that FR-RM Ss reproduced the pencil choices of the model more frequently than IR-NRM Ss ($X^2 = 4.45$, $p < .05$). This single finding may be attributed to chance. With respect to these particular incidental behaviors, then, the experimental conditions failed to influence differentially the child's imitative behavior.

DISCUSSION

Effects of Model

Observation of altruistic models increased the frequency of altruistic behavior of the Ss, a finding which confirms the results of Rosenhan and White (1967). Since frequency of altruism was highly correlated with the latency of nonaltruistic behavior, the evidence suggests that two parameters of altruism were imitated. As pointed out earlier, however, the most conservative description of the results is in terms of one altruism index, not both.

Can it be assumed that the behavior displayed by the model was construed by S as "altruism"? It is true that S was not told explicitly that he would be able to keep the trinkets in his own bowl and that those in the other child's bowl were to be given away. Nevertheless, in postsession interviews with ten Ss, all ten thought they could keep the trinkets in their own bowl, and seven thought the trinkets in the second bowl would be given to the child whose picture was attached to the bowl. Consequently, the assumption that the experiment involved imitative effects on altruism is tenable.

Among Ss who observed a model, those showing imitative altruism tended to imitate other components of the altruistic response sequence. Most of the intercorrelations among response measures were low, however, indicating that the effects of observing a model were not highly pervasive. The experimental findings are consistent with the intercorrelations. The peer reinforcement history tended to have significant effects on behavior which was central in the altruistic response sequence (frequency of "giving to other"). Borderline effects of peer reinforcement were found with respect to imitative verbalization, and no effects were obtained with respect to less central actions ("lining up" behavior or choices of hat, feather, and pencil). This failure of the treatment effects to generalize to all measures could simply have been a function of "response centrality." It is also possible that the treatment effects did not generalize to "lining up" scores and hat, feather, and pencil choices because these behaviors occurred much less frequently than trinket sorting or verbalization.

Effects of Peer Reinforcement

The relation between rewardingness of the peer model and imitative altruism was positive when S was reinforced frequently by the peer group but negative when reinforcement was infrequent. It is known that peer reinforcement is correlated with social acceptance (e.g., Hartup, Glazer, & Charlesworth, 1967; Marshall & McCandless, 1957). Therefore, the four experimental groups were contrasted with respect to the social acceptance of the models, the acceptance of the Ss, and the friendliness existing between the models and their respective Ss. Data from a picture sociometric test were used for this purpose. First, no significant differences were found in the frequency with which the models in the four groups were chosen by their peers as "liked," as "disliked," or in total times mentioned. Similarly, the social acceptance of the Ss themselves did not differ significantly among the four groups. Finally, children in group FR-RM were significantly more friendly toward their models, as revealed by the frequency with which the model was included among S's sociometric choices, than were the children in the other three groups. However, Ss in group IR-NRM, which imitated as much as group FR-RM, were less friendly toward their models than Ss in the latter group. Thus, overall, status differences among the groups do not account for the observed differences in imitation.

It is concluded that the results support Mowrer's secondary reinforcement theory of imitation when S's history includes relatively frequent reinforcement from persons resembling the model. For infrequently reinforced Ss, the influence of model rewardingness did not diminish; rather, nonrewarding models proved to be more efficacious than rewarding ones.

One explanation for these results is based on the assumption that children who receive little reinforcement are also anxious when placed in contact with other children. For them, exposure to a nonrewarding model may arouse discomfort or anxiety, adding motivation to perform the actions which the situation elicits (including, in the present instance, imitation). Exposure of such children to a rewarding model, however, could result in anxiety reduction, thereby lowering S's motivation for imitative behavior.

This argument implies a dual theory of peer imitation: (a) when reinforcement from peers is frequent, matching the behavior of a rewarding model has greater incentive value than matching a nonrewarding model (the Mowrer hypothesis); (b) when peer reinforcement is not frequent, a nonrewarding model sustains or increases anxiety, whereas the presence of a rewarding model reduces such motivation for imitation. This theory is similar to the hypothesis advanced by Hill (1967) concerning the role of anxiety in task performance under social reinforcement and, in some respects, parallels the dualism in psychoanalytic theories of identification. For example, it could be hypothesized that (a) nurturant models are emulated (anaclitic identification) when reinforcement from persons like the model has been frequent, and (b) when reinforcement has been infrequent, the model who elicits anxiety (or who does not behave in such a way as to reduce it) is defensively emulated. Thus, the present speculations contain interesting implications for predicting the conditions under which anaclitic and defensive identification operate.

It is also possible to consider the present results in terms of perceived similarity. It is known that, in the peer group, the correlation between "giving reinforcement to others" and "getting reinforcement from others" is positive and high (Charlesworth & Hartup, 1967). Thus, it is possible that FR-RM Ss perceive themselves to be similar to the model (both give as well as receive frequent reinforcements) as do IR-NRM Ss (both receive and give few reinforcements). On the other hand, perceived similarity would not be great in the other two experimental groups, FR-NRM and IR-RM. Earlier studies have shown that if S perceives himself as similar to M, conformity is enhanced (e.g., Stotland & Patchen, 1961) as well as imitation (Maccoby, 1959; Rosekrans, 1967). The perceived similarity (or reduced dissimilarity) existing for frequently reinforced Ss with rewarding models and for infrequently reinforced Ss with nonrewarding models would thus account for the greater amounts of imitation shown by these two groups than by the other groups in the experiment.

The present study helps to clarify the influence of the model's rewardingness on imitation. The generality of the results needs to be assessed in further research and theoretical implications explored. It appears, however, that the child's socialization history contributes importantly to the effects on imitation of rewards from the model.

REFERENCES

Bandura, A., & Huston, Aletha C. Identification as a process of incidental learning. *Journal of Abnormal and Social Psychology*, 1961, *63*, 311–318.

Bandura, A., & Kupers, Carol J. Transmission of patterns of self-reinforcement through modelling. *Journal of Abnormal and Social Psychology*, 1964, *69*, 1–9.

Bandura, A., Ross, Dorothea, & Ross, Sheila A. A comparative test of the status envy, social power, and secondary reinforcement theories of identificatory learning, *Journal of Abnormal and Social Psychology*, 1963, *67*, 527–534.

Charlesworth, Rosalind, & Hartup, W. W. Positive social reinforcement in the nursery school peer group. *Child Development*, 1967, *38*, 993–1002.

Clark, Barbara S. The acquisition and extinction of peer imitation in children. *Psychonomic Science*, 1965, *2*, 147–148.

Freud, S. On narcissism: an introduction (1914). In J. D. Sutherland (Ed.), *Collected papers of Sigmund Freud*. Vol. 4. London: Hogarth, 1957. Pp. 30–60.

Grosser, D., Polansky, N., & Lippitt, R. A laboratory study of behavioral contagion. *Human Relations*, 1951, *4*, 115–142.

Grusec, Joan. Some antecedents of self-criticism. *Journal of Personality and Social Psychology, 1966, 4,* 244–253.

Hartup, W. W., Glazer, Jane, & Charlesworth, Rosalind. Peer reinforcement and sociometric status. *Child Development*, 1967, *38*, 1017–1024.

Hicks, D. J. Imitation and retention of film-mediated aggressive peer and adult models. *Journal of Personality and Social Psychology*, 1965, *2*, 97–100.

Hill, K. T. Social reinforcement as a function of test anxiety and success-failure experiences. *Child Development*, 1967, *38*, 723–737.

Kobasigawa, A. Observation of failure in another person as a determinant of amplitude and speed of a simple motor response. *Journal of Personality and Social Psychology*, 1965, *1*, 626–631.

Maccoby, Eleanor E. Role-taking in childhood and its consequences for social learning. *Child Development*, 1959, *30*, 239–252.

Marshall, Helen R., & McCandless, B. R. A study in prediction of social behavior of preschool children. *Child Development*, 1957, *28*, 149–159.

Mischel, W., & Grusec, Joan. Determinants of the rehearsal and transmission of neutral and aversive behaviors. *Journal of Personality and Social Psychology*, 1966, *3*, 197–206.

Mowrer, O. H. Identification: a link between learning theory and psychotherapy. In *Learning theory and personality dynamics.* New York: Ronald Press, 1950. Pp. 69–94.

Mowrer, O. H. *Learning theory and the symbolic processes.* New York: Wiley, 1960.

Mussen, P. H. Some antecedents and consequents of masculine sex-typing in adolescent boys. *Psychological Monographs*, 1961, *75* (Whole No. 506).

Mussen, P. H., & Distler, L. Masculinity, identification, and father-son relationships. *Journal of Abnormal and Social Psychology*, 1959, *59*, 350–356.

Mussen, P. H., & Distler, L. Child-rearing antecedents of masculine identification in kindergarten boys. *Child Development*, 1960, *31*, 89–100.

Mussen, P. H., & Rutherford, E. Parent-child relations and parental personality in relation to young children's sex-role preferences. *Child Development*, 1963, *34*, 589–607.

Rosekrans, Mary A. Imitation in children as a function of perceived similarity to a social model and vicarious reinforcement. *Journal of Personality and Social Psychology*, 1967, in press.

Rosenblith, Judy F. Learning by imitation in kindergarten children. *Child Development*, 1959, *30*, 69–80.

Rosenhan, D., & White, G. M. Observation and rehearsal as determinants of prosocial behavior. *Journal of Personality and Social Psychology*, 1967, *5*, 424–431.

Sears, Pauline S. Child rearing factors related to the playing of sex-typed roles. *American Psychologist*, 1953, *8*, 431. (Abstract)

Sears, R. R. Identification as a form of behavior development. In D. B. Harris (Ed.), *The concept of development.* Minneapolis: University of Minnesota Press, 1957. Pp. 149–161.

Sears, R. R., Rau, Lucy, & Alpert, R. *Identification and child rearing.* Stanford, Calif.: Stanford University Press, 1965.

Skinner, B. F. *Science and human behavior.* New York: Macmillan, 1953.

Stein, Aletha H., & Wright, J. C. Imitative learning under conditions of nurturance and nurturance withdrawal. *Child Development*, 1964, *35*, 927–937.

Stotland, E., and Patchen, M. Identification and change in prejudice and in authoritarianism. *Journal of Abnormal and Social Psychology*, 1961, *62*, 254–274.

Vicarious Extinction of Avoidance Behavior

*Albert Bandura, Joan E. Grusec,
and Frances L. Menlove*
STANFORD UNIVERSITY

Recent investigations have shown that behavioral inhibitions (Bandura, 1965a; Bandura, Ross, & Ross, 1963; Walters & Parke, 1964) and conditioned emotional responses (Bandura & Rosenthal, 1966; Berger, 1962) can be acquired by observers as a function of witnessing aversive stimuli administered to performing subjects. The present experiment was primarily designed to determine whether preexisting avoidance behavior can similarly be extinguished on a vicarious basis. The latter phenomenon requires exposing observers to modeled stimulus events in which a performing subject repeatedly exhibits ap-

Reprinted from *Journal of Personality and Social Psychology*, 1967, *5*, No. 1, 16–23. Published by the American Psychological Association. By permission.

This research was supported by Public Health Research Grant M-5162 from the National Institute of Mental Health.

The authors are indebted to Janet Brewer, Edith Dowley, Doris Grant, and Mary Lewis for their generous assistance in various phases of this research.

proach responses toward the feared object without incurring any aversive consequences.

Some suggestive evidence that avoidance responses can be extinguished vicariously is furnished by Masserman (1943) and Jones (1924) in exploratory studies of the relative efficacy of various psychotherapeutic procedures. Masserman produced strong feeding inhibitions in cats, following which the inhibited animals observed a cage mate, that had never been negatively conditioned, exhibit prompt approach and feeding responses. The observing subjects initially cowered at the presentation of the conditioned stimulus, but with continued exposure to their fearless companion they advanced, at first hesitantly and then more boldly, to the goal box and consumed the food. Some of the animals, however, showed little reduction in avoidance behavior despite prolonged food deprivation and numerous modeling trials. Moreover, avoidance responses reappeared in a few of the animals after the normal cat was removed, suggesting that in the latter cases the modeling stimuli served merely as temporary external inhibitors of avoidance responses. Jones (1924) similarly obtained variable results in extinguishing children's phobic responses by having them observe their peers behave in a nonanxious manner in the presence of the avoided objects.

If a person is to be influenced by modeling stimuli and the accompanying consequences, then the necessary observing responses must be elicited and maintained. In the foregoing case studies, the models responded to the most feared stimulus situation at the outset, a modeling procedure that is likely to generate high levels of emotional arousal in observers. Under these conditions any avoidance responses designed to reduce vicariously instigated aversive stimulation, such as subjects withdrawing or looking away, would impede vicarious extinction. Therefore, the manner in which modeling stimuli are presented may be an important determinant of the course of vicarious extinction.

Results from psychotherapeutic studies (Bandura[1]) and experiments with infrahuman subjects (Kimble & Kendall, 1953) reveal that avoidance responses can be rapidly extinguished if subjects are exposed to a graduated series of aversive stimuli that progressively approximate the original intensity of the conditioned fear stimulus. For the above reasons it would seem advisable to conduct vicarious extinction by exposing observers to a graduated sequence of modeling activities beginning with presentations that can be easily tolerated; as observers' emotional reactions to displays of attenuated approach responses are extinguished, the fear-provoking properties of the modeled displays might be gradually increased, concluding with interactions capable of arousing relatively strong emotional responses.

If emotion-eliciting stimuli occur in association with positively reinforcing events, the former cues are likely to lose their conditioned aversive properties more rapidly (Farber, 1948) than through mere repeated nonreinforced

---

[1] A. Bandura, "Principles of Behavioral Modification," unpublished manuscript, Stanford University, 1966.

presentation. It might therefore be supposed that vicarious extinction would likewise be hastened and more adequately controlled by presenting the modeling stimuli within a favorable context designed to evoke simultaneously competing positive responses.

The principles discussed above were applied in the present experiment, which explored the vicarious extinction of children's fearful and avoidant responses toward dogs. One group of children participated in a series of modeling sessions in which they observed a fearless peer model exhibit progressively longer, closer, and more active interactions with a dog. For these subjects, the modeled approach behavior was presented within a highly positive context. A second group of children was presented the same modeling stimuli, but in a neutral context.

Exposure to the behavior of the model contains two important stimulus events, that is, the occurrence of approach responses without any adverse consequences to the performer and repeated observation of the feared animal. Therefore, in order to control for the effects of exposure to the dog per se, children assigned to a third group observed the dog in the positive context but with the model absent. A fourth group of children participated in the positive activities, but they were never exposed to either the dog or the model.

In order to assess both the generality and the stability of vicarious extinction effects, the children were readministered tests for avoidance behavior toward different dogs following completion of the treatment series, and approximately 1 month later. It was predicted that children who had observed the peer model interact nonanxiously with the dog would display significantly less avoidance behavior than subjects who had no exposure to the modeling stimuli. The largest decrements were expected to occur among children in the modeling-positive context condition. It was also expected that repeated behavioral assessments and the general disinhibitory effects of participation in a series of highly positive activities might in themselves produce some decrease in avoidance behavior.

METHOD

Subjects

The subjects were 24 boys and 24 girls selected from three nursery schools. The children ranged in age from 3 to 5 years.

Pretreatment Assessment of Avoidance Behavior

As a preliminary step in the selection procedure, parents were asked to rate the magnitude of their children's fearful and avoidant behavior toward dogs. Children who received high fear ratings were administered a standardized performance test on the basis of which the final selection was made.

The strength of avoidance responses was measured by means of a graded sequence of 14 performance tasks in which the children were required to

engage in increasingly intimate interactions with a dog. A female experimenter brought the children individually to the test room, which contained a
brown cocker spaniel confined in a modified playpen. In the initial tasks the
children were asked, in the following order, to walk up to the playpen and
look down at the dog, to touch her fur, and to pet her. Following the assessment of avoidance responses to the dog in the protective enclosure, the
children were instructed to open a hinged door on the side of the playpen,
to walk the dog on a leash to a throw rug, to remove the leash, and to turn
the dog over and scratch her stomach. Although a number of the subjects
were unable to perform all of the latter tasks, they were nevertheless administered the remaining test items to avoid any assumption of a perfectly ordered scale for all cases. In subsequent items the children were asked to
remain alone in the room with the animal and to feed her dog biscuits. The final
and most difficult set of tasks required the children to climb into the playpen
with the dog, to pet her, to scratch her stomach, and to remain alone in the
room with the dog under the exceedingly confining and fear-provoking conditions.

The strength of the children's avoidant tendencies was reflected not only
in the items completed, but also in the degree of vacillation, reluctance, and
fearfulness that preceded and accompanied each approach response. Consequently, children were credited 2 points if they executed a given task either
spontaneously or willingly, and 1 point when they carried out the task minimally after considerable hesitancy and reluctance. Thus, for example, children
who promptly stroked the dog's fur repeatedly when requested to do so
received 2 points, whereas subjects who held back but then touched the
dog's fur briefly obtained 1 point. In the item requiring the children to remain alone in the room with the dog, they received 2 points if they approached the animal and played with her, and 1 point if they were willing to
remain in the room but avoided any contact with the dog. Similarly, in the
feeding situation children were credited 2 points if they fed the dog by hand,
but a single point if they tossed the biscuits on the floor and thereby avoided
close contact with the animal. The maximum approach score that a subject
could attain was 28 points.

On the basis of the pretreatment assessment, the children in each nursery
school were grouped into three levels of avoidance behavior, with the corresponding scores ranging from 0 to 7, 8 to 17, and 18 to 20 points. There
were approximately the same number of children, equally divided between
boys and girls, at each of the three avoidance levels. The subjects from each
of these groups were then assigned randomly to one of four conditions.

Treatment Conditions

Children who participated in the *modeling-positive context* condition
observed a fearless peer model display approach responses toward a cocker
spaniel within the context of a highly enjoyable party atmosphere.

There were eight 10-minute treatment sessions conducted on 4 consecutive days. Each session, which was attended by a group of four children,

commenced with a jovial party. The children were furnished brightly colored hats, cookie treats, and given small prizes. In addition, the experimenter read stories, blew large plastic balloons for the children to play with, and engaged in other party activities designed to produce strong positive affective responses.

After the party was well under way, a second experimenter entered the room carrying the dog, followed by a 4-year-old male model who was unknown to most of the children. The dog was placed in a playpen located across the room from a large table at which the children were seated. The model, who had been chosen because of his complete lack of fear of dogs, then performed prearranged sequences of interactions with the dog for approximately 3 minutes during each session. One boy served as the model for children drawn from two of the nursery schools, and a second boy functioned in the same role at the third school.

The fear-provoking properties of the modeled displays were gradually increased from session to session by varying simultaneously the physical restraints on the dog, the directness and intimacy of the modeled approach responses, and the duration of interaction between the model and his canine companion. Initially, the experimenter carried the dog into the room and confined her to the playpen, and the model's behavior was limited to friendly verbal responses ("Hi, Chloe") and occasional petting. During the following three sessions the dog remained confined to the playpen, but the model exhibited progressively longer and more active interactions in the form of petting the dog with his hands and feet, and feeding her wieners and milk from a baby bottle. Beginning with the fifth session, the dog was walked into the room on a leash, and the modeled tasks were mainly performed outside the playpen. For example, in addition to repeating the feeding routines, the model walked the dog around the room, petted her, and scratched her stomach while the leash was removed. In the last two sessions the model climbed into the playpen with the dog where he petted her, hugged her, and fed her wieners and milk from the baby bottle.

It would have been of interest to compare the relative efficacy of the graduated modeling technique with bold displays of approach behavior from the outset. However, pretest findings showed that when modeled displays are too fear provoking, children actively avoid looking at the performances and are reluctant to participate in subsequent sessions. The latter approach would therefore require additional procedures designed to maintain strong attending behavior to highly aversive modeling stimuli.

Children assigned to the *modeling-neutral context* condition observed the same sequence of approach responses performed by the same peer model except that the parties were omitted. In each of the eight sessions the subjects were merely seated at the table and obsrved the modeled performances.

In order to control for the influence of repeated exposure to the positive atmosphere and to the dog per se, children in the *exposure-positive context* group attended the series of parties in the presence of the dog with the model absent. As in the two modeling conditions, the dog was introduced into the room in the same manner for the identical length of time; similarly, the dog was confined in the playpen during the first four sessions and placed on a leash outside the enclosure in the remaining sessions.

Children in the *positive-context* group participated in the parties, but they were never exposed to either the dog or the model. The main purpose of this condition was to determine whether the mere presence of a dog had an adverse or a beneficial effect on the children. Like the third condition, it also provided a control for the possible therapeutic effects of positive experiences and increased familiarity with amiable experimenters, which may be particularly influential in reducing inhibitions in very young children. In addition, repeated behavioral assessments in which subjects perform a graded series of approach responses toward a feared object without any aversive consequences would be expected to produce some direct extinction of avoidance behavior. The inclusion of the latter two control groups thus makes it possible to evaluate the changes effected by exposure to modeling stimuli over and above those resulting from general disinhibition, direct extinction, and repeated observation of the feared object.

Posttreatment Assessment of Avoidance Behavior

On the day following completion of the treatment series, the children were administered the performance test consisting of the graded sequence of interaction tasks with the dog. In order to determine the generality of vicarious extinction effects, half the children in each of the four groups were tested initially with the experimental animal and then with an unfamiliar dog; the remaining were presented with the two dogs in the reverse order.[2] The testing sessions were separated by an interval of 1½ hours so as to minimize any transfer of emotional reactions generated by one animal to the other.

The unfamiliar animal was a white mongrel, predominantly terrier, and of approximately the same size and activity level as the cocker spaniel. Two groups of 15 children, drawn from the same nursery-school population, were tested with either the mongrel or the spaniel in order to determine the aversiveness of the two animals. The mean approach scores with the spaniel ($M = 16.47$) and the mongrel ($M = 15.80$) were virtually identical ($t = .21$).

Follow-Up Assessment

A follow-up evaluation was conducted approximately 1 month after the posttreatment assessment in order to determine the stability of modeling-induced changes in approach behavior. The children's responses were tested with the same performance tasks toward both animals, presented in the identical order.

After the experiment was completed, the children were told that, while most dogs are friendly, before petting an unfamiliar dog they should ask the owner. This precautionary instruction was designed to reduce indiscriminate

---

[2] The authors are especially indebted to Chloe and Jenny for their invaluable and steadfast assistance with a task that, at times, must have been most perplexing to them.

approach behavior by children who were in the modeling conditions toward strange dogs which they would undoubtedly encounter.

Measurement Procedure

The same female experimenter administered the pretreatment, posttreatment, and follow-up behavioral tests. To prevent any possible bias, the experimenter was given minimal information about the details of the study and had no knowledge of the conditions to which the children were assigned. The treatment and assessment procedures were further separated by the use of different rooms for each activity.

In order to provide an estimate of interscorer reliability, the performances of 25% of the children, randomly selected from pretreatment, posttreatment, and follow-up phases of the experiment, were scored simultaneously but independently by another rater who observed the test sessions through a one-way mirror from an adjoining observation room. The two raters were in perfect agreement on 97% of the specific approach responses that were scored.

A dog's activity level may partly determine the degree of fear and avoidance exhibited by the children; conversely, timorous or unrestrained approach responses might differentially affect the animals' reactivity. Therefore, during the administration of each test item, the animals' behavior was rated as either passive, moderately active, or vigorous. The raters were in perfect agreement in categorizing the dogs' activity levels on 81% of the performance tests.

Changes in children's approach-response scores across the different phases of the experiment, and the number of subjects in each treatment condition who were able to carry out the terminal performance task, served as the dependent measures.

RESULTS

The percentages of test items in which the animals behaved in a passive, moderately active, or vigorous manner were 55, 43, and 2, respectively, for the model-positive context groups; 53, 44, and 2 for children in the model-neutral context condition; 52, 45, and 3 for the exposure-positive context group; and 57, 41, and 2 for the positive-context subjects. Thus, the test animals did not differ in their behavior during the administration of performance tasks to children in the various treatment conditions.

Approach Responses

Table 1 presents the mean increases in approach behavior achieved by children in each of the treatment conditions in different phases of the experiment with each of the test animals.

The children's approach responses toward the two dogs did not differ either in the posttreatment assessment ($t = 1.35$) or in the follow-up phase

Table 1   Mean Increases in Approach Responses as a Function of Treatment
Conditions, Assessment Phases, and Test Animals

| | Treatment Conditions | | | |
| | Modeling–
Positive
Context | Modeling–
Neutral
Context | Exposure–
Positive
Context | Positive
Context |
Phases				
Posttreatment				
Spaniel	10.83	9.83	2.67	6.08
Mongrel	5.83	10.25	3.17	4.17
Follow-up				
Spaniel	10.83	9.33	4.67	5.83
Mongrel	12.59	9.67	4.75	6.67
Combined data	10.02	9.77	3.81	5.69

$(t = .91)$ of the study. Nor were there any significant effects $(t = 1.68)$ due to the order in which the test animals were presented following completion of the treatment series. A t-test analysis also disclosed no significant change $(t = 1.50)$ in mean approach scores between measurements conducted in the posttreatment and the follow-up phases of the experiment. Moreover, analysis of variance of the posttreatment scores revealed no significant Treatment × Dogs $(F = 2.15)$ or Treatment × Order $(F = .30)$ interaction effects. The data were therefore combined across phases and test animals in evaluating the major hypotheses.

An analysis of covariance, in which adjustments were made for differences in initial level of avoidance, was computed for mean approach responses performed by children in the various groups. The results reveal that the treatment conditions had a highly significant effect on the children's behavior $(F = 5.09, p < .01)$. Tests of the differences between the various pairs of treatments indicate that subjects in the modeling-positive context condition displayed significantly more approach behavior than subjects in either the exposure $(F = 9.32, p < .01)$ or the positive-context $(F = 8.96, p < .01)$ groups. Similarly, children who had observed the model within the neutral setting exceeded both the exposure $(F = 6.57, p < .05)$ and positive-context groups $(F = 4.91, p < .05)$ in approach behavior. However, the data yielded no significant differences between either the two modeling conditions $(F = .04)$ or the two control groups $(F = .76)$.

Within-Group Analysis of Approach Responses

The approach scores obtained by the different groups of children in preexperimental and subsequent tests are summarized graphically in Fig. 1. Within-group analyses of changes between initial performance and mean level of approach behavior following treatment disclose significant increases in approach behavior for children in the modeling-positive context group $(t = 7.71, p < .001)$ and for those who observed the modeling performance

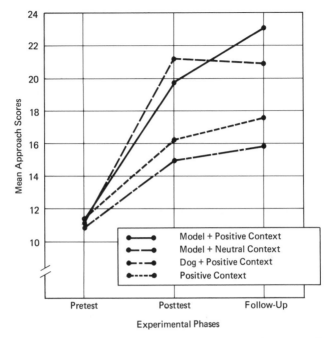

Fig. 1. Mean approach scores achieved by children in each of the treatment conditions on the three different periods of assessment.

within the neutral setting ($t = 5.80$, $p < .001$). Although the positive-context group showed an increment in approach behavior ($t = 5.78$, $p < .001$), children who were merely exposed to the dog in the positive context achieved a small, but nonsignificant ($t = 1.98$), reduction in avoidance responses.

Terminal Performances

Another measure of the efficacy of modeling procedures is provided by comparisons of the number of children in each condition who performed the terminal approach behavior at least once during the posttreatment assessment. Since the frequencies within the two modeling conditions did not differ, and the two control groups were essentially the same, the data for each of the two sets of subgroups were combined. The findings show that 67% of the children in the modeling treatment were able to remain alone in the room confined with the dog in the playpen, whereas the corresponding figure for the control subjects is 33%. The χ^2 value for these data is 4.08, which is significant beyond the .025 level.

Within the control groups, the terminal performances were attained primarily by subjects who initially showed the weakest level of avoidance behavior. The differences between the two groups are, therefore, even more pronounced if the analysis is conducted on the subjects whose pretreatment performances reflected extreme or moderately high levels of avoidance behavior. Of the most avoidant subjects in each of the two pooled groups, 55% of the children in the modeling conditions were able to perform the terminal approach behavior following the experimental sessions, while only 13% of the control subjects successfully completed the final task. The one-tailed probability for the obtained $\chi^2 = 4.74$ is slightly below the .01 level of significance.

The relative superiority of the modeling groups is also evident in the follow-up phase of the experiment. Based on the stringent criterion in which the most fearful task is successfully performed with *both* animals, a significantly larger number of children in the modeling conditions (42%) than in the control groups (12%) exhibited generalized extinction ($\chi^2 = 4.22$, $p < .025$). Moreover, not a single control subject from the two highest levels of avoidance behavior was able to remain alone in the room confined in the playpen with each of the dogs, whereas 33% of the most avoidant children in the modeling conditions successfully passed both terminal approach tasks ($\chi^2 = 4.02$, $p < .025$).

DISCUSSION

The findings of the present experiment provide considerable evidence that avoidance responses can be successfully extinguished on a vicarious basis. This is shown in the fact that children who experienced a gradual exposure to progressively more fearful modeled responses displayed extensive and stable reduction in avoidance behavior. Moreover, most of these subjects were able to engage in extremely intimate and potentially fearful interactions with test animals following the treatment series. The considerable degree of generalization of extinction effects obtained to the unfamiliar dog is most likely due to similar stimulus properties of the test animals. Under conditions where observers' avoidance responses are extinguished to a single animal, one would expect a progressive decrement in approach behavior toward animals of increasing size and fearfulness.

The prediction that vicarious extinction would be augmented by presenting the modeling stimuli within a highly positive context was not confirmed, although subjects in the latter condition differed more significantly from the controls than children who observed approach behavior under neutral conditions. It is entirely possible that a different temporal ordering of emotion-provoking modeling stimuli and events designed to induce anxiety-inhibiting responses would facilitate the vicarious extinction process. On the basis of evidence from conditioning studies (Melvin & Brown, 1964) the optimal treatment procedure might require repeated observational trials, in each of which aversive modeling stimuli are immediately followed by positively reinforcing experiences for the observers. These temporal prerequisites depend upon the abrupt presentation and termination of the two sets of stimulus events that cannot be readily achieved with live demonstrations. It would be possible, however, to study the effects of systematic variations in the temporal spacing of critical variables if modeling stimuli were presented pictorially. Apart from issues of economy and control, if pictorial stimulus material proved equally as efficacious as live modeling, then skillfully designed therapeutic films could be developed and employed in preventive programs for eliminating common fears and anxieties before they become well established and widely generalized.

Although children in both the exposure and the positive-context groups showed some increment in approach behavior, only the changes in the latter group were of statistically significant magnitude. Apparently the mere presence of a dog had some mild negative consequences that counteracted the facilitative effects resulting from highly rewarding interactions with amiable experimenters, increased familiarity with the person conducting the numerous tests of avoidance behavior, and any inevitable direct extinction produced by the repeated performance of some approach responses toward the test animals without any adverse consequences. As might be expected, the general disinhibitory effects arising from these multiple sources occurred only in the early phase of the experiment, and no significant increases in approach behavior appeared between the posttreatment and follow-up assessments.

The data obtained in this experiment demonstrate that the fearless behavior of a model can substantially reduce avoidance responses in observers, but the findings do not establish the nature of the mechanism by which vicarious extinction occurs. There are several possible explanations of vicariously produced effects (Bandura, 1965b; Kanfer, 1965). One interpretation is in terms of the informative value of modeling stimuli. That is, the repeated evocation of approach responses without any adverse consequences to another person undoubtedly conveys information to the observer about the probable outcomes of close interactions with dogs. In the present study, however, an attempt was made to minimize the contribution of purely cognitive factors by informing children in all groups beforehand that the test animals were harmless.

The nonoccurrence of anticipated aversive consequences to a model accompanied by positive affective reactions on his part can also extinguish in observers previously established emotional responses that are vicariously aroused by the modeled displays (Bandura & Rosenthal, 1966). It is therefore possible that reduction in avoidance behavior is partly mediated by the elimination of conditioned emotionality.

Further research is needed to separate the relative contribution of cognitive, emotional, and other factors governing vicarious processes. It would also be of interest to study the effects upon vicarious extinction exercised by such variables as number of modeling trials, distribution of extinction sessions, mode of model presentation, and variations in the characteristics of the models and the feared stimuli. For example, with extensive sampling in the modeled displays of both girls and boys exhibiting approach responses to dogs ranging from diminutive breeds to larger specimens, it may be possible to achieve widely generalized extinction effects. Once approach behaviors have been restored through modeling, their maintenance and further generalization can be effectively controlled by response-contingent reinforcement administered directly to the subject. The combined use of modeling and reinforcement procedures may thus serve as a highly efficacious mode of therapy for eliminating severe behavioral inhibitions.

REFERENCES

Bandura, A. Influence of models' reinforcement contingencies on the acquisition of imitative responses. *Journal of Personality and Social Psychology*, 1965, *1*, 589–595. (a).

Bandura, A. Vicarious processes: A case of no-trial learning. In L. Berkowitz (Ed.), *Advances in experimental social psychology*. Vol. 2. New York: Academic Press, 1965. Pp. 1–55 (b).

Bandura, A., & Rosenthal, T. L. Vicarious classical conditioning as a function of arousal level. *Journal of Personality and Social Psychology*, 1966, *3*, 54–62.

Bandura, A., Ross, D., & Ross, S. A. Vicarious reinforcement and imitative learning. *Journal of Abnormal and Social Psychology*, 1963, *67*, 601–607.

Berger, S. M. Conditioning through vicarious instigation. *Psychological Review*, 1962, *69*, 450–466.

Farber, I. E. Response fixation under anxiety and non-anxiety conditions. *Journal of Experimental Psychology*, 1948, *38*, 111–131.

Jones, M. C. The elimination of children's fears. *Journal of Experimental Psychology*, 1924, *7*, 383–390.

Kanter, F. H. Vicarious human reinforcement: A glimpse into the black box. In L. Krasner & L. P. Ullmann (Eds.), *Research in behavior modification*. New York: Holt, Rinehart and Winston, 1965. Pp. 244–267.

Kimble, G. A., & Kendall, J. W., Jr. A comparison of two methods of producing experimental extinction. *Journal of Experimental Psychology*, 1953, *45*, 87–90.

Masserman, J. H. *Behavior and neurosis*. Chicago: University of Chicago Press, 1943.

Melvin, K. B., & Brown, J. S. Neutralization of an aversive light stimulus as a function of number of paired presentations with food. *Journal of Comparative and Physiological Psychology*, 1964, *58*, 350–353.

Walters, R. H., & Parke, R. D. Influence of response consequences to a social model on resistance to deviation. *Journal of Experimental Child Psychology*, 1964, *1*, 269–280.

Effects of Social Reinforcement on Isolate Behavior of a Nursery School Child

K. Eileen Allen, Betty Hart, Joan S. Buell,
Florence R. Harris, and Montrose M. Wolf

UNIVERSITY OF WASHINGTON

This report presents an application of reinforcement principles to guidance in a preschool. Teachers used systematic presentation of positive social reinforcement (adult attention) to help a child showing persistent and marked isolate behavior to achieve and maintain more play relationships with peers. Adult attention was defined as: a teacher's going to, talking to, smiling to, touching, offering and/or giving assistance to the child. Play relationships were defined as interactions between the subject and one or more children, such as conversing, looking or smiling toward each other, touching, helping, or working with each other on a project.

Reprinted from *Child Development,* copyright © 1964 by The Society for Research in Child Development, Inc., *35,* No. 2, 511–518. By permission.

Of inestimable value in planning and carrying out this study were the counsel and steady support of Sidney W. Bijou, Donald M. Baer, and Jay S. Birnbrauer. Refinement of observation techniques depended heavily on the collaboration of Robert G. Wahler, who is currently exploring and developing methods for recording behavior in the child clinical situation.

397

Reinforcement principles have been established in experiments with several subhuman species, and some applications have been made to human problems. Wolf, Risley, and Mees *(7)* and Ferster and DeMeyer *(4)* have applied them to the treatment of autism in children; Brady and Lind *(3)* to functional blindness; Ayllon and Michael *(2)* and Ayllon and Haughton *(1)* to psychotic behavior; Harris, Johnston, Kelley, and Wolf *(5)* to regressed motor behavior of a preschool child; and Hart, Allen, Buell, Harris, and Wolf *(6)* to operant crying. In each instance systematic improvement in behavior was achieved.

METHOD

Subject

Ann was 4.3 years old at the start of the study. She was enrolled at the Laboratory Preschool of the University of Washington in a group of eight boys and eight girls, homogeneous in terms of age (4 to 4.5 years), intelligence levels (higher than average), and family background (upper middle class).

During the first days of school, Ann interacted freely with adults but seldom initiated contact with children or responded to their attempts to play with her. She did not seem severely withdrawn or frightened; instead she revealed a varied repertory of unusually well-developed physical and mental skills that drew the interested attention of adults but failed to gain the companionship of children. Teachers gave warm recognition to her skilled climbing, jumping, and riding; her creative use of paints and clay; her original songs and rhythmic interpretations of musical selections; her collections of nature objects; her perceptive and mature verbalizations; and her willing and thorough help-with-cleanup behaviors.

With passing days she complained at length about minute or invisible bumps and abrasions. She often spoke in breathy tones at levels so low that it was difficult to understand what she said. Her innumerable, bulky collections of rocks or leaves seemed to serve as "conversation pieces" valued only so long as they drew adult comments. She spent increasing time simply standing and looking. Frequently she retired to a make-believe bed in a packing box in the play yard to "sleep" for several minutes. Mild, tic-like behaviors such as picking her lower lip, pulling a strand of hair, or fingering her cheek were apparent.

After six weeks of school, a period considered ample for adjustment to the nursery school situation, the teachers made a formal inventory of Ann's behaviors and appraised the time she spent with children, with adults, and by herself. The evaluation revealed that Ann's behavior consisted of isolating herself from children and indulging in many varied techniques for gaining and prolonging the attention of adults. Close scrutiny further revealed that most of the adult attention given to her was contingent upon behaviors incompatible with play behavior with peers.

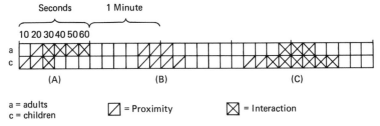

Fig. 1. A sample line from a data sheet which accommodated 12 such lines (1 hour of recording), spaced. Proximity was defined as physical closeness to adult or child (within 3 feet). Interaction was defined as conversing, smiling, or looking toward, touching, and/or helping an adult or a child. All interaction with adults was recorded in row a; interaction with children was recorded in row c. Notations were made every 10 seconds, by the observer, using a stop watch. Neither capital letters in parentheses nor time notations above the line appear on data sheets but merely facilitate explanations in the text.

A plan was instituted to give Ann maximum adult attention contingent on play with another child, and minimum attention upon isolate behavior or upon interactions with an adult when alone. Approximately the same total amount of adult attention was to be available to Ann each day provided she met the criteria for obtaining such behavior from the teachers.

Effort was made to hold all variables other than adult social reinforcement constant throughout the study: no changes were to be made in the regular nursery school program or in supervisional assignments of the three teachers. Teachers were to continue to be physically present, as usual. The only change instituted was in the conditions under which they were to give Ann attention, and this was governed by the schedule of reinforcement in effect at a given phase of the study.

Recording

In order to make assessments of changes in Ann's behavior, objective data were obtained each morning by two observers, the same throughout the study. Each observer worked half the morning. To ascertain rater reliability, they recorded jointly for two mornings. Their records showed 81 and 91 per cent agreement.

Proximity and interaction with adults and with children were recorded at 10-second intervals. A sample line from a data sheet is given in Fig. 1. The sample shows 5 minutes of recorded behaviors. In the top row (a), the single strokes indicate four intervals of proximity to adults; the X's indicate seven intervals of interaction with adults. In the bottom row (c), single strokes indicate eight intervals of proximity to children; X's indicate seven intervals of interaction with children. Blank squares indicate intervals when Ann was neither in proximity to nor interacting with an adult (upper row) or a child (bottom row). A behavioral account might read as follows: Ann stood near a child when a teacher drew near (A). Ann talked to the child, and the teacher at once smiled at her and spoke to both children. Ann turned all her attention to the teacher, following her as she moved away. The teacher busied hereslf exclusively with some other children, and Ann turned and walked to a gravel area where she started to gather pebbles alone. She moved near some children and a teacher (B), where she stayed for half a minute without interacting with them. Shortly after the teacher left the group, Ann moved away, continuing to gather pebbles by herself. A child approached her (C) and joined her in picking up pebbles. They smiled at each other. A teacher at once came and talked to both children. The teacher left after half a minute. Ann continued to play with the child for 20 seconds. After the child left, Ann continued picking up pebbles alone.

Behavior during a daily scheduled group activity which averaged about 15 minutes was excluded from the data. During this part of the nursery school program the children were expected to sit in close proximity to each other and to the teacher.

Procedures

Before reinforcement procedures were initiated, an objective record was obtained of the actual amounts of time Ann was spending with children, adults, and alone.

After five days of baseline data had been secured, teachers were instructed to give attention to Ann whenever and only when she interacted with children. To begin with, any approximations to social interaction, such as standing near another child or playing beside another in the sandbox or at a table, were followed by teacher attention. As soon as Ann interacted with a child, an adult immediately gave her direct individual attention. A sample interaction was, "Ann, you are making dinner for the whole family." When she played alone, Ann was not given attention, and when she contacted an adult she was given minimum attention unless she was with another child.

It was immediately apparent that a direct approach to Ann tended to draw her away from the play with children and into interaction with the adult. Original procedures were amended as follows: the teacher made comments and directed other attending behaviors to Ann, not individually, but as a participant in the ongoing group play; whenever possible, the adult approached the group prepared to give Ann an appropriate material or toy to add to the joint play project. A sample amended operation was, "You three girls have a cozy house! Here are some more cups, Ann, for your tea party." Whenever Ann began to leave the group, the teacher turned away from her and became occupied with some other child or with equipment. This procedure, which extended over six days, seemed to bring Ann into interaction with other children more frequently and for longer periods.

In order to substantiate whether the behavior changes effected by the above procedures had indeed been produced by the application of reinforcement principles, procedures were reversed for five days. Solitary pursuits and contacts made solely with an adult were once more made discriminative

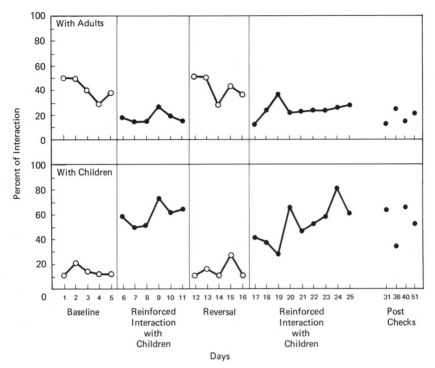

Fig. 2. Percentages of time spent in social interaction during approximately 2 hours of each morning session.

stimuli for adult attention. Ann was disregarded by adults whenever she interacted with children, and given only an unavoidable minimum of attention when she, in the company of another child, contacted them.

After this reversal, the previous contingencies were reinstated. For the next nine days teachers again gave (a) a maximum of attention for all play with children, (b) no attention when Ann was alone, and (c) a minimum of attention when she contacted adults, unless she was with a child. When she began spending longer periods in continuous interaction with children, adult reinforcement of interaction was gradually made more intermittent until she received adult attention in an amount normal for the group.

Following the last day of systematic reinforcement of interaction, the observers recorded Ann's behaviors on four days spaced at irregular intervals during the last months of school.

RESULTS

The data on interactions with adults and with children are shown in Fig. 2. Since the total observation time each morning varied slightly (average of 114 minutes, with a range from 100 to 130 minutes), each dot on the graph represents a percentage of a morning Ann spent in interaction (a) with adults and (b) with children. Open dots represent periods in which baseline and reversal procedures were carried out. Closed dots represent periods in which interactions with children were reinforced by the teachers. The percentages of interactions on a given day sometimes total more than 100 per cent, since Ann often interacted with both an adult and a child in the same 10-second interval (see C, Fig. 1).

As can be seen in Fig. 2, the baseline data collected over five days showed that Ann was spending little more than 10 per cent of the time interacting with children and 40 per cent with adults. For at least half the time she was essentially solitary. Analysis of the data indicated that her isolate behavior was being maintained and probably strengthened inadvertently by adult social reinforcement. Using traditional nursery school guidance techniques, the teachers responded warmly to Ann whenever she contacted them and remained in conversation with her for as long as she desired. When she stood about alone, they usually went to her and tried to get her into play with children. If they succeeded, they left shortly, to allow Ann to play freely with other children. All too frequently Ann was "out" again as soon as the teacher left, standing on the periphery, soliciting teacher attention, or playing alone.

On day 6, when Ann was first given teacher attention only when she was near children or interacting with them, an immediate change in her behavior took place. She spent almost 60 per cent of that morning first in approximations to interaction, and then in active play with children. Adult-child interaction, which was not followed by attention, dropped to less than 20 per cent. These levels of interactions varied little throughout the six-day period of continuous reinforcement of child-child interaction. Over the period, Ann spent increasing time in play with other children.

When procedures were reversed (12th day), Ann's previous patterns of behavior immediately reappeared. She spent the first few minutes after her arrival in close one-to-one interaction with a teacher, which was, of course, continuously reinforced. With this beginning, she spent the remainder of the morning much as she did during the baseline days. Over the five days of reversal she averaged less than 20 per cent of mornings in interaction with children and about 40 per cent in interaction with adults. She repeatedly ignored the contacts of other children and remained in some solitary activity where a teacher could attend to her. When she did enter play with children, she nearly always broke away after a few minutes to contact and remain with a teacher.

On the 17th day the final shift in contingencies was initiated and Ann was given adult attention only when she interacted with children. An immediate change in her behaviors again occurred. Less than 20 per cent of that morning was spent interacting with adults and 40 per cent interacting with children. Interaction with adults was for the most part adult-initiated, as when the teacher reinforced her play or gave routine instructions. Over the ensuing eight days of the study her interactions with adults stabilized at about 25 per cent of mornings; interactions with children rose to the previous level of about 60 per cent. During the last days of this reinforcement period, teachers gave increasingly intermittent (nonsystematic) attention for interaction with children. The schedule of nonreinforcement of adult contacts was similarly relaxed.

Six school days after the last day of reinforcement (25th day), the first post check of Ann's interactions with children and adults was made (Fig. 2: 31st day, post checks). The data showed Ann to be spending more than 60 per cent of the morning in interaction with children, and only 12 per cent in interaction with adults. Further checks taken on the 13th, 15th, and 26th days subsequent to the last reinforcement day (25th day) indicated that Ann was maintaining an average interaction rate with other children of about 54 per cent per morning. Interaction with adults on these days averaged about 18 per cent per morning. On day 38, Ann's mother was present during school hours. Her presence seemed to influence Ann's behavior in the direction of less interaction with children, although the rate was higher than during either the baseline or the reversal periods.

DISCUSSION

Within the first half hour of the first morning of reinforcing interaction with children, Ann seemed to react to the contingencies for getting teacher attention. The immediate change may be attributed to the fact that she already had a repertory of skills readily adapted to play with peers. Similar studies in progress show that the development of adequate play behavior is not always so rapid as in Ann's case. Other children who tend to be off to themselves have taken several weeks to achieve similar levels of social play. During the six days of increasing interaction with children, other changes were noticed. Her speech rose in volume, tempo, and pitch, and complaints about abrasions and bumps dropped out entirely. She appeared to enjoy her play contacts, and the other children responded well to her.

When baseline procedures were again instituted, it immediately became apparent from the decrease in percentage that Ann's play with children was not yet so reinforcing as interaction with adults. Concurrently, her speech again became slow, drawling, and frequently almost inaudible. She again sought adult attention for various minor ills.

During the final period of reinforcing interaction with children, the inappropriate vocal and complaining behaviors quickly disappeared. At times Ann even took and held a strong, give-and-take role in play with five or six other children. Occasionally she defended herself vigorously. In general, her behavior indicated she had become a happy, confident member of the school group.

During the final period of the study teachers had further evidence of the care they must continue to exercise in judging how and under what circumstances to give adult social reinforcement to Ann: on the 19th day (see Fig. 2) the children, with the help of a teacher, were making Easter baskets and dyeing eggs. Ann was in almost continuous proximity to both children and the teacher. But most of her interaction was with the adult, as can be seen from the sharp rise in child-adult interaction on this day. This tendency for Ann to gravitate readily to exclusive interaction with the reinforcing adult had been noted early in the study. Teachers had been trained to give attention and approval to Ann as a member of the group by commenting to the group on her contribution, offering some item which Ann could add to the group's play, or approving of the group activity as a unit. Such close pairing of adult reinforcement with children seemed effective in increasing the positive reinforcement values of Ann's peers.

Systematic application of reinforcement principles as a nursery school guidance technique seems to be an important advance toward more effective analysis and use of the existing knowledge about child behavior and development. Guidance measures such as "Encourage him to play with other children" are familiar to every parent and teacher. They imply that adults are to give attention to the child. Reinforcement principles offer a clear, objective guide for precisely discriminating occasions for giving and for withholding adult attention, a positive reinforcer for most young children. The only aspect of reinforcement principles that seems relatively new in nursery school guidance can be subsumed under the word *systematic*.

It seems noteworthy that this study was conducted by teachers in the course of their regular professional work with children. As they helped a child needing special guidance, they examined a guidance technique. Such a combination of the functions of research and service seems both practical and desirable.

REFERENCES

1. Ayllon, T., & Haughton, E. Control of the behavior of schizophrenic patients by food. *J. exp. Anal. Behav.,* 1962, *5,* 343–352.
2. Ayllon, T., & Michael, J. The psychiatric nurse as a behavioral engineer. *J. exp. Anal. Behav.,* 1959, *2,* 323–334.
3. Brady, J. P., & Lind, D. L. Experimental analysis of hysterical blindness. *Arch. gen. Psychiat.,* 1961, *4,* 331–339.
4. Ferster, C. B., & DeMyer, M. K. The development of performance in autistic children in an automatically controlled environment. *J. chronic Dis.,* 1961, *13,* 312–345.
5. Harris, F. R., Johnston, M. K., Kelley, C. S., & Wolf, M. M. Effects of positive social reinforcement on regressed crawling of a nursery school child. *J. Educ. Psychol.,* 1964, *55,* 35–41.
6. Hart, B. M., Allen, K. E., Buell, J. S., Harris, F. R., & Wolf, M. M. Effects of social reinforcement on operant crying. *J. exp. Child Psychol.,* in press.
7. Wolf, M., Risley, T. R., & Mees, H. L. Application of operant conditioning procedures to the behavior problems of an autistic child. *Behav. Res. & Ther.,* in press.

part V
The School as an Agent of Socialization

Once a child has entered kindergarten or first grade, school becomes the center of his extrafamilial world for more than a decade, occupying almost half his waking hours.

It would be difficult to overestimate the importance of the school's role in the child's life. Not only does it strengthen some of the social and cognitive responses that the child's parents may be teaching him; it also teaches him many new responses. The number, variety, and complexity of learned responses required of adults in our culture are so great that even the most remarkable parents could hardly accomplish the task of instilling, without assistance, all such responses in their children. As one of the principal socializing agents of our society, the school should be in a uniquely favorable position to supplement—and sometimes to compensate for—parental training. By teaching the child academic skills, by broadening his store of cultural information, by stimulating his needs for achievement and mastery, and by giving him supervised practice in social relationships both with adults and a wider range of peers, the school should make him better able to deal comfortably with the ever-widening range of challenges and opportunities, as well as problems, that lie ahead of him on the road toward psychological maturity.

How well the school succeeds in carrying out these functions will depend on a wide variety of factors: the types of teachers a child has; the structure of the learning situation itself; the kinds of textbooks and other curricular material to which he is exposed; and the characteristics of the child himself. What may be an appropriate school environment for one child may be almost totally inappropriate for another. The bright, confident child; the child who is fearful and uncertain; the perceptually handicapped child; the white middle-class suburban child; and the culturally deprived, minority-group child from an urban ghetto will have different needs, motivations, attitudes, and skills.

If we are to help every child to make the most effective use of whatever potential he possesses in dealing with an increasingly complex, demanding world, we are obligated to recognize individual differences among children, and to take them into account in designing appropriate and effective school experiences. While in many instances today's schools have succeeded remarkably well in this task, there are also a number of circumstances in which their success to date has been far from optimal (e.g., in meeting the special needs and problems of culturally deprived children; providing ade-

407

quate programs of special education for children with perceptual handicaps or minimal brain damage).

The papers in this part illustrate some of the points summarized above. Both the failure of many of our schools to meet the needs of culturally deprived, minority-group students, and the formidable difficulties in the way of attempting to do so, are illustrated in the sensitive essay that begins this part. Its author, Robert Coles, is a gifted Harvard psychiatrist who has devoted much of his professional life to working with and coming to understand the problems of minority-group children and adults both in the rural slums of the South and the big city ghettos of the North.

Possibly the most important single influence on the child in the school situation is the teacher herself (or himself). Numerous studies have indicated that certain kinds of teacher characteristics and behaviors *generally* facilitate pupil progress (e.g., fair, consistent, warm and cheerful, well-organized). It has also been shown, however, that the same teacher may not be equally effective with all kinds of students. One kind of teacher may be more effective for some students, and another kind more effective for other students.

In the second paper Regina Yando and Jerome Kagan have explored one dimension of teacher behavior, "teacher tempo," and its effects upon first grade boys and girls. Their finding that children (and especially boys) taught by experienced, reflective teachers become more measured and deliberate, and less impulsive in their responses than those taught by inexperienced or impulsive teachers appears to have practical implications for teaching. As the authors note, boys have greater difficulty than girls in mastering reading, partly as a function of their more impulsive attitudes and behavior. It may well be that placement of extremely impulsive boys with teachers who are experienced and temperamentally reflective would promote adoption of a more reflective disposition on the part of the boy and facilitate his reading progress.

While a teacher's attitudes and behavior undoubtedly exert a more profound effect upon the child's development than the textbooks she uses, the latter also play an important role. In the third paper in this part, Gaston Blom, Richard Waite, and Sara Zimet summarize a series of investigations which indicate that there is considerable room for improvement both in the content and formal characteristics of the readers to which children are exposed in the early years of school. The typical "Dick and Jane" sort of elementary school reader—with its smiling, stereotyped, white, suburban parents and children, living in a sunny and static world without conflicts or real problems—appears almost painfully irrelevant to the real life needs of flesh-and-blood children. Even for favored middle–class boys and girls, life is not a "sun-drenched Sunday afternoon," and anxieties, conflicts, and obstacles are common. For a child from an urban ghetto (such as that described by Robert Coles in the first paper), the typical current reader must seem not only irrelevant and lacking in interest, but virtually incomprehensible. These investigators also found differences in the way boys and girls (and their respective activities) are depicted in current readers. The differences obtained have interesting, and not entirely reassuring implications for the role of children's readers in the development of sex-typing.

The effectiveness of different teaching methods, as well as differences among teachers and textbooks, will vary from one child to another. In the fourth study Jesse W. Grimes and Wesley Allinsmith demonstrate that highly anxious and low-anxious children, as well as highly compulsive and low-compulsive children, differ significantly in their responses to highly structured, rather rigid teaching methods as opposed to relatively unstructured methods. Both highly anxious and highly compulsive children appeared to perform more adequately in the structured setting, at least in the early school years.

The importance of taking into account individual differences between children in school teaching is also ingeniously demonstrated in the paper by Virginia Crandall that concludes this part. It is commonly assumed by teachers and parents that successful training of children can be achieved by praising correct performances and ignoring mistakes, on the assumption that the "ignoring" (or nonreaction) is neutral in its reinforcement (i.e., reward) effect. Crandall shows that the matter is not so simple, and that the reinforcing effects of particular adult reactions and nonreactions may be influenced both by the nature of prior adult reactions in the immediate situation, and also by longer-term, generalized experience with parental proclivities toward "positive" or "negative" reactions in child rearing.

Like It Is
in the Alley

Robert Coles

HARVARD UNIVERSITY

In the alley it's mostly dark, even if the sun is out. But if you look around, you can find things. I know how to get into every building, except that it's like night once you're inside them, because they don't have lights. So, I stay here. You're better off. It's no good on the street. You can get hurt all the time, one way or the other. And in buildings, like I told you, it's bad in them, too. But here it's o.k. You can find your own corner, and if someone tries to move in you fight him off. We meet here all the time, and figure out what we'll do next. It might be a game, or over for some pool, or a coke or something. You need to have a place to start out from, and that's like it is in the alley; you can always know your buddy will be there, provided it's the right time. So you go there, and you're on your way, man.

Like all children of nine, Peter is always on his way—to a person, a place, a "thing" he wants to do. *"There's this here thing we thought we'd*

Reprinted by permission of *Daedalus,* Journal of the American Academy of Arts and Sciences, Boston, Mass. "Conscience of the City," Fall, 1968, *97,* 1315–1330.

try tomorrow," he'll say; and eventually I'll find out that he means there's to be a race. He and his friends will compete with another gang to see who can wash a car faster and better. The cars belong to four youths who make their money taking bets, and selling liquor that I don't believe was ever purchased, and pushing a few of those pills that *"go classy with beer."* I am not completely sure, but I think they also have something to do with other drugs; and again, I can't quite be sure what their connection is with a "residence" I've seen not too far from the alley Peter describes so possessively. The women come and go—from that residence and along the street Peter's alley leaves.

Peter lives in the heart of what we in contemporary America have chosen (ironically, so far as history goes) to call an "urban ghetto." The area was a slum before it became a ghetto, and there still are some very poor white people on its edges and increasing numbers of Puerto Ricans in several of its blocks. Peter was not born in the ghetto, nor was his family told to go there. They are Americans and have been here *"since way back before anyone can remember."* That is the way Peter's mother talks about Alabama, about the length of time she and her ancestors have lived there. She and Peter's father came north *"for freedom."* They did not seek out a ghetto, an old quarter of Boston where they were expected to live and where they would be confined, yet at least some of the time solidly at rest, with kin, and reasonably safe.

No, they sought freedom. Americans, they moved on when the going got *"real bad,"* and Americans, they expected something better someplace, some other place. They left Alabama on impulse. They found Peter's alley by accident. And they do not fear pogroms. They are Americans, and in Peter's words: *"There's likely to be another riot here soon. That's what I heard today. You hear it a lot, but one day you know it'll happen."*

Peter's mother fears riots too—among other things. The Jews of Eastern Europe huddled together in their ghettos, afraid of the barbarians, afraid of the *Goyim,* but always sure of one thing, their God-given destiny. Peter's mother has no such faith. She believes that *"something will work out one of these days."* She believes that *"you have to keep on going, and things can get better, but don't ask me how."* She believes that *"God wants us to have a bad spell here, and so maybe it'll get better the next time—you know in Heaven, and I hope that's where we'll be going."* Peter's mother, in other words, is a pragmatist, an optimist, and a Christian. Above all she is American:

> Yes, I hear them talk about Africa, but it don't mean anything to us. All I know is Alabama and now it's in Massachusetts that we are. It was a long trip coming up here, and sometimes I wish we were back there, and sometimes I'd just as soon be here, for all that's no good about it. But I'm not going to take any more trips, no sir. And like Peter said, this is the only country we've got. If you come from a country, you come from it, and we're from it, I'd say, and there isn't much we can do but try to live as best we can. I mean, live here.

What is "life" like for her over there, where she lives, in the neighborhood she refers to as "here"? A question like that cannot be answered by the likes of me, and even her answer provides only the beginning of a reply:

> Well, we does o.k., I guess. Peter here, he has it better than I did, or his daddy. I can say that. I tell myself that a lot. He can turn on the faucet over there, and a lot of the time, he just gets the water, right away. And when I tell him what it was like for us, to go fetch that water—we'd walk three miles, yes sir, and we'd be lucky it wasn't ten—well, Peter, it doesn't register on him. He thinks I'm trying to fool him, and the more serious I get the more he laughs, so I've stopped.
>
> Of course it's not all so good, I have to admit. We're still where we were, so far as knowing where your next meal is coming from. When I go to bed at night I tell myself I've done good, to stay alive and keep the kids alive, and if they'll just wake up in the morning, and me too, well then, we can worry about that, all the rest, come tomorrow. So there you go. We do our best, and that's all you can do.

She may sound fatalistic, but she appears to be a nervous, hardworking, even hard-driven woman—thin, short, constantly on the move. I may not know what she "really" thinks and believes, because like the rest of us she has her contradictions and her mixed feelings. I think it is fair to say that there are some things that she can't say to me—or to herself. She is a Negro, and I am white. She is poor, and I am fairly well off. She is very near to illiterate, and I put in a lot of time worrying about how to say things. But she and I are both human beings, and we both have trouble—to use that word—"communicating," not only with each other, but with ourselves. Sometimes she doesn't tell me something she really wants me to know. She has forgotten, pure and simple. More is on her mind than information I might want. And sometimes I forget too:

> Remember you asked the other day about Peter, if he was ever real sick. And I told you he was a weak child, and I feared for his life, and I've lost five children, three that was born and two that wasn't. Well, I forgot to tell you that he got real sick up here, just after we came. He was three, and I didn't know what to do. You see, I didn't have my mother to help out. She always knew what to do. She could hold a child and get him to stop crying, no matter how sick he was, and no matter how much he wanted food, and we didn't have it. But she was gone—and that's when we left to come up here, and I never would have left her, not for anything in the world. But suddenly she took a seizure of something and went in a half hour, I'd say. And Peter, he was so hot and sick, I thought he had the same thing his grandmother did and he was going to die. I thought maybe she's calling him. She always liked Peter. She helped him be born, she and my cousin, they did.

Actually, Peter's mother remembers quite a lot of things. She remembers the "old days" back South, sometimes with a shudder, but sometimes with the same nostalgia that the region is famous for generating in its white exiles. She also notices a lot of things. She notices, and from time to time will remark upon, the various changes in her life. She has moved from the country to the city. Her father was a sharecropper and her son wants to be a pilot (sometimes), a policeman (sometimes), a racing-car driver (sometimes), and a baseball player (most of the time). Her husband is not alive. He died one year after they came to Boston. He woke up vomiting in the middle of the night—vomiting blood. He bled and bled and vomited and vomited and then he died. The doctor does not have to press very hard for "the facts." Whatever is known gets spoken vividly and (still) emotionally:

> I didn't know what to do. I was beside myself. I prayed and I prayed, and in between I held his head and wiped his forehead. It was the middle of the night. I woke up my oldest girl and told her to go knocking on the doors. But no one would answer. They must have been scared, or have suspected something bad. I thought if only he'd be able to last into the morning, then we could get some help. I was caught between things. I couldn't leave him to go get a policeman. And my girl, she was afraid to go out. And besides, there was no one outside, and I thought we'd just stay at his side, and somehow he'd be o.k., because he was a strong man, you know. His muscles, they were big all his life. Even with the blood coming up, he looked too big and strong to die, I thought. But I knew he was sick. He was real bad sick. There wasn't anything else, no sir, to do. We didn't have no phone and even if there was a car, I never could have used it. Nor my daughter. And then he took a big breath and that was his last one.

When I first met Peter and his mother, I wanted to know how they lived, what they did with their time, what they liked to do or disliked doing, what they believed. In the back of my mind were large subjects like "the connection between a person's moods and the environment in which he lives." Once I was told I was studying "the psychology of the ghetto," and another time the subject of "urban poverty and mental health." It is hoped that at some point large issues like those submit themselves to lives; and when that is done, when particular but not unrepresentative or unusual human beings are called in witness, their concrete medical history becomes extremely revealing. I cannot think of a better way to begin knowing what life is like for Peter and his mother than to hear the following and hear it again and think about its implications:

> No sir, Peter has never been to a doctor, not unless you count the one at school, and she's a nurse I believe. He was his sickest back home before we came here, and you know there was no doctor for us in the country. In Alabama you have to pay a white doctor first, before he'll go near you. And we don't have but a few colored ones. (I've never seen a one.) There was this woman we'd go to, and she had gotten some nursing education in Mobile. (No, I don't know if she was a nurse or not, or a helper to the nurses, maybe.) Well, she would come to help us. With the convulsions, she'd show you how to hold the child, and make sure he doesn't hurt himself. They can bite their tongues real, real bad.

Here, I don't know what to do. There's the city hospital, but it's no good for us. I went there with my husband, no sooner than a month or so after we came up here. We waited and waited, and finally the day was almost over. We left the kids with a neighbor, and we barely knew her. I said it would take the morning, but I never thought we'd get home near suppertime. And they wanted us to come back and come back, because it was something they couldn't do all at once—though for most of the time we just sat there and did nothing. And my husband, he said his stomach was the worse for going there, and he'd take care of himself from now on, rather than go there.

Maybe they could have saved him. But they're far away, and I didn't have money to get a cab, even if there was one around here, and I thought to myself it'll make him worse, to take him there.

My kids, they get sick. The welfare worker, she sends a nurse here, and she tells me we should be on vitamins and the kids need all kinds of check-ups. Once she took my daughter and told her she had to have her teeth looked at, and the same with Peter. So, I went with my daughter, and they didn't see me that day, but said they could in a couple of weeks. And I had to pay the woman next door to mind the little ones, and there was the carfare, and we sat and sat, like before. So, I figured, it would take more than we've got to see that dentist. And when the nurse told us we'd have to come back a few times— that's how many, a few—I thought that no one ever looked at my teeth, and they're not good, I'll admit, but you can't have everything, that's what I say, and that's what my kids have to know, I guess.

What *does* she have? And what belongs to Peter? For one thing, there is the apartment, three rooms for six people, a mother and five children. Peter is a middle child with two older girls on one side and a younger sister and still younger brother on the other side. The smallest child was born in Boston:

It's the only time I ever spent time in a hospital. He's the only one to be born there. My neighbor got the police. I was in the hall, crying I guess. We almost didn't make it. They told me I had bad blood pressure, and I should have been on pills, and I should come back, but I didn't. It was the worst time I've ever had, because I was alone. My husband had to stay with the kids, and no one was there to visit me.

Peter sleeps with his brother in one bedroom. The three girls sleep in the living room, which is a bedroom. And, of course, there is a small kitchen. There is not very much furniture about. The kitchen has a table with four chairs, only two of which are sturdy. The girls sleep in one big bed. Peter shares his bed with his brother. The mother sleeps on a couch. There is one more chair and a table in the living room. Jesus looks down from the living room wall, and an undertaker's calendar hangs on the kitchen wall. The apartment has no books, no records. There is a television set in the living room, and I have never seen it off.

Peter in many respects is his father's successor. His mother talks things over with him. She even defers to him at times. She will say something; he will disagree; she will nod and let him have the last word. He knows the city. She still feels a stranger to the city. *"If you want to know about anything around here, just ask Peter,"* she once said to me. That was three years ago, when Peter was six. Peter continues to do very poorly at school, but I find him a very good teacher. He notices a lot, makes a lot of sense when he talks, and has a shrewd eye for the ironic detail. He is very intelligent, for all the trouble he gives his teachers. He recently summed up a lot of American history for me: *"I wasn't made for that school, and that school wasn't made for me."* It is an old school, filled with memories. The name of the school evokes Boston's Puritan past. Pictures and statues adorn the corridors—reminders of the soldiers and statesmen and writers who made New England so influential in the nineteenth century. And naturally one finds slogans on the walls, about freedom and democracy and the rights of the people. Peter can be surly and cynical when he points all that out to the visitor. If he is asked what kind of school he would *like,* he laughs incredulously.

> Are you kidding? No school would be my first choice. They should leave us alone, and let us help out at home, and maybe let some of our own people teach us. The other day the teacher admitted she was no good. She said maybe a Negro should come in and give us the discipline, because she was scared. She said all she wanted from us was that we keep quiet and stop wearing her nerves down, and she'd be grateful, because she would retire soon. She said we were becoming too much for her, and she didn't understand why. But when one kid wanted to say something, tell her why, she told us to keep still, and write something. You know what? She whipped out a book and told us to copy a whole page from it, so we'd learn it. A stupid waste of time. I didn't even try; and she didn't care. She just wanted an excuse not to talk with us. They're all alike.

Actually, they're all *not* alike, and Peter knows it. He has met up with two fine teachers, and in mellow moments he can say so:

> They're trying hard, but me and my friends, I don't think we're cut out for school. To tell the truth, that's what I think. My mother says we should try, anyway, but it doesn't seem to help, trying. The teacher can't understand a lot of us, but he does all these new things, and you can see he's excited. Some kids are really with him, and I am, too. But I can't take all his stuff very serious. He's a nice man, and he says he wants to come and visit every one of our homes; but my mother says no, she wouldn't know what to do with him, when he came here. We'd just stand and have nothing to talk about. So she said tell him not to come; and I don't think he will, anyway. I think he's getting to know.

What is that teacher getting to know? What *is* there to know about Peter and all the others like him in our American cities? Of course Peter and his friends who play in the alley need better schools, schools they can feel to be theirs, and better teachers, like the ones they *have* in fact met on occasion. But I do not feel that a reasonably good teacher in the finest school building in America would reach and affect Peter in quite the way, I suppose, people like me would expect and desire. At nine Peter is both young and quite old. At nine he is much wiser about many things than my sons will be at nine, and maybe nineteen. Peter has in fact taught me a lot about his neighborhood, about life on the streets, about survival:

> I get up when I get up, no special time. My mother has Alabama in her. She gets up with the sun, and she wants to go to bed when it gets dark. I try to tell her that up here things just get started in the night. But she gets mad. She wakes me up. If it weren't for her shaking me, I might sleep until noon. Sometimes we have a good breakfast, when the check comes. Later on, though, *before* it comes, it might just be some coffee and a slice of bread. She worries about food. She says we should eat what she gives us, but sometimes I'd rather go hungry. I was sick a long time ago, my stomach or something—maybe like my father, she says. So I don't like all the potatoes she pushes on us and cereal, all the time cereal. We're supposed to be lucky, because we get some food every day. Down South they can't be sure. That's what she says, and I guess she's right.
>
> Then I go to school. I eat what I can, and leave. I have two changes of clothes, one for everyday and one for Sunday. I wait on my friend Billy, and we're off by 8:15. He's from around here, and he's a year older. He knows everything. He can tell you if a woman is high on some stuff, or if she's been drinking, or she's off her mind about something. He knows. His brother has a convertible, a Buick. He pays off the police, but Billy won't say no more than that.
>
> In school we waste time until it's over. I do what I have to. I don't like the place. I feel like falling off all day, just putting my head down and saying good-bye to everyone until three. We're out then, and we sure wake up. I don't have to stop home first, not now. I go with Billy. We'll be in the alley, or we'll go to see them play pool. Then you know when it's time to go home. You hear someone say six o'clock, and you go in. I eat and I watch television. It must be around ten or eleven I'm in bed.

Peter sees rats all the time. He has been bitten by them. He has a big stick by his bed to use against them. They also claim the alley, even in the daytime. They are not large enough to be compared with cats, as some observers have insisted; they are simply large, confident, well-fed, unafraid rats. The garbage is theirs; the land is theirs; the tenement is theirs; human flesh is theirs. When I first started visiting Peter's family, I wondered why they didn't do something to rid themselves of those rats, and the cockroaches, and the mosquitoes, and the flies, and the maggots, and the ants, and especially the garbage in the alley which attracts so much of all that "lower life." Eventually I began to see some of the reasons why. A large apartment building with many families has exactly two barrels in its basement. The halls of the building go unlighted. Many windows have no screens, and some windows are broken and boarded up. The stairs are dangerous; some of them have missing timber. (*"We just jump over them,"* says Peter cheerfully.) And the landowner is no one in particular. Rent is collected by an agent, in the name of a "realty trust." Somewhere in City Hall there is a bureaucrat who unquestionably might be persuaded to prod someone in the "trust"; and one day I went with three of the tenants, including Peter's mother, to try that "approach." We waited and waited at City Hall. (I drove us there, clear across town, naturally.) Finally we met up with a man, a not very encouraging or inspiring or generous or friendly man. He told us we would have to try yet another department and swear out a complaint; and that the "case" would have to be "studied," and that we would then be "notified of a decision." We went to the department down the hall, and waited some more, another hour and ten minutes. By then it was three o'clock, and the mothers wanted to go home. They weren't thinking of rats anymore, or poorly heated apartments, or garbage that had nowhere to go and often went uncollected for two weeks, not one. They were thinking of their children, who would be home from school and, in the case of two women, their husbands who would also soon be home. *"Maybe we should come back some other day,"* Peter's mother said. I noted she didn't say *tomorrow,* and I realized that I had read someplace that people like her aren't precisely "future-oriented."

Actually, both Peter and his mother have a very clear idea of what is ahead. For the mother it is *"more of the same."* One evening she was tired but unusually talkative, perhaps because a daughter of hers was sick:

> I'm glad to be speaking about all these things tonight. My little girl has a bad fever. I've been trying to cool her off all day. Maybe if there was a place near here, that we could go to, maybe I would have gone. But like it is, I have to do the best I can and pray she'll be o.k.

I asked whether she thought her children would find things different, and that's when she said it would be *"more of the same"* for them. Then she added a long afterthought:

> Maybe it'll be a little better for them. A mother has to have hope for her children, I guess. But I'm not too sure, I'll admit. Up here you know there's a lot more jobs around than in Alabama. We don't get them, but you know they're someplace near, and they tell you that if you go train for them, then you'll be eligible. So maybe Peter might someday have some real good steady work, and that would be something, yes sir it would. I keep telling him he should pay more attention to school, and put more of himself into the lessons they give there. But he says no, it's no good; it's a waste of time; they don't care what happens there, only if the kids don't keep quiet and mind themselves. Well, Peter has got to learn to mind himself, and not be fresh. He speaks back to me, these days. There'll be a time he won't even speak to me at all, I suppose. I used to blame it all on the city up here, city living. Back home we were always together, and there wasn't no place you could go, unless to Birmingham, and you couldn't do much for yourself there, we all knew. Of course, my momma, she knew how to make us behave. But I was thinking the other night, it wasn't so good back there either. Colored people, they'd beat on one another, and we had lot of people that liquor was eating away at them; they'd use wine by the gallon. All they'd do was work on the land, and then go back and kill themselves with wine. And then there'd be the next day—until they'd one evening go to sleep and never wake up. And we'd get the Bossman and he'd see to it they got buried.

Up here I think it's better, but don't ask me to tell you why. There's the welfare, that's for sure. And we get our water and if there isn't good heat, at least there's some. Yes, it's cold up here, but we had cold down there, too, only then we didn't have any heat, and we'd just die, some of us would, every winter with one of those freezing spells.

And I do believe things are changing. On the television they talk to you, the colored man and all the others who aren't doing so good. My boy Peter, he says they're putting you on. That's all he sees, people "putting on" other people. But I think they all mean it, the white people. I never see them, except on television, when they say the white man wants good for the colored people. I think Peter could go and do better for himself later on, when he gets older, except for the fact that he just doesn't *believe*. He don't believe what they say, the teacher, or the man who says it's getting better for us—on television. I guess it's my fault. I never taught my children, any of them, to believe that kind of thing; because I never thought we'd ever have it any different, not in this life. So maybe I've failed Peter. I told him the other day, he should work hard, because of all the "opportunity" they say is coming for us, and he said I was talking good, but where was my proof. So I went next door with him, to my neighbor's, and we asked her husband, and you know he sided with Peter. He said they were taking in a few here and a few there, and putting them in the front windows of all the big companies, but that all you have to do is look around at our block and you'd see all the young men, and they just haven't got a thing to do. Nothing.

Her son also looks to the future. Sometimes he talks—in his own words —"big." He'll one day be a bombardier or *"something like that."* At other times he is less sure of things:

I don't know what I'll be. Maybe nothing. I see the men sitting around, hiding from the welfare lady. They fool her. Maybe I'll fool her, too. I don't know what you can do. The teacher the other day said that if just one of us turned out o.k. she'd congratulate herself and call herself lucky.

A while back a riot excited Peter and his mother, excited them and frightened them. The spectacle of the police being fought, of white-owned property being assaulted, stirred the boy a great deal: *"I figured the whole world might get changed around. I figured people would treat us better from now on. Only I don't think they will."* As for his mother, she was less hopeful, but even more apocalyptic: *"I told Peter we were going to pay for this good. I told him they wouldn't let us get away with it, not later on."* And in the midst of the trouble she was frightened as she had never before been:

I saw them running around on the streets, the men and women, and they were talking about burning things down, and how there'd be nothing left when they got through. I sat there with my children and I thought we might die the way things are going, die right here. I didn't know what to do: if I should leave, in case they burn down the building, or if I should stay, so that the police don't arrest us, or we get mixed up with the crowd of people. I've never seen so many people, going in so many different directions. They were running and shouting and they didn't know what to do. They were so excited. My neighbor, she said they'd burn us all up, and then the white man would have himself one less of a headache. The colored man is a worse enemy to himself than the white. I mean, it's hard to know which is the worst.

I find it as hard as she does to sort things out. When I think of her and the mothers like her I have worked with for years, when I think of Peter and his friends, I find myself caught between the contradictory observations I have made. Peter already seems a grim and unhappy child. He trusts no one white, not his white teacher, not the white policeman he sees, not the white welfare worker, not the white storekeeper, and not, I might add, me. There we are, the five of us from the 180,000,000 Americans who surround him and of course 20,000,000 others. Yet, Peter doesn't really trust his friends and neighbors, either. At nine he has learned to be careful, wary, guarded, doubtful, and calculating. His teacher may not know it, but Peter is a good sociologist, and a good political scientist, a good student of urban affairs. With devastating accuracy he can reveal how much of the "score" he knows; yes, and how fearful and sad and angry he is:

> This here city isn't for us. It's for the people downtown. We're here because, like my mother said, we had to come. If they could lock us up or sweep us away, they would. That's why I figure the only way you can stay ahead is get some kind of deal for yourself. If I had a choice I'd live someplace else, but I don't know where. It would be a place where they treated you right, and they didn't think you were some nuisance. But the only thing you can do is be careful of yourself; if not, you'll get killed somehow, like it happened to my father.

His father died prematurely, and most probably, unnecessarily. Among the poor of our cities the grim medical statistics we all know about become terrible daily experiences. Among the black and white families I work with— in nearby but separate slums—disease and the pain that goes with it are taken for granted. When my children complain of an earache or demonstrate a skin rash I rush them to the doctor. When I have a headache, I take an aspirin; and if the headache is persistent, I can always get a medical check-up. Not so with Peter's mother and Peter; they have learned to live with sores and infections and poorly mended fractures and bad teeth and eyes that need but don't have the help of glasses. Yes, they can go to a city hospital and get free care; but again and again they don't. They come to the city without any previous experience as patients. They have never had the money to purchase a doctor's time. They have never had free medical care available. (I am speaking now of Appalachian whites as well as southern blacks.) It may comfort me to know that every American city provides some free medical services for its "indigent," but Peter's mother and thousands like her have quite a different view of things:

> I said to you the other time, I've tried there. It's like at City Hall, you wait and wait and they pushes you and shove you and call your name, only to tell you to wait some more, and if you tell them you can't stay there all day, they'll

say "lady, go home, then." You get sick just trying to get there. You have to give your children over to people or take them all with you; and the carfare is expensive. Why if we had a doctor around here, I could almost pay him with the carfare it takes to get there and back all of us. And you know, they keep on having you come back and back, and they don't know what each other says. Each time they starts from scratch.

It so happens that recently I took Peter to a children's hospital and arranged for a series of evaluations which led to the following: a pair of glasses; a prolonged bout of dental work; antibiotic treatment for skin lesions; a thorough cardiac work-up, with the subsequent diagnosis of rheumatic heart disease; a conference between Peter's mother and a nutritionist, because the boy has been on a high-starch, low-protein, and low-vitamin diet all his life. He suffers from one attack of sinus trouble after another, from a succession of sore throats and earaches, from cold upon cold, even in the summer. A running nose is unsurprising to him—and so is chest pain and shortness of breath, due to a heart ailment, we now know.

At the same time Peter is tough. I have to emphasize again *how* tough and, yes, how "politic, cautious and meticulous," not in Prufrock's way, but in another way and for other reasons. Peter has learned to be wary as well as angry; tentative as well as extravagant; at times controlled and only under certain circumstances defiant:

> Most of the time, I think you have to watch your step. That's what I think. That's the difference between up here and down in the South. That's what my mother says, and she's right. I don't remember it down there, but I know she must be right. Here, you measure the next guy first and then make your move when you think it's a good time to.

He was talking about *"how you get along"* when you leave school and go *"mix with the guys"* and start *"getting your deal."* He was telling me what an outrageous and unsafe world he has inherited and how very carefully he has made his appraisal of the future. Were I afflicted with some of his physical complaints, I would be fretful, annoyed, petulant, angry—and moved to do something, see someone, get a remedy, a pill, a promise of help. He has made his "adjustment" to the body's pain, and he has also learned to contend with the alley and the neighborhood and *us,* the world beyond: *"The cops come by here all the time. They drive up and down the street. They want to make sure everything is o.k. to look at. They don't bother you, so long as you don't get in their way."*

So, it is live and let live—except that families like Peter's have a tough time living, and of late have been troubling those cops, among others. Our cities have become not only **battlegrounds,** but places where all sorts of American problems and historical ironics have converged. Ailing, poorly fed, and proud Appalachian families have reluctantly left the hollows of eastern Kentucky and West Virginia for Chicago and Dayton and Cincinnati and Cleveland and Detroit, and even, I have found, Boston. They stick close together in all-white neighborhoods—or enclaves or sections or slums or ghettos or whatever. They wish to go home but can't, unless they are willing to be idle and hungry all the time. They confuse social workers and public officials of all kinds because they both want and reject the city. Black families also have sought out cities and learned to feel frightened and disappointed.

I am a physician, and over the past ten years I have been asking myself how people like Peter and his mother survive in mind and body and spirit. And I have wanted to know what a twentieth-century American city "means" to them or "does" to them. People cannot be handed questionnaires and asked to answer such questions. They cannot be "interviewed" a few times and told to come across with a statement, a reply. But inside Peter and his brother and his sisters and his mother, and inside a number of Appalachian mothers and fathers and children I know, are feelings and thoughts and ideas —which, in my experience, come out casually or suddenly, by accident almost. After a year or two of talking, after experiences such as I have briefly described in a city hall, in a children's hospital, a lifetime of pent-up tensions and observation comes to blunt expression:

> Down in Alabama we had to be careful about ourselves with the white man, but we had plenty of things we could do by ourselves. There was our side of town, and you could walk and run all over, and we had a garden you know. Up here they have you in a cage. There's no place to go, and all I do is stay in the building all day long and the night, too. I don't use my legs no more, hardly at all. I never see those trees, and my oldest girl, she misses planting time. It was bad down there. We had to leave. But it's no good here, too, I'll tell you. Once I woke up and I thought all the buildings on the block were falling down on me. And I was trying to climb out, but I couldn't. And then the next thing I knew, we were all back South, and I was standing near some sunflowers—you know, the tall ones that can shade you if you sit down.
>
> No, I don't dream much. I fall into a heavy sleep as soon as I touch the bed. The next thing I know I'm stirring myself to start in all over in the morning. It used to be the sun would wake me up, but now it's up in my head, I guess. I know I've got to get the house going and off to school.

Her wistful, conscientious, law-abiding, devoutly Christian spirit hasn't completely escaped the notice of Peter, for all his hardheaded, cynical protestations:

> If I had a chance, I'd like to get enough money to bring us all back to Alabama for a visit. Then I could prove it that it may be good down there, a little bit, even if it's no good, either. Like she says, we had to get out of there or we'd be dead by now. I hear say we all may get killed soon, it's so bad here; but I think we did right to get up here, and if we make them listen to us, the white man, maybe he will.

To which Peter's mother adds:

> We've carried a lot of trouble in us, from way back in the beginning. I have these pains, and so does everyone around here. But you can't just die until

you're ready to. And I do believe something is happening. I do believe I see that.

To which Peter adds:

Maybe it won't be that we'll win, but if we get killed, everyone will hear about it. Like the minister said, before we used to die real quiet, and no one stopped to pay notice.

Two years before Peter spoke those words he drew a picture for me, one of many he has done. When he was younger, and when I didn't know him so well as I think I do now, it was easier for us to have something tangible to do and then talk about. I used to visit the alley with him, as I still do, and one day I asked him to draw the alley. That was a good idea, he thought. (Not all of my suggestions were, however.) He started in, then stopped, and finally worked rather longer and harder than usual at the job. I busied myself with my own sketches, which from the start he insisted I do. Suddenly from across the table I heard him say he was through. Ordinarily he would slowly turn the drawing around for me to see; and I would get up and walk over to his side of the table, to see even better. But he didn't move his paper, and I didn't move myself. I saw what he had drawn, and he saw me looking. I was surprised and a bit stunned and more than a bit upset, and surely he saw my face and heard my utter silence. Often I would break the awkward moments when neither of us seemed to have anything to say, but this time it was his turn to do so: *"You know what it is?"* He knew that I liked us to talk about our work. I said no, I didn't—though in fact the vivid power of his black crayon had come right across to me. *"It's that hole we dug in the alley. I made it bigger here. If you fall into it, you can't get out. You die."*

He had drawn circles within circles, all of them black, and then a center, also black. He had imposed an X on the center. Nearby, strewn across the circles, were fragments of the human body—two faces, an arm, five legs. And after I had taken the scene in, I could only think to myself that I had been shown *"like it is in the alley"*—by an intelligent boy who knew what he saw around him, could give it expression, and, I am convinced, would respond to a different city, a city that is alive and breathing, one that is not for many of its citizens a virtual morgue.

The Effect
of Teacher
Tempo
on the Child

Regina M. Yando and Jerome Kagan

HARVARD UNIVERSITY

A series of investigations on individual differences in decision time has revealed a stable psychological dimension called reflection-impulsivity (Kagan,· 1965a, 1965b; Kagan, Pearson, & Welch, 1966a; Kagan, Rosman, Day, Albert, & Phillips, 1964). This dimension describes a consistent tendency to display slow or fast decision times in problem situations with high response uncertainty (i.e., where S must select one hypothesis from among several possibilities). Previous research has established that the tendency to display fast or slow decision times is stable over time and predicts quality of cognitive product in a variety of areas, including reading recognition (Kagan 1965b), serial learning (Kagan 1966b), and inductive reasoning (Kagan et al., 1966a).

Reprinted from *Child Development,* copyright © 1968 by The Society for Research in Child Development, Inc., *39,* No. 1, 27–34. By permission.

This research was supported in part by research grant MH-8792 from the National Institute of Mental Health, U.S. Public Health Service. The authors appreciate the assistance and advice of Michael Ross in the analysis of the data.

424

Although this behavioral dimension appears to be relatively stable over time, it is still important to ascertain its modifiability. A recent study (Kagan, Pearson, & Welch, 1966b) reported that impulsive first-grade children could be trained to delay their offering of an answer after only 3 hours of direct tutoring. However, children often modify their behavior as a result of simple exposure to a model, and it would be of interest to determine if a child's conceptual tempo could be changed by placing him in an ecologically natural situation where he had ample opportunity to observe, and perhaps to imitate, a reflective or an impulsive model. The elementary school classroom provides an excellent natural setting to study this issue.

Casual observation of teachers reveals that some are consistently impulsive, others reflective, and it is reasonable to expect that some children might be influenced by the tempo of their teachers. There is a clear tendency for reflection to increase with age, partly because the school encourages this posture. As a result, we might expect the reflective teacher to have a greater effect in promoting a reflective attitude than an impulsive teacher would in promoting fast decision times. The present study was designed to investigate the influence of the teacher on changes in decision time in the child during the first year in school.

METHOD

Selection and Testing of Teachers

The five school districts comprising the county school system in Clark County, Ohio, provided the population initially selected for study. This population is predominantly rural, with one major city of about 150,000. Initially, all of the first-grade teachers in the county system (43 women in all) were interviewed individually and administered an adult version of the Matching Familiar Figures Test. Figure 1 illustrates a sample item from this 12-item test.

In the administration of this test, the subject is shown a picture of a familiar object (the standard) and eight similar variants. The S is instructed to select the one variant that is exactly like the standard. The mean response time to the S's first hypothesis and the total number of errors for the 12-item test are the major variables recorded. Errors and response time are combined to select reflective and impulsive Ss. Reflective Ss are those who have average response times above the median and error scores below the median for the group being tested. Impulsive Ss have average response times below the median and error scores above the median. The data permitted us to classify 15 teachers as reflective and 15 as impulsive, using the criteria described above. The remaining 13 teachers were excluded from the study. The distributions of the response time and error scores for the two groups of teachers were markedly different. The average response time for the reflective teachers was 60.9 seconds, with a range of 43–89 seconds; in contrast to the impulsive women whose mean response time was 15.7 seconds, with a range of 11–22 seconds. Thus the fastest reflective teacher had an average response time

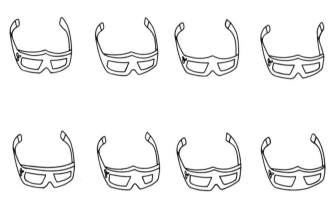

Fig. 1. Sample item from the adult version of the Matching Familiar Figures Test.

twice as long as the slowest impulsive teacher. Similarly the average error score for reflectives was 2.6, the range 0–5, and 60 per cent of the group made less than three errors on the test. In contrast, the average error score for impulsive teachers was 7.8, with a range of 7–11 errors. Thus the problem-solving behaviors of the two groups were dramatically different and characteristic of reflective or impulsive adults.

Two members of the group of 30 teachers left the district prior to the end of the school year, and four were conducting classes for "slow learners" whose IQ's were well under 80. Since the four teachers of the slow-learning classes were all reflective, it was decided to eliminate randomly an equal number of impulsive teachers. Thus 10 teachers were eliminated, leaving 10 reflective and 10 impulsive teachers in the final sample. Teacher age ranged from 22 to 63 years; years of experience, from less than 1 year to 32 years. Teachers were classified as more or less experienced by dividing them into two groups based on the median value of 8 years of teaching experience.

Selection and Testing of Children

Twelve children from each of the 20 classes were randomly selected from the class lists (six boys and six girls), and each child was administered one form of the children's version of the Matching Familiar Figures Test during the first week of school in the fall and a different form of the test during the following spring. Each form contained 10 items, and each item contained a standard and six variants, rather than eight variants used with the adults.

Attrition during the year left us with four children of each sex from each of the 20 classrooms. Thus, the final population included 80 boys and 80 girls, half of whom came from classrooms of reflective teachers, half from the classrooms of impulsive teachers. Administration of the Matching Familiar Figures Test to the children was standard. The child was required to select the one variant that was identical to the standard, and the response time to his first hypothesis and the number of errors were recorded. Scoring of the children's protocols was postponed until all of the spring testing had been completed in order to prevent knowledge of the child's psychological classification to influence any of the data gathering. Additional data collected by the school personnel included scores on the Metropolitan Reading Readiness Test, an occupational scale for social class membership, and the teacher's end-of-the-year grade evaluation of the child.

The primary question asked of the data was whether changes in response time or errors over the 7–8-month period were related to membership in the classroom of an impulsive or a reflective female teacher.

RESULTS

Table 1 presents the intercorrelations among the seven major variables for boys and girls separately. The major variables were: errors and response time on the fall and spring administrations of the Matching Familiar Figures Tests, Metropolitan Reading Readiness Test score, child's socioeconomic class, and teacher's evaluation of the child.

The general pattern of the data was concordant with findings from earlier investigations. There was a negative relation between errors and response time for teachers as well as children, and there was no relation between the child's social class and his response time or error scores on either testing. Stability of average response time on the Matching Familiar Figures Test from fall to spring was relatively high for girls ($r = .70$), but low for boys ($r = .13$). This sex difference is typical, for response time is usually more stable for girls than for boys during the early school years. Error scores showed low stability for both sexes ($r = .23$ and .24). Among the teachers, response time and errors were each independent of teacher's age of years of experience (r ranged from $- .13$ to $+ .11$). It is of interest that the teacher's evaluation was higher for girls who tended to display long response times and for boys who had low error scores. It appeared that teachers have a positive halo toward girls who normally delay and toward boys who do not make mistakes.

Effect of Teacher Tempo
The absolute differences in response time and errors between the fall and spring administrations of the Matching Familiar Figures Tests were analyzed by two separate analyses of variance, with tempo of teacher, experience of teacher (less than 8 years vs. more than 8 years), and sex of child as pri-

Table 1 Intercorrelations Among Major Variables

Variable	1	2	3	4	5	6	7
MFF fall (errors)	...	−.53[b]	.24[a]	−.15	−.36[b]	−.17	−.29[b]
MFF fall (response time)	−.58[b]	...	.24[a]	.13	.20	.01	.18
MFF spring (errors)	.23[a]	−.35[b]	...	−.37[b]	−.23[a]	.01	−.39[b]
MFF spring (response time)	−.41[b]	.70[b]	−.48[b]	...	.16	−.14	.18
Metropolitan Reading Test	−.33[b]	.27[a]	−.48[b]	.40[b]	...	.04	.36[b]
Socioeconomic class	−.02	−.12	.18	.02	.48[b]	...	.07
Teacher evaluation of child	−.12	.27[a]	−.36[b]	.33[b]	.61[b]	.25[a]	...

Note: Boys to the right and above the diagonal; girls to the left and below the diagonal.
[a] $p < .05$.
[b] $p < .01$.

Table 2 Means, Standard Deviations, and Difference Scores for MFF
Response Time in the Fall and Spring

	Teacher Type							
	Reflective				Impulsive			
	Over 8 Years Experience		Less than 8 Years Experience		Over 8 Years Experience		Less than 8 Years Experience	
	Mean	SD	Mean	SD	Mean	SD	Mean	SD
Boys:								
Fall	7.7	5.27	8.0	4.71	11.0	6.80	8.3	3.99
Spring	18.6	11.87	10.6	5.17	10.6	4.26	12.1	5.34
Change	+10.9	...	+2.6	...	−0.4	...	+3.8	...
Girls:								
Fall	8.5	4.60	8.8	4.65	7.6	5.64	8.8	5.94
Spring	15.0	6.68	12.1	6.31	10.6	8.75	11.7	7.24
Change	+6.5	...	+3.3	...	+3.0	...	+2.9	...

mary factors and classrooms as a fourth factor nested in the first two. There
were no significant main or interaction effects for errors, but there was a
dramatic effect for change in response time. Boys in the classrooms of experienced reflective teachers showed a large increase in response time (10.9
seconds) over the course of the academic year ($F = 4.26$; $p < .05$ for interaction of tempo $\times$ experience $\times$ sex). Girls with reflective experienced teachers
also displayed sizable increases in response time. The simple main effect of
teacher tempo was significant ($F = 9.44$, $p < .01$), but the critical result was
the significant interaction of tempo and teacher experience ($F = 11.72$, $p <
.001$). Neither experience nor sex alone yielded significant effects for response
time.

Table 2 presents the means and the standard deviations for response
times in the fall and spring as well as the relevant difference scores for each
of the eight groups.

There were no major differences in average response time or variability
among the eight groups on the first administration of the test during the
fall. The spring scores revealed that the children who showed the largest
increases in response time were in the classrooms of highly experienced reflective teachers. The increase of 10.9 seconds for the boys in this group is
not the result of one or two children, for 60 per cent of the boys in this
group showed increases in response time equal to or greater than 14 seconds,
in contrast to 33 per cent showing increases that large among the boys in the
remaining groups. Similarly, 50 per cent of the girls placed with experienced
reflective teachers showed gains of 14 seconds or more, in contrast to 25
per cent showing gains that large among the remaining girls.

Individual comparisons, by means of t tests, revealed two significant ratios. Boys with reflective experienced teachers showed larger increases than (a) boys in the classrooms of reflective inexperienced teachers ($t = 3.67$; $p < .05$) or (b) boys with impulsive experienced teachers ($t = 4.94$; $p < .01$). In a final analysis, children from the classrooms of impulsive or reflective teachers were matched on sex, initial response time on the fall test, and teachers' level of experience, and changes in response time from fall to spring were compared for these matched pairs. The mean gains in response time for each of the four matched groups were always larger for the children from the reflective classrooms, and the largest difference emerged for boys with experienced reflective teachers ($t = 3.17$; $p < .01$).

Although response latencies were influenced by the teacher, error scores were not altered appreciably. This finding also occurred in a previous study of first-grade children who were trained individually to inhibit rapid decisions. The training produced longer latencies but did not have a dramatic effect on accuracy (Kagan et al., 1966b). It appears that the capacity to delay or to inhibit a response is more malleable than the ability to perform perceptual discriminations. This is not too surprising, for a cognitive product reflects the combined effect of many processes. Although delay is normally associated with accuracy, when a child's strategy is being changed, it is possible to alter the delay-inhibition vector without necessarily affecting accuracy. It is obvious that specific training in scanning strategies is required.

DISCUSSION

First-grade children placed with experienced reflective teachers became more reflective during the school year than those placed with impulsive teachers. Since the school rewards delay and inhibition more consistently than it encourages impulsive spontaneity during the primary grades, it might be expected that the presence of a model who was impulsive would have less of an effect on the child's decision time than a reflective model.

It is not possible to specify the exact behaviors in the teacher that may have caused this change. It is likely that the increase in response time was mediated both by modeling effects (Bandura, 1962), as well as by direct reinforcement. It is possible, and perhaps even probable, that the reflective teacher issued more frequent social reinforcements for inhibitions and delay than the impulsive teacher, and it is not reasonable to conclude that the effect noted here was mediated solely by imitation of the model's behavior. However, observations of the classroom actions of reflective and impulsive teachers should supply information needed to decide how much variance each of these two mechanisms is contributing to the changes noted in the children.

It would appear that thought should sometimes be given to tailoring tempo of teacher to tempo of child. Boys have greater difficulty than girls mastering reading, and previous research has indicated that part of the problem can be attributed to their impulsive attitude (Kagan, 1966). Placement of extremely impulsive boys with teachers who are temperamentally reflective might promote the adoption of a more reflective disposition on the part of the boy and facilitate his reading progress.

REFERENCES

Bandura, A. Social learning through imitation. In M. R. Jones (Ed.), *Nebraska symposium on motivation,* 1962. Lincoln: University of Nebraska Press, 1962. Pp. 211–269.

Kagan, J. Impulsive and reflective children: significance of conceptual tempo. In J. D. Krumboltz (Ed.), *Learning and the educational process.* Chicago: Rand, McNally, 1965. Pp. 133–161. (a)

Kagan, J. Reflection-impulsivity and reading ability in primary grade children. *Child Development,* 1965, *36,* 609–628. (b)

Kagan, J. Reflection-impulsivity: the generality and dynamics of conceptual tempo. *Journal of Abnormal Psychology,* 1966, *71,* 17–24.

Kagan, J., Pearson, L., & Welch, L. Conceptual impulsivity and inductive reasoning. *Child Development,* 1966, *37,* 583–594. (a)

Kagan, J., Pearson, L., & Welch, L. The modifiability of an impulsive tempo. *Journal of Educational Psychology,* 1966, *57* (6), 359–365. (b)

Kagan, J., Rosman, B. L., Day, D., Albert, J., & Phillips, W. Information processing in the child: significance of analytic and reflective attitudes. *Psychological Monographs,* 1964, *78* (1, Whole No. 578).

A Motivational
Content Analysis
of Children's Primers

*Gaston E. Blom, Richard R. Waite,
and Sara G. Zimet*

UNIVERSITY OF COLORADO SCHOOL OF MEDICINE

Our initial interest in the research reported was stimulated by our clinical work with children who had difficulties in reading. We were much impressed with the greater frequency of this kind of disorder in boys than in girls. This observation, based on limited clinical data, had been made by others; indeed, the sex ratios reported by other investigators ranged from 3:1 to 10:1, boys always having a greater incidence of difficulty. These findings, however, did not hold in all countries or cultures, and this suggested that innate, sex-linked physiological variables were of limited, or at best, indirect importance. We began to wonder what variables were responsible. A variety of variables suggested themselves, including sex differences in child-rearing, instructional methods, attitudes toward school and learning, and the content of reading materials.

Our focus of attention was drawn to the materials used to teach Ameri-

Reprinted by permission of the authors.
Supported by United States Office of Education Cooperative Research Project 3094.

can children to read by a number of articles which appeared in the popular and educational press. These studies called attention to many inappropriate elements in the content and format of first grade reading textbooks. These included:

(1) Lack of recognition of ethnic, national, and cultural differences (Kline-berg, 1963; *Books for Schools and the Treatment of Minorities*, 1966; Whipple, 1964; Larrick, 1965; Whipple and Black, 1966).
(2) The nature of cultural values and attitudes (Chilcott, 1961; Klineberg, 1963; Henry, 1961; Commager, 1962).
(3) Lack of information (Bettelheim, 1961; Gray, 1960; Commager, 1962).
(4) Lack of resemblance to everyday life (Henry, 1961; Ashton-Warner, 1963; Caswell, 1964; Trace, 1965).
(5) Restricted to middle-class situations and suburban life (Klineberg, 1963; Carillo, 1964).
(6) Restricted vocabulary and unnatural language (Gates, 1962; Smith, 1962; Flesch, 1955; Loban, 1963; Strickland, 1962; Walcutt, 1961; Trace, 1965).
(7) Inappropriate theme interests (Harris, 1955; Byers, 1964; Lamb, 1955).
(8) Lack of awareness of sex differences in interests (Norwell, 1958; Peller, 1958; Edge, 1963).

These writings suggested that the reading textbooks used in the first grade were inappropriate in terms of interest value. They concealed the reali-ties of life in America, hiding not only its difficulties and problems, but also much of its excitement and joy. They featured Dick and Jane in the clean, Caucasian, correct suburbs, in houses surrounded by white fences, playing happily with happy peers and happy parents. They contained a dearth of moral content which could have high interest value. They presented a mon-strous repetition of pollyannaish family activities. They offered no new knowl-edge. They contradicted the everyday experiences of children in general, since most American children seldom if ever experienced the affect-less situ-ations depicted in the books. Some of these writers also felt that the stories were so predictable in outcome that little if any of a child's incentive to con-tinue reading was derived from the story content.

We began to look at first grade reading books in order to get a better understanding of what these writers were referring to. Was there anything about the books that could help explain the greater incidence of reading failure in boys? Gradually we arrived at three clinical "hunches" about the stories. First, we agreed that the descriptions of primers as representative of the upper middle-suburban class, unrelated to real life situations, and overly pollyannaish were essentially accurate. Second, it appeared that the stories depicted activities that in real life are most frequently engaged in by (1) children younger than first-graders and (2) girls rather than boys. Third, it appeared to us that in many stories children's attempts to plan and carry out constructive activities were frustrated by one agent or another. Moreover, from the stories we read it seemed that masculine activities were frustrated more than feminine activities.

We made the assumption that there was a relationship between the kinds of stories used to teach children to read and the development of their ability to read. This assumption is a reasonable one, although attempts to support it scientifically pose noteworthy methodological problems. The results of at least one study (Whipple, 1963) contribute to its validity, although further research is needed. Whipple found differences in measurements of word recognition, oral reading accuracy, and interest appeal between traditional primers and a new multi-ethnic reading text. The results favored the multi-ethnic reading textbooks. We also believed that the variables included in our "clinical hunches" (depiction of reality, age, sex, and outcome characteristics of the activities in the stories) were particularly important influences in the development of reading ability. Although some of the research in progress focuses on this assumption, our main interest has been the content analysis of the books themselves.

The work already completed and described below began with the analysis of traditional primers (those used most frequently in American schools) in terms of hypotheses derived from our initial impressions. That is, we sought to establish some indications as to the validity of our impressionistic observations. Following these analyses, our attention turned toward reading books which differed from traditional primers, including books used in other countries, books used in American schools prior to 1950, new series explicitly designed for particular groups of children, and books freely selected from libraries by first grade children.

Content Dimensions and Coding Manual

The selection of dimensions to be used in the content analyses was based in part on our clinical impressions. That is, particular attention was paid to those aspects of stories which were relevant to the hypotheses we made and to the criticisms of other writers. In addition, it should be noted that both the selection of content dimensions and the generation of hypotheses were based partly on knowledge of developmental factors of special importance for the five- or six-year-old child. For example, the establishment of a more clearly defined sex-role identity is of developmental importance in the six-year-old child, and thus the sex of the activities depicted in the story is of interest. Also, the tendency of children this age to identify with peers and adults suggests that the degree of similarity between the child and his environment on the one hand, and the story characters and their environment on the other, is a relevant consideration.

Seven content dimensions were selected. In addition, the stories were rated according to reading level as indicated by the publisher in terms of vocabulary range, word complexity, sentence structure, and idea comprehension. The seven content dimensions were:

1. *Characters:* Each story was coded according to its constellation of characters. Ten categories were used, such as "children only," "children and mother," "animals only."

2. *Distribution of children:* The children in each story were counted according to their family membership (primary family or other family), age (less than six years, six years, more than six years), and sex.
3. *Theme:* The predominate theme of each story was coded using seventeen categories, including "active play," "pets," "religion," etc.
4. *Age of activity:* This dimension refers to the age at which children engage in or would be interested in the main activity depicted in each story. Five categories were used, ranging from "two- and three-year-olds" to "ten- and eleven-year-olds."
5. *Sex of activity:* Each story was coded as to whether its main activity would be one performed preferentially by girls or boys, regardless of the sex of the character(s) carrying out the activity in the story. Since some activities tend to be equally preferred by both sexes, the category "boy-girl" was included in addition to "boy" and "girl."

    Forced-sex ratings: Those stories in which the main activity was coded "boy-girl" were later re-coded. The raters were asked to which sex they would assign the activity if they were forced to choose. They were instructed here to use the "boy-girl" category only if the forced sex assignment was impossible.
6. *Outcome of activity:* The main activity of each story was coded as to the nature of its conclusion. Four categories were available to the raters, "success," "failure," "help" (success achieved only with the assistance of someone not involved in the activity's initiation), and "unclassified."
7. *Environmental setting:* The geographic location of each story was coded, using the categories "urban," "suburban," "rural," "make believe," and "not clear."

When a search of the literature produced no existing scales completely appropriate to the task, four members of the research group devised a coding manual to be used by the raters. They based their judgments on data available in the developmental literature, and in addition, they made use of their own experiences. (All were parents, two had experience as elementary school teachers, one was a child psychoanalyst and one a child clinical psychologist.) Lists of activities appropriate to each age and sex category were compiled. Judgments as to the most suitable category for a given behavioral item were pooled, and for inclusion in the lists complete agreement among the four researchers was necessary.

Training the Raters
The four originators used the first edition of the coding manual to code a number of stories independently. Group discussions, revisions, and further discussions followed until the manual appeared satisfactory from the standpoint of its utility as well as its applicability. Two raters who had not been involved previously in the research and who were uninformed as to its purposes and hypotheses were trained in the use of the manual with stories not included in the subsequent studies. They then coded one publisher's series

of books (134 stories) independently, and interrater agreements were calculated. These agreements ranged from 86 per cent on one dimension to 99 per cent on another. The overall percentage of agreement at 93 per cent.

The raters then proceeded to code stories independently. Periodic re-evaluation of interrater reliability was made, using a criterion of 85 per cent agreement on each dimension. As new raters were employed, they were trained in the same way and subjected to identical evaluations of reliability.

CONTENT ANALYSIS OF A NATIONAL SAMPLE OF FIRST GRADE READING TEXTBOOKS

Selection of Books

Twelve publishers' series of first grade reading textbooks were selected on the basis of a national survey conducted by Hollins (1955). Each series consists of about five books graded by reading level, most of which are concerned with the events occurring in a primary family and its neighborhood. These twelve were the most frequently used series in American first grade classrooms, and constituted approximately 90 per cent of the books to which first-graders are exposed. In all, they contained 1307 stories. In appearance, they are very similar, and they are referred to later as "standard" or "traditional" primers or series.

Tabulation of Data

The coded data on the 1307 stories were assembled in terms of frequency distributions within each dimension and the interactions between certain dimensions. These distributions and interactions have been reported in part elsewhere (Blom, Waite, & Zimet, 1968). They provide a statistical description of the stories most American children read, or learn to read, in first grade.

The complete findings will not be reproduced here. However, several specific dimensions that were pertinent to our original interests are discussed below.

RESULTS

Theme

Table 1 lists the seventeen theme categories in rank order by frequency of ratings. The stereotyped quality of these stories and books is indicated by the large proportion of stories (47 per cent) contained in the first three categories. (In nine of the twelve publishers' series these three categories account for more than 40 per cent of the stories.)

Quiet Activities, Pranks and Humor, School, Parties, Lessons from Life, and Aesthetic Appreciation are all found infrequently. There were no stories at all in which the central theme pertained to Religion. The absence of stories about religion and the low frequency of stories about aesthetics and lessons

Table 1 Frequency Ratings: Theme

	No. of Stories	Per Cent		No. of Stories	Per Cent
Real Life with			Work Projects	76	6
Positive Emotions	303	23	Quiet Activities	41	3
Active Play	162	12	Pranks and Humor	37	3
Pets	152	12	School	35	3
Outings	107	8	Parties	20	2
Imaginative Play	95	7	Lessons from Life	14	1
Real Life with			Aesthetics	7	.5
Negative Emotions	93	7	Unclassified	3	.5
Nature	83	6	Religion	0	0
Folk Tales	78	6			

Note: Those stories coded Real Life with Positive Emotions feature happy endings, and, together with those coded Active Play are the kinds of stories frequently described as "pollyannaish."

from life is in marked contrast to the content of the McGuffey published prior to the 1830s. While the absence of religion in modern primers is "understandable," the low frequency of other kinds of stories is not. (In seven of the twelve series, no stories were coded Lessons from Life.) It is clear that the communication of moral and ethical values is avoided and, evidently, contemplative, intellectual, and creative activities are considered of less importance than active, happy events. The stories are generally bland, perhaps in an effort to teach reading more efficiently by eliminating interfering stimuli, or to avoid public controversy of any sort. Furthermore, with a strong emphasis on vocabulary control and on the mastery of basic skills, motivational issues were neglected.

Could ethical and cultural values have been represented in the 78 stories coded Folk Tales? Further inspection of these stories indicated that this was not the case. Generally, they contained few stories with human characters. The characters in 77 per cent of them were animals with human characteristics. Ten per cent featured as characters other anthropomorphized figures, including toys, flowers, trains, and pancakes.

Characters

In the character dimension there are ten categories as shown in Table 2. Again, the categories are presented in rank order of frequency. The first three categories constitute 53 per cent of the stories, and in eight of the twelve series they account for more than one-half of the stories. This indicates the degree of restriction in the range of character combination. Four of the twelve series had no stories in which only adults appear. There are fewer stories that include Children and Father as compared with Children and Mother. Thus, the emphasis is on restricted patterns of interactions, and only a limited number of stories is provided which would focus the children's attention on adults, particularly male adults.

Table 2 Frequency Ratings: Character

Children and Animals	$N = 296$	23%
Children and Mother	$N = 202$	16%
Children, Mother and Father	$N = 188$	14%
Children and Other Adults	$N = 172$	13%
Children Only	$N = 146$	11%
Children and Father	$N = 112$	9%
Adults Only	$N = 27$	2%
Make-Believe Characters	$N = 14$	1%
Inanimate Objects	$N = 11$	1%

Distributions of Children

The ratings on the distributions of children dimension are summarized in Table 3. Of the 1307 stories, 1161 include children. The codings point out the representation of family membership in most stories. The "typical" family consists of parents, a boy and a girl each of whom is about six years, and a younger sister. Older brothers and sisters appear infrequently. When other child characters appear, they tend to be about six-years-old or younger. Seldom are older neighborhood children present. If we assume that the child reader tends to identify with the characters in the story, then they would be identifying with age-identical or younger age children. When the data were examined according to combinations of age, sex, and family status (primary family or other), interesting findings emerged. Stories in which only one child is present were few (12 per cent). In slightly more than half of the stories only members of the primary family appeared. Five per cent of the stories excluded the primary family, and 31 per cent included both family and non-family char-

Table 3 Distribution of Children According to Age, Sex, Family

Categories	No. of Stories in Which Category is Represented	Percentage of Total of 1161
Boy: Age 6, Family	897	77%
Girl: Age 6, Family	837	72%
Girl: < 6, Family	389	34%
Boy: Age 6, Non-family	340	29%
Girl: Age 6, Non-family	278	25%
Boy: < 6, Family	69	6%
Boy: < 6, Non-family	64	5.5%
Boy: > 6, Non-family	38	3%
Girl: < 6, Non-family	29	2.5%
Girl: > 6, Non-family	9	.8%
Boy: > 6, Family	9	.8%
Girl: > 6, Family	4	.3%

Table 4 Interaction Between Forced-Sex and Outcome Ratings

Forced-Sex Rating	Success	Failure	Help	Unclassified	Total
Boy	379	181	56	4	620
Girl	394	135	54	2	585
Boy-Girl	64	30	4	4	102
Total	837	346	114	10	1307

acters. In general, these ratings indicated that what is depicted as age-appropriate are activities that are shared with others, a kind of other-directed reactive, yet family-oriented society of children and parents.

Sex, Age, and Outcome of Activities

Three specific hypotheses were formulated prior to the data analysis. They stemmed from our original impressions of the primers and were later stated in terms of the dimensions. The hypotheses were:

1. The activities depicted in the stories are more frequently ones which, in American culture, are engaged in by children younger than six years of age than by children older than six.
2. The activities are most frequently those in which, in American culture, girls engage.
3. The masculine activities end in failure more frequently than the feminine activities do.

The results of this particular study have been reported previously (Waite, Blom, Zimet, & Edge, 1967). Briefly, the first two hypotheses (sex and age), were not supported by the data. Approximately the same number of stories were coded "Boy" as were coded "Girl." A sizable number, 599 out of 1307, were coded "Boy-Girl," indicating a decided lack of sex-role differentiation in the stories. Forced-sex ratings failed to yield differences in frequencies of "Boy" and "Girl" ratings. The age ratings showed that there were approximately the same number of stories depicting activities appropriate to children older than six years as there were to children younger than six years.

The third hypothesis was tested by examining the interaction between sex and outcome ratings. This interaction, presented in Table 4, was statistically significant, ($x^2 = 23.8, p < .001$). Those activities judged to be masculine (using forced-sex ratings) more frequently ended in failure than those judged to be feminine.

A re-examination of the data disclosed an interesting additional finding. It was found that the first two hypotheses were in fact supported by the data contained in books published between 1956 and 1961. Indeed, these hypotheses had evolved from our original examination of primers published during that period. Thus, the six series published before 1962 tended to feature stories in which the activities were more appropriate to children younger than six years and to girls rather than boys. After 1962, these tendencies were

Table 5 Interaction Between Forced-Sex and Outcome Ratings According to Publication Date (<1962–>1962)

Forced-Sex Rating	Success		Failure		Help		Unclassified		Totals	
	<1962	>1962	<1962	>1962	<1962	>1962	<1962	>1962	<1962	>1962
Boy	182	197	77	104	18	38	3	1	280	340
Girl	262	132	61	74	26	28	1	1	350	235
Boy-Girl	42	22	12	18	4	0	3	1	61	41
Total	486	351	150	196	48	66	7	3	691	616

reversed. The interactions between sex of activity and publication date and between age of activity and publication date were statistically significant. Further analysis demonstrated that the third hypothesis (the interaction between sex and outcome) was also supported only in those stories published prior to 1962 (see Table 5).

The fact that the findings were related to the year of publication was surprising. We wondered whether this reflected a deliberate change in the content of stories selected for primers. In the absence at the moment of data relevant to this question, (inquiries directed to publishers have been answered with evasion), one might speculate that these differences reflect, directly or indirectly, the reorientation of American education in the late 1950s. During this period, the frequency of reading disability in boys was acknowledged, along with the growing public criticism of reading textbooks put forth in scholarly articles and in the popular press and television. In addition, some recent research on differences in the learning patterns of boys and girls was having an impact. The national support toward greater scientific achievement (the post-Sputnik era) stimulated greater educational efforts throughout schools.

It is also of interest that there was a large proportion of stories coded "Boy-Girl" both before and after 1962. Developmental studies demonstrate that by the sixth year most children follow interests that are generally preferred by their sex (Kagan, 1964). Boys are caught up in the pursuits of masculine activities, interests, and identifications. They choose male peers as friends and avoid girls. Girls, too, generally accept feminine interests, fantasies, and personality reaction though perhaps less strongly than boys do masculine ones. It is possible that the lack of differentiation in sex roles in the stories conflicts with the important developmental task of sex-role identification. It may be that in their efforts to provide stories that are of interest to both sexes, the authors of these primers have diminished their motivational value for all children. From the standpoint of child development it would be more consonant to present activities in stories that are clearly differentiated as to sex role. This would mean that in general when girls appear in stories, they would perform girl activities and when boys appear they would engage in boy activities. This would be consistent with the reinforcement various cultural traditions and activities provide in fostering appropriate sex-role identification.

STUDIES OF MULTI-ETHNIC FIRST GRADE READING MATERIALS

Introduction

During the past five years publishers have responded to growing social pressures for reading textbooks that include as characters children of more than one ethnic background. Prior to this time, the characters were almost exclusively limited to white middle-class people living a suburban life. The need for integrated textbooks has been stated and restated by numerous writers who emphasized not only the necessity of providing better materials for minority group children, but also for educating white children who may receive much misinformation about other ethnic groups. Most of the multi-ethnic readers currently published have been criticized on the grounds that, except for the skin color of the characters, they are essentially similar to the traditional primers. These criticisms have been mainly impressionistic, but they are important enough to warrant serious examination. Therefore, we carried out two studies of multi-ethnic series to ascertain how they are similar and different from traditional series, and one study which was a clinical analysis of characters portrayed in one multi-ethnic series.

First Study: The Sample

The first study focused on a multi-ethnic urban first grade reading series which was published in 1964 (City Schools Reading Program). This series resulted from the effort of individuals associated with a large urban school system to help urban children more readily identify with story characters that represented the types of people seen in multi-cultural neighborhoods (Marburger, 1963; Whipple, 1964). The authors attempted a deliberate departure from the traditional reading series in more than the skin color of the characters. Efforts were made to develop stories with suspense, surprise, humor and high interest. Natural, familiar speech patterns and word usage were employed. A large number of active verbs was chosen for the vocabulary. A comparison of this series with the more traditional ones in terms of the reading acquisition, interest, and preferences of children from a variety of socioeconomic and cultural neighborhoods indicated that the urban series was more effective (Whipple, 1963). Whether or not its appeal and effectiveness have continued since its introduction has not been determined.

Method of the Study

The following content analysis dimensions were used: story themes, attributes of characters in the stories, sex appropriateness of the activities, age appropriateness of the activities, and outcome of the activities. In addition, environmental setting ratings and ethnicity ratings (frequency counts of Negro, Caucasian, and other racial characters) were made. The results of this content analysis were compared to those of the previously described traditional series (Blom, Waite, & Zimet, 1967).

RESULTS

The comparisons of theme and character ratings between the two series indicated that the urban series contained the same emphasis as the standard series on pollyannaish stories, with a somewhat greater emphasis on family-centered activities. No statistically significant differences were found in the age of the activities, nor in the sex appropriateness of the activities. Ratings of the character attributes showed a greater frequency of stories in the urban series portraying family and nonfamily members together. Whereas the "typical" family constellation in the standard series consists of the parents, a boy and a girl, each of about six years, and a younger sister, in the urban series "typical" family the younger sister is replaced by a younger brother.

These ratings indicate that in many ways the urban series closely approximates the more traditional series used by schools. The environmental setting ratings support this conclusion, since in this series suburban settings predominate to an even larger degree than they do in the traditional series, although there are fewer rural stories and more urban stories. Qualitative examination of the urban stories revealed that what is being depicted is a Negro family living in a happy, stable, white suburban neighborhood. No Negroes appear other than members of the primary family. Marburger (1963) described the difficulties and frustrations of writing this first series of pre-primers that would focus on the life of a working-class family, living in a typical, racially mixed neighborhood. The two basic issues confronting this sophisticated and knowledgeable group related to: (1) whether to select stories that describe "what is" or "what should be" and (2) avoiding stereotypes in the characterizations. And yet, despite conscious efforts to avoid the problems associated with these factors, the results of our content analysis indicate that these problems were not adequately resolved.

The outcome ratings in the urban series revealed striking differences between it and the standard series sample. First, the activities in the urban stories end in "failure" nearly twice as frequently as they end in "success." None of the twelve series in the traditional series contains more "failure" stories than "success" stories. Second, in the urban series there are about as many activities ending in "help," as in "success." In the traditional series, seven times as many stories end in "success" as in "help." These differences are statistically significant ($p < .001$). Thus, in terms of the outcome dimension the urban series is distinctly different from each of the other series we studied. An investigation of the relationship between ethnicity ratings and outcome ratings showed no particular relationship between the two dimensions. That is, the preponderance of failure stories is a general phenomenon characteristic of this series, and is not correlated with the presence or absence of particular racial groups.

The clear differences between the urban series and the standard series in terms of the outcome of activities are somewhat surprising. If the development of reading skill is related to the content of the stories in reading textbooks, the presentation of a preponderance of "failure" stories raises questions about the appropriateness of the stories. The first story in the series is a case in point. One must remember that this is part of the *first* reading book a young child uses. The student opens the book and sees a picture of a Negro child sitting down to read. Before the child can begin to read his books, a second child (Caucasian) tickles him with a small branch. The story goes on

Table 6   Identification of Series A-G

Series	Publisher	Series Title	Copyright Year
A	Follett	City Schools Reading Program	1965
B	Houghton Mifflin	Reading for Meaning Series (4th Ed.)	1966
C	Scott, Foresman	The New Basic Readers Curriculum Foundation Series	1965
D	Harper & Row	The Harper & Row Basic Reading Program	1966
E	Macmillan	The Macmillan Reading Program	1965
F	Macmillan	Bank Street Readers	1965
G	Chandler	Chandler Language-Experience Readers	1966

to show the Negro child dropping his books and chasing his Caucasian friend. The story ends at that point, with the Negro child's original intention of reading completely frustrated.

CONCLUSION

We were forced to conclude as the result of our findings that the authors of this important departure from traditional reading series failed to accomplish their aims in several respects. First, they were unable to portray life in a racially mixed, urban neighborhood. What they did do was to present characters of several ethnic backgrounds living in an almost completely white middle-class neighborhood. They attempted to create early success experiences for first grade students by shortening the first pre-primer of the series. Although this goal was apparently realized, our findings indicated that in the process of meeting this goal, the authors created a series of stories that focused on children who were often unable to succeed in whatever they attempted to do.

Second Study: The Sample and Methods

A second study (Waite, 1968) expanded our investigation of multi-ethnic primers. Six additional multi-ethnic series were subjected to content analysis, using the same content dimensions described above. They are identified in Table 6 (Series A is the one investigated in the previous study). That series, together with Series F and G, represent the results of new and innovative efforts by publishers of reading textbooks. The four other series were published by companies that have marketed traditional series more widely used by school systems throughout the country. Comparisons between series were used to ascertain whether the findings obtained with Series A were characteristic of multi-ethnic series in general. In addition, where the same group of authors wrote both multi-ethnic series and a traditional series, comparisons were made between their two efforts in terms of the dimensions utilized.

RESULTS

The analysis of environmental setting ratings is shown in Table 7. Only Series F and G emphasize urban settings. Thus, the authors of the major publishing companies' series (B through E), have continued to portray children in a nonurban environment. In this respect, they are even more like the "all white" standard series sample than is Series A. The inner-city child, whatever his ethnic background, is thus reading about children in settings quite unlike those with which he is familiar. On the other hand, the two innovative series (F and G) clearly provide the inner-city child with stories about his own immediate world.

The ethnicity ratings are presented in Table 8. "WAS" signifies that *all* characters in a given story were judged to be of white, Anglo-Saxon background. Because characters of different backgrounds were introduced deliberately into these stories, readers have little or no difficulty in identifying which ethnic groups are involved. These groups would include: Negro, Spanish-surname, Oriental, and white of different national backgrounds. However, the research group experienced difficulty in grouping the characters and labelling according to ethnic background and their combinations. For example, questions arose whether characters belonged to "cultural" groups or "ethnic" groups. Neither word is adequate, according to Webster (1961) since the distinguishing attributes of one group are racial, that of another are national background, and others are defined by religion (not included in this particular study). Issues of ethnic background are currently of tremendous national, social, and frequently personal importance and it is not too surprising that concerns about equality and potential hostility reach even to such an abstract, "ivory tower" function of categorization.

The research group finally developed five categories for rating characters and character combinations to describe ethnic composition. These were: (1) "WAS Only," (2) "One Non-WAS Group Only," (3) "Negro and WAS Only," (4) "Other Combinations of Groups," and (5) "No Real People." The overriding criterion for rating was clear identifiability of the characters. The categories were selected to determine the degree of integration with particular emphasis on Negroes and whites.

The use of the label "WAS" may be somewhat misleading. (It is, of course, a form of the widely used term, WASP. We found it impossible to identify the characters' religions). A more accurate description might be Northern European White, which would encompass the many possibilities inherent in the illustrations (Nordic, Celtic, Germanic, Gaelic, Baltic, and Slavic, to name a few). However, it became apparent that one could get into trouble whichever way one turned, since the abbreviations of Northern European Whites, came out NEW, and these characters were anything but new! Rather, they were OLD (Old Line Durables)! The label "WAS" was settled on because it had existing communication values. Moreover, the

Table 7 Environmental Setting Ratings: Number and Per Cent of Stories in Each Category

Series	Urban	Suburban	Rural	Not Clear	Make-Believe	Total
A	22 (19%)	71 (60%)	4 (3%)	10 (8%)	11 (10%)	118
B	3 (2%)	87 (65%)	34 (26%)	9 (7%)	0 (0%)	133
C	8 (7%)	46 (40%)	14 (12%)	42 (37%)	4 (4%)	114
D	2 (1%)	86 (52%)	24 (15%)	40 (24%)	13 (8%)	165
E	2 (2%)	47 (38%)	50 (41%)	23 (18%)	1 (1%)	123
F	48 (70%)	2 (3%)	2 (3%)	16 (24%)	0 (0%)	68
G	80 (81%)	1 (1%)	0 (0%)	13 (13%)	5 (5%)	99
National sample	18 (2%)	499 (38%)	254 (19%)	469 (36%)	67 (6%)	1307

Table 8 Ethnic Composition Ratings: Number and Per Cent of Stories in Each Category

Series	(1) WAS Only	(2) One Non-WAS Group Only	(3) Negro and WAS Only	(4) Other Combinations of Groups	(5) No Real People	Total
A	7 (6%)	17 (14%)	46 (39%)	35 (30%)	13 (11%)	118
B	105 (79%)	0 (0%)	17 (13%)	0 (0%)	11 (8%)	133
C	56 (49%)	16 (14%)	30 (26%)	5 (4%)	7 (7%)	114
D	66 (40%)	3 (2%)	26 (16%)	50 (30%)	20 (12%)	165
E	107 (87%)	0 (0%)	12 (10%)	0 (0%)	4 (3%)	123
F	0 (0%)	3 (4%)	47 (70%)	8 (12%)	7 (10%)	68
G	3 (4%)	2 (2%)	21 (21%)	67 (68%)	5 (5%)	99

names of the characters lend credence to the supposition that they were of Anglo-Saxon heritage. There was an abundance of Dicks, Janes, and Mr. Littles, and an absence of Pierres, Gretchens, and Mr. O'Briens. Jewish names were never used. The classification "WAS Only" is self-explanatory. The second category, "One Non-WAS Group Only" includes those stories in which all characters are of the same non-WAS ethnic background. The third category, "Negro and WAS Only" contains characters only from those two groups. The fourth category, "Other Combinations of Groups" refers to those stories in which members of different ethnic groups are present, but the combination is something other than Negroes and White Anglo-Saxons. Finally, the classification "No Real People" was necessary to include stories about animals, imaginary creatures, etc., in which no humans appear.

It is obvious from Table 8 that each series approaches the issue of multi-ethnicity in its own way. In series A, F, and G, people from more than one ethnic group are seen together in most of the stories. Series A and Series F contain stories in which *only* Negroes and whites appear, while the character distribution in Series G stories is made up predominantly of several ethnic groups. Series B, C, D, and E each have a large number of stories in which only WAS characters appear. While C and D attempt to include other ethnic combinations, B and E (with only 10 to 13 per cent of their stories including characters from groups other than WAS), cannot legitimately be described as multi-ethnic nor urban. This conclusion is further supported by the environmental setting ratings in Table 7, which indicate that 91 per cent of the Series B stories, and 79 per cent of the stories in Series E, take place in suburban or rural settings. Obviously, neither of these series was designed to depict accurately children from a variety of ethnic backgrounds living in urban cultures.

Table 9 shows the outcome ratings within each series. Series A is unique. No other series had so few stories in which the main activity ended in "success." Series B and C also differ from the standard series sample in the same direction, but to a lesser degree. Series D through G approximate or exceed the frequency of success experiences in the standard series. Thus, the findings in the previous study of Series A cannot be generalized to all multi-ethnic primers.

An interesting finding appearing in Table 8 is the relatively high frequency of "Help" ratings. With the exception of Series G, every series has a greater proportion of stories rated "Help" than does the standard series sample. We compared Series B through G with the standard series in this regard. There was a significant difference between the multi-ethnic series and the standard series in the frequency of "Help" ratings ($\chi^2 = 11.4$, $p < .001$). Examination of the data indicated no correlation between outcome ratings and ethnicity ratings, a finding similar to that for Series A alone. That is, non-WAS children in the stories do not "Succeed," "Fail," or need "Help" any more frequently than other children. The general emphasis on "Help" is significant and suggests a poorly understood change in emphasis when authors write multi-ethnic primers. It may very well be, when authors attempt to write stories

Table 9 Outcome Ratings in Multi-Ethnic Series: Number and Per Cent of Stories in Each Category

Series	Success	Failure	Help	Unclear	Total
A	26 (22%)	64 (54%)	27 (23%)	1 (1%)	99
B	55 (41%)	54 (41%)	17 (13%)	7 (5%)	118
C	59 (52%)	35 (31%)	20 (17%)	0 (0%)	133
D	113 (68%)	22 (13%)	23 (14%)	7 (5%)	114
E	75 (61%)	24 (19%)	18 (15%)	6 (5%)	165
F	49 (72%)	1 (2%)	18 (26%)	0 (0%)	123
G	91 (92%)	4 (4%)	4 (4%)	0 (0%)	68
National sample	832 (64%)	340 (26%)	120 (9%)	15 (1%)	1307

about children from urban settings with different ethnic backgrounds, that attitudes of limited ability and intelligence influence the content in a general way.

Two series, B and D, were written by authors who had previously written traditional all-white series (Alice and Jerry Basic Reading Program, Harper & Row, 1957; Reading for Meaning, Houghton Mifflin, 1963) comparing B with the all-white series written by the same authors, we found that Negro characters were introduced into 13 per cent of the stories, and that the stories in general were new and different. Outcome ratings also changed, with the multi-ethnic series having a lower percentage of "Success" stories. This difference in outcome ratings was statistically significant ($\chi^2 = 16.3$, $p < .001$). The same comparison was made between Series D and the all-White traditional series written by the same authors. Sixty per cent of the stories in Series D contained non-WAS characters. Once again, the outcome ratings show a significantly lower incidence of success stories in the multi-ethnic books, ($\chi^2 = 9.5$, $p < .005$).

CONCLUSIONS

Several conclusions were drawn from the results. First, what may appear on the basis of its cover and promotional literature to be a multi-ethnic first grade reading book may, upon closer inspection, contain few significant characters of ethnic background other than White Anglo-Saxon. Second, including "other" ethnic groups does not necessarily imply that the environmental setting of the stories is any different than that of the traditional, suburban-oriented series. Third, although multi-ethnic series are not generally characterized by stories in which the main activity ends in failure, *some* authors may have a tendency to emphasize lack of success to a greater extent in their multi-ethnic series than they do in their traditional first grade reading books.

This type of study, in which the emphasis is on rating, scales, frequency distributions, and statistical comparisons, makes it almost impossible to communicate the many attributes that tend to make a reading series attractive, pallid, or unappealing. Suffice to say that Series G is new and different, depicting real children in real situations. After having read a large number of pollyannaish stories about essentially the same smiling, unreal children in the same sunshiny, idealized middle-class situations, we found Series G to be attractive, appealing, and stimulating.

A CLINICAL ANALYSIS OF SOME CHARACTER TYPES IN MULTI-ETHNIC READING SERIES

Third Study

While our original interest was on the influence of content of stories in reading textbooks on the development of reading skill, it also became apparent that cultural values and attitudes were being conveyed through the content as well. This was strikingly brought to our attention through the content analysis of multi-ethnic urban reading textbooks.

Waite (1968) approached this problem through a clinical analysis of some character types in one multi-ethnic urban reading series (Series A). He focused on comparisons of white and Negro six-year-old boys and their fathers in terms of their behavior characteristics displayed in all the stories of the series. Waite found that the Negro boy was depicted as athletic, less intelligent, impulsive, distractible, and the object of humor. In contrast, the white boy was presented as reflective, more intelligent, and socially secure. The fathers of these two boys also showed definite individual characteristics. The white father had more economic resources, displayed consistent masculine behaviors, and offered assistance to the Negro father. In comparison the Negro father had less economic resources, performed feminine tasks, or assumed feminine responsibilities in nearly half of his appearances, and accepted help from the white father.

Waite (1968) indicated that although the authors of this multi-ethnic urban series (Series A) responded to an urgent social need to write textbooks that depicted whites and Negroes in social interaction, the characteristics they chose for the Negro males reflected the stereotypes and prejudices which exist about them. While the conscious intent of the authors was socially responsive, prejudicial values and attitudes clearly emerged in spite of conscious attempts to avoid them.

Historical Study of Sex-Role Models in Primary Reading Textbooks

The large proportion of stories coded for both boys and girls together in the standard and multi-ethnic series suggested an area for further exploration by Zimet (1968). She was interested in finding out what models of sex-role behavior were portrayed in the primary reading textbooks used by previous generations of American school children.

Methods of the Investigation

Six contiguous time divisions were established, covering the years from 1600 to 1966,[1] after a careful examination of the literature describing sex-role behavior patterns and expectations for adults and children over this open span of years. The six time boundaries included: (1) trends away from a previous behavior standard; (2) the predominant behavior standard; and (3) trends towards a new standard of behavior expectancy. Using the same source of information, criterion lists were devised for each of the six periods consisting of: (1) the play activities participated in by boys, girls, and both boys and girls together; (2) the behavior expectancies for boys, girls, and boys and girls together, under and over five-years-old; and (3) behavior expectancies for male and female adults.

The coding dimensions used in the earlier studies required some modifications and expansion in order to more adequately tap the sex-role variables being investigated. In other words, in addition to those categories mentioned for the standard series,[2] each story was rated for adult male and female roles, outcome of adult roles, outcome for children characters, aggression and dependency themes, agents of help and frustration, sex-directed references to learning and school, occupational references, and ratings of the age and sex appropriateness of the content and illustrations.

Three primary reading textbooks representative of each of the six periods were selected for coding, a total of 18 readers in all. Since sex-role behavior was being coded, one male and one female were trained as raters. Interrater reliability was computed at 95 per cent agreement, after which the books were divided between the two raters and coded independently.

The findings from this analysis of the sex-role models produced some interesting results, only a few of which will be presented and discussed here.

RESULTS AND DISCUSSION

A diffuse sex-role model was presented in varying and increasing degrees from colonial days to the present. This model was expressed through the portrayal of adult males and females performing similar roles and of boys and girls playing at the same activities.

The lack of specificity in sex role is consistent with the diffuse model described in the behavior criterion lists for each of six periods. It should be noted, however, that a sex-differentiated model is also described in this list. Thus, on the one hand differences between the sexes are minimized in a society that prides itself on its egalitarianism. On the other hand, the culture continues to expect different behavior from the two sexes. The model se-

---

[1] Period I: 1600–1776; Period II: 1776–1835; Period III: 1835–1898; Period IV: 1898–1921; Period V: 1921–1940; Period VI: 1940–1966.
[2] Family composition and forced-sex ratings were not included.

lected for presentation in these textbooks has been the diffuse one and therefore such a model of behavior is incomplete.

In addition to the consistent pattern of sex-role diffusion which shows up from 1600 to 1966, another consistent and complementary pattern appears to evolve. Textbook authors began to increase the number of female characters in the stories as formal education was opened up to girls (between 1776 and 1835). This trend continued so that by 1898 and up through 1966, girl characters actually outnumbered boy characters in the texts. Despite this dominance of females in the stories, a distinct female behavior identity was avoided. The diffuse sex-role characterization prevailed.

A possible explanation for the minimizing of sex differences may be found in the desire to present materials that would be acceptable to a heterogeneous classroom grouping. It remains a curious matter, however, that other alternatives were not attempted. Thus, one might also speculate that the neutral, non-sex-linked male and female behavior described in the stories was an unconscious effort to deny the existence of sexuality in children.

This same explanation may also account for the similar treatment in our culture today of boys and girls under five-years-old. They are dressed alike, have the same toys and play together at the same activities. By presenting these less mature models of behavior in stories meant to be read by children over five-years-old, are we not also ignoring the tendency of older children to look down upon behavior which was appropriate the year before? A prime insult is to be accused of "acting like a baby."

There was an extremely high frequency of dependency themes in the total sample of books coded, especially in those from 1921 to 1966 (Periods V and VI). This behavior was rewarded overwhelmingly for both sexes and for all age levels, and thus helped to reinforce the less mature behavior model described above. A feminizing quality is also present in the positive characterization of a male dependent model. Dependency is characteristically associated with females.

Adult characters dominated the texts during Periods I and II (1600 to 1835). They were portrayed as idealized models of religious and ethical behavior and in this sense an adult-centered model was presented. Between 1835 and 1921 (Periods II through IV), adult characters practically disappeared from the texts and were displaced by children and animals. Adult characters entered the books again in sizable numbers during the last two periods (1921 to 1966) but this time they (both males and females) were presented as facilitators of their children's wishes, interests, and needs, without distinct interests and needs of their own. Thus a sex-diffuse, child-centered model of adult behavior was portrayed.

Since it is primarily from adult models that sex-role behavior is learned, it was important to examine the characterizations of adults in the books to see what standard they were communicating. The child-centered adult model communicates an attitude that the adult exists for the child's pleasure only. The sex-diffuse adult model also presents a very limited view of male and female behavior. Let us assume, however, that the adults are also being assessed by the child reader on the basis of their personality characteristics. Unfortunately, the range was limited here to those of congeniality and affability and also made no distinction between the sexes. Although these examples of behavior were consistent with the egalitarian and nurturant standards and expectations of society, they excluded the sex distinctions and the broad range of behavior manifested by adults in our culture. To this extent, the texts fell far short of fulfilling the role of an acculturation medium.

Both adults and children, males and females, were successful most of the time in whatever they set out to do in those books coded from 1835 to the present (Periods III through VI). During this time, life for both sexes and all age levels was presented as being carefree, without sorrow, pain, and conflict, and may be characterized broadly as "pollyanna." The preoccupation with pollyanna themes in the textbooks may well be a reflection of the protective attitude which developed towards children as a result of seeing them as unique beings. Keeping children from negative experiences as well as from the realities of the adult world could be accomplished through presenting this kind of vapid story content. The predominance of stories in a rural and suburban setting may be attributable to this same protective attitude, since the bad life was equated with the city and the good life with the country or the suburbs.

Aggression themes were rarely present. When they were in evidence, the aggressors were more often animals rather than humans (Periods III through VI, 1835 to 1966). This finding is a prime example of the avoidance of negative affect in the reading texts. The presence of aggression themes appeared to be for the sole purpose of convincing children that only animals experienced such feelings or exhibited such behavior. The aggressive behavior was detached enough so that the child would not copy it and yet plausible enough for him to accept the moral that aggressive behavior led to punishment.

Only one socioeconomic and cultural group was represented in the total sample of texts examined, and thus only one possible model of sex-role behavior was presented. The avoidance of socioeconomic and cultural differences is similar in a sense to the avoidance of sex differences and the denial of aggression as a human trait. We are saying in essence, that by ignoring them or diffusing them, we are doing away with the evils or inequalities associated with them. This is the old story of treating the symptom rather than the cause. By dealing with aggressive drives directly we can better understand both the direction they can take us and the direction we can take them. Similarly, the extent to which sex labels, cultural labels, and socioeconomic labels produce inequities in our society, the inequities should be eliminated, not the differences.

Perhaps in this sense, what was left out of the content of these primary reading texts is as important to examine as what was left in. The exclusion of the plurality of sex-role models that exists in American society suggests that these texts ignored the differences in cultural backgrounds and socioeconomic conditions that account for these differences. It is interesting to speculate whether this was an attempt to unify a diverse people under the White Anglo-Saxon middle-class model in the spirit of egalitarianism, or if this was a reflection of the attitude towards the role of education as a selector and sustainer of tradition.

· · ·

CONCLUSIONS

The reading textbook is the traditional means through which reading skills are taught. But more than that it is also the first text placed in the hands of the child entering first grade or possibly even school for the first time. In addition to having an instrumental purpose (that of teaching reading), its content is intended to be motivational. In other words, what is written is intended to fit the predispositions of the child so that he will want to learn to read. Thus, the motivational factors identifiable within the stories relate to motivational factors in the learning process itself.

It is assumed then that in reading a story, a child symbolically goes through the action that is described and consequently his social attitudes will be influenced by the behavior patterns portrayed in the many stories he reads. The reading text, in this sense, is a channel of acculturation and socialization, interpreting to the reader the peculiar characteristics of his culture. The effect of the stories upon the child will depend, however, upon the ease with which he is able to identify with the characters carrying through the action.

While considerable national attention has been focused on the need for providing appropriate sociocultural models in the reading materials, less attention has been given to presenting appropriate developmental models and to the motivational influence of these models on the child.

Thus, the content of reading textbooks has two functions to perform: (1) an instrumental one and (2) a socializing one. The degree of success textbooks achieve instrumentally may well depend upon their success as a socializing agent. What is needed next is an investigation into the actual effect of content on children's attitudes and reading acquisition. Once we gain more insight and understanding in this area, it may be possible to apply our knowledge of child development in writing textbooks that are equally effective as instruments of acculturation and of teaching reading.

REFERENCES

Ashton-Warner, S. *Teacher.* New York: Simon and Schuster, 1963.

Bettelheim, B. The decision to fail. *Saturday Review*, 1961, *69*, 377–412.

Blom, G. E., Waite, R. R., & Zimet, S. G. Ethnic integration and urbanization of a first grade reading textbook: A research study. *Psychology in the Schools*, 1967, *2*, 176–181.

Blom, G. E., Waite, R. R., & Zimet, S. G. Content of first grade reading books. *The Reading Teacher,* 1968, *21,* 317–323.

Blom, G. E. & Wiberg, J. L. A comparative study of primer stories from the United States, Great Britain, and West Germany, in press.

Books for schools and the treatment of minorities. Hearings before the Ad Hoc Subcommittee on De Facto School Segregation of the Committee on Education and Labor, United States House of Representatives, Eighty-ninth Congress, 1966.

Byers, L. Pupils' interests and the content of primary reading texts. *The Reading Teacher,* 1964, *17,* 277–233.

Carrillo, L. W. *Informal reading-readiness experiences.* San Francisco: Chandler Publishing, 1964.

Caswell, H. L. The nature of good teaching. In A. Crow and L. D. Crow (Eds.), *Vital issues in American education.* New York: Bantam Books, 1964.

Chilcott, J. H. An analysis of the enculturation of values as illustrated in primary readers, 1879–1960. Paper presented at California Educational Research Association Meeting, March, 1961.

Child, I. L., Potter E. M., & Levine, E. M. Children's textbooks and personality development: An exploration in the social psychology of education. *Psychological Monographs,* 1946, *60,* 1–54.

Commager, H. S. "Forward," *McGuffey's fifth eclectic reader,* 1879 ed. New York: The New American Library of World Literature (Signet Classics), 1962.

Edge, S. A review of the literature relating to sex differences and reading disability, parts I and II. Unpublished term papers, University of Denver, School of Librarianship, April, 1963.

Flesch, R. *Why Johnny can't read—and what you can do about it.* New York: Harper & Row, 1955.

Gates, A. I. On teaching young children to read. *Proceedings of a Conference on Reading,* 1962.

Gray, W. S. Physiology and psychology of reading. *Encyclopedia of Educational Research,* 3rd ed. New York: Macmillan Co., 1960. Pp. 1096–1114.

Harris, J. M. The expressed reading interests of first grade boys and girls, and the adequacy of current basic readers in meeting these interests. Unpublished doctoral dissertation, Cornell University, 1955.

Henry, J. Reading for what? *Claremont Reading Conference, Twenty-fifth Yearbook.* Claremont, California: Claremont Graduate School Curriculum Laboratory, 1961.

Hollins, W. H. A national survey of commonly used first grade readers. Unpublished data from Alabama Agricultural and Mechanical College, Normal, Alabama, 1955.

Holmes, M. B. A cross-cultural study of the relationship between values and modal conscience. In W. Muensterberger and S. Axelrad (Eds.), *The psychoanalytic study of society, Vol. 1.* New York: International Universities Press, pp. 98–181.

Kagan, J. Acquisition and significance of sex-typing and sex role identity. In M. L. Hoffman and L. W. Hoffman (Eds.), *Review of child development research, Vol. 1.* New York: Russell Sage Foundation, 1964, pp. 137–166.

Klineberg, O. Life is fun in a smiling, fair-skinned world. *Saturday Review,* 1963, *46,* 75–77.

Lamb, E. N. A study of the reading interests of poor reading achievers at the second-grade level. Unpublished data from San Diego State College, 1955.

Larrick, N. The all-white world of children's books. *Saturday Review,* 1965, *48,* 63–64, 84–85.

Loban, W. D. *The language of elementary school children.* Champaign, Ill.: National Council of Teachers of English, 1963.

Marburger, C. L. Considerations for educational planning. In A. H. Passow (Ed.), *Education in depressed areas.* New York: Teachers College Press, 1963, pp. 298–321.

McClellend, D. C. *The achieving society.* New York: D. Van Nostrand, 1961.

McKee, P., Harrison, M. L., McCowan, A., & Lehr, E. *Reading for meaning.* Boston: Houghton Mifflin, 1963.

Norvell, G. W. *What boys and girls like to read.* Morristown, N.J.: Silver Burdett, 1958.

O'Connell, M. *The Alice and Jerry basic reading program.* New York: Harper & Row, 1957.

Peller, L. Reading and daydreams in latency boy-girl differences. *Journal of the American Psychoanalytic Association,* 1958, *6,* 57–70.

Smith, R. C. Children's reading choices and basic reader content. *Elementary English,* 1962, *39,* 202–209.

Strickland, R. G. The language of elementary school children: its relationship to the language of reading textbooks and the quality of reading of selected children. *Bulletin of the School of Education, Indiana University,* 1964, *34,* No. 4.

Trace, A. S., Jr. *Reading without Dick and Jane.* Chicago: Henry Regnery, 1965.

Waite, R. R. Further attempts to integrate and urbanize first grade reading textbooks. *Journal of Negro Education,* Winter, 1968, 62–69.

Waite, R. R. Some character types in Negro primers: A psychoanalytic study. Presented to the Denver Psychoanalytic Society, February, 1968.

Waite, R. R., Blom, G. E. Zimet, S. G., & Edge, S. First grade reading textbooks. *Elementary School Journal,* 1967, *67,* 366–374.

Walcott, C. C. (Ed.). *Tomorrow's illiterates.* Boston: Little, Brown, 1961.

Webster's new collegiate dictionary. Springfield, Mass.: G. & C. Merriam Co., 1961.

Whipple, G. Appraisal of the city schools reading program. Detroit: Detroit Public Schools Division for Improvement of Instruction, Language Education Department, 1963.

Whipple, G. & Black, M. H. *Reading for children without—our disadvantaged youth.* Newark, Del.: I.R.A., 1966.

Wiberg, J. L. & Trost, M. Comparison of content of first grade primers and free choice library selections, in press.

Zimet, S. G. A historical study of sex role models, in press.

Zimet, S. G., Blom, G. E., & Waite, R. R. *A teacher's guide for selecting stories for children—the content of first grade reading textbooks.* Detroit: Wayne State University Press, 1968.

Compulsivity, Anxiety, and School Achievement

Jesse W. Grimes and Wesley Allinsmith

COORDINATOR OF LEARNING DISABILITY SERVICES,
NEWTON PUBLIC SCHOOLS, NEWTON, MASSACHUSETTS
AND HARVARD MEDICAL SCHOOL AND MASSACHUSETTS GENERAL HOSPITAL

INTRODUCTION

The problem of the child in the task of learning to read is of serious concern to psychologists, as well as to educators, parents, and children themselves. Among the many possible causes of reading retardation, some, such as physical handicaps or low intelligence, are obvious. Others are more subtle. Recent psychological research suggests that certain motivational and perceptual characteristics of children may interact with common techniques used in the

Reprinted from *Merrill-Palmer Quarterly of Behavior and Development*, 1961, *7*, 247–269. By permission.

This investigation was part of a program of studies conducted at the Harvard Laboratory for Research in Instruction under the direction of Dr. John B. Carroll, who gave much help during the collection and analysis of data. We are grateful also to Celeste T. Forbes and to Dr. Beverly Allinsmith, Dr. Leonard M. Lansky, and Dr. Judy F. Rosenblith for their deft criticisms of the manuscript.

teaching of reading. Individual differences in such factors as selective perception or emotional needs may dispose pupils to find that one or another method of teaching makes learning easier, more palatable, or more satisfying. The classroom procedure that is effective for some children may prove to be deleterious to the performance or development of others. If a clear-cut association can be shown between school achievement and an interaction of pupil personality and teaching method, the implications will be far-reaching for the psychology of learning and instruction as well as for teaching the specific skill of reading.

Each person restructures any stimulus into a unique pattern that fits his own expectations, conceptions, values, taboos, and wishes. Learning becomes a function of what the individual does to the material as well as of the actual content of the material. Studies of perceptual defense (16, 26) and clinical observations of children with learning difficulties (28) have given evidence of perceptual distortions that protect the individual from conscious recognition of unwanted or feared stimuli. Bruner (5) emphasizes the factor of expectation, interpreting his research as evidence that the individual perceives by using a set of cues which he has learned from his particular experiences to associate with certain situations.

A child's personal reconstruction of stimuli in perception may be vastly different from reality as a consequence of his unique needs, anxieties, or ambitions. For instance, when a teacher kindly remarks, "I know you will do well," some children may perceive severe threat, perhaps unconsciously generalizing from earlier traumatic experiences when an authority figure demanded performance beyond their capacities. When a teacher attempts to be democratic and permissive, some other children's conflicts over making decisions in the absence of direction may cause them to perceive only disorganization, danger, and confusion. If the teacher as well as the child is unaware that what is seen or heard is not being interpreted realistically, it is impossible for the teacher to help the pupil perceive correctly.

It seems probable that one cannot teach a single lesson in a particular manner with any assurance that *all* children will have perceived the content as intended or will attend to it as hoped, free of crippling anxiety or other preoccupation. If almost all children are to be reached and some degree of unity established in the perception of a given fact or generalization, a differentiation of teaching methods may be required. Interest in these problems led to an investigation of ways in which reading is currently taught.

Methods of Instruction in Reading

There are two major schools of thought about the teaching of reading and each group leans upon psychological principles to support the method advocated. Much controversy between the groups has been publicized in recent years, particularly as an aftermath of Flesch's *Why Johnny Can't Read* (11) which provoked a rebuttal by Carroll (7). A summary of the two systems is presented below.

One group would initiate reading instruction through systematic presentation of sounds and their letter symbols, and teaching for competence in the skill of "sounding out" the words encountered in reading. This "phonics" method is basically a system of rules; the child learns that the word symbols have been built from the letter elements in an orderly manner. Most such systems begin with a limited number of letters. The children are drilled in the sound-letter associations. Syllables and words are built by the child through the use of known word elements, with new letters and letter combinations presented systematically, followed by drill, and then by usage in word attack. The phonics approach is usually followed by an emphasis upon thought-getting when the child actually begins to read, with whole words becoming automatically recognized *after* the child establishes the skill of word analysis. Proponents of the system argue that since the child has already acquired much of the spoken language, his greatest need in learning to read is to achieve mastery of the translation of the alphabetical symbols.

In contrast to the method in which phonics is emphasized from the outset, the "whole-word" or "look-and-say" approach to initial reading instruction has been advocated by many educators in recent decades and is in wide use throughout the United States. Instruction begins with narrative reading material. The child is taught to recognize whole word configurations in association with meaning, thus developing a "sight vocabulary" through repetitive exposure to a limited but gradually expanding number of words. The original "sight vocabulary" of 50 to 200 words is learned through memorization of total word forms with little or no attention to the alphabetical details of word construction. The words that are taught are chosen for their concept and interest value rather than in accordance with any designed plan for systematizing word recognition. The whole-word approach is *followed* by instruction in a variety of word attack skills including phonics, but the latter is taught incidentally, i.e., when the teacher perceives the need during the on-going process of reading for meaning. In the procedure, generalizations are made, and used later in attempts at word analysis, but there is seldom a systematic follow-through with isolated drills to establish the learning of one generalization at a time in an ordered fashion. Other word attack techniques accompanying the sight method encourage the child to make "trial responses" on unfamiliar words, i.e., to make intelligent guesses, on the basis of clues gained from pictures, text, or configuration.

Proponents of the whole word method argue that since the only real objective of reading is to derive meaning from the printed words, skill in achieving this objective can best be attained through successful and rewarding experience in actual reading. They argue further that an early emphasis upon phonic analysis impedes the child in the process of thought-getting, and that the irregularities in spelling render this approach confusing. In contrast, advocates of phonics allege that many children taught with a sight emphasis cannot analyze new words effectively and do poorly in composition because they fail to differentiate nuances of spelling.

Of course individual teachers can be found who use a combination of techniques from both systems. Nevertheless, one emphasis has tended to exclude the other in many educational settings. The major differences between the two systems are found in (a) the timing of the introduction of phonics instruction; (b) the degree of systemization of phonics instruction; (c) the emphasis upon phonics as a basic tool in word attack; and (d) the encouragement of trial responses on the basis of clues other than letter-sound associations.

Many researchers have investigated the differential effectiveness of the two methods. The results are inconclusive and contradictory, often showing no significant differences in reading skill between groups taught one way and those taught another, but usually finding a substantial and about equal number of children in *both* systems who do not achieve satisfactorily in reading and whose under achievement or relatively poor performance is not explained by the usual "causes" of school failure, such as low intelligence or clear-cut emotional problems. After reviewing the literature, Witty and Sizemore (31) concluded that while differences in method of reading instruction may produce different qualities of reading skill, they are inconsequential when overall skill is judged. Others have voiced opinions that many children learn to read more successfully through the whole-word approach, but that certain children seem to make better progress through a systematic study of phonics.

Interaction of Personality and Methods

This latter observation suggests that there may be an interaction between children's personality characteristics and methods of teaching. Until recently there has been almost no attempt through research to discover whether one teaching method may have been more effective than another for certain students because of the students' individual characteristics.

The few relevant studies, all within the past decade, have in every case dealt with college students. Wispe (29), Smith et al. (25), and McKeachie (18) have reported experiments which suggest that teaching methods interact with student personality characteristics. In all these experiments some students were placed in recitation or lecture sections where expectations were clearly defined, while other students were placed in seminar-like sections where they were free to establish objectives and course procedures. In one instance, Smith et al., the more highly structured sections were taught in a cold, impersonal, even punitive manner, while the unstructured sections were conducted in a warm, supportive, and permissive atmosphere. In all three instances, a type of student was identified who appeared to demand a high degree of structuring in the learning situation in order to make optimum progress. Wispe describes such students as personally insecure and dependent:

> In the first place, this insecurity demands an abnormal amount of structuring of the situation, so that tensions arising out of the fear of doing the wrong

thing can be reduced. . . . When this kind of student, who is disposed toward a highly dependent type of educational system, with desires for direction that cannot be met by any "normal" amount of instructor-structuring of the situation, is placed in a permissive section, the real conflict comes to the fore. Being intensely frustrated, and lacking the personal security to make the best of a bad situation, this student becomes rigid, intropunitive, and vindictive in his evaluation of sections and instructors. To this student the permissive section meetings are "absolutely worthless," a place where intellectual confusion is heaped upon personal anxiety. [Pp. 176–177.]

Such reports suggest a promising method of attack on the problem at hand. The two methods of teaching reading described may be viewed as providing contrasting amounts of structure imposed in the definition of the task. From the above reports, two different pupil personality tendencies appear relevant: anxiety and compulsivity, tendencies for which there is much descriptive evidence in the literature. If an interaction does exist between teaching methods and these two personality types, we should find that highly anxious or highly compulsive children will perform successfully when exposed to one method of instruction while similar children will do less well or even fail when taught by the other method. Before making a prediction, we need to look at (a) structure in teaching, and (b) the nature of anxiety and compulsivity.

Structure as a Dimension in the Teaching of Reading

Structure in teaching involves the availability of cues within the whole that give certainty of meaning, definiteness of form, or clearly understood expectations. Usually this means that material is presented sequentially in such a way that when new stimuli are introduced, the learner is able to recognize familiar elements and attack each problem on the basis of prior learning of fundamental skills, facts, or principles. In structured teaching, the child is made aware of all expectations through carefully defined rules; when new situations are presented, the child is prepared to act with certainty on the basis of previously taught information.[1]

We believe that the two methods of teaching reading provide different amounts of structure. The phonics method, because of its reliance upon rules, systematic arrangement, and provision for certainty in problem-solving, appears to represent a high degree of structuring. The whole-word method, particularly in its earlier stages, can be judged as relatively unstructured

---

[1] "Structure," as a term long applied to educational practices, has recently taken on a special color as a result of Bruner's (6) writings. He uses the term with a meaning which differs somewhat from ours. To him, structure is an attribute of the curriculum concerned with the sequence of the *conceptual principles* taught and their application to the mastery of later material. (We are using "structure" in a more traditional sense as referring to the clarity of procedure to be followed in a given task and the explicitness of the connections between one task and the next. This usage does not exclude Bruner's theme.)

because of its lack of discipline in word attack, and its encouragement of "intelligent guessing" on the basis of loosely defined clues.

Personality Tendencies

Anxiety and compulsivity, the two personality characteristics chosen for the investigation of a possible interaction with methods, are discussed below to determine what evidence exists that would enable us to predict the direction of interaction.

Compulsivity. Fenichel (10) describes the need for being systematic and for clinging to known routine and clear guide-rules as it occurs in the obsessive-compulsive, as well as the tendency of such persons to classify ideas rigidly in logical categories and to think in black and white terms. Meticulous preoccupation with small, insignificant details and with the letter of the law are noted in many cases with a frequent inability to see the forest for the trees.

Murphy (19) offers a functional description of the compulsive personality: "Everything that is free, uncontrolled, spontaneous is dangerous. Papa will spank. Play safe; put the books back in the right place; rule the notepaper neatly; pay your bills on the first of the month; be good" (p. 748).

Frenkel-Brunswik (12) pursued the task of demonstrating the inhibitory and paralyzing effects of harsh discipline upon the initiative and imagination of children. In homes with a rigid orientation she found that discipline was often based upon an expectation of the quick learning of external, superficial rules. Her description of the behavior of children from such homes is typical of the syndrome of compulsivity:

> In order to reduce conflict and anxiety and to maintain stereotyped patterns, certain aspects of experience have to be kept out of awareness. . . . The clinging to the familiar and precise detail can go hand in hand with the ignoring of most of the remaining aspects of the stimulus configuration, resulting in an altogether haphazard approach to reality. [Pp. 487–489.]

Children of this type exhibited an extreme intolerance of ambiguity. Ambiguity seems to be perceived as a warning of the uncertainty of continued well-being and tends to evoke fear or anxiety. It is as though the individual would prefer to see anything "certain" rather than remain in a state of flux, often accepting superficial clarity at a cost of maladaptive behavior.

In summary, the compulsive person appears to have exaggerated conceptions about exactness and order, and is oriented motivationally and perceptually by these concerns. Compulsives are described as relatively rigid, preoccupied with small details, inhibited in spontaneity, conforming, perfectionistic, seeking certainty, and intolerant of the ambiguous or incongruous situation. Of course these adjectives apply in marked degree only to disordered personalities (or to some fairly well-adjusted people in periods of stress). But obsessive-compulsive *tendencies* can be observed in so many children who are clinically within the normal range that we found it possible to categorize our sample of "normal" public school pupils as relatively "high," "medium," or "low" in compulsivity. It seems logical to predict that the structured phonics program would facilitate school progress for children who show evidence of "high" compulsivity compared with similar children exposed to an unstructured whole-word reading program. The latter approach would probably be perceived by such children as disorganized and unsystematic, and they could be expected to have difficulty in complying with the requirement to guess in ambiguous situations.

Anxiety.   Anxiety as a universal experience of human beings and as a factor in neurosis has long been recognized as a key psychological phenomenon, but only recently has there been a concentrated attack upon it as a personality variable in normal subjects. People measured as highly anxious have been shown to perceive more intense threat in a greater variety of circumstances *(14)*. It appears that anxiety is a response to stress or to the perception of threat. When experienced at an optimum level for the subject, such anxiety *facilitates* problem-solving behavior (22), but at an intense level it exerts a disorganizing effect (8), diminishing the powers of discrimination and thinking.

Korchin and Levine (15) analyzed types of errors and rate of learning verbal material and found that the more anxious subjects differed little from non-anxious in the amount learned when dealing with simple and logically associated material, but that the differences were significant when difficult or unfamiliar material was presented, particularly if it was contradictory to previous knowledge. Their interpretation was, "In the situation in which the subject has to make a novel adjustment and cannot utilize existing behavior patterns, the possibility of failure and the consequent loss of self-esteem can further release anxiety and further reduce the subject's ability to develop appropriate behavior." (Pp. 234–240.) A similar point is made by Ausubel *et al. (3)*.

Noll (20) investigated the relation of anxiety to the learning and retention of verbal material. He found that the more difficult the task, the more difficult it was for highly anxious subjects to habituate to the learning situation, but that they were able to do so when required to master a series of tasks that aided in the structuring of the succeeding tasks. When task difficulty was thus structured, the anxious subjects performed as well as, or better than the other group.

These findings seem directly applicable to the problem of this study, and justify forecasting the direction of an interaction between anxiety and methods of teaching beginning reading. We predicted that if learning experiences are highly structured as in the phonics method of teaching reading, the child with high anxiety will make greater progress in school than similar children in the unstructured setting.

Thus the structured phonics approach should allow anxious children as well as compulsive children to do better than they would have with the unstructured, whole-word method.

RESEARCH PROCEDURE

Selection of Schools Representing Methods of Reading Instruction

Two city school systems were chosen to be representative of the methods of instruction required for this study. Trained independent observers surveyed the methods of teaching primary reading throughout the two communities, using objective checklists. Classroom observations and studies of curricula were made in the first three grades, obtaining evidence of actual practices. In one system, all schools initiated reading through teaching the alphabet, using a systematic phonics program with phonics drill held separately from reading practice, and through an emphasis upon "sounding out" as the major word-attack tool. In the other school system all primary grade teachers were using the whole-word approach as the initial instructional technique, followed by incidental phonics begun late in the first grade and continued throughout the primary grades. Objective categorizing of the data confirmed the classification of each school as structured or unstructured, according to the dimension of structure discussed earlier in this paper.

Further differences were noted in the general conditions in the classrooms in the two school systems. In the structured schools, the classroom atmosphere was found to be more authoritarian and cold, the curriculum more traditional. In the unstructured schools, child expression and meaningful experience were emphasized throughout the curriculum, and the teachers were more democratic and permissive.

Control of Socioeconomic Status

It would have been desirable for the two communities to have differed only in respect to the variable being investigated: the degree of structure in teaching method. The structured schools were in an industrial city, with three-family tenement houses typical of the residential areas, but with one rather sizable section of middle-class homes. The unstructured schools were in a large suburban community, predominantly middle- to upper-middle class, but fringed by an industrial area. In order to equate the samples on socioeconomic status, we chose schools in both cities on the basis of socioeconomic status of the neighborhoods. School principals and guidance workers made ratings of the various neighborhoods and the research team made independent observations of houses and dwelling areas. An objective scale was developed for rating school neighborhoods from these data. Equal proportions of children in each city were drawn from upper-lower and lower-middle class neighborhoods.

Subjects

Individual differences in maturation and the development of readiness for learning to read indicate that not until the third grade have most children had ample opportunity to demonstrate their capacity for school achievement. Therefore, third-grade children were chosen as subjects for this study.

For purposes of sample selection only (individual tests were given later) we obtained group test scores of reading achievement and intelligence from school records of the entire third-grade population in each school system.[2] The subjects for this study were randomly selected from stratified areas of the distribution, one-third as under-achievers, one-third medium, and one-third over-achievers. Children whose reading scores were at least one standard deviation below the regression line of each total third-grade school population were considered under-achievers for the purpose of sample selection. Over-achievers were at least one standard deviation above the regression line in their school system. The final sample was not significantly different from a normal distribution in regard to reading achievement or intelligence test scores. Twenty-four classrooms in twelve unstructured schools furnished 156 cases, 87 boys and 69 girls. Eight classrooms in three structured schools furnished 72 cases, 36 boys and 36 girls. Administrative restrictions necessitated the smaller sample size in the structured schools.

It was assumed that the sampling procedure was purely random with respect to the personality variables under investigation.

Rating Scale of Compulsivity

An interview schedule of open-ended questions and a multiple-choice questionnaire[3] were prepared, and one parent of each of the sample children was seen in the home. The parent was asked to describe the child's typical behavior in certain standard situations in which there was an opportunity to observe tendencies toward perfectionism in demands upon self and others, irrational conformity to rules, orderliness, punctuality, and need for certainty. The interviewers were instructed not to suggest answers and, as much as possible, to record the parents' actual words as they described the child's behavior in home situations.

The rating scale of compulsivity was constructed by first perusing the interview records, categorizing all evidence related to compulsivity, then arranging a distribution of such information apart from the case records. Final ratings were made on the basis of a point system which was developed after studying the distributions of actual behaviors recorded and assigning weight values to each type of behavior that was deviant from the discovered norms. Children scoring high in compulsivity were those who gave evidence of tension or emotionality in situations where there was lack of organization or conformity to standards and expectations, or who made exaggerated efforts

---

[2] In structured schools, the California Test of Mental Maturity was used as a measure of intelligence; in unstructured schools, the Kuhlmann-Anderson Intelligence Test. Reading achievement was recorded from scores on the Paragraph Meaning Subtest of Stanford Achievement Test, Form J, in both school systems.

[3] These and other instruments used in the study are given in the report of Grimes (*13*) on which this article is partly based.

to achieve these goals.[4] The low compulsive child was one who appeared relatively unconcerned about such matters. For instance, the following statement was rated low in compulsivity, "She's naturally quite neat about things, but it doesn't bother her at all if her room gets messy. But she cleans it up very well when I remind her."

Measurement of Anxiety

Castaneda et al. (9) revised the Taylor Anxiety Scale for use with children. The Taylor Scale was adapted from the Minnesota Multiphastic Personality Inventory, with item selection based upon clinical definitions of anxiety. There is much research evidence (27) to validate the use of the instrument in differentiating individuals who are likely to manifest anxiety in varying degrees. Reliability and validation work with the Children's Anxiety Scale by Castaneda et al. demonstrated results closely similar to the findings with the adult scale. Although the Taylor Scale was designed as a group testing device, in this study it was individually administered by psychologically trained workers who established rapport and assisted the children in reading the items.[5]

Relationship of Anxiety to Compulsivity

The question may be raised whether or not we are dealing with a common factor in anxiety and compulsivity. The two ratings yield a correlation of $+.04$, which is not significantly different from zero; therefore, we have measured two different characteristics. In theory, compulsive behavior is a way of diminishing anxiety, and one might expect a negative association except for the possibility that for many children the obsessive-compulsive defenses are not sufficient to quell the amount of anxiety they suffer. The issue of interaction between anxiety and compulsivity will be taken up later.

Criterion Measurement

In the primary grades, reading permeates almost every aspect of school progress, and the children's early experiences of success or failure in learning

[4] In order to fit the theoretically defined compulsive character we scored deviant behavior in either direction as compulsive: those whose need for orderliness was exaggerated, those who were rebelliously disorderly, and those who inconsistently oscillated between the extremes.

[5] The work of Alpert and Haber (1) raises the question whether a test of situational anxiety specific to schooling, e.g., one of test-anxiety, might have been more appropriate and revealing than the Taylor Children's Scale of general anxiety used in the present study. Such an instrument was not available at the time these data were collected. Since that time the Sarason (23) Scale of test anxiety for children has been developed. It is interesting to note that even though Alpert and Haber found no correlation between the Taylor Scale and academic achievement with college students, Castaneda found significant negative correlations between the Taylor Children's Scale and achievement scores, foreshadowing one aspect of the results reported below. Perhaps the contradiction arises from an absence, among those gaining entrance to college, of students whose general anxiety inhibits rather than facilitates school performance.

to read often set a pattern of total achievement that is relatively enduring throughout the following years. In establishing criterion measurements, it was therefore thought best to broaden the scope beyond the reading act itself. The predicted interaction effect should, if potent, extend its influence over all academic achievement.

The Stanford Achievement Test, Form J, was administered by classroom teachers, consisting of a battery of six sub-tests: Paragraph Meaning, Word Meaning, Spelling, Language, Arithmetic Computation, and Arithmetic Reasoning. All of these sub-tests involve reading except Arithmetic Computation. Scores are stated in grade-equivalents on a national norm. The battery median grade-equivalent was used in data analysis in this study.

The Wechsler Intelligence Scale for Children was administered to each sample third-grade child by a clinical worker. The relationship of intelligence test scores to school achievement is a well-established fact (in this case, $r = .506 \ p < .001$); therefore, in the investigation of the present hypothesis, it was necessary to control this factor.

The criterion score used in the statistical analysis is an index of over- or under-achievement. It is the discrepancy between the actual attained achievement test score and the score that would be predicted by the I.Q. For example, on the basis of the regression equation, a child with an I.Q. of 120 in this sample would be expected to earn an achievement test score of 4.8 (grade equivalent). If a child with an I.Q. of 120 scored 5.5 in achievement, his discrepancy score would be + .7, representing .7 of one year of over-achievement. A child with an I.Q. of 98 would be expected to earn an achievement test score of 3.5. If such a child scored 3.0, his discrepancy score would be − .5, representing .5 of one year of under-achievement. In this manner, the factors measured by the intelligence test were controlled, allowing discovered differences in achievement to be interpreted as resulting from other variables.

RESULTS

Test of Interaction of Compulsivity and Teaching Methods

Tables 1 and 2 present the results of the statistical analysis of the data when compulsivity is used as the descriptive variable. Figure 1 portrays the mean achievement scores of each sub-group graphically. First of all, as we had surmised, the highly compulsive children in the structured setting score significantly better ($p < .001$) on achievement than do similar children in the unstructured schools. It can be seen too that when we contrast levels of compulsivity within the structured schools, the high compulsive children do better ($p < .01$). No significant difference was found in achievement between high and low compulsive children within the unstructured school. The hypothesis of there being an interaction between compulsivity and teaching method was supported, in this case, at the .05 level.

While we had expected that compulsive children in the unstructured

Table 1 The Effect of Teaching Method on School Achievement of Children Rated Low, Medium, or High in Compulsivity

	Mean Years of Over- or Under-Achievement						
Teaching Method	*Low Compulsivity Years*	*N*	*Medium Compulsivity Years*	*N*	*High Compulsivity Years*	*N*	*t-ratio high vs. low*
Structured	+.05	17	+.45	36	+.82	19	2.89[a]
Unstructured	−.28	42	−.36	57	−.12	56	.99
t-ratio	1.65[a]				4.15[b]		

[a] $p < .01$ (2 tail).
[b] $p < .001$ (1 tail).

school setting would have difficulty when compared to those in the structured, we were surprised to find that the achievement of the high compulsives within the schools where the whole-word method is used in beginning reading compares favorably with that of the low compulsives.[6] Indeed their achievement scores were somewhat better on an absolute basis although the difference was not significant. We speculate that compulsives in the unstructured schools are under greater strain because of the lack of systemization in their school setting, but that their need to organize (for comfort) is so intense that they struggle to induce the phonic rules and achieve in spite of the lack of direction from the environment.[7]

Table 2 Analysis of Variances of High vs. Low Compulsivity

Source of Variance	S. S.	d. f.	*Mean Sq.*	F
Between method groups	40.73	1	40.73	17.12[a]
Between trait groups	21.51	1	21.51	9.04[a]
Interaction	9.26	1	9.26	3.89[b]
Error		131	2.38	

[a] $p < .01$ (2 tail).
[b] $p < .05$ (1 tail).
[c] Corrected for unequal frequencies.

[6] This could have been foretold from a careful reading of Frenkel-Brunswik (*12*) or from listening to our colleague, Dr. Leonard M. Lansky, who anticipated that the compulsive person is one who is inclined to make blind stabs at any possible solution. One might then speculate that difficulty in guessing under lack of structure would occur only in the case of those compulsive children who were also highly anxious. The achievement of such children who are anxious is compared below with those compulsive children low in anxiety. The trend is in line with the expectation although it is not significant with the small number of cases.

[7] If this is true, we would expect that high compulsives in the unstructured schools would develop skill in phonics to a greater extent than the low compulsive children. Scores were available on a test of phonics skill, and again intelligence was controlled. Analysis revealed that high compulsives in unstructured schools learned phonics significantly ($P < .01$) more successfully than low compulsives.

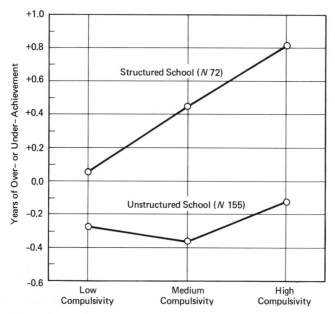

Fig. 1. Graph of test results showing mean school achievement of children categorized as to compulsivity.

It is interesting to note that medium compulsives in the unstructured schools made the lowest achievement scores (although not significantly lower). Possibly their compulsivity was not strong enough to cause them to build their own structure.

Our conjecture is, then, that regardless of the manner in which school lessons are taught, the compulsive child accentuates those elements of each lesson that aid him in systematizing his work. When helped by a high degree of structure in lesson presentation, then, and only then, does such a child attain unusual success.

Test of Interaction of Anxiety and Teaching Methods

The statistical analyses of achievement in relation to anxiety and teaching methods and the interactions of the two are presented in Tables 3 and 4. Figure 2 is a graph of the mean achievement scores of each group. As predicted, the highly anxious children in the unstructured schools score more poorly ($p < .001$) than those in the structured schools. The interaction effect, which is significant at the .01 level, can be seen best in the contrast of mean scores. While high anxiety children achieve significantly less well ($p < .01$) in the unstructured school than do low anxiety children, they appear to do at least as well as the average in the structured classroom.

The most striking aspect of the interaction demonstrated is the marked decrement in performance suffered by the highly anxious children in un-

Table 3 The Effect of Teaching Method on School Achievement of Children Rated Low, Medium, or High in Anxiety

Teaching Method	Mean Years or Over- or Under-Achievement						t-ratio high vs. low
	Low Anxiety		Medium Anxiety		High Anxiety		
	Years	N	Years	N	Years	N	
Structured	+.39	27	+.43	27	+.60	18	.80
Unstructured	+.002	51	−.24	46	−.49	59	3.34[b]
t-ratio	2.07[a]				4.88[c]		

[a] $P < .05$ (2 tail).
[b] $P < .01$ (2 tail).
[c] $P < .001$ (1 tail).

structured schools. According to the theory proposed, this is a consequence of the severe condition of perceived threat that persists unabated for the anxious child in an ambiguous sort of school environment. The fact that such a threat is potent in the beginning reading lessons is thought to be a vital factor in the continued pattern of failure or under-achievement these children exhibit. The child with high anxiety may first direct his anxiety-released energy toward achievement, but because his distress severely reduces the abilities of discrimination and memorization of complex symbols, the child may fail in his initial attempts to master the problem. Failure confirms the threat, and the intensity of anxiety is increased as the required learning becomes more difficult, so that by the time the child reaches the third grade the decrement in performance is pronounced.

The individual with high anxiety in the structured classroom may approach the learning task with the same increased energy and lowered powers of discrimination. But the symbols he is asked to learn are simple. As shown earlier, the highly anxious individual may be superior in his memorizing of simple elements. Success reduces the prospect of threat and his powers of discrimination are improved. By the time the child first attacks the actual problem of reading, he is completely familiar and at ease with all of the elements of words. Apparently academic challenge in the structured setting creates an optimum of stress so that the child with high anxiety is able to

Table 4 Analysis of Variance[c] of High vs. Low Anxiety

Source of Variance	S. S.	d. f.	Mean Sq.	F
Between method groups	54.27	1	54.27	26.22[a]
Between trait groups	1.87	1	1.87	.90
Interaction	12.09	1	12.09	5.83[b]
Error		151	2.07	

[a] $P < .01$ (2 tail).
[b] $P < .01$ (1 tail).
[c] Corrected for unequal frequencies.

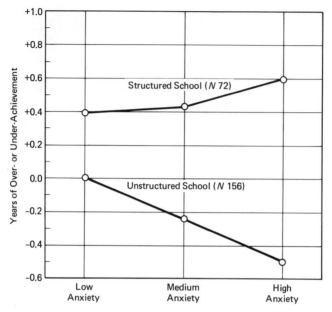

Fig. 2. Graph of test results showing mean school achievement of children categorized as to anxiety.

achieve because he is aroused to an energetic state without becoming confused or panicked.

Sarason et al. (23) present evidence that the anxious child will suffer in the test-like situation, and that his performance will be impaired unless he receives supporting and accepting treatment from the teacher. Although the present study was not a direct replication of their investigations, the results do not confirm their conclusion. Observers, in the two school systems studied here, judged the teachers in the structured schools to be more impersonal and demanding, while the atmosphere in the unstructured school was judged to be more supporting and accepting. Yet the highly anxious child suffered a tremendous disadvantage only in the unstructured school, and performed as well or better than average in the structured setting. Our results lead us to guess that the study by Sarason et al. was done entirely in "modern," unstructured schools. It seems probable to us that the child who perceives danger in the test-like situation associates that danger not only with the authoritative parent-like status of the teacher, but also with the degree of his own adequacy for mastering the situation. It is apparent that warm, understanding treatment alone does not mitigate that threat, and, indeed, may accentuate it in a situation which shifts from accustomed warm support to authoritative discipline on the day of achievement testing.

Shands (24) mentioned two factors that may be effective in relieving anxiety: (a) the availability of a pattern of behavior (the present authors assumed that a structured program should excel in offering a guide to behavior) and (b) the availability of a pattern of relationship, i.e., dependence upon some other person. Sarason *et al.* have concentrated on personal relationships and support as a means of allaying anxiety and presumably making it possible for the child to achieve. The present study shows that even in the absence of such support, the condition of structure is so potent that it will have a significant beneficial effect upon the achievement of the anxious child. But with support available and structure missing, the anxious child risks failure. The feeling the teacher imparts to such a child is evidently not so influential as the extent to which the teacher lets the child know exactly what is expected, and structures the learning in simple, logically ordered steps. Of course teachers should not exacerbate children's anxiety, but it may be that they should be less concerned with allaying anxiety on the assumption that in doing so they are providing a sufficient condition for learning, and more concerned with teaching in a manner that allows the child to make optimum "use" of his existing anxieties.

Sarason *et al.* argue well that the influence of the teacher goes well beyond what is measured in an achievement test, and that the supportive and benign attitudes and behavior they recommend would have far-reaching effects in improving mental health. This is probably true as far as it goes, but the positive value of academic success cannot be discounted, nor can the seriously disruptive effects of school failure or underachievement. We then have to raise the question: Is there any reason why teachers cannot provide both conditions prescribed by Shands?

Many complex interacting factors are at work in any classroom. While the results of a number of studies have indicated the rewarding advantages of warmth and friendliness on the part of the teacher, e.g., Withall's (30) investigations have demonstrated that a greater degree of general progress can be expected in a warm, assuring climate, yet in the present study we find that such emotional support is of little avail with highly anxious children in the absence of structure. This discovery enables us to postulate that if the highly anxious children in the structured school had experienced a greater degree of warmth and security in interpersonal relationships, they might have made even greater gains as Sarason *et al.* would expect.

The implications of these findings may reach further. Interpretations of both psychoanalytic and non-directive concepts have led many workers in the fields of counseling and educational therapy as well as remedial reading to spend months—or even years!—in establishing a "proper" relationship, with no sense of urgency about actual instruction. Meanwhile the children continue to fail in school and their anxiety mounts. It is entirely possible too that when actual tutoring itself is conducted in an unstructured, nondirective way, it cannot meet certain needs of children whose symptoms include anxiety and loss of self-esteem through continued school failure. If ways can be found to accelerate educational progress through more directive and structured teaching without hampering the work of the psychotherapist, the time and professional investment often taken to treat learning difficulties might be reduced.

Differences in the Total Samples

A highly significant difference was found between the two towns in the means of achievement criterion scores ($p < .001$), indicating that the structured school system was more successful in bringing about a generally higher level of student achievement. The magnitude of this difference in terms of grade equivalents as depicted in Figs. 1 and 2 might at first seem spectacular, and an answer to the nation's prayer for guidance in furthering early school performance, but the differences call for qualification. We raise a question first about the causation of the differences, and then state our uncertainty whether such achievement is the most important goal for education at this level.

A possible factor, other than teaching method, in accounting for the differences may be the cultural variations between the two communities. The attempt to equate socioeconomic status may not have been sufficient, based as it was on house and dwelling area. Data established that incomes were lower in the structured school community, and interviewers gained the impression that a larger proportion of income was used there to keep up residence appearances, while certain cultural values seemed less highly prized than in the other community. It is possible that school achievement in primary grades, particularly skill development, is stressed to a greater extent in the homes of the structured school community. At the same time, the conditions ordinarily expected to motivate reading growth were found more prevalent in the homes of the unstructured school community: These homes contain more books, the parents read more to their preschool children, they provide more tutoring, and have higher expectations for future academic and vocational attainments for their children. It appears that there may be two different types of achievement motivation in the two communities, and future research should control this factor.

If the achievement differences between systems are due to the differences in schooling methods, several questions may be asked regarding the desirability of such achievement, and whether or not it is attained at too great a cost. It is probable that more of the total school time in the structured schools was devoted to practice of skills, thereby producing students able to read, spell, and work arithmetic problems, but, for all we know, less advanced in other areas of development. The general scholastic superiority in the structured schools of this study may possibly be attributed to this factor of extra practice.

The achievement test used in this study essentially measures skill in fundamental tool subjects, and does not measure the breadth of the child's understanding and behavior in other respects. For instance, we have no evidence about the creativity of one set of children or the other. We do, however, have scores on the California Test of Personality. Children in the unstructured schools scored higher ($p < .001$) than in the structured schools. This fact may indicate a greater degree of social adjustment.

It may be, too, that the attainment of skill proficiency is the only reward-ing element in the school environment in these particular structured schools, i.e., perhaps the children find that they must achieve in the limited sphere of the Three R's to gain any approbation.

Anderson et al. (2) found that systematic instruction resulted in faster initial progress in skill development but that after a few years, children taught by a technique emphasizing child expression and meaningfulness of each task caught up or surpassed those who continued in the systematized learning situation. Our results, then, do not necessarily point to a clear superiority of one method over another as a recommended approach for teaching *all* chil-dren. Our goal is to call attention to the possible need for creating methods of instruction attuned to the type of pupil, or for seeking a single method that does not handicap any pupils. Indications are that many primary grade children might be helped by a more formal structure in their earlier school learnings.

Test of Interaction of Anxiety and Compulsivity

The results of the study open up several new questions, at least one of which can be investigated through further analysis of these data. When ratings in one personality factor are held constant, will the other factor exert a sig-nificant influence, or are the discovered differences a result of an interaction of anxiety and compulsivity such that neither has an effect without the other?

In this analysis, each school system, the structured and unstructured, is considered separately. Within each system four groups of children are studied: HiComp-HiAnx, HiComp-LoAnx, LoComp-HiAnx, LoComp-LoAnx. In order to obtain larger frequencies in each category, the cutting point for each extreme group was moved closer to the median score on compulsivity and anxiety than in the previous three-way categoriziation. The resulting smaller medium groups were removed from consideration. This recategorization was done without reference to achievement scores, and the cutting points then set so that one-third of the cases would fall in the excluded median group. The mean achievement score of each new group and the frequencies above and below the local medians are presented in Table 5. Results of non-para-metric tests of significance of differences between groups are shown in Tables 6 and 7. Since the overall differences between groups in each school are significant as shown in Table 6, we may interpret each specific difference in terms of the personality categorization.

At once apparent is the successful academic performance of the HiComp-HiAnx children in the structured schools. As a group they are more than a year advanced in achievement! Apparently, when the school systematizes the learning experiences for such children in accordance with their need for orderliness, their anxiety is facilitating rather than disorganizing.[8]

This interpretation is supported by the comparable data of the other groups, each of which is significantly different from the HiComp-HiAnx. The

---

[8] Their "over-achievement" may of course mask serious neurotic problems by causing them to be regarded as model children.

Table 5 Mean Achievement and Frequencies Above and Below Local Medians of Children Categorized According to Combinations of High and Low Anxiety and Compulsivity

	Structured Schools			
	HiComp-HiAnx	HiComp-LoAnx	LoComp-HiAnx	LoComp-LoAnx
Above local median	8	7	3	4
Below local median	0	7	8	9
Mean achievement Criterion scores	+1.24	+.42	+.08	+.08
	Unstructured Schools			
	HiComp-HiAnx	HiComp-LoAnx	LoComp-HiAnx	LoComp-LoAnx
Above local median	11	22	5	10
Below local median	11	11	16	11
Mean achievement Criterion scores	−.22	+.16	−.68	−.14

HiComp-LoAnx children are evidently benefited by lesson structure in satisfying their need for organization but apparently lack some of the drive of the HiComp-HiAnx group.

In the unstructured school, the data again indicate an interaction of the two personality variables. The HiComp-LoAnx group makes the best record while the LoComp-HiAnx group does poorly, and the difference is significant at the .01 level. The child with low anxiety is evidently not threatened by the lack of structure, and if he has the organizational power to systematize his own learning tasks, he is able to master the achievement problem reasonably well. However, when little structure is provided in the school experiences, children with high anxiety and no personal drive to systematize for themselves are in serious trouble. The anxiety serves to disrupt problem-solving ability to a striking degree.

Table 6 Non-Parametric Significance Tests of the Frequencies in Table 5 (Mood's Likelihood Ratio Test)

School System	Groups Compared	d.f.	x^2
Structured	HiComp-HiAnx × HiComp-LoAnx × LoComp-HiAnx × LoComp-LoAnx	3	15.336[b]
Unstructured	HiComp-HiAnx × HiComp-LoAnx × LoComp-Hi-Anx × LoComp-LoAnx	3	9.834[a]

[a] $P < .03$ (2 tail).
[b] $P < .01$ (2 tail).

Table 7 Significance of Differences Between Personality Categories Within Each School System (Tested by Chi Square, Corrected for Continuity. Probabilities are Two-Tailed)

| | Structural Schools | | Unstructured Schools | |
Groups Compared	d. f.	x^2	d. f.	x^2
HiComp-HiAnx × HiComp-LoAnx	1	5.867[b]	1	1.528
LoComp-HiAnx × LoComp-LoAnx	1	.035	1	2.593
HiComp-HiAnx × LoComp-HiAnx	1	10.455[d]	1	3.154[a]
HiComp-LoAnx × LoComp-LoAnx	1	1.033	1	1.929
HiComp-LoAnx × LoComp-LoAnx	1	1.325	1	9.42[e]
HiComp-HiAnx × LoComp-HiAnx	1	9.692[d]	1	.024

[a] $P < .10.$
[b] $P < .02.$
[e] $P < .01.$
[d] $P < .005.$

The same analyses were repeated but with sex held constant, and the results are closely similar to those shown above. We still find for both sexes the poor performance of LoComp-HiAnx in the unstructured school, and in the case of girls (there was a dearth of boys in the comparison) the marked high performance of HiComp-HiAnx in the structured school.

Alternate Interpretation of Structure

What we have really shown definitively, of course, is merely that there are interactions among compulsivity, anxiety, and school system attended. The question is: What causes these findings? Although we have chosen the matter of structure in methods of teaching reading to account for the variations, there may be, in fact, at least three meanings:

(a) The influence of teaching method may reflect *not* the structure of phonics but a generally structured manner of teaching and classroom management, if such existed in one school system more than another. Clarity of directions, explicitness about the applications of principles taught, and precise knowledge on the part of the child as to what is expected of him are characteristics of a structured manner of teaching.

(b) The findings of interaction between pupil personality and teaching method may be due to the structure provided in phonics, along with whatever structure through sequencing and rule-teaching may have existed in other subject-matter areas.

(c) Pupil personality may have been interacting with one or more attributes of teaching method other than the provision of structure.

We have no evidence that interpretation (c) is incorrect, but the concordance with personality theory of the interactions that we discovered leads us to reject it as an explanation of our findings. Our skepticism of interpretation (a) is less easy to defend: We made no measurements of structure in teaching manner. Yet it seems to us that structure of this type might be provided equally well by a teacher in either system.[9] During their three years in school, our 156 whole-word taught children had been taught by 87 different teachers, and our 72 phonics-taught children had experienced 31 different teachers. Individual differences among teachers must have been great in both school systems. We have considerable confidence that if structure in teaching manner had been constantly greater in one system than in the other, this fact would not have gone undetected by our team of observers.

The methods of teaching reading were accurately determined, and the structure of the phonics program was the only clear-cut difference that was found to be constant across school systems. Therefore, we feel justified in accepting interpretation (b) as an explanation of the interactions of personality tendencies with teaching methods. This does not rule out the possibility that if degree of structure in teaching manner were experimentally varied it would produce similar results. It seems probable that structure provided by phonics[10] in conjunction with that in the whole classroom experience would produce even more striking benefits for highly anxious or highly compulsive children.

We must acknowledge an important caution about the provision of structure in teaching. The continuance of structuring too far in later schooling may perpetuate dependence upon those in authority positions. Because of this danger McKeachie (17) wrote of structured techniques, ". . . we still may not grant that it is the most desirable method to be used in our educational system which has as its aim preparation for life in a democracy." We suggest that if particular children's desperate need for structure in certain types of learning can be satisfied during the early school years with failure prevented and their literacy assured, ways to reduce the need for continuance of such structure may be gradually introduced later.

Alternate Interpretations of Personality Characteristics

We have implied a causal relationship—that because of existing tendencies toward compulsivity or anxiety, a child may need structure in teaching. The reverse might be argued, that failure or success in learning to read contributed to or actually caused the personality characteristics that we observed. Since we have no personality measures of the children before they entered

---

[9] Earlier in this paper, it was mentioned that the team of observers had noted a more authoritarian and cold atmosphere in the structured schools. We do not consider this to be evidence of general structure in teaching manner. The more traditional curriculum that was also noted may or may not indicate a greater degree of structure in the organization of subject matter.

[10] Should further investigations show interpretation (b) to be valid, the needed structure might be provided by means other than the alphabetic or phonics approach. Brown (4) describes a method in which the rules of pronunciation and spelling are defined to children early in their study of reading, but word recognition is used from the start for necessary words like "and" and "the," without which meaningful material cannot be read. Also, Richards and Gibson (21) have prepared materials using a structured whole-word program, teaching the child in his first lessons to discriminate letter, sound, and meaning within closely similar sentences.

first grade, we cannot deny this possibility, but our examination of the results leads us to discount it as an explanation of the findings.

The reverse argument gains plausibility from the common observations that children who are retarded in reading often are emotionally maladjusted and that with wise remedial instruction and consequent success in learning to read, the signs of maladjustment may disappear. This is doubtless often true, but the argument is weakened if those signs are not the same as the ones measured by our instruments. And indeed, the behaviors exhibited by pupils and recognized by teachers as maladjustment are not those revealed by our tests of compulsivity and anxiety. Each of our sample children was placed on a five-point scale of emotional adjustment by the first-, second-, and third-grade teachers who had taught them. The scaled continuum ran from 1 (well adjusted and secure), to 5 (poorly adjusted, insecure, apprehensive). Teacher ratings were then compared with our measures of compulsivity and anxiety, and also with school achievement. Nonparametric analysis showed that teacher ratings of maladjustment were negatively related ($P < .05$) to school achievement, but not related to anxiety or compulsivity. Thus children's emotional reactions in the classroom are not indicative of the more subtle personality characteristics measured in our instruments, and the data do not confirm the supposition that the degree of school success actually causes the personality tendencies that we measured.

School failure will probably cause certain manifestations of emotional behavior in most children, but if we are reasoning soundly, it can hardly account for the interactions that we found. While low achievement in the unstructured school may heighten tension, it does not seem reasonable that high achievement would cause a *high* rating on the same test of anxiety for some children in the *structured* school! Also it is not reasonable that compulsivity, as measured by emotionality in certain homelike situations, would be changed substantially by variations of methods of teaching at school. Therefore, we feel justified in interpreting our data to mean that the differential in teaching methods (that we see in the structure provided in systematic phonics) interacts with personality characteristics such that highly anxious and/or highly compulsive children are helped in school achievement by the introduction of structure in teaching.

Possible Applications

Do we seriously envisage the differentiation of teaching methods according to pupils' personality tendencies? Upon first hearing this suggestion, educators may throw up their hands in horror! But homogeneous grouping done by means of achievement or intelligence test scores is, after all, common practice. Already the skilled teacher tries as best he can to individuate instruction for certain pupils within his classroom based upon his intuitive judgments of personal needs. When the results of studies like ours have hardened in the kiln of replication, they may foretell the wide use of personality tests to distinguish those children who will particularly benefit by increased structure (or other techniques) in their school experiences.

A final implication concerns those doing counseling or educational therapy with children afflicted by learning difficulties. In some cases where emphasis has been placed upon allaying anxiety, it may prove effective to provide concomitantly a high degree of structure in the remedial teaching.

SUMMARY

In this study we tested the hypothesis that there is an interaction between teaching method and pupils' personality characteristics in determining school achievement. We anticipated that highly anxious or highly compulsive children who are taught reading initially by "structured" methods stressing phonics will show more achievement by the third grade than similar children taught in other schools where the "unstructured" word recognition approach to beginning reading is used. Our expectation is supported by the findings.

We also examined the effects of personality variables with teaching method held constant. Under structured teaching, compulsive children do substantially better than less compulsive children, but compulsivity makes no difference in the unstructured settings. Anxiety, in contrast, makes no difference under structured conditions; it is in the unstructured settings that high anxiety impedes scholastic performance.

Anxiety and compulsivity, which are not correlated in our sample, interact with one another as well as with teaching method. Children who are both highly anxious *and* highly compulsive over-achieve strikingly in the structured environment, and those who are highly anxious but *low* in compulsivity under-achieve in the unstructured schools.

Thus choice of instructional methods makes a big difference for certain kinds of pupils, and a search for the "best" way to teach can succeed only when the learner's personality is taken into account.

REFERENCES

1. Alpert, R., & Haber, R. N. Anxiety in academic achievement situations. *J. abnorm. soc. Psychol.*, 1960, *61*, 207–215.
2. Anderson, I. H., Hughes, B. O., & Dixon, W. R. Relationships between reading achievement and method of teaching. *Univer. Michigan, sch. of educ. bull.*, 1956, *7*, 104–108.
3. Ausubel, D. P., Schiff, H. M., & Goldman, M. Qualitative characteristics in the learning process associated with anxiety. *J. abnorm. soc. Psychol.*, 1953, *48*, 537–547.
4. Brown, R. *Words and things.* Glencoe, Ill.: Free Press, 1958, 78–79.
5. Bruner, J. S. Personality dynamics and the process of perceiving. In R. Blake and G. Ramsey (Eds.), *Perception: An approach to personality.* New York: Ronald, 1951.
6. Bruner, J. S. *The process of education.* Cambridge, Mass.: Harvard Univer. Press, 1960.

7. Carroll, J. B. The case of Dr. Flesch. *Amer. Psychologist*, 1956, *11*, 158–163.
8. Castaneda, A. Reaction time and response amplitude as a function of anxiety and stimulus intensity. *J. abnorm. soc. Psychol.*, 1956, *53*, 225–228.
9. Castaneda, A., McCandless, B. R., & Palermo, D. S. The children's form of the manifest anxiety scale. *Child Develpm.*, 1956, *27*, 317–326.
10. Fenichel, O. *The psychoanalytic theory of neurosis.* New York: Norton, 1945.
11. Flesch, R. *Why Johnny can't read.* New York: Harper, 1955.
12. Frenkel-Brunswik, Else. The inhibitory effects of an authoritarian home regime on the emotional and cognitive patterns of children. In J. Frosh (Ed.), *Annual survey of psychoanalysis* (Vol. 3). New York: Internat. Univer. Press, 1952.
13. Grimes, J. W. The interaction of pupil personality with methods of teaching reading in determining primary grade achievement. Unpublished doctoral dissertation, Harvard Univer., 1958.
14. Heath, D. H. Individual anxiety thresholds and their effect on intellectual performance. *J. abnorm. soc. Psychol.*, 1956, *52*, 403–408.
15. Korchin, S. J., & Levine, S. Anxiety and verbal learning. *J. abnorm. soc. Psychol.*, 1957, *54*, 234–240.
16. Lowenfeld, J., Rubenfeld, S., & Guthrie, G. M. Verbal inhibition in subception. *J. gen. Psychol.*, 1956, *54*, 171–176.
17. McKeachie, W. J. Anxiety in the college classroom. *J. educ. Res.*, 1951, *55*, 153–160.
18. McKeachie, W. J. Students, groups, and teaching methods. *Amer. Psychologist*, 1958, *13*, 580–584.
19. Murphy, G. *Personality.* New York: Harper, 1947.
20. Noll, J. O. An investigation of the relation of anxiety to learning and retention. *Dissert. Abstr.*, 1955, 15.
21. Richards, I. A., & Gibson, Christine M. *First steps in reading English.* New York: Washington Square Press, 1957.
22. Sarason, I. G. Effect of anxiety and two kinds of motivating instructions on verbal learning. *J. abnorm. soc. Psychol.*, 1957, *54*, 166–171.
23. Sarason, S. B., Davidson, K. S., Lighthall, F. F., Waite, R. R., & Ruebush, B. K. *Anxiety in elementary school children.* New York: Wiley, 1960.
24. Shands, H. C. Anxiety, anaclitic object, and the sign function: Comments on early developments in the use of symbols. *Amer. J. Orthopsychiat.*, 1954, *23*, 84–97.
25. Smith, D. E. P., Wood, R. L., Downer, J. W., & Raygor, A. L. Reading improvement as a function of student personality and teaching method. *J. educ. Psychol.*, 1956, *47*, 47–59.
26. Spence, D. P. A new look at vigilance and defense. *J. abnorm. soc. Psychol.*, 1957, *54*, 103–108.
27. Taylor, Janet A. Drive theory and manifest anxiety. *Psychol. Bull.*, 1956, *53*, 303–320.
28. Weisskopf, Edith A. Intellectual malfunctioning and personality. *J. abnorm. soc. Psychol.*, 1951, *46*, 410–423.
29. Wispe, Lauren G. Evaluating section teaching methods in the introductory course. *J. educ. Res.*, 1951, *45*, 162.
30. Withall, J. The development of the climate index. *J. educ. Res.*, 1951, *45*, 93–100.
31. Witty, P., & Sizemore, R. A. Phonics in the reading program: A review and an evaluation. *Elem. English*, 1955, *32*, 335–371.

Reinforcement Effects of Adult Reactions and Nonreactions on Children's Achievement Expectations

Virginia C. Crandall

FELS RESEARCH INSTITUTE FOR THE STUDY OF HUMAN DEVELOPMENT

There are many times during a child's formative years when his naivete and unfamiliarity with social standards and expectations leave him wondering whether his efforts are defined by others as success or failure. Since in these novel situations he does not yet know how to discriminate the relevant cues

Reprinted from *Child Development*, copyright © 1963 by The Society for Research in Child Development, Inc., *34*, 335–354. By permission.

This study was a part of a larger project, "Parents as identification models and reinforcers of children's achievement development," partially supported by USPH Grant M-2238, Vaughn J. Crandall, senior investigator.

This report is based on a master's thesis presented to the Graduate School of Ohio State University (5). The author wishes to express her appreciation to Dr. Julian Rotter, her thesis advisor; and to Miss Rachel Dennison, principal, and Mr. David Cobaugh, teacher of for proper performance from the situation *per se*, he cannot determine for himself what it is that defines success and must depend on others for this judgment.

Social reinforcements in a *novel* task or in a new social situation, then, give the child information which helps him to select the proper response. While adult reactions to a child's behavior in a *familiar* situation may continue to strengthen a habit and maintain the child's behavior, they probably no longer have as many informative and selective properties. Parent-child interactions in the latter, familiar situations were not the focus of this study. The interest here was in the possible active, informative reinforcement properties of adult nonreaction in new situations where children cannot yet define success or failure for themselves.

It is commonly thought by parents and teachers that successful training of children can be achieved by praising correct performances and ignoring mistakes on the assumption that the "ignoring" (or nonreaction) is neutral in its reinforcement effect. It is quite possible, however, that an adult's ignoring a child's error is perceived by the child differently depending upon his previous history of reinforcement with that adult. Thus, the child who has been reared by "usually praising" parents may interpret their occasional silences as evidence of disapproval and behave as though he has been negatively reinforced. Conversely, the child who has been subjected to a "usually criticizing" adult may perceive silence as unverbalized approval and behave as though having been positively reinforced.

To examine the credibility of the above propositions, three groups of children were subjected to different treatments in the current study. One was provided a series of positive adult reactions followed by a series of nonreactions. A second received nonreactions followed by another similar series. A third group received negative reactions followed by nonreactions. The dependent variable of the investigation was the child's Expectancy-of-Success estimate assessed before and after each series of adult reactions, the interest being in whether increases or decreases in judgments of success would follow such treatments. The nature of the task involved was such that the child could not determine, without being told, the success or failure of his own performance. It was hypothesized that: "Adult nonreaction, following either positive or negative verbal reactions, will take on reinforcement value of the sign opposite to the reactions which preceded it."

In addition to experimentally manipulating positive and negative reactions preceding nonreaction, the present experiment also investigated the possible influence of the child's preexperimental history of such positive and negative reactions from his parents. A given child, depending on the particular proclivities of his parents, might have met with more positive reaction than negative reaction, or vice versa. Such a background was felt to be a

the Mills Lawn Elementary School of Yellow Springs, Ohio, and to Mr. Robert Martin, principal, and Mrs. Roger Middleswart, secretary of the Fairborn Central Junior High School of Fairborn, Ohio, for their cooperation in securing subjects for this study.

possible predictor of a child's response to more of the same adult behavior to which he was accustomed, or, on the other hand, to behavior with which he was unfamiliar. A number of previous research findings concerning satiation and sequence effects (1, 7, 9) indicate that the same reaction, given over a period of time to the same individual, begins to lose some of its reinforcing strength and also that a single new reinforcement of opposite sign introduced after a series of similar reinforcements will cause a significant change in expectancy. Thus, it was anticipated that the change in a child's Expectancy-of-Success in the experimental situation would be greater if the original verbal reactions given him, as well as the reinforcement value acquired by succeeding nonreaction, were not congruent with the kind of reactions he had come to expect from his parents.

The Ss were divided into two groups on the basis of a questionnaire which elicited their perceptions of their parents' "positiveness" or "negativeness," and half of each experimental treatment group was made up of Ss with each kind of history. The individual difference hypothesis predicted that: "The Ss who had 'positive' parents would react less to the experimenter's positive verbal reactions than Ss of 'negative' parents. Also, it was anticipated that, if nonreaction following positive verbal reactions does indeed take on negative reinforcing properties, then the Ss of positive parents should react more strongly to such experimenter nonreaction than Ss of negative parents. Conversely, the children of negative parents should react less to the experimenter's negative reactions than Ss of positive parents and more to the nonreaction following negative reaction."

METHOD

Subjects

All assessment measures were first pretested. Then, 169 eighth grade boys were given the Perception-of-Parent Questionnaire, and from that group 90 were selected to be used as the experimental sample. Forty-five of these Ss had scored at or above the medians of positive responses on both the mother and father portions of the questionnaire and were designated as the "high parent-positive" Ss. The other 45 had scores below the medians on both parts of the questionnaire and were designated as the "low parent-positive" Ss. The 45 "high" Ss were then assigned to three subgroups of 15 Ss each, as were the 45 "low" Ss, one high and one low subgroup for each of the three experimental treatments. Ss were individually matched across treatment groups on the basis of their parent questionnaire scores.

Procedure

Child's perception of amount of positive parental reaction to his behavior (antecedent variable.)   Originally, a two-part questionnaire of 60 items was devised, composed of 30 questions each pertaining to the child's mother and to his father. This was given to the pretest sample. The items represented widely varying parent-child interaction situations to which a parent might be apt to respond in some positive or negative manner.

Each of the items presented a forced choice alternative in which the child was required to make an evaluation of his parents' feelings, presumably on the basis of whether they usually reacted positively or negatively to this behavior. Some examples of the items are:

When you do school work at home, does your mother seem to:
——————— Feel you make quite a few mistakes?
——————— Feel your work is pretty good?
When you hang around the house because the weather is bad, does your mother seem to feel:
——————— You are kind of a bother and in the way?
——————— She kind of enjoys having you around?[1]

The portion of the questionnaire concerning the child's father was composed chiefly of items which were duplicates of those contained in the mother portion of the questionnaire. However, occasional substitutions of items were made where the content was not applicable to a father-son situation. Thus, of the two examples above, the first item was used in both parts of the questionnaire; the second item does not appear on the father questionnaire, and a substitute was used in its place. Of the original 60 items given the pretest sample, those which discriminated with at least an 8–16 split were retained to make up the 40 items administered to the experimental sample.

Because this was a forced-choice questionnaire, only the positive checks were needed for the statistical analysis. An S with a "low" parent-positive score had checked few of the positive alternatives and most of the negative alternatives and can be said to perceive his parents as usually reacting negatively to him.

Sequences of adult reaction and nonreaction to children's performance on an angle-matching task (experimental treatment). The task used was a revision of one devised by James (8). The present form consisted of 17 6 by 6

[1] A history of reinforcement questionnaire usually posits a list of parental reactions such as monetary rewards, deprivation of privileges, kisses, isolation, gold stars, etc., from which Ss may choose those which are used. The item stems in this case, however, were constructed to read, "How does your mother *feel* about . . ." not because it was thought that a child could somehow mystically intuit his parents' attitudes, but because such a stem was thought to allow the child to take into account *all* the cues (both obvious and minimal) by which the parent had communicated his approval or disapproval. In this way, it was hoped to tap a more inclusive sample of parental responses. By asking the questions in this form, it also seemed that the child would be more likely to assess the total range of responses his own parent used, with the relative strengths and frequencies of each, and report in his answer the reinforcement value to him of the composite of these. This method was thought to avoid the assumption present in many of the measures used to assess an individual's reinforcement history, that any particular parental reaction or combination of reactions must have the same reinforcement value to the child as it is assumed to have in the culture.

inch white cards on which were drawn angles of varying degrees of acuity. Five of these cards were used as "standards" and were mounted on a bulletin board placed 8 feet in front of the *S*s. An *S*'s task was to match each of the remaining 12 cards to the appropriate standard as *E* presented these stimuli to him one by one. The angles used as standards were 45, 55. 65, 75, and 110 degrees and were arranged in the following order from left to right on the bulletin board: 45, 75, 110, 55, and 65. Those used as stimuli for judgment were three each of 50, 60, 70, and 80 degree angles also presented to the *S* in nonconsecutive order. Thus, although the *S* was led to believe that each of the stimulus cards matched one of the standards, none were exact matches. They all fell equidistant in size between two of the standards, and the differences between the standards angles were barely discriminable. Finally, the apexes of all the angles on both the standards and the stimulus cards were at slightly differently points of the compass.

The experimental task was specifically chosen for its novel and ambiguous qualities. This made it possible to manipulate the *E*'s reactions in the desired manner because the *S* could not tell, from the task materials, whether he was right or wrong. Thus, as in everyday life, when the situation was novel to the child, he was unable to learn directly from the task what criterion or criteria define success and was made dependent on the social reinforcements given by the adult. This task also made it possible to use the same number and sequence of verbal reactions to nonreactions in the positive and negative treatments.

As each child entered the testing room, he was seated and given the following instructons:

> This is a test to see how well boys your age can match up figures. You'll see, if you look closely, that those figures up there (indicating standards) are slightly different sizes. I have some more cards here in my hand with the same size figures on them. Each of the figures on these cards in my hand matches in size one of those figures up there (indicating standards), but these figures are turned round, upside down, sideways—every which way. Those cards up there (standards) have numbers on them so that you can tell me, when I show you each figure, which one it matches. Remember, you are matching by size, not position. Do you understand?

The child's initial expectancy estimate (to be described later) was then obtained, and *E* seated herself at the side and slightly behind the *S* in order to prevent the child from observing any facial expressions or mannerisms of *E* which might contradict the verbal positive or negative reactions she administered.

E then presented the stimulus cards to the *S* one by one, and *S* attempted to match them with the standards. Various phrases, such as "Here's the first one," "Here's another," ". . . and another one," were used in a fixed sequence to introduce the cards for all groups. The reactions of the examiner to *Ss*' decisions in the positive group were, "That's right," "That one's right," "That one's right, too," etc., given in a predetermined sequence. For *Ss* in the negative reaction group the E used the negative counterparts of the positive responses, and in the same order, i.e., "That's wrong," "That one's wrong," "That one's wrong, too," etc. Following trials 3, 4, and 7 of the 12 trials, Ss in both groups received no reaction from E so that the situation would seem reasonably realistic; it was felt that the child might become suspicious if every single one of his matches were "right" or every one "wrong." For the control group, no response was given by the examiner to the attempted matches.

A second expectancy estimate was obtained from each S at the end of the first 12 trials. Then 12 additional trials were administered to all Ss using the same stimuli as well as the same introductory phrases on the presentation of each card. However, in this second series E made no reactions to any of an S's decisions.

Changes in expectancy estimates (dependent variable). Expectancy was defined as "the probability held by an individual that a specific reinforcement or group of reinforcements will occur in a given situation." In this case, the reinforcement which the S obtained was the information, provided by the E's reactions (and nonreactions), on which to base his judgment of success in comparing well with his peers in the angle-matching "test." The children's expectancy changes were thus used as a measure of the direction and strength of the reinforcement properties of the adult E's reactions and nonreactions.

Three expectancy estimates were obtained from each child in the following manner: Immediately after he was read the instructions for the angle-matching task and shown the task materials, but before he had participated in any of the matching trials, he was given a sheet of paper with 50 small stick figures drawn in a vertical line down the length of the sheet. The top figure was labeled "Does the best on this test," the bottom was labeled "Does the poorest on this test." The following directions were then read to him:

> Now before we start—I am giving this test to a lot of boys your age. Some of them are very good at this kind of thing, some are not particularly good. Here is a paper with a line of boys on it. As you see, here is the boy who does the very best on this test here at the top of the page. Here is the boy who does it the worst at the bottom, and these are all the boys in between (motioning). Now, before we start the test, put a circle around the boy you think you will turn out to be when I get all through testing everyone.

After the first set of treatment conditions (the positive and the negative reactions for the two experimental groups and the nonreaction for the control group), directions for the second expectancy estimate were read to the S. These were:

> Now that you have had a chance to actually try the test, please indicate on this fresh sheet how well you think you *actually did*, compared to the other boys. Circle the boy you think you will turn out to be.

Pretesting had revealed that many of the children had difficulty remembering where they had placed their first estimate on the sheet of stick figures. Therefore, each S was given his original estimate to look at so that he could indicate more accurately how much better or worse he felt he had done than he had originally expected. Each S was then told, "All right. Now we are going to go through the test again." They were then readministered the 12-trial series with no reactions from E to any of their attempts to match the stimuli with the standards.

The third expectancy estimate, assessed after the nonreaction series, was obtained in much the same manner as the second estimate. S was shown his second estimate, given a fresh sheet with the stick figures on it, and asked:

> Now this second time you took the test, how well do you feel you did it? Which boy do you think you will turn out to be on this second test? Circle the boy you think you will be.

In summary, the positive reaction group gave an initial expectancy estimate, was administered a 12-trial series with nine positive reactions from E, gave a second expectancy estimate, was administered 12 more trials with no reactions, and then gave a third and final expectancy estimate. The negative reaction group gave an initial expectancy estimate, was administered 12 trials with nine negative reactions from E, gave a second expectancy estimate, was administered 12 more trials with no reactions from E, and gave a third and final expectancy estimate. The control group gave an initial expectancy estimate, received 12 more trials with no reaction, and gave a final expectancy estimate.

Statistical Treatment

In order to test hypothesis I, that children's expectancy estimates would change depending on adult verbal reactions and nonreactions, change scores between each S's successive expectancy estimates were used as the measures of the dependent variable. That is, the difference between his first expectancy estimate (Ex_1) and his second (Ex_2) was computed, indicating changes in the children's expectancies in the first condition (as a result of the positive reactions, the nonreactions, and the negative reactions in the three treatment groups, respectively). In like manner, change scores between the children's second (Ex_2) and third (Ex_3) expectancy estimates were computed and used as a measure of their responses to the nonreaction trials following positive reaction for the first treatment group, of nonreaction following negative reaction for the second treatment group, and of nonreaction following nonreaction for the control group. Separate tests of difference were thus necessary for each of the two aforementioned dependent measures, first between each experimental treatment and the control group and between high and low parent-approval subgroups within each treatment for the first change scores.

Variance ratio tests of homogeneity revealed that all six subgroups were homogeneous as to variance when matched on the antecedent variable, the Perception-of-Parent Questionnaire. This was also true of their first change scores during the experiment. However, this test revealed that there were significant differences in the variances among the groups on the second change scores. Therefore, nonparametric Wilcoxon tests of difference were employed throughout.

RESULTS AND DISCUSSION

Before the tests of the hypotheses are presented, it may be of general interest to note that Ss in all three treatment groups started with absolute Ex_1 estimates which were not significantly different from one another. Then, after diverging widely on their Ex_2 estimates, their final Ex_3 estimates returned to a point where these were again not significantly different from one another. Wilcoxon matched-pairs signed-rank tests (13) indicated that there were no significant (one-tail)[2] differences between the Ex_1 scores of the three groups, nor between their Ex_3 scores.

Figure 1 presents results of the experiment as they pertain to the total experimental groups. The figure is based on the median *change* scores of the groups, rather than their absolute Ex_1, Ex_2, and Ex_3 scores, in order that the reader may better evaluate the relative slope of the rises and falls in the expectancies of the three groups of children (see p. 488).

Changes in Expectancy Resulting from Experimental Treatments
The situational hypothesis predicted that an adult's nonreaction to children's achievement efforts following that adult's positive or negative verbal reactions would produce expectancy changes in directions opposite to those produced by the adult's preceding verbal reactions.

A group of experiments by Buss and colleagues (4, 6), Buchwald (2, 3), and Meyer and Seidman (10, 11) have some relevance here because these studies investigated the possible acquisition of reinforcement value to an adult's nonreactions. However, because of the experimental paradigm they employed, the relatively consistent data obtained from acquisition series by the various investigators do not lend themselves to unequivocal theoretical interpretation. This is evidenced by the fact that three different interpretations are made by the three groups of fairly similar results. The difficulty seems to lie in the use of varying numbers and sequences of verbal reactions and nonreactions in the same acquisition series, allowing for different interpretations of the function of the verbal reactions and the nonreactions in contributing to the trials-to-criterion or errors-to-criterion used as dependent measures.

[2] Tests of significance of difference of all remaining data are two-tailed unless otherwise noted. When one-tailed tests have been used, these were the most conservative measure since Wilcoxon tests of differences were, in these cases, used to establish similarity.

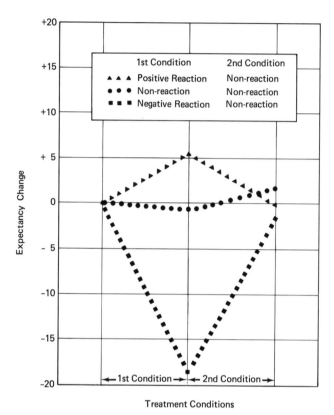

Fig. 1. Median changes in expectancy estimates for the total treatment groups.

In some of these studies, extinction series and counter-conditioning or reversal learning series were run in an attempt to better disentangle the effects of the various reactions. In these cases, however, the empirical data vary sufficiently from study to study to make it difficult for a reader to reach a consistent conclusion as to the contribution of the strength of the verbal reactions and the direction and strength of the nonreactions used in the counter-conditioning and reversal learning series and of the effect of the reactions and nonreactions used in the acquisition series run prior to the extinction conditions.

The present study attempted to investigate one of the same theoretical issues, the possible informative reinforcement properties of nonreaction, by simplifying the procedure previously used. In the present case, separate measurements were made of the effects of similar series of positive reactions as of negative reactions, and of a series of nonreactions following each of these, as well as the effects of nonreactions which were not preceded by

Table 1 Differences Between First Expectancy Changes of the Total Groups as a Function of Verbal Reaction Treatments

Treatments	Sum of Rank with Least Sign	Total No. of ds Having a Sign	p
Positive vs. Negative	.0	30	.0001
Negative vs. Nonreaction	23.5	30	.001
Positive vs. Nonreaction	54.0	28	.01

either verbal reaction. However, Expectancy-of-Success, the dependent measure of the current investigation which permitted the separation of measurement and the use of comparable numbers and sequences of reactions and nonreactions, allows only tenuous generalizations to the other kinds of learning problems previously studied by the aforementioned researchers.

In the current study, an analysis of the first change scores for the positive and negative groups, as compared with those of the control group, was initially carried out to determine whether or not the E's verbal reactions were, in fact, reinforcing. The fact that 26 of the 30 subjects in the positive reaction condition raised their expectancy estimates, and 29 of the 30 subjects in the negative condition lowered theirs, clearly indicated that these reinforcements were effective.

To determine more definitively whether each of the verbal reaction treatments was significantly different from each other treatment, Wilcoxon matched-pairs signed-rank tests were run between each possible combination of treatments since these tests account for amount of change, as well as direction of change. The results are presented in Table 1.

Table 1 shows that each verbal reaction of the E was actually reinforcing in the expected directions. E's positive reactions raised the children's expectations of success, and her negative reactions lowered their expectancy estimates in comparison with her nonreaction.

Now, the question arises as to whether the E's nonreactions following her verbal reactions were actually opposite in reinforcement value to her preceding behaviors. A crude estimate of these effects is evidenced by the fact that, of the 30 subjects in the positive-nonreaction group, 27 lowered their estimates as the result of subsequent E nonreactions. Of the 30 children in the negative-nonreaction group, 28 raised their estimates following E's nonreaction. Again, to determine whether the effects of the nonreaction treatments (following positive, negative, and nonreaction series) were significantly different from each other, Wilcoxon matched-pairs signed-rank tests between each combination of treatments were run. Table 2 presents these results.

From an inspection of Table 2, it can be seen that, not only were the nonreaction expectancy changes significantly different when they followed positive reaction from those which followed negative reaction, but each of these was also significantly different from the changes which occurred in the control group.

Table 2 Differences Between Second Expectancy Changes of the Total Groups as a Function of Nonreaction Treatments

Treatments	Sum of Rank with Least Sign	Total No. of ds Having a Sign	p
Pos.-Non. vs. Neg.-Non.	.0	30	.0001
Neg.-Non. vs. Non-Non.	1.0	30	.0001
Non-Non. vs. Pos.-Non.	10.0	30	.0001

Finally, a Wilcoxon matched-pairs signed-rank test was run between the 30 control Ss' first change scores and their own second change scores. The purpose of this analysis was to determine whether any significant difference had occurred in the expectancy change scores for those children who had received no initial verbal reactions from the E against which to contrast her nonreaction. No significant difference was found.

The situational hypothesis was thus substantiated. The data demonstrated that an adult's silence (or nonreaction) takes on reinforcement value for a child when that silence has been preceded by verbal reinforcements from that adult and fails to do so in the absence of preceding verbal reactions. The fact that the nonreaction change scores of the positive and negative experimental groups were so different from each other as well as from the control group in both direction and amount of change when all groups met with the same nonreaction from E in the second condition indicates that the children's expectancies must have been dependent on what had transpired earlier. The learning process in the child seems to be one of comparing or contrasting the meaning of the adult's silence with the adult's previous active reactions to his behavior. The children who had experienced previous positive reaction from E interpreted her subsequent nonreaction as negative; the children who had experienced previous negative reaction interpreted subsequent E nonreaction as positive.

Absolute Strengths of Reinforcement of Positive vs. Negative Reactions and of Nonreaction Following Positive and Negative Reactions

In the Buss, Buchwald, and Meyer and Seidman studies mentioned earlier, E said nothing to S's *correct* responses in "nothing–wrong" treatments and nothing to his *incorrect* responses in "right–nothing" treatments. Thus, all acquisition series were combinations of trials in which verbal reinforcements of one sign had been given and other trials to which nothing had been said. The investigators all found that the "right-nothing" reinforcement combination was less effective in concept acquisition and discrimination problems than "nothing-wrong." Whether this was due to the superior strength of "wrong" as a reinforcer or to the shifting value of "nothing" is difficult to determine since the ratio and sequence of verbal reactions to nonreactions could not be controlled. The findings of the current study are not directly comparable with those of the foregoing investigations because the dependent variable was different from those previously employed. However, the differential strength of "that's right" and "that's wrong" in changing children's expectancies of success could be assessed in the present case since the positive and negative treatments were directly comparable with one another as to number and sequence of verbally reinforced trials.

A Wilcoxon matched-pairs signed-rank test was run using the amount of change of Ss experiencing the positive reaction condition versus the amount of change of those Ss undergoing the negative reaction condition. For this test, only the *amount* of change of Ss' first expectancy change scores was considered, as long as the change was in the proper direction, i.e., rising under positive treatment and falling under negative treatment. This analysis produced a sum of rank of least sign of 6 which was significant at the .0001 level of confidence. The negative adult reaction employed in the present study was much more effective in lowering expectancy estimates than was the positive reaction in increasing expectations for success.

The above data are not intended to demonstrate the superiority of "negative" versus "positive" reinforcements in the theoretical sense. As long as we are currently limited to defining the strength of a reinforcement by the effect of the event on some dependent variable, it is impossible to determine whether such effects are actually produced by the "positiveness" or "negativeness" *per se* of the reinforcement, or whether such effects occur because of other properties of the reinforcements being studied. For example, "right" might empirically have weaker reinforcement strength in changing behavior, not because it is positive, but because it is used so much more frequently in normal social intercourse in our general culture that it has lost some of its original reinforcement value. Other possible reasons for the differing reinforcement effects of a given positive or negative reaction will occur to the reader, e.g., the sequence in which they appear, the need system involved, the individual's reinforcement history, etc. These, as well as other factors, may account for the empirical fact that a given reinforcement under investigation has a demonstrated degree of strength in changing behavior. Therefore, the present writer does not mean to imply that the data of the current study are presented as evidence of the superiority of "negative" versus "positive" reinforcements, in the theoretical sense, and there is nothing in the Buss, Buchwald, and Meyer and Seidman articles to lead one to believe that they are attempting to interpret their data as proof of this theoretical question either. Empirically, the present study has shown that "wrong" is a more potent reinforcer, but nothing can be said concerning the reasons why this is the case, nor about the attributes of "positiveness" and "negativeness" as these contribute to the strength of social reinforcements.

To determine the relative acquired reinforcement strengths of an adult's nonreaction following different kinds of verbal reactions, a Wilcoxon matched-pairs signed-rank test was run on the second change scores of Ss in the two experimental treatments. For this procedure, again, the change scores were used with the signs removed in all cases in which the change was in the predicted direction. In this case, the test resulted in a sum of rank of least sign of 45 which was significant at the .0001 level of confidence. This demonstrates that nonreaction following *negative* verbal reaction has a much greater reinforcement strength in changing expectancy estimates than does nonreaction following positive reaction. Whether the greater strength of nonreaction following negative reaction is due to the greater reinforcement strength of the predecessive negative reactions or to their negative sign is undetermined. It can only be said that, for whatever reason, the adult's nonreactions following her negative reactions produced greater changes in the boys' expectations than nonreaction following the positive reaction treatment. However, the fact that, not only does adult nonreaction acquire opposite reinforcement signs, but that it also acquires differing *amounts* of reinforcement strength depending on what has preceded it is taken as additional evidence of the active reinforcing qualities of silence.

Changes in Expectancy Relating to Differences in Perceived Parental Reaction

What can be said concerning individual differences in the Ss' reactions to the experimental treatments they encountered? Do they, as was hypothesized, react more strongly to the E's verbal reactions and/or the acquired reinforcement value of her nonreactions if these reinforcements are not congruent with reactions which they are accustomed to receiving from their parents? Wilcoxon unpaired replicates tests *(14)* between the high and low subgroups in the three treatments were run. Figure 2 represents these results graphically.

Of the three comparisons made of the high versus the low subgroups in the first condition (positive verbal reaction, negative verbal reaction, and nonreaction for the control group), only one difference was significant. The high parent-positive subgroup in the positive experimental condition obtained a lesser rank total of 180.0 which was significant at the .05 level of confidence. Those Ss who perceived their parents as responding positively to their behavior did, as hypothesized, raise their expectancy estimates less under the E's positive verbal reactions than Ss who perceived their parents as responding negatively to their actions.

Of similar comparisons made for the second experimental condition (nonreaction in all three treatment groups) using the second change scores, one significant difference also occurred. It should be remembered that the 30 Ss in the control group as a whole did not change their scores significantly between the first and second nonreaction series. However, in the second condition, when the high parent-positive Ss in the control group were compared with the low Ss, the former obtained a lesser rank total of 183.0 which was significant at the .05 level of confidence. The negative-parent boys raised their expectancies more during the second series of examiner nonreactions in the control condition than did the positive-parent boys. It appears that more of the boys in the parent-negative subgroup interpreted the experimenter's silence in the second nonreaction series as having positive reinforcement value than did the boys in the parent-positive subgroup. This would seem to

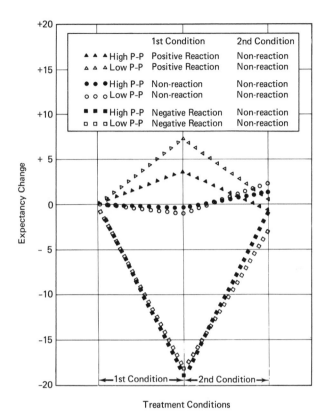

Fig. 2. Medium changes in expectancy estimates for subgroups based on high and low perception-of-parent questionnaire scores.

lend some additional support to the noncongruent hypotheses of the study, i.e., when boys who are accustomed to negative responses from their parents are met with no reaction even from a strange examiner, they seem to impute implied approval for her nonreaction. The implication seems to be that the contrast conditions necessary for the acquisition of reinforcement value to nonreaction exist or generalize *across* adult reinforcers, as well as existing within the experience of the child with one specific reinforcing agent.[3]

Thus, using the children's perceptions of their parents' positive or negative reactions to their behaviors as an antecedent predictor for individual differences in response to the experimental treatments resulted in only two

---

[3] However, a replication of the control group portion (only) of this experiment has since been completed as a separate study. Using a new but similar sample, and a different examiner, no differences between high and low parent-positive subgroups were found. Appreciation is expressed to Elinor Waters who conducted this replication experiment.

significant differences. These differences provide some slight substantiation of the noncongruent hypothesis, that boys who are unaccustomed to parent reaction of a given sign will respond more to that reaction from the examiner than boys who are accustomed to such experiences.

Changes in Expectancy Relating to Differences
in Generalized Expectancy of Success

Another possible predictor of the children's differences in response to E's reactions in the present experiment is the generalized expectancy of success in achievement situations which Ss brought to the experimental task. It was decided to reanalyze the data in reference to this predictor variable.

Generalized Expectancy as presently used is consistent with Rotter's definition of that concept. He defines Generalized Expectancy as "the generalization of the expectancies for the same or similar reinforcements to occur in a present situation as occurred in past situations for the same or functionally related behaviors" (12, p. 166). He maintains that, "It would seem logical or in accord with common-sense observations that in a relatively novel situation a person's expectancies would be largely a function of such generalizations. Or, stated differently, that the GE effect (effect of a generalized expectancy of success) will weigh more heavily in situations that might be described as novel than in those in which the subject has had a series of experiences" (12, p. 166). It will be remembered that the task presented to the Ss in the current study was especially chosen for its novel qualities. As such, it may be presumed that the first expectancy estimate the boys made (Ex_1), before they had any experience with the "test," might be representative of their generalized expectancies of success in "functionally related" past achievement situations.

In order to formulate hypotheses for the prediction of individual differences in the boys' reactions to the treatment situations on the basis of their generalized expectancies, it may be helpful to consider the possible relation between generalized expectancy for success in achievement situations and the amount of parental approval the children had reported they experienced. Perhaps it can be assumed that frequent parental praise in a number of everyday parent-child interactions will result in a child's feeling of self-confidence in new situations. In other words, it might be assumed that such consistent positive parental reactions may help to produce a high generalized expectancy of success for the many new tasks and situations which confront a growing child. A child's generalized expectancy of success might be seen then, at least partially, as a derivative of his past history of parental approval and his expectancy of success as a currently measurable personality variable which should produce similar effects on changes in expectancy in a given immediate situation as would the more-removed antecedent predictor. This enables the same predictions to be made from both predictor variables.

Because of the theoretical relationship posited between these two variables, i.e., Ss' generalized expectancy of success and their perceptions of their parents' positive reactions, a Pearson product-moment correlation was run between the children's first expectancy estimates and their scores on the

Perception-of-Parent Questionnaire. We would not, of course, expect an extremely high correlation between these two measures, since, obviously, by the time a child has reached the eighth grade level many other potent influences, such as, for example, the reactions of his peer group and of his teachers, will have affected his generalized expectancy of success. However, the product-moment correlation between parental positiveness and the child's generalized expectancy of success as first measured in this novel situation should show some relationship. The correlation obtained between the two measures was .26, significant at the .02 level of confidence for an N of 90 subjects and substantiates the moderate degree of relationship to be expected from these two predictor variables.

To proceed with the data analysis using generalized expectancy (GE) of success as an individual difference predictor, each of the treatment groups was divided at the median of the Ex_1 estimates for all 30 Ss in that treatment. This procedure resulted in six subgroups of subjects, one high in GE and one low in GE in each treatment. However, the variance in the subgroup Ex_1 estimates differed so widely that individuals could not be matched across groups. The variance ratio test yielded an F of 5.58 which indicated heterogeneity of groups at the .01 level of confidence. Therefore, parametric t tests again were not applied, and the nonparametric Wilcoxon tests of difference were used.

The high and low expectancy subgroups were compared in each of the first experimental treatments (positive reaction from the E, and negative reaction from her in the two experimental treatments and the first series of nonreactions for the control condition). In these analyses two significant differences appeared. Subjects with a low generalized expectancy of success did, in fact, change their expectancy of success more as a result of *positive* reaction treatment than did Ss with a high generalized success expectancy (the high subgroup obtained a lesser rank total of 173.5, significant at the .02 level of probability). In the *negative* reaction treatment, the high GE subgroup changed their estimates more as a result of this treatment than did subjects with low generalized expectancies (lesser rank total was 168.0, significant at the .01 level of probability).

In the second condition (nonreaction in all three treatments), Ss' second change scores showed no significant differences between subgroups in any of the treatments.

Thus, it is evident that neither the antecedent variable (amount of parent positiveness) nor the personality variable (height of generalized expectancy produced many significant individual differences in the present study. Let us summarize those which were found:

1. Low parent-approval children raised their expectancies more to the verbalized positive reactions of the experimenter than did high parent-approval children (.05 level).

2. Low parent-approval children raised their expectancies more to continued examiner nonreaction (the second series of nonreactions) in the control condition than did high parent-approval children (.05 level).

3. Children with low generalized expectancies of success raised their expectancies more as a result of adult positive reaction than did children with high generalized expectancies of success (.02 level).

4. Children with high generalized expectancies of success dropped their expectancies more as a result of adult negative reaction than did children with low generalized expectancies (.01 level).

While neither predictor resulted in many significant differences in the children's reactions to the experimental treatments, still those differences which were found seem to lend some support to the individual difference hypothesis of this study: Children who are unaccustomed to reactions of a given sign from their parents or have achieved a generalized expectancy for success in achievement situations which corresponds with the kind of parental reactions they are used to, will change their expectancies more as the result of reactions from the E which are not congruent with those they have come to expect and less when they meet with reactions with which they are familiar. A child who is used to being praised reacts more strongly to being told he is wrong than does a child who is accustomed to negative reactions, and vice versa.

Empirically, height of generalized expectancy (amount of self-confidence) was more highly associated with significant differences than was the parent measure. The differences which were obtained from GE were at somewhat better levels of confidence ($p = .01$ and $.02$) than those resulting from the parent questionnaire (both $p = .05$). This is to be expected, since previous research has indicated that better prediction is usually obtained from an immediate personality characteristic than from an historical antecedent predictor, as well as the fact that Generalized Expectancy is more closely allied to the dependent variable, changes in expectancy, than is parental approval.

A replication and extension of the present study is currently underway, using Ss who have actually been matched and divided on the empirically better predictor variable, Generalized Expectancy, to further test this "noncongruent" hypothesis. If the noncongruent hypothesis is more clearly substantiated, then we may feel that we have begun to attain some leverage on the problem of individual differences in reinforcement sensitivity to the same objectively defined social reactions.

Now, if at this point the reader will again refer to Fig. 1, inspection will reveal that both nonreaction series appear to have reinforcement effects equivalent in strength to the actual verbalized reinforcements which preceded them. While it has been predicted that nonreaction would acquire active reinforcing properties, it had seemed so improbable that the strength of such unspoken reinforcement would be as great as that of overtly verbalized reactions that this possibility had not even been considered. However, when such a result seemed apparent by inspection, it was decided to apply Wilcoxon matched-pairs signed-rank tests to the Ss' first vs. their second change scores in the positive and in the negative treatment groups to determine whether statistically there was actually no significant difference between the two. The Wilcoxon test of the first vs. the second change scores of the positive treatment group resulted in a sum of rank of at least sign of 132.0 which was not significant (one-tailed test of difference). The same test applied to the first and second change scores of the negative treatment group yielded a sum of rank of least sign of 199.0 which was also not significant (one-tailed test). Thus, it appears that nonreaction is roughly equal in reinforcement strength to the verbal reinforcement which precedes it, although, of course, opposite in direction.

While the results of this study seem to indicate that there are active reinforcing properties in nonreaction, it is also possible to conceive of the nonreaction conditions in the present study as extinction series. Usually the concept of extinction is applied to the diminution of correct *performance* previously acquired by means of reinforcement. However, in the present case, we might think of the positive reaction treatment as reinforcing a greater *expectancy for success* and of the negative reaction treatment as reinforcing a growing *expectancy of failure*. Then, in the nonreaction conditions perhaps the acquired expectancies have simply returned to their original levels. Perhaps the reinforcement effects were "washed away," or dissipated, or forgotten, as is frequently considered to take place during extinction. In other words, this may be a passive, neutral, forgetting process, rather than an active, contrasting, learning one. A current replication and extension of the present study, previously referred to, will attempt to test these two alternatives more definitively.

SUMMARY

This study was designed to test the possibility that an adult's nonreaction (silence) may acquire active reinforcing properties for children. Hypotheses tested predicted: I, that such nonreactions acquire reinforcement value of the sign opposite to that of verbal reinforcements which preceded them (situational hypothesis) and II, that children who are accustomed to reactions of one sign (e.g., positive reactions such as praise and negative reactions such as criticism) from their parents are influenced more by verbal treatments in the experimental situation which carry the opposite sign, or by nonreaction treatments which have acquired the opposite reinforcement sign, than are children who do not have these experiences (individual difference hypothesis).

The sample was composed of 90 eighth grade boys, half of whom had scored above the medians on both parts of a questionnaire designed to assess each S's perception of the amount of positive reaction he felt his mother and his father displayed toward his everyday behavior. The other half of the sample was comprised of boys who scored below the medians on both parts of the questionnaire. Fifteen "high" Ss and 15 "low" Ss were assigned to one of three experimenter-reaction treatments on an ambiguous and novel angle-matching task. The first treatment consisted of E positive reactions followed by E nonreactions; the second (control condition) consisted of a series of E nonreactions followed by another series of E nonreactions; the third treatment consisted of E negative reactions followed by E nonreactions. Expectancy-of-Success estimates were obtained from the Ss before the verbal reaction series, at the end of this series, and at the end of the subsequent nonreaction series. Two change scores, one between the Ss' first two expectancy estimates and the other between their second and third estimates, were the two measures of the dependent variable, changes in expectancy, used in this study.

The following findings substantiated hypothesis I: (a) Ss changed their expectancy estimates after adult nonreaction in directions opposite to the adult verbal reactions which had preceded them $(p = .0001)$. Nonreaction (or silence) thus appeared to have *active* reinforcing properties contingent upon the child's previous reinforcement experience with the examiner. Concerning the question of the absolute strength of the reinforcements employed in the study, it was found that: (b) negative E reactions had greater reinforcement strength in changing expectancy estimates than did positive E reactions $(p = .0001)$. (c) The E's nonreaction following negative reaction also acquired greater reinforcement strength and changed the children's expectations of success more than her nonreaction following positive reactions $(p = .0001)$. The fact that the same nonreaction could acquire differing *amounts* of reinforcement strength, as well as different directions, was interpreted as additional evidence of the active reinforcing properties of nonreaction.

Findings concerned with hypothesis II above indicated limited support, as measured in the present study. The two significant differences found, using positive parental reaction as the individual difference predictor variable, demonstrated (a) that children who were accustomed to negative parental reactions raised their expectations of success more as a result of E's positive reaction than did Ss who were accustomed to positive parental reactions $(p = .05)$ and (b) children who were accustomed to negative parental reactions raised their expectancies more to continued examiner nonreaction in the control group than did Ss who were accustomed to positive parental reactions $(p = .05)$.

A theoretical relationship was proposed between the amount of parental approval a child had received and his generalized expectancy for success, in which the latter was seen to be partially derived from the former. Therefore, additional data analyses were carried out in which generalized expectancy of success was predicted to bear the same relations to changes in expectancy in the experimental conditions as had been hypothesized for parental approval (hypothesis II above). These data analyses indicated that: (a) The children's perception of the amount of positive parental reaction to their behavior correlated .26 with their generalized expectancy of success $(p = .02)$. (b) Because of positive adult reaction, the high subgroup raised their expectancy estimates, but did not raise them as much as the low Ss $(p = .02)$. (c) As the result of negative adult reactions, the low Ss dropped their expectancy scores but did not drop them as much as the high Ss $(p = .01)$. The significant differences found, while few, do seem to substantiate the noncongruence hypothesis of this study. However, a replication and extension of this experiment is currently underway, using only Generalized Expectancy (found empirically to be the better predictor) as the variable on which children are divided and matched, to further test this hypothesis.

A comparison of the nonreaction treatment following positive verbal reactions with the positive treatment itself revealed that there was no significant difference between the reinforcement strengths of the two treatments. This was also true of negative verbal reactions and the nonreaction which followed this negative series. While these results might be interpreted as indicating that nonreaction had acquired a significant amount of active reinforcement strength, the fact that its effect had essentially returned the children's expectancies to their original levels at the beginning of the experiment also suggests the possibility that simple extinction might have occurred. The replication and extension of this study previously mentioned will also attempt to clarify this issue.

REFERENCES

1. Austrin, H. The attractiveness of activities as determined by different patterns of negative and positive reinforcement. Unpublished doctoral dissertation, Ohio State Univer., 1950.
2. Buchwald, A. Extinction after acquisition under different verbal reinforcement combinations, *J. exp. Psychol.,* 1959, *57,* 43–48.
3. Buchwald, A. Experimental alterations in the effectiveness of verbal reinforcement combinations. *J. exp. Psychol.,* 1959, *57,* 351–361.
4. Buss, A., Braden, W., Orgel, A., & Buss, E. Acquisition and extinction with different verbal reinforcement combinations. *J. exp. Psychol.,* 1956, *52,* 283–287.
5. Crandall, V. C. The effects of an adult's positive and negative reactions and nonreactions on children's expectancies of success. Unpublished master's thesis, Ohio State Univer., 1961.
6. Ferguson, E., & Buss, A. A supplementary report: acquisition, extinction and counter-conditioning with different verbal reinforcement conditions. *J. exp. Psychol.,* 1959, *58,* 94–95.
7. Gerhard, M. Changes in the attractiveness of activities; the effect of expectation preceding performance. *J. exp. Psychol.,* 1949, *39,* 404–413.
8. James, W. Internal *vs.* external control of reinforcement as a basic variable in learning theory. Unpublished doctoral dissertation, Ohio State Univer., 1951.
9. Jessor, S. The effects of reinforcement and of distribution of practice on psychological satiation. Unpublished doctoral dissertation, Ohio State Univer., 1951.
10. Meyer, W., & Seidman, S. Age differences in the effectiveness of different reinforcement combinations on the acquisition and extinction of a simple concept learning problem. *Child Develpm.,* 1960, *31,* 419–429.
11. Meyer, W., & Seidman, S. Relative effectiveness of different reinforcement combinations on concept learning of children at two developmental levels. *Child Develpm.,* 1961, *32,* 117–127.
12. Rotter, J. *Social learning and clinical psychology.* Prentice-Hall, 1954.
13. Siegel, S. *Nonparametric statistics.* McGraw-Hill, 1956.
14. Wilcoxon, F. *Some rapid approximate statistic procedures.* Amer. Cyanimid Co., 1949.

part VI
Adolescence

In most societies, adolescence is viewed as a period of special difficulty in adjustment—a "critical period" in the individual's development. This is true of the more technologically advanced societies, such as our own, as well as a substantial number of nonliterate ones.

This should not appear surprising if we stop to consider the special stresses to which the adolescent is typically subjected, in comparison to children at many other age levels. Problems of adjustment are minimal during periods when a fairly well-stabilized individual is confronted with environmental demands that are for the most part familiar, and for which he has already developed appropriate and need-satisfying responses. Neither condition characterizes adolescence in our culture.

In the first place, the onset of puberty brings with it a host of physiological changes, including increases in sex hormone and changes in body structure and function, which not only present special adjustment problems in themselves, but which also challenge the individual's basic sense of self, or what Erik Erikson has called his "ego identity." As he says, "In puberty and adolescence, all sameness and continuities relied on earlier are questioned again because of the rapidity of body growth which equals that of early childhood and because of the entirely new addition of physical genital maturity."

At the same time that the adolescent in our culture is confronted with the uncertainties brought on by rapid physical and physiological changes, and the flood of unfamiliar subjective feelings which accompany them, he is also confronted with a whole set of societal demands from which he has heretofore been protected. In the few short years between puberty and nominal adulthood, he is suddenly expected to prepare himself for a job; for changed political and social status as a citizen; for marriage; for relatively complete separation from his parents and the setting up of an independent household; and for a mature philosophy of life. The task is not made easier by the fact that we are living through a period of very rapid social change, marked by a plethora of unsolved problems—poverty, discrimination, chaotic urbanization, wars, and the breakdown of traditional cultural and family ties.

Small wonder, then, that adolescence constitutes a "critical period." Small wonder, too, that a significant minority of adolescents, unable to achieve a satisfying resolution of the various conflicting forces to which they are subjected, are turning to active rebellion against a society that they view as "phony": immoral, impersonal, hypocritical, and overly aggressive and materialistic. Or that other adolescents are forced into inadequate, and ultimately self-defeating compromises in their search for a psychological modus vivendi—some into neurosis or even psychosis, others into various forms of alienated or antisocial behavior. Perhaps the remarkable fact is that so many of today's adolescents survive their parents' and society's most extreme fears, and grow into reasonably happy, effective, and responsible adults, no worse, and quite possibly better fitted for life than their parents.

The five papers included in this part illustrate the principal issues discussed above. In the first, Paul Henry Mussen and Mary Cover Jones make clear, not only that the very fact of rapid physical change creates problems for adolescents generally, but that deviations from the average timetables for these changes pose special problems for the young people involved, often with profound psychological consequences. In their study of early- and late-maturing boys, they found that boys who mature late are likely to feel anxious and inadequate, to have stronger needs for social acceptance than early-maturing boys, while at the same time having a greater fear of rejection by others. The fact that adolescents of both sexes are intensely aware of idealized group norms in appearance, ability, and interest, and are seriously affected by deviations from them, should not seem too surprising when we realize the special importance that identification with a peer group assumes at a time when the individual is still struggling with, and is not too sure of his own identity.

Increased sexual drive, influenced by hormonal and anatomical changes is, of course, a major concomitant of the physiological changes of adolescence. However, the manner in which the adolescent adjusts—or fails to adjust—to his new-found sexual maturity will vary, depending on a wide variety of psychological and cultural forces. We hear much today about a "new morality" in youth culture. Does this new morality in fact exist, and if so, how is it manifested? In the second paper Robert Bell indicates that there are differences in sexual morality between today's adolescents and their parents, and further, that the greatest changes have occurred in the area of sexual values, rather than in behavior. In general, parents tend to express more conservative attitudes and to place greater emphasis on absolute behavioral standards of right and wrong. In contrast, today's youth tend to place greater emphasis on the meaningfulness of the interpersonal relationships involved when evaluating the morality of sexual conduct, such as premarital intimacy. While significant numbers of adolescents may experience difficulties and conflict in incorporating sexuality into their emerging ego identity, the evidence suggests that today's adolescents are probably less troubled, and more open and honest about sex than their parents were at the same age.

In the third selection in this part, Erik Erikson, a gifted psychoanalyst and writer, with a background in social anthropology and comparative education, discusses the adolescent search for a *sense of identity*—for an answer to the fundamental question, "Who am I?" which he calls the "central problem of the period." As he points out, unless the adolescent, despite the host of other demands placed upon him, can find a reasonably workable solution of this issue, he is left to drift on the sea of his own fate, subject at best to the whims of an "other-directed" culture as David Riesman has called it or, at worst, to psychological defeat.

It is fashionable these days to speak of youth who in one way or another do not "fit in" as being "alienated." However, as Kenneth Keniston notes, all we have really done by labeling is to imply that "something is wrong somewhere." Unless we can go further and specify the nature of the alienation—its source and the manner in which it is expressed—we have accomplished little. In the fourth study Keniston discusses two types of dissenting youth in contemporary society—the student activist and the culturally alienated—and points out the fallacy of popular stereotypes that fail to distinguish between them. For example, while both types find a good deal wrong with "the establishment," the activist responds to his discontent with positive action. In contrast, the culturally alienated youth "is far too pessimistic . . . to wish to demonstrate his disapproval in any organized public way. His demonstrations of dissent are private. . . . The activist attempts to change the world around him, but the alienated student is convinced that meaningful change of the social and political world is impossible; instead he considers 'dropping out' the only real option." Further, there are differences between these two types in the sources of their dissent. Culturally alienated students are more likely to be disturbed psychologically, and to reveal a history of conflict-ridden parent-child relationships. In contrast, and contrary to popular stereotypes, the activist student, rather than being in rebellion against his parent's values, is likely to be "living out expressed but unimplemented parental values."

Another manifestation of alienation in contemporary society, with both psychological and sociological roots, is the rising rate of juvenile delinquency. Delinquency is by no means a new problem, but there seems little doubt that it is an increasingly serious social concern in our ever more complex, fragmented society. And just as a *sense of identity* has its earliest roots in what Erikson calls the "basic trust" of infancy, so too does adolescent delinquency often find antecedents in the early years of childhood. In the concluding paper of this part, John Janeway Conger, Wilbur Miller, and Charles Walsmith show that the personality characteristics of future delinquents differ from those of nondelinquents even in the early school years, and even after the possible effects of such factors as socioeconomic status, sex, intelligence, residence area, school background, and ethnic group membership have been controlled through a matching technique. Perhaps most importantly, they demonstrate that it may be relatively meaningless to speak of overall personality differences between delinquents and nondelinquents, without first taking into account the social class background and intelligence of the individual studied.

Self-Conceptions, Motivations, and Interpersonal Attitudes of Late- and Early- Maturing Boys

Paul Henry Mussen and Mary Cover Jones

University of California, Berkeley

While intensive case studies show that personal and social adjustment during adolescence may be profoundly influenced by rate of physical maturation, there is a scarcity of systematic data on the relationship between the adolescent's physical status and his underlying motivations, self-conceptions, and interpersonal attitudes. There is, however, a small body of evidence which demonstrates that greater physical maturity is associated with greater maturity of interest among girls (10) and that early-maturing boys differ from their late-maturing peers in both overt behavior and reputational status. In one study (8) in which a staff of trained observers assessed a large group of adolescents on a number of personality variables, boys who were consistently retarded in physical development were rated lower than those who were

Reprinted from *Child Development*, copyright © 1957 by The Society for Research in Child Development, Inc., *28,* 243–256. By permission.

consistently accelerated in physical attractiveness, grooming, and matter-of-factness; and higher in sociability, social initiative (often of a childish, attention-getting sort), and eagerness. Reputation Test (11) data indicated that classmates regarded the late-maturing boys as more attention-getting, more restless, more bossy, less grown-up and less good-looking than those who were physically accelerated.

On the basis of these findings, it may be inferred that adult and peer attitudes toward the adolescent, as well as their treatment and acceptance of him, are related to his physical status. This means that the sociopsychological environment to which late-maturers are subjected—and consequently the social learning situations they encounter—may be significantly different from that of their early-maturing peers. As a consequence, according to the ratings summarized above, they acquire different patterns of overt social behavior. It seems reasonable to hypothesize that groups differing in physical status will also differ in more covert aspects of behavior and personality.

Indirect evidence relevant to this hypothesis comes from an investigation of the long-term consequences of physical acceleration or retardation during adolescence. Jones (6) found that group differences in physique had practically disappeared by the time her early- and late-maturing subjects reached their early thirties. Nevertheless, young adults who had been physically retarded adolescents differed from those who had been accelerated in several important psychological characteristics. In general, it appeared that the adult subjects could be described much as they had been during adolescence. Thus, those who had been early-maturers scored higher on the good impression, socialization, dominance, self-control (low score on impulsivity), and responsibility scales of the California Psychological Inventory, while those who had been slow in maturing scored higher on the flexibility scale. On the Edwards Personal Preference Schedule, early-maturers scored significantly higher on the dominance scale, while the late-maturing were high in succorance. Jones concludes that the early-maturing "present a consistently favorable personality picture with regard to . . . important social variables" (6). Moreover, there was some evidence that these men had attained more stable vocational adjustments than those who had been late in maturing. These group differences in later adjustment suggest that the sociopsychological atmosphere in which the adolescent lives may have profound immediate and enduring effects on his personality structure as well as on his overt behavior.

The present study was designed to investigate the relationship between maturational status and certain important covert aspects of personality during late adolescence. Personality structure was assessed by means of the Thematic Apperception Test (TAT) which seems to be the most appropriate and sensitive instrument for this purpose. More specifically, on the basis of the literature reviewed above and other general works on the psychology of adolescence (1, 4, 5), we formulated and tested a series of propositions relating to differences between the physically retarded and accelerated in self-conceptions, underlying motivations, and basic interpersonal attitudes. These variables were translated into TAT categories—needs (n), Press (p), and descriptions (defined briefly in Table 1)—and the scores of early- and late-maturers in each of these categories were compared. The propositions and the rationale underlying them, together with the TAT variables involved, follow.

1. In view of their obvious physical retardation, relatively unfavorable reputations and disadvantageous competitive position in many activities, the late-maturing boys are more likely to have feelings of inadequacy. Hence, more boys in this group than in the early-maturing group are likely to have negative self-conceptions (TAT category: *negative characteristics*).

2. The adolescent in our culture generally desires some independence and adult status. This may be the source of a major problem for the late-maturer, however, since he is often regarded and treated as a small boy by adults and peers and is not likely to be granted independence as early as physically accelerated boys. Therefore, it may be anticipated that more late- than early-maturers regard adults, particularly their parents, as dominating, forcing them to do things they don't want to or preventing them from doing things they want to do (high scores in *p Dominance*). Moreover, the parental treatment these boys experience and parental refusal to grant them independent status may be interpreted as personal rejection. Hence we predicted that more late-maturing boys would score high in *p Rejection*.

3. These feelings of being dominated and rejected may result in attitudes of rebellion against the family and in feelings of hostility. We therefore expected that more of the late-maturing group would reveal strong aggressive needs (high scores in *n Aggression*) and desires to escape from (*n Autonomy* —leaving parents), or to defy, the family (*n Autonomy*—defying parents).

4. On the basis of the data indicating that slow-maturers showed a great deal of social interest (although often of an immature kind), we hypothesized that more members of this, than of the early-maturing group would reveal strong interests in friendly, intimate interpersonal relationships (high scores in *n Affiliation*).

5. Assuming that, as Jones and Bayley (8) suggest, the social initiative and attention-getting devices of the late-maturers are of a compensatory nature, we would expect this group to be basically dependent and to have strong needs for support from others. These should be manifest by higher scores in TAT *n Succorance* and *p Nurturance*. The latter may be considered a more indirect measure of dependence, a kind of wish-fulfilling view of the world as helpful and friendly.

6. The early-maturer, being regarded and treated as more adult, is more likely to become self-confident, and to acquire high status goals. For these reasons, we predicted that more of the physically accelerated would give evidence of high achievement goals (high scores in *n Achievement*) and concern with personal recognition (high scores in *n Recognition*).

7. Late-maturing boys in our culture probably face more problems of personal adjustment than do their early-maturing peers. As a result of this, they may become more aware of their problems, and, as the high degree of flexibility of young adults who had been retarded in maturing suggests, more

insightful. Hence we predicted that they would be more willing and able than early-maturers to face their own feelings and emotions (low score in the TAT variable *denial of feeling*).

In summary, we attempted to test seven propositions related to difference in the personalities of early- and late-maturing boys. It was hypothesized that more late-maturers would score high in variables relating to negative self-conceptions, dependence, aggression, affiliation, rebelliousness, and feelings of being dominated and rejected. More early-maturers, on the other hand, were expected to reveal strong achievement and recognition needs, feelings of personal success, and tendencies toward denial of feelings.

PROCEDURE

The thirty-three 17-year-old male subjects of this investigation were members of the Adolescent Growth Study which included a normal sample of boys in an urban public school system (3). The subjects of the present investigation represented two contrasting groups, selected on the basis of their physical maturity status: 16 of them had been among the most consistently accelerated throughout the adolescent period; the other 17 had been among the most consistently retarded.[1] All of them took the Thematic Apperception Test, which provides the basic data of this study, at age 17.

The TAT consisted of 18 pictures: nine from the Murray set which is now standard (cards, 1, 5, 6, 7BM, 10, 11, 14, 15, 17); five pictures from the set generally used in 1938 when these data were collected (a man and woman seated on a park bench; a bearded old man writing in an open book; a thin, sullen, young man standing behind a well-dressed older man; a tea table and two chairs; an abstract drawing of two bearded men); and four designed especially for this investigation (the nave of a large church; a madonna and child; a dramatic view of mountains; a boy gazing at a cross which is wreathed in clouds).

The tests were administered individually. Each card was projected on a screen while the subject told a story which was recorded verbatim. Standard instructions were given for the Murray cards, and subjects were asked to describe the feelings elicited by the other four pictures. Most of the stories were brief, consisting of only one or two sentences.

As we noted earlier, each of the personality variables involved in the seven propositions was translated into a TAT scoring category. The scoring scheme involved counting the relevant needs, press, and descriptions of the heroes of the stories, the assumption being that the storyteller has identified

---

[1] The present sample includes 27 of Jones and Bayley's (8) 32 subjects (the 16 most consistently retarded and 16 most consistently accelerated boys in the study). The other five boys had not taken the TAT at age 17. The six subjects who were in the present study but not in Jones and Bayley's study are the three "runners-up" from each end of the physical maturity distribution, i.e., the three who were closest to the 16 most accelerated cases and the three cases next to the 16 most retarded.

Table 1 Number of Early- and Late-Maturers Scoring High in TAT Variables

TAT Variable	Definition of Variable	High Early-Maturers	High Late-Maturers	Chi-Square Value	P
Proposition 1					
Negative characteristics	H is described in negative terms (e.g., imbecile, weakling, fanatic)	5	13	6.80	<.01
Proposition 2					
p Dominance 1	H forced by parents to do something he doesn't want to do	4	8	1.73	.09
p Dominance 2	H prevented by parents from doing something he wants to do	6	8	.31	>.30
p Dominance 3	Total instance of H's being forced by parents to do something and/or prevented from doing something	7	11	1.46	.11
p Rejection	H rejected, scorned, or disapproved of by parents or authorities	5	11	3.69	.03
Proposition 3					
n Aggression 1	H is aggressive in physical, asocial way	8	3	3.88	.02
n Aggression 2	H is mad at someone, argues	7	4	1.52	.10
n Aggression 3	Total of all H's aggressive actions	11	8	1.26	.10
n Autonomy 1	H leaves home	7	10	.75	.20
n Autonomy 2	H disobeys or defies parents	7	11	1.46	.11
n Autonomy 3	Total of instances in which hero leaves and/or defies his parents	3	9	4.16	.02

Table 1   (Continued)

TAT Variable	Definition of Variable	High Early-Maturers	High Late-Maturers	Chi-Square Value	P
Proposition 4					
n Affiliation 1	H establishes good relations with his parents	8	8	.00	>.50
n Affiliation 2	H falls in love, has a romance, marries	9	14	2.66	.05
n Affiliation 3	Total instance in which H establishes and/or maintains friendly relations	8	12	1.46	.11
Proposition 5					
n Succorance	H feels helpless, seeks aid or sympathy	7	12	2.43	.06
p Nurturance 1	H is helped, encouraged, or given something by parents	5	8	.93	.18
p Nurturance 2	H is helped, encouraged, or given something by someone else (not parents)	8	14	3.88	.02
Proposition 6					
n Achievement	H attempts to attain a high goal or to do something creditable	9	10	.02	>.50
n Recognition	H seeks fame and/or high prestige status	9	8	.28	>.30
Proposition 7					
Denial of feeling	S states that picture elicits no thoughts or feelings	9	5	2.43	.06

with the hero: the hero's needs are the same as the boy's; the press that impinge upon the hero are the ones that affect the boy telling the story. A total of 20 needs, press, and descriptive categories, each defined as specifically as possible, was developed in the analysis of the protocols. A score for each subject for each TAT category was derived by counting the number of stories in which it appeared. A list of the categories used, together with brief descriptions of them, is found in Table 1.

To test the reliability of this analysis, one of the authors (PM) and another psychologist[2] independently scored 15 complete protocols (300 stories). The percentage of interrater agreement was 90, computed by the usual formula (number of agreements divided by number of agreements plus number of disagreements).

In order to eliminate bias, the scoring used in the present study was done "blind," that is, independent of knowledge of the subject's maturational status.

RESULTS

Frequency distributions of the scores of all subjects were made for all the TAT variables. Each distribution was then dichotomized at the point which most nearly enabled the placing of half of the 33 subjects above, and half of them below, the dividing point. Subjects having scores above this point were considered high in this particular variable; those with scores below this point were considered low in this variable. Chi-square tests were used to test the seven propositons, i.e., to ascertain whether or not high scores in certain TAT variables were in fact more characteristic of one group (late- or early-maturers) than of the other.

Table 1 lists the TAT variables, the number of late- and early-maturers with high scores in the variable, the chi-square value obtained and the level of significance. It should be noted that the hypotheses tested were one-sided hypotheses, while the chi-square value is in terms of a two-sided hypothesis. When chi-square has only one degree of freedom, the square root of chi-square has a distribution which is the right hand half of a normal distribution. In order to test a one-sided hypothesis, the chi-square test must be converted into the equivalent value in terms of a unit normal deviate (2). The levels of significance reported in Table 1 were evaluated in these terms.

Table 1 shows that, as had been predicted, more late-maturing than early-maturing boys revealed feelings of inadequacy and negative self-concepts, i.e., scored high in the TAT variable *negative characteristics*. Hence proposition 1 was confirmed. This finding is consistent with the frequently made clinical observation that retardation in physical maturation may be an important source of personal maladjustment and attitudes of inferiority.

Proposition 2 stated that more late-maturers regard their parents as highly dominating and rejecting. The evidence summarized in Table 1 substantially supported this proposition. While the difference was not statistically significant, more late- than early-maturers scored high in *p Dominance by parents* (total). There was a marked difference between the groups in the variable which involves parental domination by forcing the child to do something he does not want to do (*p Dominance by parents, forcing*). However, examination of the data with respect to the variable *p Dominance by parents*

---

[2] We are indebted to Dr. Virginia B. Ware for her participation in this aspect of the study.

(*prevention*) makes it necessary to reject that part of the proposition which maintains that late-maturers are more likely to view their parents as highly restrictive of their activities.

That aspect of proposition 2 which deals with feelings of rejection was confirmed by our data. Compared with the early-maturing group a significantly greater proportion of the late-maturers told stories in which the hero was rejected by parents or authority figures. These feelings of rejection may stem from different sources. In some cases, the parents' behavior may make it clear that they are disappointed in their physically retarded son whom they regard as immature. The boy, perceiving this attitude, may interpret it as rejection. In other cases, parental reluctance to allow the late-maturing boy to establish his independence may lead to considerable tension in the family and the boy's feelings of rejection may simply reflect the ongoing parent-child conflict.

It is possible that earlier in their teens, soon after the physical changes of adolescence became apparent, many of the early-maturing boys also experienced conflicts with their parents, arising from difficulties in establishing their independence or in handling emerging heterosexual interests. At that time they too may have felt dominated or rejected. However, by the age of 17, when these data were collected, these boys were ordinarily treated as adults and granted more freedom. Hence, they were more likely to have resolved many of their conflicts with their parents and to feel accepted and independent.

The hypothesis (part of proposition 3) that more late-maturers would be highly aggressive was rejected on the basis of the evidence given in Table 1. In fact, the differences between the two groups on all the TAT aggression variables were in the opposite direction from the prediction. High scores in the variables relating to aggression of the most overt and violent type were significantly more frequent among the early-maturers, and more members of this group also scored high in measures of milder (verbal) aggression and of total aggression. While late-maturers may experience more problems of adjustment and greater frustrations than their early-maturing peers, they apparently do not manifest greater aggressive motivation. It may be that their own feelings of inadequacy or fears of retaliation and punishment for aggression inhibit their expression of hostile feelings, even in fantasy. On the other hand, the early-maturers who feel more secure personally, and recognize their own relatively advantageous physical and social status, may feel freer to express their aggressive needs. Since aggression is a culturally stereotyped masculine trait, it seems possible that the physically accelerated, being accepted as mature and identifying readily with adult males, are more likely to acquire this characteristic. In any case, the finding that early-maturers express higher aggressive motivation during late adolescence seems consistent with Jones' finding that, as young adults, they score high on the dominance scale of the Edwards Personal Preference test (6). Perhaps the relatively strong aggressive motivation of the early-maturer, or the mature sex-role identification it may imply, serves as a basis for the development of later qualities of leadership and persuasiveness (7).

As Table 1 indicates, the other aspect of proposition 3 was confirmed: a significantly greater proportion of late- than of early-maturers displayed strong motivations to escape from, or defy, their parents. These may be essentially aggressive reactions, stemming from feelings of parental domination and rejection, or they may reflect the late-maturers awareness of their strife with their parents whom they perceive as blocking their drives for independence. These strong needs for escape and defiance may also be considered evidence of a generally immature way of handling parent-child conflicts. Perhaps, by the age of 17, the early-maturers have already resolved many of their conflicts with their families and/or have learned to handle these in less rebellious and in more direct and mature ways.

Proposition 4 stated that, compared with their early-maturing peers, more late-maturers would manifest strong needs for establishing close social contacts with others. While there was some confirmatory evidence, the results were not clear-cut. When all affiliative needs were considered together (score for n Affiliation—total), the group differences were in the predicted direction, but not statistically significant. Examination of the protocols revealed that almost all instances of affiliation concerned either parents or the opposite sex; there were very few stories involving close, friendly associations between like-sexed peers. The two major types of affiliation were scored separately. As Table 1 shows, late-maturers did not differ from early-maturers with respect to need for affiliation with parents, but a significantly greater proportion of the former group displayed strong motivation for heterosexual affiliation.

In view of the late-maturers' strong feelings of inadequacy and dependent needs (see below), it is surprising that a greater proportion of this group did not exhibit strong needs to establish and maintain close bonds with their parents. This may be due to the late-maturers' more intense conflicts with their parents at this age (17 years), their fears of being rejected and dominated by them, and their generally defiant attitudes which prevent them from admitting, even in fantasy, their strong underlying needs to form close contacts with them.

The significant difference between groups in n Affiliation (love, romance, marriage) is subject to several possible interpretations. For one thing, this category may refer to general needs to establish close relations with others (with peers or adults other than parents) and not merely to desire for contact with the opposite sex. The set of stimulus cards may not have been adequate to elicit responses indicative of more general affiliative needs; hence, these were expressed through responses in the heterosexual affiliation category. If this is true, proposition 4 was confirmed, and the late-maturers' high scores in this variable indicate their greater general interest in establishing and maintaining friendly relationships.

It is also possible that the late-maturers' strong affiliative needs are actually directed only toward members of the opposite sex, i.e., that n Affiliation (love, romance, marriage) measures specifically heterosexual interests. Assuming that this is true, there is another plausible explanation for the discovered difference. As we saw earlier, the late-maturer may be afraid to admit that he desires close associations with his parents. He may also feel that his immaturity and poor reputational status prevent him from establishing successful social relationships with like-sexed peers. Hence, he may "displace" his affiliative needs to members of the opposite sex, who in his fantasies, may seem more responsive.

A third possible explanation of the difference is based on Jones and Bayley's findings that the late-maturers show less overt interest in girls and are regarded as less good-looking (8). From these data, it may be inferred that the physically retarded probably do not have successful and rewarding experiences with girls. Hence their heightened need for affiliation with the opposite sex, expressed in the TAT, may reflect their attempts to satisfy in fantasy needs which they cannot satisfy adequately in reality.

The data were generally supportive of proposition 5 which stated that late-maturers are likely to have strong underlying dependent needs. A higher proportion of this group than of their early-maturing peers scored high in *n Succorance,* the difference between the two groups approaching statistical significance ($p = .06$). Furthermore, high scores in the category involving receiving help and support from others (not including parents) (*p Nurturance —nonparents*)—an indirect measure of dependent needs—were significantly more characteristic of the physically retarded than of the physically accelerated. In view of the late-maturers' attitudes toward their parents, discussed above, it is not surprising to find that perceptions of parents as kindly and supportive (high scores in *p Nurturance-parents*) were not significantly more common in this group than in the early-maturing group.

On the basis of the data involving the TAT variables *n Achievement* and *n Recognition,* we rejected proposition 6 which stated that more early-maturers would be self-confident and have high needs for achievement and personal recognition. In our culture there is strong pressure to develop needs for achievement and personal recognition, and, according to our results, these needs and feelings may become intense regardless of—or perhaps in spite of —the child's maturational status, feelings of personal adequacy, dependency, and adjustment to parents.

Two interesting incidental findings from the TAT data seem to be consistent with the proposition that more early- than late-maturers are likely to be self-confident. Seven boys in this sample of 33 adolescents told stories in which the hero was helpful or kind to someone else (*n Nurturance*). Of this group, six were early-maturers, while only one was a late-maturer ($\chi^2 = 2.09$, $p = .07$). Insofar as *n Nurturance* may be a measure of the storyteller's own feelings that he can accept an active, mature role, more of the accelerated group feel self-assured with respect to having attained mature status.

The other incidental finding which seems to support proposition 6 is based on responses only to card 1 of the Murray series which depicts a young boy contemplating a violin which rests on a table in front of him. Eight of the subjects spoke of the boy (the hero) as a prodigy or a genius. Of these, seven were early-maturers; only one was physically retarded ($\chi^2 = 5.25$, $p = .01$). If the attribution of this prestige status and accomplishment to the hero reflects the subject's own feeling that he has been an achiever, it follows that more of the physically accelerated have positive self-concepts. In view of the small number of cases involved, both of these findings must be considered tentative, but they do offer some evidence in support of proposition 6.

Proposition 7, which stated that relatively few of the physically retarded boys are unwilling or unable to face their own feelings and emotions, received some support from the TAT data summarized in Table 1. A smaller proportion of the members of this group than of the physically accelerated group specifically denied that the pictures evoked any feelings or emotions (e.g., "It doesn't make me think of anything."). While this variable may not adequately measure *denial of feeling* as a major defense mechanism, this result seems to indicate that late-maturers are more sensitive to their own feelings and more ready to admit and face them openly. Since these qualities are basic to the development of psychological insight, it may be inferred that late-maturers, as a group, are more likely to become insightful individuals.

DISCUSSION

The results of the study support the general hypothesis that, in our culture, the boy whose physical development is retarded is exposed to a socio-psychological environment which may have adverse effects on his personality development. Apparently, being in a disadvantageous competitive position in athletic activities, as well as being regarded and treated as immature by others, may lead to negative self-conceptions, heightened feelings of rejection by others, prolonged dependent needs, and rebellious attitudes toward parents. Hence, the physically retarded boy is more likely than his early-maturing peer to be personally and socially maladjusted during late adolescence. Moreover, some of his attitudes are likely to interfere with the process of identification with his parents, which is generally based on perceptions of them as warm and accepting (9). This, in turn, may inhibit or delay the acquisition of mature characteristics and attitudes which are ordinarily established through identification with parents. Fortunately for the late-maturers' subsequent adjustments, they seem more willing and able to face their feelings and emotions. This may be a result of their awareness of others' attitudes toward their immaturity or their feelings of personal inadequacy and dependency.

The physically accelerated boys, on the other hand, are likely to experience environmental circumstances which are much more conducive to good psychological adjustment. Hence, their psychological picture, as reflected in their TAT stories, is much more favorable. By the time they were 17, relatively few early-maturers harbored strong feelings of inadequacy, perceived themselves as rejected or dominated by parents or authorities, or felt rebellious toward their families. As a group, they appeared to have acquired more self-confidence and had probably made stronger identifications with mature adults. Hence, they perceived themselves as more mature individuals, less dependent and in need of help, and more capable of playing an adult male role in interpersonal relationships.

These findings assume additional, probably greater, importance when they are considered in the light of Jones' findings on the early adult (age 33) adjustments of boys who had been retarded or accelerated in physical maturing (6). It should be recalled that by this age physical differences between the two groups had practically disappeared. Certain important psychological differences were noted, however, and these were consistent with the differences at age 17, reported in the present study. For example, the responses of the early-maturing group to two paper-and-pencil tests revealed that, as young adults, they were more dominant, more able to make a good impression, and more likely to be turned to for advice and reassurance; more self-controlled; and more willing and able to carry social responsibility. In short, they present a general picture of psychological maturity. Moreover, more of the early-maturers seemed to have made successful vocational adjustments. In contrast to this, when the late-maturers became adults, they tended to be highly dependent individuals who could be described, on the basis of their test responses, as tending to be rebellious, touchy, impulsive, self-indulgent, and insightful. Most of these characteristics are indicative of poor adjustment and psychological immaturity. Fewer of this group had made good vocational adjustments.

The striking correspondence between the two descriptions of the groups, derived from different kinds of tests and collected at widely separated periods of time, lends further support to Jones' conclusion that "the adolescent handicaps and advantages associated with late- or early-maturing appear to carry over into adulthood to some extent" (6). It seems clear that many attributes of adolescent personality (patterns of motivation, self-conceptions, and attitudes toward others) characteristic of late- and early-maturing boys are relatively stable and durable rather than situational and transitory. This may be attributable to the fact that in our culture adolescence is generally a critical and difficult period of adjustment. Within a relatively brief interval of time, the child must work out numerous complex and vitally important personal problems, e.g., adaptation to his changed biological and social status, establishment of independence, vocational adjustment. In dealing with these problems, he may acquire new behaviors and personality attributes which have broad ramifications, not only on his current adjustment, but also on his subsequent development. If the adolescent can cope with his problems without too much inner stress and turmoil, his self-esteem, feelings of adequacy, and consequently his subsequent adjustment, are likely to be enhanced. On the other hand, if his problems induce great tension and anxiety, he is likely to feel frustrated and inadequate, and, if these feelings are maintained, to adjust less satisfactorily as an adult.

Obviously, the adolescents' success or failure, as well as ease or tension, in handling his problems will be determined to a large degree by the socio-psychological forces to which he is subjected during this time, and these, as we have seen, may be significantly related to his rate of maturation. Thus, physical status during adolescence—mediated through the sociopsychological environment—may exert profound and lasting influences on personality. For this reason, many aspects of the adult's behavior and personality seem consistent with his adolescent adjustments, attitudes and motivations.

Insofar as our results permit generalization, they suggest that some important aspects of motivation, such as needs for achievement and personal recognition, are not significantly affected by maturational status. It may be that among subjects whose achievements are strongly encouraged and rewarded from very early childhood, the need to achieve becomes powerful and resistant to change even in the face of feelings of helplessness and inadequacy. The latter may inhibit the achievement-oriented overt behavior of some late-maturers, but the underlying motivation to achieve seems as strong in this group as it is among the physically accelerated.

In conclusion, it should be noted that, although rate of maturing and associated factors may affect personality development, the relationship between physical status and psychological characteristics is by no means simple. A vast number of complex, interacting factors, including rate of maturation, determine each adolescent's unique personality structure. Hence, in any specific instance, the *group* findings of the present study may not be directly applicable, for other physical, psychological, or social factors may attenuate the effects of late- or early-maturing. For example, an adolescent boy who is fundamentally secure and has warm, accepting parents and generally rewarding social relationships may not develop strong feelings of inadequacy even if he matures slowly. Analogously, the early-maturing boy who has deep feelings of insecurity, for whatever reasons, will probably not gain self-confidence simply because he matures early. In summary, in understanding any individual case, generalizations based on the data of the present study must be particularized in the light of the individual's past history and present circumstances.

SUMMARY

The present investigation was designed to test seven propositions concerning the relationship between rate of physical maturation and important aspects of personality structure, specifically, self-conceptions, underlying motivations, and basic interpersonal attitudes. The TAT protocols of thirty-three 17-year-old boys—16 who had been consistently physically accelerated throughout adolescence and 17 who had been consistently retarded—were analyzed according to a scoring schema involving 20 needs, press, and descriptive categories. The scores of early- and late-maturers in each of the categories were compared.

An earlier study (8) demonstrated that late-maturing boys are more likely than their early-maturing peers to encounter a generally unfavorable sociopsychological environment. Analysis of the data of the present study indicates that this situation may have adverse effects on the personalities of the physically retarded. These boys are more likely to have negative self-conceptions, feelings of inadequacy, strong feelings of being rejected and dominated, prolonged dependency needs, and rebellious attitudes toward parents. In contrast, the early-maturing boys present a much more favorable psychological picture during adolescence. Relatively few of them felt inadequate, rejected, dominated, or rebellious toward their families. More of them appeared to be self-confident, independent, and capable of playing an adult role in interpersonal relationships. Early- and late-maturing groups did not differ significantly from each other in needs for achievement or personal recognition.

These findings make it clear that rate of physical maturing may affect personality development in crucially important ways. However, it is important to note that in any particular case, the effects of early- or late-maturing may be significantly modified by the individual's psychological history and present circumstances.

REFERENCES

1. Farnham, M. L. *The adolescent.* New York: Harper & Row, 1951.
2. Fisher, R. A. *Statistical methods for research workers.* (7th ed.) Oliver & Boyd, 1938.
3. Jones, H. E. Observational methods in the study of individual development. *J. consult. Psychol.,* 1940, *4,* 234–238.
4. Jones, H. E. *Development in adolescence: approaches to the study of the individual.* Appleton-Century-Crofts, 1943.
5. Jones, H. E. Adolescence in our society. In Anniversary Papers of the Community Service Society of New York, *The family in a democratic society.* Columbia Univ. Press, 1949. Pp. 70–82.
6. Jones, M. C. The later careers of boys who were early- or late-maturing. *Child Develpm.,* 1957, *28,* 113–128.
7. Jones, M. C. A study of socialization patterns at the high school level. *J. genet. Psychol.,* 1959, *93,* 87–111.
8. Jones, M. C., & Bayley, N. Physical maturing among boys as related to behavior. *J. educ. Psychol.,* 1950, *41,* 129–148.
9. Payne, D. E., & Mussen, P. H. Parent-child relations and father identification among adolescent boys. *J. abnorm. soc. Psychol.,* 1956, *52,* 358–362.
10. Stone, C. P., & Barker, R. G. The attitudes and interests of premenarcheal and postmenarcheal girls. *J. genet. Psychol.,* 1939, *54,* 27–71.
11. Tryon, C. M. Evaluations of adolescent personality by adolescents. *Monogr. Soc. Res. Child Develpm.,* 1939, *4*(4).

Parent-Child Conflict in Sexual Values

Robert R. Bell

Temple University

The old cliché that as one grows older he becomes more conservative may be true, if premarital sexual values held by parents are compared with the values they held when they were younger. In this paper, the interest is in the nature of sex value conflict between parents and their unmarried late adolescent and young adult children. Our discussion will focus on values held by parents and by their unmarried children toward premarital sexual intimacy.

Conceptually, our approach focuses upon values related to a specific area of sexual behavior held by individuals from two very different role perspectives. The perspectives differ because parents and children are always at different stages in the life cycle, and while parents are highly significant in the socialization of their children, other social forces increasingly come to influence the child as he grows older. The various social values that influence

Reprinted from *The Journal of Social Issues*, XXII, No. 2, 34–44. By permission.

the child's sexual behavior are often complementary, but they may also be contradictory. Furthermore, various types of influences on the acceptance of a given set of values may operate on the child only during a given age period. For example, the youngster at age fifteen may be influenced by his age peers to a much greater extent than he will be at age twenty.

Given their different stages in the life cycle, parents and children will almost always show differences in how they define appropriate behavior for a given role. Values as to "proper" premarital sexual role behavior from the perspective of the parents are greatly influenced by the strong emotional involvement of the parent with his child. Youth, on the other hand, are going through a life cycle stage in which the actual behavior occurs, and they must relate the parent values to what they are doing or may do. There is a significant difference between defining appropriate role conduct for others to follow and defining proper role conduct to be followed by oneself. Even more important for actual behavior, there is often more than one significant group of role definers to which the young person can turn to as guides for his sex role behavior. Therefore, our discussion will focus more specifically on parent values related to premarital sexual intimacy, the peer group values of youth, and how these two different age groups, as role definers, influence the sexual values and behavior of unmarried youth.

Limits of Discussion

For several reasons, our discussion will center primarily on the middle class. First, this class level has been highly significant in influencing changes in general sexual values and behavior. Second, and on a more pragmatic level, what little research has been done on parent-child conflict over sexual values has been done with middle-class groups. Third, the general values of the middle class are coming to include an increasing proportion of the American population. This also suggests that the values and behavior of college youth are of increasing importance as this group continues to expand in size and influence within the middle class.

A further limit is that our main focus is on the generational conflict between mother and daughter. The history of change in sexual values in the United States has been complexly interwoven with the attainment of greater sex equality and freedom by the female (2). Also, the relationship between the mother and daughter tends to be the closest of the possible parent-child relationships in the family socializing of the child to future adult sex roles. Furthermore, whatever the value system verbalized and/or applied by the girl, she often has more to gain or lose personally than the boy by whatever premarital sexual decisions she makes.

We also believe that any analysis of conflict over premarital sex between generations should center on *value* changes rather than *behavioral* changes. On the basis of available evidence, it appears that there have been no significant changes in the *frequency* of premarital sexual petting or coitus since the 1920's. Kinsey has pointed out that "there has been little recognition that the premarital petting and coital patterns which were established then (1920's) are still with us" (15, 300). Therefore, it is important to recognize that the parents and even some of the grandparents of today were the youth who introduced the new patterns of premarital sexual behavior about forty years ago.

PARENT VALUES ABOUT PREMARITAL SEX

The transmission of sexual values by parents to their children is only a small part of all parent values passed on during the family socialization process. Most parents do a more deliberate and comprehensive job of transmitting values to their children in such areas as educational attainment, career choice, religious beliefs, and so forth than they do with reference to any aspect of sexual values. Often when parents do discuss sex with their children it may be from a "clinical, physiological" perspective with overtones of parental embarrassment and a desire to get a distasteful task over with.

But perhaps more important than the formal confrontation between the parent and child in sexual matters are the informal values transmitted by the parent. In the past girls were often taught that premarital sexual deviancy was dirty and shameful, and that nonconformity to premarital sexual chastity values would mean suffering great personal and social shame. This highly negative view of premarital sex is undoubtedly less common today, but the newer, more "positive" values may also have some negative consequences. Very often today the mother continues to place great value on the daughter's virginity, and stresses to the daughter the great virtues of maintaining her virginity until marriage. But the "romantic" view of the rewards for the girl who waits for coitus until after marriage are often highly unrealistic and may sometimes create problems by leading the girl to expectations that cannot be realistically met in marital sex. Morton Hunt writes with regard to this approach that "if the woman has been assured that she will, that she ought, and she *must* see colored lights, feel like a breaking wave, or helplessly utter inarticulate cries, she is apt to consider herself or her husband at fault when these promised wonders do not appear" (13, 114). Whether or not the "romantic" view of marital sex is presented by her mother the girl often encounters it in the "approved" reading list suggested by the adult world, which tells her about the positive delights of waiting for sex until after marriage. So, though premarital sexual control may be "positive" in that it is based on rewards for waiting, it can be "negative" if the rewards are unrealistic and unobtainable.

For many parents, a major problem as their child moves through adolescence and into early adult years centers around how much independence to allow the child. Because they often recall the child's younger dependency, it may be difficult to assess the independency of the same child who is now older. Also, over the years the growing child has increasingly become involved with reference groups outside—and sometimes competing with—the family. In other words, the self-role definitions by the child and the parents' definitions of the child's role undergo constant change as the child grows older. For example, "The daughter in her younger years has her role as daughter defined to a great degree by her mother. But as she grows older she is influenced by other definitions which she internalizes and applies to herself in her movement toward self-determination. The mother frequently continues to visualize the daughter's role as it was defined in the past and also attaches the same importance to her function as mother in defining her daughter's role. But given the rapid social change associated with family roles the definer, as well as the definitions, may no longer be institutionally appropriate" (5, 388).

Parents may also be biased in their definitions of their child as less mature than they, the parents, were when they were the child's age. One cannot recall experiences earlier in the life cycle free from influence by the events that have occurred since. This may result in many parents' thinking of their younger selves as being more mature than they actually were. At the same time the parents' view of their child's degree of maturity may be biased by their recall of him when he was younger and less mature. Thus, from the parents' perspective they may recall themselves as youngsters within the context of what has occurred since (more mature) and may see their offspring within the context of their earlier childhood (less mature).

There also may be some symbolic significance for parents who must define their children as having reached the age when something as "adult" as sexual behavior is of relevance. In part, viewing one's children as too young for sexual involvement may contribute to the parents' feeling young, while seeing their children as old enough to be involved in sexual activity may lead to some parents feeling forced to view themselves as aging. For example, the comment about a man seen out with a young woman that "she is young enough to be his daughter" may have implications for his self-role image if the young woman *is* his daughter. We have little research data on how the aging process of parents influences their definitions of appropriate behavior for their young adult children.

In general, it is probable that most parents assume that their children, especially their daughters, accept the traditional restrictive values about premarital sexual behavior unless they are forced to do otherwise. Also, because of the great emotional involvement of parents with their own children, there is a common parental tendency to attribute sexual "immorality" to other youngsters. For many parents to face the possibility that their children do not conform to their values is to suggest some failure on the part of the parents. Often, rather than admit failure, the parents may define their children as having been forced to reject the parent values by other social influences or that their children have willfully let them down.

YOUTH VIEWS ABOUT PREMARITAL SEX

The importance of age peer group influence on the values and behavior of young people has been shown by a number of social scientists (see: 6, 9, 10, 11, 12, 14, 19, 20, 21, 22). Because youth subcultures are to some degree self-developing, they often have conflict points in relation to some dominant adult values. However, the inconsistency and lack of effective adult defini- tions for adolescent behavior have also contributed to the emergence of youth subcultural values. That adults often view the adolescent with indeci- sion as to appropriate behavior means that sometimes given adolescent be- havior is treated one way at one time and in a different way at another time. Since the young person desires some decisiveness and precision in his role definitions, he often develops his own role pretscriptions. Often when he creates his own role expectations, he demands a high degree of conformity by other adolescents as "proof" of the rightness of his definitions. It is ironical that the adolescent often thinks of himself as a social deviant. What he fails to realize is that his adolescent group deviates from the adult world, but that the requirements for conformity within his youth subculture are very strong (1, 369–374).

Youth subcultures have developed great influence over many aspects of premarital male-female interaction. The patterns of dating and courtship, ap- propriate behavior, success and failure are for the most part patterns defined by the youth group and not by the adult world. Yet, heterosexual relation- ships of youth are often based on adult role patterns, and they are therefore an important part of the youth world because they are seen by the youth as symbolizing adult status. To many young people, who are no longer defined by the adult world as children, but are not yet given full status as adults, their involvement in what they see as adult roles is important to them in seeking for adult status and recognition.

A part of the American youth subculture has been the development of new values related to premarital sexual intimacy. Reiss suggests that "It might well be that, since the 1920's, what has been occurring is a change in attitudes to match the change in behavior of that era" [premarital sexual behavior] (16, 233). The evidence suggests that for at least some college students new sex norms are emerging at the various stages of dating and courtship. One study found that "on the dating level necking is the norm for females and petting for males. During going steady and engagement, petting seems to be acceptable for both sexes. This would suggest that the young people both act and accept a higher level of intimacy than has generally been suggested by courtship norms" (3, 63).

In the past, emphasis was placed on the girl's virginity at the time of marriage; but today, many young people may only emphasize her being a virgin until she is in love, which may mean at the stage of going steady or engagement (8, chap. 5 and 16, chap. 6). If the girl is in love, some premarital sexual relations may be acceptable by peer group standards, although the dominant adult values—that love and marriage are basic prerequisites for coitus—continue. In the United States love as a prerequisite for sexual rela- tions has long been a necessary condition for most middle-class females. The condition has not changed; rather, the point in the courtship-marriage process where it may be applied to sexual involvement has shifted. Hence, the major point of parent-child conflict over premarital sex centers around the parent value that one should be in love *and* married before entering coitus and the modified value system that an emotional and interpersonal commitment is important, but that this may occur before marriage.

There are two recent studies that provide some evidence on the nature of generational conflict; one study is of youth and adults in general and the other study is specifically concerned with mothers and their daughters. Reiss, in his extensive study of premarital sexual permissiveness, provides data on values held by adults as contrasted with values in a sample of high-school and college students. The respondents were asked to express their beliefs about different combinations of intimacy and degree of interpersonal commitment for both unmarried males and females. Respondents were asked if they believed petting to be acceptable when the male or female is engaged. In the adult sample the belief that petting during engagement was acceptable for the engaged male was the response of 61 per cent, and for the engaged female the response was 56 per cent. Of the student responses 85 per cent approved for the engaged male and 82 per cent for the engaged female (17, 190–191); thus adult attitudes about petting during engagement were more conservative than those of the student population. It may also be noted that for both the adult and student groups there was a single standard—that is, the acceptance rates were essentially the same for both males and females.

Reiss also asked his respondents if they believed full sexual relations to be acceptable if the male or female were engaged. Approval was the response given by 20 per cent of the adult group for males and 17 per cent for females. In the student group acceptance was given by 52 per cent for the male and 44 per cent for the female (17, 190–191). Here, as with petting, there are significant differences between the adult and the student samples, and once again both respondent groups suggest a single standard of acceptance or rejection for both males and females.

A study by Bell and Buerkle compared the attitudes of 217 coeds with those of their mothers. Both mothers and daughters were asked to respond to the question, "How important do you think it is that a girl be a virgin when she marries?" Of the mothers, 88 per cent answered "very important," 12 per cent "generally important," and 0 per cent "not important"; compared to 55 per cent, 34 per cent, and 13 per cent of the daughters (4, 391). Both the mothers and daughters were also asked: "Do you think sexual intercourse during engagement is: very wrong; generally wrong; right in many situations?" The percentages for each response category were 83 per cent, 15 per cent, and 2 per cent for the mothers; and 35 per cent, 48 per cent, and 17 per cent for the daughters (4, 391).

Both of the above questions show sharp differences between the value responses of the mothers and daughters with reference to premarital chastity. Many mothers were undoubtedly influenced in their responses by having a daughter in the age setting where the questions had an immediate and highly emotional application. Nevertheless, the differences in mother and daughter responses indicate that the area of premarital sexual behavior is one of potentially great conflict. One means of minimizing conflict is for the daughter not to discuss her sexual values or behavior with her mother. In the Bell and Buerkle study it was found that only 37 per cent of the daughters, in contrast with 83 per cent of the mothers, felt daughters should freely answer questions from their mothers in regard to attitudes toward sexual intimacy (4, 392).

The area of sexual values appears to be highly influenced by emotion, especially for the mother with reference to her daughter. Generational conflict with regard to premarital sexual intimacy has a variety of implications. First, the conflict in values clearly suggests that the traditional morality is often not socially effective as a meaningful determinant of behavior. Social values have behavioral influence when they emerge as social norms with significant rewards and punishments. In the case of sexual norms, however, there are rarely clearly-articulated rewards, or positive consequences, for the conforming individual. In almost all situations the effectiveness of sexual norms is dependent upon their negative sanctions, or punishments. For example, the traditional norm of female premarital chastity bases its behavioral influence primarily on negative consequences for the girl who fails to conform. This negative means of control is most commonly found as a part of the adult value system. In effect, the major sanctions over premarital chastity are based upon punishments for the girl and for her family if she deviates. Yet, in most cases the girl who has premarital coitus is not discovered by her parents or by the community. The real danger for the girl often centers around premarital pregnancy, because if that occurs and becomes known there can be no denying premarital coitus. Vincent has suggested that an important part of the negative sanction toward premarital pregnancy is not the pregnancy itself, but rather that it symbolizes premarital coitus *and* getting caught (12, chap. 1).

The available studies indicate that fear of pregnancy is not the major deterrent for most girls (7, 344 and 15, 315). The personal values of the girl appear far more important in restricting her from engaging in premarital coitus. Yet, within the privacy of the youth world, there may operate for some girls certain values positive toward premarital coitus. For example, there may be a strong emotional desire and commitment to the boy and a positive feeling by the girl of wanting to engage in greater sexual intimacy.

There is a tendency by parents, as well as by many who give professional advice, to overlook the pleasurable aspects of sex at all ages, especially for the young who are experiencing sexual pleasure for the first time. Undoubtedly many girls engage in premarital sexual intimacy to "compensate" for some need and many may suffer some negative consequences. But it is foolish to state categorically that the "artificial" setting of premarital sex always makes it negative and unpleasant for the girl. We would be much more honest if we recognized that for many girls premarital coitus is enjoyable and the participants suffer no negative consequences. This was illustrated in the Kinsey research; it was found that "69 per cent of the still unmarried females in the sample who had had premarital coitus insisted they did not regret their experiences. Another 13 per cent recorded some minor regrets" (15, 316). Kinsey also found that "77 per cent of the married females, looking back from the vantage point of their more mature experience, saw no reason to regret their premarital coitus" (15, 316).

THE EXTENT OF GENERATIONAL CONFLICT

With the evidence suggesting strong conflict between generations with regard to premarital sexual values, our final consideration is: how permanent is this generational conflict? We can provide some evidence on this question by examining the values of college-educated females of different ages. This appears justified because higher educated females are generally the most liberal in their views about sexual rights and expectations for women.

The evidence suggests that the premarital sexual liberalism of the college girl may be a temporary phenomenon. The coed's sexual liberalism must be seen as related to the interactional context of her being emotionally involved, and to a future commitment to an ongoing paired relationship. The Bell and Buerkle study (4) found that the values of daughters toward the importance of premarital virginity were very similar to those of their mothers, until they had spent some time in college. However, at "around age 20 there emerge sharp differences between mothers and daughters in regard to premarital sexual attitudes. Behavioral studies indicate that it is at this point that sexual activity is greatly intensified, perhaps because it is at this age that college girls are entering engagement. A suggested pattern is that the college girl of 20 or 21 years of age, in her junior or senior year and engaged, has a strong 'liberal' pattern toward premarital sexual behavior and attitudes" (4, 392 and 18, 696).

We can get some indication of the persistence of premarital sexual liberalism by comparing the values of mothers by education. In the mothers' views as to the importance of premarital virginity it was found that the college educated mothers were actually as "conservative" as those mothers with lower levels of education (4, 392). It is quite possible that in the future the coeds will become as conservative as the college educated mothers. This may occur when the coed's attitudinal rationales are not related to herself, but as a mother to her own daughter. It is therefore possible that the "sexual emancipation" of the college girl exists only for a short period of time, centering mainly around the engagement years.

Yet, even if the girl becomes more conservative as she grows older, and especially with reference to her own daughter, her temporary "liberalism" probably is contributing to some shift in adult values about premarital sexual intimacy. Certainly, today's parental generation accepts greater sexual intimacy as a part of the premarital heterosexual relationship. Probably most parents assume that their adolescent and young adult children are engaging in necking and even some petting. Most parents, as long as they don't actually see the sexual intimacy, don't concern themselves about it. However, to suggest that parents may be more liberal (or tolerant) of premarital sexual intimacy does not necessarily suggest that parents are liberal if the intimacy reaches coitus.

It also appears that there has been some reduction in the severity of negative sanctions by parents if the daughter deviates and is caught. Among middle-class parents today it may be less common to reject the unwed daughter if she becomes pregnant than in the past, and more common for the parents to help her. This is not to suggest that today's parents offer any positive sanctions for premarital pregnancy, but that they may be able to adapt (often painfully) to it, rather than respond with high rejection and anger.

If our suggestion is correct (that parents take a less totally negative view of "discovered" premarital coitus), then this further suggests that traditional sexual values are being altered, since, as we have suggested, in the past the values of premarital chastity were primarily based on the negative consequences for those who deviated and were caught. If these negative consequences have been reduced, then the social force of the traditional values has been reduced as a means utilized by parents to control premarital sexual deviancy.

CONCLUSIONS

Based on the available evidence, there are several general speculations that may be made about future generational conflict over premarital sex. In general we would suggest that conflict between parents and their adolescent-young adult children with regard to premarital sexual intimacy may decrease in the future, because of several trends.

1. The trend in the United States is toward a more liberal view of sexual behavior in general. This is reflected in the generally accepted professional opinion that the woman has a right to sexual satisfaction, and that sexual satisfaction is a desirable end in itself. The trend toward a belief in a single sexual standard for both men and women, even though within the setting of marriage, is bound to influence the beliefs and behavior of the unmarried. For the unmarried, there may be an increasing tendency to attach less importance to the marriage act as the arbitrary dividing line between socially approved and socially disapproved sexual intimacy.

2. Since the evidence suggests that over the past three or four generations the rates of female premarital coital experience have not changed, and since the younger generation has developed some value frameworks for its behavior, modification of traditional values and behavior may increasingly influence the values of parents to be more liberal. That is, it may become increasingly difficult for many parents to hold their children to a set of conservative values which they, the parents, did not hold to when they were younger.

3. Parents seem increasingly unwilling to strongly punish their daughters who sexually deviate and are caught. This parental reduction of punishment

may be influenced by the increasing public attention directed at such social problems as illegal abortion. For example, many parents may be more willing to accept and help an unmarried pregnant daughter than take the risk of her seeking out an illegal abortion. The possible negative consequences of abortion may appear more undesirable than the premarital pregnancy.

4. Less generational conflict will occur if parents know less about the sexual activities of their children. A great part of the social activity of young people is carried out in the privacy of their age peer setting; what they do in the way of sexual intimacy is increasingly less apt to be noted by their parents. With the development and marketing of oral contraceptives, the risks of premarital pregnancy will be greatly reduced. In the future the rates of premarital coitus may remain the same, but with the chances of pregnancy reduced, parents may be less aware of their children's premarital coitus.

Over time, then, the values of parents and the adult community in general may become more liberal and the conflict between generations reduced (There seems little possibility that the opposite will occur; i.e., the younger generation's reducing the conflict by becoming more conservative.) But in the meantime, and certainly in the near future, it appears that parents and their children will continue to live with somewhat different value systems with regard to premarital sexual values. Parents will probably continue to hold to traditional values, and assume that *their* child is conforming to those values unless his actions force them to see otherwise. The youth generation will probably continue to develop their own modified value systems and keep those values to themselves, and implicitly allow their parents to believe they are behaving according to the traditional values of premarital sexual morality. For many parents and their children, the conflict about premarital sex will continue to be characterized by the parent's playing ostrich and burying his head in the sand, and the youth's efforts to keep the sand from blowing away.

REFERENCES

1. Bell, Robert R. *Marriage and family interaction.* Homewood, Ill.: The Dorsey Press, 1963.
2. Bell, Robert R. *Premarital sex in a changing society.* Englewood Cliffs, N.J.: Prentice-Hall (in press).
3. Bell, Robert R. & Blumberg, Leonard. Courtship stages and intimacy attitudes: *Family Life Coordinator,* 1960, *8,* 60–63.
4. Bell, Robert R. & Buerkle, Jack V. Mother and daughter attitudes to premarital sexual behavior: *Marriage and Family Living,* 1961, *23,* 390–392.
5. Bell, Robert R. & Buerkle, Jack V. Mother-daughter conflict during the 'launching stage.' *Marriage and Family Living.* 1962, *24,* 384–388.
6. Bernard, Jessie (Editor). Teen-age culture. *Annals of the American Academy of Political and Social Science,* November, 1961, 338.
7. Burgess, Ernest & Wallin, Paul. *Engagement and marriage.* Chicago: J. B. Lippincott, 1953.

8. Ehrmann, Winston. *Premarital dating behavior.* New York: Henry Holt, 1959.
9. Ginsberg, Eli. *Values and ideals of American youth.* New York: Columbia University Press, 1962.
10. Gottlieb, David & Ramsey, Charles. *The American adolescent.* Homewood, Ill.: The Dorsey Press, 1964.
11. Grinder, Robert. *Studies in adolescence.* New York: Macmillan, 1963.
12. Hechinger, Grace & Hechinger, Fred. *Teen-age tyranny.* New York: Crest, 1962.
13. Hunt, Norton M. *The natural history of love.* New York: Alfred A. Knopf, 1959.
14. Kelley, Earl C. *In defense of youth.* Englewood Cliffs, N.J.: Prentice-Hall, 1962.
15. Kinsey, Alfred C., Pomeroy, Wardell B., Martin, Clyde E. & Gebhard, Paul H. *Sexual behavior in the human female.* Philadelphia: W. B. Saunders, 1953.
16. Reiss, Ira L. *Premarital sexual standards in America.* Glencoe, Ill.: The Free Press, 1960.
17. Reiss, Ira L. The scaling of premarital sexual permissiveness. *Journal of Marriage and the Family,* 1964, *26,* 188–98.
18. Reiss, Ira L. Premarital sexual permissiveness among Negroes and Whites. *American Sociological Review,* 1964, *29,* 688–698.
19. Remmers, H. H. & Radler, D. H. *The American teenager.* New York: Charter, 1957.
20. Seidman, Jerome. *The adolescent.* New York: Holt, 1960.
21. Smith, Ernest A. *American youth culture.* New York: The Free Press, 1963.
22. Symonds, P. M. *From adolescent to adult.* New York: Columbia University Press, 1961.
23. Vincent, Clark. *Unmarried mothers.* Glencoe, Ill.: The Free Press, 1961.

Identity
Versus Identity
Diffusion

Erik H. Erikson
HARVARD UNIVERSITY

I

With the establishment of a good relationship to the world of skills and to those who teach and share in the new skills, childhood proper comes to an end. Youth begins. But in puberty and adolescence all sameness and continuities relied on earlier are questioned again because of a rapidity of body growth which equals that of early childhood and because of the entirely new addition of physical genital maturity. The growing and developing young people, faced with this physiological revolution within them, are now primarily concerned with attempts at consolidating their social roles. They are sometimes

Reprinted from "Growth and Crises of the Healthy Personality: VI. In M. J. E. Senn (Ed.), *Symposium on the healthy personality. II: Problems of infancy and childhood.* New York: Josiah Macy, Jr. Foundation, 1950, pp. 134–140. By permission. This paper was prepared for the White House Conference of 1950.

morbidly, often curiously, preoccupied with what they appear to be in the eyes of others as compared with what they feel they are and with the question of how to connect the earlier cultivated roles and skills with the ideal proto-types of the day. In their search for a new sense of continuity and sameness, some adolescents have to refight many of the crises of earlier years, and they are never ready to install lasting idols and ideals as guardians of a final identity.

The integration now taking place in the form of the ego identity is more than the sum of the childhood identifications. It is the inner capital accrued from all those experiences of each successive stage, when successful identifi-cation led to a successful alignment of the individual's *basic drives* with his *endowment* and his *opportunities*. In psychoanalysis we ascribe such success-ful alignments to "ego synthesis"; I have tried to demonstrate that the ego values accrued in childhood culminate in what I have called a *sense of ego identity*. The sense of ego identity, then, is the accrued confidence that one's ability to maintain inner sameness and continuity (one's ego in the psycho-logical sense) is matched by the sameness and continuity of one's meaning for others. To go back into early childhood once more: a child who has just found himself able to walk, more or less coaxed or ignored by those around him, seems driven to repeat the act for the pure enjoyment of func-tioning and out of the need to master and perfect a newly initiated function. But he also acts under the immediate awareness of the new status and stature of "one who can walk," although different peoples and different people may express this according to a great variety of expectations: "one who will go far," "one who will be able to stand on his own feet," "one who will be up-right," "one who must be watched because he might go too far," or some-times "one who will surely fall." At any rate, to become "one who can walk" is one of the many steps in child development which suddenly give an experi-ence of physical mastery and of cultural meaning, of pleasure in activity and of social prestige; it thus is one building stone of self-esteem. This self-es-teem, confirmed at the end of each major crisis, grows to be a conviction that one is learning effective steps toward a tangible future, that one is developing a defined personality within a social reality which one understands. The growing child must, at every step, derive a vitalizing sense of reality from the awareness that his individual way of mastering experience is a success-ful variant of the way other people around him master experience and recog-nize such mastery.

In this, children cannot be fooled by empty praise and condescending encouragement. They may have to accept artificial bolstering of their self-esteem in lieu of something better, but what I call their accruing ego identity gains real strength only from wholehearted and consistent recognition of real accomplishment, that is, achievement that has meaning in their culture. A child has quite a number of opportunities to identify himself, more or less experimentally, with habits, traits, occupations, and ideas of real or fictitious people of either sex. Certain crises force him to make radical selections. However, this historical era in which he lives offers only a limited number of socially meaningful models for workable combinations of identification fragments. His usefulness depends on the way in which he simultaneously meets the requirements of his maturational stage and his habits of adjustment. But, should a child feel that the environment tries to deprive him too radically of all the forms of expression which permit him to develop and to integrate the next step in this ego identity, he will resist with the astonishing strength encountered in animals who are suddenly forced to defend their lives. Indeed, in the social jungle of human existence, there is no feeling of being alive without a sense of ego identity. To understand this would be to understand the trouble of adolescents better, especially the trouble of all those who cannot just be "nice" boys and girls, but are desperately seeking for a satisfactory sense of belonging, be it cliques and gangs here in our country or in inspiring mass movements in others.

Ego identity, then, develops out of a gradual integration of all identifications, but here, if anywhere, the whole has a different quality than the sum of its parts. Under favorable circumstances children have the nucleus of a separate identity in early life; often they must defend it against any pressure which would make them overidentify with one of their parents. This is difficult to learn from patients, because the neurotic ego has, by definition, fallen prey to overidentification and to faulty identifications with disturbed parents, a circumstance which isolated the small individual both from his budding identity and from his milieu. But we can study it profitably in the children of minority-group Americans who, having successfully graduated from a marked and well-guided stage of autonomy, enter the most decisive stage of American childhood: that of initiative and industry.

Minority groups of a lesser degree of Americanization (Negroes, Indians, Mexicans, and certain European groups) often are privileged in the enjoyment of a more sensual early childhood. Their crises come when their parents and teachers, losing trust in themselves and using sudden correctives in order to approach the vague but pervasive Anglo-Saxon ideal, create violent discontinuities; or where, indeed, the children themselves learn to disavow their sensual and overprotective mothers as temptations and a hindrance to the formation of a more American personality.

On the whole, it can be said that American schools successfully meet the challenge of training children of play-school age and of the elementary grades in a spirit of self-reliance and enterprise. Children of these ages seem remarkably free of prejudice and apprehension, preoccupied as they still are with growing and learning and with the new pleasures of association outside their families. This, to forestall the sense of individual inferiority, must lead to a hope for "industrial association," for equality with all those who apply themselves wholeheartedly to the same skills and adventures in learning. Many individual successes, on the other hand, only expose the now overly encouraged children of mixed backgrounds and somewhat deviant endowments to the shock of American adolescence: the standardization of individuality and the intolerance of "differences." The emerging ego identity, then, bridges the early childhood stages, when the body and the parent images were given their specific meanings, and the later stages, when a variety of social roles become available and increasingly coercive. A lasting ego identity cannot begin to exist without the trust of the first oral stage; it cannot be completed without a promise of fulfillment which from the dominant image of adulthood reaches down into the baby's beginnings and which creates at every step an accruing sense of ego strength.

II

The danger of this stage is *self-diffusion;* as Biff puts it in Arthur Miller's *Death of a Salesman,* "I just can't take hold, Mom, I can't take hold of some kind of a life." Where such a dilemma is based on a strong previous doubt of one's ethnic and sexual identity, delinquent and outright psychotic incidents are not uncommon. Youth after youth, bewildered by some assumed role, a role forced on him by the inexorable standardization of American adolescence, runs away in one form or another; leaving schools and jobs, staying out all night, or withdrawing into bizarre and inaccessible moods. Once "delinquent," his greatest need and often his only salvation, is the refusal on the part of older friends, advisers, and judiciary personnel to type him further by pat diagnoses and social judgments which ignore the special dynamic conditions of adolescence. For if diagnosed and treated correctly, seemingly psychotic and criminal incidents do not in adolescence have the same fatal significance which they have at other ages. Yet many a youth, finding that the authorities expect him to be "a bum," or " a queer," or "off the beam," perversely obliges society by becoming just that.

In general it is primarily the inability to settle on an occupational identity which disturbs young people. To keep themselves together they temporarily overidentify, to the point of apparent complete loss of identity, with the heroes of cliques and crowds. On the other hand, they become remarkably clannish, intolerant, and cruel in their exclusion of others who are "different," in skin color or cultural background, in tastes and gifts, and often in entirely petty aspects of dress and gesture arbitrarily selected as the signs of an in-grouper or out-grouper. It is important to understand (which does not mean condone or participate in) such intolerance as the necessary *defense against a sense of identity diffusion,* which is unavoidable at a time of life when the body changes its proportions radically, when genital maturity floods body and imagination with all manners of drives, when intimacy with the other sex approaches and is, on occasion, forced on the youngster, and when life lies before one with a variety of conflicting possibilities and choices. Adolescents help one another temporarily through such discomfort by forming cliques and by stereotyping themselves and their ideals.

It is important to understand this because it makes clear the appeal which simple totalitarian doctrines have on the minds of the youth of such countries and classes as have lost or are losing their group identities (feudal, agrarian, national, and so forth) in these times of world-wide industrialization, emancipation, and wider intercommunication. The dynamic quality of the tempestuous adolescences lived through in patriarchal and agrarian countries (countries which face the most radical changes in political structure and in economy) explains the fact that their young people find convincing and satisfactory identities in the simple totalitarian doctrines of race, class, or nation. Even though we may be forced to win wars against their leaders, we still are faced with the job of winning the peace with these grim youths by convincingly demonstrating to them (by living it) a democratic identity which can be strong and yet tolerant, judicious and still determined.

But it is increasingly important to understand this also in order to treat the intolerances of our adolescents at home with understanding and guidance rather than with verbal stereotypes or prohibitions. It is difficult to be tolerant if deep down you are not quite sure that you are a man (or a woman), that you will ever grow together again and be attractive, that you will be able to master your drives, that you really know who you are,[1] that you know what you want to be, that you know what you look like to others, and that you will know how to make the right decision without, once and for all, committing yourself to the wrong friend, girl, or career. Religions help the integration of such identity with "confirmations" of a clearly defined way of life. In many countries, nationalism supports a sense of identity. In primitive tribes puberty rites help to standardize the new identity, often with horrifying, impressive rituals.

Democracy in a country like America poses special problems in that it insists on *self-made identities* ready to grasp many chances and ready to adjust to changing necessities of booms and busts, of peace and war, of migration and determined sedentary life. Our democracy, furthermore, must present the adolescent with ideals which can be shared by youths of many backgrounds and which emphasize autonomy in the form of independence and initiative in the form of enterprise. These promises, in turn, are not easy to fulfill in increasingly complex and centralized systems of economic and political organization, systems which, if geared to war, must automatically neglect the "self-made" identities of millions of individuals and put them where they are most needed. This is hard on many young Americans because their whole upbringing, and therefore the development of a healthy personality, depends on a certain degree of choice, a certain hope for an individual chance, and a certain conviction in freedom of *self-determination*.

We are speaking here not only of high privileges and lofty ideas but also of psychological necessities. Psychologically speaking, a gradually accruing ego identity is the only safeguard against the *anarchy of drives* as well as the *autocracy of conscience*, that is, the cruel overconscientiousness which is the inner residue in the adult of his past inequality in regard to his parent. Any loss of a sense of identity exposes the individual to his own childhood conflicts—as could be observed, for example, in the neuroses of World War

---

[1] On the wall of a cowboys' bar in the wide-open West hangs a saying: "I ain't what I ought to be, I ain't what I'm going to be, but I ain't what I was."

ll among men and women who could not stand the general dislocation of their careers or a variety of other special pressures of war. Our adversaries, it seems, understand this. Their psychological warfare consists in the determined continuation of general conditions which permit them to indoctrinate mankind within their orbit with the simple and yet for them undoubtedly effective identities of class warfare and nationalism, while they know that the psychology, as well as the economy, of free enterprise and of self-determination is stretched to the breaking point under conditions of long-drawn-out cold and lukewarm war. It is clear, therefore, that we must bend every effort to present our young men and women with the tangible and trustworthy promise of opportunities for a rededication to the life for which the country's history, as well as their own childhood, has prepared them. Among the tasks of national defense, this one must not be forgotten.

I have tentatively referred to the relationship of the problem of trust to matters of adult faith; to that of the problem of autonomy to matters of adult independence in work and citizenship. I have pointed to the connection between a sense of initiative and the kind of enterprise sanctioned in the economic system, and between the sense of industry and a culture's technology. In searching for the social values which guide identity, one confronts the problem of aristocracy, in its widest possible sense, which connotes the conviction that the best people rule and that that rule, as defined in society, develops the best in people. In order not to become cynically or apathetically lost, young people in search of an identity must somewhere be able to convince themselves that those who succeed acquire not only the conviction that they have proven to be better than others, but also the obligation of being the best, that is, of personifying the nation's ideals. In this country, as in any other, we have those successful types who become the cynical representatives of the "inside track," the "bosses" of impersonal machinery. . . . In a culture once pervaded with the value of the self-made man, a special danger ensues from the idea of a synthetic personality: as if you are what you can appear to be, or as if you are what you can buy. Here the very special influence of the entertainment industry must be considered. This can be counteracted only by a system of education that transmits values and goals which determinedly aspire beyond mere "functioning" and "making the grade."

The Sources
of Student Dissent

Kenneth Keniston
YALE UNIVERSITY

The apparent upsurge of dissent among American college students is one of the more puzzling phenomena in recent American history. Less than a decade ago, commencement orators were decrying the "silence" of college students in the face of urgent national and international issues; but in the past two or three years, the same speakers have warned graduating classes across the country against the dangers of unreflective protest, irresponsible action and unselective dissent. Rarely in history has apparent apathy been replaced so rapidly by publicized activism, silence by strident dissent.

This "wave" of dissent among American college students has been much discussed. Especially in the mass media—popular magazines, newspapers and television—articles of interpretation, explanation, deprecation and occasionally applause have appeared in enormous numbers. More important, from the first beginnings of the student civil rights movement, social scientists have

Reprinted from *Journal of Social Issues*, 1967, 23, No. 3, 108–137. By permission.

been regular participant-observers and investigators of student dissent. There now exists a considerable body of research that deals with the characteristics and settings of student dissent (see Lipset and Altbach, 1966; Block, Haan and Smith, forthcoming; Katz, 1967; Peterson, 1967 for summaries of this research). To be sure, most of these studies are topical (centered around a particular protest or demonstration), and some of the more extensive studies are still in varying stages of incompletion. Yet enough evidence has already been gathered to permit tentative generalizations about the varieties, origins and future of student dissent in the nineteen sixties.

In the remarks to follow, I will attempt to gather together this evidence (along with my own research and informal observations) to provide tentative answers to three questions about student dissent today. First, what is the nature of student dissent in American colleges? Second, what are the sources of the recent "wave of protest" by college students? And third, what can we predict about the future of student dissent?

TWO VARIETIES OF DISSENT

Dissent is by no means the dominant mood of American college students. Every responsible study or survey shows apathy and privatism far more dominant than dissent (see, for example, Newsweek, 1965; Katz, 1965; Reed, 1966; Peterson, 1966; Block, Haan and Smith, forthcoming). On most of our twenty-two hundred campuses, student protest, student alienation and student unrest are something that happens elsewhere, or that characterizes a mere handful of "kooks" on the local campus. However we define "dissent," overt dissent is relatively infrequent and tends to be concentrated largely at the more selective, "progressive," and "academic" colleges and universities in America. Thus, Peterson's study of student protests (1966) finds political demonstrations concentrated in the larger universities and institutions of higher academic calibre, and almost totally absent at teachers colleges, technical institutes and non-academic denominational colleges. And even at the colleges that gather together the greatest number of dissenters, the vast majority of students—generally well over 95%—remain interested onlookers or opponents rather than active dissenters. Thus, whatever we say about student dissenters is said about a very small minority of America's six million college students. At most colleges, dissent is not visible at all.

Partly because the vast majority of American students remain largely uncritical of the wider society, fundamentally conformist in behavior and outlook, and basically "adjusted" to the prevailing collegiate, national and international order, the small minority of dissenting students is highly visible to the mass media. As I will argue later, such students are often distinctly talented; they "use" the mass media effectively; and they generally succeed in their goal of making themselves and their causes highly visible. Equally important, student dissenters of all types arouse deep and ambivalent feelings in non-dissenting students and adults—envy, resentment, admiration, repulsion, nostalgia and guilt. Such feelings contribute both to the selective over-attention dissenters receive and to the often distorted perceptions and interpretations of them and their activities. Thus, there has developed through the mass media and the imaginings of adults a more or less stereotyped—and generally incorrect—image of the student dissenter.

The Stereotyped Dissenter

The "stereotypical" dissenter as popularly portrayed is both a Bohemian and political activist. Bearded, be-Levi-ed, long-haired, dirty and unkempt, he is seen as profoundly disaffected from his society, often influenced by "radical" (Marxist, Communist, Maoist, or Castroite) ideas, an experimenter in sex and drugs, unconventional in his daily behavior. Frustrated and un-happy, often deeply maladjusted as a person, he is a "failure" (or as one U. S. Senator put it, a "reject"). Certain academic communities like Berkeley are said to act as "magnets" for dissenters, who selectively attend colleges with a reputation as protest centers. Furthermore, dropouts or "non-students" who have failed in college cluster in large numbers around the fringes of such colleges, actively seeking pretexts for protest, refusing all compromise and impatient with ordinary democratic processes.

According to such popular analyses, the sources of dissent are to be found in the loss of certain traditional American virtues. The "breakdown" of American family life, high rates of divorce, the "softness" of American liv-ing, inadequate parents, and above all, overindulgence and "spoiling" con-tribute to the prevalence of dissent. Brought up in undisciplined homes by parents unsure of their own values and standards, dissenters channel their frustration and anger against the older generation, against all authority, and against established institutions.

Similar themes are sometimes found in the interpretations of more scholarly commentators. "Generational conflict" is said to underly the moti-vation to dissent, and a profound "alienation" from American society is seen as a factor of major importance in producing protests. Then, too, such factors as the poor quality and impersonality of American college education, the large size and lack of close student-faculty contact in the "multiversity" are sometimes seen as the latent or precipitating factors in student protests, regardless of the manifest issues around which students are organized. And still other scholarly analysts, usually men now disillusioned by the radicalism of the 1930's, have expressed fear of the dogmatism, rigidity and "authori-tarianism of the left" of today's student activists.

Activism and Alienation

These stereotyped views are, I believe, incorrect in a variety of ways. They confuse two distinct varieties of student dissent; equally important, they fuse dissent with maladjustment. There are, of course, as many forms of dissent as there are individual dissenters; and any effort to counter the popu-lar stereotype of the dissenter by pointing to the existence of distinct "types" of dissenters runs the risk of over-simplifying at a lower level of abstraction. Nonetheless, it seems to me useful to suggest that student dissenters generally fall somewhere along a continuum that runs between two ideal types—first, the political activist or protester, and second, the withdrawn, culturally alienated student.

The activist. The defining characteristic of the "new" activist is his participation in a student demonstration or group activity that concerns itself with some matter of general political, social or ethical principle. Characteristically, the activist feels that some injustice has been done, and attempts to "take a stand," "demonstrate" or in some fashion express his convictions. The specific issues in question range from protest against a paternalistic college administration's actions to disagreement with American Vietnam policies, from indignation at the exploitation of the poor to anger at the firing of a devoted teacher, from opposition to the Selective Service laws which exempt him but not the poor to—most important—outrage at the deprivation of the civil rights of other Americans.

The initial concern of the protester is almost always immediate, ad hoc and local. To be sure, the student who protests about one issue is likely to feel inclined or obliged to demonstrate his convictions on other issues as well (Heist, 1966). But whatever the issue, the protester rarely demonstrates because his *own* interests are jeopardized, but rather because he perceives injustices being done to *others* less fortunate than himself. For example, one of the apparent paradoxes about protests against current draft policies is that the protesting students are selectively drawn from that subgroup *most* likely to receive student deferments for graduate work. The basis of protest is a general sense that the selective service rules and the war in Vietnam are unjust to others with whom the student is identified, but whose fate he does not share. If one runs down the list of "causes" taken up by student activists, in rare cases are demonstrations directed at improving the lot of the protesters themselves; identification with the oppressed is a more important motivating factor than an actual sense of immediate personal oppression.

The anti-ideological stance of today's activists has been noted by many commentators. This distrust of formal ideologies (and at times of articulate thought) makes it difficult to pinpoint the positive social and political values of student protesters. Clearly, many current American political institutions like de facto segregation are opposed; clearly, too, most students of the New Left reject careerism and familism as personal values. In this sense, we might think of the activist as (politically) "alienated." But this label seems to me more misleading than illuminating, for it overlooks the more basic *commitment* of most student activists to other ancient, traditional and credal American values like free speech, citizen's participation in decision-making, equal opportunity and justice. In so far as the activist rejects all or part of "the power structure," it is because current political realities fall so far short of the ideals he sees as central to the American creed. And in so far as he repudiates careerism and familism, it is because of his implicit allegiance to other human goals he sees, once again, as more crucial to American life. Thus, to emphasize the "alienation" of activists is to neglect their more basic allegiance to credal American ideals.

One of these ideals is, of course, a belief in the desirability of political and social action. Sustained in good measure by the successes of the student civil rights movement, the protester is usually convinced that demonstrations are effective in mobilizing public opinion, bringing moral or political pressure to bear, demonstrating the existence of his opinions, or, at times, in "bringing the machine to a halt." In this sense, then, despite his criticisms of existing political practices and social institutions, he is a political optimist. Moreover, the protester must believe in at least minimal organization and group activity; otherwise, he would find it impossible to take part, as he does, in any organized demonstrations or activities. Despite their search for more truly "democratic" forms of organization and action (e.g., participatory democracy), activists agree that group action is more effective than purely individual acts. To be sure, a belief in the value and efficacy of political action is not equivalent to endorsement of prevalent political institutions or forms of action. Thus, one characteristic of activists is their search for new forms of social action, protest and political organization (community organization, sit-ins, participatory democracy) that will be more effective and less oppressive than traditional political institutions.

The culturally alienated. In contrast to the politically optimistic, active, and socially concerned protester, the culturally alienated student is far too pessimistic and too firmly opposed to "the System" to wish to demonstrate his disapproval in any organized public way.[1] His demonstrations of dissent are private: through nonconformity of behavior, ideology and dress, through personal experimentation and above all through efforts to intensify his own subjective experience, he shows his distaste and disinterest in politics and society. The activist attempts to change the world around him, but the alienated student is convinced that meaningful change of the social and political world is impossible; instead, he considers "dropping out" the only real option.

Alienated students tend to be drawn from the same general social strata and colleges as protesters. But psychologically and ideologically, their backgrounds are often very different. Alienated students are more likely to be disturbed psychologically; and although they are often highly talented and artistically gifted, they are less committed to academic values and intellectual achievement than are protesters. The alienated student's real campus is the school of the absurd, and he has more affinity for pessimistic existentialist ontology than for traditional American activism. Furthermore, such students usually find it psychologically and ideologically impossible to take part in

---

[1] The following paragraphs are based on the study of culturally alienated students described in *The Uncommitted* (1965). For a more extensive discussion of the overwhelmingly anti-political stance of these students, see Keniston (1966) and also Rigney and Smith (1961), Allen and Silverstein (1967), Watts and Wittaker (1967), and Wittaker and Watts (1967).

organized group activities for any length of time, particularly when they are expected to assume responsibilities for leadership. Thus, on the rare occasions when they become involved in demonstrations, they usually prefer peripheral roles, avoid responsibilities and are considered a nuisance by serious activists (Draper, 1965).

Whereas the protesting student is likely to accept the basic political and social values of his parents, the alienated student almost always rejects his parents' values. In particular, he is likely to see his father as a man who has "sold out" to the pressures for success and status in American society: he is determined to avoid the fate that overtook his father. Toward their mothers, however, alienated students usually express a very special sympathy and iden-tification. These mothers, far from encouraging their sons towards indepen-dence and achievement, generally seem to have been over-solicitous and limiting. The most common family environment of the alienated-student-to-be consists of a parental schism supplemented by a special mother-son alliance of mutual understanding and maternal control and depreciation of the father (Keniston, 1965a).

In many colleges, alienated students often constitute a kind of hidden underground, disorganized and shifting in membership, in which students can temporarily or permanently withdraw from the ordinary pressures of college life. The alienated are especially attracted to the hallucinogenic drugs like marijuana, mescaline and LSD, precisely because these agents combine withdrawal from ordinary social life with the promise of greatly intensified subjectivity and perception. To the confirmed "acid head," what matters is intense, drug-assisted perception; the rest—including politics, social action and student demonstrations—is usually seen as "role-playing."[2]

The recent and much-publicized emergence of "hippie" sub-cultures in several major cities and increasingly on the campuses of many selective and progressive colleges illustrates the overwhelmingly apolitical stance of alienated youth. For although hippies oppose war and believe in inter-racial

---

[2] The presence among student dissenters of a group of "nonstudents"—that is, drop-outs from college or graduate school who congregate or remain near some academic center—has been much noted. In fact, however, student protesters seem somewhat *less* likely to drop out of college than do nonparticipants in demonstrations (Heist, 1966), and there is no evidence that dropping out of college is in any way related to dissent from American society (Keniston and Helmreich, 1965). On the contrary, several studies sug-gest that the academically gifted and psychologically intact student who drops out of college voluntarily has few distinctive discontents about his college or about American society (Suczek and Alfort, 1966; Pervin et al., 1966; Wright, 1966). If he is dissatisfied at all, it is with himself, usually for failing to take advantage of the "rich educational opportunities" he sees in his college. The motivations of students dropping out of college are complex and varied, but such motivations more often seem related to personal questions of self-definition and parental identification or to a desire to escape relentless academic pres-sures, than to any explicit dissent from the Great Society. Thus, although a handful of students have chosen to drop out of college for a period to devote themselves to political and societal protest activities, there seems little reason in general to associate the drop-out with the dissenter, whether he be a protester or an alienated student. The opposite is nearer the truth.

living, few have been willing or able to engage in anything beyond occasional peace marches or apolitical "human be-ins." Indeed, the hippies' emphasis on immediacy, "love" and "turning-on," together with his basic rejection of the traditional values of American life, inoculates him against involvement in long-range activist endeavors, like education or community organization, and even against the sustained effort needed to plan and execute demonstrations or marches. For the alienated hippie, American society is beyond redemption (or not worth trying to redeem); but the activist, no matter how intense his rejection of specific American policies and practices, retains a conviction that his society can and should be changed. Thus, despite occasional agreement in principle between the alienated and the activists, cooperation in practice has been rare, and usually ends with activists accusing the alienated of "irresponsibility," while the alienated are confirmed in their view of activists as moralistic, "up-tight," and "un-cool."

Obviously, no description of a type ever fits an individual perfectly. But by this rough typology, I mean to suggest that popular stereotypes which present a unified portrait of student dissent are gravely oversimplified. More specifically, they confuse the politically pessimistic and socially uncommitted alienated student with the politically hopeful and socially committed activist. To be sure, there are many students who fall between these two extremes, and some of them alternate between passionate search for intensified subjectivity and equally passionate efforts to remedy social and political injustices. And as I will later suggest, even within the student movement, one of the central tensions is between political activism and cultural alienation. Nonetheless, even to understand this tension we must first distinguish between the varieties of dissent apparent on American campuses.

Furthermore, the distinction between activist and alienated students as psychological types suggests the incompleteness of scholarly analyses that see social and historical factors as the only forces that "push" a student toward one or the other of these forms of dissent. To be sure, social and cultural factors are of immense importance in providing channels for the expression (or suppression) of dissent, and in determining which kinds of dissenters receive publicity, censure, support or ostracism in any historical period. But these factors, cannot, in general, change a hippie into a committed activist, nor a SNCC field worker into a full-time "acid-head." Thus, the prototypical activist of 1966 is not the "same" student as the prototypical student bohemian of 1956, but is rather the politically aware but frustrated, academically oriented "privatist" of that era. Similarly, as I will argue below, the most compelling alternative to most activists is not the reach for kicks or sentience but the quest for scholarly competence. And if culturally sanctioned opportunities for the expression of alienation were to disappear, most alienated students would turn to private psychopathology rather than to public activism.

Stated more generally, historical forces do not ordinarily transform radically the character, values and inclinations of an adult in later life. Rather, they thrust certain groups forward in some eras and discourage or suppress other groups. The recent alternation in styles of student dissent in America is therefore not to be explained so much by the malleability of individual character as by the power of society to bring activists into the limelight, providing them with the intellectual and moral instruments for action. Only a minority of potential dissenters fall close enough to the midpoint between alienation and activism so that they can constitute a "swing vote" acutely responsive to social and cultural pressures and styles. The rest, the majority, are characterologically committed to one or another style of dissent.

THE SOURCES OF ACTIVISM

What I have termed "alienated" students are by no means a new phenomenon in American life, or for that matter in industrialized societies. Bohemians, "beatniks" and artistically inclined undergraduates who rejected middle-class values have long been a part of the American student scene, especially at more selective colleges; they constituted the most visible form of dissent during the relative political "silence" of American students in the 1950's. What is distinctive about student dissent in recent years is the unexpected emergence of a vocal minority of politically and socially active students.[3] Much is now known about the characteristics of such students, and the circumstances under which protests are likely to be mounted. At the same time, many areas of ignorance remain. In the account to follow, I will attempt to formulate a series of general hypotheses concerning the sources of student activism.[4]

It is abundantly clear that no single factor will suffice to explain the increase of politically motivated activities and protests on American campuses. Even if we define an activist narrowly, as a student who (a) acts together with others in a group, (b) is concerned with some ethical, social, ideological or political issue, and (c) holds liberal or "radical" views, the sources of student activism and protest are complex and inter-related. At least four kinds of

[3] Student activism, albeit of a rather different nature, was also found in the nineteen thirties. For a discussion and contrast of student protest today and after the Depression, see Lipset (1966a).

[4] Throughout the following, I will use the terms "protester" and "activist" interchangeably, although I am aware that some activists are not involved in protests. Furthermore, the category of "activist" is an embracing one, comprising at least three sub-classes. First, those who might be termed *reformers*, that is, students involved in community organization work, the Peace Corps, tutoring programs, Vista, etc., but not generally affiliated with any of the "New Left" organizations. Second, the group of *activists proper*, most of whom are or have been affiliated with organizations like the Free Speech Movement at Berkeley, Students for a Democratic Society, the Student Non-violent Coordinating Committee or the Congress on Racial Equality or the Vietnam Summer Project. Finally, there is a much publicized handful of students who might be considered *extremists*, who belong to doctrinaire Marxist and Trotskyite organizations like the now-defunct May Second Movement. No empirical study with which I am acquainted has investigated the differences between students in these three sub-groups. Most studies have concentrated on the "activist proper," and my remarks will be based on a reading of their data.

factors seem involved in any given protest. First, the individuals involved must be suitably predisposed by their personal backgrounds, values and motivations. Second, the likelihood of protest is far greater in certain kinds of educational and social settings. Third, socially directed protests require a special cultural climate, that is, certain distinctive values and views about the effectiveness and meaning of demonstrations, and about the wider society. And finally, some historical situations are especially conducive to protests.

THE PROTEST-PRONE PERSONALITY

A large and still-growing number of studies, conducted under different auspices, at different times and about different students, presents a remarkably consistent picture of the protest-prone individual (Aiken, Demerath and Marwell, 1966; Flacks, 1967; Gastwirth, 1965; Heist, 1965, 1966; Lyonns, 1965; Somers, 1965; Watts and Whittaker, 1966; Westby and Baungart, 1966; Katz, 1967; and Paulus, 1967). For one, student protesters are generally outstanding students; the higher the student's grade average, the more outstanding his academic achievements, the more likely it is that he will become involved in any given political demonstration. Similarly, student activists come from families with liberal political values; a disproportionate number report that their parents hold views essentially similar to their own, and accept or support their activities. Thus, among the parents of protesters we find large numbers of liberal Democrats, plus an unusually large scattering of pacifists, socialists, etc. A disproportionate number of protesters come from Jewish families; and if the parents of activists are religious, they tend to be concentrated in the more liberal denominations—Reform Judaism, Unitarianism, the Society of Friends, etc. Such parents are reported to have high ethical and political standards, regardless of their actual convictions.

As might be expected of a group of politically liberal and academically talented students, a disproportionate number are drawn from professional and intellectual families of upper middle-class status. For example, compared with active student conservatives, members of protest groups tend to have higher parental incomes, more parental education, and less anxiety about social status (Westby and Braungart, 1966). Another study finds that high levels of education distinguish the activist's family even in the grandparental generation (Flacks, 1967). In brief, activists are not drawn from disadvantaged, status-anxious, underprivileged or uneducated groups; on the contrary, they are selectively recruited from among those young Americans who have had the most socially fortunate upbringings.

Basic Value Commitments of Activists

The basic value commitments of the activist tend to be academic and non-vocational. Such students are rarely found among engineers, future teachers at teachers colleges, or students of business administration. Their over-all educational goals are those of a liberal education for its own sake, rather than specifically technical, vocational or professional preparation. Rejecting careerist and familist goals, activists espouse humanitarian, expressive and self-actualizing values. Perhaps because of these values, they delay career choice longer than their classmates (Flacks, 1967). Nor are such students distinctively dogmatic, rigid or authoritarian. Quite the contrary, the substance and style of their beliefs and activities tends to be open, flexible and highly liberal. Their fields of academic specialization are non-vocational —the social sciences and the humanities. Once in college, they not only do well academically, but tend to persist in their academic commitments, dropping out *less* frequently than most of their classmates. As might be expected, a disproportionate number receive a B.A. within four years and continue on to graduate school, preparing themselves for academic careers.

Survey data also suggest that the activist is not distinctively dissatisfied with his college education. As will be noted below, activists generally attend colleges which provide the best, rather than the worst, undergraduate education available today. Objectively then, activists probably have less to complain about in their undergraduate educations than most other students. And subjectively as well, surveys show most activists, like most other American undergraduates, to be relatively well satisfied with their undergraduate educations (Somers, 1965; Kornhauser, 1967). Thus, dissatisfaction with educational failings of the "impersonal multiversity," however important as a rallying cry, does not appear to be a distinctive cause of activism.

In contrast to their relative satisfaction with the quality of their educations, however, activists *are* distinctively dissatisfied with what might be termed the "civil-libertarian" defects of their college administrations. While no doubt a great many American undergraduates distrust "University Hall," this distrust is especially pronounced amongst student protesters (Kornhausen, 1967; Paulus, 1967). Furthermore, activists tend to be more responsive than other students to deprivations of civil rights on campus as well as off campus, particularly when political pressures seem to motivate on-campus policies they consider unjust. The same responsiveness increasingly extends to issues of "student power": i.e., student participation and decisions affecting campus life. Thus, bans on controversial speakers, censureship of student publications, and limitations on off-campus political or social action are likely to incense the activist, as is arbitrary "administration without the consent of the administered." But it is primarily perceived injustice or the denial of student rights by the Administration—rather than poor educational quality, neglect by the faculty, or the impersonality of the multiversity—that agitates the activist.

Most studies of activists have concentrated on variables that are relatively easy to measure: social class, academic achievements, explicit values and satisfaction with college. But these factors alone will not explain activism: more students possess the demographic and attitudinal characteristics of the protest-prone personality than are actually involved in protests and social action programs. Situational, institutional, cultural and historical factors (discussed below), obviously contribute to "catalysing" a protest-prone personality into an actual activist. But it also seems that, within the broad demographic group so far defined, more specific psychodynamic factors contribute to activism.

Activists . . . Not in Rebellion

In speculating about such factors, we leave the ground of established fact and enter the terrain of speculation, for only a few studies have explored the personality dynamics and family constellation of the activist, and most of these studies are impressionistic and clinical (e.g., Coles, 1967; Ehle, 1965; Draper, 1965; Fishman and Solomon, n.d., 1964; Gastwirth, 1965; Newfield, 1966; Schneider, 1966; Solomon and Fishman, 1963, 1964; Zinn, 1965). But certain facts are clear. As noted, activists are *not*, on the whole, repudiating or rebelling against explicit parental values and ideologies. On the contrary, there is some evidence that such students are living out their parents' values in practice; and one study suggests that activists may be somewhat *closer* to their parents' values than nonactivists (Flacks, 1967). Thus, any simple concept of "generational conflict" or "rebellion against parental authority" is clearly oversimplified as applied to the motivations of most protesters.

Activists . . . Living Out Parental Values

It does seem probable, however, that many activists are concerned with *living out expressed but unimplemented parental values*. Solomon and Fishman (1963), studying civil rights activists and peace marchers, argue that many demonstrators are "acting out" in their demonstrations the values which their parents explicitly believed, but did not have the courage or opportunity to practice or fight for. Similarly, when protesters criticize their fathers, it is usually over their fathers' failure to practice what they have preached to their children throughout their lives. Thus, in the personal background of the protester there is occasionally a suggestion that his father is less-than-"sincere" (and even at times "hypocritical") in his professions of political liberalism. In particular, both careerism and familism in parents are the objects of activist criticisms, the more so because these implicit goals often conflict with explicit parental values. And it may be that protesters receive both covert and overt support from their parents because the latter are secretly proud of their children's eagerness to implement the ideals they as parents have only given lip-service to. But whatever the ambivalences that bind parents with their activist children, it would be wrong to overemphasize them: what is most impressive is the solidarity of older and younger generations.

ACTIVISTS . . . FAMILY STRUCTURE

While no empirical study has tested this hypothesis, it seems probable that in many activist-producing families, the mother will have a dominant psychological influence on her son's development. I have already noted that the protester's cause is rarely himself, but rather alleviating the oppression of others. As a group, activists seem to possess an unusual *capacity for nurturant identification*—that is, for empathy and sympathy with the underdog, the oppressed and the needy. Such a capacity can have many origins, but its most likely source in upper-middle-class professional families is identification with an active mother whose own work embodies nurturant concern for others. Flacks' finding that the mothers of activists are likely to be employed, often in professional or service roles like teaching and social work, is consistent with this hypothesis. In general, in American society, middle-class women have greater social and financial freedom to work in jobs that are idealistically "fulfilling" as opposed to merely lucrative or prestigious. As a rule, then, in middle-class families, it is the mother who actively embodies in her life and work the humanitarian, social and political ideals that the father may share in principle but does not or cannot implement in his career.

Given what we know about the general characteristics of the families of protest-prone students, it also seems probable that the dominant ethos of their families is unusually equalitarian, permissive, "democratic," and highly individuated. More specifically, we might expect that these will be families where children talk back to their parents at the dinner table, where free dialogue and discussion of feelings are encouraged and where "rational" solutions are sought to everyday family problems and conflicts. We would also expect that such families would place a high premium on self-expression and intellectual independence, encouraging their children to make up their own minds and to stand firm against group pressures. Once again, the mother seems the most likely carrier and epitome of these values, given her relative freedom from professional and financial pressures.

The contrast between such protest-promoting families and alienating families should be underlined. In both, the son's deepest emotional ties are often to his mother. But in the alienating family, the mother-son relationship is characterized by maternal control and intrusiveness, whereas in the protest-promoting family, the mother is a highly individuating force in her son's life, pushing him to independence and autonomy. Furthermore, the alienated student is determined to avoid the fate that befell his father, whereas the protesting student wants merely to live out the values that his father has not always worked hard enough to practice. Finally, the egalitarian, permissive, democratic and individuating environment of the entire family of the protester contrasts with the overcontrolling, over-solicitous attitude of the mother in the alienating family, where the father is usually excluded from major emotional life within the family.

These hypotheses about the family background and psychodynamics of the protester are speculative, and future research may prove their invalidity. But regardless of whether *these* particular speculations are correct, it seems clear that in addition to the general social, demographic and attitudinal factors mentioned in most research, more specific familial and psychodynamic influences contribute to protest-proneness.

THE PROTEST-PROMOTING INSTITUTION

However we define his characteristics, one activist alone cannot make a protest: the characteristics of the college or university he attends have much to do with whether his protest-proneness will ever be mobilized into actual activism. Politically, socially and ideologically motivated demonstrations and activities are most likely to occur at certain types of colleges; they are almost unknown at a majority of campuses. The effects of institutional characteristics on protests have been studied by Cowan (1966) and Peterson (1966), and by Sampson (1967) and Brown (1967).

In order for an organized protest or related activities to occur, there must obviously be sufficient *numbers* of protest-prone students to form a group, these students must have an opportunity for *interaction* with each other, and there must be *leaders* to initiate and mount the protest. Thus, we might expect—and we indeed find—that protest is associated with institutional size, and particularly with the congregation of large numbers of protest-prone students in close proximity to each other. More important than sheer size alone, however, is the "image" of the institution: certain institutions selectively recruit students with protest-prone characteristics. Specifically, a reputation for academic excellence and freedom, coupled with highly selective admissions policies, will tend to congregate large numbers of potentially protesting students on one campus. Thus, certain institutions do act as "magnets" for political activists, but not so much because of their reputations for political radicalism as because they are noted for their academic excellence. Among such institutions are some of the most selective and "progressive" private liberal arts colleges, major state universities (like Michigan, California at Berkeley and Wisconsin) which have long traditions of vivid undergraduate teaching and high admissions standards (Lipset and Altbach, 1966) and many of the more prestigious private universities.

Once protest-prone students are on campus, they must have an opportunity to interact, to support one another, to develop common outlooks and shared policies—in short, to form an *activist sub-culture* with sufficient mass and potency to generate a demonstration or action program. Establishing "honors colleges" for talented and academically motivated students is one particularly effective way of creating a "critical mass" of protest-prone students. Similarly, inadequate on-campus housing indirectly results in the development of off-campus protest-prone sub-cultures (e.g., co-op houses) in residences where student activists can develop a high degree of ideological solidarity and organizational cohesion.

But even the presence of a critical mass of protest-prone undergraduates in an activist sub-culture is not enough to make a protest without leaders and issues. And in general, the most effective protest leaders have not been undergraduates, but teaching assistants. The presence of large numbers of exploited, underpaid, disgruntled and frustrated teacher assistants (or other equivalent graduate students and younger faculty members) is almost essential for organized and persistent protest. For one, advanced students tend to be more liberal politically and more sensitive to political issues than are most undergraduates—partly because education seems to have a liberalizing effect, and partly because students who persist into graduate school tend to be more liberal to start than those who drop out or go elsewhere. Furthermore, the frustrations of graduate students, especially at very large public universities, make them particularly sensitive to general problems of injustice, exploitation and oppression. Teaching assistants, graduate students and young faculty members also tend to be in daily and prolonged contact with students, are close enough to them in age to sense their mood, and are therefore in an excellent position to lead and organize student protests. Particularly at institutions which command little institutional allegiance from large numbers of highly capable graduate students (Lipset and Altbach, 1966) will such students be found among the leaders of the protest movement.

The Issues of Protest

Finally, issues are a necessity. In many cases, these issues are provided by historical developments on the national or international scene, a point to which I will return. But in some instances, as at Berkeley, "on-campus" issues are the focus of protest. And in other cases, off-campus and on-campus issues are fused, as in the recent protests at institutional cooperation with draft board policies considered unjust by demonstrating students. In providing such on-campus issues, the attitude of the university administration is central. Skillful handling of student complaints, the maintenance of open channels of communication between student leaders and faculty members, and administrative willingness to resist public and political pressures in order to protect the rights of students—all minimize the likelihood of organized protest. Conversely, a university administration that shows itself unduly sensitive to political, legislative or public pressures, that treats students arrogantly, ineptly, condescendingly, hypocritically or above all dishonestly, is asking for a demonstration.

Thus one reason for the relative absence of on-campus student protests and demonstrations on the campuses of private, non-denominational "academic" colleges and universities (which recruit many protest-prone students) probably lies in the liberal policies of the administrations. As Cowan (1966) notes, liberal students generally attend non-restrictive and "libertarian" colleges. Given an administration and faculty that supports or tolerates activism and student rights, student activists must generally find their issues off-campus. The same students, confronting an administration unduly sensitive to political pressures from a conservative board of regents or State legislature, might engage in active on-campus protests. There is also some evidence that clever administrative manipulation of student complaints, even in the absence of genuine concern with student rights, can serve to dissipate the potentialities of protest (Keene, 1966).

Among the institutional factors often cited as motivating student protest is the largeness, impersonality, atomization, "multiversification," etc., of the university. I have already noted that student protesters do not seem distinctively dissatisfied with their educations. Furthermore, the outstanding academic achievements and intellectual motivations of activists concentrate them, within any college, in the courses and programs that provide the most "personal" attention: honors programs, individual instruction, advanced seminars, and so on. Thus, they probably receive relatively *more* individual attention and a *higher* calibre of instruction than do non-protesters. Furthermore, protests generally tend to occur at the best, rather than the worst colleges, judged from the point of view of the quality of undergraduate instruction. Thus, despite the popularity of student slogans dealing with the impersonality and irrelevance of the multiversity, the absolute level of educational opportunities seems, if anything, positively related to the occurrence of protest: the better the institution, the more likely demonstrations are.

Nor can today's student activism be attributed in any direct way to mounting academic pressures. To be sure, activism is most manifest at those selective colleges where the "pressure to perform" (Keniston, 1965b) is greatest, where standards are highest, and where anxieties about being admitted to a "good" graduate or professional school are most pronounced. But, contrary to the argument of Lipset and Altbach (1966), the impact of academic pressure on activism seems negative rather than positive. Protest-prone students, with their superior academic attainments and strong intellectual commitments, seem especially vulnerable to a kind of academic professionalism that, because of the enormous demands it makes upon the student's energies, serves to cancel or preclude activism. Student demonstrations rarely take place during exam periods, and protests concerned with educational quality almost invariably seek an improvement of quality, rather than a lessening of pressure. Thus, though the pressure to perform doubtless affects *all* American students, it probably acts as a deterrent rather than a stimulus to student activism.

Deprivation of Expectations

What probably does matter, however, is the *relative* deprivation of student expectations. A college that recruits large numbers of academically motivated and capable students into a less-than-first-rate education program, one that oversells entering freshmen on the virtues of the college, or one that reneges on implicit or explicit promises about the quality and freedom of education may well produce an "academic backlash" that will take the form of student protests over the quality of education. Even more important is the gap between expectations and actualities regarding freedom of student expression. Stern (1967) has demonstrated that most entering freshmen have extremely high hopes regarding the freedom of speech and action they will be able to exercise during college: most learn the real facts quickly, and graduate thoroughly disabused of their illusions. But since activists, as I have argued above, are particularly responsive to these issues, they are apt to tolerate disillusion less lightly, and to take up arms to concretize their dashed hopes. Compared to the frustration engendered by disillusionment regarding educational quality, the relative deprivation of civil libertarian hopes seems a more potent source of protests. And with regard to both issues, it must be recalled that protests have been *fewest* at institutions of low educational quality and little freedom for student expression. Thus, it is not the absolute level either of educational quality or of student freedom that matters, but the gap between student hopes and institutional facts.

THE PROTEST-PROMPTING CULTURAL CLIMATE

Even if a critical mass of interacting protest-prone students forms in an institution that provides leadership and issues, student protests are by no means inevitable, as the quiescence of American students during the nineteen fifties suggests. For protests to occur, other more broadly cultural factors, attitudes and values must be present. Protest activities must be seen as meaningful acts, either in an instrumental or an expressive sense; and activists must be convinced that the consequences of activism and protest will not be overwhelmingly damaging to them. During the 1950's one much-discussed factor that may have militated against student activism was the conviction that the consequences of protest (blacklisting, F.B.I. investigations, problems in obtaining security clearance, difficulties in getting jobs) were both harmful to the individual and yet extremely likely. Even more important was the sense on the part of many politically conscious students that participation in left-wing causes would merely show their naiveté, gullibility and political innocence without furthering any worthy cause. The prevailing climate was such that protest was rarely seen as an act of any meaning or usefulness.

Academic Support . . .
Today, in contrast, student protesters are not only criticized and excoriated by a large segment of the general public, but—more crucial—actively defended, encouraged, lionized, praised, publicized, photographed, interviewed and studied by a portion of the academic community. Since the primary reference group of most activists is not the general public, but rather that liberal segment of the academic world most sympathetic to protest, academic support has a disproportionate impact on protest-prone students' perception of their own activities. In addition, the active participation of admired faculty members in protests, teach-ins and peace marches, acts as a further incentive to students (Kelman, 1966). Thus, in a minority of American colleges, sub-cultures have arisen where protest is felt to be both an important existential act—a dignified way of "standing up to be counted"—and an effective way of "bringing the machine to a halt," sometimes by disruptive acts (sit-ins, strikes, etc.), more often by calling public attention to injustice.

Universalism . . .
An equally important, if less tangible "cultural" factor is the broad climate of social criticism in American society. As Parsons (1951, 1960), White (1961), and others have noted, one of the enduring themes of American

society is the pressure toward "universalism," that is, an increasing extension of principles like equality, equal opportunity, and fair protection of the law to all groups within the society (and in recent years, to all groups in the world). As affluence has increased in American society, impatience at the slow "progress" of non-affluent minority groups has also increased, not only among students, but among other segments of the population. Even before the advent of the student civil rights movement, support for racial segregation was diminishing. Similarly, the current student concern for the "forgotten fifth" was not so much initiated by student activists as it was taken up by them. In this regard, student activists are both caught up in and in the vanguard of a new wave of extension of universalism in American society. Although the demands of student activists usually go far beyond the national consensus, they nonetheless reflect (at the same time that they have helped advance) one of the continuing trends in American social change.

A contrasting but equally enduring theme in American social criticism is a more fundamental revulsion against the premises of industrial—and now technological—society. Universalistic-liberal criticism blames our society because it has not yet extended its principles, privileges and benefits to all: the complaint is injustice and the goal is to complete our unfinished business. But alienated-romantic criticism questions the validity and importance of these same principles, privileges and benefits—the complaint is materialism and the goal is spiritual, aesthetic or expressive fulfillment. The tradition of revulsion against conformist, anti-aesthetic, materialistic, ugly, middle-class America runs through American writing from Melville through the "lost generation" to the "beat generation" and has been expressed concretely in the bohemian sub-cultures that have flourished in a few large American cities since the turn of the century. But today, the power of the romantic-alienated position has increased: one response to prosperity has been a more searching examination of the technological assumptions upon which prosperity has been based. Especially for the children of the upper middle-class, affluence is simply taken for granted, and the drive "to get ahead in the world" no longer makes sense for students who start out ahead. The meanings of life must be sought elsewhere, in art, sentience, philosophy, love, service to others, intensified experience, adventure—in short, in the broadly aesthetic or expressive realm.

Deviant Views . . .

Since neither the universalistic nor the romantic critique of modern society is new, these critiques affect the current student generation not only directly but indirectly, in that they have influenced the way many of today's college students were raised. Thus, a few of today's activists are children of the "radicals of the 1930's" (Lipset and Altbach, 1966); and Flacks comments on the growing number of intellectual, professional upper-middle-class families who have adopted "deviant" views of traditional American life and embodied these views in the practices by which they brought up their children. Thus, some of today's activists are the children of bohemians, college professors, etc. But in general, the explanation from parental "deviance" does not seem fully convincing. To be sure, the backgrounds of activists are "atypical" in a statistical sense, and thus might be termed empirically "deviant." It may indeed turn out that the parents of activists are distinguished by their emphasis on humanitarianism, intellectualism and romanticism, and by their lack of stress on moralism (Flacks, 1967). But it is not obvious that such parental values can be termed "deviant" in any but a statistical sense. "Concern with the plight of others," "desire to realize intellectual capacities," and "lack of concern about the importance of strictly controlling personal impulses"—all these values might be thought of as more normative than deviant in upper-middle-class suburban American society in 1966. Even "sensitivity to beauty and art" is becoming increasingly acceptable. Nor can the socio-economic facts of affluence, freedom from status anxiety, high educational levels, permissiveness with children, training for independence, etc. be considered normatively deviant in middle-class America. Thus, the sense in which activists are the deviant offspring of sub-culturally deviant parents remains to be clarified.

Psychological Flexibility . . .

Another explanation seems equally plausible, at least as applied to some student activists—namely that their activism is closely related to the social and cultural conditions that promote high levels of psychological flexibility, complexity and integration. As Bay (1966) has argued, social scientists may be too reluctant to entertain the possibility that some political and social outlooks or activities are symptomatic of psychological "health," while others indicate "disturbance." In fact, many of the personal characteristics of activists —empathy, superior intellectual attainments, capacity for group involvement, strong humanitarian values, emphasis on self-realization, etc.—are consistent with the hypothesis that, as a group, they are unusually "healthy" psychologically. (See also Heist, 1966.) Similarly, the personal antecedents of activists— economic security, committed parents, humanitarian, liberal and permissive home environments, good education, etc.—are those that would seem to promote unusually high levels of psychological functioning. If this be correct, then former SDS president Tom Hayden's words (1966) may be a valid commentary on the cultural setting of activism:

> Most of the active student radicals today come from middle to upper middle-class professional homes. They were born with status and affluence as facts of life, not goals to be striven for. In their upbringing, their parents stressed the right of children to question and make judgments, producing perhaps the first generation of young people both affluent and independent of mind.

In agreeing with Bay that activists may be more psychologically "healthy" as a group than nonactivists, I am aware of the many difficulties entailed by this hypothesis. First, complexity, flexibility, integration, high levels of functioning, etc., are by no means easy to define, and the criteria for "positive mental health" remains vague and elusive. (See Jahoda, 1958.) Second, there are obviously many individuals with these same "healthy" characteristics who are not activists; and within the group of activists, there are many individuals with definite psychopathologies. In any social movement, a variety of individuals of highly diverse talents and motivations are bound to be involved, and global descriptions are certain to be oversimplified. Third, the explanation from "psychological health" and the explanation from "parental deviance" are not necessarily opposed. On the contrary, these two arguments become identical if we assume that the preconditions for high levels of psychological functioning are both statistically and normatively deviant in modern American society. This assumption seems quite plausible.

Whatever the most plausible explanation of the socio-cultural sources of activism, the importance of prevailing attitudes toward student protest and of the climate of social criticism in America seems clear. In the past five years a conviction has arisen, at least among a minority of American college students, that protest and social action are effective and honorable. Furthermore, changes in American society, especially in middle-class child rearing practices, mean that American students are increasingly responsive to both the universalistic and romantic critique of our society. Both strands of social criticism have been picked up by student activists in a rhetoric of protest that combines a major theme of impatience at the slow fulfillment of the credal ideals of American society with a more muted minor theme of aesthetic revulsion at technological society itself. By and large, activists respond most affirmatively to the first theme and alienated students to the second; but even within the student protest movement, these two themes coexist in uneasy tension.

THE PROTEST-PRODUCING HISTORICAL SITUATION

To separate what I have called the "cultural climate" from the "historical situation" is largely arbitrary. But by this latter term I hope to point to the special sensitivity of today's student activists to historical events and trends that do not immediately impinge upon their own lives. In other nations, and in the past, student protest movements seem to have been more closely related to immediate student frustrations than they are in America today. The "transformationist" (utopian, Marxist, universalistic or democratic) aspirations of activist youth in rapidly developing nations often seem closely related to their personal frustrations under oppressive regimes or at "feudal" practices in their societies; the "restorationist" (romantic, alienated) youth movements that have appeared in later stages of industrialization seem closely connected to a personal sense of the loss of a feudal, maternal, and "organic" past. (See Lifton, 1960, 1963, 1964.) Furthermore, both universalistic and romantic youth movements in other nations have traditionally been highly ideological, committed either to concepts of universal democracy and economic justice or to particularistic values of brotherhood, loyalty, feeling and nation.

Anti-ideological . . .

Today's activists, in contrast, are rarely concerned with improving their own conditions and are highly motivated by identification with the oppressions of others. The anti-ideological bias of today's student activists has been underlined by virtually every commentator. Furthermore, as Flacks notes, the historical conditions that have produced protest elsewhere are largely absent in modern America; and the student "movement" in this country differs in important ways from student movements elsewhere. In many respects, then, today's American activists have no historical precedent, and only time will tell to what extent the appearance of organized student dissent in the 1960's is a product of locally American conditions, of the psychosocial effects of a technological affluence that will soon characterize other advanced nations, or of widespread changes in identity and style produced by psychohistorical factors that affect youth of all nations (thermonuclear warfare, increased culture contact, rapid communications, etc.).

Sensitivity to World Events

But whatever the historical roots of protest, today's student protester seems uniquely sensitive to historical trends and events. In interviewing student activists I have been impressed with how often they mention some world-historical event as the catalyst for their activism—in some cases, witnessing via television of the Little Rock demonstrations over school integration, in another case, watching rioting Zengakuren students in Japan protesting the arrival of President Eisenhower, in other cases, particularly among Negro students, a strong identification with the rising black nationalism of recently independent African nations.

Several factors help explain this sensitivity to world events. For one, modern means of communication make the historical world more psychologically "available" to youth. Students today are exposed to world events and world trends with a speed and intensity that has no historical precedent. Revolutions, trends, fashions and fads are now world-wide; it takes but two or three years for fashions to spread from Carnaby Street to New York, New Delhi, Tokyo, Warsaw, Lagos and Lima. In particular, students who have been brought up in a tradition that makes them unusually empathic, humanitarian and universalistic in values may react more intensely to exposure via television to student demonstrations in Japan than to social pressures from their fellow seniors in Centerville High. Finally, this broadening of empathy is, I believe, part of a general modern trend toward the *internationalization of identity*. Hastened by modern communications and consolidated by the world-wide threat of nuclear warfare, this trend involves, in vanguard groups in many nations, a loosening of parochial and national allegiances in favor of a more inclusive sense of affinity with one's peers (and non-peers) from all nations. In this respect, American student activists are both participants and leaders in the reorganization of psycho-social identity and ideology that is gradually emerging from the unique historical conditions of the twentieth century (Lifton, 1965).

A small but growing number of American students, then, exhibit a peculiar responsiveness to world-historical events—a responsiveness based partly on their own broad identification with others like them throughout the world, and partly on the availability of information about world events via the mass media. The impact of historical events, be they the world-wide revolution for human dignity and esteem, the rising aspirations of the developing nations, or the war in Vietnam, is greatly magnified upon such students; their primary identification is not their unreflective national identity, but their sense of affinity for Vietnamese peasants, Negro sharecroppers, demonstrating Zengakuren activists, exploited migrant workers, and the oppressed everywhere. One of the consequences of security, affluence and education is a growing sense of personal involvement with those who are insecure, non-affluent and uneducated.

THE FUTURE OF STUDENT ACTIVISM

I have argued that no single factor can explain or help us predict the future of the student protest movement in America: active expressions of dissent have become more prevalent because of an *interaction* of individual, institutional, cultural and historical factors. Affluence and education have changed the environment within which middle-class children are raised, in turn producing a minority of students with special sensitivity to the oppressed and the dissenting everywhere. At the same time, technological innovations like television have made available to these students abundant imagery of oppression and dissent in America and in other nations. And each of these factors exerts a potentiating influence on the others.

Given some understanding of the interaction of these factors, general questions about the probable future of student activism in America can now be broken down into four more specific questions: Are we likely to produce (a) more protest-prone personalities? (b) more institutional settings in which protests are likely? (c) a cultural climate that sanctions and encourages activism? and (d) a historical situation that facilitates activism? To three of the questions (a, b and d), I think the answer is a qualified yes; I would therefore expect that in the future, if the cultural climate remains the same, student activism and protest would continue to be visible features on the American social landscape.

Consider first the factors that promote protest-prone personalities. In the coming generation there will be more and more students who come from the upper middle-class, highly educated, politically liberal professional backgrounds from which protesters are selectively recruited (Michael, 1965). Furthermore, we can expect that a significant and perhaps growing proportion of these families will have the universalistic, humanitarian, equalitarian and individualistic values found in the families of protesters. Finally, the expressive, permissive, democratic and autonomy-promoting atmosphere of these families seems to be the emerging trend of middle-class America: older patterns of "entrepreneurial-authoritarian" control are slowly giving way to more "bureaucratic-democratic" techniques of socialization (Miller and Swanson, 1958). Such secular changes in the American family would produce a growing proportion of students with protest-prone personalities.

Institutional factors, I have argued, are of primary importance in so far as they bring together a critical mass of suitably protest-predisposed students in an atmosphere where they can interact, create their own subculture, develop leadership and find issues. The growing size of major American universities, their increasing academic and intellectual selectivity, and the emphasis on "quality" education (honors programs, individual instruction, greater student freedom)—all seem to promote the continuing development of activist sub-cultures in a minority of American institutions. The increasing use of graduate student teaching assistants in major universities points to the growing availability of large numbers of potential "leaders" for student protests. Admittedly, a sudden increase in the administrative wisdom in college Deans and Presidents could reduce the number of available "on-campus" issues; but such a growth in wisdom does not seem imminent.

Cultural Climate May Change
In sharp contrast, a maintenance of the cultural climate required for continuation of activism during the coming years seems far more problematical. Much depends on the future course of the war in Vietnam. Continuing escalation of the war in Southeast Asia will convince many student activists that their efforts are doomed to ineffectuality. For as of mid-1967, anti-war activism has become the primary common cause of student protesters. The increasing militancy and exclusivity of the Negro student civil rights movement, its emphasis on "Black Power" and on grass-roots community organization work (to be done by Negroes) is rapidly pushing white activists out of civil rights work, thus depriving them of the issue upon which the current mood of student activism was built. This fact, coupled with the downgrading of the war on poverty, the decline of public enthusiasm for civil rights, and the increasing scarcity of public and private financing for work with the underprivileged sectors of American society, has already begun to turn activists away from domestic issues toward an increasingly single-minded focus on the war in Vietnam. Yet at the same time, increasing numbers of activists overtly or covertly despair of the efficacy of student attempts to mobilize public opinion against the war, much less to influence directly American foreign policies. Continuing escalation in Southeast Asia has also begun to create a more repressive atmosphere towards student (and other) protesters of the war, exemplified by the question, "Dissent or Treason"? Already the movement of activists back to full-time academic work is apparent.

Thus, the war in Vietnam, coupled by the "rejection" of white middle-class students by the vestigial black civil rights movement is producing a crisis among activists, manifest by a "search for issues" and intense disagreement over strategy and tactics. At the same time, the diminution of support for student activism tends to exert a "radicalizing" effect upon those who remain committed activists—partly because frustration itself tends to radicalize the frustrated, and partly because many of the less dedicated and committed activists have dropped away from the movement. At the same time, most activists find it difficult to turn from civil rights or peace work toward "organizing the middle-class" along lines suggested by alienated-romantic criticisms of technological society. On the whole, activists remain more responsive to universalistic issues like peace and civil rights than to primarily expressive or aesthetic criticisms of American society. Furthermore, the practical and organizational problems of "organizing the middle-class" are overwhelming. Were the student movement to be forced to turn away from universalistic issues like civil rights and peace to a romantic critique of the "quality of middle-class life," my argument here implies that its following and efficacy would diminish considerably. Were this to happen, observations based on student activism of a more "universalistic" variety would have to be modified to take account of a more radical and yet more alienated membership. Thus, escalation or even continuation of the war in Vietnam, particularly over a long period, will reduce the likelihood of student activism.

Yet there are other, hopefully more permanent, trends in American culture that argue for a continuation of protests. The further extension of affluence in America will probably mean growing impatience over our society's failure to include the "forgotten fifth" in its prosperity: as the excluded and underprivileged become fewer in number, pressures to include them in American society will grow. Similarly, as more young Americans are brought up in affluent homes and sub-cultures, many will undoubtedly turn to question the value of monetary, familistic and careerist goals, looking instead toward expressive, romantic, experiential, humanitarian and self-actualizing pursuits to give their lives meaning. Thus, in the next decades, barring a major world conflagration, criticisms of American society will probably continue and intensify on two grounds: first, that it has excluded a significant minority from its prosperity, and second, that affluence alone is empty without humanitarian, aesthetic or expressive fulfillment. Both of these trends would strengthen the climate conducive to continuing activism.

World-Wide Protest-Promoting Pressures . . .

Finally, protest-promoting pressures from the rest of the world will doubtless increase in the coming years. The esteem revolution in developing nations, the rise of aspirations in the impoverished two-thirds of the world, and the spread of universalistic principles to other nations—all of these trends portend a growing international unrest, especially in the developing nations. If young Americans continue to be unusually responsive to the unfulfilled aspirations of those abroad, international trends will touch a minority of them deeply, inspiring them to overseas activities like the Peace Corps, to efforts to "internationalize" American foreign policies, and to an acute sensitivity to the frustrated aspirations of other Americans. Similarly, continuation of current American policies of supporting anti-communist but often repressive regimes in developing nations (particularly regimes anathema to student activists abroad) will tend to agitate American students as well. Thus, pressures from the probable world situation will support the continuance of student protests in American society.

In the next decades, then, I believe we can forsee the continuation, with short-range ebbs and falls, of activism in American society. Only if activists were to become convinced that protests were ineffectual or social action impossible is this trend likely to be fundamentally reversed. None of this will mean that protesters will become a majority among American students; but we can anticipate a slowly-growing minority of the most talented, empathic, and intellectually independent of our students who will take up arms against injustice both here and abroad.

IN SUMMARY . . .

Throughout this discussion, I have emphasized the contrast between two types of students, two types of family backgrounds, and two sets of values that inspire dissent from the Great Society. On the one hand, I have discussed students I have termed alienated, whose values are apolitical, romantic, and aesthetic. These students are most responsive to "romantic" themes of social criticism; that is, they reject our society because of its dehumanizing effects, its lack of aesthetic quality and its failure to provide "spiritual" fulfillment to its members. And they are relatively impervious to appeals to social, economic or political justice. On the other hand, I have discussed activists, who are politically involved, humanitarian and universalistic in values. These students object to our society not because they oppose its basic principles, but because it fails to implement these principles fully at home and abroad.

In the future, the tension between the romantic-alienated and the universalistic-activist styles of dissent will probably increase. I would anticipate a growing polarization between those students and student groups who turn to highly personal and experiential pursuits like drugs, sex, art and intimacy, and those students who redouble their efforts to change American society. In the past five years, activists have been in the ascendant, and the alienated have been little involved in organized political protests. But a variety of possible events could reverse this ascendency. A sense of ineffectuality, especially if coupled with repression of organized dissent, would obviously dishearten many activists. More important, the inability of the student protest movement to define its own long-range objectives, coupled with its intransigent hostility to ideology and efficient organization, means that ad hoc protests are too rarely linked to the explicit intellectual, political and social goals that alone can sustain prolonged efforts to change society. Without some shared sustaining vision of the society and world they are working to promote, and frustrated by the enormous obstacles that beset any social reformer, student activists would be likely to return to the library.

How and whether this tension between alienation and activism is resolved seems to me of the greatest importance. If a growing number of
activists, frustrated by political ineffectuality or a mounting war in Southeast
Asia, withdraw from active social concern into a narrowly academic quest
for professional competence, then a considerable reservoir of the most
talented young Americans will have been lost to our society and the world.
The field of dissent would be left to the alienated, whose intense quest for
personal salvation, meaning, creativity and revelation dulls their perception
of the public world and inhibits attempts to better the lot of others. If, in
contrast, tomorrow's potential activists can feel that their demonstrations and
actions are effective in molding public opinion and, more important, in
effecting needed social change, then the possibilities for constructive change
in post-industrial American society are virtually without limit.

REFERENCES

Aiken, M., Demrath, N. J., & Marwell, G. Conscience and confrontation: some preliminary findings on summer civil rights volunteers. University of Wisconsin, 1966
(mimeo).

Allen, M., & Silverstein, H. Progress report: creative arts—alienated youth project.
New York: March, 1967.

Bay, Christian. Political and apolitical students: facts in search of theory. *Journal of
Social Issues,* 1967, 23(3).

Bernreuter, Robert G. The college student: he is thinking, talking, acting. *Penn State
Alumni News,* July, 1966.

Block, J., Haan, N., & Smith, M. B. Activism and apathy in contemporary adolescents.
In J. F. Adams (Ed.), *Contributions to the understanding of adolescence.* Boston:
Allyn and Bacon, in press.

Coles, Robert. Serpents and doves: non-violent youth in the South. In Erik H. Erikson
(Ed.), *The challenge of youth.* New York: Basic Books, 1963.

Coles, Robert. *Children of crisis.* Boston: Little, Brown, 1967.

Cowan, John Lewis. Academic freedom, protest and university environments. Paper
read at APA, New York, 1966.

Draper, Hal. *Berkeley, the new student revolt.* New York: Grove, 1965.

Ehle, John. *The free men.* New York: Harper & Row, 1965.

Erikson, Erik H. (Ed.), *The challenge of youth.* New York: Basic Books, 1963.

Fishman, Jacob R., & Solomon, Frederic. Psychological observations on the student
sit-in movement. *Proceedings of the Third World Congress of Psychiatry.* Toronto:
University of Toronto/McGill, n.d.

Fishman, Jacob R., & Solomon, Frederic. Youth and social action. *The Journal of Social
Issues,* 1964, 20(4), 1–28.

Flacks, Richard E. The liberated generation: an exploration of the roots of student
protest. *Journal of Social Issues,* 1967, 23(3).

Gastwirth, D. Why students protest. Unpublished paper, Yale University, 1965.

Hayden, T. Quoted in *Comparative Education Review,* 1966, 10, 187.

Heist, Paul. Intellect and commitment: the faces of discontent. *Order and freedom on
the campus.* Western Interstate Commission for Higher Education and the Center for the Study of Higher Education, 1965.

Heist, Paul. The dynamics of student discontent and protest. Paper read at APA, New York, 1966.

Jahoda, Marie. *Current concepts of positive mental health.* New York: Basic Books, 1958.

Katz, J. The learning environment: social expectations and influences. Paper presented at American Council of Education, Washington, D. C., 1965.

Katz, J. The student activists: rights, needs and powers of undergraduates. Stanford: Institute for the Study of Human Problems, 1967.

Keene, S. How one big university laid unrest to rest. *The American Student,* 1966, *1,* 18–21.

Kelman, H. D. Notes on faculty activism. *Letter to Michigan Alumni,* 1966.

Keniston, Kenneth. American students and the "political revival." *The American Scholar,* 1962, *32,* 40–64.

Keniston, Kenneth. *The uncommitted.* New York: Harcourt Brace & World, 1965a.

Keniston, Kenneth. The pressure to perform. *The Intercollegian.* September, 1965b.

Keniston, Kenneth. The faces in the lecture room. In R. S. Morison (Ed.), *The American university.* Boston: Houghton Mifflin, 1966a.

Keniston, Kenneth. The psychology of alienated students. Paper read at APA, New York, 1966b.

Keniston, Kenneth, & Helmreich, R. An exploratory study of discontent and potential drop-outs at Yale. Yale University, 1965 (mimeo).

Kornhauser, W. Alienation and participation in the mass university. Paper read at American Ortho-Psychiatric Association, Washington, D.C., 1967.

Lifton, Robert Jay. Japanese youth: the search for the new and the pure. *The American Scholar,* 1960, *30,* 332–344.

Lifton, Robert Jay. Youth and history: individual change in post-war Japan. In Erik H. Erikson (Ed.), *The challenge of youth.* New York: Harper & Row, 1963.

Lifton, Robert Jay. Individual patterns in historical change. *Comparative Studies in Society and History.* 1964, *6,* 369–383.

Lifton, Robert Jay. Protean man. Yale University, 1965 (mimeo).

Lipset, Seymour M. Student opposition in the United States. *Government and Opposition,* 1966a, *1,* 351–374.

Lipset, Seymour M. University students and politics in underdeveloped countries. *Comparative Education Review,* 1966b, *10,* 132–162.

Lipset, Seymour M., & Altbach, P. G. Student politics and higher education in the United States. *Comparative Education Review,* 1966, *10,* 320–349.

Lipset, Seymour M., & Wolin, S. S. (Eds.), *The Berkeley student revolt.* Garden City, New York: Doubleday, 1965.

Lyonns, G. The police car demonstration: a survey of participants. In S. Lipset and S. Wolin (Eds.), *The Berkeley student revolt.* Garden City, New York: Doubleday, 1965.

Michael, Donald Nelson. *The next generation, the prospects ahead for the youth of today and tomorrow.* New York: Vintage, 1965.

Miller, Michael, & Gilmore, Susan (Eds.), *Revolution at Berkeley,* New York: Dell, 1965.

Miller, Daniel. R. & Swanson, Guy E. *The changing American parent.* New York: Wiley, 1958.

Newfield, Jack. *A prophetic minority.* New York: New American Library, 1966.

Newsweek. Campus, 1965. March 22, 1965.

Parsons, Talcott. *The social system.* Glencoe. Ill.: Free Press, 1951.

Parsons, Talcott. *Structure and process in modern societies.* Glencoe, Ill.: Free Press, 1960.

Paulus, G. *A multivariate analysis study of student activist leaders, student government leaders, and non-activists.* Cited in Richard E. Peterson, *The student Left in American higher education.* Draft for Puerto Rico Conference on Students and Politics, 1967.

Pervin, Lawrence A., Reik, L. E., & Dalrymple, W. (Eds.), *The college drop-out and the utilization of talent.* Princeton: Princeton University, 1966.

Peterson, Richard E. *The scope of organized student protest in 1964–65.* Princeton: Educational Testing Service, 1966.

Peterson, Richard E. The student Left in American higher education. Draft for Puerto Rico Conference on Students and Politics, 1967.

Reed, M. Student non-politics, or how to make irrelevancy a virtue. *The American Student,* 1966, *1*(3), 7–10.

Rigney, Francis J., & Smith, L. D. *The real bohemia.* New York: Basic Books, 1961.

Schneider, Patricia. A study of members of SDS and YD at Harvard, Unpublished B.A. thesis, Wellesley College, 1966.

Solomon, Frederic, & Fishman, Jacob R. Perspectives on the student sit-in movement. *American Journal of Ortho-Psychiatry,* 1963, *33,* 873–874.

Solomon, Frederic, & Fishman, Jacob R. Youth and peace: a psycho-social study of student peace demonstrators in Washington, D. C. *The Journal of Social Issues,* 1964, *20*(4), 54–73.

Somers, R. H. The mainsprings of the rebellion: a survey of Berkeley students in November, 1964. In S. Lipset and S. Wolin (Eds.), *The Berkeley student revolt.* Garden City, New York: Doubleday, 1965.

Stern, G. Myth and reality in the American college. *AAUP Bulletin,* Winter, 1966, 408–414.

Suczek, Robert Francis, & Alfert, E. Personality characteristic of college dropouts. University of California, 1966 (mimeo).

Trow, Martin. Some lessons from Berkeley. Paper presented to American Council of Education, Washington, D. C., 1965.

Watts, William Arthur, & Whittaker, D. Some socio-psychological differences between highly committed members of the Free Speech Movement and the student population at Berkeley. *Applied Behavioral Science,* 1966, *2,* 41–62.

Watts, Wiliam Arthur, & Whittaker, D. Socio-psychological characteristics of intellectually oriented, alienated youth: a study of the Berkeley nonstudent University of California, Berkeley, 1967 (mimeo).

Westby, D., & Braungart, R. Class and politics in the family backgrounds of student political activists, *American Social Review,* 1966, *31,* 690–692.

White, Winston. *Beyond conformity.* Glencoe, Ill.: Free Press, 1961.

Whittaker, D., & Watts, W. A. Personality and value attitudes of intellectually disposed, alienated youth. Paper presented at APA, New York, 1966.

Wright, E. O. Student leaves of absence from Harvard College: A personality and social system approach. Unpublished paper, Harvard University, 1966.

Zinn, Howard. *SNCC, the new abolitionists.* Boston: Beacon, 1965.

Antecedents of Delinquency: Personality, Social Class, and Intelligence

John Janeway Conger, Wilbur C. Miller and Charles R. Walsmith

UNIVERSITY OF COLORADO SCHOOL OF MEDICINE
AND UNIVERSITY OF DENVER

A considerable number of studies have examined the relationship between delinquency and such variables as social class, intelligence, and residence area (2, 3, 5, 6, 9, 10, 11, 12, 13, 16). Many others, including such pioneering efforts as those of Healy and Bronner (8) and the Gluecks (6), have investigated the relationship of personality traits to delinquency within various populations (1, 7, 14, 15, 16).

It may well be, however, that the relationship of these variables to delinquency cannot properly be considered independently of their relation to one another. Thus, it is perfectly possible that personality characteristics which

Reprinted by permission of the authors.

This study, and the more extended research project of which it is a part, was made possible by a grant (MH-03040) from the National Institute of Mental Health. We would like to express our indebtedness to the following colleagues and research assistants for their help in the conduct of this study: Joan Happel, Rosamond Putsch, Robert V. Rainey, Ann A. Shenefield, Joan Searles, and Donald Stilson.

are related to delinquency in some intelligence and social-class subgroups may not be related in other subgroups. For example, traits which differentiate delinquents from nondelinquents in a high-IQ, socioeconomically favored subgroup may fail to be differentiating in a deprived subgroup of average intelligence.

If this is the case, it is not enough, in studying the relationship of antecedent personality characterstics to later delinquency, simply to control for the possible effects of other factors, such as socioeconomic status, residence area, intelligence, sex, educational background, and ethnic group membership. This is clearly a necessary step, and one which the more adequate studies in this field have attempted to take, but it is not a sufficient step.

The study reported here in condensed form is a part of a larger, longitudinal study of personality, social class, and delinquency (4). The principle aims of the present study were to determine (1) whether personality traits manifested by boys in the period from kindergarten through the third grade are significantly related to future delinquency after the potential effects of other factors have been controlled through a matching technique, and (2) whether the nature, extent, and direction of such relationships may vary, depending on the intelligence and social class status of the child.

The population from which the subjects of this study were drawn comprised all males in the tenth grade of all high schools in a large Western city ($N = 2,348$). Subjects actually employed met several additional requirements, including presence in the school system of this city in the period from kindergarten through the third grade (K-3) and continued residence in this city, at least through age 18.

Teacher ratings of "personal-social behavior," made on a three-point scale twice yearly during the early school years, were available for use as antecedent variables, as were more informal, unstructured comments made by teachers about their pupils during the same period. The latter were subjected to a content analysis, from which the investigators derived a "Teacher Comment Check List," consisting of 97 discrete behavioral traits and environmental influences (e.g., "good attention, concentration," "distractable, poor attention, daydreams," "independent, self-sufficient," "resents and rejects authority," "parent interest and cooperation"), reflecting the principle kinds of statements which teachers tended to make spontaneously about their pupils at this age. Two trained judges, with experience both in psychology and in elementary education, then applied the check list independently to a sample of 100 sets of teacher comments. For purposes of the present study, a set comprised all of the comments made by teachers about a particular child in the K-3 period. Only those check list items showing interjudge reliabilities of .65 and above at this age level were employed in the study.

Delinquency Criterion

All boys in the population who became delinquent prior to age 18 were subsequently identified. The criterion for delinquency employed in this study was formal acceptance of the case by the Juvenile Court. As we have noted elsewhere (4), and as Bandura and Walters (1) also note, delinquency as such is a sociolegal, rather than a psychological phenomenon. In fact, a primary purpose of this investigation was to determine what, if any, were the relationships of psychological variables to this sociolegal phenomenon. As a result, any operationally defined criterion of delinquency had to involve some degree of contact with law enforcement officials—either police or judicial.

Because of the organization of juvenile authorities in this particular city, we were faced with these alternatives: we could have defined as delinquent all youths who had any contact either with the court or juvenile bureau of the police department. This, however, would have meant including as "delinquents" a large number of boys who were involved in very trivial incidents, such as minor pranks, and who were talked to briefly, turned over to their parents or sent home, and never seen again. The local juvenile bureau of the police department has estimated that out of every five cases seen, only two are eventually considered serious enough, either because of the gravity of the offense or because of recidivism, to be turned over to the juvenile court.

In turn, of the youths carried on the records of the juvenile court, only about one in eight is brought to trial, convicted, and sentenced to an institution—either because of failure to respond to assistance by probation workers, or because of the gravity of the offense.

It was our belief that to have used the first of these possible criteria would have diluted the meaning of the term delinquency to the point of absurdity (e.g., calling a child delinquent because he was once involved in a minor bit of mischief which came to the attention of the police). On the other hand, we were convinced that it would be equally inappropriate to designate as delinquent only those youths whose offenses were extremely serious or chronic, and who proved completely refractory to help from juvenile workers. Not only would such a definition exclude many youths in considerable trouble with the law, but it would also render subsequent comparisons between repeaters and nonrepeaters, or treatable and refractory cases, impossible.

It was our conclusion that selecting the middle ground, and defining delinquency as acceptance of the case by the juvenile court, had the greatest promise for this investigation, and was also in closest accord with common usage. The distribution of offenses and ages of offenses for males in our population are shown in Fig. 1 and Table 1. As may be seen, the highest incidence of delinquent offenses occurs at age 15.5, with a marked decline in number of offenses below age 14 and above age 16.

Selection of Study Samples

After identifying the delinquent males in our population for whom relatively complete records were available ($N = 271$), each was investigated individually to determine the following relevant characteristics: age, socioeconomic status (three levels: high, medium, low) residence area characteristics, IQ (seven levels: very superior, superior, bright normal, average, dull normal, borderline, mentally defective), school background (schools at-

Table 1   Distribution of 184 Male Delinquents by Age in Half-Years at Time of Offense, and by Type of Offense

Type of Offense	Age									
	9.5	10	10.5	11	11.5	12	12.5	13	13.5	14
Aggravated assault										2
Aggravated robbery										
Arson				1		1	1			
Assault and battery									1	3
Attempted car theft										
Burglary	1	2	1	2	1	3	3	5	7	4
Car prowl										
Car theft							1			2
Carrying concealed weapon										1
Cruelty to animals										
Curfew violation					1		1			1
Destroying city property										
Disturbances										
Escape from Juvenile Hall									1	
False fire alarm										
False registration										
Forgery										
Gangs										
Hit and run									1	1
Incorrigible	1	2	1	1		2	3	2	8	4
Indecent acts										1
Indecent language						1			1	1
Joyriding							1		1	1
Larceny	1			1	1	1	1	2	6	7
Loitering										
Malicious mischief	1					1	3	2	5	5
Receiving stolen goods						1	1			
Resisting arrest										
Runaway		1				1			2	2
Sex offenses						1			1	
Threats										1
Traffic violation										
Truancy		1					2		2	1
Vandalism						1				
Wearing women's clothing										
Witness to stabbing			1							
Total	4	6	3	5	3	13	17	11	36	49

Table 1   (Continued)

Type of Offense	14.5	15	15.5	16	16.5	17	17.5	18	Total
Aggravated assault	1	1	5	1					10
Aggravated robbery	1	1	1						3
Arson									3
Assault and battery									4
Attempted car theft			2						2
Burglary	2	10	7	3	4		1		56
Car prowl	3	1							4
Car theft		5	5	6	1		1	1	22
Carrying concealed weapon	3	1							5
Cruelty to animals		1							1
Curfew violation	2	2	6				2		15
Destroying city property	1								1
Disturbances		1	3	1		1			6
Escape from Juvenile Hall			1						2
False fire alarm	1	1							2
False registration				1					1
Forgery					1	1			2
Gangs		1							1
Hit and run	2	2	1						7
Incorrigible	13	9	7	5	3	1	2		64
Indecent acts			1						2
Indecent language									3
Joyriding	17	18	12	5	3	1			71
Larceny	10	5	7	2	2	1			47
Loitering			2						2
Malicious mischief	3	3	5				1		29
Receiving stolen goods			1		1	1			5
Resisting arrest			1						1
Runaway	2	3	1	3					15
Sex offenses		1	2	3					8
Threats									1
Traffic violation		1	3						4
Truancy	1			1					8
Vandalism									1
Wearing women's clothing							1		1
Witness to stabbing									1
Total	62	67	73	31	15	6	8	1	N 410

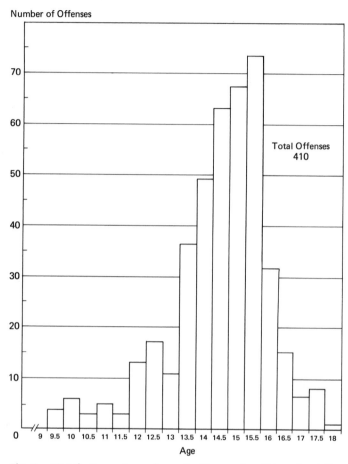

Fig. 1. Distribution of number of offenses for 184 male delinquents, by age in half years, at time of offense.

tended) and ethnic group membership. More detailed information regarding the techniques employed in determining such characteristics as socioeconomic status is available elsewhere (4).

Each delinquent was then matched *individually* with a nondelinquent on all the above variables. Because of the obvious impossibility of finding complete matches for all delinquents, this procedure reduced the number of potentially usable delinquents from 271 to 184.

Absence of teacher ratings or teacher comments on some of these boys during the K-3 period further reduced this number to 86. Thus, the final number of subjects employed in this study was 172, divided equally between delinquents and nondelinquents.

Table 2   Number of Pairs in Which Both Delinquent-Nondelinquent Pair Members Received Ratings for Each Item of Personal-Social Behavior at Grade 3

Teacher Rating	Number of Delinquent-Nondelinquent Pairs
Physical skill	22
Creativeness	25
Clear thinking	20
Openmindedness	25
Leadership ability	50
Regard for persons	48
Sense of responsibility	52
Response to authority	49
Social acceptability	48
Work habits	49
Interests	15
Appreciations	4
Ideals (ambitions, wishes)	7
Physical health resources	12
Physical health problems	9
Home resources	5
Home problems	5
Overall	0

STUDY I: PERSONAL-SOCIAL BEHAVIOR OF FUTURE DELINQUENTS AND NONDELINQUENTS DURING THE EARLY SCHOOL YEARS

The first, and statistically much the simpler, of the two analyses presented in this paper involved a comparison of the personality characteristics of future delinquents and their nondelinquent matches in the period from kindergarten through the third grade. As noted above, two kinds of developmental personality measures were available in this period: teacher ratings of personal-social development and the Teacher Comment Check List. Each will be discussed in turn.

1. Ratings of Personal-Social Development

The behaviors rated here are listed in Table 2, and described in more detail elsewhere (4). Each behavior was rated on a three-point scale: low (lower 25 percent), middle (middle 50 percent), and high (upper 25 percent). For purposes of statistical analysis, these ratings were given numerical values of 1, 2, and 3, respectively. Teachers were permitted to omit ratings where they did not feel that they had sufficient evidence to justify a judgment. While these same behaviors were rated at all elementary school grade levels, we selected the children's third grade ratings to represent the early school years. This was done for two reasons: (1) analyzing the ratings at all grade levels would have been prohibitive in terms of time and expense; (2) teachers apparently felt capable of rating more behaviors at this grade level than at earlier ones (though still less capable than at later grade levels). Thus, we had a greater total number of ratings with which to work at grade three.

It was our hypothesis, in view of the operational descriptions of these behaviors which were provided to teachers, that future nondelinquents would obtain higher scores on each of the traits rated. In testing this hypothesis we wanted to preserve the benefits of individual matching of delinquent and nondelinquent subjects and also to be able *later* to analyze for the effects, separately and in interaction, of social class-IQ subgroup membership. Consequently, for reasons to be described in more detail later in this paper, a 2 × 5 analysis of variance design for matched pairs (main effect for delinquency) was employed to test for the significance of delinquent-nondelinquent differences. For present purposes, and for the benefit of nonstatistically oriented readers, it is sufficient to note that this technique permitted us to test for the statistical significance of delinquent-nondelinquent differences on each personality measure.

Table 2 shows the number of times teachers rated *both* members of delinquent-nondelinquent pairs for each of the 18 traits rated at grade three. As may be seen, it appears that teachers felt little confidence at grade three in making ratings for most children on such variables as physical skill, creativeness, clear thinking, and open-mindedness (less than 30 pairs rated on each of these traits); and virtually no confidence in rating interest, appreciations, ideals, physical health resources, physical health problems, home resources, home problems, and overall adjustment (15 or fewer pairs rated).

On the other hand, they seemed to feel relatively confident (more than 45 pairs rated at this grade level) in rating: leadership ability, regard for persons, sense of responsibility, response to authority, social acceptability, and work habits. It is interesting to note that each of these six variables involves readily identifiable, relatively objective behaviors, common to the classroom situation; while many of the other variables involve behaviors or information not necessarily observable or known in the classroom, or they involve clinical inferences or unusually subtle judgments (e.g., "creativeness").

Nondelinquents scored higher than delinquents on 15 of the 18 traits, although, of course, in a fair number of instances the total number of ratings was too small to make statistical analysis possible. (Only on *interests, physical health resources,* and *physical health problems* did the delinquents obtain higher scores, and on none of these traits were more than 15 ratings made.)

However, as may be seen in Table 3, which presents means and significance levels for each rating involving over 45 pairs, of the six most commonly (and presumably most confidently) rated traits at the third grade level, three (*regard for persons, sense of responsibility,* and *social acceptability*) significantly differentiate nondelinquents from delinquents in the predicted direction at the .05[1] level or better, despite relatively small numbers. A fourth trait, *response to authority,* shows a possible trend toward significance (ap-

---

[1] A word of explanation for the nonstatistically oriented reader may be in order. A significance level of .025 simply means that there are only 25 chances in 1,000 that differ-

Table 3 Mean Scores of Male Delinquents and Nondelinquents on
Teacher Ratings (Grade 3)

Teacher Rating	Delinquent Mean	Non-delinquent Mean	Number of Matched Pairs	F Ratio
Leadership	2.10	2.10	50	.00
Regard for persons	1.95	2.22	48	5.64[a]
Sense of responsibility	1.80	2.11	52	8.40[b]
Response to authority	2.10	2.28	49	2.48
Social acceptability	2.04	2.37	48	6.67[a]
Work habits	1.93	2.04	49	.62

[a] Significant at .05 level.
[b] Significant at .01 level.

proaching the .10 level). Only two of the six variables, *work habits* and *leadership,* clearly fail to show any trend toward significance.[2]

2. Teacher Comment Check List

It may be recalled that only those items on the Teacher Comment Check List which had an interjudge reliability coefficient of .65 or higher at this age level were employed in the present study. These are listed in Table 4, and are described in more detail elsewhere (4).

The data emerging from the check list were analyzed in two ways. On the basis of a priori hypotheses about the relation to delinquency of specific personality traits, each trait was postulated as more likely to be associated with delinquency or more likely to be associated with nondelinquency. All instances of the former in a record were arbitrarily scored + 1, and all instances of the latter − 1. By summing all instances of the former and subtracting all instances of the latter, a hypothetical "D" (or delinquency) score was obtained for each subject. This procedure has, of course, both advantages and disadvantages. On the positive side, items occurring sufficiently infrequently that their individual validity cannot be assessed have an opportunity, if they are in fact valid, of contributing to the discriminating power of the overall D-score. On the other hand, even though the D-score itself proves capable of discriminating delinquents from nondelinquents, one cannot be

---

ences this large or larger would be obtained by chance alone. Similarly, a significance level of .01 indicated that there is only 1 chance in 100 that such results would occur by chance alone.

[2] *Statistical note:* These same data were also analyzed using a nonparametric sign test, based on the number of times the score of the nondelinquent member of a pair exceeded his match for each trait. Similar results were obtained, except that *respons to authority,* discriminated in this latter analysis at the .05 level, rather than simply showing a possible trend. *Sense of responsibility* and *social acceptability* showed somewhat higher significance levels (.001 and .004, respectively) and *regard for persons* remained about the same (.035). *Work habits* and *leadership* continued to be nondiscriminating.

Table 4 Distribution of Reliable Teacher Comment Categories for Matched Pairs of Male Delinquents and Nondelinquents, and D-Score Ratings for Each Category

Teacher Comment Category	D-Score Ratings	Delinquent Only	Non-delinquent Only	Both	Neither	Significance Level (if p<.10)
1. Special ability or interest	−	7	15	5	59	.067
2. Below average ability	+	1	2[a]	0	83	
3. Slow learner	+	1	2	0	83	
4. Works up to capacity	−	2	4	0	80	
5. Underachieving	+	12	14	1	59	
6. Good reader	−	7	6[a]	3	70	
7. Poor reader	+	11	17[a]	9	49	
8. Good work habits	−	9	7[a]	1	69	
9. Careful worker	−	7	8	0	71	
10. Careless worker	+	6	4	3	73	
11. Good attention, concentration	−	6	8	0	72	
12. Distractible, poor attention, daydreams	+	21	9	4	52	.003
13. Shows effort to improve	−	16	23	11	36	
14. Lacks persistence, gives up easily	+	9	7	0	70	
15. Conscientious, dependable	−	9	11	2	64	
16. Cooperative	−	11	13	1	61	
17. Poor attitude toward school	+	2	2	1	81	
18. Good attendance	−	1	1	0	84	
19. Attendance problem	+	7	7	0	72	
20. Parent interest and cooperation	−	10	18	4	54	.093
21. Stable home	−	1	3	0	82	
22. Disturbed home environment	+	21	5	1	59	.002
23. Friendly, pleasant	−	11	26	6	43	.011
24. Considerate, fair to others	−	3	13	0	70	.011
25. Aggressive	+	10	4	1	71	.090
26. Resents and rejects authority	+	13	2	0	71	.004
27. Influenced by others	+	4	1	0	81	
28. Active group participation	−	6	13	3	64	.084
29. Well liked, accepted, gets along with peers	−	16	32	12	26	.027
30. Not well accepted, doesn't get along with peers	+	15	5	2	64	.021
31. Attention seeking	+	8	12[a]	0	66	

Table 4   (Continued)

Teacher Comment Category	D-Score Ratings	Delin- quent Only	Non- delin- quent Only	Both	Neither	Signifi- cance Level (if p<.10)
32. Well-behaved	−	2	4	0	80	
33. Unstable, insecure	+	12	7	2	65	
34. Nervous, restless	+	8	5	0	73	
35. Mature (emotionally)	−	0	4	0	82	
36. Immature (emotionally)	+	6	17[a]	1	62	.017
37. Quiet, shy, tends to withdraw	−	12	11	2	61	
38. Physical defects	+	21	15	11	39	

[a] Not in predicted direction.

sure just which rare items are making a valid (as opposed to a chance) contribution to this discrimination.

One can, however, test the individual significance of D-score items which occur frequently enough to make a statistical test of their discriminating power possible.

Table 4 shows the D-score rating (+1, or −1) for each of the reliable teacher comment categories, as well as the distribution of these categories for matched pairs of delinquents and nondelinquents, for the period kindergarten through third grade. The D-score for all subjects were obtained, means for delinquents and nondelinquents were computed, and the significance of the delinquent-nondelinquent difference was run.[3] A mean D-score of +.23 was found for delinquents and −1.23 for nondelinquents. The difference is clearly significant ($p < .001$).[4]

Among individual D-score items, 29 fell in the predicted direction, while eight fell in the opposite direction (Table 4). Of 26 cases where more than 15 ratings of delinquents and nondelinquents combined were made, *12 discriminated delinquents from nondelinquents at the .10 level or better, of which 8 were significant below the .05 level (sign test).*

SUMMARY OF FINDINGS

It appears that even at the third grade level future delinquents and nondelinquents as a group are viewed differently by their teachers. It should be stressed that we are speaking here only of differences above and beyond those which might be due to the effects of such variables as socioeconomic status, intelligence, and ethnic group membership, since the potential effects

[3] Based on the main effect for delinquency in an analysis of variance design for D-score.
[4] A nonparametric sign test, based on the number of instances in which delinquent pair members exceeded their nondelinquent matches, yielded similar results ($p = .003$).

of these variables have already been controlled through matching. Had these not been controlled, even larger differences would be anticipated, in view of the known relationship between these variables and both personality and delinquency, a relationship confirmed in this research (4).

Nevertheless, even with such controls the differences are impressive, particularly at this early age—as evidenced, for example, by the fact that the overall D-score enabled us to discriminate future delinquents and nondelinquents at the .001 level of significance.

In the period from kindergarten through third grade, future delinquent boys already appeared more poorly adapted than their classmates. They appeared to have less regard for the rights and feelings of their peers; less awareness of the need to accept responsibility for their obligations, both as individuals and as members of a group; and poorer attitudes toward authority, including the failure to understand the need for rules and regulations in any well-ordered social group, and to abide by them. They both resented and rejected authority in the school situation. Their overall social behavior was simply less acceptable; they had more difficulty in getting along with peers, both in individual 1-to-1 contacts and in group situations, and were less willing or able to treat others courteously and tactfully and less able to be fair in dealing with them. In return, they were less well liked and accepted by their peers.

In the academic situation itself, they were more easily distracted, daydreamed more, and, in general, had greater difficulty in maintaining attention and sticking to the task at hand until it was completed. They were less likely to display any special ability or interest.

Not surprisingly, these social and academic problems frequently appeared to reflect underlying emotional problems. In the opinion of teachers, as manifested by the ratings and teacher comments, future delinquents more often came from a disturbed home environment and were considered overly aggressive.

Future nondelinquents appeared in many ways as the other side of the coin. Socially, they were rated significantly more cooperative, dependable, friendly, pleasant, considerate, and fair. They were better liked by their peers and more accepted as members of the group.

In the school situation, they showed a considerably greater sense of individual and group responsibility, greater acceptance of constituted authority, and more acceptable social behavior generally.

Their parents appeared more often to show interest in the child's academic and social progress, and to cooperate more readily with school authorities. Emotionally, these boys appeared less aggressive.

STUDY II: SOCIOECONOMIC STATUS AND INTELLIGENCE

The question arising in our minds at this juncture was whether or not the general picture described above was equally applicable to all subgroups,

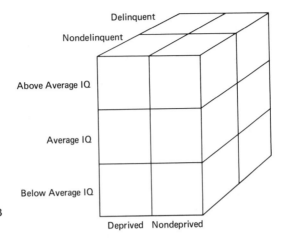

Fig. 2. The basic 2 x 2 x 3 design.

or whether the picture might change as we proceeded from one social class-IQ subgroup to another. However, to approach this problem, it was necessary to subdivide our subjects, not only into the two matched groups of delinquents and nondelinquents employed in Study I, but also along the dimensions of socioeconomic status and intelligence.

For reasons which are elaborated elsewhere (4), it appeared most appropriate, both for statistical reasons and because of the socioeconomic and IQ distributions of residents of this predominantly middle-class city, to employ two levels of socioeconomic status ("deprived" and "nondeprived"), and three levels of intelligence (below average, average [90–109 IQ], and above average). As may be seen in Fig. 2, this, yielded a 2 × 2 × 3 design. The number of subjects falling into each of the cells of this design is shown in Table 5.

As statistically oriented readers are aware, the optimal method of analyzing a design of this sort involves a 2 × 2 × 3 analysis of variance. Such an analysis would permit us simultaneously to determine not only if there are differences on a personality measure between delinquents and nondelinquents, between IQ categories, and between deprived and nondeprived sub-

Table 5 Distribution of Subjects According to Socioeconomic Levels, IQ, and Delinquency Status (K-3)

	Delinquents			Nondelinquents		
Socioeconomic Level	Below Average IQ	Average IQ	Above Average IQ	Below Average IQ	Average IQ	Above Average IQ
Deprived	5	20	0	5	20	0
Nondeprived	13	33	15	13	33	15

jects, but also whether there are *interaction effects* among two or more of these variables (i.e., in nonstatistical terms, and for present purposes, whether there are variations in the relationships of personality characteristcs to delinquency as we proceed from one social class-IQ subgroup to another).

However, use of this one, maximally efficient method of analysis requires a basic minimum number of subjects in all cells of the design. Unfortunately, as Table 5 makes clear, this is not the case in our sample, since no subject fell in the above average IQ-deprived-delinquent cell. Apparently it is very unusual for a subject to be delinquent, socioeconomically deprived, and still obtain an above average IQ score. (Examination of a *representative sample* of our entire population indicates that the combination of high IQ-deprived-nondelinquent is somewhat more common in the general population, but still relatively rare.)

The absence of above average IQ-deprived cells forced us to modify our methods of analysis. This will become clear as we proceed. *The important fact for the reader (whether statistically oriented or not) to realize at this point is simply that the actual distribution of our subjects made it impossible to include an above average IQ-deprived subgroup in our comparisons of the personality characterstics of delinquents and nondelinquents.*

Teacher Comments and D-Score

Breaking down individual teacher comment check list items into social class-IQ subgroups was not feasible, because too few entries would have appeared in the various cells for any one trait to make statistical analysis meaningful. On the other hand, since a fairly large number of children (N-172) had D-scores, it was possible to analyze them further. Figure 3 shows the actual distribution of mean D-scores at this age level for future delinquents and nondelinquents in each of the social class-IQ subgroups, as well as in the group as a whole.

As may be seen, saying that delinquents have a mean D-score of +.23 while nondelinquents average −1.23, may be quite misleading when we come to a consideration of the various subgroups. Thus, for example, in the non-deprived-below average IQ subgroup, nondelinquents are actually closer to the overall delinquent mean than to the nondelinquent. Conversely, delinquent youngsters in the nondeprived-above average and the deprived-below average IQ subgroups come much closer to the overall nondelinquent mean than to the delinquent. Such results appear to lend support to one of the basic tenets of this study, namely, that *personality factors may be differentially related to delinquency, depending on the social class and IQ status of the child.*

Analyses of Variance

Are the kinds of differences shown in Fig. 3 meaningful, however, or do they simply reflect the effects of chance? In attempting to determine the statistical significance of the social class-IQ subgroup differences seen in Fig. 3, it was not possible for reasons already stated, to use a straightforward

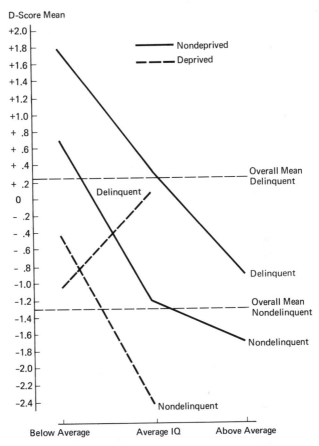

Fig. 3. Distribution of mean D-scores for delinquents and matched nondelinquents by social class-IQ subgroup. N-172; K-3.

2 × 2 × 3 analysis of variance. Instead, we were forced to employ three partial analyses of variance in order to achieve as nearly as possible the same degree of information (pp. 577–578). These analyses will be described briefly in this section, although nonstatistically oriented readers may wish to proceed immediately to the next section, *Teacher Ratings*.

In the first place, a 2 × 5 analysis of variance was performed. This design involved two independent variables: (1) delinquency-nondelinquency, and (2) five combinations of IQ level and socioeconomic status (e.g., "Deprived-below average IQ"). This analysis yielded significant differences between delinquents and nondelinquents as a group ($p < .001$, as previously noted) and between the various social class-IQ subgroups ($p < .001$). Interpreting these results in terms of Figure 3, it appears that an individual's D-score may be significantly elevated both by delinquency and by lower social class-IQ status, except in the case of deprived delinquents, where D-score actually decreases from average to below average IQ.

However, since this design confounds IQ and social class (each subgroup used in the preceding analysis involved a combination of the two), it did not permit an evaluation of the significance of each of these variables separately. In order to deal, at least partially, with this latter problem, two additional analyses of variance were performed. First, a $2 \times 2 \times 2$ analysis of variance was carried out involving two levels of IQ (average, below average), two levels of socioeconomic status (deprived, nondeprived), and two levels of delinquency (delinquent, nondelinquent). This analysis yielded a significant overall difference between delinquents and nondelinquents ($p < .05$) and socioeconomic status ($p < .05$). In addition, there was some suggestion ($p < .20$) of an interaction effect between delinquency and intelligence, with the largest differences between delinquents and nondelinquents occurring in the average IQ range.

This type of analysis (unlike the 2×5 analysis) permitted us to consider the effects of intelligence and social class separately from one another at the average and below average IQ levels. However, it did not allow us to include above average IQ subjects. For this reason, one additional 2×3 analysis of variance was performed, involving only nondeprived subjects. This permitted us to include the above average IQ subjects and hence to cast additional light on the possible effects of IQ considered separately among nondeprived subjects. After the exclusion of deprived subjects, this analysis yielded a significant overall difference between delinquents and nondelinquents ($p < .025$), as in previous analyses. It also indicated that the D-score was strongly affected by intelligence ($p < .005$).

Teacher Ratings

It will be recalled that six items of personal-social behavior were noted fairly frequently by teachers at this age-grade level. These were: *work habits, social acceptability, response to authority, sense of responsibility, regard for persons,* and *leadership.* It has already been shown that three of these traits (*social acceptability, sense of responsibility,* and *regard for persons*) differentiated delinquents from nondelinquents at better than the .05 level.

There was no assurance, however, that each of these traits would discriminate in the same direction or to the same extent as we proceeded from one social class-IQ subgroup to another.

In fact, the findings from the D-score analysis suggested the likelihood that at least some of them would not. It appeared desirable, therefore, to subject each of these traits to the same series of complementary analysis of variance designs that we had employed for D-scores, and this was done. Unfortunately, however, the results (or in some cases, the lack of results) at this age level have to be interpreted more cautiously, and also less fully for

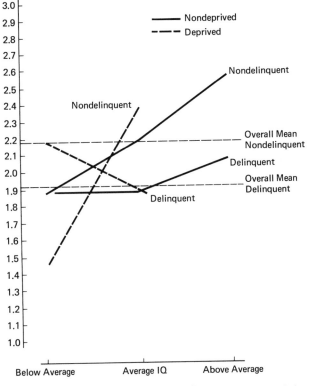

Fig. 4. Distribution of mean teacher ratings of "regard for persons" for delinquents and matched nondelinquents by social class-IQ subgroup. N-96; K-3.

the following reason: The total number of pairs involved for each of these traits was consistently smaller than for D-score (ranging between 96 and 104, as contrasted with 172 for D-score). As it turned out, this had its greatest effect in the below average IQ-deprived subgroups, limiting the number of subjects to four in these analyses, as compared to ten in the D-score analysis. Other subgroups, while also reduced in number, still contained reasonable numbers of subjects.

At this age-grade level, therefore, the results of the D-score analysis appear deserving of greater confidence. Nevertheless, despite smaller numbers (both overall and particularly in the below average IQ-deprived subgroup), several traits still showed effects of variables other than delinquency status, and the statistically significant findings on these traits will be summarized briefly. Detailed results of the various analyses of variance supporting these statements are available elsewhere (4).

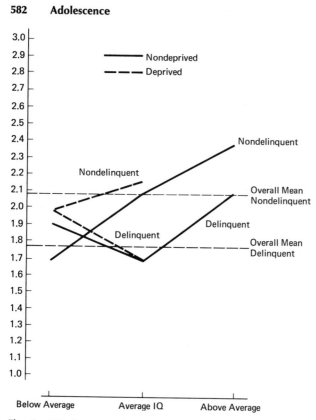

Fig. 6. Distribution of mean teacher ratings of "social responsibility" for delinquents and matched nondelinquents by social class-IQ subgroup. N-104; K-3.

Regard for Persons

Figure 4 shows the distribution of ratings for the five subgroups on this trait. As may be seen, as one progresses from below average to above average IQ among nondeprived subjects, favorableness of rating shows a (statistically significant) increase for both delinquents and nondelinquents, with the greatest increase occurring in the nondelinquent group. This has the effect of placing nondelinquents in the below average IQ subgroup closer to the actual delinquent mean, while playing above average IQ delinquents closer to the overall nondelinquent mean.

It may be observed that in the below average IQ-deprived subgroup, delinquents scored more favorably than nondelinquents. This is interesting, since it corresponds to the findings for the D-score analysis and several other teacher ratings. However, in view of the small number of subjects in this subgroup, this observation must be viewed merely as suggestive; not surprisingly, it fails to find support in any of the analyses of variance.

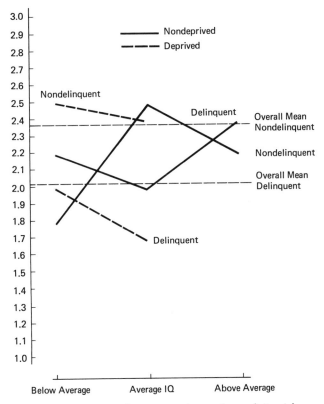

Fig. 6. Distribution of mean teacher ratings of "social acceptability for delinquents and matched nondelinquents by social class-IQ subgroup. N-96; K-3.

Sense of Responsibility

Figure 5 shows the distribution of ratings on this triat. What appears to be reflected here, according to the various analyses of variance, is a significant tendency for delinquents and nondelinquents (deprived and nondeprived) to show few differences at the below average IQ level, but marked differences at the average IQ level. Furthermore, among nondeprived subjects, there appears to be at least a tendency for favorableness of rating to increase with increases in IQ from below average to above average.

Again, as in the case of *regard for persons*, it would appear presumptuous to conclude that overall delinquent-nondelinquent differences on this trait are likely to be equally applicable to all subgroups. For example, as may be seen, among nondeprived subjects, *delinquents* of above average IQ fell at the overall *nondelinquent* mean and *nondelinquents* of below average IQ actually fell below the overall *delinquent* mean. Furthermore, while fairly wide differences separating nondelinquents and delinquents occurred among all subgroups at the average and above average IQ levels, at the below average IQ level there were either no differences or the direction of differences was actually reversed (though not significantly so).

Social Acceptability

Figure 6 shows the distribution of teacher ratings on this trait. In this case, it will be recalled from Study I that the significance level for overall delinquent-nondelinquent differences fell at the .025 level. As Fig. 6 suggests, the failure to obtain a larger level of significance appears to have been due primarily to reversals in the direction of delinquent-nondelinquent differences among nondeprived subjects at the below average and above average IQ levels. This interpretation finds support in the various analyses of variance conducted for this trait.

Certainly, it would appear incautious, on the basis of these findings, to assume that overall delinquent and nondelinquent means for *social acceptability* could be applied to nondeprived subgroups of below average and above average intelligence, although they appear quite applicable to the other subgroups, both deprived and nondeprived.

Work Habits

The distribution of teacher ratings for this trait is shown in Fig. 7. It will be recalled that this trait, unlike those discussed above, showed no significant overall mean difference between delinquents and nondelinquents. When one examines Fig. 7, these results do not appear surprising. While in a number of subgroups fairly wide delinquent-nondelinquent differences are seen (considerably wider than the *overall* mean difference), in the case of two of the three greatest differences, the delinquent scored more favorably.

These findings would appear to raise a warning of a different sort from those previously suggested. While the numbers of subjects involved in the subgroups showing reversals is quite small, making definitive statements suspect, it is at least possible (as a delinquency-intelligence *interaction effect* suggests) that the failure to obtain a significant overall delinquent-nondelinquent difference may have been due, not to the possibility that there were, in fact, no differences, but that the nature and distribution of these differences varied from one subgroup to another.

Obviously, this may be true of a number of personality characteristics. If so, investigations which confine themselves to studying only *overall* delinquent-nondelinquent differences (and this includes the great majority) may be ruling out as unrelated to delinquency, traits which, in some subgroups at least, and conceivably in all, actually may be strongly related to it.

The remaining two traits, *leadership* and *response to authority*, had originally shown no significant overall mean differences between delinquents and nondelinquents, and also showed no other main or interaction effects in the various analyses of variance.

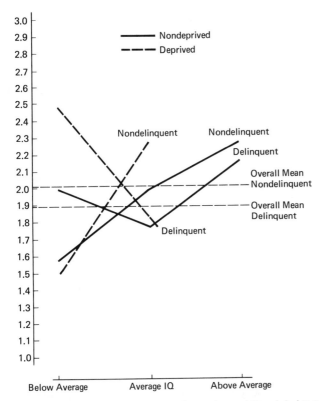

Fig. 7. Distribution of mean teacher ratings of "work habits" for delinquents and matched nondelinquents by social class-IQ subgroup. N-98; K-3.

SUMMARY OF TEACHER RATINGS AND D-SCORE FINDINGS

Viewed together, the findings from the D-score analysis, supplemented by the more limited findings on individual teacher rating analyses, suggest that:

1. Personality trait ratings may be differentially related to delinquency, depending on socioeconomic status and IQ. As a result, *overall* means and mean differences between delinquents and nondelinquents may be quite misleading when applied to a particular social class-IQ subgroup. In many instances, delinquents in a particular subgroup scored closer to the overall nondelinquent mean than to the delinquent; conversely, in other subgroups nondelinquents scored closer to the overall delinquent mean than to the nondelinquent. This fact alone would appear to lend support to one of

the basic hypotheses of this study; namely, that personality factors may be differentially related to delinquency, depending on the particular personality factor involved and on the social class and IQ status of the child.

2.   On overall D-score, and on most individual traits, nondelinquents obtained more favorable mean ratings than delinquents in most subgroups. This would be expected, in view of the fact that significant overall differences between delinquents and nondelinquents (with nondelinquents scoring more favorably) were obtained for D-score, *social acceptability, sense of responsibility,* and *regard for persons.*

3.   The largest mean differences between delinquents and nondelinquents occurred without exception among socioeconomically deprived children, either in the average IQ or below average IQ subgroups.

4.   In some instances (e.g., *work habits*) where significant overall differences between delinquents and nondelinquents are *not* found, in this and other investigations, this may be due, at least partly, to variations in the direction of delinquent-nondelinquent differences from one social class-IQ subgroup to another.

5.   In the case of boys of below average IQ, future delinquents *tended* to receive *more favorable* ratings than nondelinquents. This was especially likely to be true in the case of socioeconomically deprived subjects, although this observation must be viewed with considerable caution, due to the small number of subjects frequently present in the below average-IQ-deprived subgroups.

It would appear that in those instances where significant interaction effects between delinquency and intelligence were found on either the 2 × 2 × 2 or 2 × 3 analyses of variance, absence of delinquent-nondelinquent differences, or reversals in the direction of these differences, among children of below average IQ were primarily responsible.

It should also be obvious that in *all* instances where delinquent subjects received the same or more favorable scores than nondelinquents, it would be a mistake to consider overall delinquent-nondelinquent differences as applicable to these subgroups, since the latter did not contribute to the size and significance of the overall difference, and in at least some cases (i.e., those where significant interaction effects were found) substantially reduced them.

6.   There is some tendency among *nondeprived* subjects for favorableness of rating to increase with increases in IQ. This observation is supported by the fact that a highly significant main effect for intelligence was obtained on the 2 × 3 analysis of variance for D-score. Among individual teacher ratings on the 2 × 3 analysis, considerable variation was found, with significance levels for main effect for intelligence ranging from .05 to nonsignificance, with most traits showing a *trend* toward significance. No such tendency for favorableness of rating to increase with intelligence could be observed among *deprived* subjects.

7.   Except in the case of D-score, there is little *direct* relation between

favorableness of teacher ratings and socioeconomic status, and even in the case of D-score, the expected direction of the difference is reversed, with deprived children scoring *more favorably* at both IQ levels, as the accompanying figures indicate. These statements are supported by the absence of a main effect for socioeconomic status in the 2 × 2 × 2 analyses, except in the case of D-score where a significant effect was found.

This finding is of considerable general interest, in view of the contention of many sociologists and psychologists that teachers tend to rate lower-class children more unfavorably than middle-class children on personal-social traits in the school situation as a result of bias stemming from the average teacher's membership in middle-class culture. At least in this age-grade period, the most *favorable* teacher comments and ratings at the average IQ level characteristically were given to *deprived* nondelinquents.

It would appear that the apparent bias of teachers noted by some investigators may be due to a greater incidence of delinquent trends among socioeconomically deprived children. But where a deprived child, even though he may be identified with lower-class culture, appears capable of average intellectual performance and socially responsible future behavior, he tends to be rated, at least according to this investigation, as or more favorably than his middle-class peer.

SUMMARY

Even in the period from kindergarten through the third grade, future delinquents generally appeared more poorly adapted than nondelinquent peers of the same age, sex, IQ, socioeconomic status, residential background, and ethnic group membership, as measured by teacher ratings and a content analysis of informal teacher comments. As a group, they manifested less acceptable social behavior, more academic difficulty, and a greater incidence of emotional problems.

However, these general findings cannot be applied indiscriminately to all subgroups in the population. There were marked differences in the relationship of various personality traits to delinquency status from one social class-IQ subgroup to another. While in most subgroups nondelinquents received more favorable ratings from teachers on most traits, the size of delinquent-nondelinquent differences and the ranges in which these differences occurred varied considerably.

Furthermore, on some traits even the direction of delinquent-nondelinquent differences changed as one proceeded from one social class-IQ subgroup to another. Thus, on a majority of traits, future delinquents of below average IQ received more favorable teacher ratings than their nondelinquent peers. In short, ratings of personal-social behavior at this age were related, not only to future delinquency status, but also to socioeconomic status and intelligence, whether directly or through interaction with delinquency status.

REFERENCES

1. Bandura, A., & Walters, R. H. *Adolescent aggression.* New York: Ronald, 1959.
2. Cloward, R. A., & Ohlin, L. *Delinquency and opportunity: a theory of delinquent groups.* Glencoe, Ill.: Free Press, 1960.
3. Conger, J. J., Miller, W. C., Gaskill, H. S., & Walsmith, C. R. *Progress report.* (Grant no. M–3040) National Institute of Mental Health, U.S.P.H.S., Washington, D. C., 1960.
4. Conger, J. J., & Miller, W. C., *Personality, social class, and delinquency.* New York: Wiley, 1966.
5. Glueck, S., & Glueck, E. T. *One thousand juvenile delinquents.* Cambridge: Harvard Univer. Press, 1934.
6. Glueck, S., & Glueck, E. T. *Unraveling juvenile delinquency.* New York: Commonwealth Fund, 1950.
7. Hathaway, S. R., and Monachesi, E. D. (Eds.) *Analyzing and predicting juvenile delinquency with the MMPI.* Minneapolis: Univer. Minnesota Press, 1953.
8. Healy, W., & Bronner, A. F. *New light on delinquency and its treatment.* New Haven: Yale Univer. Press, 1936.
9. Maccoby, Eleanor E., Johnson, J. P., & Church, R. M. Community integration and the social control of juvenile delinquency. *J. soc. Issues,* 1958, *14,* 38–51.
10. Merrill, M. A. *Problems of child delinquency.* Boston: Houghton Mifflin, 1947.
11. Salisbury, H. E. *The shook-up generation.* New York: Harper (Crest Books), 1959.
12. Shaw, C. R. *Delinquency areas.* Chicago: Univer. Chicago Press, 1929.
13. Shaw, C. R., McKay, H. D., et al. *Juvenile delinquency and urban areas.* Chicago: Univer. Chicago Press, 1942.
14. Wattenberg, W. W. *The adolescent years.* New York: Harcourt Brace, 1955.
15. Werner, E. & Gallistel, E. Prediction of outstanding performances, delinquency, and emotional disturbance from childhood evaluations. *Child Developm.* 1961, *32,* 255–260.
16. Wirt, R. D., & Briggs, P. F. Personality and environmental factors in the development of delinquency. *Psychol. Monogr.,* 1959, *73,* No. 15, 1–47.

Index
of Names

Index
of Subjects

Adolescence, deliquency in, 505, 535, 570–587; *see also* Delinquency
historical awareness in, 556–558
identity search in, 504 f., 532–537
maturation rates in, 507–520
nature of, 503 f.
physical changes in, 503 f., 507–520, 532
political attitudes in, 505, 541 f., 545 ff., 551 f., 559 ff.
psychological flexibility in, 555 f.
sexual morality in, 504, 521–530
social alienation in, 505, 541, 542–545, 561 f.
stereotyped dissenter in, 540
student activists in, 541 f., 544–562
student dissent in, 538–562
Arithmetic, 292
Asthma, allergies and, 348 f., 353
description of, 346
mother-child relationship in, 302, 345–354

rapidly remitting, 345, 347 ff., 352
steroid dependant, 345, 347 ff., 352

Behavior, developmental research on, 248 ff., 258
linguistic, *see* Concept formation; Language
theory, 261 f.
therapy, in nursery school, 360, 397–404
Behavior, child, altruism in, 380 ff.
by age: three-year-old, 251 ff., 277, 369 f.; four-year-old, 251 ff., 257 f., 335, 369 f., 398–404; five-year-old, 251 f., 258, 261, 267, 269, 272–277, 328 ff., 335, 369 f.; six-year-old, 252 f., 258, 261, 335; seven-year-old, 251, 253, 257, 267, 269, 273, 277, 296 f.; eight-year-old, 252, 261; ten-year-old, 252, 255 f., 261, 267, 269, 274 f.; twelve-year-old, 297 f.
continuity and stability in, 361, 364 f., 369 f.

discontinuity and stability in, 361, 365–370
ego identification in, 533 ff.
expectancy estimates in, 484–490, 497 ff.
of future delinquents, 571–576, 587
language abilities in preschool, 207–209, 211–227; *see also* Language
preschool; 260, 264, 289 f., 359 f., 397–404
personality tendencies in, 459 ff., 464–478
in unfamiliar situations, 481–499
See also Adolescence; Class, social; Cognition; Compulsivity; Concept formation; Delinquency; Ghetto, northern urban; Identification; Infants; Intelligence; Intelligence Quotient; Learning; Memory; Roles; Sex; Socialization

Children, deprived, 280–283, 286–290

70 71 72 73 7 6 5 4 3 2 1

22-302

Date Due

NO 30 '70	MR 24 '72				
JUL 26 '70	MR 30 '73				
AUG 5 '70	AP 24 '73				
SEP 28 '71	JY 10 '74				
OCT 19 '71	DE 3 '76				
NOV 18 '71	OCT. 23 1982				
JA 24 '72					
FE -8 '72					
MR 10 '72					

PRINTED IN U.S.A.   CAT. NO. 23 231

71365

136.7
M989r   2nd ed.

Mussen,Paul Henry
   Readings in child develop. & person.

LIBRARY
OHIO DOMINICAN COLLEGE
COLUMBUS, OHIO 43219